The Miegunyah Press

The general series of the
Miegunyah Volumes
was made possible by the
Miegunyah Fund
established by bequests
under the wills of
Sir Russell and Lady Grimwade.

'Miegunyah'
was Russell Grimwade's home
from 1911 to 1955
and Mab Grimwade's home
from 1911 to 1973.

H.M. Bark
Endeavour

Her place in Australian History

With an Account of her Construction, Crew and Equipment and a Narrative of her Voyage on the East Coast of New Holland in the Year 1770

Ray Parkin

With Plans, Charts and Illustrations by the Author

THE
MIEGUNYAH
PRESS

For Thelma, my wife, who wished me well in this before she died — yet somehow stayed to see it done.

The Miegunyah Press
An imprint of Melbourne University Publishing Ltd
Level 1, 715 Swanston Street, Carlton, Victoria 3053, Australia
mup-contact@unimelb.edu.au
www.mup.com.au

First published 1997
Second edition published 2003
Paperback edition published 2006
Third edition published 2020

Edited by Sally Moss
Text design by Mark Davis
Cover design by Pfisterer + Freeman
Printed in China by 1010 Printing Asia Pty Ltd

NATIONAL LIBRARY OF AUSTRALIA
A catalogue record for this book is available from the National Library of Australia

ISBN 9780522876444 (box set)
ISBN 9780522876437 (hardback)

Foreword

Alan Frost

Lieutenant James Cook's *Endeavour* is one of the most famous ships in European history and his circumnavigation in it—which included observing a transit of Venus across the face of the sun at Tahiti, the charting of New Zealand's two large islands and the charting of almost the entire eastern coast of Australia—was one of the defining voyages of the modern era. Effectively, it dispelled the age-old notion of a huge land mass, *Terra Australis Incognita*, stretching across the southern hemisphere, went a good way to showing the empty vastness of the Pacific Ocean and delineated the hitherto unknown eastern coast of New Holland. In the process, Cook somehow survived 'the most dangerous navigation that perhaps ever Ship was in', what with the Great Barrier Reef on the right hand side—'a wall of Coral Rock rising all most perpendicular out of the unfathomable Ocean, . . . [on which] the large waves of the vast Ocean . . . make a most terrible surf breaking mountains high'; and inside which were scattered a myriad smaller reefs waiting to tear the bottom out of the ship, which one nearly did.

Ray Parkin's exhaustive study of the *Endeavour* and its voyage is comprised of three classes. The first are extracts from Cook's daily log which, as it were, show the 'bare bones' of circumstances. Then, there are extracts from journals kept by members of the ship's company. Of these, those by Cook and Joseph Banks are by far the most important, together with (to a lesser extent) that of Sydney Parkinson. At points, Parkin has augmented these with details from three classes of records kept on the voyage. Finally, there are Parkin's own analyses and comments. Some of these are brief, but others are quite lengthy; and in them Parkin draws on his extraordinary knowledge of the details of the ship, of the routes it took, and of sea circumstances more generally.

For example, while repairing the ship at Endeavour River (Cooktown), on 9 July Cook send a boat out to reconnoitre a safe passage away. In his log, he wrote: 'The master return'd, having been 7 leagues out sounding without being able to bring in a satisfactory account of the passage.' Banks expanded on this somewhat in his journal: 'At night the Pinnace . . . returnd, she had been unsuccessful in her main errand. Shoals innumerable she had met with.' Parkin explains how it was not feasible at this point for Cook to get out to sea again by returning southwards until he found an end to the Great Barrier Reef:

> Working to windward against the prevailing south-easters, they well knew, was out of the question, even in clear water in which to make substantial tacks. The Captain had already recognised that in these constricted shoal-strewn waters, short of a reversal of the seasonal wind, it was hopeless. Therefore if no passage to the north could be found they would have to face a protracted period of delay when, already, the state of the provision was critical. The ship had been absent from England now for two years all but a month, most of which had been spent at sea. She had been under considerable stress of weather on the coast of South America, in the Forties approaching New Zealand, and particularly during her six months charting and circumnavigating the two islands. So that, at this present time, she had to work on this challenging coast with worn and deteriorated gear: with sails and rigging that had to be nursed by the sailmakers and riggers with a vigilance that involved everybody onboard.

Repeatedly, Parkin emphasises Cook's diligence, attention to detail and perseverance: 'danger was always imminent. It takes a special sort of man to be able to live with this responsibility, day and night for months on end. It takes a devotion to one's calling not cheaply bought.'

A similar characterisation can be made of Ray Parkin's endeavour. Since the shipwrights who built it and the Navy Board artificers who fitted it out for its long and arduous voyage, no one has known so much about the *Endeavour* as he did. His account is a monument to diligent and persevering scholarship.

Note

Since he published *H. M. Bark Endeavour* in 1997, further research has shown Tupaia,[1] the Ra'iatean priest and navigator who joined the *Endeavour* at Tahiti, in a considerably more interesting light than Ray Parkin was able to do. First, it is now clear that Tupaia was the person who painted the eight watercolours of Tahitian and New Zealand scenes in the British Library, which were previously ascribed, first to 'The Artist of the Chief Mourner', and then to Banks.[2] We may wonder at Tupaia's capacity to adapt to a new cultural medium. Second, a recent very lengthy and detailed analysis of a third copy of Tupaia's chart of Polynesian islands has increased our understanding of the extraordinary extent of his geographical knowledge.[3] Had he known these things, I am confident that Ray Parkin would have given Tupaia a greater role in his story of the *Endeavour's* voyage.

1 This is now the preferred spelling. Parkin used that in Cook's and Banks's journals.

2 Glyndwr Williams, 'Tupaia, Polynesian Warrior, Navigator, High Priest', in *The Global Eighteenth Century*, ed. Felicity Nussbaum (The Johns Hopkins University Press, Baltimore Md, 2003), pp. 38–51.

3 Lars Eckstein and Anja Schwarz, ' The making of Tupaia's Map: A Story of the Extent and Mastery of Polynesian Navigation, Competing Systems of Wayfinding on James Cook's *Endeavour*, and the Invention of an Ingenious Cartographic System', *The Journal of Pacific History*, vol. 54, no. 1, pp. 1–95.

CONTENTS

Foreword by Alan Frost *v*
Acknowledgements *viii*
Weights and Measures *viii*
Preface *ix*

PART I: THE WORLD OF THE SHIP

Introduction *3*
1 The Sailor and His Environment *41*
2 The Captain *58*
3 The Ship *68*
4 Scurvy and Provisions *85*
5 The Ship's Company *96*
6 From Misfortune, and by Their Sins *110*
7 Peradventure *131*

PART II: THE VOYAGE

Introduction *141*
1 The Decision *147*
2 Towards New Holland *150*
3 Towards Botany Bay *159*
4 Botany Bay *180*
5 Port Jackson to Sandy Cape *205*
6 Sandy Cape to Thirsty Sound *235*
7 Thirsty Sound to Trinity Bay *267*
8 Endeavour Reef *299*
9 Endeavour River: June *324*
10 Endeavour River: July *345*
11 Departure *382*
12 Escape to Sea *391*
13 The Breadth of One Wave *412*
14 Keeping the Main on Board *424*
15 *L'envoi* *444*

Notes to Part I *455*
Bibliography *459*
Index of Individuals and Locations *461*

Acknowledgements

My thanks to Commander A.C.F. David for providing me with a copy of the original letter from Major Samuel Holland to Lieutenant Governor Simcoe held by Metropolitan Toronto Library Board, Toronto, reproduced on page 62.

Compilation of my own 'Compleat Log', on which I based my reconstruction of the voyage that is the subject of this book (see Part II), was made possible by a Special Purposes Grant from the Literature Board of the Australia Council.

R.P.

The publishers express their gratitude to Andrew David and Richard Campbell for their advice and assistance during the preparation of this book.

Weights and Measures

Conversions are approximate. Abbreviations and symbols used in the text are included in parentheses.

acre	=	4,050 square metres, or 4,840 square yards
degree (°)	=	1/360 of the circumference of a circle
fathom	=	1.82 metres, or 6 feet
foot (ft, ')	=	0.305 metres
gallon	=	4.55 litres
hundredweight (cwt)	=	112 pounds, or 50.8 kilograms
inch (in., ")	=	2.54 centimetres
knot	=	1 sea-mile (or nautical mile) per hour
league	=	1/20 of a degree, or 3 international sea-miles
mile	=	1.61 kilometres
minute (')	=	1/60 of a degree
ounce (oz.)	=	28.35 grams
point	=	(of compass) 11¼ degrees
pound (Ib)	=	0.45 kilograms
quarter (qr)	=	28 pounds, or 12.7 kilograms
sea-mile	=	1 minute of latitude
second (")	=	1/60 of a minute
ton	=	1.016 tonnes

Preface

I was drawn to the subject of H.M. Bark *Endeavour* some twenty-five years ago, and have been trying ever since to find answers to a constantly growing list of questions posed by the records of her 1768 voyage.

It all began innocently enough. I had simply wanted to engrave a true image of *Endeavour* Bark on my greeting card for 1967/8, her bicentennial year. Though she was said to be one of the best recorded vessels in history, I could find nothing really reliable from which to work, and was more than surprised by this. So it was, with nothing more than curiosity, that I began the research that led to this book.

It soon became apparent that a mere physical reconstruction, however accurate, would not be sufficient for a proper understanding—for an anatomy without its physiology is no more than a corpse. And I wanted her alive, not dead.

For me, there was a link of tradition and service because, when young, I had been a very ordinary sailor for some seventeen years in His Majesty's ships. I was affected by discovering how little many basic things in a sailor's life had changed over one hundred and sixty years—and so deeply affected that much of my impressionable youth at sea came back to remind my older head of things I had apparently forgotten.

We all live in a Perpetual Present. Behind us we have our own *envisaged* Past; with us is our own *confusing* and *imperative* Present, subject to compulsive expedient; ahead of us we have only our *surmised* Future of unsure prophecy and expectation. With these we make our way, doing what we must and constantly bending to demanding necessity, while trying to hold fast to our best intentions.

This is the human condition, in which the Past is made up only of the echoes that reach the Present by inheritance or acquisition. And it is the ability or otherwise of these echoes to affect our Present that gives us a nice paradox: the Dead can bring the Living to life, because the Dead are only as dead as the Living allow them to be.

It occurred to me, during my research, that, by tuning in to the echoes bequeathed us, we might all achieve a more vital understanding of the *Endeavour*, of the men who sailed in her, and of the place of the whole saga in Australian history.

James Cook did not discover Australia, nor did he ever claim to have done so. From the outset of the voyage in 1768, he knew, and had maps of, what mariners had seen and recorded, as well as what philosophical geographers had limned-in, each according to his own fancy. And he understood perfectly the difference between the two.

Having circumnavigated New Zealand (and thus having more than fulfilled his instructions), Cook chose to return to England by way of New Holland rather than by Cape Horn. This decision was based upon two major considerations. The first was the state of his badly worn and weathered gear, which was unlikely to withstand the boisterous winter passage of the Southern Ocean, despite favourable winds. The second, and I suspect more compelling, reason was Cook's own dedication to geography and navigation. For ten years before this voyage, he had been intimately and professionally concerned with sea surveys—the quality of which was marking the beginning of a new era of excellence and standards in exploration, navigation and chart-making. Thus the whole inclination of his talent and sense of obligation towards this unmapped eastern portion of New Holland was to resume where Abel Tasman had left off one hundred and twenty-eight years previously. The weather took him a little north of Tasman's point of departure from Van Diemen's Land. But, for the rest, from Point Hicks to Cape York, he laid down the coast with unprecedented accuracy and skill that continue to amaze modern mariners.

Endeavour was armed only defensively. The voyage was a voyage after knowledge, not conquest. The instructions were explicitly humanitarian, and the men demonstrably inclined to compassion and fellow-feeling. On quitting the coast of New Holland, Cook wrote with a rare empathy on the Aborigines of this land:

> From what I have said of the Natives of New-Holland they may appear to some to be the most wretched people upon Earth, but in reality they are far more happier than we Europeans; being wholy unacquainted not only with the superfluous but the necessary Conveniences so much sought after in Europe, they are happy in not knowing the use of them. They live in a Tranquillity which is not disturb'd by the Inequality of Condition: The Earth and sea of their own accord furnishes them with all things necessary for life, they covet not Magnificent Houses, Household-stuff &c[a], they live in a warm and fine Climate and enjoy a very wholsome Air, so that they have very little need of Clothing and this they seem to be fully sencible of, for many to whom we gave Cloth &c[a] to, left it carlessly upon the Sea beach and in the woods as a thing they had no manner of use for. In short they seem'd to set no Value upon any thing we gave them, nor would they ever part with any thing of their own for any one article we could offer them; this in my opinion argues that they think themselves provided with all the necessarys of Life and that they have no superfluities.[1]

There is little doubt that this contact of *Endeavour* with New Holland, together with the confluence of foreign and domestic policy on the other side of the world, brought white settlement to New Holland some eighteen years later to begin the history of what is now Australia as a Western civilisation. Therefore it would seem most important that the nature of this voyage, as it touches Australia, be properly understood—so that this innocent beginning is not confused with subsequent events and exploitation, over a great deal of which hangs the tragic shadow of the Mark of Cain. And how better to understand it than by allowing the voyagers to speak for themselves, directly to the reader and without any after-the-event theoretical intrusion?

So, I have brought all this material together in the hope that it may tell its own true tale of the vessel, of the men who sailed in it, and of the voyage.

PART I

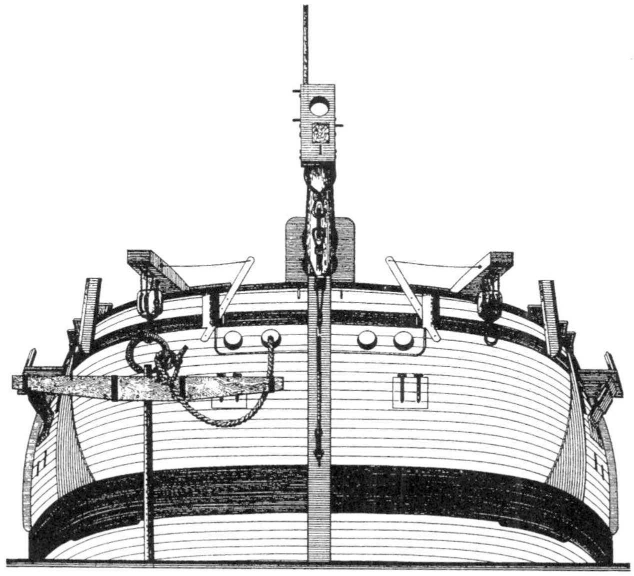

THE WORLD OF THE SHIP

CONTENTS: PART I

Introduction *3*
The plans *7*
The Parkinson drawings *12*
The boats *27*
Rigging and sail plans *34*
1 The Sailor and His Environment *41*
2 The Captain *58*
3 The Ship *68*
4 Scurvy and Provisions *85*
5 The Ship's Company *96*
6 From Misfortune, and by Their Sins *110*
7 Peradventure *131*

INTRODUCTION

When I set out on my quest for information about H.M. Bark *Endeavour*, I, like many people, had only a vague and generalised concept of her, and I was soon to realise just how abysmal my ignorance was.

During the bicentenary of the *Endeavour*'s voyage, there was a flood of opportunistic journalese upon this subject. Even authors with a reputation for sea-writing were, it would seem, more intent upon catching a market than on a conscientious consideration of their material. Popular misconceptions and fallacies were being made even more popular by their not allowing simple fact to interfere with a 'good story'. Later, in the course of my research, I was astonished when a leading maritime museum offered me one of these books as a reliable source of reference.

I could not help feeling that there was something very impoverishing in this superficial presentation. Too many questions were not being addressed. Historical theories, opinions and conclusions were far easier to come by than the facts which they cloaked in one guise or another to fit an author's occasion. This put me on my guard and acted as a spur to try to get at the facts. Gradually I emerged from a plain ignorance, which did not even know which questions to ask, to an informed ignorance—an understanding of exactly what needed to be asked and how important these questions were.

My first contact with solid fact was in a copy of an article obtained for me from the State Library of Victoria. It was 'H.M. Bark *Endeavour*' by C. Knight.[1] This informative article was accompanied by reproductions of the ship's plans[2] and deck plans[3] of 1768 and 1771 respectively. There was also an extract of a letter from the Deptford Yard Officers to Navy Board, dated 27 March 1768.[4] This report gave the complete scantlings—that is, dimensions as to breadth and thickness—of each piece of timber in the whole ship's carcase. It began:

> Pursuant to your warrant of the 23rd instant we have surveyed and measured the undermentioned ships[5] recommended to your Honours to proceed on Foreign

Service and send you an amount of their quantities, condition, age and dimensions with our opinion of the value of the hull, masts and yards as may be proper to purchase with them, viz:

Earl of Pembroke

Length on the lower deck from the after side of the rabbet of the stem to the foreside of the rabbet of the post	97ft. 7in.
Length of the keel for tonnage	81ft. 0 3/8 in.
Breadth extreme	29ft. 3in.
Depth of Hold	11ft. 4in.
Burthen in tons	368 71/94
Height between decks: afore	7ft. 6in.
midships	7ft. 9in.
abaft	7ft. 11in.
Length of fo'castle	18ft. 8in.
Height of ditto: afore	4ft. 8in.
abaft	4ft. 6in.
Length from the after side of the stem to the first rise aft	51ft. 4in.
Height of ditto	2ft. 1in.
Length from the after side of the stem to the second rise aft	74ft. 10 1/2 in.
Height of ditto	11in.
Height between plank and plank on the steerage: afore	4ft. 7 1/2 in.
abaft	5ft. 0in.
Height of waist in midships	11in.
Length of great cabin	14ft. 4 1/2 in.
Height of ditto: afore	6ft. 8in.
abaft	7ft. 2 1/2 in.
Room and space of timbers	2ft. 5in.
Floor timbers sided	1ft. 2in.
Height of cutting down	1ft. 4in.
Lower futtocks sided	11in.
Timbers at the breadth: sided	9in.
moulded	7 1/2 in.
In Hold—hooks under deck: Nos.	3
sided	1ft. 3in.
moulded	1ft. 6in.
No. of bolts	11.
Transome knees on each side: hooks Nos.	3
sided	1ft. 11in.
moulded	1ft. 10in.
No. of bolts	13
Lower deck beams: sided	1ft. 1in.
moulded	1ft. 1in.
spaced	5ft. 6in.
No. of bolts	14
Knees lodging at each side: No.	2
sided	11in.
moulded	1ft. 2in.
No. of bolts	4
Upper deck beams: No.	8
sided	10in.
moulded	9in.
Knees with one hanging and one lodging knee: sided	8in.
moulded	1ft. 0in.
No. of bolts	6
Quarter deck beams: sided	9in.
moulded	7in.

Knees with one hanging and one lodging knee: sided	6in.
moulded	9in.
No. of bolts	4
Fore hatch: fore and aft (Main Hatch 8ft. 3in.)	3ft. 11in.
athwartships (" " 5ft. 11in.)	4ft. 11in.
Raft port in hold: fore and aft	2ft. 8in.
athwartships	2ft. 7in.
Raft port between decks: up and down	2ft. 8in.
athwartships	2ft. 7½in.
Keel in two pieces one on the other: depth	2ft. 10½in.
Keel below rabbet	11in.
Plank of bottom under wales to floorheads	4in.
From thence to keel	3in.
Main wale	5½in.
Fir strakes above wales	3in.
Topsides	2½in.

This was like coming out of a fog into clear sunlight, and marked the material beginning of my whole search for H.M. Bark *Endeavour*.

I had been fortunate enough to obtain a copy of *The Voyage of the* Endeavour *1768–1771*, being one of the journals of James Cook, edited by J.C. Beaglehole.[6] This masterly work by such an able and dedicated scholar has virtually been the cornerstone of my research because, in its introduction and appendices, it has directed me to the major sources of prime evidence for what I was seeking. As Malcolm Letts wrote in his preface to this work, 'the publication of his [Cook's] Journals in a version which can be used with confidence is not to be considered an end in itself. Let us look upon it rather as the beginning of a fresh phase in Cook studies, in which, upon the basis of a reliable text, historical investigation may with new vigour define and clarify the work of this man, great alike as a seaman, as an explorer, as a practical scientist, and as a leader of men.'

In having Professor R.M. (Max) Crawford[7] as a close friend and neighbour, I was most fortunate. It was his copy of *Endeavour's Voyage* that I had. It was he who got me the photocopy of Knight's article. Both of these gave me my first firm footing in the subject. He obtained for me a Reader's Ticket for the Manuscript Room of the British Library. Never did he direct me; but, in that quiet gentle manner all his own, he simply encouraged and reassured along the way. Throughout the whole ten years of the process, he was always there to discuss with me at any length my problems and doubts. He personally put me in touch with Professor J.C. Beaglehole, whom he knew. Without his support I am sure that I would not have had the courage (temerity?) to persevere beyond that first engraving I made of *Endeavour*.

I wrote to Professor Beaglehole of what I was trying to do. He replied, 'I received . . . your exceedingly interesting letter and drawings; & if at this moment I merely say thank you, you must understand that my thanks are real, and that I do not feel gratitude for most of the communications that I get. I cannot do any sort of justice to either the letter or the drawings immediately . . . and this is just a holding note till I can assemble my thoughts. When I am able to do that, I shall certainly write again.'[8] I met him when he came to lecture in Melbourne in 1970. Not long after this he died. His encouragement meant a great deal to me, and his thoroughness and integrity set me a formidable standard.

Thus fired, I set about collecting all the microfilms of the known journals and logs (I had already obtained full-size photocopies of the plans from the Greenwich Maritime Museum). The microfilms I had printed out to full size[9]—yielding some 1160 metres—which I cut into pages and bound in a separate volume for each log keeper. Whereas one can look at only one microfilm at a time, I could now lay the volumes side by side for comparison. From these I compiled a complete handwritten journal in which the events of each day were described by all of the writers, one after the other. To this manuscript (which I called 'The Compleat Log') I added, at the head of each day, a reproduction of the Ship's Log, which served as a backbone of information. Finally, I added to the accounts for each day photocopies of all available correspondence. In this way I made for myself a convenient historical tool. The process was time-consuming: eventually I had ten large volumes, each of some two hundred pages, of material in chronological order. I was now able to comb the volumes for more particular information about the ship herself. This I entered into another volume indexed for ready reference under the headings: 'Anchors & Cables', 'Boats', 'Hull', 'Rigging', 'Spars', 'Sails', 'Wood & Water', 'Provisions', 'Tacking, Wearing, etc.', 'Sounding and Log Lines', 'Hygiene', 'Discipline', 'Guns, etc.', 'Casualties & Personnel'. I wanted to tread on sure ground.

Fortunately for me, a number of eighteenth-century nautical publications were being reissued around this time. Those of special interest to me became invaluable reference to the practices of the era. Frederik af Chapman's *Architectura Navalis Mercatoria* (1768) set a standard of plan-making which has never been surpassed. He was not called the Genius of the Drawing Board for nothing. He was using, even then, testing tanks for testing the resistance of various designs of ships' hulls through the water, and calculating displacement and waterlines on the drawing board. He had studied under Simpson of the famous Simpson's Rule for finding volume or area of irregular bodies. Chapman more than anyone else influenced my drawings of reconstruction. Also being reissued were Steel's *Elements of Mastmaking, Sailmaking and Rigging* (1794); *Falconer's Marine Dictionary (1780)*, enlarged 1815; Rees's cyclopædia *Naval Architecture (1819–20)* which deals with ship-building from the first mark on the drawing board to the last bolt in the hull, together with rigging; mast and yards; sail; and rope making; Darcy Lever's *Young Sea Officer's Sheet Anchor* (1819): *key to the leading of rigging and to practical seamanship*; and Röding's *Allgemeines Wörterbuch der Marine* (1793). The value of this last work was its demonstration of the international nature of so much of the then marine practices. Lastly there was *A Sea Grammar* (1627) by Captain John Smith (of Pocohontas fame), giving an insight into origins. I also had at my disposal a facsimile first edition of *Encyclopædia Britannica* (1771). This gave me a good idea of what was then present knowledge so that I might avoid anachronistic judgements.

I kept these references constantly by my side. I also read omnivorously anything else which might, however obliquely, offer further clues to what I was looking for.

~ THE PLANS ~

There are six Admiralty plans of *Endeavour* in the Greenwich Maritime Museum. Four of them (NMM ADM. 3814, 3814a, 3814b and 3814c) are complete draughts, each comprising the conventional Profile or Sheer Plan, below which is the scale of one-quarter of an inch to the foot. Set off to the left of this is the Body Plan, sometimes called the Projection, which represents the vessel viewed end-on, with the left half as from astern, and the right half as from ahead; while below the Sheer Plan is the Half-breadth Plan, sometimes called the Horizontal Plane, which, as the name implies, is of one side of the vessel only (for the other is its mirror image), showing the waterlines. The two remaining plans (NMM ADM. 3819 and 3819a) are Deck Plans of 1768, when the vessel was being fitted for the South Seas, and of 1771, when being fitted for the Fleet Auxiliary (as a store ship 1771–75). Of course, plans are of little significance unless one can 'read' them. This I had to learn to do, and, in the process, I developed nothing less than total admiration for the craft and knowledge of this era.

Ships were built from either half-models or draughts. For shipwrights who could not read plans, the half-model gave them all they needed to know: the stem, the sternpost, the keel, the wing transom, and the fashion pieces which give the shape of the stern. Also from the model they could take cross-sections at intervals to shape their frames-of-timbers. Thus they could 'raise' their vessel with practical experience and skill which has been aptly termed as 'art-and-eye'. However, the half-model led to variations in vessels built from the same model by different craftsmen. Plans did much to curtail this variation, and made it possible to construct identical 'sister-ships' with more certainty than previously.

The first ship plans in England appear to have been introduced in Elizabethan times. *Fragments of Ancient English Shipwrightry*, circa 1586, came to England at the time of Henry VIII, or even earlier. A master shipwright of Elizabeth's, Mathew Baker, is accredited with the major part of this writing. It is in this publication that we find the introduction of mathematical curves to form transverse sections of the hull, with preconceived longitudinal curves and heights shown in profile. These plans still demanded a great deal of art-and-eye to reconcile them, but, as time went by and knowledge increased, they became more comprehensive.

About the middle of the seventeenth century, the Admiralty ruled that plans of all ships were to be filed in records; but it seems that this was not fully complied with until about 1675.[10] By the beginning of the next century, well-drawn plans were being produced. By 1690, drawing instruments had reached a standard little changed until the first quarter of the twentieth century. The right-line pens, scale rules, squares, compasses (ink and pencil), dividers and possibly proportional compasses, boxwood curves and flexible battens for variable curves were all in use. Parchment was used at first, but was later replaced by handmade paper spliced to required sizes. Plans were normally drawn at one quarter of an inch to one foot. Fresh

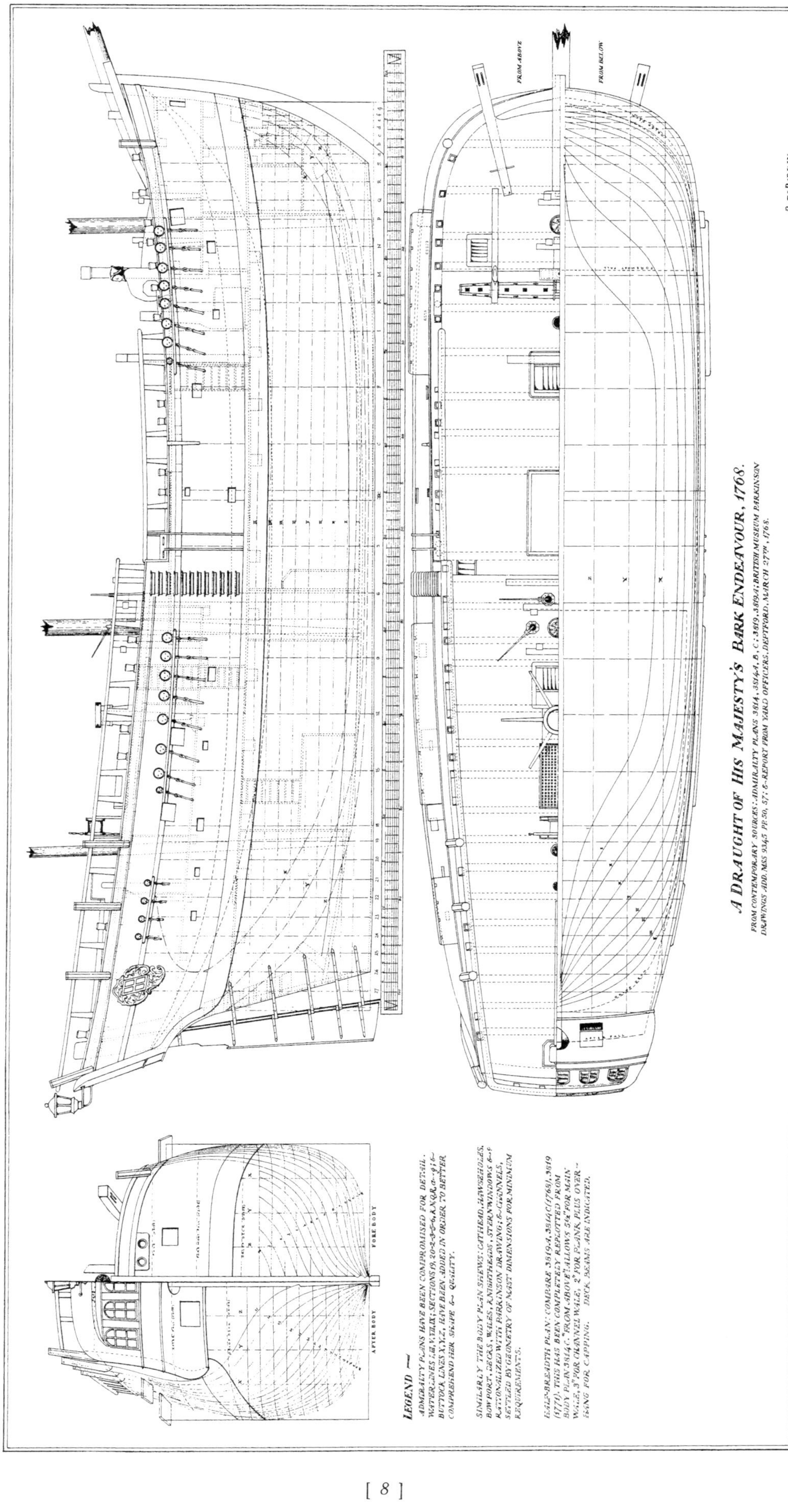
AFTER BODY
FORE BODY
LEGEND —
ADMIRALTY PLANS HAVE BEEN COMPROMISED FOR DETAIL. WATERLINES I, III, V, VII, IX; SECTIONS 19, 20-2-3-5-6, K, N, Q, R, a—g; & BUTTOCK LINES X, Y, Z, HAVE BEEN ADDED IN ORDER TO BETTER COMPREHEND HER SHAPE & QUALITY.
SIMILARLY THE BODY PLAN SHEWS: CATHEAD, HAWSEHOLES, BOW PORT, DECKS, WALES, KNIGHTHEADS, STERNWINDOWS & RATIONALIZED WITH PARKINSON DRAWING; & CHANNELS, SETTLED BY GEOMETRY OF MAST DIMENSIONS FOR MINIMUM REQUIREMENTS.
HALF-BREADTH PLAN: COMPARE 3819A, 3814C(1768), 3819 (1771). THIS HAS BEEN COMPLETELY REPLOTTED FROM BODY PLAN 3814C. "FROM ABOVE" ALLOWS 5½" FOR MAIN WALE, 3" FOR CHANNEL WALE, 2" FOR PLANK PLUS OVERHANG FOR CAPPING. DECK BEAMS ARE INDICATED.
FROM ABOVE
FROM BELOW
A DRAUGHT OF HIS MAJESTY'S BARK ENDEAVOUR, 1768.
FROM CONTEMPORARY SOURCES: ADMIRALTY PLANS 3814, 3814A, B, C; 3819, 3819A; BRITISH MUSEUM PARKINSON DRAWINGS ADD. MSS 9345 PP. 50, 57; & REPORT FROM YARD OFFICERS, DEPTFORD, MARCH 27TH, 1768.
RAY PARKIN

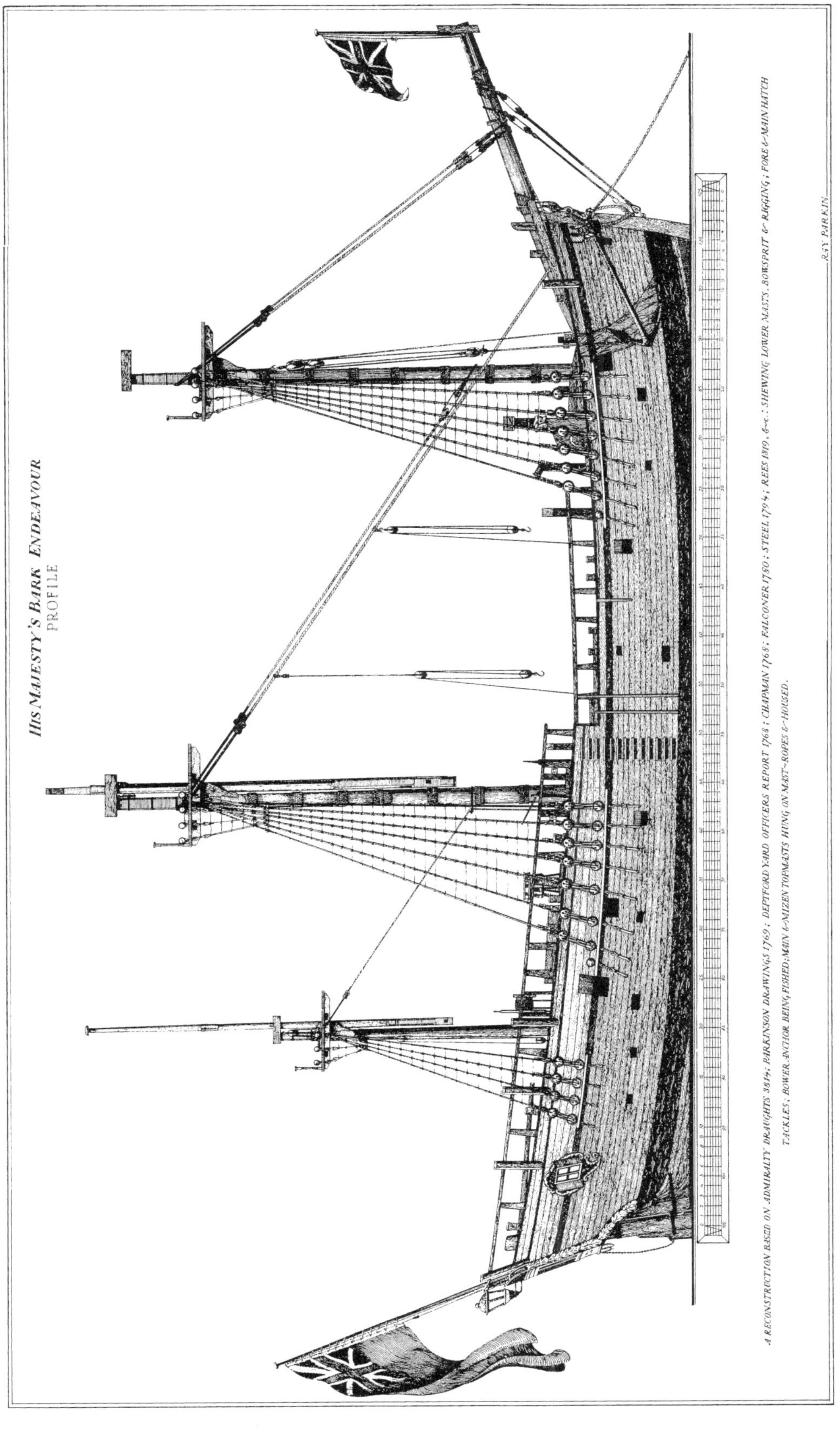
HIS MAJESTY'S BARK ENDEAVOUR
PROFILE
A RECONSTRUCTION BASED ON ADMIRALTY DRAUGHTS 3814; PARKINSON DRAWINGS 1769; DEPTFORD YARD OFFICERS REPORT 1768; CHAPMAN 1768; FALCONER 1780; STEEL 1794; REES 1819, &c.: SHEWING LOWER MASTS, BOWSPRIT & RIGGING; FORE & MAIN HATCH
TACKLES; BOWER ANCHOR BEING FISHED; MAIN & MIZEN TOPMASTS HUNG ON MAST-ROPES & HOUSED.
R. G. PARKIN

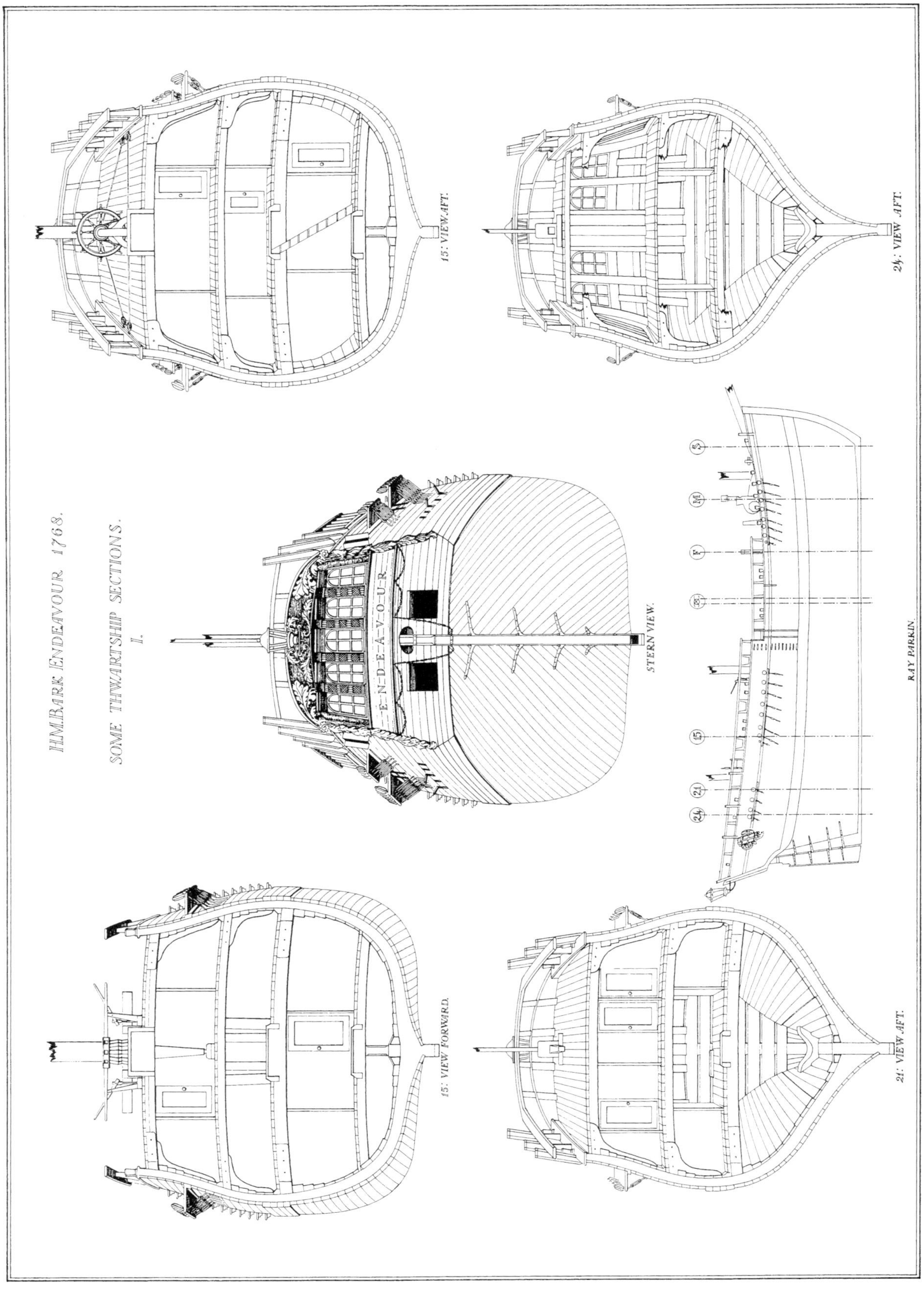
H.M.BARK ENDEAVOUR 1768.
SOME THWARTSHIP SECTIONS.
I.
15: VIEW AFT.
24: VIEW AFT.
STERN VIEW.
E-N-D-E-A-V-O-U-R
RAY PARKIN.
15: VIEW FORWARD.
21: VIEW AFT.

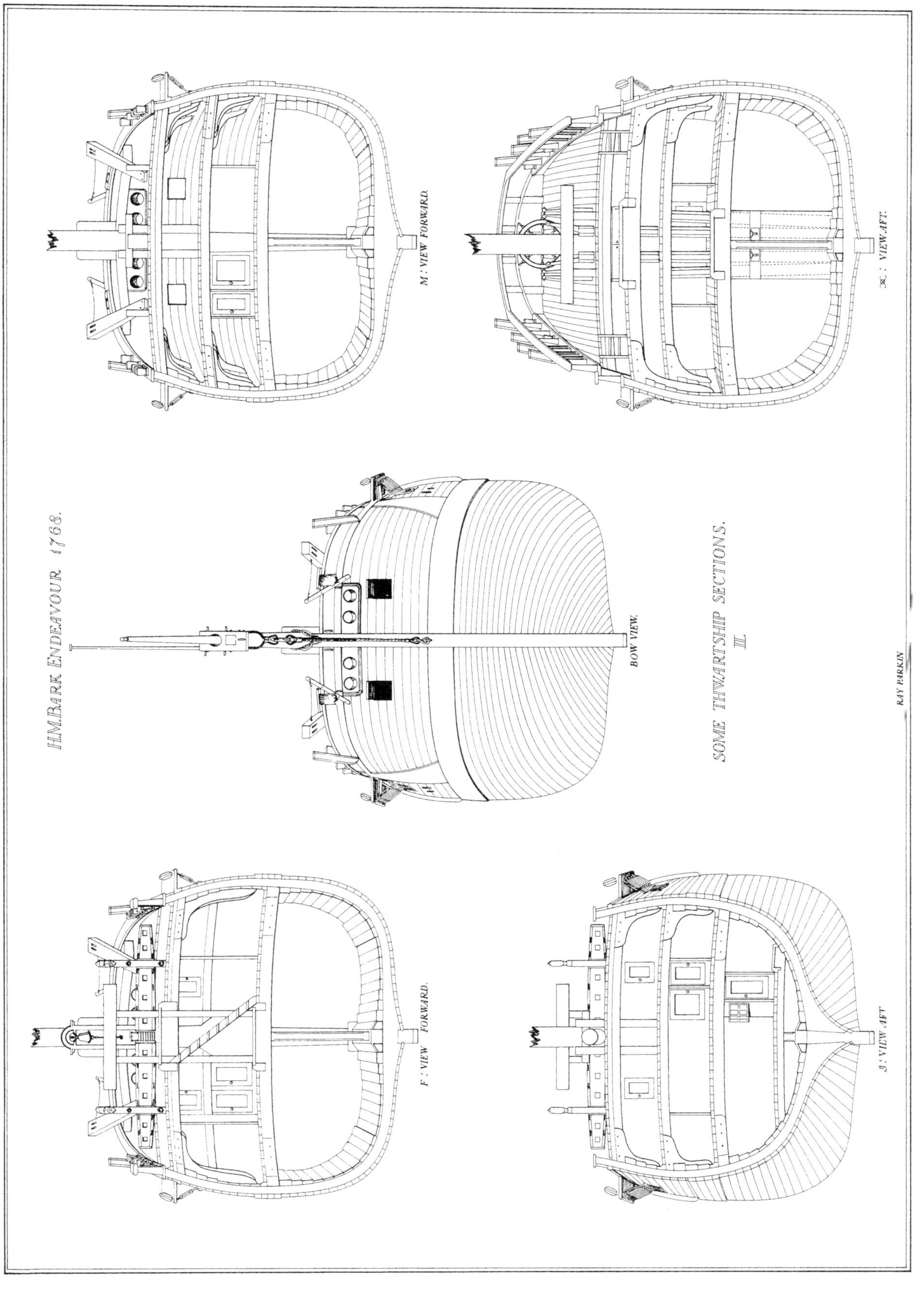
H.M.BARK ENDEAVOUR 1768.
SOME THWARTSHIP SECTIONS.
II
M: VIEW FORWARD.
⊗: VIEW AFT.
BOW VIEW.
F: VIEW FORWARD.
3: VIEW AFT
RAY PARKIN

bread was used (as it is today) to erase pencil lines, while ink (which was China or India and came in sticks) was scraped with a sharp knife, with bone or spoon burnishers being used to re-lay the fibres to prevent runs. Cook's drawing instruments would be indistinguishable from those with which I began this work—even to the shape of the bone handles.

In the eighteenth century, the standard of plan-making was very high indeed—one glance at the work of Frederik af Chapman shows that. To quote Howard Chapelle, a noted American naval architect and historian, 'it is not surprising to find the naval draughtsmen of the eighteenth century capable of producing plans of great accuracy and beauty of workmanship. In fact, the marine draughtsman of the eighteenth century was capable of producing drawings of greater beauty than have since been seen in this field.'[11]

So, for me, these plans can never be cold documents, for they have grown out of a tradition devoid of pretension—in which the proof of the pudding was *always* in the eating. They are the work of men trying to express facts clearly, concisely and unequivocally. Each plan carries something of its draughtsman, and is redolent of the time. For instance, on plan 3814 is the notation 'April 16th. This draught was sent to Deptford to fitt her out for the South Sea. Returned the 18th D.°' Here is a glimpse of the efficiency and industry of these men. In two days, the plan was sent, accepted, copied and returned, with the working time of probably no more than one day. There is no humbug in these draughts. No line is without significance; the veracity of each is always tested. So, if one learns to read these draughts, the door is opened to a rewarding understanding.

These are only preliminary remarks. It should become apparent throughout the rest of this book that *Endeavour* was a vessel soundly designed for her original service and proved eminently suitable for discovery; and it was James Cook who judged her so—to the point where he stuck to this design for all of his voyages. For those who can see only her limitations, let them lay these alongside Cook's achievements in her. This may also adduce a healthy homily for all such counsellors of 'perfection'.

~ The Parkinson Drawings ~

Sydney Parkinson's sketches of *Endeavour*[12] are the only eyewitness records of her living appearance that we have.

Yet, when I came to this work, they were being treated as little more than curiosities of 'artistic licence'. They had been dismissed as providing no credible evidence of the actual structure or appearance of the vessel. In the replies I was getting from reputable 'authorities', there seemed to be a curious perversity and a consistency which indicated a common entrenchment of opinion. When questioned more closely, those who held such opinions seemed to have based them on a first impression of 'poor drawing' (their own words), and they had not bothered to study the work further, being apparently hemmed in by their own wall of prejudice.

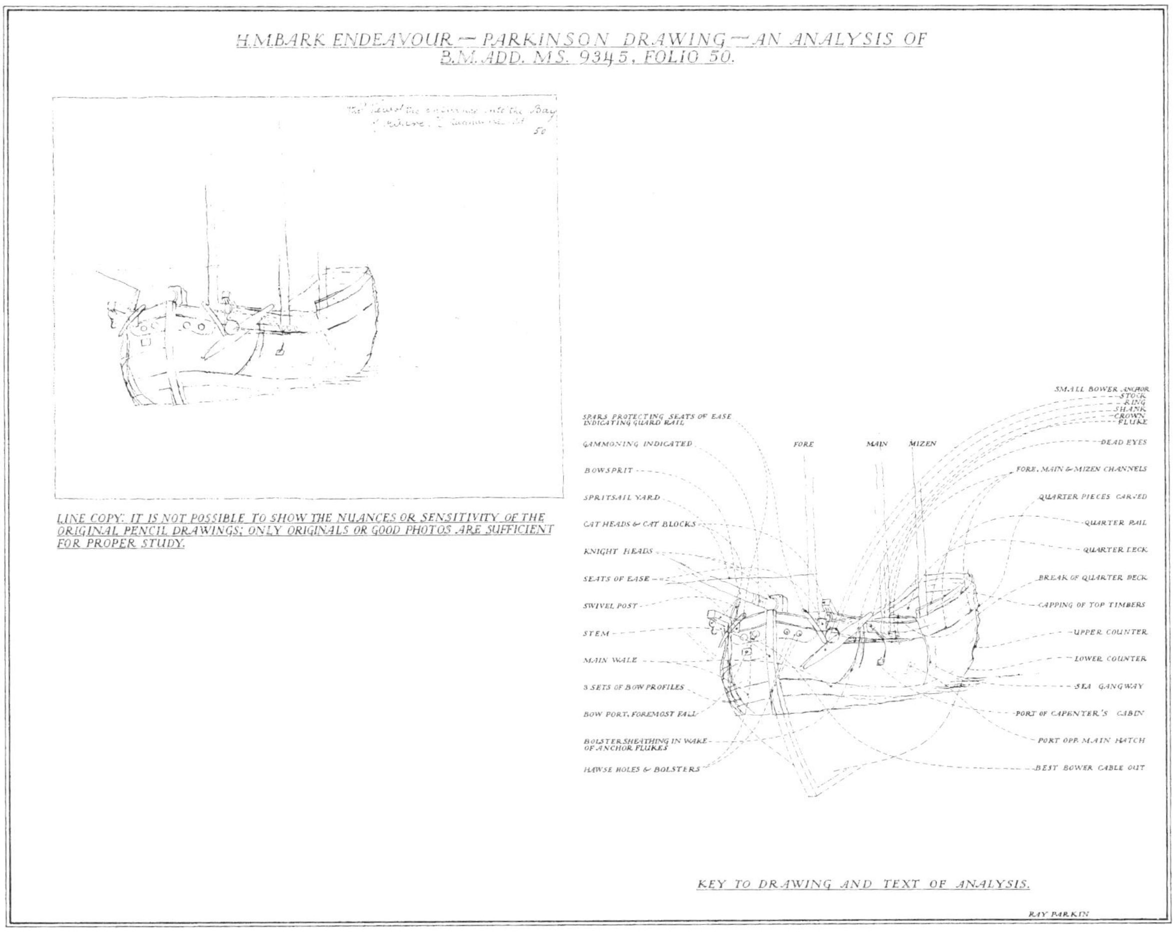

I was particularly concerned with folios 50 and 57, which were views from off the larboard (port) bow and the larboard quarter respectively, for they contained details of the vessel of which these were the only records. Yet they were being ignored in a very studied way: the case was closed. I decided to find what sort of a witness the young Quaker Parkinson could prove himself to be.

For some three years I had been studying these two drawings and already they had yielded me a great deal of information that undeniably refuted previous judgements. But was this merely an uninformed opinion of my own, or was there substance to back it? These drawings are contained in a sketchbook of Parkinson's[13] of some seventy pages. In 1976, I spent a week at the British Library, from opening time to closing time each day, scrutinising these drawings. The effect they had on me was profound: I found in them more than I had ever dreamed to confound the superficial assessments that had been made of folios 50 and 57 (see above and page 17).

Sydney Parkinson had joined *Endeavour* as a botanical draughtsman in the retinue of Joseph Banks. By the time the ship had reached Rio, a bare two and a half months into the voyage, he had completed one hundred finished drawings as well as many other sketches, as he told his brother in a letter. Banks wrote of him, 'In

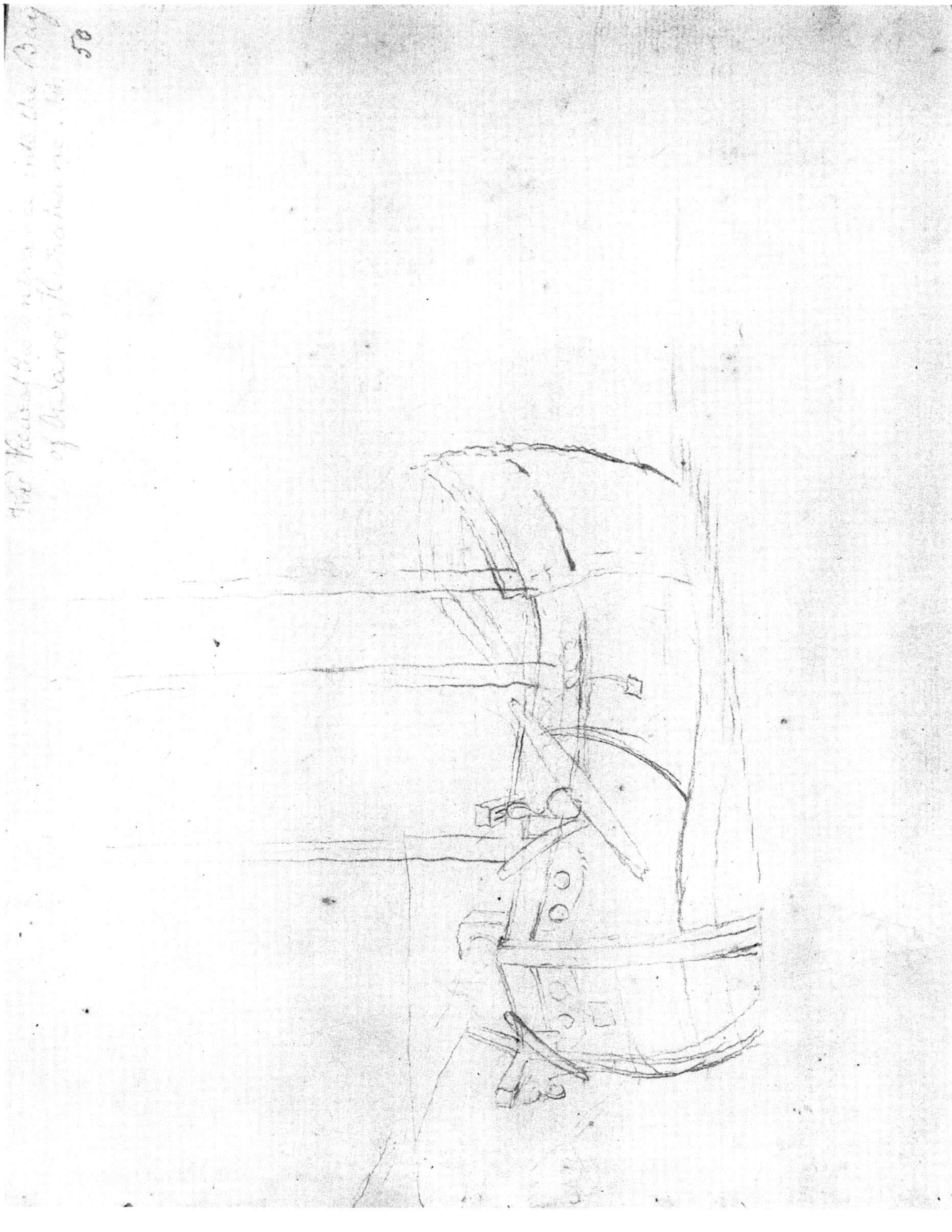

Parkinson, BM9345/f.50

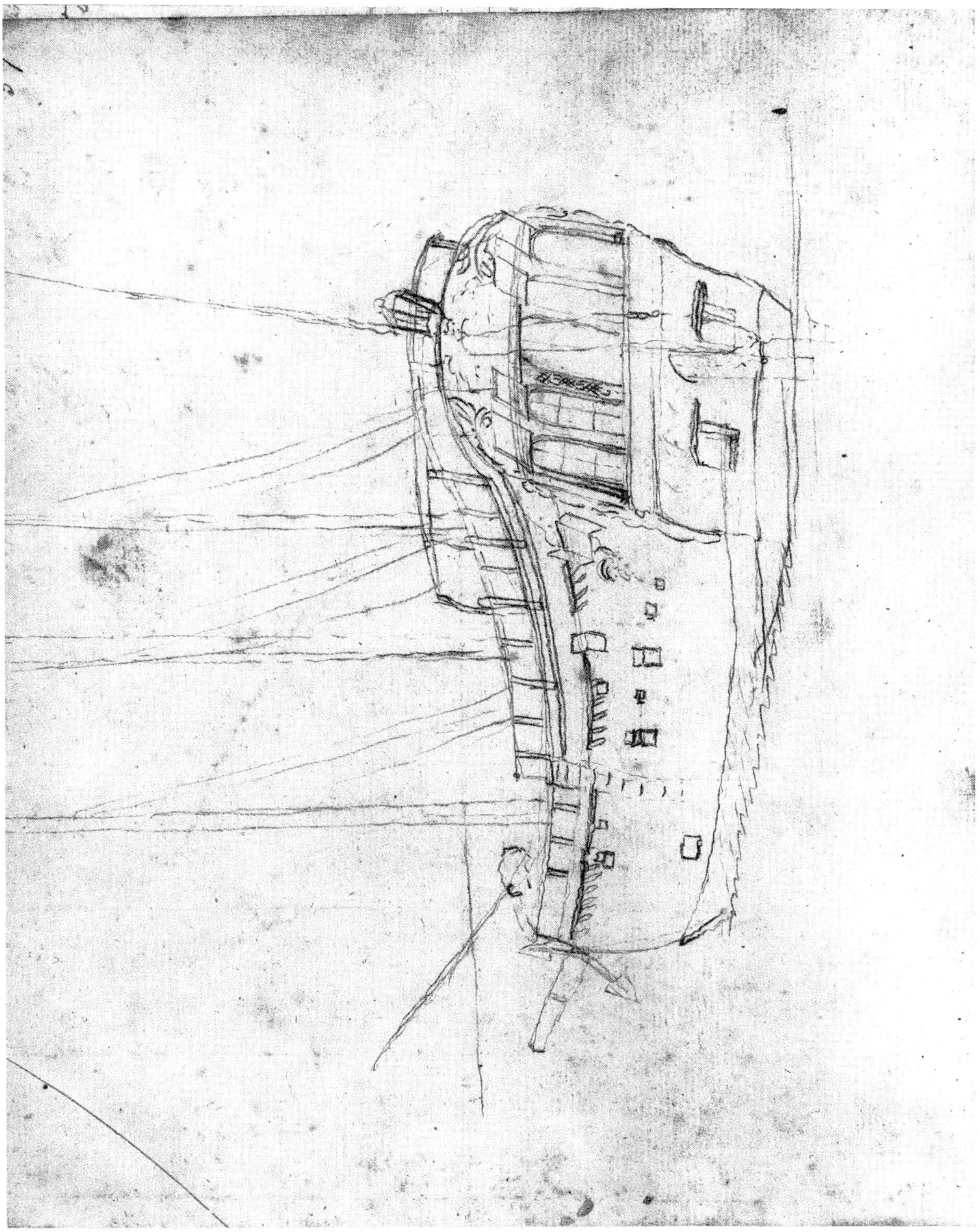

PARKINSON, BM9345/F.57

14 days just, one draughtsman has made 94 sketch drawings, so quick a hand has he acquired by use.' Parkinson's sketchbook shows his personal and wider interests, beyond mere botanical draughtsmanship, indicating a lively, intelligent and enquiring mind.

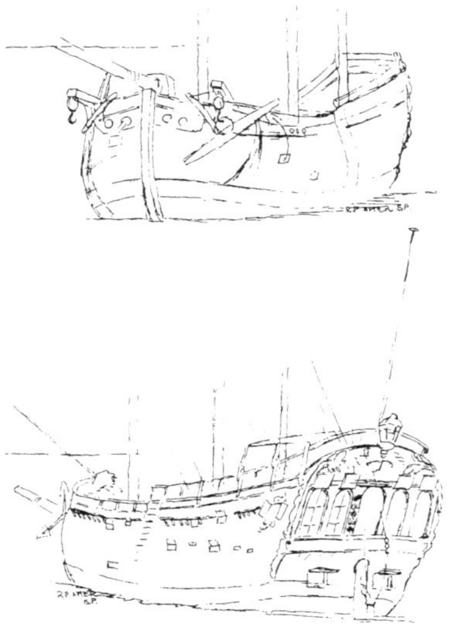

DRAWINGS AFTER SYDNEY PARKINSON'S NOTATION SKETCHES OF H.M. BARK *ENDEAVOUR*, SHOWN HERE TOGETHER TO DEMONSTRATE THEIR COMPLEMENTARY NATURE.

Sydney's brother Stanfield Parkinson, into whose hands the journals survived, wrote in the preface to the 1773 edition, *A Journal of a Voyage to the South Seas*:

> His recommendation being so effectually confirmed by these proofs of ingenuity and industry, Joseph Banks made him the proposal of going in the capacity of botanical draughtsman, on the then intended voyage to the South-seas. An insatiable curiosity for such researches prevailed over every consideration of danger, that reasonably suggested itself, as the necessary attendant of so long, so perilous, and, to my poor brother, so fatal a voyage . . . And here let me be indulged in the spontaneous effusions of a heart still affected with the loss of a loving and beloved brother, while I declare how I have heard many of the surviving companions of this amiable young man dwell with pleasure on the relation of his singular simplicity of conduct, his sincere regard for truth, his ardent thirst after knowledge, his indefatigable industry to obtain it, and his generous disposition in freely communicating, with the most friendly participation, to others, that information which perhaps none but himself could have obtained.

Far from mere brotherly effusion, this judgement is amply supported by other sources. This does not sound like a man who would allow the vanity of artistic licence to override his dedication to truth. As for 'poor drawing', it is hard indeed to explain to some people that drawing is an understanding of *form* and has nothing to do with 'prettiness', 'tidiness' or 'finish', for not one of these things can hide bad drawing even though they may beguile the viewer. As a botanical draughtsman Parkinson had that acute observation necessary to untangle confused pattern and structure and render it clearly, with the exotic as with the familiar.

The sketchbook that contains his ship and boat sketches has many others as well, all set down with an immediacy and penetration that are still valid today. There is no trace of that European vision here which would push everything into its own mould. Here the vision is fresh, with a childlike freedom from any preconceptions, showing the artist's direct empathy with his subjects. Nowhere do these sketches become slick or stylised. A nervous ingenuous line tentatively feels for that link of understanding with the subject. This sketchbook, like the sketchbooks of all artists of integrity, is probably the most personal and intimate communication Parkinson ever makes, for here he is communing with himself and recording those

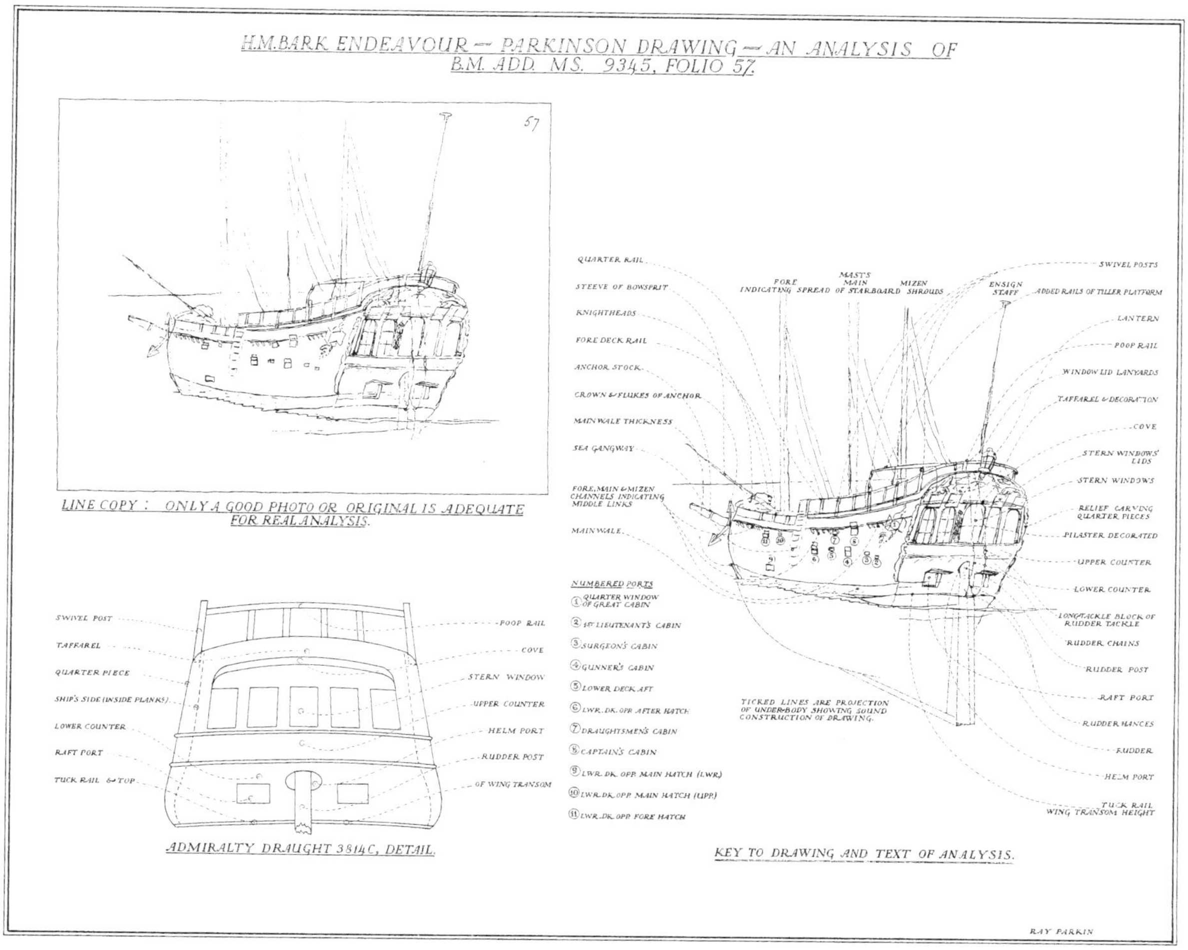

thoughts as he goes, self-confessing and unselfconscious. Such a personalised calligraphy has to be understood before the sketch may be deciphered and what is *not* drawn be appreciated. The images are the artist's notes, his mnemonic, his stored memory of an experience that has affected him. We must not mistake their 'unfinished' appearance for 'poor drawing'; nor must we expect them to inform our uninformed glance, for this can be no more than a measure of our own conceit. Without some humility and patience they will yield nothing but the superficial which will be a measure of our *own* understanding. Two things have become clear to me in studying these sketches: they will not yield to our ignorance; and the artist was anything but ignorant of his subject.

But, more narrowly, what of folios 50 and 57? What was Parkinson trying to express through them? Parkinson was an excellent example of the dictum of William James which said 'Let *expression* equal *impression*', for this seemed to be the whole unconscious motivation of the impressionable young man. Parkinson would have been concerned not with great art but with the expression of spontaneous impressions with which this new adventure was so alive. And these two drawings were part of that release, surely. He was in daily contact with the ship and with the men whose livelihood and vocation were ships and the sea. The men and the ship

H.M. BARK ENDEAVOUR.

ELEMENTS USED FOR THE DERIVATION OF THE APPEARANCE AND STRUCTURE OF HER STERN.

PRELIMINARY DRAWINGS PLOTTING UNDERLYING STRUCTURES: BASED ON ADMIRALTY DRAUGHTS.

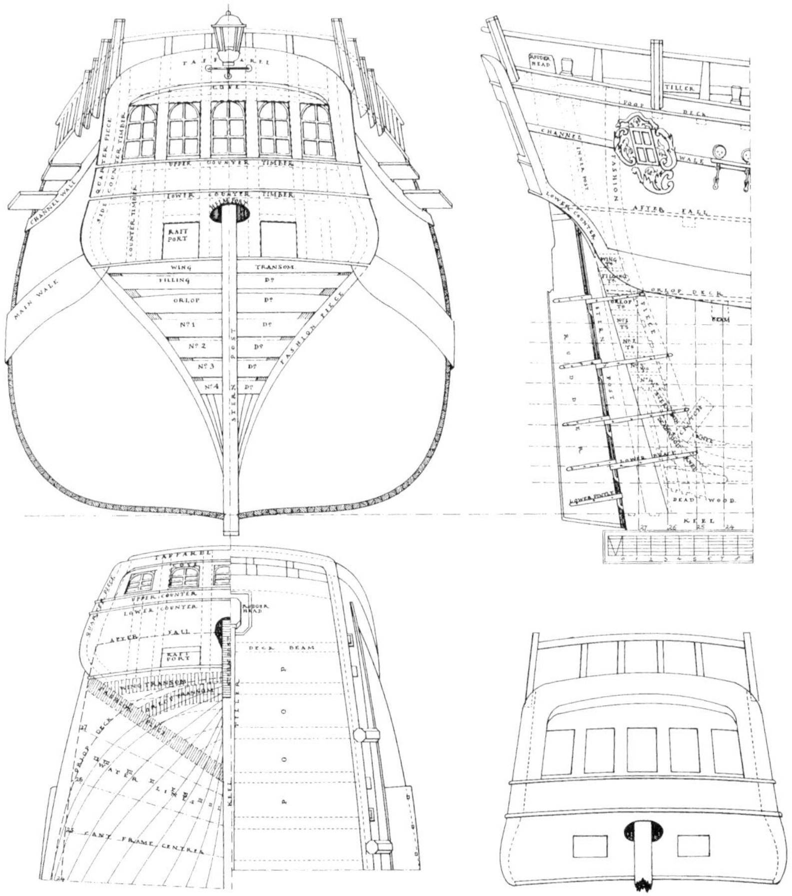

DETAIL OF ADMIRALTY DRAUGHT 3814C.

COPY OF PARKINSON'S DRAWING, BRITISH MUSEUM, ADD. MS. 9345, FOL. 57. THIS IS THE MOST COMPLETE PIECE OF KNOWN CONTEMPORARY SURVIVING EVIDENCE OF THE ACTUAL APPEARANCE OF ENDEAVOUR'S STERN.

STERN BOARD OF AMERICAN WHALER EUNICE H. ADAMS WHICH SHEWS CONCISE DETAIL OF TAFFAREL CARVING SUGGESTED IN THE PARKINSON DRAWING ABOVE.

RAY PARKIN

in action all around him were his daily norm, giving him the same conditioned reflexes to all the changing circumstance. His journal shows this clearly, as does his eager participation in it whenever he could. In Rio, with the shore guard boat lying off the ship day and night, he could slip out through the stern raft ports with the others into the boat beneath the counter, to cast off and drift silently with the tide until beyond notice. Mixed with a curiosity for research was also a boyish readiness for adventure. Later they would get back to the ship equally unnoticed. He was on the voyage of his life, and fully aware of it, with a youthful zest to lap up everything that came his way. He knew the ship and her company in a close, testing association for almost three years. I suggest that he must have known more about the ship and her men than all the historians who have ever written about her. What such credentials can the detractors of these two drawings bring to support their singular claims? I could find none, and I used these drawings as prime evidence for reconstruction—in spite of one seemingly unanswerable contradiction of Parkinson which appears in no less a place than on ship's draught ADM. 3814c—the only one to give an aspect of *Endeavour*'s stern. I could not see how this *could* be wrong, yet, for reasons I have just explained, my predeliction remained towards Parkinson. It will emerge later just how this turned out.

A problem on which I spent more than three years was to try to determine the actual appearance of *Endeavour*'s stern. This really boiled down to a resolution of the marked differences between 3814c and Parkinson.

From their positions in the sketchbook, the bow and stern drawings cannot be seen together. It was not until I got my photocopies of them that I could compare them side by side. I was immediately struck by their complementary inseparability. I doubt that anyone had realised this before, because, for my copy of the bow view, a negative had to be made, which indicated that it had not previously been closely examined. Thus I saw these as a deliberate effort on Parkinson's part to record for himself the significant details of the ship that was his home, and to which he had applied the same curiosity and interest as he had to his botanical subjects. From my own experience it seemed to me that he had made these while in a boat (the shore being too far from a ship at anchor) stationed just far enough off to avoid sharp and distorting perspective from such a low eye-level. I thought that he made the stern view first, then, realising what else he needed to note, shifted to the bow to get it. He would seem to have made this decision on the spur of the moment, as this bow view is superimposed over another lightly drawn sketch with the title 'The View of the Entrance into the Bay of Aware', as if done in a hurry. Sparse though these drawings may appear, there are deft touches of notation born of underlying knowledge such as is seen in the work of the Van de Veldes (elder and younger) before him, and in Turner after him. And it is possibly this very element in the drawings that has caused them to be so misjudged. It was only as I learned more about eighteenth-century seamanship and shipbuilding practices that they began to speak to me—but then only in proportion to my knowledge. Yet all this peroration would be pointless if it could not deliver the goods.

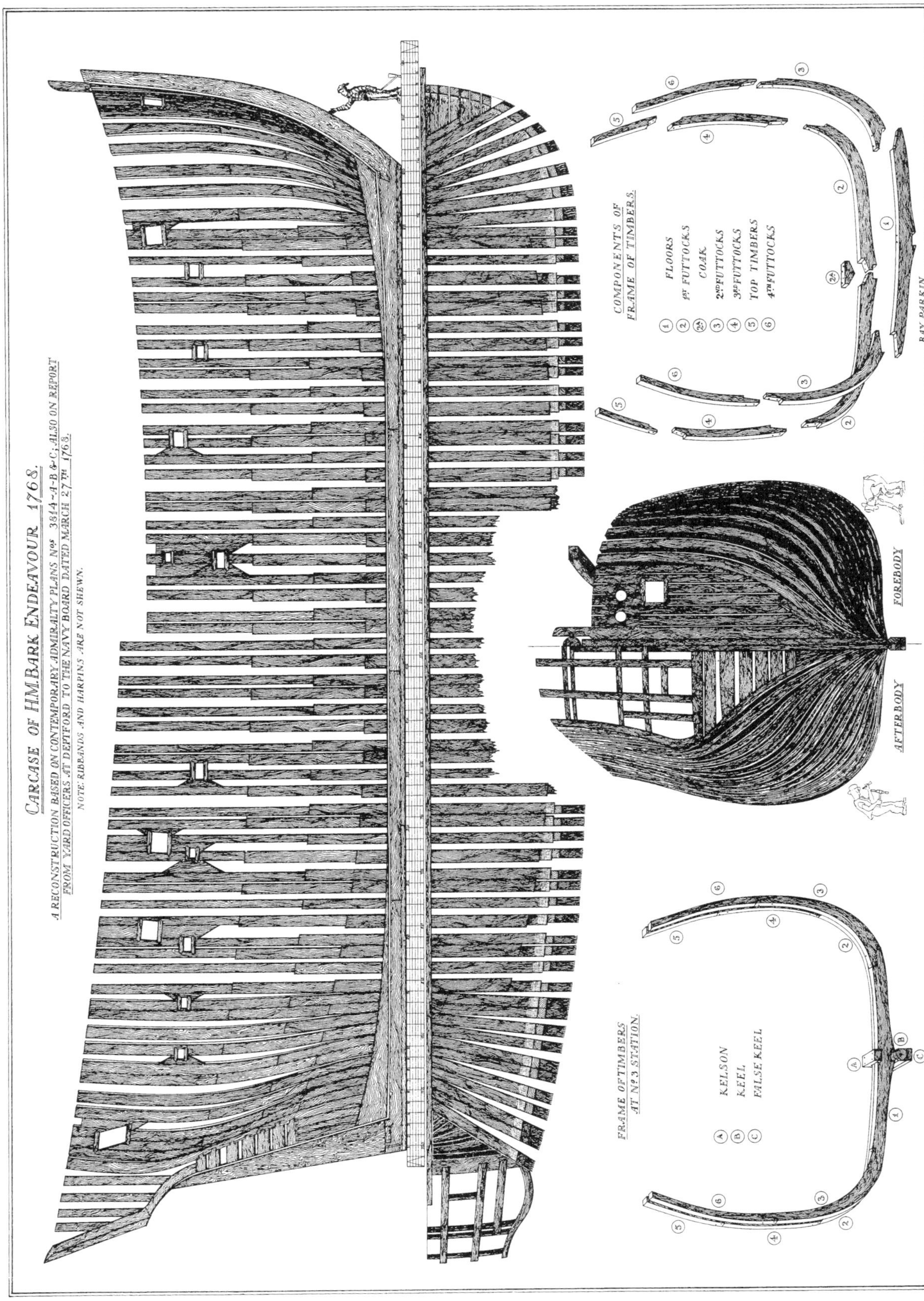
CARCASE OF H.M.BARK ENDEAVOUR 1768.
A RECONSTRUCTION BASED ON CONTEMPORARY ADMIRALTY PLANS Nos 3814-A-B & C; ALSO ON REPORT FROM YARD OFFICERS AT DEPTFORD TO THE NAVY BOARD DATED MARCH 27TH 1768.
NOTE: RIBBANDS AND HARPINS ARE NOT SHEWN.
COMPONENTS OF FRAME OF TIMBERS.
1 FLOORS
2 1st FUTTOCKS
2A COAK
3 2nd FUTTOCKS
4 3rd FUTTOCKS
5 TOP TIMBERS
6 4th FUTTOCKS
FOREBODY
AFTERBODY
FRAME OF TIMBERS AT No 3 STATION.
A KELSON
B KEEL
C FALSE KEEL
RAY PARKIN

First, concerning the real appearance of *Endeavour*'s stern . . . Parkinson shows the stern windows to be tall, with rounded tops; 3814c shows them shorter with square tops. This, I suspect, brought the accusation of 'artistic licence' on Parkinson. What I wanted to know was whether these round-topped windows would in fact fit within the structure of the ship's framework. There was only one way to find out, and that was to reconstruct the whole skeleton of the carcase of the vessel (see page 20). This, though involved, I managed, thanks to the draughts combined with that letter of detailed dimensions which the Deptford Yard Officers had sent to Navy Board in March 1768. The round-topped windows fitted perfectly. Also, it must be remembered that Parkinson worked continually at the table in the Great Cabin under the light of those very windows, so he literally knew them inside out. There was one other point that might have explained the difference in 3814c: draughts did not always indicate the final appearance as the craftsmen often applied their own 'finish' to the basics, and this was especially true of the carvings (which often were not shown at all). There was another point, however, which showed in favour of Parkinson and against 3814c. It concerned the raft ports in the stern. In the 3814c detail these ports are shown as rectangular—2′ 6″ (2 feet 6 inches) wide and 1′ 5″ deep. Parkinson shows them square. The Deptford Yard Officers make them 2′ 7½″ wide by 2′ 8″ deep—virtually square. Besides this, the practice with these ports is always to have the sills on the *wing transom* so that logs and spars, which they are designed to take into the ship (the hatches being too small), are loaded with a solid sill to support them. Now 3814c, at 1′ 5″ deep, is above the wing transom; if extended down to, it would be 2′ 8″. Here the 'irrefutable' was proven wrong, and Parkinson right. I then went ahead and reconstructed the stern according to Parkinson (see pages 18 and 22).

If we take each of these drawings separately we can see what positive information they do contain. First, I have found by exhaustive experiment that no amount of 'fairing' or 'prettying-up' can improve the basic drawing. Also, there is something of the character of the vessel in the drawings. Furthermore, they will stand up to two rigorous tests. A projection of each below the waterline develops an underbody most agreeable to the draughts; and a series of drawings may be made, as I have done, upon which to erect masts, spars, rigging and sails in a variety of settings—and this without one line of the drawings being unduly modified. Finally, the ensign staff and the underbody come close to actual scale in a way that is remarkable in such a free drawing (see page 17).

The drawing from off the port bow is executed with an amazing economy, yet it includes all significant information subtly but precisely (see pages 13 and 24). What looks like a tangle of lines on the profile of the starboard bow holds a particular insight. This is a very critical observation angle, because any minute change in it will alter the profile appreciably. So these lines show the ship not as tide-rode but swinging gently this way or that to the catspaws of wind fanning the surface of the sea. And here Parkinson has given us three valid sets of lines: the position and limits of the spritsail yard are shown by a single horizontal line; the stive of the bowsprit

HIS MAJESTY'S BARK ENDEAVOUR

THE STERN

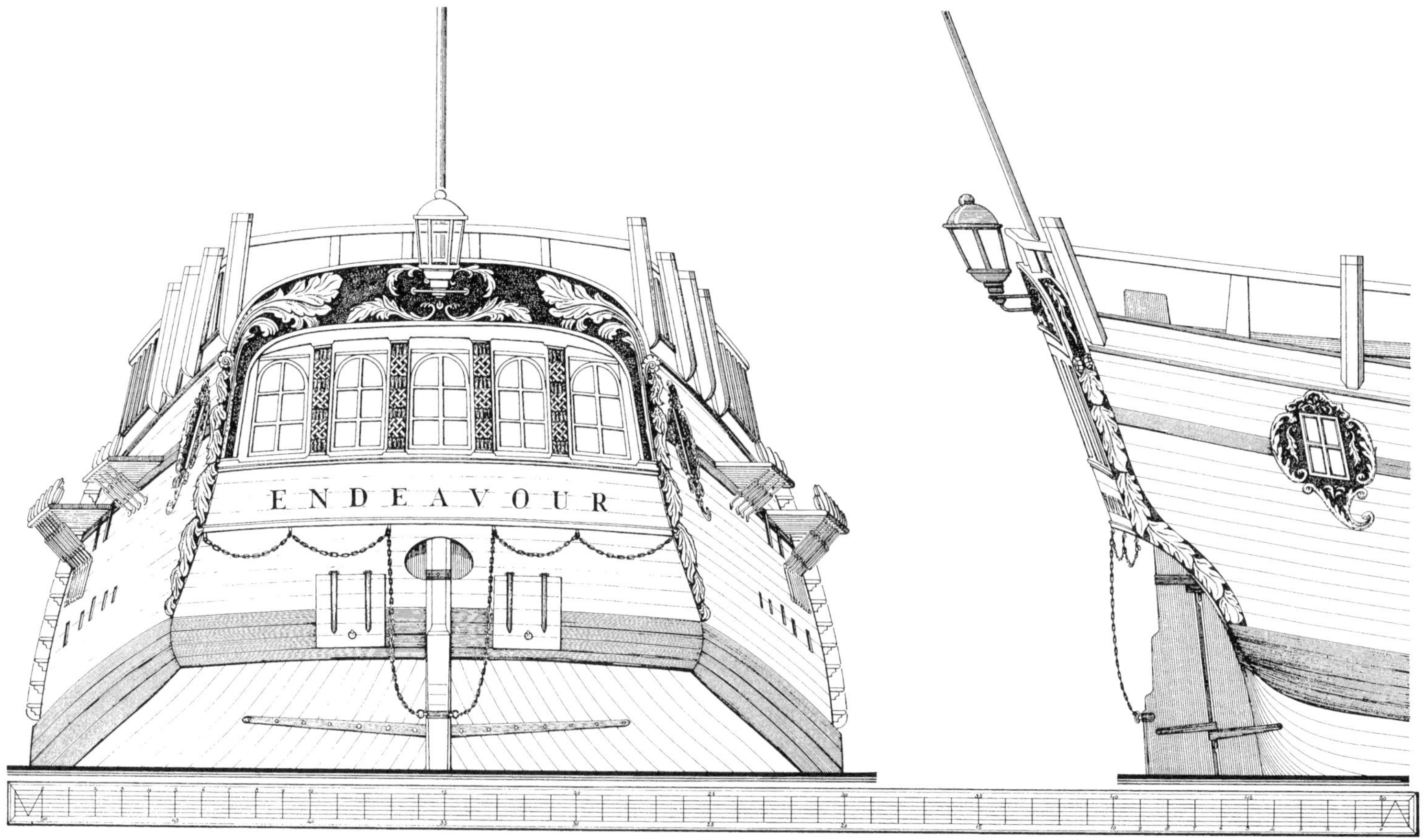

A RECONSTRUCTION BASED ON: ADMIRALTY DRAUGHT 3814 C, 1768; PARKINSON DRAWINGS 1769, B.M., ADD. MS 9345, FOLIOS 57 &-15V; DEPTFORD YARD OFFICERS' REPORT MARCH 27, 1768; EUNICE H. ADAMS' STERNBOARD.

RAY PARKIN

is clear and there are two double ticks near its heel to indicate the position of the gammoning which bowses it down to the stem; and two ticks at the starboard inner hawse hole are sufficient to mark the size and direction of the best bower cable without confusing or obscuring any other detail, and tell us that the ship *is* at anchor. The profile of the stern at this angle seems little more than a scribble, but a closer look shows the carved quarter pieces clearly indicated, and the precise position of the upper and lower counters. The mast positions and diameters are clearly shown, with the three channels which take their lower shrouds indicated by darkened accents on the channel wale. The knightheads, which have received 'artistic licence' in many renditions I have seen, are here shown just as they were at the heel of the bowsprit. The swivel post just abaft the starboard cathead, with its octagonal section, is clear. The sea gangway is shown by two parallel lines which give the contour of the hull there at the same time. The quarter rails and the capping of the top timbers are there. The break of the quarterdeck, and the proportions of the stem . . . all there. But there is much more.

Now concerning the ports which were cut into the ship . . . Not one draught shows them all, so that an aggregate must be totalled from various sources. Nor do the draughts show which ports had lids and which had dead-lights. Yet these two humble sketches do! Elsewhere, we are not shown where the ship's heads (latrines) are. But they are clearly identified in Parkinson's bow view by two vertical lines descending from just before the catheads on either side, and connected at the bottom by a ragged line. This represents the canvas cylinders below the circular hole of the seats, designed (very practically) to circumvent the up-draughts off the bows, especially if the weather side had to be used. There are also two spars nailed to the hull at an angle on the forward side of the platforms with a lifeline/guardrail running to the cathead for the safety of the occupant during devotions.

Nowhere else but in these drawings do we get a look at the ship's anchors. Though Parkinson drew them ashore with the ship careened at Endeavour River, his drawing has been lost and we are left only with what the engravers have made of it. The result is somewhat banal when compared with the liveliness of the original sketches. But in both these drawings we have excellent details of an anchor—the small bower. It is almost as if this particular anchor was destined for history, not only in picture but in fact. It was this very anchor which had to be cut away to a full cable at Endeavour Reef in June 1770. And it was this anchor which, on 28 December 1971, was recovered from under five feet of sand after two hundred years, giving us the real thing to compare with Parkinson's drawing of it. Having had the opportunity to handle, take detailed measurements and make scale drawings of it, I have become reasonably familiar with this anchor. When I examined the drawings and took comparative measurements, I was again amazed at the precision in this apparently casual sketch. The bow view is full of information on the anchor work of the ship. The anchor is hanging by the ring from the cat hook of the cat block. The cathead clearly shows two sheaves, so we see that the anchors of a ton and a quarter each were worked with two-fold purchases. The crown of the anchor is triced up to a

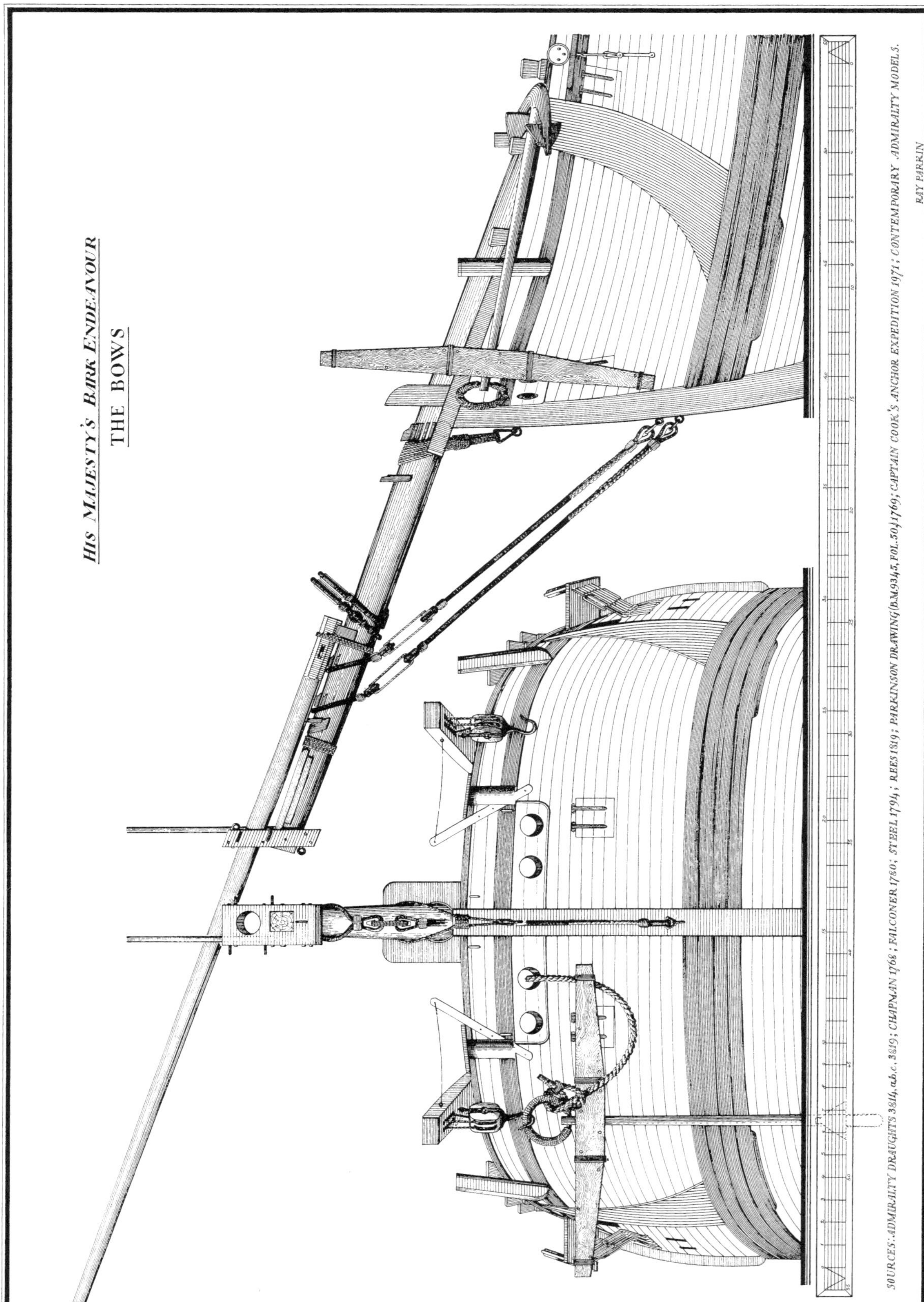
HIS MAJESTY'S BARK ENDEAVOUR
THE BOWS
SOURCES: ADMIRALTY DRAUGHTS 3814, a.b.c. 3819; CHAPMAN 1768; FALCONER 1780; STEEL 1794; REES 1819; PARKINSON DRAWING (B.M.9345, FOL.50) 1769; CAPTAIN COOK'S ANCHOR EXPEDITION 1971; CONTEMPORARY ADMIRALTY MODELS.
RAY PARKIN

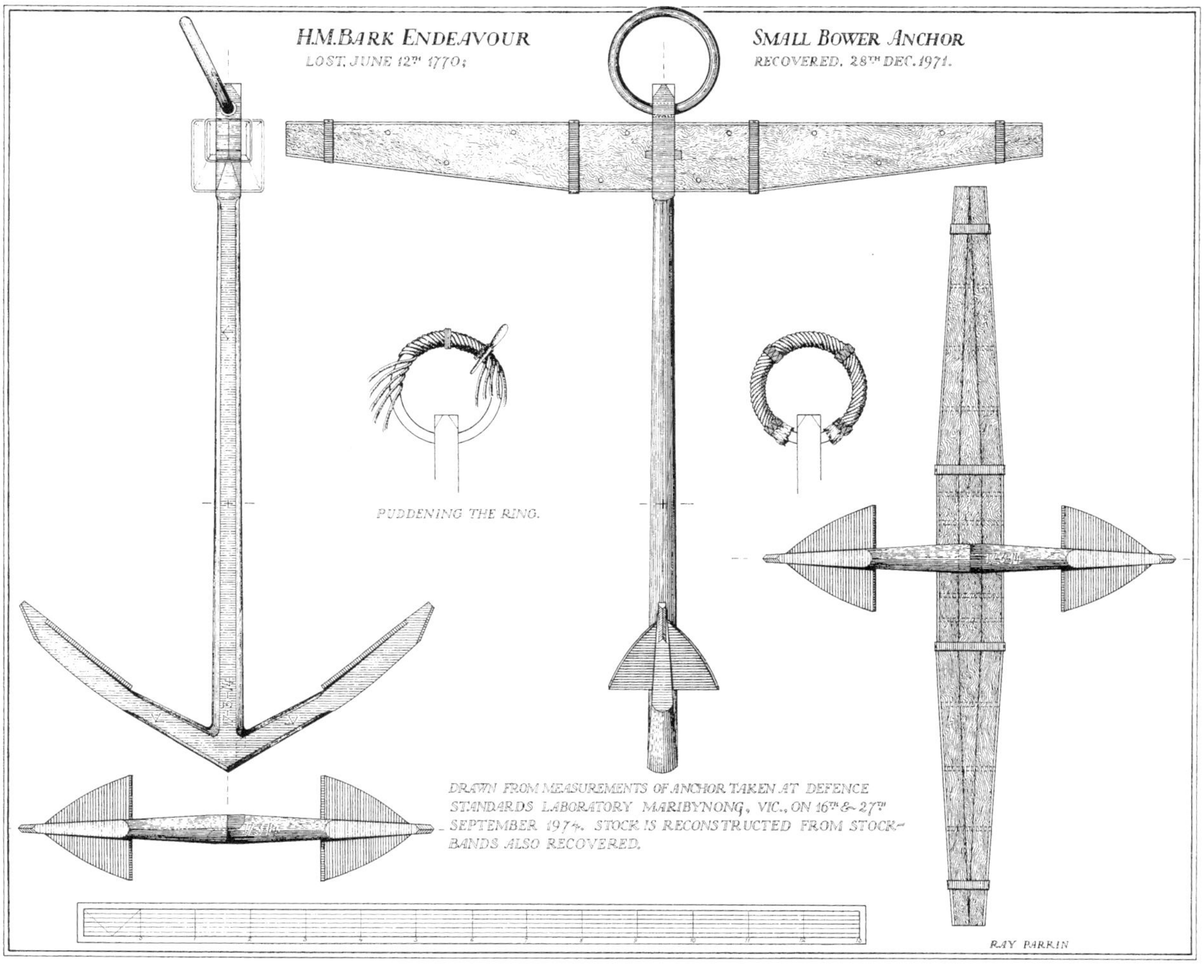

timberhead at the fore-end of the forechains. When this is lowered the ship's side is protected from bruising by the anchor flukes with a panch of timber nailed in the quadrant of their wake. This too is shown here, but nowhere else has it been recorded. We can see the bolsters outside the hawse holes to give the cable a fairer lead to prevent undue nip and chafe. The main wale shows the sheer of the vessel as it intersects the waterline and gives an excellent idea of her 'seat' in the water. All this is there, within the economy of these lines, for those with eyes to see.

The drawing of the stern, like the other, does not leave out one significant detail. Furthermore, it contains information that is nowhere else recorded—and I am afraid that *this* is what the uninformed have called 'artistic licence'. For instance, we are shown the stern lantern and the braces by which it was secured to the taffarel; we are shown the carving of the pilasters between the stern windows, as well as the divisions of panes in those windows and the lids which protected them in bad weather; we are shown the decorative carving of the taffarel, and the carving on the nine-inch-square quarter-pieces; we are shown the ensign staff with its truck in accurate length; we are shown the extra rails which had to be added when the platform was built over the tiller 'for the convenience of the Gentlemen'; and, as has already been mentioned, we are shown which ports had deadlights and which had lids. Of these, one in particular is of interest: the quarter window surrounded by the decorative quarterbadge. This quarterbadge was quite often put on vessels purely as a decoration, as a dummy. Nowhere on the plans is it shown as a penetration through the hull, so that it may fairly be thought to be merely a decoration. But here it is shown with lids, indicating that there was an opening to protect. Further, the lids are carefully observed, for the window's rhomboid shape requires that one lid hinges up and one downward, as is shown. That this is indeed a window is confirmed in Banks's journal when he records how, off the north of New Zealand in heavy weather, they were shipping water through the windows. Also, as evidence of Parkinson's acute observations, there are the little loops he shows immediately below the channels of the rigging. This is the correct aspect of the middle link of the three-link system of the chains securing the shrouds.

Parkinson's knowledge of his subject as selector of the significant is indicated in a nice illustration by a small squiggle which I doubt that anyone has noticed for what it is. We see the rudder pendants unrove and hanging idly from the stern rail above the tafferel down to where they are secured to the rudder hance. Just where the starboard one crosses the lower counter are two little loops and a hook, somewhat like a pair of spectacles. One day their significance dawned on me. This was the long-tackle block of the rudder tackle. This was a specialised block whose use is apparent only to the seamanship-minded. The rudder tackles were rove so that the rudder might still be worked if the tiller should break. They led from the rudder hance to the mizen chains on either side of the Quarter Deck with the hauling parts leading in to the deck where they were manned. If this system had a normal two-fold block with its sheaves side by side, with the tight lead there would be a danger that the block would capsize and choke itself, and be unworkable, putting the ship in extreme danger. But the long-tackle block that Parkinson indicates puts the two sheaves *in line* so that they cannot capsize, thus averting the danger. And this indeed was one of the specified uses for the long-tackle block.

Plainly, in these drawings, Parkinson was intelligently aware of his subject and knew it, he had a keen interest in it and he was able to transfer his observations adequately to paper. On these grounds I consider that he has provided absolutely reliable evidence. For my purposes his drawings have been paramount to any final resolution of *Endeavour*'s living appearance.

And finally a footnote . . . While I was studying the sketchbook at the British Library, I was introduced to Dr Helen Wallis of the Map Room because of her great professional interest in the Cook voyages. By this time—1976—I had completed most of my reconstructions of the hull and had them with me. On seeing these, Dr Wallis said, 'I think you should meet George Naish of the Greenwich Maritime Museum. He would be most interested.' So I met him in his office at Greenwich. He had been Keeper of Ships there for twenty-seven years, and was a noted maritime antiquarian as well as being one of the most helpful and friendly men that I have met. I explained to him the seeming contradiction between Parkinson and 3814c with its apparent authority, and I showed him my redrawing of it. He said that he did not know that plan. Straightaway he took me over to the Plan Room where the Admiralty draughts were. He had the keeper produce the plan and with it spread before us he asked, 'What can you tell us about this one?' The keeper told us that, from internal evidence, this was not one of the original plans but a nineteenth-century reconstruction; and that it looked so much more complete because it had been a collation of all the others, with the *addition* of the draughtsman's own reconstruction of the aspect of the stern. Though the draughtsman had undoubtedly done this in good faith it was plain that two vital pieces of evidence had escaped him. For it was apparent from his raft ports that he had seen neither the letter from the Deptford Yard Officers to Navy Board nor Parkinson's drawings, or else he had dismissed them. But, perhaps more importantly, he had not seen the ship herself, while Parkinson had. My last doubt had been dispelled by a lucky chance meeting.

~ THE BOATS ~

There are no contemporary plans or detailed descriptions of *Endeavour*'s boats. Such information as I have been able to uncover is contained in the logs and journals of the voyage, as well as on the five pages of Parkinson's sketchbook.[14] The Admiralty draughts of the ship helped me deduce the length of the boats from the stowage available for them.

Boat-handling was a common theme in the logs and journals, and what was practical and what was not became apparent. This, backed up by my own experience, caused me to question what others had given as their estimation of the sizes of the longboat, pinnace and yawl—an estimation made apparently on the assumption that the boats would have to be stowed on the booms. (The booms were two sets of gallows arms, one set at the break of the poop and the other twenty-three feet forward of it. *Booms* was the term used because all spare masts and spars and booms were stowed there.) So the boats had been thought to be at least twenty-three feet in length. My first objection to this was that, if a boat of that length had been so stowed, its bows would have been right over the galley funnel, the heat of which would have harmed the boat's planking. In fact, the boats were stowed not on the booms but on the main hatch. Now if these boats, at the lengths given, had been stowed there they would have blocked off the fore hatch which was the crew's only access to their quarters—the distance from the break of the poop to the fore hatch being a bare nineteen feet. The stowage of the larger boats on the main hatch, and of the yawl on the quarter deck, is made plain quite often in the logs and journals. A further obstacle to stowing the boats on the booms was that this would have raised the ship's centre of gravity too much. That balance was critical is demonstrated by Molyneux, the Master, in his log when he writes that, as the fresh water was emptied from the casks in the hold, it was replaced with salt water so that the ship would not become 'crank' (unstable). As well, if the boats had been stowed nested on the booms (as was the case in the three models built for Australia,

Great Britain and New Zealand) this would have required that a large gore be cut out of the foot of the main course to clear them, unduly reducing the sail area. There was one further point about these other reconstructions of the boats: they had all been made carvel-built—that is, with the planks butted into a smooth skin. However, every one of Parkinson's sketches of the boats shows them as clinker-built—that is, with overlapping planks like a weatherboard house.

On 12 April 1768, a Navy Board Warrant was issued: 'Long boat, pinnace and yawl to be built by Mr Burr for the Endeavour Bark.'[15] And this is the only official communication we have of the boats themselves. The Naval Dockyards built their own boats, but only carvel-built ones. The fact that the *Endeavour* boats were contracted out at least hints at a difference. I do not know whether Mr Burr was a Deal boatbuilder, but Deal was the home of clinker-built boats in England, so it is possible. There was also a good reason for the differing choice of clinker-built: the ship would be spending much time on coasts in exploration, so the boats would be in for long bouts of arduous work, and this build had a strength–weight ratio much better than carvel. And, for me, Parkinson was incontrovertible evidence. Therefore I was obliged to reject previous estimates and begin to make my own.

At first it seemed that the space available for stowage would make the boats unduly small. Could a longboat (so exaggerated in popular conception) be practical at eighteen feet or so? She had to be able to carry out an anchor. *Endeavour*'s small, best and sheet anchors were all, including the heavy oaken stocks, some twenty-five hundredweight. Could she carry sufficient water when watering ship?

I discovered that, in 1761, a new scale of boats for smaller vessels was laid down in which sloops were given longboats of between 16 and 19 feet. This made it evident that boats of this size could do the work. A 19′ boat with a beam of 6′ 4″ could carry six hogsheads of water. A hogshead is one-quarter tun (or ten cubic feet), weighing 625 pounds when filled; thus a capacity of six hogsheads is 1½ tun measurement and 1 ton 13 cwt 1 qr 26 lb deadweight. Each anchor was 1 ton 5 cwt 2 qr 16 lb. So this made a smaller boat practical.

In Chapman's *Architectura Navalis Mercatoria*, I found the lines of a longboat of 18′ 1″, pulling four pairs of oars. From these lines I reconstructed a longboat of 18′ overall with a beam of 7′, having a full form and a depth at the sternpost of 3′ 2″. Her capacity would be approximately the same as the 19′ boat.

The pinnace (sometimes called the barge) was a boat the officers used on official occasions, but it was also used in other work. On 11 June 1770, when *Endeavour* had struck on Endeavour Reef, Banks recorded, 'About one AM the water was fallen so low that the pinnace touched ground as she lay under the ship's bows ready to take in an anchor.' This would be the smaller kedge or stream anchor. Her lines were not as full as the longboat and her beam was less. I made her 18′ × 5′ 9″ × 3′ at the sternpost. From Parkinson I knew that she pulled three pairs of oars (see opposite).

The length of the yawl was more open to question. We know that she was a handy seaworthy boat of great utility. While the ship lay in Endeavour River, she went out turtling to the reef regularly, only twice being prevented by bad weather in the

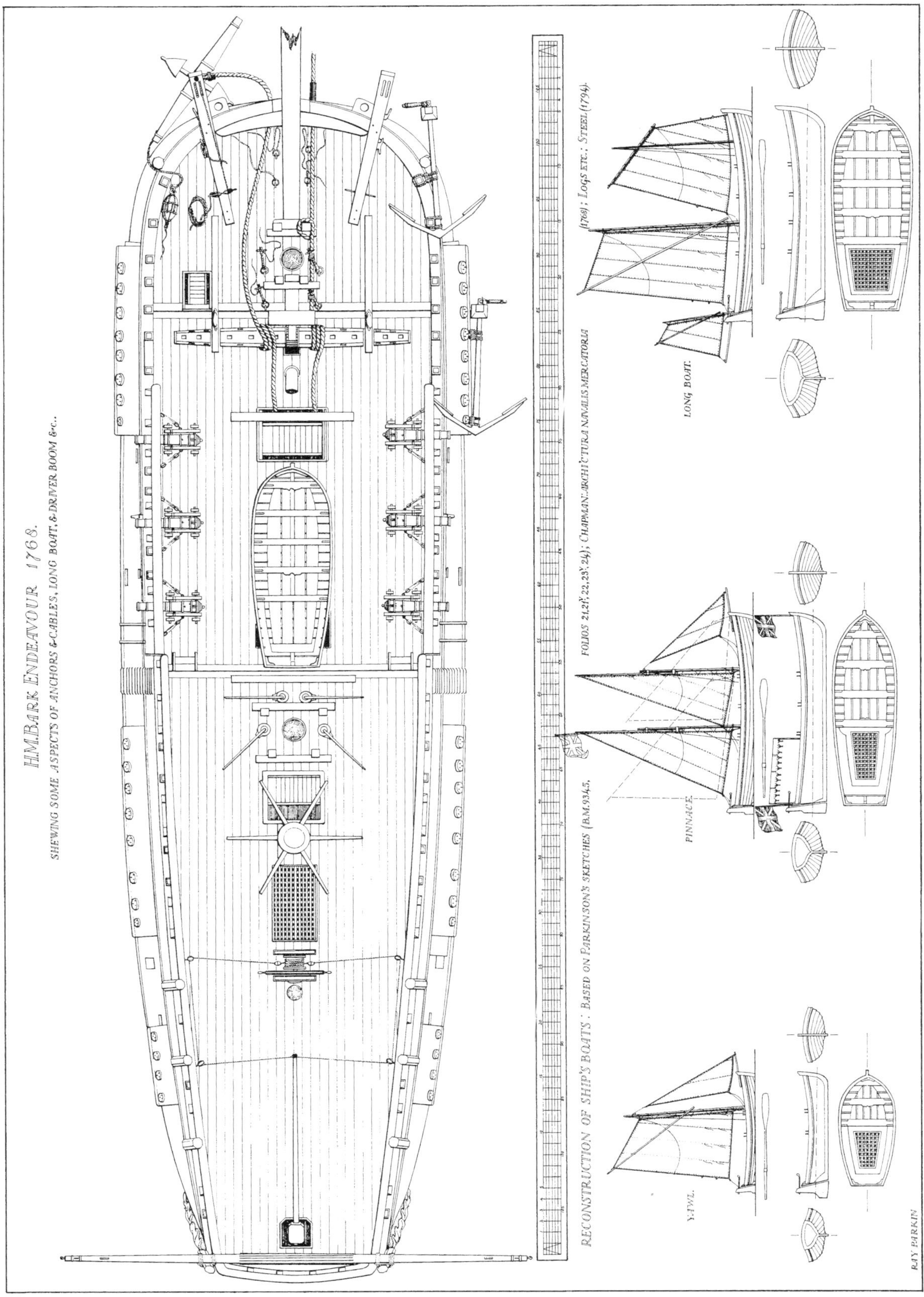
H.M.BARK ENDEAVOUR 1768.
SHEWING SOME ASPECTS OF ANCHORS & CABLES, LONG BOAT, & DRIVER BOOM &c..
RECONSTRUCTION OF SHIP'S BOATS: BASED ON PARKINSON'S SKETCHES (B.M.934.5, FOLIOS 21,21V,22,23,23V,24); CHAPMAN: ARCHITECTURA NAVALIS MERCATORIA (1768); LOGS ETC.; STEEL (1794).
LONG BOAT.
PINNACE.
YAWL.
RAY PARKIN

The yawl (f. 21)

The longboat (f. 21v)

After Sydney Parkinson's action sketches of *Endeavour*'s boats.

season of fresh south-easterlies. My first clue came from Banks in Rio de Janeiro: '. . . we now had no boat onboard but a small 4 oard yawl.' Once again, I was able to find in Chapman a 10-foot yawl pulling two pairs of oars. This seemed to marry well with Banks's description. I made her 10′ × 5′ × 2′ 3″ at the sternpost. There was a specific reason for the smallness of this boat. Cook himself remarks on the importance of a ship carrying a small boat as a necessity for 'trying' the current in the ocean out of sight of land.

The ship also carried two other small boats. One belonged to the boatswain, Mr Gathrey. But, as early as 1 September 1768, by reckoning about 330 miles S, 28° 15′ W from the Lizard, 'Very hard gales which brought us under our two courses . . . washed overboard a small boat belonging to the Boatswain and drowned between 3 or 4 dozen of our poultry which was worst of all . . .' The other small boat belonged to Mr Banks which, one gathers, was not much more than a cockleshell used only in calm weather. She appears to have survived the whole voyage.

There are some interesting remarks in the logs and journals which give us a closer look at the boats.

On 24 May 1769, Cook writes, 'Having found the Long-boat leakey for these few days past we haled her ashore to stop the leakes, when to our great surprize we found her bottom so much eaten by the worms that it was necessary to give her a new one, and all the Carpenters were immidiatly set to work on her.'[16] While Banks writes, '. . . being [found] very leaky was hauld dry and her bottom found to be eat intirly through by the worm, which surprizes us much as Dolphins boats met with no such inconvenience . . . The pinnace which has been in the water as long as her is totaly untouchd which we attribute to hers being painted with white lead and oil.'[17] On the 30th, he records, 'Carpenters employd today in repairing the long boat which is eat in a most wonderfull manner, every part of her bottom is like a honey-comb and some of the holes $\frac{1}{8}$th of an inch in diameter, such a progress has this destructive insect made in six weeks.'[18] Thereafter the logs record, 'Carpenters painting the boats.' So we may assume that the boats were white, though the Parkinson sketches indicate that they also had a black wash strake at the gunwale, as well as square transoms with a full bearing aft.

It may surprise the modern reader, but the establishment (or number) of boats to any ship had nothing at all to do with their life-saving capacity. It was based solely upon the work they had to do. On 11 June 1770, when *Endeavour* struck on the reef and they were about to attempt to haul her back into deep water, Banks writes, 'The most critical part of our distress now aproachd: the ship was almost afloat and every thing ready to get her into deep water but she leakd so fast that with all our pumps we could just keep her free: if (as was probable) she should make more water when hauld off she must sink and we well knew that our boats were not capable of carrying us all ashore, so that some, probably the most of us, must be drownd'.[19]

On 16 August 1770, *Endeavour* was probably in the most critically dramatic situation of her whole career. Becalmed, she was being relentlessly carried on to the outer edge of the Barrier Reef which was steep-to with no bottom able to be reached with 150 fathoms of line, so that there was no hope of checking her with the anchors. The ship was within forty yards (almost thirty-seven metres) of the breakers. Banks wrote:

> Every method had been taken since we first saw our danger to get the boats out in hopes that they might tow us off but it was not yet accomplishd; the Pinnace had had a Plank strippd off her for repair and the longboat under the Booms was lashd and fastned so well from our supposd security that she was not yet got out. Two large Oars or sweeps were got out at the stern ports to pull the ships head round the other way in hopes that might delay till the boats were out. All this while we were approaching and came I beleive before this could be effected within 40 yards of the breaker [this distance—some 36 metres—confirmed by other logs]; the same sea which washd the side of the ship rose in a breaker enormously high the very next time it did rise, so between us and it [Cook writes 'that between us and destruction'] was only a dismal valley the breadth of one wave . . . Now was our case truly desperate, no man I beleive but who gave himself intirely over, a speedy death was all we had to hope for and that from the vastness of the Breakers which must quickly dash the ship all to peices was scarce to be doubted. Other hopes we had none: the boats were in the ship and must be dashed to peices with her and the nearest dry land was 8 or 10 Leagues distant.[20]

They were freakishly delivered, however, by a couple of fortuitous slants of a faint breeze used with superb seamanship by Cook and the assistance of the boats keeping her heading right, and possibly a back current from the sheer wall of the reef itself.

Of this occasion, Alan Villiers writes in his *Captain Cook, the Seamen's Seaman*, '. . . but even with twenty stout men in each of the two best [boats and] The combined pulling power of sixty men in all the boats would not hold the ship . . .'[21] This seems to be an unwarranted and pointless exaggeration ignoring simple facts. To begin with, the Watch Bill could not find that many men to spare from the ship; nor could the boats accommodate them, for sixty men would mean thirty pairs of oars. Parkinson clearly shows the pinnace as pulling just 3 pairs; Banks has clearly stated that the yawl pulled 2 pairs; and Chapman's longboat of this size pulled 4 pairs, making only 9 pairs in all, pulled by 18 men. Now there would seem to be an

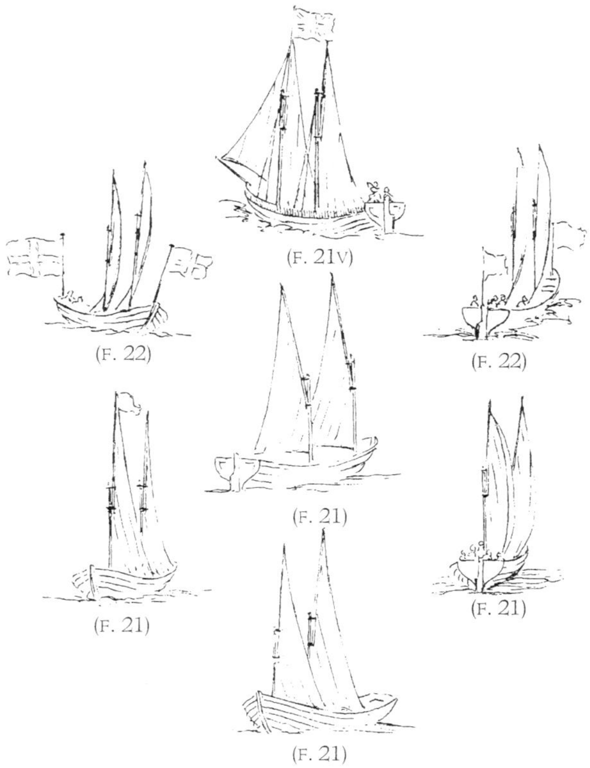

After Sydney Parkinson's action sketches of *Endeavour's* pinnace.

oblique confirmation of this number in the Admiralty instruction to Navy Board on 21 July 1768: 'The Board is to cause twenty Cork Jackets to be purchased and sent on board the Endeavour Bark for the use of the men that it may be necessary to employ in boats in the course of her present intended voyage.'[22]

As an indication of the pinnace's capacity, on 3 September 1770, Banks writes, 'The Captn, Dr Solander and myself with the Boat's crew and my servants, consisting in all of 12 men well armd, went in her [the pinnace] and rowd directly towards the shore [of New Guinea] but could not get nearer than about 200 yards on account of the shallowness of the water . . .'[23] This would mean six boat's crew plus the coxswain; Banks's two servants, Briscoe and Roberts; and the three gentlemen. Briscoe and Roberts would probably be up forward on the unmanned bow thwart, the six crew on the three pulling thwarts, the coxswain on the dickie on the transom quarter, and the three gentlemen in the stern sheets on the benches either side. This would leave seating room there for only another three or four.

At first I found the identification of the boats in Parkinson's boat sketches confusing, but then I discovered folios 23v and 24. As negatives had to be made for my copy of this, it seemed that no one else had been interested enough in it. But, for me, it proved a vital key to the rest of the drawings, for in its foreground there were two studies of what was undoubtedly the pinnace, and the detail contained in them identified this boat in the other drawings. By a process of elimination it was then not difficult to distinguish the longboat from the yawl. Of the yawl there are three and of the longboat only one but this is absolutely clear in its sail plan.

Folios 23v and 24 are a double-page panorama of Rio harbour as evidently seen from the ship at anchor: for all the salient features of the harbour line up in bearings from the anchorage as shown on both Cook's and Molyneux's plans of the harbour. The topography is faint but in the foreground are boat studies. There is a boat with an ensign and a jack flying, under six oars and with an awning spread on stanchions over the sternsheets. In the stern is an officer in cocked hat, and the mainmast is stepped and the sail brailed to the mast. This is undoubtedly the pinnace on her way ashore on official business. The boat is stern to the observer and just to the left of this is another study with the boat end-on and stern-to, showing six oars, the awning and the officer, and the sail unbrailed. With such details I could then identify the pinnace in the other sketches. The top three on folio 22 were certainly the pinnace with ensign and jack being worn, both masts stepped and six oars. On folio 21, the four top sketches are again undoubtedly the pinnace under sail. It shows her to be two-masted and clearly to be a sliding gunter rig—that is, a spar laced to the luff of the sail which slides up when hoisted to form a kind of topmast. At the bottom of this page are two more of her end-on but with a jib or foresail set on a small bowsprit. On folio 21v, at the top, we have two more sketches of this boat with an ensign at the peak. The left-hand one shows the fore and main sliding gunters, and again, the short bowsprit and the jib set. The other shows her lying-to under oars with the sails brailed to the mast. She has an ensign at the peak and only four oars out. The ensign could be a signal to the ship, 'Have found safe anchorage.'

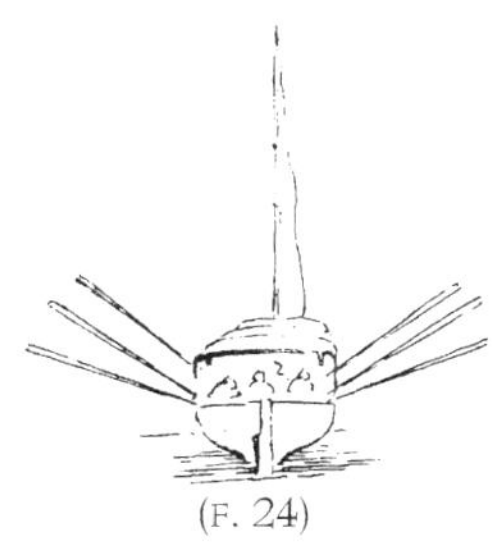

(F. 24)

(F. 24)

(F. 22)

(F. 21V)

PINNACE UNDER *SETEE* RIG (F. 21V)

AFTER SYDNEY PARKINSON'S ACTION SKETCHES OF *ENDEAVOUR*'S PINNACE.

There was one sketch in the centre of folio 21v of a two-masted boat with settee sails. These sails are triangular but with a short fore-leech which makes them quadrilateral. And there is also a 'ghost' of the same boat in the bottom left-hand corner. For years this puzzled me. It could not be the yawl, for she would be unable to step two masts. One day it dawned on me that the settee sails could be set on the same short masts of the pinnace as were the sliding gunters! The settee sail is particularly efficient, especially when lying close to the wind. It would not be unusual for a keen coxswain with a pride in his boat thus to vary the rig for differing circumstances—and good officers were always tolerant and encouraging of such efforts, as I well know from experience. Nowhere else can I find any mention of this variation, and though Parkinson is unique in his recording of it, I am convinced that he only drew what he saw. I find it an intriguing insight into the flexibility and commonsense of their seamanship, unconstricted by hidebound regulation within the practices of the ship. There would seem no doubt that Cook was open to sensible innovation and would always listen to the ideas of others—as he did to Jonathan Munkhouse, one of his midshipmen, for fothering the ship to check the leaks after they had hauled off from Endeavour Reef. Munkhouse had had experience of the same situation in a merchant ship in the West Indies, so Cook put him in charge of the whole operation without once interfering.

The three sketches of the yawl, occupying the centre line of folio 21, are so clear that no doubt can remain of any of her rig: single mast with spritsail, and a small jib set on a short bowsprit.

Likewise, though there is only one drawing of the longboat (the left-hand boat on the centre line of folio 21v), the whole sail plan is perfectly clear. The fullness of her hull is shown by the amount of lee bow showing beyond the stem. She has three masts stepped. The foremast carries a quadrilateral lug sail on a yard with two rows of reef points at the foot of the sail. On the main is a square spritsail with two rows of reef points. And on the small mizenmast stepped on the transom is a spritsail with its sheet led in from the end of a short bumkin out over the stern. This sail is only to balance the boat so that, on the wind, she does not carry too much dangerous weather helm.

From all this and David Steel's proportions in his *Elements of Mastmaking, Sailmaking and Rigging* (1794) I was able to create the hull and sail plans of the boats reproduced on page 29.

Once again Parkinson had supplied the reliable and indispensable key.

~ Rigging and Sail Plans ~

The key to my research into the rigging and sails was a list of dimensions of *Endeavour*'s masts and yards added to the Deck Plan No. 3819, given in yards and inches, and signed by Wm Gray:

Woolwich Yard 16th October 1771

Bark Endeavour

	Masts			Yards		
	Length		Dia.	Length		Dia.
	Yds	Ins	Ins	Yds	Ins	Ins
Main Mast	23	4	21	15	34	13
Topmast	13	19	12	13	15	10 1/8
Gall.^{t} to H..^{ds}	6	10	6	10	20	5 7/8
Pole	3	3				
Fore Mast	21	28	19 3/4	14	26	11 3/4
Topmast	12	28	12	12	1	9
Gal..^{nt} to H..^{ds}	5	26	5 3/4	9	21	5 1/2
Pole	2	27				
Mizon Mast	16	29	14 1/8	8	12	6 1/2
Topmast	8	10	8	10	25	5 1/8
Pole	3	26				
Bowspreet	11	12	19 5/8	12	33	8 1/4
Crossjack yard				13	14	7 3/4
Fly.^{g} Jibb Boom	11	15	9 7/8	10	20	5 5/8

W^{m}. Gray.[24]

Having a positive knowledge of these dimensions allowed a comparison with the tables in Steel's *Elements* for vessels of this size. I found the coincidences almost too

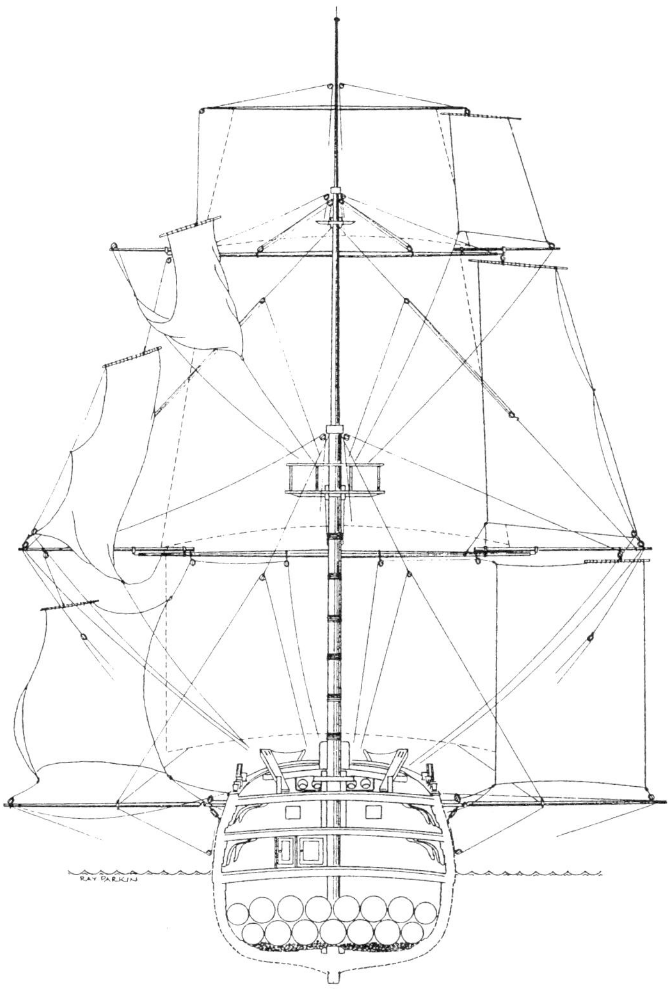

good to be true, there being virtually no difference. On comparing these with Steel for vessels from 360 to 300 tons (*Endeavour* was 366 49/94th tons) I found them so close as to make no real difference. This meant, to me, that *Endeavour* was no freak and that I could rely upon Steel for other information. I went to his 'Table of the dimensions of the standing and running rigging: with the species, size and number, of blocks, hearts, deadeyes, etc.'

Under a column headed 'Ships from 22 to 24 Guns or from 400 to 250 tons' I found, in exhaustive detail, an account of every piece of standing and running rigging. But this was for a naval vessel; how far, if at all, had she been modified from the merchant vessel which she was? I then went to the tables for merchant vessels. The nearest I found was 330 tons, but as the next column was for vessels of 544 tons I felt that the former came well within the requirements of *Endeavour* at 366 tons. Between this table and that for the naval vessel, I found that there was only the most minor of differences in the specifications. So I have taken Steel as my benchmark for this reconstruction (see pages 36–40).

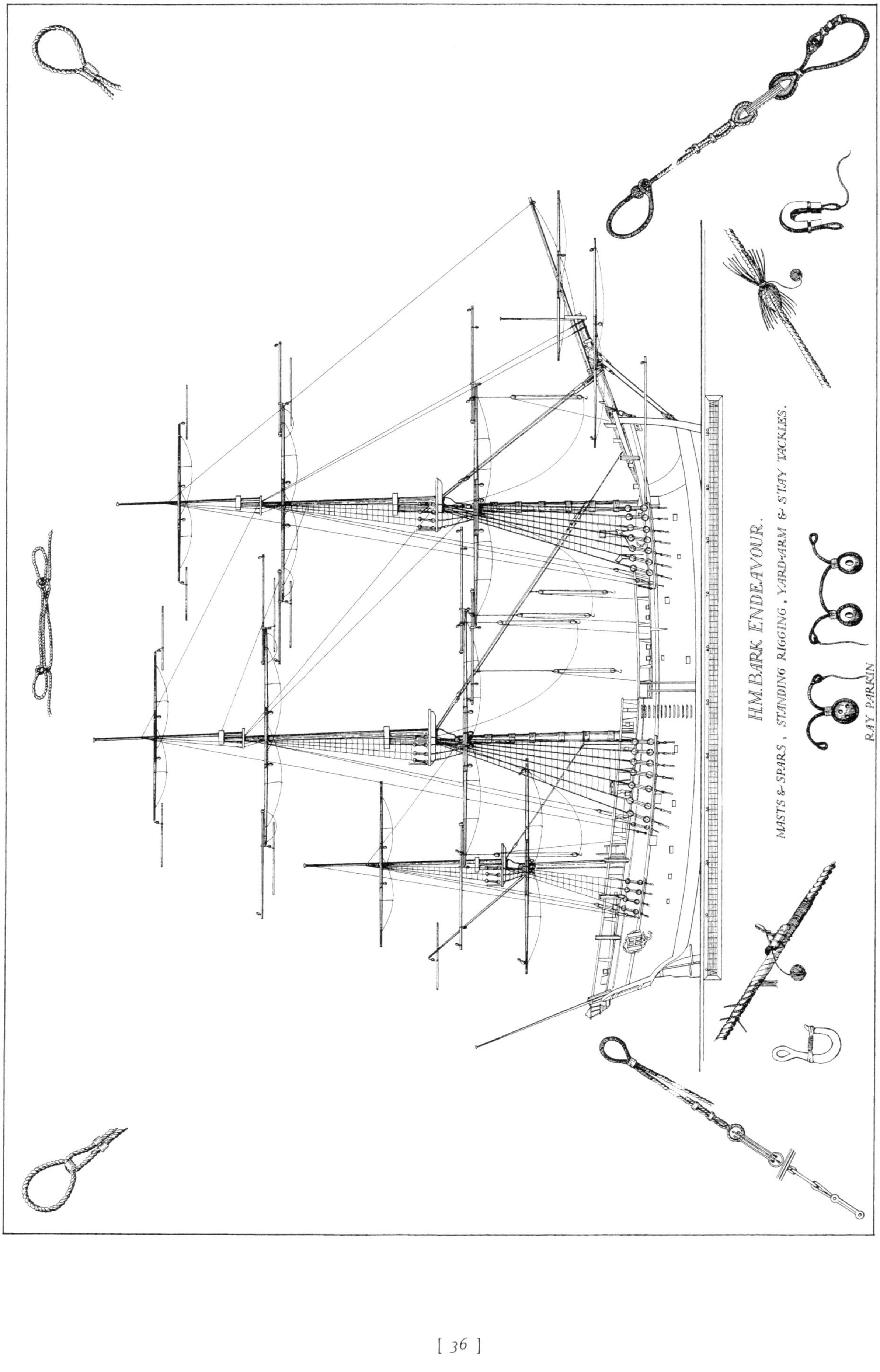
H.M. BARK ENDEAVOUR.
MASTS & SPARS, STANDING RIGGING, YARD-ARM & STAY TACKLES.
RAY PARKIN

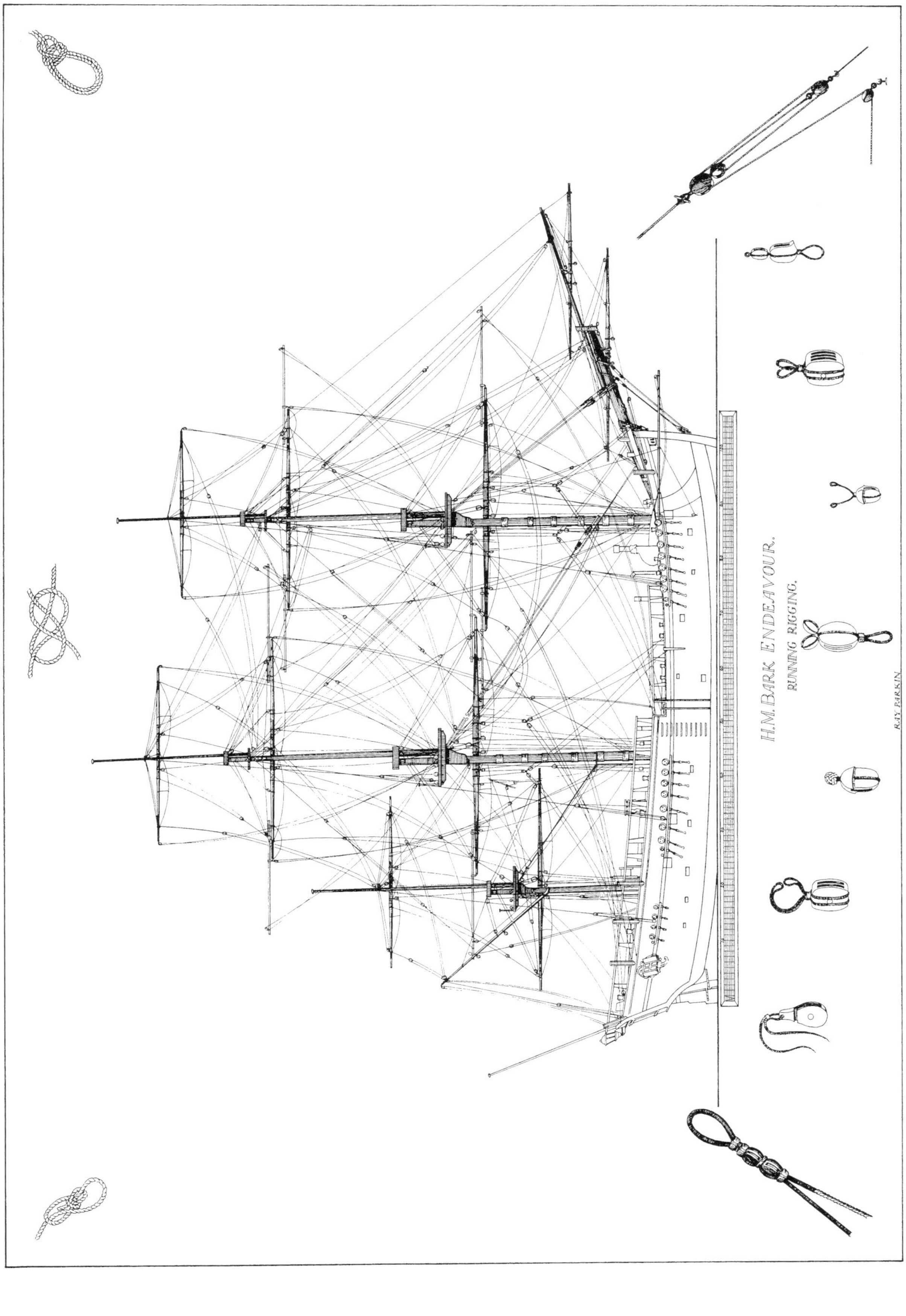
H.M. BARK ENDEAVOUR.
RUNNING RIGGING.
RAY PARKIN

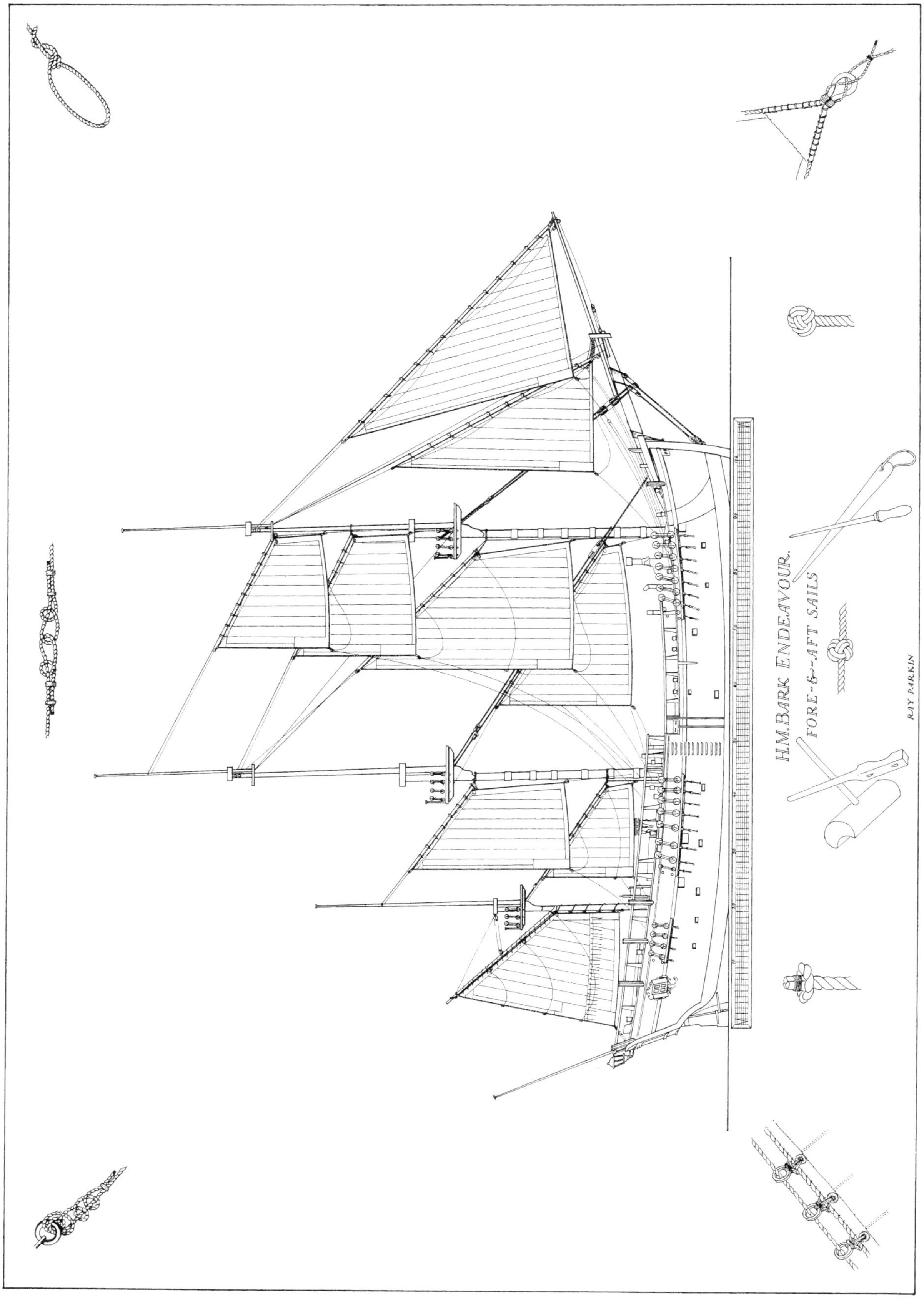
H.M.BARK ENDEAVOUR.
FORE-&-AFT SAILS
RAY PARKIN

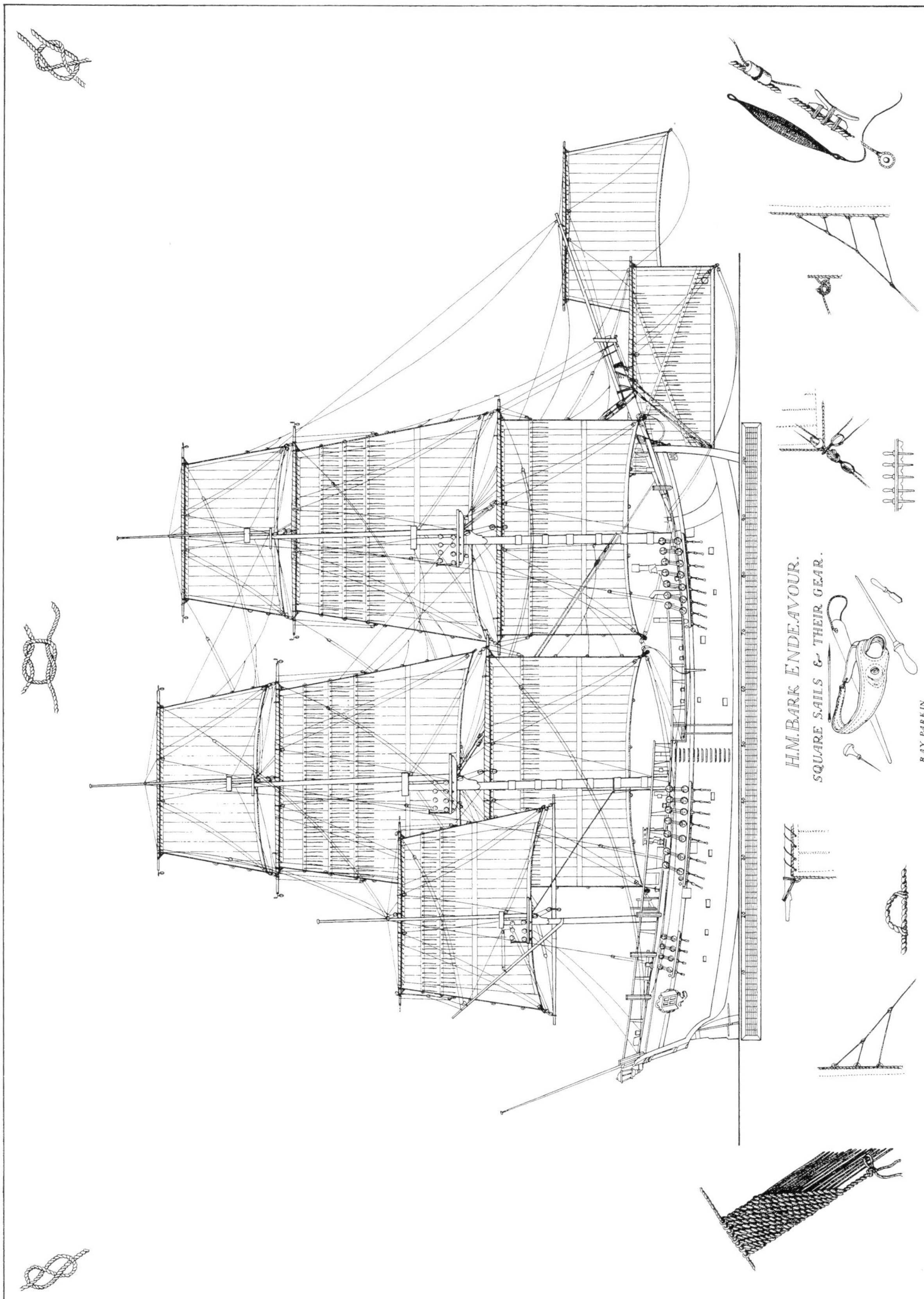
H.M.BARK ENDEAVOUR.
SQUARE SAILS & THEIR GEAR.
RAY PARKIN

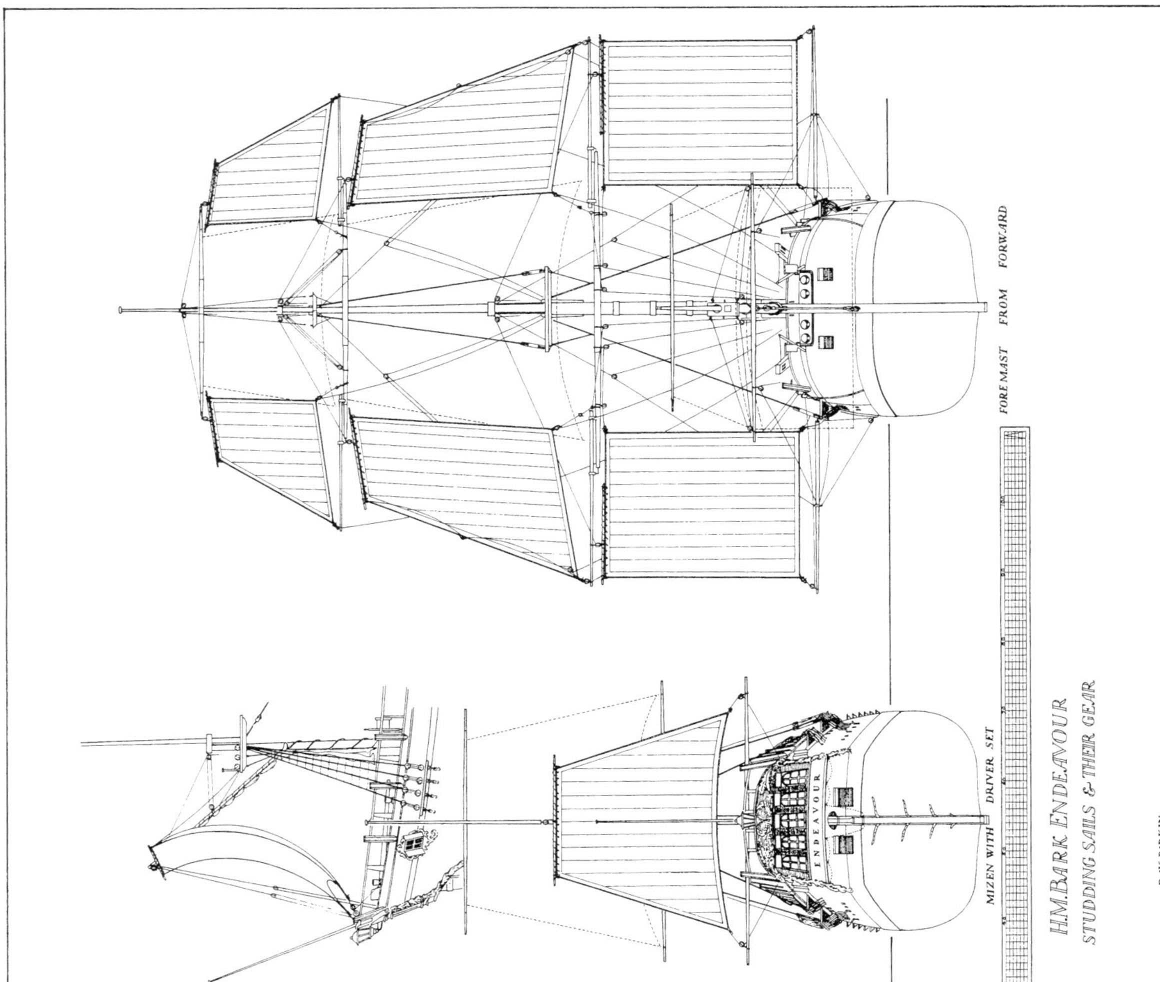
FOREMAST FROM FORWARD
MIZEN WITH DRIVER SET
ENDEAVOUR
MAINMAST FROM AFT
H.M.BARK ENDEAVOUR
STUDDING SAILS & THEIR GEAR
RAY PARKIN

CHAPTER 1
THE SAILOR AND HIS ENVIRONMENT

A first reading of the journals shows us, more than anything, the gaps in our understanding of *Endeavour*'s voyage. If we are to reverse this situation, we first need to know something of the sailor's tools and ways, especially since the quality that Cook brought to the usage of his tools leads one to a contemplation of the tools themselves, out of a curiosity for their real relationship with the men and their times.

Perhaps no tool has ever influenced the user more throughout history than the ship. It is not a hand-held device to be taken up and put down at will. Paradoxically it is a tool by which *the user* is held. It will serve him only in proportion to *his* service to *it*. It sustains the disciple, not only in his normal daily existence, but even to the point where destruction is imminent. The ship can call forth qualities above and beyond the norm. It explores the ultimate in the user and may give him in return a lasting self-respect—or a terrible insight. It may call forth his unsuspected best, or reveal his worst: as if administering the Judgement of Doomsday. Thus, comparatively few men were unaffected by the usage of this tool, whatever the capacity in which they served it. A profound relationship between man and ship is not the least tenable of all psychological propositions.

The sailor had few illusions about life in a ship. He knew it involved hard work, long hours, short broken sleep, small wages and real peril. He could be exposed to gross human cruelty and injustice at the whim of another. This sort of thing, no doubt, led Dr Johnson to prefer gaol to going to sea. Yet, despite all this, the sailor could find that he was not quite stripped of everything. It was in his private and personal relationship with his vessel that he finally found himself with a peculiar selflessness. In this way he found a quality of life unknown and unsuspected by much of the shorebound and pedestrian human race.

The sailor's experience was direct: with the ship and the world in which she swam. The word *soul* has been used with ships; but if the sailor ever used it, he meant *essence*—the distillation of experiences shared. He had no metaphysical intention, for his experiences were physical in the purest sense of dealing with the properties of matter and energy. But there is a world of difference between 'old Tarry Breeks' of the eighteenth century and the modern physicist with his everyday alchemy and technical wizardry. Perhaps the outstanding difference is individuality.

The ship is a mass interaction of complex mathematical formulae. It has volume; spars supporting variable planes at changing angles to variable and capricious forces; rigging to support and compensate for these forces and to convert them into a calculated notion of the vessel herself; above and beneath her the interaction of changing and opposing forces, further modifying the vessel's action. The old sailor calculated this tolerably well—yet it seems to call forth no wonder in us, beguiled as we are by the immaculate conception of the modern computer—which, after all, is not even as complex as the humble worm.

Two hundred years ago in the Bark *Endeavour*, these rag-wrapped, parent-begotten human computers would go aloft on dark nights to take in or make sail; they would stand on the gyrating deck and divine the state of the all-but-invisible sails and rigging complex and make swift sure decisions. Within the labyrinth of the mind they sensed relations and reactions between the ship and the sea, anticipated crises and how best she would live. In all this the sailor was being attuned to the forces of which, for him, the ship was the centre. He became ever more sensitive. On the darkest nights he felt, through the soles of his mostly bare feet, or through his hands-grip's changing grasp aloft, the roll, scend and pitch of the whole fabric. Last instant, this instant, the next instant—these plotted an intuitive graph within him that became a usable rhythm. Just as he knew where to scratch himself accurately in the dark, so he developed this wider proprioceptive sense about the ship herself. The tension on a rope, the spring of a spar, the creak of a block, the heel of the ship, the wind in his face, its tune in the rigging, the signs of the sea and sky, the centrifugal force on deck or aloft as the stars flew by—all this, and more, flowed through him. He watched endless seas approach, lift, and run under the ship; or break and swirl and scatter onboard. He watched the march of cloud, rain, hail, snow; moving sea-mountains or still sea-plains. He sensed the wind as if he saw it. All within his horizon fed into him. It affected his senses until he knew and knew not that he knew. Then, and then only, was his intuition well-served and able to serve him well. His computer was fully programmed.

So, as the forces played about the ship and on her, reaction became predictable and there was a feeling of rightness even in a desperate situation. It was not so much that he gave the ship a soul, but that he felt in her the distilled essence of all this experience which gave to it a sublimating unity. This insight was the thing the sailor could not be stripped of. But, as sailor Herman Melville wrote in *Moby Dick*: 'Wonderfullest things are ever the unmentionable; deep memories yield no epitaphs.'

The sailor could see this incommunicable world of his in contrast to the profane one to which he was outwardly chained but from which he was released by this insight. He was able to see in just proportion. He learned to accept the inevitable and, more importantly, to recognise it. He could objectively perceive circumstance. Simple directness nurtured the sensitivity to proper intuitive function: that of being intelligent without being intellectual. And all the while he remained essentially of this world.

There is a conception that the sea is a living force, a personality, a demon, a fickle She of malicious whimsy making sport of men in their brave defiance of her. But man is ever the self-justifying animal who has to compensate for his inadequate acceptance of reality with transference and fatal inventions of his own. The sailor, by experience, knows that the sea is no more and no less than he is himself. Left to itself without sun, moon, wind or earthquake, the sea would be still. The air, but for changing heat and pressure, would be calm. But with change it is made gale, storm, hurricane and so on. It does not matter what you call these forces in some subjective self-assumed drama to be acted out to the bitter end—it can only be futile. Sheer defiance of wind and sea is in vain. Many sailors over many hundreds of years, without ever arguing it, have known this simple fact: that the sea, the ship and the wind are not in conflict but are merely trying to live together under common circumstance. This is not to argue a fine philosophical point; it is choosing between sanity and megalomania. The sea smashing against the ship is as much smashed against by the ship; the wind howling through the rigging is powerless to do otherwise, and may just as well be howling in anguish as in anger. The sea, the air, and the ship are only seeking equilibrium.

The sailor sees his job within the ship as continuing to live with the elements without declaring war on them; not to be insensible to prime causes; not to lay indiscriminate blame. He recognises self-pity as fatal.

On the morning of 19 August 1768, when *Endeavour* was almost ready to sail from Plymouth, Cook wrote:

> Read to the Ships Company the articles of War and the Act of Parliament, they likewise were paid two Months Wages in advance. I also told them that they were not to expect any additional pay for the performance of our intended Voyage [as had some other ships previously] they were well satisfied and express'd a great chearfullness and readyness to prosecute the Voyage.[1]

This 'readyness' was in full realisation of the work they would have to do, which is more constant and diverse than a landsman may readily appreciate. But the work is done with such involvement that, though still hard, it is also a psychological salvation. The ship of this period was often alluded to as a 'noble fabric' (though not necessarily by the sailor) and, like any fabric, she needed maintenance and attention. Looking up through her web of rigging she may have looked most complex; yet, basically, she was astonishingly simple. Except for a minimum of iron, she was made wholly of trees and grass. The hull, masts and spars were of wood, and the rigging and sails of grass. This was little more or no more than early humans used for their first shelters. And it meant that the sailor, with his bare hands, could maintain her.

It may be thought that the rigging was neatly spliced into place and there it stayed for a 'full-due', to use a sailor's phrase. But, with rigging made of grass, this was not so. Splices, except for joining, were quite few. Hempen rope shrinks and stretches with wet and dry and constant strain, so that it has to be continually set up. Because of this, it was not spliced, but secured by bends and hitches and seizings which could be readily cast off and remade. The strain of a whole mast and sails upon the rigging of a rolling ship was very great, and set up movement which caused not only strain but chafe at critical points. Movement, strain and chafe were everywhere, demanding supervision and anticipation at all times.

Replacement and repair were not a simple matter of going to the boatswain's store, cutting off a piece of rope, and installing it in place of the defective stuff. Rope for the standing and running rigging, as well as the cables for the anchors, came readymade in coils. For the two bower anchors and the sheet anchor, seven cables were supplied, each 13½" in circumference[2] by 120 fathoms.[3] For the kedge and stream anchors, which are smaller, there were 5" and 6" hawsers. The sails, however, came with a lot of work still to be done before they could be bent to the yards and set. This meant that a multitude of things had to be made and fitted by sailors themselves, and all of this handmade stuff had constantly to be overhauled and mended—one might almost say, with the frequency of a darned sock. The safety of both men and material depended upon its good condition.

All of this most essential stuff was made from 'junk': lengths of condemned cable cut out as it wore and chafed. The word *junk* would seem to come from the Latin *juncus*: a rush, perhaps signifying rope returned to its original fibre. This was issued to ships, like any new stores, and had to be signed for. Shortage of junk in a ship on a long voyage could place the vessel in very serious jeopardy for want of vital replacements. (This was the case with *Swallow*, a ship still struggling round the world even as *Endeavour* was fitting out.[4])

There is a difference between cable and rope (see opposite). Cable is *cable-laid*, ordinary rope *hawser-laid*. Rope is made by being laid (twisted) in stages: the *fibres* are spun into *yarns*; several yarns are laid into a *strand*; and several (usually three) strands are laid into a *rope*—said to be hawser-laid. A cable-laid rope is then made by laying three or four hawser-laid ropes into one. This kind of rope was used for the lower shrouds and the larger fore-stays of the ship. The cables of a line-of-battle ship could be twenty-five inches around and contain 2,500 yarns. Although cables as supplied were 120 fathoms long, to make them thus the initial yarns had to be 200 fathoms long. Each of *Endeavour*'s 13½" cables contained 954 yarns, weighed 2 tons 5 cwt 2 qr, and had a breaking strain of around 55½ tons. They were preserved with Stockholm tar.

Without the yarn from the junk, the sails would have been useless. They came to the ship from the sail loft only as bare canvas ringed with their bolt ropes and fitted

H.M.BARK ENDEAVOUR — HER BOWER CABLES
BOWER CABLE : LIFE SIZE
THREE-STRAND HAWSER-LAID ROPE
STRAND OF 106 YARNS
YARN
HEMP FIBRE
INCHES
1 2 3 4 5 6 7 8 9 10 11
METHODS OF 'LAYING PLATTS' : PROTECTING THE CABLES
POINTING
WORMING
KECKLING
ROUNDING
LEGEND
SHIP SUPPLIED WITH SEVEN CABLES EACH 13½ INCHES CIRCUMFERENCE, 120 FATHOMS (720 FEET) IN LENGTH, COMPOSED OF 954 YARNS EACH 200 FATHOMS OF RUSSIAN HEMP TARRED WITH GOOD STOCKHOLM TAR, AND WEIGHING 2 TONS 5 CWT. 2 QRS. : BREAKING STRAIN 55½ TONS APPROX (UNTARRED). TARRING WEAKENS ROPE BY ABOUT ONE-TENTH; ONE-QUARTER OF ORIGINAL WEIGHT IS OF TAR.
THIS RECONSTRUCTION BASED ON 'ENDEAVOUR' LOGS; FALCONER 1771, 1815; STEEL 1794; RÖDING 1793-8; REES 1819.
RAY PARKIN

with no more than the cringles of the earings, clews, reef bands and bowline bridles. There was nothing to fasten them to the yards with, nothing to secure them when furled, and no reef points to reduce the sail area in heavy weather. All of these things had to be made onboard from yarn plaited into various multiple plaits called sennit. Rope bands, known colloquially by the sailor as robands, robbens or robins, were plaited to fasten the head of the sails to the yards. To secure the sails to the yards when furled, longer plaits called gaskets were made and fixed to the yards. When the sails were set, these were coiled up and thrown over the foreside of the sails. The reef points were put in rows across the sails where strengthening strips were sewn. The topsails had three rows, except the mizen which had only two; the courses (fore and main) each had one row. These points were plaits tapered from the middle to the ends and were long enough to tie round the yard and the sail which they partially bundled up when it was reefed. They were pushed through eyelets in the reef bands, middled, and knotted on each side of the sail. When reefing was required, the sail was hauled up to the yard by a tackle in the reef earing on the leech of the sail, while the men went up onto the yard, hauled the sail to the yard by the reef points and secured them there with a reef knot.

Yarn was the most important thing to come from junk, but what was unfit for re-use was teased out to make oakum. To tease this out properly by hand is a tedious job—enough to make a tough man weep—and, ashore, it was a job given to convicts and paupers. Men confined onboard as offenders also had it given to them as a task of so many pounds a day to be unpicked. Oakum was used for caulking the plank seams before they were payed with pitch. It was also used as stuffing where a padding was required; and, because of the content of Stockholm tar, to put between one's toes to help heal painful sea cracks.

The junk was first reduced to strands which were then unlaid to yarns. This required a special knack, developed only with much practice, to stop the yarn untwisting and falling apart or else writhing into a hopeless mess of kinks alluded to by the sailor as a 'bunch of bastards'. The various lengths of yarn were then knotted together with a cunning little knot, called a rope-yarn knot, which is half-splice, half-knot—it makes a join that will lay nicely if necessary. The joined yarn, known as spunyarn, was rolled into balls for later disposal.

As needle and thread were to the housewife, so was spunyarn to the sailor. Three or four balls were laid out on deck where there was enough space. A simple rotating spindle was fastened to some convenient place in the rigging and the ends of the yarn attached to a spoke in it. The spinner would walk back to a suitable distance and, holding the yarns clear in his hands, twirl them over rapidly to the left. This action served to spin the winch and twist the yarns firmly together with a tension opposite to that in the yarns, which had been twisted in the opposite direction. The spinner would then walk to the winch, wind the completed part on and hitch it afresh for the next twirl. This was repeated until all the yarn was spun. Spunyarn in the hands of a sailor felt as comforting to him as a rosary in the hands of a monk.

Spunyarn was also used to 'serve', or bind over closely, those parts of the rigging subject to chafe. This used enormous quantities. To take but one example: the foremost lower shrouds, or mast stays, on each mast were served over their whole length of some 38'. First, they were *wormed*—that is, the 'cuntlines' (grooves between the strands) were filled with spunyarn; then this was *parcelled* or bound over with strips of old canvas; finally it was *served*. As these shrouds had a circumference of 7½" and were very closely bound, the length of spunyarn required is almost incalculable. As well, to preserve the rigging and spars from chafe, various *coats, puddenings, dolphins, platts* and *matts* had to be made and fitted. Spunyarn seizings were constantly renewed. The indispensable *salvagee strop*, used in setting up the rigging and a dozen other jobs, was made wholly of spunyarn.

And so it was that the fabric of the ship was constantly preserved—by means of junk and spunyarn, and a goodly commitment of sailors' labour.

There are watches to be kept while at sea, which, on this voyage, was most of the time. The norm is *watch and watch*—that is, one watch on and one watch off. This means never more than four hours' straight sleep. In lower latitudes, where the weather was generally fairer, *Endeavour*'s sailors were in three watches, which gave them up to eight hours between watches on deck. This was not only humane, but meant a great deal to the health of the crew. An article in a near-contemporary marine dictionary on this point gives the following:

> It has been remarked, 'that the order of nature was never inverted with impunity; and whatever we detract from the natural period of our sleep, will be deducted in the end from the natural range of our existence. Those whose rest is regularly broken by watch-duty, generally put on an appearance of premature old age, that a person unacquainted with them would be liable to err several years in forming a calculation of their ages from their exterior physiognomy, owing principally to their abridged and broken sleep at night.'[5]

Cook seems to have managed very well, for nowhere in the logs is there a call for 'all-hands' at night. Any sail changes needing more than one watch were made at the change of watch, when both watches were on deck. Sail was reduced at nightfall, and made again at first light. The sailor has, under these circumstances, one of the finest therapies yet devised: his hands and mind are co-ordinated in a sensible and satisfying action pertinent to his existence.

When the ship comes into harbour, two things take priority: wood and water. The ship's endurance at sea is governed by these two things, and the ship's boats become the workhorses (see page 29). The longboat was the boat supplied especially for the watering of the ship. But, on occasion, the others could assist. Wooding was carried on at the same time and often wood and water were brought off to the ship together. It was the job of the carpenter's crew to cut the fuel for the galley fire. But watering was more involved than the wood-cutting. It had to be brought off in casks which were hoisted into the hold to fill the butts (large casks) of the ground and second tiers. The salt water used to refill empty casks, for the stability of the ship, then had to be pumped out before the next fresh water was taken in. The largest of the casks were butts each of 126 gallons or half a ton (see illustration page 53). There were also hogsheads, one quarter ton; half hogsheads, one eighth ton; and puncheons, one quarter ton. (All of these *tons* are, of course, the wine *tun*.)

The cask used to bring off the water in the boats had to be able to stow between the thwarts (seats) of the boat. As we have seen, the longboat was so designed with the maximum buoyancy to length, and no larger than the ship can conveniently stow or hoist. Water in a cask is heavy and awkward, especially off a beach and into a boat. It requires considerable work and experience. At times, with a surf running onto a beach, the boat had to lie outside the surfline to a grapnel, or an anchor. The cask was then hauled through the surf by a line and parbuckled into the heaving boat at some risk to skin and fingers. On board, the Master's Mates and quartermasters supervised the stow. All this work—the beaching and lying alongside in choppy water—caused heavy wear and tear on the boats. Thus, when the ship was under way again, the log often read, 'Carpenters about the boats.'

Cook's instructions to *Endeavour*'s boats' crews:

> Whenever a Boat or Boats are sent in Shore to examine any coast and that I would have them proceed along shore keeping pace with or going before the Ship, I will hoist an Ensign at the Miz^{n} Peek. Upon the discovering any Bay or harbour that I would have the Boats examine I will hoist a Jack at the Ensign Staff and if they are to land I will haul down the Sig^{l} from the Miz^{n} Peek and fire a Gun for while this Sig^{l} is out the Boats are not to land on any account whatever. Whenever the Boats finds safe Anchorage for Shipping they are to hoist a Jack which will be answer'd by the Ship with either an Ensign or a Jack hoisted where it can best be seen, Topg^{t} mast head Ensign Staff and Miz^{n} Peek excepted, and if the Ship intends to anchor the Signal will be kept out.
>
> Upon discovering of Danger the Boats are to hoist a flag which is to be kept out until they see that the Ship stears from it.
>
> Upon landing on any unknown coast or Island a sufficient guard is always to be left in the Boat or boats to keep them afloat, the party landed are to keep in one Body unless from circumstances the officer finds it necessary to divide into two one of which is to remain as a reserve both to succer the advanc'd party if attack'd and to secure the communication to the Boats which upon all occasions is to be very carefully attended to.
>
> Where ever thier are any Inhabitants every oppertunity is to be taken at our first coming among them to convince them of the use of fire arms by killing of Birds &c^{a} that may come in the way, but in the doing of this care must be taken not to fire at random least the natives should Conceve that they do no execution.[6]

On anchoring, the boatswain and his crew set to work overhauling any rigging that could not be repaired at sea. But occasionally he had a party ashore to cut brooms, searching for any indigenous bushes suitable to his purpose. Parties ashore were always covered by a file (two men) or so of marines, a precaution that was certainly necessary in New Zealand. The cooper and his mate went ashore with the watering parties to set up the casks on the beach. These had been 'shaken' (dismantled) on board to save space. Coopering was necessary not only for the water but also because much of the provisions were in cask. The armourer's forge was brought on deck to repair the iron work. This burned coal which had been embarked at Deptford. Amongst other things he made nails and, at Tahiti, he made hatchet heads for trade purposes.

The ship's and officer's cooks had their regular work and had to adapt to anything that might be brought to them—as, no doubt, did the eaters of their handiwork. The Captain was a great innovator, collecting any local product he thought might be edible and never afraid to encourage by his own example. The ship carried a butcher and a poulterer. Mr Banks and Mr Gore gave the latter plenty to do, never missing an opportunity to shoot birds for the table. A tailor and a barber were also carried. All of these men were able seamen just the same.

The ship's bottom had to be kept as clean as possible. On calm days at sea, a small boat was got overside and the ship scrubbed around the waterline 'between wind and water', helped by the slight roll of the ship to reach further down. In harbour she could be put on the careen by shifting weight to one side and heeling her, but neither of these methods got right under the ship. To do this the men 'hogged' the ship. A hog was a kind of sledge fixed with rows of scrubbers made with strong twigs clamped between planks. It was given buoyancy with small casks lashed to it so that, as it was hauled under the ship, it bore against the bottom. It was pushed under the ship with poles from a boat alongside and hauled about with lines from above.

Hot weather and the working of the ship made re-caulking a frequent job for the carpenters. Defective caulking often let water into the forward sail room. The spare sails had to be aired regularly and looked at for mildew and rot, and the bent sails loosed to dry whenever possible after rain because fresh water is worse than salt in causing mould. Before bending sails to the yards, they were often dipped over the side in the salt water to inhibit moulding. Sails and canvas were all-important to the ship for she would not move without them. Sail canvas was so important that it had to be made to standards laid down by Acts of Parliament of William III and George II:

> Every piece or bolt of twenty-four inches in breadth [shall have] at least 560 double threads of yarn . . . Every sailmaker, or other person who shall make or work up sail-cloth into sails or tarpawlins, shall cause this Act, or an abstract thereof, to be put up or affixed, there to continue, in some public part of the loft, shop, or workhouse, where his said trade is carried on, or his workmen employed, under the penalty of forty shillings.[7]

Insisting on certain minimum standards was part of the legislative effort being made for the safety of vessels at sea. But the sailmaker on board, the half-century-old John Ravenhill, was fully occupied, with his mate and other helpers in emergencies, in keeping the sails in one piece as wind and wear took their toll.

All of this amounted to the general housekeeping of the ship, but there were also those repetitive routine evolutions carried out for the working of the ship in making a passage. The scant phrases recording them in the logs do not tell the uninformed reader much at all, and, without some explanation, important implications might go unappreciated.

When *Endeavour* came out of the single dock at Deptford, she went alongside the 'sheer hulk' in the river (see illustration page 89). This was the hull of a hulked vessel upon which powerful sheer legs had been erected so that she became a floating crane and was used to lift the heavy lower masts into or out of ships. *Endeavour* went alongside to be masted. Her main lower mast was 69′ 4″ long, and 21″ in diameter, and weighed about 3 tons. The fore lower mast was 65′ 4″, $19\frac{3}{4}$″ in diameter; the mizen 50′ 5″ and $14\frac{1}{8}$″ in diameter. The bowsprit was 34′ long with a diameter of $19\frac{5}{8}$″ and weighed about one and a quarter tons. Once these were in the ship, the other masts and spars were placed onboard. From this point the rest of the rigging and masting was done without further outside aid.

Remembering that what was done here, in the flat calm of a river estuary, had to be done at sea in boisterous weather, to relieve the ship, brings us to the point of imagining the tangle of flailing rigging and the spasmodic lurching of masts the men had to deal with then. It is not for the faint-hearted, yet it is but part of the sailor's daily work . . .

The lower masts are stayed in position by sets of ropes called shrouds. There are seven on each side of the fore and main masts, each of four-stranded cable-laid $7\frac{1}{2}$″ rope (see page 9). A complete 'mast' is made up of three masts: the lower mast, the topmast, and the topgallant mast which incorporates the polemast on top. The *Endeavour*'s mizen was made up of only a lower mast and a topmast (with polemast). When the lower mast is rigged and the top (a platform to support the topmast rigging) is fitted, it is ready to have the topmast sent up.

To take the mainmast as an example, we have a topmast 40′ 7″ long and 12″ in diameter, weighing about 1200 pounds. This is placed vertically in front of the lower mast with its head through the opening in the platform of the top. A cap has been placed over the head of the lower mast which juts forward with a hole in it for the topmast to slide up through. A rope is fastened to this cap and taken down to the heel of the topmast where it is rove (threaded) round a sheave (pulley wheel) and brought back up the opposite side to a block (pulley) on the cap. Going through this block the rope leads down to the deck where, through a leading block, it is brought to the capstan. Thus the topmast is raised by hauling on this mast rope, as the bight (loop) in which the mast now hangs is shortened. This is a kind of parbuckling, a method used by brewery workers to lower barrels into cellars, and by the boat's crew when hauling water casks into the boat. When the mast has been hoisted high enough, a wooden or iron square fid is pushed through the fid-hole in the heel of the mast which is then eased back so that the mast now rests on the fid which rests across the trestle-trees of the top. The topmast overlaps or 'doubles' the lower mast by some six to eight feet for stability. This mast is then rigged with its trestle- and cross-trees and cap, and the shrouds, backstays and forestay.

A similar evolution is carried out for the raising of the topgallant mast, which is 38′ 1″ long and 6″ thick. Following this, the yards are sent up and crossed, and the rigging is completed. The lower yard (main yard) is 47′ 10″ long and 13″ thick at the bunt (middle), weighing 1760 pounds; the topsail yard is 41′ 1″ long and 10½″ thick, weighing 974 pounds; the topgallant yard is 31′ 8″ and almost 6″ thick, weighing about 248 pounds. All of these weights are without sails, rigging or gear. The general mass of rigging may be seen in the various illustrations, and it is to be remembered that, whenever a mast or spar is struck (taken down) or sent up, all of this rigging and gear has to be taken care of (see illustration page 93). None of this is ever more than implied in those deceptively simple log entries. (A log, ostensibly a complete record, is ever a masterpiece of understatement to the uninitiated.)

The working of anchors and cables also takes some visualising. It constitutes a great part of the work when the ship is within soundings—that is, within the hundred-fathom line (see illustration page 53). In a vessel entirely dependent on the wind, her anchors may well be the one thing between her and destruction. In a calm they will stop her drifting ashore; or, caught on a lee-shore, they may yet save her. They may act as an emergency brake. This was never more true than during the prolonged period when Cook was continuously taking calculated risks along the whole length of the unknown and uncharted Great Barrier Reef (see illustration p.408). He wrote on 14 August 1770, when (temporarily) clearing the reef for the open sea through Cook's Passage:

> . . . which made us quite easy at being free'd from fears of Shoals &c[a]—after having been intangled among them more or less ever sence the 26th of May, in which time we have saild 360 leagues [1,080 miles] without ever having a Man out of the cheans [chains] heaving the Lead when the Ship was under way, a circumstance I dare say never happen'd to any ship before and yet here it was absolutely necessary.[8]

The *chains* is a general term for that part of the channels. The channels stand out from the ship's side some two feet and their purpose is to spread the base of the shrouds wider to give greater support to the masts. Fitted at their outer edges are dead-eyes, a foot in diameter, each with three holes like the monkey-face in a coconut. There is a dead-eye for each shroud, each encircled with an iron band which has an eye at its lower part going through to the underside of the channel. This attaches to a long middle link, which in turn is attached to the toe link bolted to the ship's side through the timbers. All the great strain of the masts comes on these through the rigging. It is these iron links that give the name of *chains* to this outer part of the channels, and it is from this outboard platform that the leadsman can lean out to clear the ship as he heaves the lead.[9] The lead weighs 14 pounds on a line 25 fathoms long, marked with knots, coloured bunting and leather. The lead is swung in a grand vertical circle over the leadsman's head with a scope of one or two fathoms (depending on his height above the water and his skill). When he has enough momentum he lets go at the precise moment which will take the lead ahead and down at the best angle to get the lead to the bottom by the time the ship reaches it. He lets the coils in his hand go freely, then quickly gathers in the slack as the ship comes ahead. When the lead is right beneath him, he has the line taut enough to 'feel' the bottom and he notes where the surface of the water is on the line. If one of the marks is there he calls 'By the mark [so and so]'. If it is an exact fathom, but no mark, he calls 'Deep [so and so]'. Otherwise he calls 'And a half [so and so]', 'A quarter less [so and so]' or 'And a quarter [so and so]'. He calls to the nearest quarter-fathom. He is supported by a breast rope which allows full use of both hands. This is a broad flat sennit passing around his chest and back under each arm, secured to two separate shrouds above and behind him. When the ship is coming to an anchor, the leadsman gives them the depth of water so that the right scope can be allowed for on the buoy-rope of the anchor. Also, with his lead touching bottom, he can tell what is not always apparent to the eye: whether the ship has stopped, is swinging to larboard or starboard, or going astern. It is a way of telling whether the ship should be dragging her anchor when there is nothing on which to take a bearing.

Heaving the lead is a minor art. One begins by taking a couple of turns around the hand at the proper scope. The cast has to be made left-handed in the larboard chains, and right-handed in the starboard chains. The lead is started with a fore-and-aft pendulum swing until it almost reaches shoulder height, then, at the next swing and at the forward end of it, the hand is brought in sharply to the shoulder (a critical moment) so that the lead is carried up and over in a full circle. As the lead passes overhead the bent arm is allowed to straighten behind with the pull of the flying 14-pound lead for the swing forward again, when the same movements are repeated until the lead has enough momentum to let go. It is essential that no slack comes into the line during these swings; otherwise, as the lead falls behind, the leadsman will receive a shoulder-dislocating wrench and the cast will be aborted. However great the temptation, the leadsman should never look up at the lead overhead, for this, more often than not, will bring it down on his head. Sailors are apt to make games out of their work; for example, competing to see who can bring the lead overhead with the greatest scope.

The purpose of the anchor buoy is to tell where the anchor is bearing from the ship. If the buoy rope is too long for the depth of water it will drift the buoy and not give a proper bearing. If the rope becomes too short, such as during a high tide, then the buoy is dragged under. This is termed 'buoy sleeping'. When it is on the surface it is 'buoy watching'. If the buoy makes water and has to be drained this is called bleeding the buoy. The buoy and buoy rope are thrown over just before letting the anchor go, with the way still on the ship—this is streaming the buoy (see opposite).

The ship has three bower anchors, so called because they are stowed at the bows (pronounced *boughs*). All are identical except for their stowage. The 'best' bower is stowed on the starboard side forward. The 'sheet' anchor is stowed just

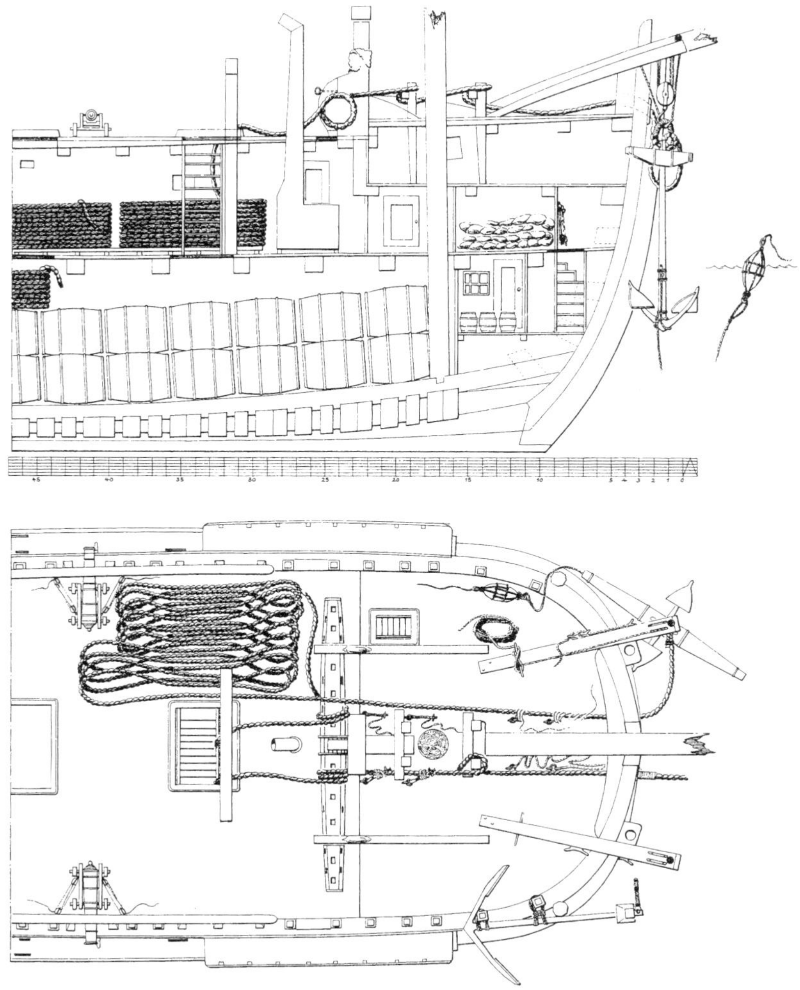

HIS MAJESTY'S BARK ENDEAVOUR.
SOME ASPECTS OF BOWER ANCHORS & CABLES

RAY PARKIN

abaft it on the starboard fore chains. This is a reserve anchor and usually has the best cable bent to it. The 'small' bower is stowed on the larboard side forward, and is just as big as the others.

When the ship comes within soundings, about the one-hundred-fathom line, the cables are bent and the bower anchors unstowed and brought to the cat-head, which is a strong baulk of timber projecting over the bows on which the anchors may hang clear. The cables have been led out through the hawse holes in the bows and bent to the two-foot rings of the anchors with an inside clinch seized back on itself. No matter how great the strain, this will never jam or slip and can always easily be cast off. Inboard, enough of the cable is flaked on deck so that the anchor will take it freely to the bottom and get a good bite into it with its broad flukes. Three turns are taken round the barrel of the windlass for further controlled surging out or heaving in. The anchor is hung on a ring painter led inboard and turned up on a cleat at the side of the cat-head. The anchor is let go by casting this off the cleat (see illustration page 53). The cable is veered to a half or third cable, depending upon the depth of water or the strength of the wind and tide and the nature of the bottom. The nature of the bottom has been found by the leadsman; he has a hollow in the bottom of his lead armed with tallow which picks up samples from the sea bottom. A general rule for the amount of cable to be veered when anchoring is six times the depth of water. A service is put on the cable to protect it from chafe at the hawse hole. There are usually permanent ones at the one-third, half and whole-cable marks. In hard weather it is not uncommon to have a whole cable, a cable-and-a-half, or two cables out, the second cable being bent on as required.

Each cable being 120 fathoms long means that, with two cables out, there is the best part of 1440 feet of wet 13½″ rope to be hauled back onboard with the weight of the ship against wind or tide. If the ship is lying to the wind, she is said to be 'wind-rode'; and if to the tide, 'tide-rode'. In *Endeavour* the job of weighing the anchors was performed by the windlass in a way that was traditional in this class of vessel. Generally naval vessels used a 'capstan and voyol' method. A capstan is a vertical barrel with bars shipped around its upper circumference like the spokes of a wheel. With these against their chests, the men walk it round reeling in any rope that has been brought to it (see page 29). *Endeavour* had a capstan on the Quarter Deck just abaft the after hatch, to which the various falls (hauling parts) of the rigging could be brought. But the windlass was a horizontal barrel which spanned almost the whole width of the fore end of the Main Deck just below the break of the Forecastle. It was 21′ long and 1′ 9″ in diameter amidships. It was octagonal in section. Three feet from each end it was supported by strong, well-braced, windlass bitts, each with a carved sou'westered head of a bearded mariner on top. At its centre was a strong rack or ratchet slotted every 7″, into which a heavy pawl, hinged on the pawl bitts, engaged. This permitted the men to hold on to everything they gained in weighing. Square holes are cut at regular intervals on each of the octagonal surfaces of the barrel but staggered on each succeeding face. These are the slots into which the handspikes are inserted as levers to turn the windlass. Ten men at a time ship their bars and heave down together with a practised rhythm to overcome the weight of the ship and cable resisting them. As one group heaves down, another deftly withdraws their handspikes and, with a practised skill, ships them in the next face and brings their weight to bear precisely as the others end their heave. Each group has to do this four times to make one revolution, which gains them five feet of the 720 or 1,440 feet they have to bring home.

Sir Walter Runciman, who had served some time himself in 'some of the colliers built in the middle of the last [eighteenth] century', in his *Collier Brigs and their Sailors* writes:

> . . . having to let go and weigh the anchor at every turn of the tide. This was a great mental and physical strain on everybody, though there was rarely any complaining. Many of the coasters' windlasses were worked with handspikes. Each of the sailors had their own, and handled it with an astonishing facility. In those days the rope cable was only slowly giving way to chain. No rush for the patent windlass handles, that displaced handspikes, was shown, partly because of the power of traditional prejudice that the sailor had against innovation . . . It should never be forgotten, however, that it was the sailing-ships and sailors of the eighteenth and nineteenth centuries that created the unsurpassed supremacy of the British mercantile marine.[10]

Men must be physically fit to endure this long heavy job, which they do with not only acceptance but a pride of attainment. The windlass is more powerful, man for man, than the capstan, but requires more skill. It is in the exercise of such simple skills that the sailor finds so much of his satisfaction—not a self-satisfaction, that is, but healthy fulfilment. How unrepresentative of all this sweat and labour is the understatement in the Log: 'Weighed and made sail.'

As the cable is brought home it is coiled down in the cable tiers in the Lower Deck to share its accommodation with the men. From time to time these are brought on deck to dry and air, and returned in heavy coils to bed at dusk. Though they are broomed off as they come onboard they are stowed wet, adding their distinction to the smells below.

When the ship again leaves soundings the anchors are 'fished' and stowed. This fishing is getting the anchors back to stowage in the fore chains. A fish tackle (pronounced *taykle*) has its upper block made fast with a pendant in the foretop (see page 9). The anchors are of a considerable size, and the heavy oaken stock fixed to the shank at right angles to the flukes makes them cumbersome. The small bower, virtually the same as the others, weighs 17 cwt 3 qr 14 lb and is 12′ 6″ from crown to ring; each arm is 4′ 10″ long, with a large two-foot triangular fluke (see illustration page 25). The oaken stock is 15″ square and 13′ 6″ long, tapering to 7½″ at its ends. At 58 lb per cubic foot, this adds considerable weight. But the large stock ensures that the anchor itself will always be capsized on the bottom so that one of the flukes will bite. Yet, despite this cumbersomeness, the men can secure an anchor outside the longboat and carry it out from the ship (see illustration page 313).

Seven whole cables were supplied. As well as these three main anchors, there are two spares in the hold with spare stocks. There are also the 'kedge' and 'stream' anchors, lighter ones, used to steady the ship from swinging, or to anchor her by in light conditions, when either of them became known as the 'coasting' anchor. They were used with 5″ or 6″ hawsers.

The job that demands perhaps the most continuous care from the sailor is steering the ship. During the whole time the ship is at sea this has to be closely attended to. The Master depends upon the helmsman to steer accurate and consistent courses to be able to make better dead reckoning (deduced reckoning) when no observations are possible. The helmsman may be any able seaman, as his qualification is the ability 'to reef, hand and steer'. But he is always under the close supervision of the watch quartermaster. During the times when extra skill and experience are required, only the best men take the wheel.

The good helmsman uses an absolute minimum of rudder to control the ship. There are two reasons for this. First, any angle put on the rudder retards the ship, as well as turning it. Secondly, if the helm is left on unduly the ship will begin to swing past her course and have to be brought back with opposite helm. The good helmsman knows when to ease the wheel and avoid the continuous correction of correction. The bad helmsman often develops a snaking course which shows up in the tell-tale trailing wake and is likely to induce the quartermaster to proclaim: 'an eel will break his bloody back trying to follow this ship.'

Steering becomes the art of anticipation, of checking a tendency before it has begun, and before there is any hint of it on the compass card. There is a tendency of a ship to 'luff' or 'gripe' (come up to the wind) with a freshening puff of wind or the heave of a passing sea, when close-hauled and steering 'full-and-by'. Again the art is to feel for the ship so that the helm is eased smoothly in time. On relieving the wheel the helmsman is told the course, if steering by compass, and how much weather or lee helm she carries (generally expressed as so many spokes of the wheel). The officer of the watch attempts to balance the sails so that the helm carried will be a minimum.

When the wind is coming from the direction in which the ship is to go she must 'tack', making larboard and starboard boards towards it. She is then 'close-hauled', or 'on a scant wind', but never any closer than six points. Then she will be steering full-and-by, being careful to keep the sails full.

The terms *larboard* and *starboard* for the left and right hands of the ship sound confusingly similar and it was not until 1844 that *larboard* was finally abandoned for *port*. *Port*, however, had always been used when referring to the helm, to avoid confusion in so vital a matter.

By way of clearing up another possible confusion, it is necessary to point out that the helm is actually the rudder, but the term is also made to include the tiller and the wheel. But when the helm is mentioned in steering orders, it always alludes to the tiller. The wheel is a form of windlass to apply extra leverage to the tiller. Paradoxically the top of the wheel moves in the opposite direction to the tiller; the tiller also moves in the opposite direction to the rudder and the ship's head. But this is understood by the helmsman. With smaller ships, in earlier times, all steering was done with the tiller. Now the tiller has a vital and immediate relationship with the ship's movements and the wind. When these were reduced to orders relating to the tiller they were always consistent and unambiguous—the ultimate aim of all naval terminology. So, even after the wheel was introduced, there was sound reason for this to be carried on and the helmsman acted as if he had the tiller in his hand.

As the most relevant thing to a sailing ship is the wind and its direction, most of the helm orders have a close relationship to it. Only when the ship is sailing 'large' is the helmsman directed to *port* or *starboard*. At other times the orders are those which keep the wind and the tiller in close relationship. The side from which the wind blows is the weather side; the side away from the wind is the lee. As the wind cants the ship, the decks slope down to the lee side, and up to the weather. All the people in the ship unconsciously register this, asleep or awake so that their reaction to it is automatic. The helmsman knows without thinking that up-helm or weather-helm will always take the ship's head *away* from the wind; while down-helm or lee-helm will always bring her *towards* the wind. Each of these movements may have to be carried out as a split-second decision on which the safety of the ship will depend—'port' and 'starboard' are not constants when related to the wind.

The helmsman has a box called the binnacle in which he can see the compass. (It was formerly called the bittacle, which probably derived from the French *habitacle*: a small habitation. But the sailor, with time, tailors words to his own economical euphony as, for instance, making *topgallantsail* into *t'gans'l*. So *binnacle* was better on his tongue.) Inside this little house are six rooms. Two of them house a compass each, while the one in between holds a lamp to shine a light on them in the darkness. The rest are stows for the watch glasses and log glasses, and the logline on its reel. The watch glasses are half-hour sand glasses turned as the last grain runs through and the bell is struck to mark the passage of time every half-hour. The half-minute log glasses are used to time the running out of the log-line, streamed every hour to help estimate the distance run. The line is marked with knots at such a distance from each other[11] that, if this were run in thirty seconds, it would correspond to a speed of one sea-mile per hour. (Thus the speed of one sea-mile per hour was called a *knot*.) In the logs the speed of *Endeavour* is shown in knots and fathoms, a fathom representing one-eighth of a knot. A helmsman spends at the wheel not a whole watch but generally only an hour or two hours of it. This period is called his trick; but for all other jobs it is known as a spell.

For the sailor, work is almost as diverse as it is endless. He is on call every hour of every day and night, and it all has a direct bearing on his own survival and that of the ship.

CHAPTER 2
THE CAPTAIN

History, it may be said, is a tapestry woven to our own design. This weaving, however, may conceal the very matrix upon which it is formed, and history has so often been rewoven to serve some present expedient. This book is concerned with revealing the matrix underlying a crucial part of Australia's history.

During the bicentennial year of *Endeavour*'s voyage it seemed that James Cook and his vessel were in danger of being buried under mountains of landslide words. All-too-ready platitudes steeped in misconceptions were binding Cook, mummy-like, in a thoughtless mould. Suppose the values we now rate so highly were not the ones paramount in Cook's cosmology . . . Suppose he was sensitive to something we have overlooked . . . Undoubtedly Cook had clear insights of his own.

Captain James Cook has generally been celebrated for the practical results of his work. 'The angle of incidence equals that of reflection.' This is a simple law of the physics of light that was so important to Cook in finding his way about the surface of the earth. With his instruments he calculated the angles to find his position.

Cook was one of those in that long line of explorers who had painfully endeavoured to inform their fellows just where they stood in relation to the rest of the world. It was Cook's good fortune to have lived when methods and accumulated knowledge available to the mariner were sufficiently advanced to have allowed his potential the scope it required. Whatever else, Cook was a competent user of tools. His instruments in action were the extension of his enquiring and calculating mind—a mind incessantly seeking the order in things. He was not a theorist who had to subvert evidence to his theories. He was an observer with a never-failing and just humility which only attempted to adduce that which was immanent, and which, naturally, avoided the tendency to make superficial intellectual impositions. This sanity is seen in his observations of the exotic and unusual. It hints at something far subtler than the mere mathematical ability for which he has become so celebrated.

It has been said that his contact with Banks on this first voyage had 'improved' his mind. It may have been that Banks was but the catalyst for Cook's mind which may have distilled from Banks's discourses more than Banks ever suspected was in them. This is not to say that Banks may not have assisted him to some freer expression in words acquired in their conversations. Yet so much of Cook's expression was in action which found its outlet in the quality of his work and in the high moral fibre of his unaffected conduct.

Professor J.C. Beaglehole presented a paper to the Cook Bicentenary Symposium of the Australian Academy of Science in May 1969. It was titled 'Cook the Man'. In this he confessed that the private man was difficult to come at under the professional one:

> Searching around, as I do, for the man—some leading characteristic, some not very secret spring—I light on what I shall call not perseverance or resolution or even determination, but stubbornness: stubbornness because I see some sort of element of native aboriginal rock in his make-up . . . At the same time I won't go so far as to say obstinacy . . .[1]

Towards the end of the paper he said:

> Literature, learning, science: can we say that he was devoted to any of the arts? We cannot. He was appreciative of the efforts of Hodges, whom he thought an 'indefaticable gentleman', on the second voyage: 'The Views are all by Mr Hodges and are so judiciously chosen and executed in so Masterly a manner as will not only show the judgement and skill of the artist but will of themselves express their various designs.'
>
> In other words, Hodges was a good hand at a landscape, and Cook had no capacity for the higher reaches of criticism . . . So far as I can see, he had no religion and no politics. He mentions Providence once or twice.[2]

Cook may not have attempted the higher reaches of criticism and I feel that he was more concerned with originating his own insights than with chewing the cud of other people's cropping. But there is a suggestion that he was more penetrating in this than Beaglehole suspected. This inference can, I think, be fairly made from Cook's use of the word *design*. He looked for those things which 'will of themselves express their various designs'. He seems strongly moved to seek ways to externalise the deep internal impressions made on him in his search of the world-without—each thing had its design, in the most fundamental sense. There is this suggestion in the way in which Cook made his drawings, as well as his charts and plans. Humbly enough he could copy others as if he would learn from them some of the facility he needed for expression. He also had some natural feeling for design in its decorative sense. This may have been an intuitive complement to his inner feeling for this deeper unifying design.

If one looks at the title page to his charts and plans, it is interesting to note the Ikebana-like arrangements of the straight elements of the flagstaffs, muskets,

H.M. Bark *Endeavour*: Quarter view. Developed from a contemporary hull sketch by Parkinson.

anchors, pikes, ramrod, and so on; the stabilising horizontal of the cannon; and the disposition of the round elements. One would have thought that, with no capacity for the higher reaches, he would have been capable of nothing more than a mechanical symmetricality. Yet here there is something more.

Cook, as Beaglehole so ably points out, repeatedly uses the phrase 'Geography and Navigation'. This, I sense, is the professional externalisation of the inner man constantly observing and evaluating as part of his nature and naturalness: reflecting on origins in the deep but never quite still waters of his being, and mirroring some expressions of those 'various designs'. One suspects this from his observations surfacing in plain words, or what is implicit in that which he specifically leaves unsaid. Expressions which, in the eighteenth century, were almost obligatory in deference to higher powers, are eschewed so consistently as to suggest a particular design of Cook's own intrinsic integrity. Perhaps it was this integrity that was the 'native aboriginal rock' which Beaglehole had glimpsed and inadequately, as he admits, called 'stubbornness'.

From these brief indications of the man, and a weather-eye lifted, we may find a little more in the narrative. It would be impossible to ignore the professional—the navigator and the explorer—for this is a revealing measure of the man, his endeavours, and his purpose through which he found his expression. Cook was immeasurably indebted to the past and he freely acknowledged it. He honoured the debt by using what it had bequeathed to the very best of his ability. Therefore, to understand his position better, we should know something of this valuable bequest.

Pythagoras, in the sixth century B.C., had said that the world was round; two centuries later Plato and Aristotle reaffirmed this. Before another century had passed, Eratosthenes, an Alexandrian, had measured the world at Syene and said that it was 25,000 miles around. (In the Geophysical Year of 1956–57, modern measurement deemed it to be 24,902 miles.) These calculations were not available to Columbus who, with other mariners of his time, was working on a smaller globe. Columbus wrote: '. . . determined by careful calculation that the degree corresponds to 56⅔ terrestrial miles' (eleven miles short). Newton had detected that the earth was not a true sphere, but slightly oblate (modern measurement tells us that the difference between the two axes is but 27.6 miles).

More narrowly, in the navigational field to which astronomy was becoming more significant, we find: In 1541, Mercator had produced globes with global projections; to Mercator's projections, in 1599, Edward Wright introduced mathematical calculations with 'meridional parts' which gave straight rhumbs (courses) on a plane chart; the quadrant was in use at the end of the fifteenth century; the backstaff was introduced by John Davis towards the end of the sixteenth century, replacing the cross staff; the quadrant, to sight along the side of a quarter-circle with a plumb line suspended from its apex, was not much use at sea. In 1731, John Hadley read his paper on his 'Reflecting Telescope', which came to be known as the 'Hadley octant' or sometimes the 'Hadley quadrant'. This was tried at sea and refined by Captain Campbell and Mr Bird to produce, in the 1750s, the 'sextant' much as we have it today. It became vital for Cook's navigation. In 1581 the dipping needle was known; in 1594 latitude was being calculated by double altitudes; variation was known and recognised, and seen to be a cause of present chart errors; in 1625 logarithms were applied to problems and in 1633 a slide rule was made. In 1635 there were discourses on the determination of variation; in 1637 trigonometry was applied, travers tables were made and methods of discovering currents evolved. The division of the logline was made in relation to the half-minute glass. (This required earth measurement[3] and an accurate division of time.) In 1668 Mr Bond forecast the variation for London for the forty-nine years to follow. Previously he had forecast that, in 1657, London would have a no-variation, after which it would increase the other way. He was proven correct. By 1768 Frederik Chapman was working on the resistance of ships' hulls through the water using testing tanks with models. Franklin had flown his kite, electricity was known, and lightning conductors were in use. *Endeavour* carried a lightning chain which performed effectively in an electrical storm in Batavia, when a Dutch vessel nearby was partially dismasted, while *Endeavour*'s marine sentry merely had his musket knocked out of his hands.

Cook therefore had at his disposal the material results of this hard-won knowledge. Further, the emergence of very fine instrument makers provided him with tools from which he could expect the very best results. But it was a little known German astronomer, Tobias Mayer, who was instrumental in Cook receiving one of the most important tools he was to have. Mayer, working for the Homann Cartographic Bureau in Nuremburg, had written in 1747:

> It is only too well known in geography that very many, indeed most, of the numerous known and noteworthy places need to have their latitude and longitude more accurately determined. *To achieve this is one of the most important objects of astronomy . . .*[4]

By 1753 he had produced the first reasonably accurate lunar tables. Ten years later the Reverend Nevil Maskelyne, astronomer, pointed out their practical utility in his *British Mariner's Guide*. Mayer's widow sent an improved set of tables to the British Admiralty in 1763. These were used by Maskelyne to calculate the lunar distance tables in the *Nautical Almanac for 1767*.[5] Cook carried no chronometer on this first voyage, and it was to these tables that he owed the accuracy of his longitudes.

This, however, was not something that many mariners of the time could manage. To quote Professor E.G.R. Taylor:

> But there is always the exceptional man, the man if [*sic*] independent mind and thought who is ready to break away, and such a man was James Cook. Nothing less than the most efficient methods and procedures available would satisfy him, whether for marine surveying, charting or navigating. He was alive to all that was going on around him, to all that was new in his profession. And he was willing, when already in adult life, to set himself to the daunting task of mastering the necessary preliminaries . . . disciplining himself to handle instruments of precision, to make the tedious records of innumerable delicate observations.[6]

Cook, in reference to Mr Green, the astronomer with him, gives a further indication of the significance of this method to navigation:

> In justice to Mr Green, I must say that he was Indefatigable in making and calculating these observations which otherwise must have taken up a great deal of my time, which I could not at all times very well spare. Not only this, but by his Instructions several of the Petty officers can make and Calculate these observations almost as well as himself: it is only by such means that this method of finding the Longitude at Sea can be put into universal practice—a method that we have generally found may be depended upon to within half a degree; which is a degree of accuracy more than Sufficient for all Nautical purposes.[7]

Later, in a report to the Admiralty, he wrote:

> The Charts and Plans I have drawn of the places we have been at were made with all the care and accuracy that time and circumstances could admit of. Thus far I am certain that the Latitude & Longitude of few parts of the world are better settled than these.[8]

Again Cook speaks to the problem:

> Would Sea officers once apply themselves to the makeing and calculating these observations they would not find them so very difficult as they at first imagine,

> especially with the assistance of the Nautical Almanac and Astronomical Ephemeris, by the help of which the calculations for finding the Long^{de} takes up but little more time than that of an Azimuth for find[ing] the Vari^{n} of the compass; but unless this Ephemeris is publish^{d} for some time to come more than either one or two Years it can never be of general use in long Voyages . . .[9]

This is not a technical treatise of Cook's work, for such is beyond my competence. What is offered here is some hint of the large background of work continually going on (largely unrecorded, except in workbooks) besides the problems of seamanship, survival and the hazards of exploration. These latter have never been better demonstrated than on the Coast of New Holland where James Cook pushed the limits of prudence into the realm of calculated risk. It was this which carried Cook beyond his contemporaries, yet which was, to him, but the simple obligation of his job.

One last word which may show why Cook-trained men were afterwards so eminent in exploration. This is from astronomer William Wales who sailed with Cook again on his second voyage and wrote in 1788 on the three voyages as a whole:

> But those who will give themselves the trouble to look into the *Astronomical Observations*, made in Captain Cook's last voyage, will find, that there were few, even of the petty officers, who could not observe the distance of the moon from the sun or a star, the most delicate of all observations, with sufficient accuracy. It may be added, that the method of making and computing observations for finding the variation of the compass is better known and more frequently practised by those who have been on those voyages than by most others. Nor is there, perhaps, a person who ranks as an officer, and has been concerned in them, who would not, whatever his real skill may be, feel ashamed to have it thought that he did not know how to observe for, and compute the time at sea, though but a short time before these voyages were set on foot, such a thing was scarcely ever heard of among seamen: and even first-rate astronomers doubted the probability of doing it with sufficient exactness.[10]

But how did James Cook come to the position we now find him in as First Lieutenant, Purser and Commander of H.M. Bark *Endeavour*?

He went to sea at the age of seventeen in the East Coast colliers. For nine years he served as a seaman, apprentice and mate. He was about to be offered a command of his own by the owners when, at the age of twenty-six, he volunteered for the Royal Navy on 17 June 1755.

He joined the sixty-gun *Eagle* as an Able Seamen (A.B.), but was soon appointed Master's Mate. The Master was responsible for the navigation in the ship as well as the water, stowage of holds and other duties. He was assisted by his Mates. Soon after, Captain Hugh Palliser became his captain. Palliser later went on to become Commander-in-Chief at Newfoundland, then Comptroller of the Navy, a Baronet, an Admiral of the White, and one of the Lords of the Admiralty. He recognised Cook's ability quite early. It was with his help and that of Bisset, the Master, that Cook obtained his Trinity House certificate in Pilotage and Practical Seamanship which qualified him for Master, in 1757.

On his twenty-ninth birthday, 27 October 1757, he joined the 64-gun *Pembroke*. This brought him to North American waters. Here began the education and experience which qualified him for his later appointments. Captain John Simcoe of *Pembroke* encouraged Cook to study mathematics and astronomy, lent him books and helped him by exposition. The severe winter of that year gave Cook the opportunity for detailed study. He had also met the military surveyor, Major Samuel Holland, who taught him, amongst other things, the use of the Plane Table. Holland wrote later to Captain Simcoe's son, who was Governor at the time:

> . . . I remained that night on Board and in ye morning landed to continue my survey at White Point, attended by Cap[t] Cook and two Young Gentlemen who your father ever attentive to the Service wished should be instructed in the Business. From that Period, I had the honor of a most intimate and Friendly acquaintance with your Worthy Father, and During our stay at Halifax, whenever I could get a moment of time from my Duty, I was on Board the Pembrook where the Great Cabbin Dedicated to scientific purposes and mostly taken up with Drawing Table, furnished no room for Idlers; here under Cap[t] Simcoe's eye, M[r] Cook and myself compiled materials for a chart of the Gulf and River S[t] Lawrence, which Plan at his decease was dedicated to Sir Charles Saunders; with no other alterations than what M[r] Cook and I made coming up the River . . . these charts were of much use, as some copies came out prior to our sailing from Halifax for Quebec in '59; By the Drawing of these Plans under so able an instructor, M[r] Cook could not fail but improve & thoroughly brought in his hand, as well in Drawing as protracting, etc., and by Your Father's finding the Latitudes; & Longitudes: along the Coast of America principally Newfoundland; & Gulf of S[t] Lawrence, so Erroneously heretofore laid Down, he was convinced of the propriety of making accurate Surveys of these parts. In Consequence he told Cap[t] Cook that as he had mentioned to Several of his Friends in power the necessity of having Surveys of these parts & astronomical observations made as Soon as Peace was restored, he would recommend him to make himself Competent to the business by learning Spherical Trigonometry; with the practical part of Astronomy; at the Same time giving him Leadbitter's works; with which M[r] Cook assisted by his explanations of Difficult passages made infinite use and fulfilled the expectations entertained of him by Your Father, in his Survey of Newfoundland: Mr Cook frequently expressed to me the obligations he was under to Cap[t] Simcoe; and on my meeting him in London in the year 1776 after his Several Discoveries, he confessed most Candidly that the Improvements; and Instructions he had received on Board the Pembrook had been the Sole Foundation of the Services he had been enabled to perform . . .[11]

When the ice had melted, Cook with the other Masters of the Fleet had the arduous job of charting and surveying the St Lawrence River from which the French had removed all marks. They were harrassed by the enemy and Cook once narrowly escaped capture as they were working in enemy territory. After the

BOATS TOWING.

Battle of the Plains of Abraham was over, Cook was transferred to *Northumberland*, under Lord Colville, Commodore of the North American Station. For the next few years he continued his surveys from this ship.

The war ended in 1762. In October, *Northumberland* was back in England. On 3 December, the declaration of the cessation of hostilities was read and on the 8th the ship was paid off.[12] Lord Colville struck his Commodore's Broad Pendant and was promoted to Rear Admiral of the White. But he was not so involved with his own affairs as to forget his late Master. He wrote to the Secretary of Admiralty:

> Sir,
>
> Mr Cook late Master of the Northumberland acquaints me that he has laid before their Lordships all his Draughts and Observations, relating to the River St Lawrence, Part of the Coast of Nova Scotia, and of Newfoundland.
>
> On this Occasion, I beg leave to inform their Lordships, that from my Experience of Mr Cook's Genius and Capacity, I think him well qualified for the Work he has performed, and for greater Undertakings of the same kind.—These Draughts being made under my own Eye I can venture to say, that they may be the means of directing many in the right way, but cannot mislead any.[13]

At the age of thirty-four, on 21 December in this same year, James Cook married Elizabeth Batts, aged twenty-one. Cook did not wear his heart on his sleeve, yet of the depth and strength of this relationship there can be no doubt.

'BROUGHT-TOO, MAIN TOPSAIL TO THE MAST.'

In April 1763, he sailed for North America and was given the schooner *Grenville* (ex *Sally*)—68 tons. From 1763 to 1767 he spent the summers in her, surveying, and the winters in London compiling and drawing his charts. At the conclusion of the 1763 season he returned to London in the *Tweed*, which also carried despatches from Governor John Graves Simcoe to Admiralty. One of these read:

> . . . The Tweed sails with these dispatches and I hope to leave the country about the same time. As Mr Cook whose Pains and attention are beyond my description, can go no farther in surveying this year I send him home in the Tweed in preferance to keeping him onboard [the *Antelope*], that he may have the more time to finish the diff^t surveys allready taken of it to be layn before their Lordships—and to copy the different sketches of ye Coasts and Harbours by ye ships on the several stations by which their Lordships will perceive how extreamly erroneous ye present draughts are, & how dangerous to ships that sail by them—and how generally beneficial to Navigation the work now in hand will be when finished . . .[14]

Cook was welcomed home by Elizabeth and a seven-week-old son, James. He sailed again for St Johns, 7 May 1764, to rejoin *Grenville*. The first entry in the Log was for 14 June:

> The first and middle parts moderate and Hazy weather the later foggy, at 1 PM His Majesty's ship the Lark anchor'd here from England, on board of which came the Master and Company of this Schooner, went on board and took possession of her—Read over to the Crew the Master's Warrant, Articles of War, and Abstract of the Late act of Parliament.[15]

Cook now had a permanent command. On 6 August the log reads:

> 2 pm Came on board the Cutter with the Master [Cook] who unfortunately had a Large Powder Horn blown up & Burst in his hand which shatter'd it in a Terrible manner and one of the people that stood hard by suffered greatly by the same accident and having no Surgeon on board Bore away for Noddy Harbour where a French fishing ship Lay, at 8 sent the Boat in for the French surgeon at 10 the boat returned with the Surgeon, at 11 Anchord in Noddy Harbour in 6 fathom water.[16]

Cook could not actively survey for about a month, but retained command. A gash between the thumb and forefinger of his right hand healed, leaving a broad scar as far as the wrist. He was back in Woolwich at the conclusion of this season on 12 December.

Again he was welcomed home by Elizabeth, young James and a second son, Nathaniel.

Grenville underwent an extensive refit and, on Cook's recommendation, had her rig changed to that of a brig 'for schooners are the worst of vessels to go on any discovery . . . for want of sail to Lay aBack [square sail] they run themselves ashore before they wear'. Because of this sail change, her complement was increased from ten to twenty. On 28 April 1765, she sailed from the Downs for another season's work and was back in Deptford by the middle of December.

Cook was once more fully engaged in working up the season's surveys and seeing to the publication of finished charts. (Admiralty was not yet publishing charts. The Hydrographic Office was not established until 1795.)

Again in April *Grenville* sailed from the Thames and was on her station by May 1766. During this season Cook made very good observations of an eclipse of the sun. These he forwarded to a Fellow of the Royal Society and the results for Cook were significant. He was published in the *Philosophical Transactions* of the Royal Society. It was upon this that he was later chosen as one of the Society's observers, with Green, for the Transit of Venus. On 30 November *Grenville* returned to Deptford. Cook was with Elizabeth and his two young sons and hard at work on his charts.

By the middle of May 1767, he was on his station again. When he returned in November it was the close of this phase of Cook's work. He was just 39 years old. He was welcomed home by Elizabeth, James, Nathaniel and a newly born daughter, Elizabeth.

There is no doubt that Cook's work over this period had set new high standards in hydrography, in both quantity and quality. His reputation had not been lightly gained and resulted only from work of the highest integrity and energy. There can be little surprise, therefore, that James Cook was appointed to *Endeavour*, which was to mark a new era in exploration, navigation and sea surveys.

By the simple fulfilment of his nature he had laid the foundation for what we, with hindsight, might call his destiny.

CHAPTER 3
THE SHIP

The naval vessel *Rose* was being fitted out for the voyage to the South Seas when Navy Board expressed its

> doubt of her being able to stow the quantity of provisions required on such an occasion, but if their Lordships incline to make choice of a cat-built vessel for the said service which in their kind are roomly and will afford the advantage of stowing and carrying a large quantity of provisions so necessary on such voyages, and in this respect preferable to a ship of war, a vessel of this sort of about 350 tons, may now be purchased in the River Thames if wanted.[1]

In late March 1768, Navy Board purchased the *Earl of Pembroke* and informed the Admiralty who, on 5 April, replied:

> Whereas you have represented to us by your letter of the 29th. of last month that, in pursuance of our directions of the 21st., you have purchased a cat-built bark of the burthen of 368 tons, for conveying to the southward such persons as shall be thought proper for making observations on the passage of the planet Venus over the sun's disk, we do hereby desire and direct you to cause the said vessel to be sheathed, filled, and fitted in all respects proper for that service, and to report to us when she will be ready to receive men. And you are to cause the said vessel to be registered on the list of the Royal Navy as a bark by the name of the *Endeavour*, and to cause her to be established with six carriage guns of four pounds each and eight swivels.[2]

She was bought from Thos Milner for £2,800, was three years and nine months old, and had been built at Whitby. She was described as 'a square stern bark, single bottom, full built'. She was entered on the Navy List as '*Endeavour* Bark'. 'Bark' was an essential part of the name, to distinguish her from *Endeavour* Cutter, which was in commission at the same time and was soon in the hands of the Deptford Yard Officers.

'Bark' alluded to the build of her hull, and not to her rig as is the common practice today. Cat-built barks were a popular and very successful type of vessel, especially around the Baltic and North seas. Ships of this type were still operating half-way through the nineteenth century. Somewhat unmindful of the sound design of these vessels, we compare them, perhaps thoughtlessly, with the glamorised clipper. The clippers were comparatively few, over-specialised and, as a class, of short duration. At best they carried only a very small proportion of the world's sea trade of their time. Vessels like *Endeavour* carried a great deal of it and, as a type, persisted so long that, in my youth I knew of living men who had served in them. Cook gave to this ship much of the credit for his achievements, and continued to use her type on all his voyages.

The convex lines of her hull and her bluff bows may seem to be perverse—but how many con*cave* lines can be found on a supersonic aircraft? She had her concave lines, but just where they counted: in the run towards the rudder to make her steer well. Ship design is always a compromise. In the eighteenth century Falconer explained it thus:

> . . . the qualities required in a ship ought to determine the figure of the bottom: a ship of war therefore should be able to sail swiftly, and carry her lower tier of guns sufficiently out of the water. A merchant-ship ought to contain a large cargo of merchant-goods, and be navigated with few hands; and both should be able to carry sail firmly; steer well; drive little to leeward; and sustain the shocks of the sea without being violently strained . . .
>
> Shipwrights differ extremely in determining the station of the midship-frame; some placing it at the middle of the ship's length, and others further forward. They who place it before the middle alledge, that if a ship is full forward, she will meet with no resistance after she had opened a column of water; and that the water so displaced will easily unite abaft, and by that means force the ship forward; besides having more power on the rudder, in proportion to its distance from the centre of gravity: this also comes nearer the form of fishes, which should seem the most advantageous for dividing the fluid.[3]

The more one learns of these times the less one is patronising.

The place of the ship in history is significant. Its proven utility as an instrument of peace and war, of survival, of commerce and expansion, of exploration and endeavour and, above all, of communication, has supported so many of the aspirations of humankind and extended its dreaming.

Endeavour was well proportioned, being about 3.3 breadths to her length (see page 8). She was built with flat floors, which meant that she could take the ground without fear of falling over when the water left her. She proved this at Endeavour River, though she had already done it in tidal ports as a merchantman. It was part of her design. 'She is a good roader and careens easy without the least danger,' Cook wrote. (A good 'roader' had the ability to lie easy at an anchor, particularly in hard weather. 'Roads' are those places where ships anchor, and a 'roader' is a ship riding at anchor.)

She was sea-kindly, or easy in a seaway. She was also described as a good sea-boat. 'Rolls easy in the trough of the Sea' and 'No sea can hurt her laying too under a Mainsail or Mizon ballanc'd' are two of Cook's opinions. Banks spoke of how well she behaved and quoted the seamen as saying that she was as good a sea-boat as ever they had been in. Cook wrote:

H.M. BARK *ENDEAVOUR*: IN THE SINGLE DOCK, DEPTFORD, 'TO CAUSE HER TO BE SHEATHED, FILLED AND FITTED FOR THAT SERVICE.'

> It was upon these considerations [that the *Endeavour* was chosen for the enterprise]. It was to these Properties in her, those onboard owe their Preservation. Hence I was enabled to prosecute Discoveries in those Seas so much longer than any other Man ever did or could do. And altho' discovery was not the first object of that Voyage, I could venture, to traverse a far greater space of Sea, before then unnavigated; to discover greater Tracks of Country in high and low South Latitudes; and even explore and Survey the extensive Coasts of those new discover'd Countries, than was ever performed before during one Voyage.[4]

Her construction was as sound as her design. Her 91′ keel was 1′ broad, and, together with the keelson (internal keel), was 2′ 10½″ deep. The stem and sternposts were equally stout. This was her spine. The floor timbers crossed and were fixed to the keel to begin the formation of the ribs which, with the stern framing, completed her carcase (see page 20). The floor timbers were 1′ 2″ wide and nowhere any less deep. These formed the bottom of the ship. Fitted to these, and curving upwards, were the futtocks; and to them the top timbers. A complete set of these parts was bolted together in pairs and called a 'frame of timbers'. Every third rib was such a frame. The two ribs in between them were called 'filling timbers' and were only single. Nowhere on the floor was there a space between timbers greater than 6″.

The planking was wrought over this strong fabric fore and aft. The main wale at the waterline was composed of four planks 5½″ thick and 7½″ wide. The channel wale, just below the upper deck level, was of thick plank 10″ wide. This supported the channels, which were platforms projecting from the ship's side to which the lower rigging was secured, giving it extra spread. The wales were for added strength, thus banding the ship. The bottom plank was 3″, below the main wale it was 4″. The ship's sides were 3″ and the topsides 2 ½″.

Within the ship, running right across between the main wale on either side, were fourteen powerful beams each 1′ 3″ square; at the upperdeck was another set 9″ square. More heavy plank was wrought inside the ship, and the whole united by large strong knees (angle brackets) of grown or compass timber in which the grain followed the change of angle from one member to another (see pages 10 and 11). All was well fitted and secured with iron bolts or treenails. Treenails were oaken dowels from 1″ to 1 ½″ thick and up to 3′ 6″ long, driven in as bolts. They were considered superior to iron because they remained swollen tight and did not induce 'iron sickness' (rust rot) into the timber. *Endeavour*, within the hundred-foot length, would have had treenails of 1″ diameter.

The above description is but a very broad sketch of *Endeavour*'s hull. The craftsmanship of eighteenth-century shipwrights has to be seen to be fully appreciated. They had reached the limits of design that their materials would allow. The result was something which, to this day, has not been surpassed.

After purchase, *Endeavour* was put into the single dock at Deptford. Here she was 'sheathed' and 'filled'. Sheathing involved covering the bottom with boards up to ⅞″ thick. First, the bottom was tarred and matted with hair or some other substance in an effort to inhibit the intrusion of the shipworm—which was to be expected, especially in tropical waters. Filling meant completely covering the sheathing with broad-headed nails, making her almost ironclad on the bottom. These were wrought-iron nails and did not rust.

Although the frigate *Alarm* had been copper-sheathed in 1758 (the first in the Royal Navy to receive such protection), there had been some trouble with electrolysis between the copper and iron fittings especially about the rudder where iron pintles and gudgeons were now being replaced with copper. But *Endeavour*'s rudder fittings and fastenings were of iron, and, as she would be on a long voyage away from dockyards, sheathing and filling was a practical procedure.

Considerable alterations and additions had to be made to the ship to make her more serviceable for the work she had in front of her. The Quarter Deck had a step taken out of it, giving more headroom below. The After Fall was re-subdivided for new accommodation for the ship's officers. But, with the late advent of Mr Banks and his retinue, all the ship's officers were moved below, except the Captain, and further alterations were made to suit Mr Banks. The displaced officers were reberthed on the Lower Deck. This was a completely new deck running the full length of the ship and built on the fourteen beams over the holds. Originally the only decks in the ship had been the Foremost Fall and the After Fall, with the rest of her space given over to cargo. A magazine was built forward in the eyes of the ship before the Forward Hold. Store rooms were built in abaft the After Hold, making a complete thwartship bulkhead which separated the holds from the bread room (see page 77).

Some interesting sidelights are provided by the following letter dated 19 April 1768, from Deptford Yard Officers to Navy Board.[5]

Honble Sirs,

Pursuant to your Warrant of the 7th inst. to fitt His Maj^{s} Ship Endeavour, we humbly propose for the Quicker dispatch thereof, that the following Works may be done by Task by the Joyners.

(Viz.)

	N^{o} of Men	Single Days
Four Stern Sashes to be made New, fitted & hung in their places compleat	1	18.
Companion on the Quarter Deck to be framed with sash Light all round & sash & Grating on the Top	1	30.
Repairing the Steerage Bulkhead & removing the Starb^{d} Door further into Midships & Building a New Bulkhead a thwart the Steerage	1	6.
Repairing the Ship's side & Roof Pannels	1	3.
Building six Cabbins between Decks with Bed-places, Lockers, and sash as usual	£ s. d. 2. 5. 0.	Each.
Building three Cabbins in the Steerage with settle Lockers all round, a sash & shutter & Cott Frame to each Cabbin	1. 16. 0.	Each.
Steps to the Side	0. 0. 8.	Each.
Waste and Drift Rails	0. 0. 1½	p^{r}f^{t}.
Penshire in the Waste and on the Quarter Deck	0. 0. 2	

. . . We are Honble Sirs
Your most Obed^{t} humble servants
AH RB MN [initials]

The cost of the total refit was quoted as follows:

Hull, masts and yards:	Materials:	£1357. 17. 11.
	Workmanship:	935. 19. 8.
Furniture and stores:	Materials:	3043. 11. 2.
	Workmanship:	57. 6. 7.
	TOTAL	£5394. 15. 4.

But she was not to get out of dock until 18 May, and was forced to lie these last three weeks dry, through very hot weather which was detrimental to the hull and caulking. The delay, as described in one of the newspapers of the day, was caused by the 'tumults and riots of the seamen on the river'. This was complicated by other industrial troubles concurrent with that of the seamen.

On 25 May, Cook was promoted from Master to Lieutenant. He took command of *Endeavour* two days later and hoisted the long whip-like Commissioning Pendant of Independant Command, with its red St George's cross towards the mast and its red, white and blue tail outwards from this. The ship was masted, rigged, stored and provisioned, then dropped down to Gallions Reach for her guns, powder and shot and other gunner's stores.

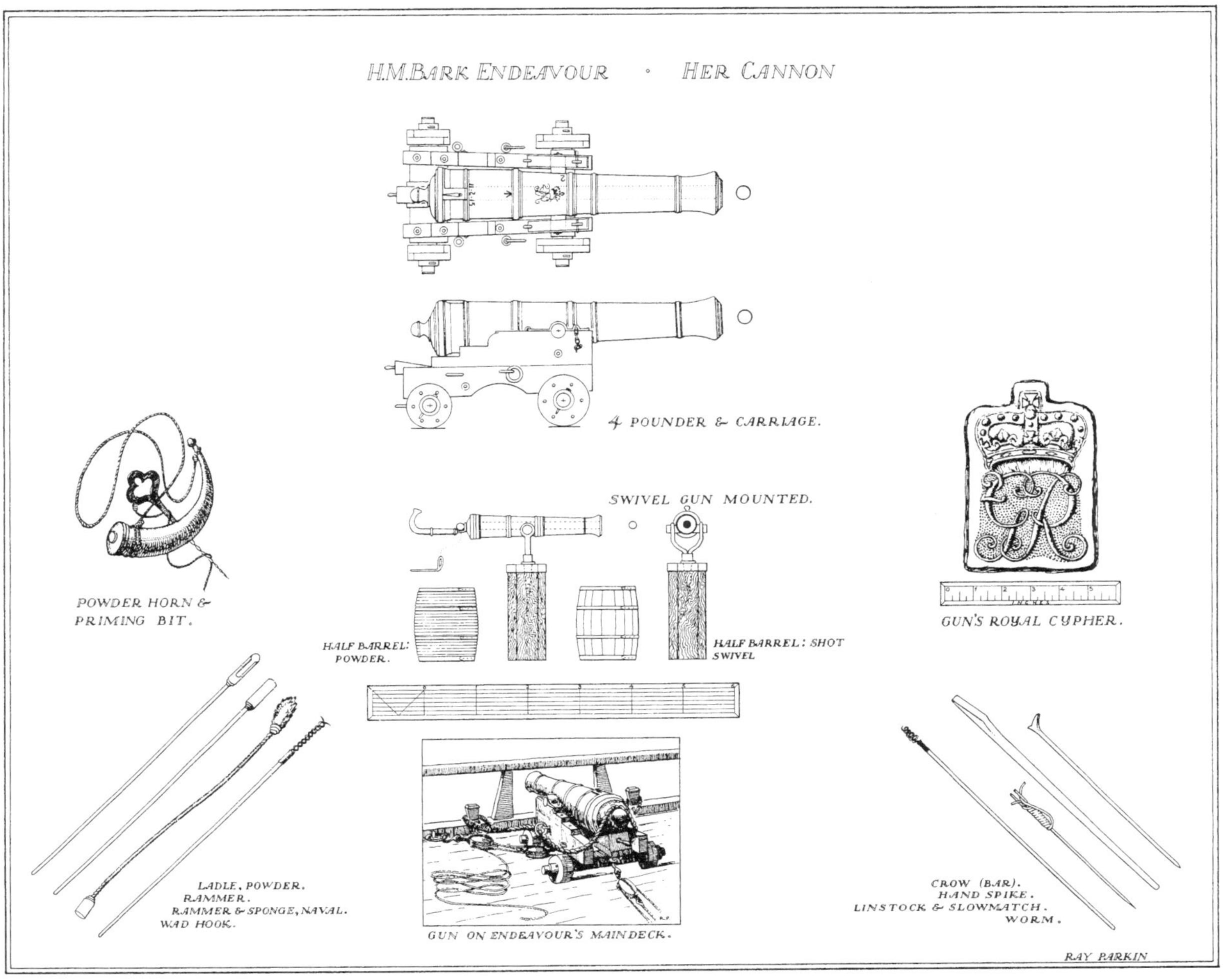

Her final establishment of guns was ten four-pounder carriage guns; and twelve swivels or blunderbusses, which could also be mounted on swivel posts in the boats. She did not get her last four carriage guns until she came to Plymouth. Only six four-pounders were mounted on the Main Deck between the mainmast and the foremast (see page 29). These were struck down below into the hold for the passage round Cape Horn, and finally jettisoned when the ship struck Endeavour Reef. After two hundred years under the sea they were recovered and restored at the end of 1969. Each gun was 6 feet long and had a bore of 3.25 inches. In 1768 the average weight of each gun had been about 1300 pounds, but after restoration each weighed only about 1200 pounds. There had been no loss of external dimensions, only of internal molecular structure which had broken down to leave virtually a graphite shell instead of iron. The remaining four guns were brought out of the hold at Endeavour River and mounted on the Quarter Deck where they remained.

At the end of the voyage, on 3 August 1771, Cook gave to Admiralty his own assessment of the qualities of this vessel, with which he had become so familiar. The printed questions are given here in italics, Cook's replies in roman type.[6]

Observations of the Qualities of His Majesty's Bark *the* Endeavour.

Her best Sailing Draft of Water, when Victualed and stored for Channel Service, Afore 13 Ft. 6 Ins. Abaft 13 Ft. 10 Ins. or as much lighter (at the same Difference) as she is able to bear Sail.

Query the 1st. How she behaves close haul'd and how many Knots she runs.	*In a Top Gallant Gale*	Steers well and runs about 5 Knots.
	In a Topsail Gale	Six Knots.
	How she Steers and how she Wears and Stays	Steers and Wears very Well.
	Under her Reef Topsails	Keep her rack full and she goe's as well as with whole Topsails.
	Under her Courses	She behaves as well under her courses as most ships.
	And Query, Whether she will stay under her Courses	I do not remember that this was every [*sic*] tried.
2d.	*In each Circumstance above-mentioned (in Sailing with other Ships) in what Proportion she gathers to Windward, and in what Proportion she forereaches, and in general her Proportion of Lee-way.*	We never but once had an oppertunity to try her with other Ships and then she fell to Lee-ward, her proportion of Lee-way is a Point or a Point and a half.
3d.	*How she proves in Sailing thro'all the Variations of the Wind from its being a Point or two Abaft the Beam, to its veering forward upon the* Bow-line *in every Strength of Gale, especially in a stiff Gale and a head Sea; and how many Knots she runs in each Circumstance; and how she carries her Helm.*	Her best sailing is with the Wind a point or two abaft the beam she will then run 7 or 8 Knots and carry a weather Helm.
4th.	*The most Knots she runs before the Wind; and how she Rolls in the Trough of the Sea.*	Eight Knots, and Rolls easy in the Trough of the Sea.
5th.	*How she behaves in lying Too or a Try, under a Main-Sail, and also under a Mizon ballanc'd.*	No Sea can hurt her laying Too under a Main Sail or Mizon ballanc'd.
6th.	*What for a Roader she is, and how she Careens?*	She is a good Roader and Careens easy and without the least danger.
7th.	*If upon Trial the best sailing Draft of Water given as above should not prove to be so, what is the best sailing Draft of Water?*	*Afore* / *Abaft* — As above.
8th.	*What is her Draft of Water when victualed to six Months, and stored for Foreign Service?*	*Afore* 14 . . 8. *Abaft* 15 . . 0.
9th.	*What Height is her lowest Gundeck-Port then above the Surface of the Water?*	Under water.
10th.	*The Trim of the Ship.*	Three or four Inches by the Stern.

Imagine, if you will, the scene in 1768 . . .

Hove-to and waiting, *Endeavour* has a simple beauty arising from her service and her class. She has a good sheer which makes her sea-kindly and makes her sit well in the water (see page 9). Her simply decorated stern overhangs her rudder above the lower counter nine feet from the water. Across the upper counter and just beneath the stern windows is ENDEAVOUR evenly spaced in eight-inch capitals (see page 22). Five round-topped stern windows spread across the stern. They are four feet high to the cove and are separated by carved pilasters and flanked on either side by the carved nine-inch square quarterpieces which frame the stern. The glazed windows, inclined towards the water, reflect the movement of the foam-flecked wake. That part of the stern above the cove of the windows is the taffarel and is carved with a design of acanthus leaves which flow up from the carving of the quarterpieces. In the centre of the taffarel are the braces which support the stern lantern raked at the same angle as the stern and a full three feet high. Just ahead of it and rising from the deck inboard is the 25′ ensign staff wearing the 12′ 6″ by 25′ red ensign[7] which is waving its crimson breadth in the light breeze like a magician's cloak and casts a bat-like shadow on the indigo sea.

Along her sides the sea swirls, a restless broken white water, sharp against the glossy black of the main wale which runs in a single sweep from stem to stern. Six feet above this broad black band runs the narrower one of the channel wale, repeating the same swan-like swoop of the sheer which flows forward to merge with the twenty-degree stive of the powerful black bowsprit, whose cap is more than twenty feet beyond the stem. But its spiritedness does not end here, for the flying jib boom soars again for another twenty-three feet until its tip is thirty-two feet above the sea. This eager reaching forward of these spars extends the tack of the large jib almost half the length of the ship ahead of it, like an impatient pathfinder. The standing and running rigging from these stretch back to the bows of the ship like intricate bridle reins whose very function contributes to the intrinsic design of the whole; there is not one unnecessary strand. Like three conifers, which they once were, the masts grow up from the deck along her length and the tapering foliage of rigging enhances them and supports them with a preplanned nicety. The small mizen, between the main and the stern, is like a younger sapling. From the main topgallant truck, long and whiplike, the red, white and blue commissioning pendant streams with the floating grace of an alighting bird. The wind-curved canvas of the sunlit sails is painted with the slanting luminous shadows interlacing from the other sails and rigging. Her main truck is just over one-hundred feet above the deck, which is greater than her length.

The way has been taken off her by bracing the main topsail yard aback so that the topsail takes the wind on its fore-side and blows back against the mast, acting as a brake to counter the other sails which are kept drawing. The log would show: 'Brought-too, main topsail to the mast.' (See illustration page 66.) It may also be done with the fore topsail. The fore and main courses (the lower square sails) (see page 39) are clewed up and hang loosely festooned in the buntlines. With the way off the ship she rides with an intimate acquiescence to the waves and the boat may now come alongside. Skids, nailed vertically a few feet apart up the ship's side, allow the boat to ride there with the scend of the sea or the languid roll of the ship without fouling any projections. Just abaft these skids is the sea gangway of thirteen wooden cleats nailed to the ship's side (at the cost, as we have seen, of eight pence each) by which we enter the ship aided by the manropes passed down from inboard. The ship rides with an easy fore-and-aft pitch as the waves pass under her and does not roll much to windward because of the steadying of the filled sails.

Only the boatkeepers are left in the boat to rig the boat's slings and hook on the falls which drop from the yardarms and from the mainstay to get the boat inboard on deck (see illustration page 93). The hauling parts are led down on deck through leading blocks and the hands tally on and hoist away until the shrill boatswain's call (whistle) signals 'high enough'. Then the boat is swung in on the midship tackle and settled into its chocks and securely griped down.

The buntlines of the courses are slacked away, the sheets and tacks hauled down, the backed yards braced up again. As the sails all draw together, the ship gathers way, surging forward and picking up the rhythm of the sea coming with almost metronomic regularity from off the starboard bow, as she is close-hauled to six points off the wind.

Standing on deck by the sea gangway near the break of the Quarter Deck abreast the main mast, the ship is seen to be divided into three main areas (see page 29). Forward is the Forecastle, 19′ long. Down a step or so is the Main Deck, 33′ long to the Quarter Deck, and the widest part of the ship. From here to the stern is the Quarter Deck, 54′ long, and narrowing as it goes aft. The masts, the three most obvious features on deck, which looked so slender from the boat, now, at closer range, look more like columns. The fore-mast is 19¾″ diameter, the main is 21″ and the mizen 14⅛″—that is, the lower masts. Around each mast, and coming down from its convergence above, a complex cluster of rigging drops in a cascade of rope with the running rigging ending in eddies of swirling coils neatly encircling their cleats or belaying pins. From the head of the lower masts, the spread of the cable-laid 7½″ lower rigging to the channels outboard stands athwart each mast like a straight Gothic arch casting a net of coarse shadows across the deck and enclosing it with a cloister-like atmosphere (see pages 9 and 29).

Right aft on the Quarter Deck, at the foot of the ensign staff, is the rudder head which comes up from the lower counter through the Great Cabin (where a casing has been built around it). From this a sixteen-foot tiller projects forward. From the forward end of the tiller, the tiller ropes lead out to the ship's side, forward, then into the wheel drum just before the mizen. Over the tiller, at the request of Mr Banks, a platform has been built with extra rails, to give them a short promenade clear of the tiller and tiller ropes. Under this platform, pens have been built for the sheep and goat.[8]

Just before the wheel (towards the bow) is a companionway, 8′ by 4′, with a grating over it giving ventilation and light to the After Fall below. Before this again is

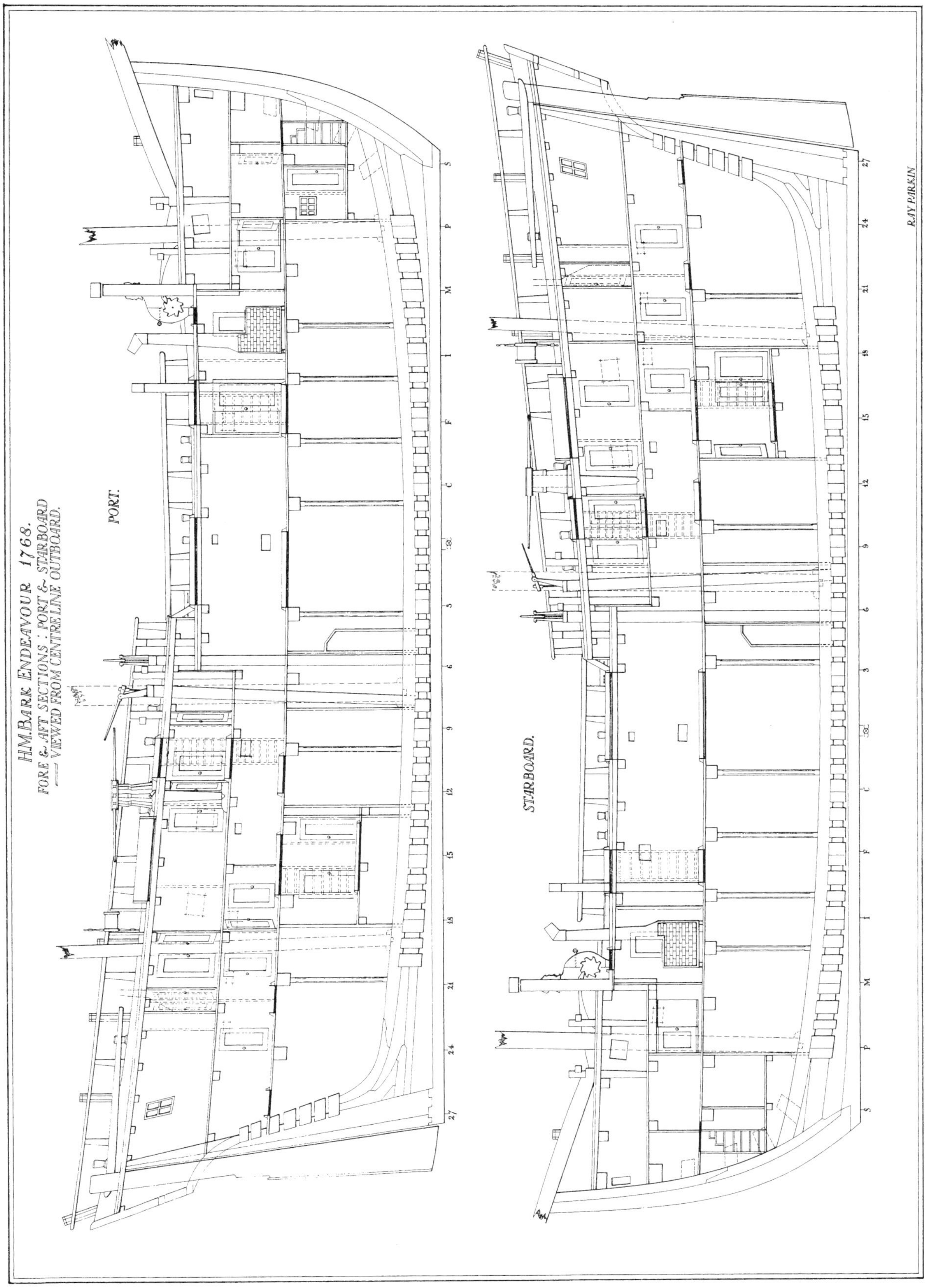
H.M.BARK ENDEAVOUR 1768.
FORE & AFT SECTIONS : PORT & STARBOARD
— VIEWED FROM CENTRELINE OUTBOARD.
PORT.
STARBOARD.
RAY PARKIN

the capstan, used to bring extra power to the working of the heavier gear. Its heel goes through the deck and revolves in its bolster in the After Fall. Forward of this is the after hatch with its ladder leading to the After Fall and Lower Deck. Then, around the column of the main lower mast, the heads of the four pumps stand up about three feet, and, unless in use, their brakes (handles) are unshipped. The shafts of these pumps run right through the Lower Deck to the pump well in the bottom of the ship. Each was made of a single elm tree bored straight through its 23-feet length by skilled tradesmen with hand augers (see page 77).

A couple of feet short of the fore end of the Quarter Deck, supported by two posts five feet apart, is a gallows eleven feet wide running athwartships (across), some three feet above the deck. This gallows is matched by another, supported by samson posts coming from the Lower Deck at the fore end of the fore hatch, and six feet clear of the Main Deck, bringing it level with the after one. Upon these are lashed the spare masts and yards and other spar timber. This is collectively known as the booms.

From the break of the Quarter Deck to the Forecastle is a drop in the upper deck known as the Main Deck. Aft, under the booms, is the main hatch, 8′ 6″ by 6′. Except in bad weather this is covered only by a grating which gives light and air to the Lower Deck. Seven feet six forward of this is the fore hatch, about 5′ square, housing the ladder which gives the crew access to their mess deck below in the Lower Deck. Close under the break of the Forecastle, on this Main Deck, is the windlass, spanning within a few feet of the rails on either side. Standing amidships, immediately before the windlass, nine feet high, is the coted belfry in which hangs the ship's bell. This is struck every half hour, as the half-hour watch glass runs out and is turned: each time with an additional bell stroke. A complete hour is tolled by a double stroke, and a half hour by a single one. The four-hour watch is finished with eight bells. Shortening one's watch by turning the glass early before all the sand has run is called 'warming the bell', a grave offence.

Between the fore hatch and the windlass the black iron galley chimney comes through the deck, standing with its revolving bent neck able to turn away from the wind to avoid downdraught.

The nineteen-foot Forecastle is almost a semi-circle. It contains not only the gear for working the fore-mast and the headsails, but also that for the evolutions concerning the anchors and cables. Right forward, on either side, the two cat-heads splay outwards over the bows, crossing the bulwarks 5′ 6″ each side of the centre-line to overhang the water. From the ends of these are rove the large cat tackles with a hook in their lower blocks on which to suspend the catted anchors by their rings. When a stopper is passed and made fast to a cleat on the cat-head, and the cat tackle unhooked, the anchor is ready to be let go by slipping the stopper from the cleat (see illustration page 53).

Just inside the cat-heads, fastened to them and the top rail of the bulwarks, is a small platform with a one-foot hole in it. Close-by, a spar is nailed to the ship's side and from this to the cat-head a rope guard-rail is rigged, by which the occupant of

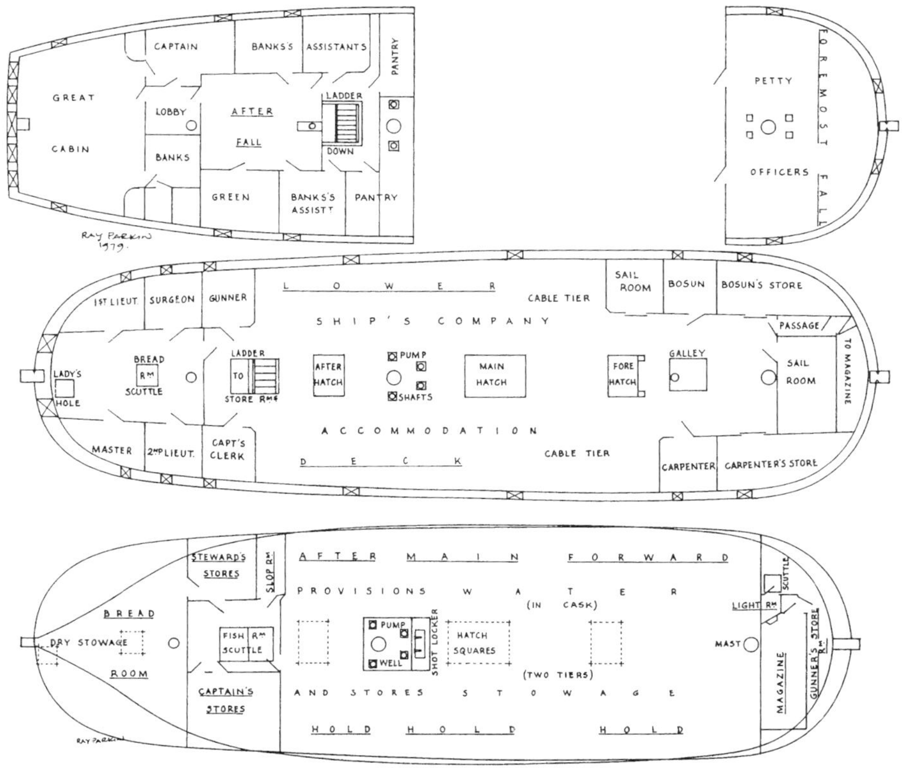

the platform may support himself. These two platforms are the ship's 'heads' or latrines. They are shown on ship's plans of this period as 'seats of ease'—this was not always true. The term *head* comes from the proximity of these seats to the figurehead, in such ships as carried one.

Now to visit below decks (see illustration above).

When this ship was built as the *Earl of Pembroke* she had but two part decks below for accommodation, and the rest was a single space for cargo. These were the Foremost Fall and the After Fall.

The Foremost Fall could at first be entered from a scuttle on the larboard side of the Forecastle, and now through two doors in the after bulkhead opening onto the Lower Deck. It is the same size and shape as the Forecastle, and its deck makes a deckhead five feet high at the forward end of the Lower Deck. In itself it is quite a shallow deck, having only 4′ 6″ headroom between the beams, yet to sailors of this period it is quite habitable. It has good ventilation with two bow ports and two side ports. Here live the Master's mates and midshipmen. These are the petty officers. Sailors, like nature, have a way of abhoring a vacuum and occupy every last niche wherein St Stylites himself might feel a little cramped. Down the ages they have learned, generally, to live cheek by jowl without too much abrasiveness.

The After Fall has far more headroom and stretches fifty-five feet from the mainmast to the stern. Apart from two pantries forward, two lobbies, the Captain's cabin and the Great Cabin, the rest is occupied by Mr Banks and his retinue, having displaced the ship's officers to new-built cabins in the Lower Deck. The After Fall is reached through the after hatch, from either the Quarter Deck above or the Lower Deck below. All cabins have a port of their own, excepting Dr Solander's and Mr Banks's. The Captain's and Mr Banks's open directly into the Great Cabin but the Captain has a second door opening into the small lobby by the mizen. The Great Cabin is the last 14′ 6″ of this deck, taking up its whole width, with the four stern windows lighting it. The midship window is partly obscured by the rudder casing which runs from deck to deckhead, from the lower counter below to the Quarter Deck above. This cabin is 22′ wide forward and 16′ aft. In the ship's side aft there is a quarter window on each side ornamented about outside with a quarter-badge carving. The Captain's cabin is to larboard and Mr Banks's to starboard forward.

The Great Cabin is the meeting and working place for meals and the consolidation of the field work. It is frequently alive with theory and argument from contending schools of thought. Between the chart-makers, the botanists and their draughtsmen, and the diners (which most unite all factions) the large table has little rest and is seldom bare. At the forward end amidships is a stove with its flue projecting on deck just abaft the mizen.

The officers sleep in 'cots' which are really modified hammocks. A hammock is suspended at each end by a lanyard with a ring or eye from which radiate sixteen nettles (or small lines) to eyelets in the head and foot of the canvas hammock. By having the outside nettles shorter or longer than the inner ones, the sailor has his 'sling' shallower for warmer weather, or deeper for colder. Some use a wooden spreader to keep the gunwales of the hammock apart, but the real sailor scorns this for a lubberly sling. The officer's cot is simply a hammock kept open by a wooden frame 6′ by 2′, giving it a flatter sling, with a strip of canvas from head to foot either side to prevent the occupant rolling out of such a shallow sling. One suspects that some of the officers would prefer the sailors' way.

The majority of the ship's company inhabits the Lower Deck (see illustration page 79), often familiarly alluded to as the 'Tween Decks, making it a small cosmopolitan village. To give the ship the necessary accommodation for her increased complement as a naval vessel, a complete new deck has been built. This was done by building over the fourteen main beams of the hold, 11′ 3″ above the keelson, running the full fore-and-aft length of the ship, 97′ 8″. It was on this level, between perpendiculars, that her length for tonnage was measured: 81′. The headroom amidships is good—7′ 6″—but, at each end, under the Foremost and After falls, it is a bare 5′. There is access down either the after hatch or the fore hatch.

Coming down the fore hatch and turning forward, one is faced with the Galley Range standing amidships just 4′ away. It is 5′ square, flat-topped and brick-lined, with its black iron flue going up through the deck above. There is a 5′ clear space all around it. Opposite this, on the larboard side, is the cabin of Mr Gathrey (bosun), and on the starboard side is that of Mr Satterly, the carpenter. Abaft the bosun's cabin is the After Sail Room, with a sliding door. On the foreside of both cabins are the bosun's and carpenter's stores respectively. The cabins are 7′ square with full head-room. The store rooms have only 5′, being under the Foremost Fall. All have their own ports. Between the two store rooms, and just before the fore-mast, runs a thwartship bulkhead behind which was the Forward Sail Room. A narrow 2′ passageway is left on the larboard side by the boatswain's store, which leads to the ladder down to the magazine. Going down this cramped ladder one doubles back to larboard, coming to two doors, one leading to a tiny compartment called the light room. This is a sealed-off place where lamps may be safely lit to shine through a projecting window to light the magazine. Naked lights in a magazine can be fatal, so no chance is taken. Shoes are covered with felt slippers before going into this compartment, to minimise friction. And the thirty-six half-barrels of powder for the carriage guns and small arms have hoops of copper and hazelwood to avoid accidental sparks. The magazine is 5′ by 14′, with 6′ headroom. The after bulkhead is only 9′ from the stem, and the whole is sealed off completely from the hold abaft it. In the cramped space outside the magazine by the ladder, Mr Forwood, the gunner, keeps his other stores. Climbing back up this ladder and stooping along the passageway one is again out in the Lower Deck in a clear space of about 14′ square around the galley. Here John Thompson, the one-handed cook, works with a cook's boy who helps him keep up the wood supply from the lower holds and other sundry tasks. John Thompson sees to the cooking of what the mess cooks prepare, as well as the general messes of wheat, portable soup, oatmeal, etc.

From the galley to the main mast is a space of about 36′ and the headroom is 7′ 6″, but for the next 42′ right to the stern it is only 5′ under the After Fall. It is in this low after end that the six displaced ship's officers have their cabins. Each cabin is 6′ square—except the after ones, which are 6′ wide, tapering an awkward wedge 10′ aft. The two forward cabins are in the open deck adjacent to the marines' mess: Mr Forwood the gunner on the larboard side, and Mr Orton the captain's clerk on the starboard. Between the after end of these cabins is a bulkhead with a door to a lobby 11′ wide running right to the two raft ports in the lower counter, each 2′ 8″ square (see page 22). It was through these raft ports, in her Baltic trading days, that the ship loaded the long spar logs for mast-making, etc. This was the only way to get such long stuff into the holds. Now they give valuable ventilation, as well as clandestine entry into the boats moored astern, to take some runs ashore in darkness under the very noses of the Port Guard Boat in Rio de Janeiro.[9] The mizen mast comes down through the forward end of the lobby and a few feet abaft it is the square of the bread room scuttle. Right aft, close to the transom, is another small one known familiarly as the Lady's Hole. The forward cabin on the larboard side is that of Mr Munkhouse, Surgeon; opposite, to starboard, is that of Mr Gore, Second Lieutenant. The after larboard one is occupied by Mr Hickes, First Lieutenant; and the starboard one by Mr Molyneux, Master. Each of these cabins has a small port and was built in complete, during the refit, at a cost of £2/5/– each.

The rest of this Lower Deck, allocated to the remaining seventy people of the ship, is some 45′ long, 26′ wide and 7′ 6″ high, excepting for some 18′ aft. It has clear deck space, except along the centre line which is taken up at intervals by the fore hatch, main hatch, mainmast and four pump shafts, after hatch and the hatch to the captain's and steward's store rooms. Also, forward, either side, between the fore and main

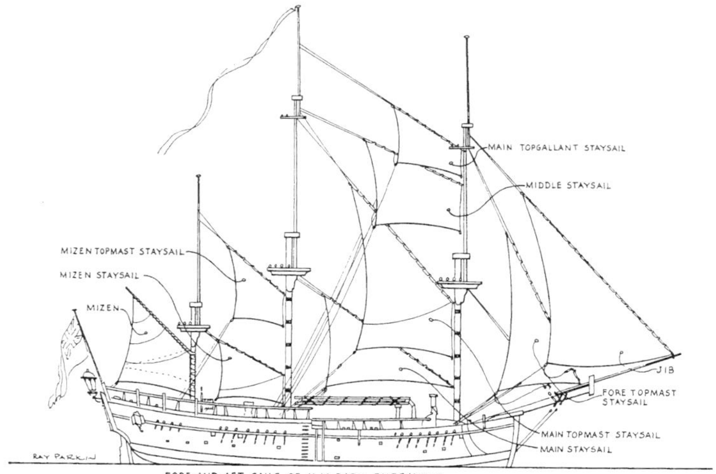

FORE-AND-AFT SAILS OF H.M. BARK ENDEAVOUR

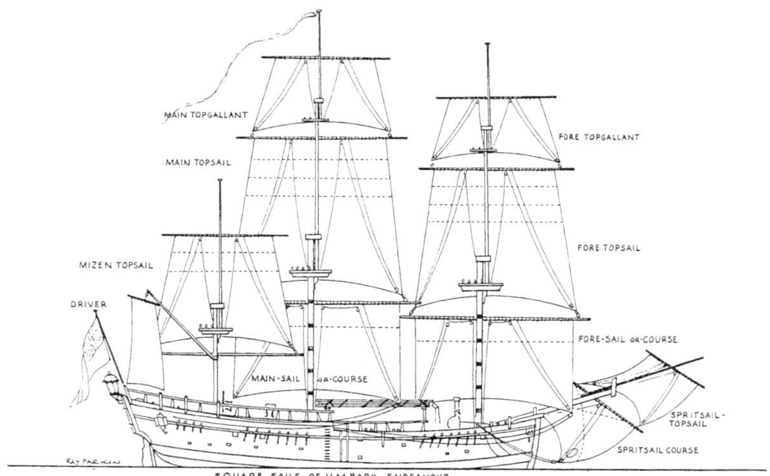

SQUARE SAILS OF H.M. BARK ENDEAVOUR

hatch, are the cable tiers. This is the space taken up by the coiling down of the working cables—thick cable-laid ropes 13½″ in circumference (see illustration page 53). Hammocks may be slung above them, but that is all. The logs tell us that the spare main [lower] mast and spare mainyard are also stowed here. During the passage round Cape Horn this deck had the additional stowage of two months' provisions to hand, to avoid the hazard of working in the holds in bad weather.

Nevertheless, the space remaining is not at all bad by naval standards of the time. The ready adaptability of the men conditioned by custom and commonsense soon make the best of any situation. They are settled into messes of six or eight men each, by mutual arrangement and compatibility or, failing this, of necessity. Tables and stools are suspended from the deckhead and have no legs. Hammocks are slung from cleats on the deck beams, being allowed officially 14″–16″ per sling. (It would still be only 15″ in the 1930s.) Some of the sailors 'sling' their hammocks on the deck, simply laying them down—but they have to find a temporary sling somewhere in the morning to lash them up to stow. Hammocks have to be lashed up with seven regular turns marlin-hitched, and the lanyards and nettles must be well tucked in beneath the lashing.[10] When slung, the hammock becomes the sailor's private world in which he may find consoling isolation and security: from the simple fact that, for a few hours, he is his own man, having at hand all that he most ardently desires—the bliss of a deep sleep. A hammock forms an unconscious refuge from the immediate in such a way that, as the sailor swings up into his own and settles down, he would not then 'call the King his uncle'.[11] That a hammock may become a refuge in a sadder way is shown by the action of William Greenslade, the distraught young marine with nowhere else to go, whose tragic tale is told later.

This deck is at once the communal and private world of the sailor, possible because of common experience, common understanding and commonsense, shared values freed from Freudian fears. It is permeated with common smells to which the men are comfortably conditioned.

The smell of the ship herself is of paint, Stockholm tar, flax and hemp, of sails and rope. Stockholm tar is also on the sailors' hands in the cracks of horny palms and nails—it is redolent in all their other smells. One quarter of the total two-and-a-quarter-ton weight of each cable in the cable tiers consists of this tar made from smoked pine pitch. When the cables are brought home and stowed, they bring up the fresh tang of the sea bottom as well. The smell of salt water in the bilges on the iron and stone ballast is distinctive. There is an acrid residue from the vinegar-washed beams and ship's side within, as well as that of the curling smoke from the brimstone stirred with a red-hot loggerhead to fumigate. There is the mustiness of untarred rope and canvas. The film of ocean-deposited salt on things, the cooking smells and the whiff of wood smoke (varying with each kind of wood got from different places, like the eucalyptus of New Holland) all haunt the memory. Then there are the boiling beef and pork, and the slush pots of the cook, containing the fat he has scooped off (his 'perks') which he must reluctantly share with the bosun for his tallowing. These are the smells of the floating world, cut and swirled by fresh sea winds above, yet undisturbed below.

The ship also has her familiar repertoire of noises: the creak and snap of the ship talking, heard in the quieter hours; the hearty slap and punch of a boisterous sea, or the wash and hiss of the more orderly skimming the ship's side; the wind making tunes here and there about the hull and rigging. These are sounds which talk to the subconscious in the men and tell them about their day. And there are also the sounds that they make themselves, talking unsecretively to each other close-by, or in cross-talk reaching the length and breadth of the mess deck in banter or abuse, usually without malice. There is unfettered skylarking and fooling; quarrels among the few, generally squashed by the many for the sake of peace and harmony. Hoarse songs—from the sentimental to the scandalous. Amid all this is a traditional acceptance by which the individual finds his own privacy of thoughts and dreams undisturbed. Those who cannot adjust to this are seen as lacking normal balance, in need of a good purgative to sweeten them. Life here is not for the hypochondriac.

Below this alive place is the world of the inanimate (see illustration page 79). The place where, except for occasional squeaks and creaks or collective groaning against the movement of the ship, the provisions and stores quietly await their disposal. One climbs down to the holds by the step cleats nailed to the hatchway stanchions. The fore hold begins at the magazine bulkhead. The fore, main and after holds comprise one common space ending at the foreward store room bulkhead about halfway between the main and mizzen masts. It is 55′ long, 25′ wide and 11′3″ deep, and is in the 'block' of the ship—that is, where the dimensions change the least. The holds take their names from their proximity to the hatches above. There is only one occluded space in this whole area, and that is the pump well surrounding the main mast and four pump shafts. On the forward side of this is attached the shot locker for the shot of the four-pounder carriage guns, known on board as the 'great guns', as opposed to the swivels and muskets. Beneath the round-shot are stowed some of the pigs of iron ballast.

Most of the fore and main hold area is taken up with the ground and second tiers of water casks permanently stowed and reaching a height of some seven feet (see illustration page 53). All have to be stowed 'bung up and bilge free', for filling and pumping out—that is, on their sides, and well-chocked with quoins. Around these there is some broken stowage like firewood, barrel staves, odd stores and cordage which does not interfere with the watering. The remainder of the after end is stowed with stores and provisions, hopefully in the order in which they will be required. The spare, unstocked anchors are stowed upright and lashed to the hatch stanchions handy for hoisting out when required. The sailors describe bad stowage as 'like a Midshipman's chest: everything on top, and nothing handy'.

The store rooms are enclosed by two bulkheads, ten feet apart, at the after end of the after hold, running right across the ship and containing the captain's store, steward's store and slop room. In a lobby between them is a scuttle opening down to the fish room, which possibly is the spirit room, though some spirits are stowed in the after hold. The slop room contains the ready-made clothing, shoes, etc. for the ship's company. These clothes are known as 'slops'—hence the term *a sloppy fit*.

Abaft these store rooms, right aft, is the bread room, which, with its rising floors and deadwood, is well drained and one of the driest stowages available for the bread (biscuit), in bags as well as cask. It is used for anything requiring a dry stow, such as the malt, wheat, etc. Mr Banks has made use of it for his dried botanical specimens.

To help the trim and stability of the ship, stone and iron ballast is stowed at various places along the centre-line of the ship. Her best sailing is with the stern trimmed a few inches deeper than the bow. But this is not always possible, even after taking on extra stone ballast in New Zealand and stowing it aft in the bread room, together with some of the iron pigs.[12]

Chapter 4
Scurvy and Provisions

Eighteenth-century sea surgeons, surgeons' mates and others had been deeply concerned with scurvy at sea over a long period and had done what they could empirically, though constantly pestered by the proliferating theories of the erudite 'Gold Headed Canes'[1] at the top of the professional pyramid. All experience at that time led them to believe that this condition was brought about by a positive cause, such as some miasma in the air only to be guessed at.

Yet the effects of scurvy were plain enough, though baffling and contradictory:

> This distemper chiefly affects the inhabitants of cold northern countries, and especially those who live in marshy, low, fat [*sic*] and moist soils, near stagnating water, whether fresh or salt. Those who live idle sedentary lives are most subject, chiefly in the winter, to the attacks of this disease; as also those who feed upon salted and smoak-dried flesh or fish, sea-biscuit, stinking water, unfermented farinaceous vegetables, pease, beans, sharp salt old cheese: likewise those who are subject to melancholic, maniacal, hysteric, or hypochondriacal disorders.
>
> It is known by spontaneous weariness, heaviness of the body, difficulty of breathing, especially after bodily motion: rottenness of the gums, a stinking breath, frequent bleeding of the nose, difficulty of walking; sometimes a swelling, sometimes a falling away of the legs, in which there are always livid, plumbeous, yellow, or violet-coloured spots; the colour of the face is generally of a pale tawney.
>
> The first state of this disease begins with unusual laziness, spontaneous weariness; the patient loves to be in a sitting or lying posture; there is a pain in all the muscles, as if he was over tired, especially the legs and loins; when he wakes in the morning, all his joints and muscles seem to be tired and bruised.
>
> In the second state, the gums swell, grow painful, hot and itching, and bleed upon the least pressure; the roots of the teeth become bare and loose; he feels pains in all the external and internal parts of the body, imitating distempers proper to the various parts.

> In the third state, the gums at length grow putrid, with a cadaverous smell; when they are inflamed, blood distils from them, and a gangrene ensues; the loose teeth by degrees grow yellow, black, and rotten; the sublingual veins become varicose, and like rings; there are often fatal haemorrhages, which break out from the external skin, without any appearance of a wound from the lips, gums, mouth, nose, lungs, stomach, liver, spleen, pancreas, intestines, womb, kidneys &c. Obstinate ulcers arise, of the very worst kind, which no applications will cure, and which are apt to turn to a gangrene; they break out in all parts, but especially the legs, and are attended with a stench. There is a kind of an itch and dry scabs, with a dry and mild leprosy. The blood drawn from a vein is black, grumous, thick, and yet wants its due consistence in the fibrous part; the serum is salt, sharp, and abounding with a yellowish green mucus on its surface. There are gnawing, rending pains, quickly shifting from place to place, which grow more violent in the night, affecting all the joints, bones, and viscera.
>
> In the fourth state, there are fevers of various kinds, which bring on an atrophy; sometimes diarrhoeas [*sic*], dysenteries, or violent stranguries; as also faintings and mortal anxieties, a dropsy, consumption, convulsions, trembling, a palsy, contractions, black spots, voiding of blood upwards and downwards, a putrefaction and consumption of the liver, spleen, pancreas, mesentery. Now the contagion spreads very quick.[2]

This baffling confusion of symptoms was well observed and described by Richard Walter, who had been with Lord Anson, the so-called Father of the Navy. He had speculated upon a number of things as being the cause, but was always faced with the contradiction of symptoms. The appalling losses on that voyage had brought the problem of scurvy at sea dramatically to the public concern. In 1747, aboard *Salisbury*, Doctor Lind took twelve patients each with well-established scurvy. Of the number of things with which he treated his various groups, the most effective were oranges and lemons, followed by cider. But it was not until Holst and Frolich carried out their experiments in 1912 that the concept of a *deficiency* disease was established. As late as 1932 King and Waugh isolated ascorbic acid—the vitamin C we all know so much about today. (Back in 1593, Sir Richard Hawkins had noted the utility of oranges and lemons in the sailor's diet. The North American Indians had also shown him how to distill spruce beer to relieve the scurvy. Anson knew the value of these things, but for him they had been unobtainable except at Tinian.) Captain John Smith gives a routine instruction in his *Sea Grammar* of 1627:

> *The petty Tally*. Fine wheat flower, close and well packed; Rice, Currands, Sugar, Prunes, Cynamon, Ginger, Pepper, Cloves, greene Ginger; Oyle, Butter, Holland cheese or old Cheese; Wine vineger, Canarie sacke, *Aqua vitæ*, the best Wines, the best waters, the juyce of Limons for the scurvy . . .[3]

There was probably enough known to have cured it, but the right people were not always in the right place. The preoccupation with theories to satisfy the mind rather than the body interfered greatly with the application of commonsense. The learned often pushed the practical aside with a strange vanity. But the sea surgeons and their mates and some of the commanders had plenty of genuine concern among them and devoted more to practical results than to theory. John Knyveton, a surgeon's mate then a surgeon in the Seven Years War, wrote:

> 'Tis a pity he did not make port; fresh fruit and vegetables might have saved him. Three men with scaliness of the skin in the sick bay after breakfast: the scurvy is breaking out.[4]

Later he wrote:

> A rare treasure has this day fallen into my hands; a book I bought at Charles Rivington's at the Bible and Crown, against the North Door of St. Paul's Church, in St. Paul's Churchyard; entitled
>
> A Treatise Upon the Scurvy
> In Three Parts; containing
> An Inquiry into the Nature, Causes, and Cure
> Of that Disease
> by
> James Lind
>
> whom I learn is a very famous man, and appointed physician to the Haslar Hospital for Seamen near Portsmouth only last year. On reflection, his name is not wholly unfamiliar to me; but there is little doubt (I think) that this treatise is destined for immortality. It is inscribed to the Right Honourable George Lord Anson, as it should of course be, and on the very first page, strikes at once to the heart and marrow of the matter.[5]

But even Lind seems to have to justify his findings in a theory spelt out in a passage from his book:

> Summer fruits in the present case become eminently serviceable, since they consist of a great quantity of water, whereby they dilute; of mucilaginous parts, whereby they obtund the stimulating putrefactive acrimony; and of a fine penetrating salt, antiseptic in the human body. Moreover, as by the scorbutic putrefaction, the crasis of the blood was broken and dissolved, these gave a homogeneous and saponaceous quality to the whole mass. At the same time they prove greatly aperient, in scouring and cleansing the furred and obstructed passages of the machine.
>
> A mixture of vegetable substances seems quiesquisite towards the composition of a good chyle, and to correct the continual putrescent tendency of the animal humours.[6]

This was written in 1753. Yet, in 1905, Captain Scott wrote: 'I understand that scurvy is believed to be the ptomaine poisoning caused by the virus of the bacterium of decay in meat.'[7] Tragically, in March 1913, Scott and his four companions died in Antarctica, most probably of a fatal misunderstanding of this disease. And even as late as 1973, a medical lecture stated: 'The biological role of ascorbic acid may not be fully understood [—*still*—] but its essential nature is beyond dispute.'

John Knyveton gave his point of view, after admitting that Lind's classical references go over his head:

> When we passed to putrid belchings and alkaline crassamenta, however, there was clear water under my forefoot; to the sailor presenting foul breath, spongy gums, swellings of the extremities, pimples, and thighs discoloured with purple maculæ as to the Surgeon who must treat him, it is Scurvy, whether Dutch, English, or that of Eugalenus . . . I must however state, that being of a limited intellect, I find it comforting that as Surgeon my work is of a practical nature; these dissertations and theoretical speculations of the physicians, debating the varied Schools of the Vitalistic, Iatro-Chemical, or Iatro-Physical Beliefs, are far beyond my comprehension and it is as well that they are of no service to those I attend. My arena is a bloody cockpit, not the lofty halls where Herman Boerhaave discourses upon the ultimate constitution of the human particle to a gathering of *Gold Headed Canes*—the miserable patient meanwhile expiring unnoticed!
>
> But James Lind is not one of those who consider the disease more important than the patient, and is evidently a man with a broad sympathetic outlook, and sound grasp of his subject . . .[8]

Knyveton's opinion notwithstanding, and almost exactly at the same time, the Sick and Hurt Board rejected Lind's findings. Lind remarked, 'The province has been mine to deliver precepts, the power is in others to execute.'[9] And so it was, fifteen years later, that Cook was given a number of supposed anti-scorbutics to try out, which were based largely on the ideas of Dr David McBride who was a proponent of malt. Meanwhile, ironically, the Sick and Hurt Board persisted in supplying *Endeavour* with orange juice which had been concentrated by evaporation *under heat* —as we now know, a sure means of destroying vitamin C. By 1953, the relative vitamin C content of the following had been calculated: orange juice, 50 units; lemon juice, 40; lime juice, 20; sauerkraut, 10; malt, trace only.[10]

Of itself, the subject of scurvy is one of vast human drama. Its relevance to *Endeavour*'s story is rather in its avoidance than its incidence. It is when one understands the minatory nature of this disease in long sea voyages that one appreciates Cook's earnest preventive preoccupation with it. It would seem that Cook used instinctive hunches arising out of his own experience. His approach was broad and empirical, leaving no stone unturned and no green thing that could be eaten unharvested. At the same time he dutifully carried out the instructions of the Sick and Hurt Board on Dr McBride's ideas. It was Cook's practice, and not Dr McBride's, nor any other theories, which kept scurvy at bay in *Endeavour*. But at least in the supply of provisions for the ship a great deal of thought had been given to the problem of scurvy and the health of the men, and experiments were attempted.

The standard daily individual allowance of provisions, if in good condition, contained 4450 calories at least, which was ample. Of the actual nature of scurvy,

H.M. BARK *ENDEAVOUR*: ALONGSIDE THE SHEER HULK OFF DEPTFORD, RIVER THAMES. 'EMPLOYED RIGGING THE LOWER MASTS.'

now well understood, there was some doubt. But Admiralty were very conscious of the need for an antiscorbutic. They instructed Victualling Board on 30 May 1768 that 'a quantity of well-dried malt is to be put on board the Endeavour Bark at Deptford, for treatment against scurvy, as recommended by Dr McBride in his book *Experimental Essays on the Scurvy and other objects*.'[11] Nine days later the Admiralty Minutes read, 'Letter from Commissioners of the Victualling, and one from Commissioners for Sick and Hurt. Proper Quantities of sour Krout and Robs [orange or lemon juice] to be sent on board the Endeavour Bark, that trial may be made of their efficacy. Resolved that the Endeavour Bark be supplied with an additional quantity of stores as necessary.'[12] On the same day, Admiralty to Navy Board: 'The Endeavour Bark is to be supplied with such an additional quantity of stores and provisions as may be necessary and she can stow. Minute, to send instructions to Deptford Officers and Commissioners of Victualling.'[13] The next day, 10 June, Admiralty Secretary to Sick and Hurt Board: 'Reply to their letter of 1 July [*sic*] 1767, concerning the use of robs prepared from the juice of lemons and oranges as a cure for scurvy. A proper quantity of the said robs, from their store at Hasler, is to be put on board the Endeavour, as her voyage will provide the opportunity they seek for testing its efficacy [which Lind had adequately demonstrated in 1753]. They are to give her surgeon the necessary instructions for its use and report the success of the experiment on her return.'[14] On the same day, Admiralty Secretary to Victualling Board: 'With reference to letter of 1 June 1767. A proper quantity of Sour Krout is to be put on board the Endeavour Bark, and a report made on her return how the same shall have been found to answer.'[15]

Thirteen days later, Cook made a request to Admiralty: 'Please to move my Lords Commissioners of the Admiralty to order the Endeavour Bark under my command to be supplied with a sufficient quantity of Portable Soup for her intended Voyage.'[16] Permission was given him to be supplied with whatever amount he should apply for, to 'make farther trial of the good effects of it.' Later the Sick and Hurt Board advised Cook, together with instructions for the use of portable soup, that 'One Ounce of the Soup is thought sufficient for a man a day.'[17] Portable soup was introduced in the 1750s and was said to have been invented by a Mrs Dubois. It was made of vegetables mixed with liver, kidney, heart and other offal boiled to a pulp. It was later dried, hardened and cut into slabs. Mrs Dubois had been awarded an Admiralty contract to supply the soup to the fleet. An order of the Board of Admiralty laid down that all the offals of oxen killed in London for the use of the Navy should be applied to this service. In 1757, the ration for foreign-going ships was 50 lb for every 100 men.

27 June. Victualling Board Minutes: 'Lieut James Cook 27th [June]. Let the provisions therein mentioned be sent, in addition to what are already ordered and acquaint him. Ordered that Mr. Soley, Mr. St. Barbe and Mr. Dixon do purchase on the best terms they can to be paid for in ready money, one hundred pounds of the newest and best mustard seed, unground and that the same be packed in tight cask.'[18]

4 July. Cook to Victualling Board: 'Victualling Office. Please to order His Majesty's Bark Endeavour under my command to be supply'd with the undermentioned Wine and Water Cask, those for Wine must be Gauged, for what was prepared before for that purpose are most of them filled with provisions; which cannot be consumed before the ship Arrives at Madeira. I understand that you have Arrack in store. Please to order her to be supply'd with One Hundred Gallons in addition to what Spirits she has already been supply'd with and likewise with the Saloup in the same proportion as the other Ships employ'd in the Southern Latitudes where supply'd . . .'[19]

Saloup was a powdered root of an orchis from Turkey and, made into broth, was a favourite dish of the working class of the eighteenth century. It is apparently still sold in Eastern bazaars. Modern opinion is that it has no medicinal value. It had been recommended by Lind to complement portable soup.

1 August. Victualling Board Minutes: 'Mr Stephens [Admiralty Secretary] 30 May last. That a quantity of well dried malt packed up in small casks is to be put on board the Endeavour Bark in order to try an experiment in her intended voyage, read: and 80 Bushells had been put on board her before the receipt of the said order, in pursuance of a verbal message from Mr Stephens.'[20]

12 August. Victualling Board Minutes: 'Mr Stephens 10th. To cause a proper quantity of Saloup to be put on board the Endeavour, read. Ordered that Mr.

Soley do provide on the best terms he can forty pounds of Saloup, and that he do cause the same to be sent on board the Endeavour Bark now fitting out at Deptford [*sic*] and place the expense thereof to his account of Disbursements.'[21]

15 June. Victualling Board Minutes: 'Lieut. James Cook, Endeavour Bark, Deptford. Let the following provisions be sent to the said Bark, as desired, viz. Bread in Bags, 21,226 pounds. Ditto in Butts, 13,440 pounds. Flour for Bread in Barrells 9,000 pounds. Beer in Puncheons 1,200 gallons. Spirits, 1,600 gallons. Beef 4,000 pieces. Flour in lieu of ditto in half barrells, 1,400 pounds. Suet—800 pounds. Raisins—2,500 pounds. Pease in Butts 187 Bushells. Oatmeal 10 ditto. Wheat 120 Bushells. Oil 120 gallons. Sugar 1,500 pounds.—Vinegar 500 gallons. Sour Krout 7,860 pounds. Malt in Hogsheads 40 bushells. Salt 20 ditto. Pork 6,000 pieces. Mustard seed 160 pounds. And acquaint him, and write the Commissioners of the Excise and Customs for leave to send the Spirit as soon as it arrives from Plymouth. Ordered in addition to minute of 10th instant, that Mr. Soley, Mr. St. Barbe and Mr. Dixon do purchase on the best terms they can to be paid for by Bill in course, five quarters of the newest and best wheat that can be got, and that the same be kiln dried at the Redhouse as soon as may be and packed in tight casks, letting the Board know their proceedings therein.

'Order Admiralty 10th That His Majestys Bark the Endeavour at Deptford being fitted out for a distant voyage it will afford an opportunity for a fair Tryal to be made of the efficacy of Sour Krout against the Scurvy [etc], read again. Write the Commanding Officer a proportion for twelve months for seventy men will be sent aboard at the rate of two pounds per man per week; desire he will let us know how the same shall be found to answer for our reporting of it to their Lordships accordingly.'[22]

The mainstay of the sailors' food was bread (hard ship's biscuit), salt beef and salt pork. Three days of the week were meatless ones called Banyan Days. On these days bread, oatmeal, sugar, butter and cheese were issued instead of the meat.

Bread was issued at the rate of one pound per man per day; beer, when available, one gallon a day; beef, two pounds on Tuesdays and Saturdays; pork, one pound on Sundays and Thursdays; pease, half pint on Mondays, Wednesdays, Thursdays and Fridays; oatmeal, half pint on Mondays, Wednesdays and Fridays; sugar and butter, each two ounces on the same days, as well as four ounces of cheese. This was the laid-down scale, but it could be varied.

> Captains may shorten this allowance, if necessity requires it, taking due care that the men be paid for the deficiency; nor is any officer to have a whole allowance while the company is at short.
>
> In foreign voyages, some of the above species may be changed; that is, half a pint of brandy, rum, or arrack, for a gallon of beer. Four pounds of flour, sometimes three pounds, with a pound of raisins, or half a pound of currants, with half a pound of beef suet pickled, are equal to a four pound piece of beef, or a two pound piece of pork with pease; half a pound of rice, or two ounces of sugar, for a pint of oatmeal.

> Prisoners of war, on board any of his Majesty's ships, have only two thirds of the aforesaid allowance of provisions.[23]

Beef and pork were supplied in cask, and each cask was required to have the contents, in pieces and weight, marked on its head. Beef was cut into four-pound pieces, and pork into two-pound pieces. The casks were to be opened in the presence of two or more warrant officers, to be weighed and counted and any deficiency by weight or number noted.

> If there be want of pork, the captain may order three pounds of beef to be given out in lieu of two pounds of pork.
>
> One day in every week there shall be issued out a proportion of flour and suet in lieu of beef [becoming known as Duff Days], but this not to extend beyond four months victualling at one time.
>
> Only three months butter and cheese shall be supplied for foreign voyages, the remainder to be made up in olive oil.
>
> Fresh meat is to be allowed every day (when it can be conveniently done), instead of salt meat; three pounds of mutton accounted for a four pound piece of beef, or a two pound piece of pork with pease.[24]

The exploitation of ships by dishonest contractors and sharp pursers was legendary. Knyveton gives an example:

> When one of the last barrels of pork was opened today 'twas found to be filled mostly with pigs' heads and feet, the heads still having iron rings through their noses and the hide and hair still on the legs. A deputation waited on the Captain, who after damning their eyes, ordered the contents to be thrown into sea, but the iron to be kept for use by the armourer and his mates.[25]

But Cook himself was purser of *Endeavour*. He provided fresh beef at Madeira, Rio, Timor, Batavia and at the Cape of Good Hope. Fresh pork he was able to get at Tahiti. At Madeira he bought on his own account 3845 pounds of onions which he issued to the men in ten- and twenty-pound lots per man. The general quality of provisions in *Endeavour* was well above the naval average. Banks gives an interesting insight into the victualling generally. On 23 September 1769, in the South Pacific between Tahiti and New Zealand, he wrote:

> Dr Solander has been unwell for some days so today I opend Dr Hulm's Essense of Lemon Juice, Mr Monkhouse having prescribd it for him, which provd perfectly good, little if at all inferior in taste to fresh lemon juice. We also today made a pye of the North American apples which Dr Fothergill gave me, which proved very good, if not quite equal to the apple pyes which our freinds in England are now eating, good enough to please us who have been so long deprivd of the fruits of our native Countrey. In the main however we are very well off for refreshments and provisions of most species: our ships *beef* and *Pork* are excellent as are the *peas*; the *flour* and *oatmeal* which have sometimes faild us are at present and have in general been very good. Our *water* is as sweet and has rather more spirit than it had when drank out of the river at Otahite. Our *bread* indeed is but indifferent, occasiond by the quantity of

'HOISTED OUT ALL BOATS.'

Vermin that are in it, I have often seen hundreds nay thousands shaken out of a single bisket. We in the Cabbin have however an easy remedy for this by baking it in an oven, not too hot, which makes them all walk off, but this cannot be allowed to the private people who must find the taste of these animals very disagreable, as they every one taste as strong as mustard or rather spirits of hartshorn. They are of 5 kinds, 3 *Tenebrios*, 1 *Ptinus* and the *Phalangium cancroides*; the last is however scarce in the common bread but was vastly plentyfull in white Deal bisket as long as we had any left.

Wheat was allowd to the ships company which has been boild for their breakfasts 2 or 3 times a week in the same manner as firmity [Furmety or frumenty: hulled wheat boiled in milk and seasoned] is made; this has I beleive been a very usefull refreshment to them as well as an agreable food, which myself and most of the officers have constantly breakfasted upon in the cold weather; the grain was originaly of a good quality and has kept without the least damage. This however cannot be said of the *Malt* of which we have plainly had two kinds, one very good but that has been some time ago us'd; that that is at present in use is good for nothing at all, it has been originaly of a bad light grain and so little care has been taken in the making of it that the tails are left in with innumerable other kinds of Dirt; add to all this that it has been damp'd on board the ship so that with all the care that can be usd it will scarce give a tincture to water. *Portable Soup* is very good, it has now and then requird an airing which has hinderd it from moulding. *Sour Crout* is as good as ever and I have not the least doubt of it remaining so.

Pinnace under sail with alternative *settee* sails (after Parkinson).

So much for the Ships Company. We ourselves are hardly as well of as them; our live stock consists of 17 sheep, 4 or 5 fowls, as many S.Sea hogs, 4 or 5 Muscovy ducks, an English boar, and a sow with a litter of piggs; in the use of these we are rather sparing as the time of our Getting a supply is rather precarious. Salt Stock we have nothing worth mentioning except a kind of Salt Beef which was put up by one *Mellish* a butcher at New Crane Stairs, which is much the best salt meat I have ever tasted, and Our Salted Cabbage . . . which is now as good as it was then.

Our Malt Liquors have answerd extreemely well: we have now both small beer and Porter upon tap as good as I ever drank them, especialy the latter which was bought of *Sam. & Jno. Curtiss* at Wapping New Stairs. The Small beer had some art usd to make it keep, it was bought of *Bruff & Taylor* in Hog Lane near St Giles's. Our wine I cannot say much for tho I beleive it to be good in its nature, we have not a glass fine these many months I beleive cheifly owing to the Carelessness or ignorance of the Steward.[26]

On 9 April 1769, as they were approaching Tahiti, Banks wrote:

As we have found no Island I shall employ the time and paper which I had allotted to describe one ['lucubration'] in a work which I am sure will be more usefull at [*sic*], if not more entertaining to all future navigators, by describing the method which we took to cure Cabbage in England; which Cabbage we have eat every day since we left Cape Horne and have now good store of, remaining as good at least to our palates and full as green and pleasing to the eye as if it was brought fresh every morning at Covent Garden market. Our Steward has given me the receipt which I shall copy exactly false spelling exceptd.[27]

Take a strong Iron bound cask for no weak wooden bound one should ever be trusted in a long voyage, take out the head and when the whole is well cleand cover the bottom with salt. Then take the Cabbage and stripping off the outside leaves take the rest leaf by leaf till you come to the heart which cut into four; these leaves

> and heart lay upon the Salt about 2 or 3 inches thick and sprinkle Salt pretty thick over them and lay cabbage upon the salt stratum super thick till the cask is full. Then lay on the head of the cask with a weight which in 5 or 6 days will have pressd the cabbage into a much smaller compass. After this fill up the cask with more cabbage as before directed and Head it up. N.B. the Cabbage should be gatherd in dry weather some time after sun rise that the dew may not be upon it. Halves of cabbages are better for keeping than single leaves.[28]

On 28 February 1770, in New Zealand, Banks again wrote: 'Opend today a Cask of Cabbage put up by the receipt p. 210 of this Journal which provd most excellently good, scarce at all worse for keeping in my opinion.'[29]

It is worth a passing thought as to how, amid all the sailorising that had to be done, the stock mentioned by Mr Banks was husbanded and kept alive. The provision of fodder and other food for these animals during the long periods at sea must have been no less an art than a problem. The South Sea hogs from Tahiti began to die of cold as they approached the latitude of 40° south on the way to New Zealand.

Food was supplemented as much as possible from the shore to extend the sea provisions. At Tahiti, this was considerable. The fish and fowl of the sea all went to the table when they could be got. Celery grass or any other edible green was gathered and boiled with the wheat, pease or portable soup.

All of these were part of the Captain's empiric approach to the maintenance of good health and the prevention of scurvy. He had received a few valuable pointers from Captain Wallis of the *Dolphin*—just returned, before *Endeavour* sailed, from the discovery of Tahiti. The ultimate acceptance of Cook's innovative feeding, and the generally high standard of the provisions supplied both contributed to, and are assessments of, the high morale of people content with their leader.

CHAPTER 5
THE SHIP'S COMPANY

The following is a list, compiled from several sources, of the people who took part in the voyage.

SHIP'S BOOK NO.	NAME	AGE	RATING	DUTY	REMARKS
1	COOK, James.	39	1st Lieut.	Commander & Purser.	
40	HICKES, Zachary.	29	2nd Lieut.	[1st Lieut.]	D.D. 26/5/'71
90	GORE, John.	38	3rd Lieut.	[2nd Lieut]	Ex *Dolphin*
64	MOLYNEUX, Robert.	22	Master		Ex *Dolphin* D.D. 16/4/71
32	BOOTIE, John	—	Midshipman		D.D. 4/2/71
74	MUNKHOUSE, Jonathon.	—	Midshipman		D.D. 6/2/71
78	SAUNDERS, Patrick.	—	Midshipman		A.B. 23/5/70 Run 25/12/70
72	MUNKHOUSE William Brougham	—	Surgeon		D.D. 5/11/70
56/105	PERRY, William	21	Surgeon's Mate		Surgeon 6/11/70
3	SATTERLY, John	—	Carpenter		D.D. 12/2/71
62	FORWOOD, Stephen	—	Gunner		
47	GATHREY, John	—	Boatswain		D.D. 4/2/71
54	TAYLOR, Robert	—	Armourer		
59	RAVENHILL, John	49	Sailmaker		D.D. 27/1/71
57	THOMPSON, John	—	Cook		D.D. 31/1/71
80	ORTON, Richard	—	Captain's Clerk		
51/139	PICKERSGILL, Rich[d].	19	Master's Mate		Ex *Dolphin* Master 26/5/71
61/141	CLERKE, Charles.	25	Master's Mate		3rd Lieut. 26/5/71 Ex *Dolphin*
79	WILKINSON, Francis	—	A.B. to 19/8/68 then Master's Mate		Ex *Dolphin* Died Eng. Aug. 71
5	WEIR, Alexander	35	Quarter Master		Drowned Funchal 14/9/68
95	EVANS, Samuel	—	Quarter Master. BOATSWAIN 5/2/71		Also Bos'ns Mate & Cox'n of Pinnace
44	ANDERSON, Robert	—	Quarter Master.		
30	READING, John Kinsale	24	Bos'ns Mate & Yeo, Sheets.		D.D. 28/8/69

SHIP'S BOOK NO.	NAME	AGE	RATING	DUTY	REMARKS
10	HARDMAN, Thomas.	33	Bos'ns Mate to 25/3/69 A.B. to 1/2/71		Ex *Grenville* Sailmaker 1/2/71
67	HUTCHINS, Richard	27	A.B. to 1/9/69 Bos'ns Mate.		Boatswain 5/2/71
26	PARKER. Isaac.	27	A.B. to 25/3/69 Bos'ns Mate		Yeo. Sheets 28/8/69
36	HUGHES, Richard.	22	A.B.	Carpenter's Mate (Joiner)	Carpenter 15/8/71 (after voyage)
87	NOWELL, George	—	A.B.	Carpenter's Crew	Carpenter 12/2/71
4/101	TERREL, Edward.	19	A.B.	Carpenter's Mate or Servant.	
14	HAITE, Francis.	42	A.B.	Carpenter's Crew	Ex *Dolphin* D.D. 30/1/71
42	MOODY, Samuel.	40	A.B.	Carpenter's Crew (Joiner)	D.D. 30/1/71
97	THURMAN or THURMOND, John	20	A.B.	Sailmaker's Mate	D.D. 3/2/71
2/103	HOWSON, William	16	Captain's Servant	Ex *Grenville* A.B. 30/4/70	D.D. 1/12/70
104	CHARLTON, John.	15	Captain's Servant		from 1/5/70 Ex *Grenville*
41/99	HARVEY, William	17	1st Lieut.'s Servant A.B. 7/4/69		
91	MOREY, Nathaniel	—	2nd Lieut.'s Servant		
65/118	MANLEY, Isaac George	12	Master's Servant		Midshipman 5/2/71 Admiral 1837 & last *Endeavour* survivor
73/s68	JONES (1st) Thomas	—	Surgeon's Servant		Astronomer's Svt 19/12/70
58	MATHEWS, Thomas	—	Ship's Cook's Servant		
48/119	JORDAN, Thomas	—	Boatswain's Servant A.B. from 5/2/71		RUN Thames 12/9/71
63	ROBERTS, Daniel	—	Gunner's Servant		D.D. 2/2/71
143	STILL, John	—	Gunner's Svt 1/7/71 No previous record.		
8	REARDON, Timothy	25	A.B. Bos'ns Yeoman		D.D. 24/12/70
43	JOHNSON, Isaac	26	A.B. Cooper		D.D. 18/12/70
88	GOODJOHN, John	—	A.B. Cooper's Mate		
12	DAWSON, William	19	A.B. Cooper's Steward		
70	CHILDS, Josiah	29	A.B. Captain's Cook		Ship's Cook 1/2/71
75	KNIGHT, Thomas	—	A.B. Lieut's Cook		
55	COLLETT, William	20	A.B. Barber		
60	WOLFE, Archibald	39	A.B. Tailor		D.D. 31/1/71
46	JEFFS, Henry	—	A.B. Butcher		D.D. 27/2/71
25	SUTHERLAND, Forby	29	A.B. Poulterer		D.D. 1/5/70
6	SMITH, Isaac	16	A.B.		Ex *Grenville* Ret. Rear Admiral 1807
7	FLOWER, Peter	18	A.B.		Ex *Grenville* Drowned 2/12/68
93	MAGRA, James Maria	—	A.B.		Midshipman 27/5/71
53	GRAY, James	24	A.B.		Quarter Master 5/2/71

Ship's Book No.	Name	Age	Rating	Duty	Remarks
11	RAMSAY, John	21	A.B.		
15	JORDAN, Benjamin	30	A.B. Carpenter's Mate		D.D. 31/1/71
18	JONES, Samuel	22	A.B.		
24	NICHOLSON, James	21	A.B.		D.D. 31/1/71
29	SIMMONDS, Thomas	24	A.B.		
52	STAINSBY, Robert	27	A.B.		Tattooed at Tahiti
66	COX, Mathew	22	A.B.		
68	WILLIAMS, Charles	38	A.B.		
71	SIMPSON, Alexander	—	A.B.		D.D. 21/2/71
76	STEPHENS, Henry	28	A.B.		
77	JONES (2nd) Thomas	27	A.B.		
82	PONTO, Antonio.	24	A.B.		Born Venice
83	DOZEY, John	20	A.B.		(Brazil) D.D. 3/4/71
85	TUNLEY, James	24	A.B.		
86	LITTLEBOY, Michael	20	A.B.		
89	WOODWORTH, John	—	A.B.		D.D. 24/12/70
92	PECKOVER, William	21	A.B.		
94	LITTLEBOY, Richard	25	A.B.		
98	PERIERA, Manoel	—	A.B. (Joined at Rio)		D.D. 27/2/71
106/S61	YOUNG, Nicholas	—	BOY. (Supernumerary with Banks. Taken on strength 6/11/70 as Surgeon Perry's servant)		

NOTE: D.D. = Discharged Dead. RUN = Deserted.
19 more men were entered at Batavia from November 1770; 10 more at the Cape of Good Hope, March–April 1771.

List of Marines

No.	Name	Rating	Remarks
M1	EDGECUMBE, John	Sergeant	
M2	TRUSLOVE, John	Corporal	D.D. 24/1/71
M3	ROSSITER, Thomas	Drummer	
M4	JUDGE, William	Private	
M5	PAUL, Henry		
M7	PRESTON, Daniel		D.D. 15/2/71
M8	WILTSHIRE, William		
M9	GREENSLADE, William		Lost Overboard 26/3/69
M10	GIBSON, Samuel		
M11	DUNSTER, Thomas		D.D. 25/1/71
M12	WEBB, Clement		Gun Room Steward [Master]
M13	Bowles, John		

List of Supernumeraries of HM Bark *Endeavour*

No.	Name	Age	Remarks
S2	BANKS, Joseph, Esquire.		Naturalist
S3	SOLANDER, Daniel Carl	35	Naturalist
S4	GREEN, Charles	33	Astronomer D.D. 29/1/71
S5	REYNOLDS, John	—	Green's Servant D.D. 18/12/70
S6	PARKINSON, Sydney	23	Botanical Artist D.D. 26/1/71
S7	BUCHAN, ALEXANDER	—	Landscape Artist D.D. 17/4/69
S8	SPÖRING, Herman Dietrich		Asst. Naturalist D.D. 25/1/71
S9	ROBERTS, James		Banks's Footman*
S10	BRISCOE, Peter		Banks's Footman*
S11	RICHMOND, Thomas		Banks's Negro Servant D.D. 16/1/69
S12	DALTON, George		Banks's Negro Servant D.D. 16/1/69
S65	TUPIA (Tahitian)		Interpreter &c. Joined 18/4/69; D.D. 11/12/70
S66	TARHETO (Tiato)		Tupia's Boy Servant. Do. 18/4/69; D.D. 9/10/11/70

*Both Briscoe and Roberts give this designation of themselves in their own crew lists.

By the time the ship reached England, 25 of the 76 ship's company, 4 of the 12 marines, and 9 of the 13 supernumeraries were dead.

The complement of *Endeavour* had been laid down as: First Lieutenant (being Cook as commander and purser) Second Lieutenant, Master, Surgeon, Boatswain, Gunner,

Carpenter, and a cook. Each of these was to have a servant. Then there were the Master's Mates (2), Midshipmen (3), Surgeon's Mate (1), Clerk (1), Steward (1), Quartermasters (2), Boatswain's Mates (2), Carpenter's Mate (1), Armourer (1), Sailmaker (1) and Able Seamen (40), making a total of seventy-one in all.

On 20 July, a Third Lieutenant with servant was added. On the 30th, Admiralty Minutes noted that the complement was to be increased to a total of eighty-five. On 3 August, at Plymouth, Cook was told to embark one sergeant, one corporal, one drummer, and nine private marines. At the same time he received instructions to pay the ship's company two months' advance of pay. The complement was then eighty-five.

Under the Act of Parliament of 1751, every naval vessel in commission was directed to bear on its books a certain number of fictitious men, to be carried as able seamen, 'the produce of whose wages and the value of whose provisions [were] to be applied to the poor widows of commissioned and warrant officers of the royal navy.' These were known as 'widows' men'. *Endeavour* was already carrying one, but now, with the complement over seventy-five, she was entitled to another. This would then bring the strength to eighty-six—one over complement. So Robert Brown was discharged and sent to H.M.S. *Cornwall*. Five had already been discharged sick or due to other causes; a further eighteen had been 'run men' (deserters); but all had been replaced.

The ship carried Mr Green, an astronomer who, together with Cook, was an observer for the Royal Society for the Transit of Venus. Mr Banks and his retinue of ten (officially) embarked on Friday 26 August 1768, at Plymouth, from whence *Endeavour* sailed with ninety-six people (including eleven supernumeraries on board and two 'ghosts' whose numbers on the ship's books were 16 and 96, the widow's men).

It is difficult to get to know most of these people as individuals because so little has been left of them. At best we gather some general impressions, with—here and there—a few particulars. From the listing of the ship's company we have perhaps begun to form some idea of their various duties. There is information in the ship's muster lists, now in the Public Records Office, as well as that given at times by the journal- and log-keepers. James Roberts and Peter Briscoe, both Banks's servants, preface their logs with a useful list of ship's company occupations not detailed elsewhere: boatswain's yeoman, carpenter's crew, joiner, cooper and cooper's mate, armourer's mate, sailmaker's mate, yeoman of the sheets, coxswain, captain's cook, lieutenants' cook, and a cook's boy. Several extra stewards are mentioned as well as a barber, a butcher and a poulterer.

'The man you have been pleased to appoint Cook of His Majestys Bark Endeavour, is a lame infirm man, and incapable of doing his Duty without the assistance of others . . .,' the Captain wrote to Navy Board, who appointed John Thompson in his place. The Captain then further submitted, 'as this man hath had the misfortune to loose his right hand . . . I am very desirous of having no one on board but what is fully able to do their duty in their respective stations . . .' To which Navy Board replied, '. . . there being no ship Vacant to provide for John Thompson Cook of the Endeavour Bark, We cannot comply with your request . . .'[1] Thus *Endeavour* sailed with a one-handed cook who seems to have performed well and drawn no complaints.

From *Grenville,* Cook had brought five of his shipmates with him. It is most probable that these men would spread the word on the mess deck in answer to that first question sailors ask, 'What's the Old Man like?' Cook must have had a good reason for bringing each of these men with him.

Isaac Smith, able seaman, aged sixteen, was to become a midshipman, then master's mate, in *Endeavour*. He was a cousin to Elizabeth Cook. The Captain remarks that he was: 'of great use to me in assisting to make Surveys, Plans, Drawings &c[a], in which he is very expert.'[2] He eventually became a rear-admiral and was to write of Cook, 'As for my self, who was with him the first two voyages as a petty officer, a youngster, I never thought him severe, and he was both loved and properly feared by the ship's company; and when he was very ill, the first question asked by officers and men on the relief of the watch at night was "How does the Captain do, is he better?"' Others, too, have testified as to how paternal Cook could be to the youngsters, especially when away in boats, when he would ponder the ways of the world with them.

Peter Flowers, Able Seaman, aged eighteen: 'He was a good hardy seaman and sailed with me above five years.'[3] Cook was greatly affected when Peter fell overboard leaving Rio and was drowned.

Thomas Hardman, aged thirty-three, joined *Endeavour* as boatswain's mate and later was to become her sailmaker. He had sailed with Cook for a year.

John Charlton, aged fifteen, had been Cook's servant in *Grenville* since 1765.

William Howson, aged sixteen, joined *Endeavour* as captain's servant until 30 April 1770, when he was mustered as able seamen again. He had been a year in *Grenville*.

That Cook saw fit to bring these five men with him must be testimony enough of their character and ability. But experience also came to *Endeavour* from another common source. The copper-bottomed, 32-gun frigate *Dolphin* had just completed her second circumnavigation of the world under Captain Wallis, discovering Tahiti on the way. This was to provide *Endeavour* with the ideal place from which to observe the Transit of Venus; otherwise, *Endeavour* would have had to search for such a platform herself. Thus, *Dolphin* provided six previous circumnavigators (plus the goat).

Francis Haite, Able Seaman, aged 42, had been on *Dolphin's* first voyage (Captain Byron) but not the second, and joined *Endeavour* as carpenter's yeoman.

Charles Clerke, aged twenty-five, had been an able seaman and midshipman in *Dolphin,* also only on her first voyage, and joined *Endeavour* as master's mate. Clerke was known as a lively young man who, as a boy in the Seven Year's War, was aloft in one of the mast tops and went over the side with it as it was shot away in action, but was still able to clamber back onboard up the shattered rigging, trailing from the chains. He was to remain with Cook on all three voyages, and, after Cook's death, was to take charge of the expedition. He persevered with Cook's intended programme despite illness and was to die before the ships could be brought home.

John Gore was the man who finally brought the ships back. He joined *Endeavour* as third lieutenant at the age of thirty-eight. He had been at sea since he was 25, had already been twice around the world in *Dolphin* and was about to make his third circumnavigation in *Endeavour*. He was an excellent practical seaman, a close natural observer and a keen hunter, shooting the first kangaroo at Endeavour River.

Robert Molyneux, aged twenty-two, had been master's mate in *Dolphin* with Wallis, and joined *Endeavour* as her master.

Richard Pickersgill, aged nineteen, had also been in *Dolphin*, joining *Endeavour* as master's mate.

Francis Wilkinson, also from *Dolphin*, joined *Endeavour* as an able seaman but, in a few months, was master's mate.

Thus we have the third lieutenant, the master and three master's mates all with pertinent experiences to share. Cook wrote that both Molyneux and Pickersgill were valuable assistants in his chart-making. All left us good journals.

There may be some confusion over the ranking of the lieutenants. Officially, from Cook down, they were first, second and third. But in practice, with Cook taking the title 'Captain' as the commanding officer, Hickes (his own spelling) became first lieutenant, and Gore became second lieutenant.

Zachary Hickes was twenty-nine years old and had served as master's mate and acting lieutenant before joining *Endeavour*. He was a very stable and reliable man, but he was to die before the voyage was over. On 19 May 1771, Cook sadly records in his journal, 'Hoisted out a boat and sent on board the *Houghton* for the Surgeon Mr Carret in order to look at Mr Hicks who is so far gone in a Consumption that his Life is despaired of.' He died on the 26th, when Cook further writes, 'He died of a Consumption which he was not free from when we sailed from England so that it may be truly said that he hath been dieing ever sence, tho he held out tollerable well untill we got to Batavia.'

William Brougham Munkhouse (his own spelling) was the surgeon. He was a good professional man and an excellent observer, as is evidenced by those fragments of his journal which survive.

William Perry, aged twenty-one, was surgeon's mate. He became surgeon when Munkhouse died at Batavia. He stood high in Cook's opinion.

Jonathon Munkhouse was the surgeon's younger brother and a midshipman to whom Cook entrusted responsible jobs. He survived his brother by only a couple of months.

Charles Green, the astronomer, had come from *Aurora*, in which he had been purser. He was appointed an assistant at the Royal Observatory, Greenwich, in 1761. In 1763, he had sailed with Nevil Maskelyne in the *Princess Louisa* for the historic second test of Mr Harrison's chronometer. He was very dedicated to his profession and somewhat impatient towards those not so dedicated. He gave a great deal of valuable instruction to the petty officers of the ship. As Cook remarked,

Green was of great assistance to him. Green's attitude as an instructor is revealed in one of the entries in his log: 'The Obs^{ns} of this Day are pretty good, the air being very clear, but might have made more and better, if *Proper Assistance* could have been had from the Young Gentlemen on Board with pleasure to themselves; otherwise their Obs^{ns} cannot be depended upon, when made a fatigue instead of a pleasure.'

By his naming of those who assisted with the daily observations an insight is gained into some of the actions and reactions that make up the running of the ship. The carpenter attended on occasions. Also Richard Orton, the captain's clerk: 'The Watch was stopped by Mr Horton by taking off the case to see the seconds more distinctly. Therefore the time must be had by the Obs^{n} of Pollux taken by self.'

All were not Britishers in the crew. Antonio Ponto, aged twenty-four, came from Venice and had joined the ship in July. John Dozey, aged twenty, came from the Brazils and had also joined as an able seaman in July. James Magra came from New York and joined as an able seaman. Manoel Periera, an able seaman, was taken on in Rio de Janeiro in December 1768 to replace the drowned Peter Flowers.

Mr Banks and his party were borne on the ship's books for victuals but not for pay, which was at Mr Banks's own expense. Banks's right-hand man was Dr Daniel Carl Solander, born at Piteå, in Northern Sweden, in 1733. He was one of Carl Linnaeus's most able pupils. Linnaeus, the great figure of European science in the eighteenth century, inspired a Swedish tradition of scientific travel. 'The "apostles" of Linneaus went to all corners of the world. They became victims of pirates and plague, hunger, thirst and poverty. Some of them died far from home. But the harvest of knowledge brought home was, nevertheless, enormous,' to quote a Swedish pamphlet. Professor J.C. Beaglehole tells us that Solander was 'a charming fellow . . . he was 35 [on leaving England], rather portly, radiant with good feeling; constitutionally almost incapable of answering a letter—or even of opening a good many—but by no means [the] lazy fellow . . .'[4] In 1762, the botanist John Ellis wrote to Linnaeus of him, 'He is exceedingly sober, well behaved and very diligent, no way expensive; so that I hope he will do very well. I can assure you, the more he is known, the more he is liked.' He had trained in medicine before becoming a naturalist. We hear him speak in a letter to Linneaus:

Rio de Janeiro
on board the *Endeavour*

Honourable Herr Archiater and Knight,
my well-disposed promoter,

. . . When this ship was equipped to make discoveries in the southern part of the *mare pacifico* [Pacific Ocean] and to bring out an astronomer to observe the transit of the sun [*sic*] across the disc of the sun on the next 3rd of June, a young rich gentleman named Joseph Banks decided to go too for the sake of Natural History; I have been well acquainted with him for many years and he proposed to me to go with him at his expense. I thought that such an offer and such an opportunity should not be turned down; We therefore made an application together to the King of England to obtain passage on the ship, which was so well received by the government that the captain was ordered to give us the best cabins and to receive as well 3 draughtsmen and 6 hands who all belong to Herr Banks. The astronomer's name is Green. The ship was called *Endeavour*, the captain's name is James Cook . . . Our intention is to sail around the southern point of the Magellanic land, that is called Cape Horn, and from there make our course through the South Seas to a big island that was discovered 3 years ago by an English Captain Wallis and named George's Land; it is inhabited by a very kind-hearted, civilized and well-shaped people. The island is situated in the South Seas under the Southern Tropic approximately halfway between America and Asia (139 degrees west of London). There we plan to perform our astronomic observations and maybe stay 4 to 6 months; if afterwards our ship and crew are in a good state I believe we will try to see if there are no unknown countries left for us to discover; our ship's name alludes to that, Endeavour meaning Attempt. Our return home is no doubt likely to take place through the East Indies, probably we will see Batavia and *Caput bonae spei*. We will probably not return home before 1771. And if Mr Banks then is in the same spirit as now to follow up his studies of Natural History we will probably directly undertake together a journey to Sweden to ask Herr Archiater to be muster master of our recruits . . .

Mr Banks calls upon me to report his best respect.

I have the honour to persist continuously with the
greatest humility
Honourable Herr Archiater's and Knight's
most honourable servant
Dan. C. Solander[5]

Mr Banks at this time was about twenty-five years of age.

Sydney Parkinson, aged twenty-two, was the Botanical Draughtsman. It is to him that we owe most of the pictorial records of this voyage. And it is from him that we have the only contemporary sketches of the ship herself. His industry was amazing and it continued to within a very short time of his miserable death from dysentery after the ship left Batavia.

Alexander Buchan was Banks's landscape artist. He was esteemed by all on board, but he has left little behind, as he died from complications following an epileptic fit taken a few days after arrival in Tahiti.

Herman Dietrich Spöring, assistant naturalist and draughtsman, was also a Swede. Born about 1733, his father was a professor of medicine, and he studied surgery. He was an able naturalist and instrument maker. He left us many exquisite topographical drawings of the coasts, as well as of natural history.

James Roberts, aged sixteen, and Peter Briscoe were Banks's 'footmen', by their own designation, and both kept journals which we have today. In this it would seem that they had been on good terms with one or another of the master's mates.

Thomas Richmond and George Dalton were negro servants to Banks.

Nicholas Young, a boy, is a small mystery for he does not appear on the ship's books until 18 April 1769, yet he must have been in the ship all the time. He took the place of Alexander Buchan on the ship's books, and would appear to have been one of Banks's people for he stayed with him after this voyage. He was the first to sight New Zealand from the masthead, and thus has left his name on the map at Young Nick's Head. That he was not universally liked we learn from midshipman Bootie's log, with an irreverent note written in it: 'Evil communications corrupt good manners. N Young is a son of a Bitch.' Bootie also classes himself as 'Master's Brute.'

Banks had two greyhounds with him, one of which was Lady.

We get only occasional glimpses of the personalities from the journals and logs, for it must be remembered that these were deliberately written in a laconic and impersonal style with the author often appearing in the third person. But to compensate for this a little let us consider the sailor generally.

It is fashionable to search out those Freudian flaws which make for sensational journalism and pseudo-drama. 'All history is conflict,' says one historian; but I think that your average sailor would look askance at this assumption. He, like the sea, the wind, and the ship, seeks only equilibrium. He suspects that looking for the chinks in another's armour gives only that restricted view through one's own.

Something in the sailor's way of life makes him simple. He becomes uncomplicated and direct. His psychiatrist's couch is the crowded mess deck. Here, group therapy dissolves his inhibitions and sorts him out. If inconvenience is an adventure viewed wrongly, and adventure an inconvenience viewed rightly, then here are men with enough inconveniences to make oceans of adventure, and who are able to keep their normality afloat in it. Their traditional right to grumble, crying thus out of the depths, was a major bulwark between them and an overwhelming feeling of absolute impotence—as in the case of the abysmally sea-sick ordinary seaman grinding out in defiance, 'Roll! Roll, you bastard. Roll! *You'll* get tired before *I* do!' It was with such self-mocking braggadocio that *Endeavour*'s sailors faced the worst, to keep intact what they knew were small and vulnerable identities. They were much too occupied with the larger issues of survival and existence, health and sleep, to be overly concerned with those inner personal problems we now have so much time to invent, cultivate, and dwell upon until the sum of the parts becomes greater than the whole—having experts in this field to help us, as a benefit of progress, that we may in supine position pay our tribute to it. While the sailor had his private problems and desires, his privacy had a two-way obligation: it was not intruded upon by others; nor was it to obtrude upon others. Together with the general environment and this code, he remained contained, and much of the problem was resolved by self-absorption and dispersal.

Language, tailored to the situation, was the jargon of their dispersal. It was rich in nautical flavour and frank in anatomical reference. It was horrid to the uninitiated, mistaking for obscenities what were but incantations with inherent liturgical rhythms to soften the impact of circumstance and necessity with humour. The result, although not short on bluntness, cultivated its own euphony. Mr Forster, the German botanist on Cook's second voyage, tells of what he heard during a storm:

> The voices of the sailors louder than the blustering winds or the raging of the ocean itself, uttering horrible volleys of curses and oaths. They execrated every limb in varied terms, piercing and complicated beyond the power of description. Inured to dangers from their infancy, they were insensible to its threats, and not a single reflection bridled their blasphemous tongues. I know of nothing comparable to the dreadful energy of their language.[6]

The sailor could mock, bitterly enough, with irreverence, many vaunted values and social pretensions, slapping them in the face with the facts of life. Yet he could also remain loyal to a deeper code of obligation and duty. Dr Johnson may have said, 'They are happy as brutes with a piece of fresh meat—with the grossest sensuality . . .', but they were generally *true* brutes: that is (in the terms of the strange inversion of our self-serving language) like the *lower* animals—for the only *inhuman* of all animals is man himself. We must not neglect, either, his sexuality in this age of voyeurism and vicariousness.

There was a simple way practised by countless normal people before the mere mechanics and plumbing of sex became its all. It was a process that may fairly be called sublimation, in the dictionary sense of the word. But, despite this label, it had more to do with plain commonsense than with morality or things transcendent. The sailor did not make of his mess decks the wholesale Sodom and Gomorrah of popular conception.

To the extent to which nature has decreed that the male shall ever be the gallant to the female, the sailor makes his ship his female, unconsciously circumventing frustration and repression with sublimated service. At sea there are clear insights which negate most of the cultivated characteristics of sex so exaggerated by social pressures of the civilised shore-bound world.

In unconsciously following this line, the sailor of yore may be thought to be an idealist. Perhaps it is not so much to his credit, for he had powerful aids. He had fresh air and work. He had demands upon all his waking hours in the exercise of which he had some professional pride. Because these calls could so constantly be made upon him, he had the perpetual longing to lie only in the voluptuous arms of Morpheus to find his fulfilment. This he expressed in a simple dictum when at sea: 'All time not spent in sleep is wasted'. In the dog watches, on deck or below, he could invent and occupy himself with the most childish and energetic games or dances which were often parodies of the actual work he did. Bawdy and ribald, maybe, but not salacious. He could get drunk when he got the chance and go to sleep without giving his sexuality a thought. If many psychological problems arise out of leisure and lack of direction, of necessity the sailor was delivered from this. Of course, the ship's company was as human and as fallible as any shore group, but, like the hard-worked captives of the Imperial Japanese Army during World War II, they had a powerful salutary therapy wrought upon them by their situation. Life on board was no idyll, for no man reaches his Utopia; yet these men had ways of making their condition tolerable.

There was some discontent and grousing at first over Cook's anti-scorbutic and dietary ideas, as well as over his trading regulations which 'oligopolized' (as one journal keeper put it) the trade to appointed officers (usually Banks and the surgeon). This was to keep the value of their trade goods stable for the getting of provisions from ashore, and which was vital for the ship to be able to eke out their own supplies for the prolonged voyage. Cook, however, was not acting out of self-interest, and the men had a way of knowing this. They could accept a just cause while in no way giving up their right to grumble, if only to show that Britons never shall be slaves. Thus were floggings accepted when, as in Cook's case, they had to be given as part of that inevitable system of discipline to which the Captain was as bound as the sailors themselves were. A catalogue (given later) of their venial sins and punishment offers further insight into the minds of these men.

The picture is rather of morale and discipline than of a ferment of discontent and mutiny. The reaction on the mess decks to punishments was pretty realistic. The victim may be told, 'Bad luck, Matey'; 'You daft bastard'; 'Was it worth it?'; 'You showed 'em!'; 'You can't fart against thunder, Mate'; 'Don't get caught next time—that's all, Mate'; and so on. But all of this was said with a fellow-feeling that was not open to any outsider, and it was as cautionary to themselves as to the victim. They all knew the game and its rules. Just officers were respected, and even loved at times. Early lectures given to new entries into the service in the first half of this century told them that the word *discipline* is formed from 'disciple', a *willing* follower. All knew that a slack ship is an unhappy ship.

The Lower Deck understood the folly, stupidity or plain cussedness of a victim, but they also understood the position of the Captain. For them, psychological trauma had little meaning.

Samuel Gibson, marine, was given two dozen lashes for desertion, but he became Cook's corporal of marines on his second voyage, and his sergeant of marines on the third. Robert Anderson, able seaman, was twice punished, but became Cook's gunner on his second and third voyages. There were others heavily censured by Cook who later received recommendations and promotion from him. Cook, aside from his natural humanity, understood the people, having lived on the Lower Deck himself. On arrival in Tahiti in April 1769, he wrote:

> At this time we had but a very few men upon the Sick list and these had but slite complaints, the Ships compney had in general been very healthy owing in a great measure to the Sour krout, Portable Soup and Malt; the first two serve'd to the People, the one on Beef Days and the other on Banyan Days, Wort was made of the Malt and at the descrition of the Surgeon given to every man that had the least symptoms of Scurvy upon him, by this Means and the care and vigilance of Mr Munkhous the Surgeon this disease was prevented from geting a footing in the Ship. The Sour Krout the Men at first would not eate untill I put in practice a Method I never once knew to fail with seamen, and this was to have some of it dressed every Day for

the Cabbin Table, and permitted all the Officers without exception to make use of it and left it to the option of the Men either to take as much as they pleased or none atall; but this practice was not continued above a week before I found it necessary to put every one on board to an Allowance, for such are the Tempers and disposissions of Seamen in general that whatever you give them out of the Common way, altho it be ever so much for their good yet it will not go down with them and you will hear nothing but murmurings gainest the man that first invented it; but the Moment they see their Superiors set a Value upon it, it becomes the finest stuff in the World and the inventer an honest fellow.[7]

'HER BEST SAILING IS WITH THE WIND A POINT OR TWO ABAFT THE BEAM, SHE WILL THEN RUN 7 OR 8 KNOTS AND CARRY WEATHER HELM.'
— COOK

Later he wrote:

Whatever refreshment we got that would bear a division I caused to be equally divided amongest the whole compney generally by weight, the meanest person in the Ship had an equal share with my self or any one on board, and this method every commander of a Ship on such a Voyage as this ought ever to observe.[8]

On Christmas Day, 1768, he wrote, 'Yesterday being Christmas Day the people were none of the Soberest.' While Banks, from the outside and lacking some of the rapport, wrote 'Christmas Day: All good Christians that is to say all hands get abominably drunk so that at night there was scarce a sober man in the ship, wind thank God very moderate or else the lord knows what would have become of us.' One may be sure that Cook, nevertheless, had a weather eye lifted.

1 August 1771. Admiralty Minutes:

> Resolved that he [Cook] be acquainted the Board extremely well approve of the whole of his Proceedings, and have great satisfaction in the account he gives of the good behaviour of his officers and men, and the chearfulness and alertness with which they went through the fatigues and dangers of the Voyage.[9]

On 23 October 1770 Cook had written a letter to the Admiralty from Batavia:

> In Justice to the officers and the whole crew I must say that they have gone through the fatigues and dangers of the whole voyage with that cheerfullness and allertness that will always do honour to British Seamen, and I have the satisfaction to say that I have not lost one man by sickness during the whole Voyage.[10]

Here he must allude only to scurvy, but the pestilent port of Batavia was to take a frightful toll. This commendation of the people was from a man as competent as any man in the ship in the practical skills of the common sailor, as well as his own more professional ones, and who asked a high standard. But he *understood*. He could encourage and praise as well as censure, forgive as well as charge. The skills of his mind were inseparable from those of his hands, and complementary, making a Whole Man, as Spinoza had termed the phenomenon two hundred years before.

On the return to England in 1771, he did not give a bad report of one man, even commending several for advancement. Nor did he forget the youngsters. 'Mr Isaac Smith & Mr Isaac Manly, both too young for perferment, yet their behavour merits the best recomendation. The former was of great use to me in assisting to make Surveys, Plans, Drawings &c^a^ in which he is very expert.'[11]

As an admiral in 1837, Manley was the last *Endeavour* survivor. Smith retired rear-admiral in 1807. Manley is an example of the paternal instinct that is strong among sailors. He was Molyneux's servant and it is obvious that Molyneux, as master, gave good instruction to the boy. Many began their careers as 'servants' to interested officers who tutored them in a *noblesse oblige* way. Nor was this unique to the officers, for the Lower Deck had its tradition of experience tutoring inexperience in the young. An older man in experience, though not necessarily in years by so much, would take a youngster under his wing and assume the responsibility for his sea education with many of the characteristics of a parent. This led them to be called Winger, and Sea Daddy, and skills were passed on that could not be written in books. It was part of the normal anatomy of ship life.

The sailor's environment taught him acceptance—to make the best of what was there. Nelson once wrote to his wife about a lieutenant, 'He is too nice in his dress and fidgetty and has not the *knack of being contented with his situation*.' Charles Darwin, at the end of the five-year voyage of *Beagle* in 1836, wrote of the effect of the voyage upon himself:

> In a moral point of view, the effect ought to be to teach him goodhumoured patience, unselfishness, the habit of acting for himself, and of making the best of everything,

> or contentment: in short, he should partake of the characteristic qualities of the greater number of sailors.[12]

Henry Fielding, the author of *Tom Jones*, and a practising eighteenth-century magistrate, had an unrivalled knowledge of life in depth at that time. He wrote, in an account of a voyage he had made:

> To say the truth, from what I observed in the behaviour of the sailors in this voyage, and comparing it with what I have formerly seen of them, at sea, and on shore, I am convinced that on land there is nothing more idle and dissolute; but in their own element, there are no persons, near the level of their degree, who live in the constant practice of half so many good qualities.[13]

CHAPTER 6

FROM MISFORTUNE, AND BY THEIR SINS

Amongst these men there are those who are glimpsed only by some misfortune overtaking them. There had been a number of these by the time the ship arrived off the coast of New Holland.

On 14 September 1768, at Funchal, Madeira, while laying out the kedge anchor from a boat in mooring the ship, Alexander Weir, aged 35, and one of the master's mates, became fouled in the bight of the buoy rope as the anchor was cast out of the boat. He was dragged to the bottom and drowned, before help could be given. The anchor was at once weighed, his body still tangled in the rope. Cook gives the circumstances in his journal:

> In the night the bend of the Hawsers of the stream Anchor slip'd, owing to the carelessness of the person who made it fast. In the morning hove up the Anchor in the Boat and carried it out to the Southward, in heaving the Anchor out of the Boat Mr Weir Masters mate was carried over board . . . Hove up the anchor by the Ship as soon as possible and found his body intangled in the Buoy-rope.[1]

Phrases from other logs are his obituary. 'Weighed the kedge and found Mr Ware's corps intangled in the buoy rope 5 fathom from the anchor.' 'Mr Ware mate, having charge of the boat.' 'Mr Ware, one of the mates, got himself in the bite of the buoy rope.' '. . . was snatched overboard and drowned . . . got on board the kedge and Mr Weir's Corps.' '. . . to the utter grief of the Ships Company.' And Sydney Parkinson records: 'While the ship lay in this harbour, we had the misfortune of losing Mr Ware, the chief-mate, who was a very honest worthy man, and one of our best seamen . . . The buoy-rope happening to entangle one of his legs, he was drawn over board and drowned before we could lend him assistance.'

At 10 o'clock the next morning, his body was taken out to the offing in the small ten-foot yawl, and buried with weighted feet to stand on the bottom like a silent sentinel, as do all sea-dead thus shrouded. While, to replace him and keep the ship up to complement, John Thurmond, an able seaman, aged twenty, was impressed into His Majesty's service from a New York sloop in the harbour.

At Rio de Janeiro on 2 December, 'In turning down the harbour Peter Flower Seaman fell overboard [from the main chains] and before assistance could be given him was drown'd, he was a good hardy seaman, and had sailed with me [Cook] above five years. In his room we got a Portuguese.' This was Manoel Pereira, able seaman, who became number 98 on the ship's books. John Thurmond was number 97, following the second widow's man, 96.

While in the Bay of Good Success at Tierra del Fuego on 16–17 January 1769, Mr Banks, Dr Solander, Mr Buchan and their four servants Roberts, Briscoe, Dalton and Richmond, with Surgeon Munkhouse, Mr Green and two seamen, 'set out from the ship to try to penetrate into the country as far as we could, and if possible to gain the tops of the hills where alone we saw places not overgrown with trees.' The weather was fine, 'much like a sun-shiny day in May, so that neither heat nor cold was troublesome.' But the way became more difficult than they had imagined because of the dense, stunted birch. They were about two-thirds of the way to their objective when Mr Buchan, who was an epileptic, took a fit. They lit a fire and only Mr Banks, Dr Solander, Mr Green and Mr Munkhouse 'advanced to the alp.'

There were frequent flurries of snow and Banks gave up all hope of being able to return to the ship that night, and could think of nothing but of getting into the thick wood and making a fire. The cold increased. It was then about eight o'clock, but still light. They proceeded to a rendez-vous in the nearest valley 'where the short Birch, the only thing we now dreaded, could not be ½ a mile over. Our people seemd well tho cold and Mr Buchan was stronger than we could have expected. I [Banks] undertook to bring up the rear to see that no one was left behind. We passd about half way very well when the cold seemd to have an effect infinitely beyond what I have ever experienced.'

Dr Solander was the first affected and could think of nothing but lying down, despite all of Banks's protests. Next affected was Richmond, one of the black servants. Banks sent a party forward, of whom Buchan was one, to make a fire at the first convenient place. Banks stayed to goad Solander and Richmond and had got through the worst of the birch when they both gave out. Richmond was told that if he did not go on he would 'be froze to death'. He answered that he would lie there and die. The Doctor said that he 'must sleep a little before be could go on, and actually did a full quarter of an hour.' They then got word of a fire about a quarter of a mile ahead. Banks was able to get the doctor on the move, but Richmond would not stir. So two hands least affected by the cold were left with him, promising to send two more to relieve them when they reached the fire.

Banks tells the rest of the story:

> . . . as soon as two people were sufficiently warmed sent them out in hopes that they would bring Richmond and the rest; after staying about half an hour they returnd bringing word that they had been all round the place shouting and hallowing but could not get any answer. We now guess'd the cause of the mischeif, a bottle of rum the whole of our stock was missing, and we soon concluded that it was in one of their

Knapsacks and that the two who were left in health had drank immoderately of it and had slept like the other.

For two hours now it snowd almost incessantly so we had little hopes of seeing any of the three alive: about 12 however to our great Joy we heard shouting, on which myself and 4 more went immediately and found it to be the Seaman who had wakd almost starvd to death and come a little way from where he lay. Him I sent back to the fire and proceeded by his direction to find the other two, Richmond was upon his leggs but not able to walk the other [Dalton] lay on the ground as insensible as a stone. We immediately calld all hands from the fire and attempted by all the means we could contrive to bring them down but finding it absolutely impossible, the road was so bad and the night so dark that we could scarcely ourselves get on nor did we without many Falls. We would then have lit a fire upon the spot but the snow on the ground as well as that which continualy fell renderd that as impracticable as the other, and to bring fire from the other place was also impossible from the quantity of snow which fell every moment from the branches of the trees; so we were forc'd to content ourselves with laying out our unfortunate companions upon a bed of boughs and covering them over with boughs also as thick as we were able, and thus we left them hopeless of ever seeing them again alive which indeed we never did.

In these employments we had spent an hour and a half expos'd to the most penetrating cold I ever felt as well as continual snow. Peter Briscoe, another servant of mine, now began to complain and before we came to the fire became very ill but got there at last almost dead with cold.

Now might our situation truely be calld terrible: of twelve [11?] our original number 2 were already past all hopes, one more was so ill that tho he was with us I had little hopes of his being able to walk in the morning, and another very likely to relapse into his fitts either before we set out or in the course of our journey: we were distant from the ship we did not know how far, we knew only that we had been the greatest part of a day in walking it through pathless woods: provision we had none but one vulture which had been shot while we were out, and at the shortest allowance could not furnish half a meal: and to compleat our misfortunes we were caught in a snow storm in a climate we were utterly unaquainted with but which we had reason to believe was as inhospitable as any in the world, not only from all the accounts we had heard or read but from the Quantity of snow which we saw falling, tho it was very little after midsummer . . .

The Morning now dawnd and shewd us the earth coverd with snow as well as all the tops of the trees, nor were the snow squalls at all the less Frequent for seldom many minutes were fair together . . .

About 6 O'Clock the sun came out a little and we immediately thought of sending to see whether the poor wretches we had been so anzious about last night were yet alive, three of our people went but soon returnd with the melancholy news of their being both dead.[2]

The two dead were Richmond and Dalton, both the negro servants. Molyneux tells us that, when they were found, Banks's faithful greyhound, Lady, was lying close-by mournfully watching her late friends.

Banks continues:

> Peter continued very ill but said he thought himself able to walk. Mr Buchan thank god was much better than I could have expected, so we agreed to dress our vulture and prepare ourselves to set out for the ship as soon as the snow should be a little more gone off: so he [the vulture] was skinnd and cut into ten equal shares, every man cooking his own share which furnishd about 3 mouthfulls of hot meat, all the refreshment we had had since our cold dinner yesterday . . .[3]

Arriving on the beach about 1 pm, 'with what pleasure then did we congratulate each other on our safety no one can tell who has not been in such circumstances.'[4] But Banks was irrepressible. Molyneux tells us, 'as soon as they came on board and were refreshed they were put into warm beds, Mr Banks excepted who considering our short stay and the uncertainty of the weather, applied for a boat to haul the sane [seine net] which was done without success the foul ground and the depth of water rendering the sane useless.'[5]

On passage from the Bay of Good Success, round Cape Horn to Tahiti, at about latitude 21° 30′ S, longitude 127° 43′ W, on 26 March 1769, Cook records, 'At 7 Wm Greenslade Marine either by Accident or design went over board and was drownded . . .'[6]

Banks gives a more circumstantial account:

> This even one of our marines threw himself overboard and was not miss'd till it was much too late even to attempt to recover him. He was a very young man scarce 21 years of age, remarkably quiet and industrious, and to make his exit the more melancholy was drove to the rash resolution by an accident so trifling that it must appear incredible to every body who is not well acquainted with the powerfull effects that shame can work upon young minds.
>
> This day at noon he was sentry at the Cabbin door and while he was on that duty one of the CaptS servants being calld away in a hurry left a piece of seal skin in his charge, which it seems he was going to cut up to make tobacco pouches some of which he had promisd to several of the men; the poor young fellow it seems had several times askd him for one, and when refusd had told him that since he refusd so trifling a thing he would if he could steal one from him, this he put in practise as soon as the skin was given into his charge and was of course found out immediately as the other returnd, who was angry and took the piece he had cut off from him but declared he would not complain to the officers for so trifling a cause.
>
> In the mean time the fact came to the ears of his fellow soldiers, who stood up for the honour of their Core 13 in number so highly that before night, for this hapned at noon, they drove the young fellow almost mad by representing his crime in the blackest coulours as a breach of trust of the worst consequance: a theft committed by a sentry upon duty they made him think an inexcusable crime, especialy when the thing stole was given into his charge: the Sargeant particularly declard that if the person acgreivd would not complain he would, for people should not suffer scandal from the ill behaviour of one. This affected the young fellow much, he went to his hammock, soon after the Sargeant went to him calld him and told him to follow him upon deck. He got up and slipping the Sargeant went forward, it was dusk and the

people thought he had gone to the head [latrine] and were not convincd that he was gone over till half an hour after it hapned.[7]

This was a saddening shock in such a small close-knit ship.

On 13 April *Endeavour* anchored in Matavai Bay, Tahiti, where *Dolphin* had anchored on her discovery of the place they named Port Royal Bay, George's Island. On the 17th, Cook entered in his log:

> At 2 oClock this Morning departed this Life Mr Alex Buchan Landscip Draftsman to Mr Banks, a Gentleman well skilld in his profession and one that will be greatly miss'd in the course of this Voyage, he had long been subject to a disorder in his Bowels which had more than once brought him to the Very point of death and was at the same time subject to fits of one of which he was taken on Saturday morning, [this was Monday] this brought on his former disorder which put a period to his life. Mr Banks thought it not so adviseable to Enterr the Body a shore in a place where we was utter strangers to the Customs of the Natives on such Occations, it was therefore set out to Sea and committed to that Element with all the decencey the circumstance of the place would admit of.[8]

Banks wrote:

> At two this morn Mr Buchan died, about nine every thing was ready for his interment he being already so much changd that it would not be practicable to keep him even till night. Dr Solander, Mr Sporing, Mr Parkinson and some of the officers of the ship attended his funeral. I sincerely regret him as an ingenious and good young man, but his Loss to me is irretrevable, my airy dreams of entertaining my freinds in England with the scenes that I am to see here are vanishd. No account of the figures and dresses of men can be satisfactory unless illustrated with figures: had providence spard him a month longer what advantage would it have been to my undertaking but I must submit.[9]

Buchan's loss placed an extra burden upon Sydney Parkinson who was then expected to fill this gap as well as his own demanding job of botanical draughtsman.

The logs of Monday 28 August were headed 'In search of land to the Southward, in the South Seas.' Below was the entry, 'At 10 AM, departed this life Jwo Radon [John Reading, 24 years] Boatswains Mate, his death was occasioned by the Boatswain, out of mere good nature, giving him part of a Bottle of rum last night, which it is supposed he drank all at once, he was found to be very much in Liquor last night, but as this was no more than what was common with him when he could get any, no farther notice was taken of him then to put him to Bed where this morning about 8 oClock he was found speechless and past recovery.'[10] This was written by the Captain.

The First Lieutenant, Zachary Hickes, entered, 'his death was occasioned by drinking three half pints of rum.'[11] While Banks says, 'One of the seamen Rayden by name was this morn found so drunk that he had scarce any signs of life and in about an hour he expird. Where he could have got this liquor is a mystery which however nobody seems to enquire into, probably not fairly. I have more than once had occasion to congratulate myself on my prudence in not taking wine on board in Madera, as I beleive I may safely say that there is not a cask on board the ship that has not been tap'd to the great dissatisfaction of the owners, who in general have had the comfort to find the gentlemen honest enough not to have filld up with salt water; in those cases however this was not a Consideration of much comfort as many of the casks were ⅔ empty and some quite.'[12]

As well as being boatswain's mate, John Reading had also been yeoman of the sheets. Both of these were responsible jobs. Yeoman of the sheets was 'a petty officer whose duty is to see that the fore or main sheets [of the courses—the lower square sails] are properly belayed on the working of the ship, and that they are kept clear for running.' His frailty was human rather than professional. On Reading's death, Isaac Parker, able seaman, aged 27, was made boatswain's mate and yeoman of the sheets in his place.

This was the last death before Botany Bay. Live men had been lost to the ship by accident, but the muster list had been increased by the addition of two ghosts of people still alive. One joined on 7 April 1769, as a servant to Mr Hickes; the other on 1 September as an able seaman. These were James Cook, aged 6 years; and Nathaniel Cook, aged 5. This was a commonly practised device of the time, though not strictly legal. There was no peculation of pay or provisions in this act, but it was simply to give the lads extra sea-time for promotion when they should be finally entered into the service.

Amongst these men there are those who are brought to our notice only by conduct contravening regulations, and the brief recital of their offence is their only epitaph for posterity to read.

'Read to the Ships Company the Articles of War and the Act of Parliament . . .' This was an entry of some regularity in the logs. The Articles of War[13] were, in fact, the Abstract of the Act of Parliament of 1749, which began: 'That, for the regulating and better government of his Majesty's navies, ships of war, and forces by sea, whereon, under the good providence of God, the wealth, safety, and strength of the kingdom chiefly depend. . .'

> Article I. All commanders, captains, and officers, in or belonging to any of his Majesty's ships or vessels of war, shall cause the public worship of Almighty God, according to the liturgy of the church of England established by law, to be . . . performed . . . and shall take care . . . that the Lord's Day be observed according to law.

The first logged record of this having been carried out in *Endeavour* is on Sunday 14 May 1769; it then took place on the following two Sundays as well. The services were held ashore in the tents at Fort Venus, Tahiti. Banks reports:

> It being Sunday Cap^{tn} Cooke proposd that divine service should be celebrated but before the proper time of doing it most of our Indian freinds were gone home to eat. I was resolvd however that some should be present that they might see our behaviour and we might if possible explain to them (in some degree at least) the reasons of

it. I went therefore over the river and brought back Tubourai and Tomio and having seated them in the tent plac'd myself between them. During the whole service they imitated my motions, standing setting or kneeling as they saw me do, and so much understood that we were about something very serious that they calld to the Indians without the fort to be silent; notwisthstanding this they did not when the service was over ask any questions nor would they attend at all to any explanation we attempted to give them. We have not yet seen the least traces of religion among these people, maybe they are intirely without it.[14]

Wilkinson, one of the master's mates, tells that 'This day [14 May] the most of the Ships Company attended with the officers attended [*sic*] Devine Service on Shore in one off the Large Tents Number of Indians being Preasent who Behaved all very well.'[15]

On the 21st, Molyneux records, 'This day Divine Service was perform'd as on Past Sunday & much the same Congregation present.' Other logs mention the fact, but Cook not at all. On the 28th, Molyneux again tells us that, as well as serving fresh pork to the ship's company as usual, 'this day Divine Service was perform'd as before our most Intimate Friends being present.'[16] Neither Cook nor Banks mentions this service, nor did they attend, for they were away in the pinnace paying Tootaha a visit. There is only one subsequent mention of a service, and that on 25 June. The services seem to have been taken by the surgeon, Mr Munkhouse. From the sailors' point of view, the Lord's Day was best celebrated by putting the people 'at their own leisure' or 'at their own disposal', as it was entered in the logs. This Cook allowed on Sundays as often as possible when in harbour, so that the men could get ashore to recreate.

John Knyveton has a log entry during the Seven Years War: 'This being our first Sunday at sea, all hands were mustered after breakfast and sitting on buckets and barrels and spars on the main deck, the officer of the watch and the master conning the ship; Captain Gardiner reads to the men the Articles of War, and the Chaplain afterwards to preach a prosy sermon about God's benefits, the which are doubtless obscure to the seamen . . .'[17]

Church was rigged on deck by making seats for the congregation with wooden buckets and capstan bars placed across them, and sometimes mess stools. At the beginning of the present century one still heard the sailors lustily singing: 'The Church's one foundation/is Capstan bars and Buckets . . .' which was echoed until World War II.

Some latitude must also have been allowed for Article II.

Article II. All flag officers, and all persons in or belonging to his Majesty's ships or vessels of war, being guilty of profane oaths, cursings, execrations, drunkenness, uncleanness, or other scandalous actions, in derogation of God's honour, and corruption of good manners, shall incur such punishment as a court-martial shall think fit to impose, and as the nature and degree of their offence shall deserve.

The Articles most generally affecting the men ran more or less to a formula beginning 'every person in the fleet' and, after specifying the offence, would end with 'and being convicted shall suffer death, or such other punishment, as from the nature and degree of the offence the court martial shall deem him to deserve.' These Articles, as well as being hung up in some prominent place in the ship, were ordered to be read to the ship's company at least once a month. The appropriate Article would also be read at the sentencing of an offender when the hands had been called to witness punishment. The mustered hands, including officers, would stand with heads bare, whenever any Article of War was being read—namely, thirty-six Articles, but, at the routine readings, only a selection would be read. These were those that, in the opinion of the Captain, were most pertinent to the time. This practice was still in force up to, and after, World War II. With bared head one regularly heard (and witnessed the resignation of the unfortunate offender to his lot): 'Every person subject to this Act who shall . . .', ending with 'shall suffer death or such other punishment as in hereinafter mentioned or as the Admiralty shall from time to time prescribe.'

'Ship's Company . . . On Caps! Stand at ease!'

Then the offence was read out: 'Wherein it has been represented to me that on the day of . . .' And the prisoner was sentenced and marched away under escort. In the past, floggings were carried out on the spot.

Quite a number of these Articles were still in much the same phrases as in 1749. A substantial amount had been added in the passing years until a large manual, called *King's Regulations and Admiralty Instructions*, had evolved to address every conceivable situation. It covered the destiny of the serving man from the time of his entry to his utter end, always having due regard to his station, as evidenced in the regulation on coffins. 'Coffins, Officers: brass handles, eight holding-down screws for lid, one pillow. Coffins, Ratings: imitation brass handles, six holding-down screws, no pillow.'

These methods of promulgation of the Articles made ignorance of them no excuse, and the men knew pretty well where they stood—except with vindictive officers. If Cook had any rancour against an offender, it would have been because of his having put the welfare or the safety of the ship at risk, and having a due regard for common justice. One feels that at times he must have been saddened by the foolishness of an offender before him, and about whom he had no option. His thoughts would probably have paralleled those of the Lower Deck expressions, for he had lived there himself. Flogging was no pleasant business, but it was obligatory on a commander in certain circumstances in which he was left no alternative. The men understood the position of a just commander, and both were subject to the mores of the period. To see Cook's punishments in a better perspective consider two floggings on board *Ramillies*, a first-rater, in the Seven Years War, taken from the journal of John Knyveton:

> May 11: Woke during the night by a wild uproar on the lower gun deck, whose bully strove to possess himself by force of the coats of two men, his own being wet with the spray flying through the ports, which the men must keep open if they are not to stifle. They were all three overcome, and dragged half conscious to self and Mr. Westrall,

we being nearer than the cockpit, when it was found the bully had a seven inch gash in the groin, and of the two men one had three broken ribs and his mate a crushed hand, which the bully had bitten and from which I removed a broken tooth. Today all three were flogged with thirty lashes, and the bully clapped in irons since he is violent, and his two foes set to chipping rust off the cannon shot. Since the wight with the broken ribs is spitting blood, do not think he will live.

May 12: The man with the broken ribs had a hæmorrhage and died last night, and today Captain Gardiner sat upon the bully, the court finding him guilty of High Treason since during hostilities he had aided the French by destroying a subject of the armed forces of the Crown [not to mention of the Court having been an accessary by the infliction of thirty lashes on the said subject], and a notice to this effect, and that the penalty was death, written out by the clerk and nailed to the main-mast to a roll of drums. But the court being merciful and the ship short of men, he was given instead only a hundred lashes at the gangway, our Doctor Payne standing by to see that he took his full punishment, and now lies in the sick-bay in a stupor, his two floggings having taken the most of the flesh off his back so that his spine and ribs are exposed in three places.[18]

Also from Knyveton, the case of the young deserter:

November 27: The deserted sailor being found guilty of attempted escape, was today flogged round the fleet, I attending him in the cutter as Doctor Payne is on attendance on the Admiral. The man was tied face downwards to the thwarts, and gagged with an iron bar, whilst our captain read the sentence from the gang-way, and a boat manned with a file of marines put off from each ship. I inserted a stocking between the man's wrists and his lashings, lest his struggles tore the flesh off 'em; and then with the ship's bell sounding at half minutes, and the ship's drummer beating the rogue's march beside the man, we rowed to each ship followed by the other boats manned by the musketeers; and from each ship he received twenty lashes from the boatswain's mate, who stood upon the ladder of each ship. After five ships had thus been visited, he was insensible, and though I plied him with rum, the master-at-arms with difficulty roused him to take further punishment; and after we left the eighth ship his backbone and ribs were bare and his mouth tore open by the gag; but the law being that he must receive a flogging from each vessel of the flotilla concerned, twenty lashes were given until the eleventh was reached; he dying at the ninth ship we hailed, the Trident of sixty four guns, and I glad that he was no more able to feel pain, being a slender youth of twenty two years of age; and so they bore him ashore and buried him, as the custom is, without religious rites in the mud below tide mark as example to the rest; and some grumbling from the sailors told off to wash down the longboat, at the muck in it.[19]

Cook was given over to nothing else but the maintenance of discipline for the good and safety of the whole, for a ship needs firm, just discipline to preserve her from that dissolution any number of sea tragedies will testify to.

Nevertheless, the following calendar of offences may tell a little more about the men, the ship and the Captain.

Friday, 16 September 1768: 'Read the Articles of War and punished Henry Stevens seaman and Thomas Dunster with a dozen lashes each for mutiny' (Ship's Log). 'For refusing to take their allowance of fresh beef' (Cook). 'Mutiny and disrespect' (Wilkinson). 'For mutinous expressions' (Bootie).

> Article XXI: If any person in the fleet shall find cause of complaint of the unwholesomeness of the victuals, or upon other just ground, he shall quietly make the same known to his superior, or captain, or commander in chief, as the occasion may deserve, that such present remedy may be had as the matter may require; and the said superior, captain, or commander in chief, shall, as far as he is able, cause the same to be presently remedied; and no person in the fleet, upon any such or other pretence, shall attempt to stir up any disturbance, upon the pain of such punishment as a court-martial shall think fit to inflict, according to the degree of the offence.

Saturday, 19 November 1768: 'Read the Articles of War and punished John Thurmond for mutiny' (Ship's Log). 'Punished John Thurman seaman with 12 lashes for refusing to assist the Sailmaker in repairing the sails' (Cook). 'Mutiny and disrespect' (Wilkinson).

> Article XXII: If any officer, mariner, soldier, or other person in the fleet shall strike any of his superior officers, draw, or offer to draw, or lift up any weapon against him, being in the execution of his office, on any pretence whatsoever, every such person being convicted of any such offence by the sentence of a court-martial, shall suffer death; and if any officer, mariner, soldier, or other person in the fleet, shall presume to quarrel with any of his superior officers, being in the execution of his office, or shall disobey any lawful command of any of his superior officers; every such person being convicted of any such offence by the sentence of a court-martial, shall suffer death, or such other punishment as shall, according to the nature and degree of his offence, be inflicted upon him by the sentence of a court-martial.

Wednesday, 30 November (Still in Rio de Janeiro—Cook): 'Read the Articles of War. Punished Robert Anderson seaman and William Judge marine with twelve lashes each, the former for leaving his duty ashore and attempting to desert from the ship, the latter for abusive language to the officer of the watch, and John Readon [Reading] Boatswain's Mate with twelve lashes for not doing his duty in punishing the above men.'

> For Robert Anderson:
>
> Article XVI: Every person in or belonging to the fleet, who shall desert, or entice others so to do, shall suffer death, or such other punishment as the circumstances of the offence shall deserve, and the court-martial shall judge fit: and if any commanding officer of any of his Majesty's ships or vessels of war shall receive or entertain a deserter from any other of his Majesty's ships or vessels, after discovering him to be such a deserter, and shall not with all convenient speed give notice to the captain of the ship or vessel to which such deserter belongs, or if the said ships or vessels are at any considerable distance from each other, to the secretary of the

SEPTEMBER 1ST, 1768: 'VERY HARD GALES . . . WHICH BROUGHT US UNDER OUR TWO COURSES. WASHED OVER BOARD A SMALL BOAT BELONGING TO THE BOATSWAIN.' — COOK

Admiralty, or to the commander in chief; every person so offending, and being convicted thereof by the sentence of the court-martial, shall be cashiered.

For William Judge:

Article XXIII: If any person in the fleet shall quarrel or fight with any other person in the fleet, or use reproachful or provoking speeches or gestures, tending to make any quarrel or disturbance, he shall, upon being convicted thereon, suffer such punishment as the offence shall deserve, and a court-martial shall impose.

For John Reading:

Article XXVII: No person in or belonging to the fleet shall sleep upon his watch, or negligently perform the duty imposed on him, or forsake his station, upon pain of death, or such other punishment as a court-martial shall think fit to impose, and as the circumstances of the case shall require.

There was an important principle involved in this last instance. The theory of punishment vehemently held at this time by authority was that it was a deterrent, and was absolutely necessary for the maintenance of order among such people as the navy was perforce composed of. Therefore it was essential that the punishment be *seen* to be given—which was the whole purpose for having the ship's company 'witness punishment'. The harshness of the sentence was normally related to this deterrent theory. Abnormally, it could be related to the savagery and viciousness in prosecuting officers, or from a rabid fear of the overturn of authority. This theory, sincerely held as the only solution by many reasonable men who did not lack humanity, was the reason why flogging was not abandoned until late in the nineteenth century. Even that humane man, Captain Robert FitzRoy, wrote in 1831 whilst in *Beagle*:

> Individual misconduct, arising out of harbour irregularities, obliged me to have recourse to harsh measures before we had been two days at sea; but every naval officer knows the absolute necessity of a certain degree of what inexperienced persons might think unnecessary coercion, when a ship is recently commissioned. Hating, abhorring corporal punishment, I am nevertheless fully aware that there are too many coarse natures which cannot be restrained without it, (to a degree required on board a ship,) not to have a thorough conviction that it could only be dispensed with, by sacrificing a great deal of discipline and consequent efficiency. . . . where so much often depends upon immediate decision, upon instant and implicit obedience.[20]

Men were being flogged as late as 1874. In 1865, one seaman complained, 'I say why not flog an officer as well as a man? If it teaches a lesson to men why not an officer? What is good for the goose is surely good for the gander.'

On 12 April 1769, Samuel Jones, seaman, was punished with twelve lashes for disobedience of orders. On the 16th, Richard Hutchins, seaman, also received twelve lashes for disobedience of command—both under the shadow of Article XXII.

On the 29th, Henry Jeffs, seaman, received one dozen lashes for theft. Cook does not make mention of this in his journal, but Banks and Molyneux do.

Banks was personally involved:

> My first business this morning was to see the promise I had made to Tubourai and Tomio of the butchers [Jeffs] being punishd performd, a promise they had not faild to remind me of yesterday when the croud of people who were with us hinderd it from being performd. In consequence of this I took them on board of the ship where Capt Cooke immediately orderd the offender to be punishd; they stood quietly and saw him stripd and fastned to the rigging but as soon as the first blow was given interfered with many tears, begging the punishment might cease a request the Cap^{tn} would not comply with.[21]

Molyneux relates: 'AM Punish'd Henry Jeffs seaman with a dozen lashes for ill Behaviour on shore [Tahiti]. He had been rude to a mans wife yesterday of which the Indian Complain'd & Jeffs was Confin'd immediately the Captain had the Fact Plainly prov'd & next Morning the Captain invited the offended Parties on Board who were Ignorant of his Intention; all Hands being call'd & the Prisoner brought aft the Captain Explain'd the Nature of his Crime in the most lively manner &

made a very Pathetick speech to the Ships Company, during his Punishment the women was in the greatest Agonies & strongly Interceded for him, the mans name was Tuburi & his wifes Tamide I remember them both last Voyage [in *Dolphin*]. I should have mention'd Tuburi being sorry to see Jeffs punish'd.'[22]

'The Captain Explain'd the Nature of his Crime in the most lively manner & made a very Pathetick speech . . .' This one sentence of Molyneux's gives perhaps one of the closest glimpses on record of Cook the inner emotional man. Reflecting, and relating it to other times and places in his life, reveals much by implication. Cook was pleading not the Articles of War but the code from whence sprang his own deep convictions, hinting at the quality of his own relationship with Elizabeth.

He was covered legally by:

> Article XXXVI [the last of them all]: All other crimes not capital, committed by any person or persons in the fleet, which are not mentioned in this act, or for which no punishment is hereby directed to be inflicted, shall be punished according to the laws and customs in such cases used at sea.

Unfortunately, it was this very Article that gave unscrupulous and tyrannical officers the opportunity to inflict almost unlimited punishments for almost any offence they chose to invent. But not Cook.

4 June 1769 (Cook): 'Punished Arch[d] Wolf with two Doz[n] Lashes for theft, having broken into one of the Store rooms and stolen from thence a large quantity of spike Nails, some few of them were found upon him.'[23] Roberts, Banks's footman, tells us in his nominal list that Wolfe was 'Captain's Tailor', which could have given him the opportunity, as he may have been allowed to work in one of the store rooms on occasion when tailoring. He probably sewed for others as well, earning himself some extra spirits or tobacco, the usual currency at sea. In this situation his offence was serious (larceny as a bailee), though the temptation was understandable, the more so when one realises that nails were the most ready currency for Tahitian women's favours. But perhaps Cook was more concerned with the devaluation of his trade goods. The breadfruit season was coming to an end and provisions were becoming more difficult to get. It was important that the ship should get as much from shore as possible to reserve the sea provisions so that endurance at sea could be extended for exploration. When Wallis had been here in *Dolphin*, the men had actually pulled nails out of the ship herself to exchange for fair favour ashore. He was virtually obliged to sail before the ship came apart. The Article which provided for Wolf's punishment was:

> Article XXIV: There shall be no wasteful expence of any powder, shot, ammunition, or other stores in the fleet, nor any embezzlement thereof, but the stores and provisions shall be carefully preserved, upon pain of such punishment to be inflicted upon the offenders, abettors, buyers, and receivers (being persons subject to naval discipline) as shall be by a court-martial found just in that behalf.

On Sunday 11 June, most of the *Endeavour's* company were ashore 'at their own leisure'. On Monday, James Nicholson and John Thurmond, seamen, were punished with one dozen and two dozen lashes respectively for 'disobedience of orders' or 'disobedience of Commitances' as two entries have it. Cook relates, 'Yesterday a complaint was made by some of the natives that Jn^O Thurman and Jam^S Nicholson seam^N had taken by force from them several bows and arrows and plaited hair. And the fact being proved upon them they were this day punished with two dozen lashes each.' Probably again under Article XXXVI.

On Sunday 9 July, when the ship was preparing for sea, the ship's log remarks: 'In the evening Clement Webb and Samuel Gibson marines were missing from the fort.' Cook enters in his journal:

> When sometime in the Middle Watch [midnight to 4 AM] Clement Webb & Saml Gibson both Marines & young Men found means to get away from the Fort (which was now no hard matter to do) & in the morning were not to be found, as it was known to every body that all hands were to go on board on monday morning & that the ship would sail in a day or 2, there was reason to think that these 2 Men intended to stay behind, However I was willing to wait one day to see if they would return before I took any steps to find them.[24]

Mr Molyneux adds:

> In the PM Clement Webb and Samuel Gibson Marines Elop'd from the Fort & can't be heard off. Webb is a sober man & was steward of the Gunroom which Office he faithfully perform'd but being very extravagantly fond of a young women with whom he has been connected for some time. Gibson is a wild young man & a sworn Brother to Webb he has no other reason than the pleasure of living in a fine Country without controul they both had large Promises from some of the Principal men & was to have Lands and servants assighn'd them.[25]

Sydney Parkinson tells:

> . . . two of our marines being enamoured with a girl, one of the natives deserted from the fort, and fled to the west part of the island, and intended to have staid there. On the same day one of the natives stole a knife from one of our sailors, and wounded him with it in the forehead, almost through his skull:—a fray ensued, and the Indians ran away.[26]

Despite this, Cook still gave the ship's company liberty that afternoon. During the morning of Monday 10th, the last of the gear from the fort was taken onboard. The ship was unmoored—she had been riding to two anchors. When the small bower was hove up and brought to the bows, so eaten was the stock by the teredo worm that it broke off. The unpainted bottom of the longboat had had to be replaced in May because of the same worm, and was now painted. The quartermasters were employed in the hold getting up two spare anchor stocks.

Molyneux informs us that the Captain 'Detained Tutuhah & Obreea & several other Principal persons in order to induce their dependents to return our two men, this struck general Terror through the Island & the Prisoners ('tho very well Treated) were inconsoleable.'[27]

Cook explains his problems:

> The 2 Marines not returning this morning I began to enquire after them & was inform'd by some of the Natives that they were gone to the Mountains & that they had got each of them a Wife & would not return, but at the same time no one would give us any Certain intelligence where they were, upon which a resolution was taken to seize upon as many of the Chiefs as we could, this was thought to be the readiest method to induce the other natives to produce the two men. We had in our Custody Obarea, Toobouratomita and two other Chiefs but as I know'd that Tootaha would have more weight with the Natives than all these put together, I dispatch'd Lieut[t] Hicks away in the Pinnace to the place where Tootaha was to endeavour to decoy him into the boat and bring him on board which M[r] Hicks perform'd without the least disturbance. We had no sooner taken the other Chiefs into Custody in M[r] Banks's Tent [ashore in Fort Venus] than they became as desireous of having the men brought back as they were before of keeping them, and only desire'd that one of our people might be sent with some of theirs for them; accordingly I sent a Petty Officer [Jonathon Munkhouse, midshipman] and the Corporal of Marines [John Truslove] with three or four of their people not doubting but what they would return with the two Men in the evening, but, they not coming so soon as I expected I took all the Chiefs on board the Ship for greater safety. About 9 oClock in the evening Web the Marine was brought in by some of the Natives and sent on board, he inform'd me that the Petty officer & the Corporal that had been sent in quest of them were disarm'd and seiz'd upon by the Natives and that Gibson was with them. Immediatly on geting this information I dispatch'd M[r] Hicks away in the Long boat with a Strong party of men to resque them but before he went, Tootaha and the other Chiefs was made to understand that they must send some of their people with M[r] Hicks to shew him the place where our men were, and at the same time to send orders for their immidiate releasement for if any harm came to these men they, the Chiefs, would suffer for it, and I believe at this time they wished as much to see the Men return in safty as I did, for the guides conducted M[r] Hicks to the place before daylight and he recover'd the men without the least oposission and return'd with them about 7 oClock in the Morning of [Tuesday 11].[28]

Banks gives more details: 'We are told by the Indians this morn that . . . one is already married and become an inhabitant of Otahite,' and to recover them,

> one certain method remaind however in our power, the seizing of some of their principal people and detaining them, which was immediately resolvd upon. Oborea, Potattow, Pototheara, Tubourai, Tamio, Tuarua, Otheothea and Tehiuatea and Nuna were in the fort and were told that they would not be permitted to go from it till our people returnd. At first they were not at all alarmd, they hardly believed us in earnest till they saw the Pinnace come ashore and soon after go away to the westward, the[y] immediately suspected what was the case, that she was gone to fetch Dootahah. They were now alarmd but depending on our having used them well on all occasions shewd but little signs of either discontent or fear, but assurd us that the people should be brought back as soon as possible. In the evening Dootahah was brought on board, Lieutenant Hickes who had been sent on the service found him at Tettahah and

easily took him or rather stole him from the people. Night came on, it was thought unsafe to let the prisoners remain in the fort, which was totally dismantled; Oborea, Potattow and Tubourai were ordered to the ship; in going into the boat they expressd much fear and shed many tears. The Cap^{tn} staid on board with them, I slept ashore and the rest of the prisoners in my tent. At about 8 our Indians came back with the two deserters but brought the disagreeable news of one of the people who had been sent after them being seizd by the Indians, who declard that they would not release them till Dootahah had his liberty. The news was sent aboard and a boat came off immediately for Nuna and Tuanne matte. They were sent to the ship, a boat armd went immediately in search of the people and in her the latter and Tupia who was our voluntary prisoner.[29]

Cook:

I then told the Chiefs that there remaind nothing more to be done to regain their liberty but to deliver up the Arms the people had taken from the petty Officer and Corporal and these were brought on board in less than half an hour and then I sent them all a Shore, they made but a short stay with our people there before they went away and most of the Natives with them but they first wanted to have given us four Hogs, these we refus'd to accept as they would take no thing for them. Thus we are likly to leave these people in disgust with our behavour [*sic*] towards them, owing wholy to the folly of two of our own people for it doth not appear that the natives had any hand in inticeing them away and therefore were not the first agressors, however it is very certain that had we not taken this step we never should have recoverd them.

The Petty officer whom I sent in quest of the deserters told me that the Natives would give him no intellingence where they were nor those that went along with him, but on the contrary grew very troublesome and as they were returning in the evening they were suddenly Siezed upon by a number of arm'd men that had hid themselves in the woods for that purpose; this was after Tootaha had been seized upon by us so that they did this by way of retaliation in order to recover their Chief, but this method did not meet with the approbation of them all, a great many condem'd these proceedings and were for having them set at liberty, while others were for keeping them until Tootaha was relase'd. The desputes went so far that they came from words to blowes and our people were several times very near to being set at liberty but at last the party for keeping them prevail'd; but as they had still some friends no insult was offer'd them; a little while after they brought Web and Gibson the two deserters to them as prisoners likewise but at last they agree'd that Web should be sent to inform us where the others were.

When I came to examine these two men touching the reasons that induce'd them to go away, it appear'd that an acquentence they had contracted with two Girls and to whome they had stron[g]ly attache'd themselves was the sole reason of their attempting to Stay behind.[30]

Again Banks supplements:

The night was spent tolerably well, the women cryd a little at first but were soon quieted by assurances that at all events they should not be hurt. At day break a large number of people gatherd about the fort many of them with weapons; we were intirely without defences so I made the best I could of it by going out among them. They wer[e] very civil and shewd much fear as they have done of me upon all occasions, probably because I never shewd the least of them [and Banks was a big man] but have upon all our quarrels gone immediately into the thickest of them. They told me that our people would soon return. Accordingly about 8 they did safe and sound, we saw them through our glasses go up the [ship's] side and immediately dischargd our prisoners, making each such a present as we though[t] would please them with which some were well content. The prisoners from the ship were by this time coming ashore. They were receivd with much joy by the multitude; I met them from the boat but no sign of forgiveness could I see in their faces, they lookd sulky and affronted. I walkd with Oborea along the beach: 4 hoggs were soon offerd me, two from her and as many from Dootahah, I refusd them however positively unless they would sell them which they refused to do. The rest of the morning was employd in getting the tents aboard, which was done by dinner time and we dind on board.[31]

Jonathon Munkhouse shows how impersonal log-keeping can be. His complete entry for the day reads:

> Tuesday 11: [wind] East, ENE, D^{o} Weather. Employed getting an anchor stock out off the main hold. Carp^{trs} Stocking the Anchor. At 9 PM. Clem^{t} Webb returned, informed us that Mr Munkhouse Midsh^{n} and the Corporal of Marines were seized by the Natives while they were endeavouring to find out about the Deserters—D^{o} sent the Long-boat with the 1st Lieut^{t} and a party to recover them. AM. The Long-Boat returnd with the afforesaid & and the other Deserter. D^{o} Released the Chiefs.[32]

While Hickes's simply reads:

> D^{o} Weather. got another anchor stock up at 9 C. Webb one of the men that deserted, arrived at the tent, and said that the inhabitants had detained Mr Monkhouse & the Corporal of Marines that had been sent in pursuit of the deserters. Captain sent away the Long boat with the first Lieutenant to release them—who seized upon some of the Principal chiefs of the Island and brought them on board and in the Evening went again to the W^{d} and returned with Mr Monkhouse the Corporal and the two marines that deserted on which we released the chiefs. Carpenters employd making a new spare anchor stock—discharged ye canoes that had been seized.[33]

On the 12th, a small anchor which was intended for a coasting anchor was let go and the best bower weighed. The stock of this was so worm-eaten that half of it fell off before it came to the bows. Parkinson tells us that the making and fitting of the stocks held the ship up for two days.

According to the muster lists, two Tahitians were entered on the ship's books on 18 April. They were Tupia, a man, and Tarheto (Tiato), a boy, his servant. But it is not until 13 July, on the point of this departure from Tahiti, that any of the logs mention them as joining the ship. This back-dating of their service must have been a bonus. On the 13th, Cook writes:

> For some time before we left this Island several of the natives were daily offering themselves to go away with us, and as it was thought that they must be of use to us in our future discoveries, we resolved to bring away one whose name was *Tupia*, a Cheif and a Priest: This man had been with us the most part of the time we had been upon the Island which gave us an oppertunity to know some thing of him: we found him to be a very intelligent person and to know more of the Geography of the Islands situated in these seas, their produce and the religion laws and customs of the inhabitants than any one we had met with and was the likeliest person to answer our purpose; for these reasons and at the request of Mr Banks I received him on board together with a you[n]g boy his servant.[34]

Banks records:

> The Cap^tn refuses to take him on his own account, in my opinion sensibly enough, the government will never in all human probability take any notice of him; I therefore have resolvd to take him. Thank heaven I have a sufficiency and do not know why I may not keep him as a curiosity, as well as some of my neighbours do lions and tygers at a larger expence than he will probably ever put me to . . . and the benefit he will be to the ship, as well as what he may be if another should be sent into these seas, will I think fully repay me.[35]

As soon as Tupia had decided to sail with them he went ashore saying that he would return in the evening and make a signal for a boat. He took with him a miniature picture belonging to Banks to shew his friends as well as several little things to give them as parting presents. Later Banks also went ashore to farewell his friends, telling them that the ship was to sail before noon. That night Tupia returned to the ship where he took up his lodgings for the first time.

Banks describes the departure, as a great number of his friends came down to farewell them:

> . . . when the anchor was weighd; they took their leaves tenderly enough, not without plenty of tears tho intirely without that clamourous weeping made use of by the other Indians, several boats of whoom were about the ship shouting their lamentations, as vyeing with each other not who should cry most but who should cry loudest—a custom we had often condemnd in conversation with our particular friends as savouring more of affected than real greif.
>
> Tupia who after all his struggles stood firm at last in his resolution of accompanying us parted with a few heartfelt tears, so I judge them to have been by the Efforts I saw him make use of to hide them. He sent by Otheothea his last present, a shirt to Potomai, Dootahah's favourite mistress. He and I went to the topmast head where we stood a long time waving to the Canoes as they went off, after which he came down and shewd no farther signs of seriousness or concern.'[36]

Parkinson writes, 'On our leaving the shore, the people in the canoes set up their woeful cry, Awai, Awai; and the young women wept very much. Some of the canoes came up to the side of the ship, while she was under sail, and brought us many cocoas.'[37]

Tupia and Tiato were the last to join the ship until she got to Batavia, where, sadly, they were both to die. Molyneux tells us more about them:

> We have on Board a Native of an Island nam'd Uliateah, his Name is Tobia he was a Principal Man in his own Country but the Incursions of the Bola Bola men (an Island adjacent) drove him from his Possessions & Oblig'd him to Fly to Queen Obree[a] for shelter, with her he has liv'd some time in the Quality of High Preist, he is Attended by one servant only who is an Indian Boy about 12 years old his name is Tioto. Tobia during our accquaintance with him has appear'd always to be infinitely superior in every Respect to any other Indian we have met with, he has conceiv'd so strong a Friendship for Mr Banks that he is Determined to Visit Britannia.[38]

At 8 AM on 14 July, with the ship at sea, Clement Webb and Samuel Gibson were punished with two dozen lashes each for all the trouble they had caused, and were released from confinement. Neither of them seems to have harboured much resentment. In 1808, Clement Webb wrote to Sir Joseph Banks for some assistance, frankly identifying himself: 'to bring my person to your recollection I beg leave to mention that I am one of the two men who were desirous of remaining at Otaheite.'[39]

Only two more offences remain by which to get a glimpse of the men's propensity for misdemeanour. The first is an incident which happened in the Bay of Islands, New Zealand, on Saturday 2 December 1769. It involved the gunner and three seamen. It shows Cook's immediate reaction to breaches of good order and discipline, and his inability to hold a grudge.

In his holograph journal of this date we find:

> Between 12 and 4 AM the Gunner having the Charge of the watch, he together with Alex^r Simpson, Richd Littleboy and [Thos Rossiter] found means to take out of the Spirit Cask on the quarter deck between 10 and 12 Gallons of Rum being the whole that was in the Cask they were caught in the very fact and part of the Rum was found in the Gunners Cabbin. The three men I punished with 12 lashes each, but as to the Gunner who richly deserved the whole upon his back is from his Drunkenness become the only useless person on board the Ship.[40]

This was then altered to: 'part of the Rum was found in their possession for which crime I not only punished them with 12 lashes each but stoped their allowance untill it amounts to the quantity stolen.' This entry was finally deleted, leaving no reference to this incident in the holograph journal. At the end of the voyage, Cook recommended Forwood for promotion. Certainly Forwood's log does not give the impression of professional incompetence, whatever his private weaknesses.

A couple of days before this, on 30 November, the other incident occurred at the same place, but ashore. At 3 in the afternoon the Captain and gentlemen went ashore in the pinnace and yawl with some marines and the boats' crews who were armed. They had not been long there when they were surrounded by about three

hundred Maori. Muskets loaded with small shot were fired by the gentlemen to discourage the natives. The situation began to look serious and threatening.

Cook writes, 'I avoided killing any one of them as much as possible and for that reason withheld our people from fire-ing.'[41] And Banks writes:

> We were in a sandy cove behind the two heads of which most of them landed [natives in canoes], one or 2 only in sight; out of these they came running with every man his arms, others appear on the tops of the hills and numbers from behind each head of the Cove so that we were in a moment surrounded by (the gentlemen in the ship say) 5 or 600 men tho we I beleive never saw more than 200 of them. We now every man expected to be attackd but did not chuse to begin hostilities so the Cap^{tn} and myself marchd up to meet them.[42]

On the coast of New Zealand: 'they brandished their arms and showed signs of contempt, while the rest paddled hard to overtake us.'
— Parkinson

By this time the alert first lieutenant, Mr Hickes, on board had become alarmed and had put a spring on the cable. When this spring was brought in on the quarter deck, led to the capstan and heaved in while veering on the cable, the ship came on a yoke, like a kite, and was turned so that her broadside came to bear on the trouble spot ashore. This was termed *pointing ship*. The three four-pounders of the complete broadside were fired and three cannon balls passed over the heads of the Maori on the hills, giving warning by the sound of their passage. On this the Maori retired. It was then about 4 o'clock. The landing party re-embarked and rowed to another cove on the same island, near which was a high hill. Banks and Cook climbed the hill so that the Captain could get a good view of the bay. It was here that 'some of the inhabitants came to [them] as meek as lambs.' The boats were loaded with celery grass 'which here we found in great plenty.' They returned to the ship at 7 pm. Banks says that 'around us we could see large Indian towns, houses and cultivations . . . as this one was very near to us, from whence several Indians came to us taking however great pains to shew us that they were unarmed.'

It was evidently while Cook and Banks were away that three men left the boats and dug up some potatoes from a nearby plantation. The next morning, the ship being wind-bound and unable to sail, Cook:

> sent the Master with two Boats to sound the harbour, but before this I order'd Math^{w} Cox, Hen^{ry} Stevens and Man^{l} Paroyra to be punished with a doz^{n} lashes each for leaving their duty when a shore last night and digging up Potatoies out of one of the Plantations, the first of the three I remited back to confinement because he insisted that there was no harm in what he had done.[43]

The following day Cox was given another half-dozen lashes and released. In this case Mathew Cox did harbour resentment and, on his return to England in 1771, brought a civil action against Cook which an Admiralty solicitor was detailed to defend. Nothing seems to have come of this action.

This much we learn of human frailty, but a little more knowledge may be had from some small adventures—to show us something of the nature of the sailors' job in exploration.

CHAPTER 7
PERADVENTURE

A strong spirit was endemic in the plain understatements of *Endeavour*'s log-keepers; superlatives were only ever used as a testimony to fact, not as an affectation.

From the first landing at Poverty Bay, Cook found the conduct of the Maori in complete contrast to that of the Tahitians. Lieutenant John Gore sets the scene with his entry for 9 October 1769:

> The Boats were all hoisted out when Mr Cook in the Pinnace and myself in the Yawl landed on the North side of the Bay near a small rivulet. We had with us the Marines all properly Arm'd and likewise the Boats crews and ourselves. Mr Banks, Doctor Solander and Mr Green were with us [also Surgeon Munkhouse], when we Landed Mr Cook left the Boats in charge of the Coxwain [Samuel Evans] and a proper number of men to defend them with orders not to fire upon any of the Natives should any appear unless the[y] offer'd violence. We crossed the Rivulet in search of fresh water and the Natives some of whom we had just seen before we landed who on our appearance ran away. Whilst we were hunting about a small distance from and out of sight of the Boats heard some firing as from them. We immediately went to know the meaning of it and found that some of the Natives armed had been down and athreatening made signs to the Coxwain to be gone. He not complying one of them brandishing a Lance and was just on the point of throwing it when the Coxwain fir'd and kill'd one of them, the rest help'd him to some distance took his arms and ran off. Our Long boat having carried out an anchor to steady the ship came to us with empty casks for fresh water which we as yet found none, we saw some empty hutts several sorts of wild fowl and wild sellery. It now being near dark we all set off for the Ship and all got on board.
>
> In the morning about 8 oclock Mr Cook in the Pinnace, and myself in the Long boat and a Petty Officer in the Yawl all properly man'd and arm'd, the same gentlemen in Company as before. We set off from the ship. Mr Cook's intention being to go Quite Round the Bay in Search of a watering place, about 9 we landed at the place we left over night when about an hundred of the Natives all arm'd came down on the opposite side of the salt river, drew themselves up in lines. Then with a regular jump

from left to right and the reverse they brandished their weapons, distended their mouths, lolling out their tongues and turned up the whites of their eyes, the whole accompanied with strong hoarse song, calculated in my opinion to chear each other and intimidate their enemies and may be call'd perhaps with propriety a Dancing War Song [*Haka*]. It lasted 3 or 4 minutes, after which Mr Cook and the other gentlemen together with the help of Toobiah [Tupia] whose language they seem'd to understand, used every method they could think of to draw some of the natives over to us. At last some of them came over and took very greedily sundry things that were given them. In the meantime one of them snatching a hangar from Mr Green's back, a skirmish ensued. Some of them were kill'd and the rest ran off, after which we set off on our journey round the bay.[1]

Cook gives some more details of this last skirmish:

soon after this about 20 more came over all armd they would willingly have exchanged their arms for ours but would not part with them on any other condition and several attempts [to] snatch ours out of our hands. I got Tobia to tell them that we was their friends and only come to get water and to trade with them and that if they offer'd to insult us we could with ease kill them all, but Tobia told us plainly that [they] were not our friends and and [*sic*] told us several times to take care of our selves, and it appeared very plane that all they came for was to seize some of our arms, they several times snatched hold of my musquet, and one of them at last Tore Mr Green's hanger from his side and was making off with it when I orderd him to be fired upon. Mr Banks first fired with only small shot which the fellow did not seem to mind but turnd about and flowrished the hanger about I then ordered Dr Munkhouse whose piece was load with a ball to fire at him and the man fell upon this some of the others who had retreated to the rock before mentioned return'd and attempted to seize the hanger and actily made them selves master of the mans own arms, and this Mr Munkhouse who was close by could not prevent unless he had run his Bagnet [bayonet] into them upon the men return from the rock I fire'd so did Mr Green and Tobia we all three being load with small shot, yet three more was wounded, but got a Cross the River and lead off by the others. The man who I thought at first was dead recovered so far as talk to Tobia—yet their was great probability of the wound being Mortal, finding nothing was to be done here, with the natives and the river affording no fresh water, I embark'd with an intent to row round the whole Bay in search of some and if possible to surprise some of the natives and bring them on board and by good treatment endeavour to gain their friendship.[2]

With what the surgeon, Mr Munkhouse, has to tell us the situation is brought into a sharper focus. Of the previous afternoon, he writes:

. . . on which repairing instantly to the boats we recieved the following account of the cause from the Coxswain—that soon after we left them, the boys in the yawl had gone upon the beach to divert themselves, that they had not remained long so before four of the Natives descended from an Ambush a little removed from the river on the same side we had landed on armed with very long lances, and marched towards the yawl; that the boys on observing this, instantly got into the Yawl and endeavoured to make their escape: meanwhile, the Coxswain attending to what had passed and fearing the boys might be cut off fired a musket in the air, which our friends payed no other reguard to than brandishing their weapons—he fired a Musketoon [one of the swivels mounted in the longboat] with no better effect. He then levelled at the headmost of the party and shot him: the others instantly retired a few paces then returned to lead off their fallen comrade—they bore him about fifty yards and now finding him dead they left him and retired tho' in no kind of haste. After hearing this Story we pursued the blood-track and found the body. He was a short, but very stout bodied man—measured about 5 f. 3 I. Upon his right cheek and nose were spirals of tattaou or punctuation of the skin—he had three arched tattaous over his left eye drawn from the root of his nose towards the temple; each arch about four lines broad [$^{4}/_{12}$, ie $\frac{1}{3}$, of an inch]—the interval between each about a line broad; this was an exceeding new and singular appearance and seem[ed] meant to give fierceness to the Visage; his hair, coarse and black, was tied upon the crown of his head—his teeth were even and small but not white—his features were large but proportional—his nose well formed—ears bored—his beard short . . . The ball had passed from the sixth rib on the left side thro' the right shoulder blade. Some nails and beads were put upon the body, and we took our leave of the shore.[3]

Of the latter skirmish the surgeon is far more circumstantial than the others:

. . . we found they understood his [Tupia's] language—A long conversation ensued, which seem^{d} to consist on their part of inquirys from whence we came, of complainings that we had killed one of their people, and of many expressions of doubt of our friendship—their pronounciation was very guttural, however Tupia understood them and made himself understood so well that he at length prevailed on one of them to strip of his covering and swim across—he landed upon a rock surrounded by the tide, and now invited us to come to him. C. Cook finding him resolved to advance no farther, gave his musket to an attendant, and went towards him, but tho' the man saw C. Cook give away his weapon to put himself on a footing with him, he had not courage enough to wait his arrival, retreating into the water, however he at last ventured forward, they saluted by touching noses, and a few trinkets put our friend into high spirits—at this time another was observed to strip and enter the river but he very artfully concealed his weapon under the water—he joined his countryman and was presently set a dancing striking his thighs, and shewing the baubles he had receiv^{d} to his friends on the other side. The ice was broke, and we had in a moment six or eight more over with us all armed, except the first visiter, with short lances—a kind of weapon we took for a paddle—and a short hand weapon which was fastned by a string round the wrist . . . this weapon, we afterwards learnt, was called *Pattoo* . . . But our new visiters kept us now in sufficient employment—Active and alert to the highest degree . . . every moment jumping from one foot to the other; and their eyes and hands as quick as those of the most accomplished pickpocket. I happened to be most forward of our company, and was engaged with three of these young active heroes at one time: this new manoeuvre disconcerted me for a moment, but my situation presently taught me to play the counterpart in these curious gesticulations, added to which, having my bayonet fixt, I was frequently obliged to call this to my aid—on bidding them sit down, one or other would obey for a Moment—to keep them in employment, I offered to barter for a paddle, which he was very ready to exchange for my musket, and my refusal drew a reproach from him.

Whilst I was thus engaged my friends behind me were not less busied; but one of the natives having expressed a desire to have Mr [Green's] hanger, to avoid being too much teased Mr [Green] had turned about to retire, which the man no sooner observed than he laid hold of the hanger and tore it away, and, contented with his prize, instantly retreated towards the river. The sufferer snapt his musket then fired a pistol—a charge of small shot was thrown into his back but he continued to make his escape until a musket ball dropt him—two others instantly flew to him, I presented my bayonet thinking they meant to carry off the hanger, but they soon convinced me that it was a green stone pâttoo they only wanted, which one of them tore from his wrist and retreated, while the other endeavoured to keep me at bay.

Matters were now in great confusion—the natives retiring across the river with the utmost precipitation, and some of our party unacquainted with the true state of things begun to fire upon them by which two or three were wounded—but this was put a stop to as soon as possible. The Natives now set up a most lamentable noise and retired slowly upon the beach. The Shot man had a human tooth hanging at one ear and a girdle of Matting about four inches broad was passed twice round his loins & tied. He had a paddle [? *pouwhenna*] in his hand which, tho' drawing his last breath, he would not part with without the greatest reluctance.

In this interview we had not leasure to examine the persons and dress of these people . . .[4]

The surgeon now sets the scene for the next incident in their search for water around the bay:

We got round to the South side without meeting with any such situation [a watering place] when two Canoes were observed coming in from Sea, the headmost of which was under sail: they stood toward us, that is, it seemed that we lay in their route home; the pinnace stood to meet them, and now they endeavoured to get inshore of her, but finding this impracticable, they lowered their Sail and begun to strip as if they meant to jump overboard—before they put this in practise, however, they chose to hazard an engagement, and as soon as the Pinnace got pretty nigh them one of them threw a large Stone which fell short; they then threw sticks and paddles, and seemed resolved to stand on their defence so long as they had any thing Missile left.

In a word, there were seven people in this boat four of whom were wounded: two of these took to the water and hung by the boat till they were drowned—two young boys were taken out of the boat—a third, a young Man about twenty, jumpt overboard and gave the Yawl a very good chase after him for as she got up with him he instantly dived, and thus kept them in play for at least ten minutes: at last he was caught but would not come into the boat till they brought him to the long boat where after recieving repeated assurances that he would not be killed, he consented to be taken in; the Canoe with the remaining two wounded Men was allowed to drive ashore—I omitted mentioning that when these poor wretches had spent their ammunition and found themselves over matched they attempted to hoist their mast and sail again to get off. The other Canoe was larger and had more people, availed herself of the present state of matters and paddled in shore very briskly.[5]

Cook was dismayed at these developments and writes:

> Tupia called to them to come along side and we would not hurt them, but instead of doing this they endeavoured to get away, upon which I order'd a Musquet to be fire'd over their heads thinking that this would either make them surrender or jump over board, but here I was misstaken for they immidiatly took to their arms or whatever they had in the boat and began to attack us, this obliged us to fire upon them and unfortunatly either two or three were kill'd, and one wounded, and three jumped over board, these last we took up and brought on board, where they were clothed and treated with all immaginable kindness and to the surprise of every body became at once as cheerful and as merry as if they had been with their friends; they were all three young, the eldest not above 20 years of age and the youngest about 10 or 12.
>
> I am aware that most humane men who have not experienced things of this nature will cencure my conduct in fireing upon the people in this boat nor do I my self think that the reason I had for seizing upon her will att all justify me, and had I thought that they would have made the least resistance I would not have come near them, but as they did I was not to stand still and suffer either my self or those that were with me to be knocked on the head.[6]

Molyneux tells us that the three boys were 'at first much terrified but finding we understood something of their Language they asked if they should be eat but being informed that we detested such a thing that we intended to carry on board & in the Morning Land them amongst their friends. This made them happy'.[7]

And Banks goes on:

> this good usage had such an effect that they seemd to have intirely forgot every thing that had happned, put on chearfull and lively countenances and askd and answerd questions with a great deal of curiosity. Our dinner came, they expressed a curiosity to taste whatever they saw us eat, and did; salt pork seemd to please them better than any thing else, of this they eat a good deal. At sunset they eat again an enormous quantity of Bread and drank above a quart of water each; we then made them beds upon the lockers [in the Great Cabbin] and they laid down to sleep with all seeming content imaginable. After dark loud noises were heard ashore as last night. Thus ended the most disagreeable day My life has yet seen, black be the mark for it and heaven send that such may never return to embitter future reflection . . .
>
> In the middle of last night one of the boys seemed to shew more reflection than he had done before, sighing often and loud; Tupia who was always upon the watch to comfort them got up and soon made them easy. They then sung a song of their own, it was not without some taste, like a Psalm tune and containd many notes and semitones; they sung it in parts which gives us no indifferent Idea of their taste as well as their skill in musick. The oldest is about 18, the middlemost 15, the youngest 10; the middlemost especialy has the most open countenance and agreable manner . . . the two first [are] brothers.
>
> In the morning they were all very chearfull and eat an enormous quantity, after that they were dressd and ornamented with bracelets, ancklets and necklaces after their own fashion. The boats were then hoisted out and we all got into them: the boys express'd much joy at this till they saw that we were going to land at our old

Landing place . . . where they said were Enemies of theirs who would kill and eat them. The Captn resolved to go ashore at that place and if the boys did not chuse to go from us, in the evening to send a boat with them to the part of the bay to which they pointed and calld their home. Accordingly we went ashore and crossd the river. The boys at first would not leave us. No method was usd to persuade them; it was even resolvd to return and carry them home when on a sudden they seemd to resolve to go and with tears in their eyes took leave. We then went along the swamp intending to shoot some ducks of which there was great plenty; the countrey was quite flat; the Sergeant and 4 marines attended us walking upon the bank [the sand dunes between them and the sea] abreast of us which overlookd the countrey. We proceeded about a mile when they Calld out that a large body of Indians was marching towards us, we drew together and resolvd to retreat; before we had put this in execution the 3 boys rose out of a bush in which they were hid and put themselves again under our protection. We went upon the beach as the clearest place and walkd briskly towards the boats. The Indians were in two parties, one marchd along the bank before spoke of, the other came round by the morass where we could not see them; on seing us draw together they ceasd to run as they had done and walkd but gently on, a circumstance most fortunate for us, for when we came to our boats the pinnace was a mile at least from her station, (sent their [*sic*] by the officer ashore to pick up a bird he had shot); the small boat [yawl] only remaind, which was carried over the river, and without the midshipman who was left to attend her: the consequence of this was that we were obligd to make 3 trips before we were all over to the rest of the party. As soon as we were well drawn up on the other side the Indians came down, not in a body as we expected, but 2 and 3 at a time, all armd and soon increasd to a considerable number; we now despaird of making peace with men who were not to be frightned with our small arms. As the ship lay so far from the shore that [she] could not throw a shot there, we resolvd to reembark as our stay would most likley be the cause of killing still more people: we were beginning to go towards the boats when on a sudden one of the boys calld out that the people there were their freinds and desird us to stay and talk with them, we did and much conversation past but neither would the boys swim over to them nor they to the boys. The bodys of both of the man who was killd yesterday, and he who was killd the day before, were left upon the beach. The first lay very near us, to it the boys went and coverd it with part of the cloths we had given them; soon after a single man unarmd swam over to us (an uncle of Maracouete, the younger boy), he brought in his hand a green bough, probably emblem of peace; we made him many presents after having receivd his bough which he presented to Tupia our interpreter. We askd him to go onboard of the ship but he refusd so we left him, but all the 3 boys chose rather to return with us than stay with them.[8]

Cook now writes, 'I now thought proper to take every body on board to prevent any more quarrels and with us came the [three natives], whome we could not prevail upon to stay behind and this appear'd the more strange as the Man who came over to us was uncle to one of them.'[9]

Although the boys wanted to stay with the ship, they were landed safely the next morning. Molyneux concludes that, seeing that this place would not serve their present purpose, the Captain resolved to embark and proceed southward, naming this bay Poverty Bay as it furnished neither provisions nor water. The place of this encounter was where Gisborne now stands.

Such confrontations were continued along the coast and were always explosive. Cook and his men were almost always outnumbered and the possibility of a massacre was constant. Moral force and the show of firearms were the only bulwark; yet it was ever possible that this could be shattered by any chance cause amongst those who, from the European point of view, were amoral. Much has been written upon the reasons and causes of Cook's final murder. Some have suggested that it came from some failing faculty within Cook the Man. Yet, it was always an inherent possibility in these ever-recurring encounters, and Cook himself must have known this. Thus we may gain a further insight into the quiet undemonstrative high courage he so constantly sustained as an explorer. He faced the elements and his fellow humans with the same equable humanity, calmly accepting his calculated risks as an onus of duty.

The Bay of Islands incident already related had been immediately preceded by another threatening one. The ship had just anchored. The boats had been sent away, sounding when the pinnace found herself in danger of being boarded by the surrounding canoes. Two musket balls were fired short of the canoes to keep them at a distance as they returned to the ship. At two o'clock there was a heavy shower of rain. The ship was surrounded by thirty-seven canoes in which they estimated there were over three-hundred Maori. A few of these had been allowed on board and given some presents, and the ship bought some mackerel from them. But, suddenly, at a signal from one of the chiefs, some of the canoes shot ahead of the ship and laid hold of the anchor buoy, got it into one of their canoes and began to cast off the seizings. They were called upon to let it go, but to no purpose. Some muskets were fired wide of them, but, this not succeeding, a musket was levelled at the man who had hold of the buoy and a ball went through his arm. They withdrew a little and took this opportunity to fire a four-pounder over the natives, which made them leave.

'This I beleive,' Cook wrote, 'would have sent them quite off, if it had not been for Tupia who soon preavaild upon them to return to the Ship, when their behaver was such as gave us no room to susspect that they meant to give us any farther trouble.'[10]

But, as has been told, Cook was wrong.

Not only were these people truculent and deceitful on shore, but they acted with the same rashness at sea. At eight in the morning of 15 October 1769, several canoes came off to the ship which was then under way off the southern end of Hawkes Bay. Some trafficking was being carried on with reasonable fairness when a large well-armed canoe containing twenty men with painted faces came under *Endeavour*'s stern and flung a lance at her. These began to cheat in trading, particularly over the exchange of a dog-skin cloak. The canoes of the fishermen continued to trade alongside. The men in the armed canoe were lying off but it was hoped to entice them near enough to be able to drop a running bowline over their bows and haul them to the anchor in the fore chains. Just as this canoe had been lured ahead and almost into position, there was an unexpected development. At this time several of *Endeavour*'s men were over the side, standing on the steps of the sea gangway so as to pass the trade goods up and down from canoe to ship. Tiato, Tupia's boy, was at the bottom of the main wale near the water, and the captain's steward, Robert Stainsby (who had been tattooed at Tahiti), was immediately above him. At first the fishermen grabbed at the steward and failed, then they managed to snatch Tiato and, hauling him into their canoe, shoved off, two holding him down in the forepart and three paddling. The marines who were on deck and armed were ordered to fire into the canoe. One of the men holding the boy was hit and Tiato, struggling free, jumped over the side and began to swim towards the ship. The ship had at once been put about by wearing (turning stern to wind). The large canoe began to close in on the boy but musketry and a great gun fired over them turned them aside and they paddled inshore. A boat, which was already outboard, lashed to the gunwale, was lowered and was quickly in the water. They took up the boy, frightened, but not hurt. Through their glasses they saw the canoes go ashore and it was noticed that three men had to be carried up the beach. Tiato told them that the man who held him was shot through the body.

Later, when the boy had got over his fright, he brought a fish to Tupia, telling him he intended it as an offering to his *Etua*, or god, in gratitude for his escape. Tupia approved of this and told him the way was to throw it into the sea. Tiato went solemnly on deck and followed his instructions. Cape Kidnappers was the name Cook gave to the headland off which this had taken place.

On a number of occasions these large canoes had come off the coast to challenge and insult the visitors in their own manner with war chants, stone throwing, spear hurling and vociferous taunts.

In a way, the *Endeavour* voyage in the Pacific may be divided into three phases: Tahiti had been near-idyllic, with both the natives and nature hospitable; in New Zealand, the natives were certainly not hospitable, while the sea and weather there had issued challenges; New Holland was to be something quite different from both . . .

There the people, somewhat gentle and fey, strangely eluded the comprehension of the voyagers. Though their physical presence was at times close, real contact was not there. The philosophical gulf was insuperable for the Anglo-saxon. Even the land itself, age-worn and unresisting, silently called on the greatest resources of the inner James Cook, and placed upon him the choice that was the to-be-or-not-to-be of the man.

What he wrote when well-tried by this dry remote land, and finding his way through the labyrinth of the Great Barrier Reef, bears witness to this:

> The world will hardly admit of an excuse for a man leaving a Coast unexplored he has once discover'd, if dangers are his excuse he is then charged with *Timorousness* and want of Perseverance and at once pronounced the unfitest man in the world to be employ'd as a discoverer; if on the other hand he boldly incounters all the dangers and obstacles he meets and is unfortunate enough not to succeed he is than charged with *Temerity* and want of conduct.[11]

Part II

The Voyage

CONTENTS: PART II

Introduction *141*
Notes on presentation *142*
Notes on the charts *143*
Primary sources of the narrative *145*
1 The Decision *147*
2 Towards New Holland *150*
3 Towards Botany Bay *159*
4 Botany Bay *180*
5 Port Jackson to Sandy Cape *205*
6 Sandy Cape to Thirsty Sound *235*
7 Thirsty Sound to Trinity Bay *267*
8 Endeavour Reef *299*
9 Endeavour River: June *324*
10 Endeavour River: July *345*
11 Departure *382*
12 Escape to Sea *391*
13 The Breadth of One Wave *412*
14 Keeping the Main on Board *424*
15 *L'envoi* *444*

INTRODUCTION

The true story of *Endeavour*'s voyage can be told only by the men who made it—and then, ideally, only when they are brought together.

This narrative is constructed from the original logs and journals of the ship's company, interpolated where sense requires by my own modern voice in *italic* type. The narrative is concerned not so much with showing the impact of an event upon history as with telling the tale. Hearing straight from the voyagers themselves enables us, without any obstruction, to partake in an adventure which, deep within, we may wish to have made ourselves. Here we can savour the language of which our own words and phrases are descendants, listen to thoughts and ideas that anticipated our own, see an ancient land and its children as it was first seen by the culture we have inherited. Through the words of these men, things we have forgotten or unlearned might be recaptured, and the voyage might become an ever-present one that we are all embarked upon.

> . . . But take you off his utmost weed, and beholde the comelinesse, beautie, and riches which lie hid within his inward sense and sentence; . . . that needes you must acknowledge, that more matter and substance could in no wise be comprised in so little a roome. And notwithstanding (as I said) his stile be unpolished, and his phrases somewhat out of use; yet, so neere as the written copies would give me leave, I have most religiously without alteration observed the same: thinking it farre more convenient that himselfe should speake, then that I should bee his spokesman; and that the Readers should enjoy his true verses, then mine or any other mans fained prose.
>
> Richard Hakluyt (1553–1616), Elizabethan historian
> Preface to second edition of *Voyages* (1598).

> To sit in the lamplight, with a book spread out before you, and hold intimate converse with men of unseen generations—such is a pleasure beyond compare.
>
> Yoshida Kenko (1283–1350), Japanese poet

~ NOTES ON PRESENTATION ~

The narrative presented here is drawn from the 'Compleat Log' referred to on page 6 of the Introduction to Part I of this book. I compiled this composite log of the *Endeavour*'s voyage by transcribing numerous primary sources, and any variations from the originals are therefore my responsibility.

In matters of typography and physical presentation, this transcription does not purport to reproduce faithfully the source journals and logs; it was originally made for my own interest, not for publication. Readers wishing to access the originals are directed to the sources listed at the end of this section. I have chosen to concentrate on the content, the flavour, of the story rather than on presentation. Most original spellings have therefore been kept, while others, and some punctuation and abbreviations, have been altered slightly so that the modern reader may not be diverted by novelty from the intention of the writers. In the language of the time, 'y' was a written abbreviation of 'th'. Hence, the log keepers used 'y^{e}' as a written, but not spoken, abbreviation for 'the'. They also wrote 'oy^{er}' for 'other'. Abbreviations were a convention for some writers, but these have all been expanded in the narrative. Text underlined by its author for emphasis has been set in italic type.

I have framed the narrative within Ship's Time—a system of time-keeping used on the ship by all her journal- and log-keepers other than Banks and Parkinson (civilians), and Green (the astronomer). In Ship's Time a new day and date began at noon and was divided into three parts: the PM (the first part of the ship's day), the middle, and the AM (the last part of the ship's day). Ship's Time was twelve hours ahead of Civil Time, which began at midnight. The day and date for the ship finished at noon, on the same day and date as Civil Time. Banks and Parkinson kept their journals in Civil Time; whereas Green kept his in Astronomical Time, which was twenty-four hours behind Ship's Time. However, for this narrative, all times have been converted to Ship's Time, with the day and date running from noon to noon.

Each day, as presented here, begins with the Ship's Log, the official daily record of events on *Endeavour*'s voyage, kept by the officer of the watch. Reproduced here from the original, this at once gives a complete skeletal structure of the coming day, which is then fleshed out by all subsequent entries. The six-column format of the log makes the chronology of the day's events quite clear. We can immediately see from it what the ship herself is doing at any given time during the whole twenty-four hours: her speed, her course, the set of her sails as well as the wind direction, and, where necessary, the depth of water.

The first column on the left gives the hour of the day (H.); the next two, (K.) and (F.), give the speed in knots and fathoms (a knot is one sea-mile per hour; a fathom, in this context, is one-eighth of a knot). In the next column is the course: the direction of the ship's heading. This is given through every thirty-two points of the compass, down to half- and quarter-points, as is the direction from which the wind blows, in the fifth column. This fifth column also shows, when required, the soundings in fathoms—a fathom being six feet, or not quite two metres. The last column on the right consists of remarks, written as concisely and precisely as can be devised in nautical terms. When the ship is in harbour there is no need for columns one to four; the log becomes a consecutive list of remarks only, with the day and date, and the winds, occupying the first and second columns respectively.

The ship's routine was divided into watches, a watch being defined by *Falconer's Marine Dictionary* of 1780 as 'the space of time wherein one division of the ship's crew remains upon deck, to perform the necessary services, whilst the rest are relieved from duty, either when the vessel is under sail or at anchor.' Timetabling of the ship's day was therefore as follows, beginning at noon with the new date: noon till 4 PM, Afternoon Watch; 4 PM to 6 PM, First Dog Watch; 6 PM to 8 PM, Last Dog Watch; 8 PM to midnight, First Watch; midnight to 4 AM, Middle Watch; 4 AM to 8 AM, Morning Watch; 8 AM to noon, Forenoon Watch—the last of the day. The purpose of the two two-hour dog watches was to ensure that no one sailor was committed to the same watch on succeeding days. The only exception was the first lieutenant, who always kept the Morning Watch. This freed him, as executive officer, to supervise the daylight duties of the daymen (those who did not keep watches) as well as those of the watchkeepers. Hence the name Point Hicks given to the first part of this continent to be sighted on the voyage; First Lieutenant Zachary Hickes (his own spelling) was keeping the Morning Watch when it came into view.

The Deck Log was written up each watch, as near to the events as possible, by the officer of the watch. From this, the captain's clerk wrote up the Fair Copy as the official report to Authority of the ship's conduct. At the same time, all the ship's officers, midshipmen and petty officers were required to write up their own separate logs and journals. These were a recognised account of their own sea service and competence, taken into consideration for advancement or promotion. Each of these in its own way helps to depict the events and circumstances of the voyage for our more detailed understanding.

The journals of Cook and Banks form the main body of the narrative. The central facts, of course, are also given in others' logs and journals but are not quoted here unless they add information, or are alternative or variant versions which throw additional light on particular occasions. The intention has been to build up the most complete picture possible from what these men wrote in response to a common experience felt by each in his own way, so that we may, even at this distance, palpably share something of their feelings and their times.

~ NOTES ON THE CHARTS ~

My own plottings of the ship's track, which accompany the narrative, are intended to inform where words alone cannot, to explain better what the men are talking about and visually to represent the situation. I am neither a cartographer nor a navigator, and I have based my work on present-day Admiralty charts.

I have attempted to keep the whole as clear and as simple as possible. The modern outlines of coasts, islands, reefs, and so on, may be taken to represent fairly the actual physical facts which confronted *Endeavour*, even though her own chart was blank and just being laid down from these confrontations. What was charted and named is shown in the appropriate places. The features that were Cook-named, but which are no longer thus known, are shown as, for example, 'Cook's "Long Nose"' (which is now Perpendicular Point—underlined on the chart). Some modern-named features are also shown, underlined, to give the present-day reader some reference and orientation. A scale of distance may be had by referring to the latitude beside the part wanted. One minute (1′) of latitude equals one sea-mile.

Concerning the ship's track as shown: at various points I have marked a nought ('o') to denote a fix of a position one could settle on with a reasonable amount of certainty or by approximation. Each of these fixes has a time and a date beside it. Pecked lines, running from land features to these positions, are bearings upon which the fixes are based. Some are based on given latitudes and distances offshore.

In deciding on the best approach to plotting the ship's track, I faced a number of imponderables, worth explaining here.

Some intermediate courses and distances are based on those given hourly in the logs for wind direction, speed and course; but it is both impossible and impractical to reconcile every change of course and distance run. Generally it is the course made good that is shown between fixes.

The distance run is estimated by the log being hove every hour, or at each radical alteration of course. As the wind seldom blows with constancy throughout any hour, the mariner has to assist calculation by art, the latter so dependent upon experience and intuition.

The course steered is not always the course made good. This is due to a combination of four factors. The first factor is leeway, resulting from deflection of the wind across the ship's heading, as well as the direction of the sea. This can be estimated by using the angle of the wake to the ship's fore-and-aft line, in addition to some art.

The second factor is compass error—deflection of the compass needle because the earth's magnetic field varies from place to place. In *Endeavour* this was calculated by azimuths and amplitudes taken as often as practicable, and the correction was allowed for. But deviation caused by magnetism within the ship, which varied with each heading, had not yet been recognised as it finally was by Matthew Flinders; thus, this remained an undetected error.

The third factor is the skill and concentration of the helmsman, upon which depended the final calculation of the course made good; and the fourth factor is the existence of currents and tides, some unsuspected and some observed, tested for and estimated.

Bearings were also affected by compass errors. A true bearing is one with the errors eliminated, but as deviation had not yet been recognised, *Endeavour*'s 'true' bearings still contained this error. A ship has to be swung through 360 degrees in order to tabulate what it is on the various headings. However, it is assumed that the bearings given have all been reduced to true insofar as this was possible at the time.

Anyone tracing the ship's movements must continually rationalise and compromise to accommodate these variables. The longitudes are not reliable alone in such close pilotage waters and Cook claimed no more accuracy for his lunar distance method than half a degree, though at times his accuracy was astounding. Latitude, though generally quite accurate, has sometimes been compromised to bearings and distance, or cross-bearings, having due regard to particular circumstances. The present knowledge of currents, many of which Cook suspected but could not then calculate with certainty, help to position the ship and confirm Cook's suspicions.

In the areas of the Barrier Reef one cannot be certain that shoals and soundings have remained constant over the intervening two hundred years, so that soundings alone were no infallible guide.

I have attempted to keep all of these things in mind when laying down this present track, feeling that it bears some close relation to the situation as it was then, always allowing for my own limitations. Aside from the modern reference on them, these charts set out simply to represent what existed during Cook's voyage: a mass of newly seen, unnamed and undelineated coast, islands, reefs and shoals, indicating the shapes his men would have seen above the surface, while beneath the surface we see what they could not, and what put them in constant danger. It may give us pause to wonder at the art, experience and skill which kept them off the bottom—for luck alone could not have sufficed against such odds.

~ Primary Sources of the Narrative ~

Logs and journals by Cook:	
Holograph Log, incomplete	British Library (Add. MSS 27955 & 27885)
Holograph MS Journal	National Library of Australia, Canberra
Other logs and journals:	
Ship's Log, MS	British Library, Add. MS 8959s
Hickes, Holograph MS Journal	PRO Adm. 51/4546/147–8
Gore, Holograph MS Journal	PRO Adm. 51/4548/145–6
Molyneux, Holograph MS Journal	PRO Adm. 51/4546/152
Molyneux, MS Log transcript	PRO Adm. 55/39
Pickersgill, Holograph MS Journal	PRO Adm. 51/4547/140–1
Pickersgill, Fair copy	PRO Adm. 51/4547/142
Wilkinson, Holograph MS Journal	PRO Adm. 51/4547/149–50
Forwood, Holograph MS Journal	PRO Adm. 51/4545/133

Bootie, Holograph MS Journal	PRO Adm. 51/4546/134–5
Clerke, Holograph MS Journal	PRO Adm. 51/4548/143–4
Anon. 153, MS Journal unsigned	PRO Adm. 51/4547/153
Anon. 155, MS Journal unsigned	PRO Adm. 51/4547/155
Green, Holograph MS Log	PRO Adm. 51/4545/151
W.B. Munkhouse, fragment MS Journal	British Library, Add. MS 27889
J. Munkhouse, Holograph MS Journal	Mitchell Library, Sydney
Banks, Holograph MS Journal	Mitchell Library, Sydney
Roberts, Holograph Log	Mitchell Library, Sydney
Briscoe, Holograph Log	Dixson Library, Sydney
Anon. MS3, Holograph (? Green)	National Library of Australia, Canberra

Parkinson, *A Journal of a Voyage to the South Seas . . . Faithfully transcribed from the papers of the late Sydney Parkinson*. London, 1773; facsimile edition: the Libraries Board of South Australia, Adelaide, 1972.

Chapter 1
The Decision

SHIP'S LOG:

SATURDAY, MARCH 31ST, 1770

On the Coast of New Zealand. Admiralty Bay. Moderate and pleasant weather. PM: Employ'd getting the wood on board. Compleated the water to 78 tons. At 7 the Captain returned. Cleared ship for sea. Draught of water forward: 13′ 11″, aft: 13′ 11″. At 6 AM weighed and made sail out of the Bay. At 7 hoisted in all boats. At 10 was abreast of the outermost island of the Sound or Bay . . . Unbent the Stream and Small Bower cables.

COOK:

Upon my return to the ship in the evening I found the water &[ca] all on board and the ship ready for sea and being now resolved to quit this country altogether and bend my thought toward returning home by such a route as might conduce most to the advantage of the service I am upon, I consulted with the officers upon the most eligible way of putting this into execution. To return by way of *Cape Horn* was what I most wished because by this route we should have been able to prove the existence or nonexistence of a Southern Continent which yet remains doubtful; but in order to ascertain this we must have kept in high latitude in the very depth of winter but the condition of the ship in every respect was not thought sufficient for such an undertaking. For the same reason the thoughts of proceeding directly to the Cape of Good Hope was laid aside especially as no discovery of any moment could be hoped for in that route. It was therefore resolved to return by way of the East Indies by following route [but as the state of the ship's provisions was more than sufficient to carry us thither it was agreed (deleted)]: upon leaving this coast to steer to the westward until we fell in with the East Coast of New Holland and then to steer the direction of that coast to the northward or what other direction it may take until we arrive at its northern extremity, and if this should be found impractical then to endeavour to fall in with the lands or islands discovered by Quiros. With this view

at daylight in the morning we got under sail and put to sea having the advantage of a fresh gale at SE and clear weather.

BANKS:

Having now entirely circumnavigated New Zealand and found it, not as generally has been supposed part of a continent, but 2 Islands: and having not the least reason to imagine that any countrey larger than itself lays in its neighborhood, it was resolved to leave it and Proceed upon further discoveries in our return to England being determined to do as much as the state of the Ship and provisions would allow. In consequence of this resolution a consultation was held and three schemes proposed: One, much the most eligible, to return by Cape Horn keeping all the way in high Latitudes, by which means we might certainly determine whether or not a Southern Continent existed; but this was unanimously agreed to be more than the condition of the ship would allow. Our provisions indeed might be equal to it—we had six months at ⅔ allowance but our Sails and rigging, with which the former especially we were at first but ill provided, were rendered so bad by the blowing weather that we had met with off New Zealand that we were by no means in a condition to weather the hard Gales that must be expected in a winter passage through high latitudes. The second was to steer to the southward of Van Deimens Land [Tasmania] and stand away directly for the Cape of Good Hope, but this likewise was immediately rejected: if we were in too bad a condition for the former we were in too good a one for this. 6 Months provision was much more than enough to carry us to any Port in the East Indies and the over plus was not to be

H.M. BARK *ENDEAVOUR*: BOW VIEW. DEVELOPED FROM A CONTEMPORARY HULL SKETCH BY PARKINSON.

thrown away in a Sea where so few navigators had been before us: the third we therefore unanimously agreed to, which was to stand immediately to the Westward, fall in with the coast of New Holland as soon as possible, and after following that to the northward as far as seemed proper, to attempt to fall in with the Lands seen by Quiros in 1606. In doing this, although we hoped to make discoveries more interesting to trade at least than any we had yet made, we were obliged intirely to give up our first grand object, the Southern Continent: this for my own part I confess I could not do without much regret.—That a Southern Continent realy exists, I firmly believe; but if ask'd why I believe so, I confess my reasons are weak; yet I have a preposession in favour of the fact which I find difficult to account for . . .

Our rout being settled in the manner above mentioned we this morn weighed and sailed with a fair breeze of wind inclined to fall in with Van Deimens Land as near as possible to the place where Tasman left it.

PARKINSON:

The captain having fulfilled his orders, it was at his option to stay as much longer in these seas as the safety of the ship and provisions would admit; and to return home either by the East-Indies or Cape Horn. Considering that Cape Horn was at a great distance from this bay; that the season of the year was at hand which is the most unfavourable for going into so high a latitude; and that at the present time, and for five months past, the monsoons prevailed in the Chinese Seas; it was thought best to proceed west to the coast of New Holland, and so to the northward along it, in order to find a convenient refreshing place; then to search for the supposed Straits between New Holland and New Guinea (which, it is thought, admiral Torrey [Torres] went through;) and along the north coast of New Holland, to the island of Java; but, if these could not be found, it was proposed to proceed along the coast to Dampier's Straits, which lie between New Guinea and New Britain; then to cross the line, and sail down along the spice islands to Java, as we were in want of many kinds of provisions, particularly sugar, salt, oil, tea and tobacco: our spirits also very low; and, as to the bread, we had not had any for upwards of six months, and our sails were nearly worn out . . .

in the morning, we weighed anchor, having a fine breeze from the S.E. left the coast of New Zealand, and steered our course toward New Holland, taking our departure from a point of land near Blind Bay, which point we named Cape Farewell.

CHAPTER 2
TOWARDS NEW HOLLAND

When Endeavour *departed New Zealand on March 31st, Cook wrote: 'I have before made mention of our quitting* New Zealand *with an intention to steer to the westward which we accordingly did taking our departure from* Cape Fare-well *in Latitude 40° 30′ s and Longitude 185° 58′ w from Greenwich . . .' By noon on April 13th they were 'by observation in the Latitude of 39° 23′ s and Longitude 204° 2′ w. Course and distance sence yesterday noon s 62° West, 26 miles and Longitude made from Cape Farewell 18° 4′ w.'*

SHIP'S LOG:

SATURDAY, APRIL 14TH, 1770

H.	K.	F.	Courses.	Winds.	Remarks, &c.
1	..	5	W.S.W.	N.W.	Light airs and fair weather.
2	..	5	..	..	
3	..	5	..	..	
4	..	5	..	..	
5	..	4	..	..	Variation by an ampli'd, 11° 28′ easterly
6	..	4	..	..	Unbent the old and bent a new foretopsail.
7	..	5	..	..	
8	..	5	..	..	
9					
10					
11					
12					
1	Calm, head to ye W's'ward.				Fair wea'r.
2					
3					
4					
5					
6	1	..	W.b.S	No.	Light airs and clear.
7	1	..	..	..	

H.	K.	F.	Courses.	Winds.	Remarks, &c.
8	1	. .	. .	. .	Variation by azymuths, 11° 30′ easterly.
9	1	4	. .	. .	The spritsail topsail being found on survey unfitt for its proper use, condemn'd it to repair the top-gall't sails, also took 50 yards out of one of the ship's tents to repair the second best jibb, there being neither canvas nor twine in the ship to spare for that purpose.
10	1	5	. .	. .	
11	1	2	. .	. .	
12	1	6	. .	. .	Lat'de obs'd, 39° 25′ So.

COOK:
Calm serene weather with sometime light airs from the northward. At sunset found the Variation to be 11° 28′ East and in the morning to be 11° 30′ E. The Spritsail topsail be [ing] wore to rags it was condem'd as no longer fit for its proper use and taken to repair the two topgallant sails they being of themselves so bad as not to be

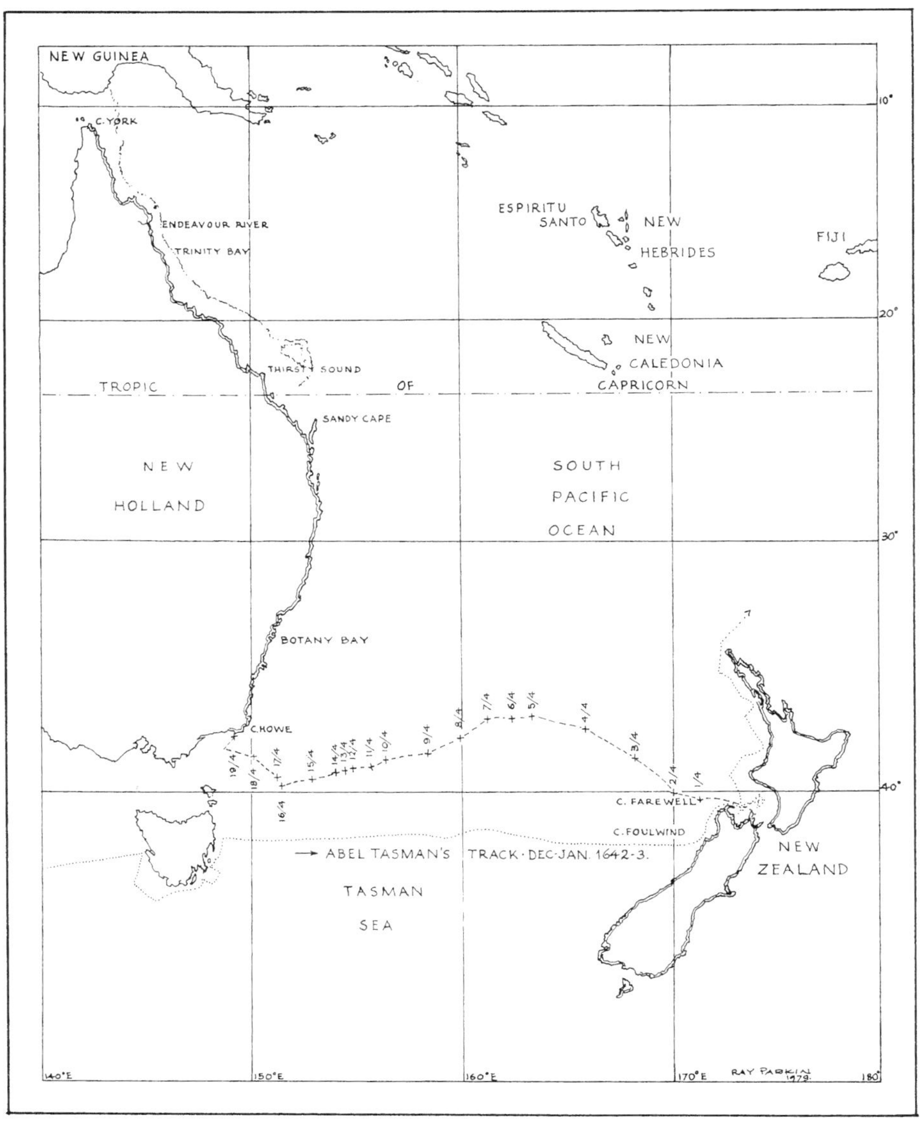

worth the expence of new Canvas but with the help of this sail may be made to last some time longer. At Noon Latitude in 39° 25′ s. Longitude made from Cape Farewell 18 21′ w. Course and distance sence yesterday noon s 81° w, 13 miles.

BANKS:

In the evening saw several fish much resembling Bonitos. The weather we have had for these nine days past and the things we have seen upon the sea are so extraordinary that I cannot help recapitulating a little. The weather in the first place which till the fifth was cool or rather cold became troublesomely hot bringing with it a mouldy dampness such as we have experienced between the tropicks: the Thermometer at this time although it showed a considerable difference in the degree of heat was not near so sensible as our bodies, which I believe is generally the case when damp air accompanies warmth. During the continuance of this weather the inhabitants of these seas between the tropicks appeared: the tropic bird, flying fish, and *Medusa porpita* are animals very seldom seen out of the influence of the trade winds, several others also are such as I have never seen in so high a latitude and never before in such perfection as now except between the tropicks.

All these uncommon appearances I myself can find no other method of accounting for than the uncommon length of time the wind had remained in the eastern quarter before this, which possibly had all that time blown home from the trade wind, and at the same time as it kept the sea in a quiet and still state had brought with it the Produce of the Climates from whence it came. A great dew this morn and Weather as calm as ever.

SHIP'S LOG:

SUNDAY, APRIL 15TH, 1770

H.	K.	F.	Courses.	Winds.	Remarks, &c.
1	1	..	W't	N.b.E.	Light airs and fair wea'r.
2	1	2	..	..	
3	1	3	..	..	
4	1	4	..	..	
5	1	6	..	..	
6	1	6	..	..	
7	2	..	..	..	
8	2	2	..	..	Ditto weather.
9	2	4	..	..	
10	2	5	..	..	
11	3	..	..	..	
12	3	6	..	..	Mod. breezes and fair weather.
1	4	2	..	N.b.W.	
2	4	2	..	N.N.W.	
3	4	..	W.½S.	..	
4	4	..	W.b.S.	..	
5	4	..	..	..	
6	4	..	..	..	Fresh breezes and fair wea'r.

H.	K.	F.	Courses.	Winds.	Remarks, &c.
7	4	..	..	..	
8	4	3	W.b.S.	..	
9	5	..	..	..	
10	5	..	..	..	In 1st reef topsails.
11	5	4	..	..	Saw some flying fish.
12	5	6	..	..	Lat. obs'd, 39° 30' So.

COOK:

In the PM had light airs at North which in the AM increased to a fresh gale with which we made the best of our way to the westward and by noon had run sence yesterday upon a S 86° 15′ West Course 79 miles. Lat[de] in by Observation 39° 30′ S and Longitude made from Cape Farewell 20° 2′ West. Some flying fish seen to day.

BANKS:

In the afternoon however a small breeze sprang up and increased gradually until towards night when a large quantity of porpoises were seen about the ship. AM: little or no dew this morn; the breeze freshened and came to WNW which soon raised a sea. Several flying fish were seen to day, tho I was not fortunate enough to see any of them yet they were seen by people who I am sure could not be mistaken.

SHIP'S LOG:

MONDAY, APRIL 16TH, 1770

H.	K.	F.	Courses.	Winds.	Remarks, &c.
1	5	4	W.b.S.	N.W.b.N.	Fresh gales and cloudy weather.
2	5	6	..	..	
3	5	6	..	..	
4	5	6	..	..	
5	6	..	..	..	Lost a log and two lines.
6	5	..	..	..	
7	4	5	..	..	
8	4	4	..	N.N.W.	Sounded 130 fa'm; no ground.
9	4	4	..	..	
10	4	..	..	..	
11	4	3	..	..	
12	4	2	..	..	Do. do.; no do.
1	4	2	..	..	
2	4	3	..	..	Do. 100 do.; no do.
3	4	4	..	..	
4	4	3	.	..	Do. 80 do.; no do.
5	4	..	..	..	
6	3	..	..	..	
7	3	2	..	No.	Out 1st reef, foretopsail.
8	3	2	..	..	
9	4	..	W't	..	
10	4	4	..	N.b.W.	
11	4	3	W.b. S.½S.	N.W.b.N.	A fresh breeze and cloudy hazy wea'r.
12	4	3	W.½S	..	Lat'de obs'd, 39° 45'.

COOK:

Fresh gales at NNW with Clowdy hazey weather. In the PM saw an Egg Bird and yesterday a Gannet was seen, these are the birds that we reckon never go far from land. We kept the lead going all night but found no soundings with a line of 100 and 130 fathoms. At Noon we were in the Latitude of 39° 45′ S and had made 22° 2′ of Longitude from Cape Farewell, Course and distance saild sence yesterday at Noon S 82° West 108 miles.

BANKS:

After dinner a small bird of the *Sterna* kind came about the ship much like Sterna of New Zealand but browner upon the back; it stayed a long time about the ship and seemed to me as if it had lost its way. At night the wind moderated but with it came a kind of invisible spray or mist which thoroughly wetted my hair as I walked the deck. AM: No dew this morn: weather moderate and cloudy. In the morn Tupia saw a large float of seaweed and shewed it to another man; it was however so far from the ship that no one else saw it. At noon, our Second Lieutenant [Gore] observed a small butterfly as he thought.

SHIP'S LOG:

TUESDAY, APRIL 17TH, 1770

H.	K.	F.	Courses.	Winds.	Remarks, &c.
1	4	4	W.S.W.	N.W.	Mod't gales and cloudy, hazy weather; at 1 in 1st reef main and mizen tops'ls; sounded with 80 fam's of line, no ground.
2	4	4	S.S.W.	Variable.	
3	1	..	S.	..	Thunder to the so'ward; wore ship.
	2	2	N.W.	W.S.W.	
4	3	4	..	..	Do. weather.
					Fresh gales with hard squalls; close-reef'd the fore and main and handed the mizen topsails; sounded—no ground at 140 f'm.
5	4	..	..	..	
6	3	..	..	..	
7	3	..	..	..	
8	3	..	N.W.b.N.	W.b.S.	Wore ship.
9	3	2	S.	W.S.W.	
10	3	3	..	..	
11	3	4	S.b.W.	W.b.S.	
12	3	2	..	..	Fresh gales, with passing squalls of light rain, lightning to the northward; wore ship.
1	3	2	N.W.b.N.	..	
2	3	..	..	..	
3	3	..	N.N.W.	West.	
4	3	2	..	..	Do. weather; wore ship.
5	3	..	S.b.E.	Variable.	
6	4	..	S.S.E.	..	
7	4	..	S.	..	
8	3	..	..	..	Dark, cloudy, hazy, variable weather; sometimes fresh puffs, others light airs and rain; a heavy swell from the westward.
9	..	..	..	..	
10	1	..	W.N.W.	Variable.	Calm; head from N. to W.
11	1	..	N.W.b.N.	..	Out all reefs, fore and 3rd and 2nd reef main topsails and sett mizen tops'l, single-reef'd; mod't breezes and fair wea'r; swell from the w'tward.
12	1	4	N.W.	..	Lat'd obs'd, 39° 36′ So.

COOK:

At 2 PM the wind came to WSW at which time we tack'd and stood to the NW, before 5 oClock we was obliged to close reef our topsails having a strong gale with heavy squalls. About this time a small landbird was seen to pearch upon the riging, we sounded but had no ground with 120 fathoms of line. At 8 oClock we wore and stood to the Southward until 12 at night than wore and stood to the NW until 4 AM when we again stood to the South^{d} having a fresh gale at WSW attend[ed] with squals and dark hazey unsettled weather until 9 oClock, at which time it fell little wind and the weather soon after clear'd up, which a little after 11 gave us an opportunity of takeing several observations of the Sun and Moon the mean result of which gave 207° 56′ West Longitude, from the Meridion of Greenwich. From these observations the longitude of the ship at Noon was 207° 58′ and by the Log 208° 20′ the difference being only 22′ and this error may well lay in the one as the other. Our Latitude at noon was 39° 36′ S and Long^{de} made from Cape Farewell 22° 22′ W.

ENDEAVOUR WATERING IN QUEEN CHARLOTTE SOUND, WITH PARKINSON'S 'FEATHER-HATTED FISHING FOLK'.

BANKS:

At night a fresh gale and some thunder at SW with a heavy swell which seemed to keep rather to the westward of the wind. Many albatrosses and black shearwaters were about the ship. At night a small land bird came on board the size of a sparrow. Some of the boys tried to catch it but it got away from them in the rigging and was never seen after.

AM: During the night and this morn the weather was most variable with continual squalls and wind shifting all round the compass; such weather is often met with in the neighborhood of land so that with this and former signs our seamen began to prophecy that we were not now at any great distance from it. A gannet was seen which flew to the NW with a steady uninterrupted flight as if it knew that the road it was going led to the shore.

SHIP'S LOG:

WEDNESDAY, APRIL 18TH, 1770

H.	K.	F.	Courses.	Winds.	Remarks, &c.
1	4	4	W.N.W.	S.W.	Squally, with rain.
2	4	5	W.b.N.	S.W.b.S.	Strong gales; close-reef'd the topsails.
3	4	..	W.	S.	Handed the main topsail.
4	4	..	..	..	Got down top-gall't yards.
5	4	..	..	..	Saw a Port Egmont hen.
6	4	..	..	..	Handed the mainsail; carried away the coller of the main topmast staysail stay.
7	2	6	..	..	Hard gales and squally, with rain; sailing with the foresail, mizen staysail, and mizen sett.
8	2	4	..	..	
9	3	2	..	..	
10	3	..	..	..	Swell from the S.S.W.
11	2	6	..	S.b.W.	
12	2	4	..	..	Do. weather; sounded; no ground with 120 fa'm line.
1	3	..	..	S.	
2	3	..	..	..	Do. do. with do. of do.
3	3	..	..	S.b.E.	
4	3	2	..	..	Do. do. do.
5	3	3	..	..	Set the mainsail; saw a pintada bird and sev'l black sheerwaters and albatrosses.
6	3	3	..	..	
7	3	3	..	..	Set the foretopsail.
8	3	3	W.b.N.	S.b.W.	
9	3	4	..	..	This day the carp'rs finished the yawl, having been employ'd ever since the 9th this instant.
10	4	.	W.N.W.	S.W.b.S.	
11	4	2	W.b.N.	S.S.W.	Set the main topsail.
12	4	5	..	..	Lat. obs'd, 38° 45' S.

COOK:

Winds southerly a hard gale with heavy squals attended with showers of rain and a great sea from the same quarter. At 3 PM Close Reef'd the topsails, handed the Main and Miz^{n} topsail & got down top gallant yards. At 6 oClock the gale increased to such a height as to Oblige us to take in the Fore topsail and Main sail and run under Fore sail and Mizen all night sounding every 2 hours but found no ground with 120 fathoms. At 6 AM set the Main-sail and soon after the fore topsail and before noon the Main-topsail both close reef'd. At Noon our Latitude by Obser^{n} was 38° 45' S. Longitude from Cape Farewell 23° 43' W and Course and distance run sence yesterday noon N 51° West 82 Miles. Last night we saw a Port Egmont Hen and this morning two more, a Pintado bird several Albatrosses and black shearwaters. The first of these birds are certain signs of the nearness of land, indeed we cannot be far from it for by our Longitude we are a degree to the westward of the East side of Vandieman Land according to *Tasmans* the first discoverers Longitude of it, who could not err so much in so short a run as from this land to Newzeland and by our Latitude we could not be above 50 or 55 Leagues to the northward of the place where he took his departure from.

PARKINSON:
We were becalmed nine days, from the 9th to the 17th, and then the wind blew from the s.s.w. and s.w. and we had a broken sea that caused the ship to pitch and roll very much; at the same time we shipped a sea fore and aft, which deluged the decks, and had like to have washed several of us overboard: we were then in latitude 38° 46′ and 22 degrees west of Cape Farewell, out of sight of land: so that the land of Van Dieman, if not an island, must have tended away abruptly to the east [west?] or we should have seen it before this time.

SHIP'S LOG:

THURSDAY, APRIL 19TH, 1770

H.	K.	F.	Courses.	Winds.	Remarks, &c.
1	5	..	W.	S.b.W.	Fresh gales and squally, with a great sea from the S'ward.
2	5	..	..	S.S.W.	
3	6	..	W. ½ N.	..	A great number of porposeses about the ship.
4	6	..	..	..	
5	6	..	..	..	
6	5	4	..	..	Handed the topsails.
7	2	5	W.b.S.	S.b.W.	
8	2	4	..	..	
9	3	..	Wd.	S.S.W.	
10	3	..	W. ½ N.	..	
11	3	..	Wd.	..	
12	3	..	..	..	Squally, with flying showers of rain; haul'd up the mainsail and lay too. Sounded, no ground at 130 f'm of line. At 1 set the mainsail.
1	..	..	{ lay too up W.b.S. }	off W.N.W.	
2	3	..	W.b.N.	S.S.W.	
3	3	..	..	..	
4	3	..	..	..	Fresh gales and fair wea'r.
5	3	..	..	..	Sett the topsails.
6	3	4	..	..	Saw the land making high, bearing from N.E.b.N. to W.b.S.; dist'ce off the nearest shore, 7 or 8 leagues; out all reefs and made sail.
7	4	5	..	..	
8	4	2	..	..	Bore up for the land.
9	5	2	N.E.	..	Variation p'r sev'l azymuths, 8° 07′ E.
10	4	..	N.E.b.E.	..	Bent the best mainsail and main topsail.
11	4	..	..	..	Att noon { A fresh gale and cloudy squally wea'r, with some small rains; the ext's of the land in sight from N.W.b. W. to E.b.N.; a remarkable point N. 12° E. Lat'd observ'd, 37° 50′ So.
12	4	3	E.N.E.	..	

COOK:

In the PM had fresh gales at SSW and Clowdy Squaly weather with a large Southerly Sea. At 6 took in the Topsails and at 1 AM brought too and sounded but has no ground with 130 fathoms of line. At 5 set Topsails Close reef'd and at 6 saw land extending from NE to West at the distance of 5 or 6 Leagues having 80 fathom water a fine sandy bottom. We continued standing to the westward with the wind at SSW until 8 oClock at which time we got topg[t] yards aCross, made all sail and bore away along shore NE for the Easternmost land we had in sight, being at this time in the Latitude of 37° 58′ S and Long[d] of 210° 39′ West. The Southernmost Point of land we had in sight which bore from us W ¼ S I judged to lay in the Latitude of 38° 0′ S and in the longitude of 211° 07′ W from the Meridion of Greenwich. I have named it *Point Hicks*, because Lieut[t] Hicks was the first who discovered this land.

To the Southward of this point we could see no land and yet it was very clear in that quarter and by our Longitude compared with that of Tasmans the body of Vandiemens land ought to have bore due south from us and from the soon falling of the Sea after the wind had abated I had reason to think it did, but as we did not see it and finding this coast to trend NE and SW or rather more to the westward makes me doubtfull whether they are one land or no: however every one who compares this Journal with that of Tasmans will be as good a judge [as] I am, but it is necessary to observe that I do not take the situation of Vandiemans from the present Charts but from the extract of Tasmans *Journal* published by *Dirk Rembrantse*.

At Noon we were in the Lat[de] of 37° 50′ and Long[d] 210° 29′ W, the extremes of the land extending from NW to ENE, a remarkable Point bore N 20° East distant 4 Leagues. This point rises to a round hillick, very much like the *Ram Head* going into Plymouth Sound on which I called it by the same name. Lat[d] 37° 39′, Londitude 210° 22′ W. The variation by an Azimuth taken this morning was 8° 7′ East. What we have as yet seen of this land appears rather low and not very hilly the face of the Country green and woody, but the sea shore is all white sand.

BANKS:

At night the weather became a little more moderate and a shoal of porpoises were about the ship which leapd out of the water like Salmons, often throwing their whole bodies several feet above the surface. With the first daylight this morn the Land was seen, at 10 it was pretty plainly to be observed; it made in sloping hills covered in Part with trees or bushes, but interspersed with large tracts of sand. At noon much the same.

PARKINSON:

We continued on our course, but nothing worthy of note occurred till the 19th, in the morning, and then we dicovered the land of New Holland, extending a great way to the south and to the eastward. It is moderately high: part of it appeared to be flat, and covered with sand; but, the weather being foggy, we had not a good view of it. We were obliged to steer E.N.E. to clear it.

Chapter 3

Towards Botany Bay

Endeavour was now sailing northwards and plotting the first accurate outline of the east coast of New Holland that we are aware of.

SHIP'S LOG:

FRIDAY, APRIL 20TH, 1770

H.	K.	F.	Courses.	Winds.	Remarks, &c.
1	5	..	E.b.N.	S.W.	Fresh gales and cloudy, with passing squalls and small rains; at 1 sett steering sails.
2	6	..	..	..	
3	5	3	N.N.E.	..	
4	6	2	..	..	
5	5	..	..	..	Squally, rainy weather.
6	5	5	..	..	Sound'd in 56 fa'm; ye northermost, N. ½ E., an island, W. 6 miles.
7–10	..	..	up S.b.W.	off S.S.E.	Bro't too, main tops'l to ye mast. Sound'd, 69 fa'm. Wore ship.
11–12	..	..	up N.W.b.W.	off N.N.W.	Sounded, 63 fa'm; fresh gales and cloudy, with flying squalls of rain.
1–4	..	..	up W.N.W.	off N.W.	70 fa'm. 68 fa'm; made sail.
5	4	1	N.N.W.	S.W.b.W.	Fresh breezes and clear wea'r; saw land making like an island, bearing N.N.W.
6	5	2	..	..	
7	5	6	N.W.b.N.	..	Variat'n p'r azymuths, 10° 20′ East.
8	6	..	..	W.S.W.	The buoys being all expended, the capt'n order'd the coopers to make casks for that purpose.

H.	K.	F.	Courses.	Winds.	Remarks, &c.
9	5	3	. .	. .	
10	5	. .	N.N.W.	S.W.b.S.	Set the steering sails; a swell from the S.S.W.
11	4	4	. .	. .	Cross'd strong rippling of a tide or current.
12	3	2	. .	. .	Ext's of the land from N. 10 W. to S ½ W.; shore dist. 4 or 5 leagues; lat. obs'd, 36° 51′ So.

COOK:

In the PM and most part of the night had a fresh gale westerly with squalls attended with showers of rain. In the AM had the wind at SW with serene weather. At 1 PM, saw three watersprouts at once, two were between us and the shore and one at some distance on our larboard quarter. At 6 oClock shortened sail and brought-too for the night having 56 fathoms and a fine sandy bottom, and the northermost land in sight bore NbE ½ E and a small island [Gabo] lying close to a point on the main bore west distant 2 leagues. This point I have named Cape Howe. It may be known by the trending of the coast which is north on one side and SW on the other (Latitude 37° 28′ S, Long^{de} 210° 3′ west) it may likewise be known by some round hills upon the main just within it. Having brought-too with her head off shore we at 10 oClock wore and lay her head in until 4 AM at which time we made sail along shore to the Northward. At 6 oClock the northermost land in sight bore North being at this time about 4 leagues from the land. At noon we were in the latitude of 36° 51′ S, and longitude 209° 53′ west and 3 leagues from ye land. Courses sailed sence yesterday noon was first N 52° E, 30 miles then NbE & Nbw, 41 miles. The weather being clear gave us an opportunity to view the country which had a very agreeable and promising aspect, the land is of a moderate height diversified with hills, ridges, plains and vallies with some small lawns but for the most part the whole was covered with wood, the ridges and hills rise with a gentle slope, they are not high neither are there many of them.

PICKERSGILL:

AM: Saw a high land called the Dromedary from its resemblance to that animal bearing NNW.

BANKS:

We were now sailing along shore 5 or 6 leagues from it, with a brisk breeze of wind and cloudy unsettled weather, when we were called on deck to see three water spouts, which at the same time made their appearance in different places but all between us and the land. Two of which were very distant soon disappeared but the third which was about a league from us lasted full a quarter of an hour. It was a column which appeared to be about the thickness of a mast or middling tree, and reached down from a smoak coloured cloud about two thirds of the way to the surface of the sea; under it the sea appeared to be much troubled for a considerable space and from the whole of that space arose a dark coloured thick mist which reached the bottom of the pipe. When it was at its greatest distance from the water the pipe itself

was perfectly transparent and much resembled a tube of glass or a column of water, if such a thing could be supposed to be suspended in the air; it very frequently contracted or dilated, lengthened and shortened itself and that by very quick motions, it very seldom remained in a perpendicular direction but generally inclined either one way or the other in a curve as a light body acted upon by wind is observed to do. During the whole time that it lasted smaller ones seemed to attempt to form in its neighborhood; at last one did about as thick as a rope close by it and became longer than the old one which at that time was at its shortest state; upon this they joined together in an instant and gradually contracting into the cloud disappeared.

APRIL 20TH, 1770: 'FRESH GALES AND CLOUDY WITH PASSING SQUALLS AND SMALL RAIN. SET STEERING SAILS. [SPEED 6 KNOTS]. SAW THREE WATERSPOUTS.'

AM: The country this morn rose in gentle sloping hills which had the appearance of the highest fertility, every hill seemed to be clothed with trees of no mean size; at noon a smoke was seen a little way inland and in the Evening several more.

PARKINSON:
And we saw three water spouts, one of which continued near a quarter of an hour. On the 20th we sailed along shore with a fine brisk breeze, but we found no harbour. The land appeared rather level, with here and there a gentle ascent, covered entirely with wood, some of which appeared to be large. About noon we saw smoke ascending out of a wood near the sea side.

The point that the Captain named Cape Howe and described as adjacent to the island (Gabo) would appear to be what is now known as Telegraph Point, though his

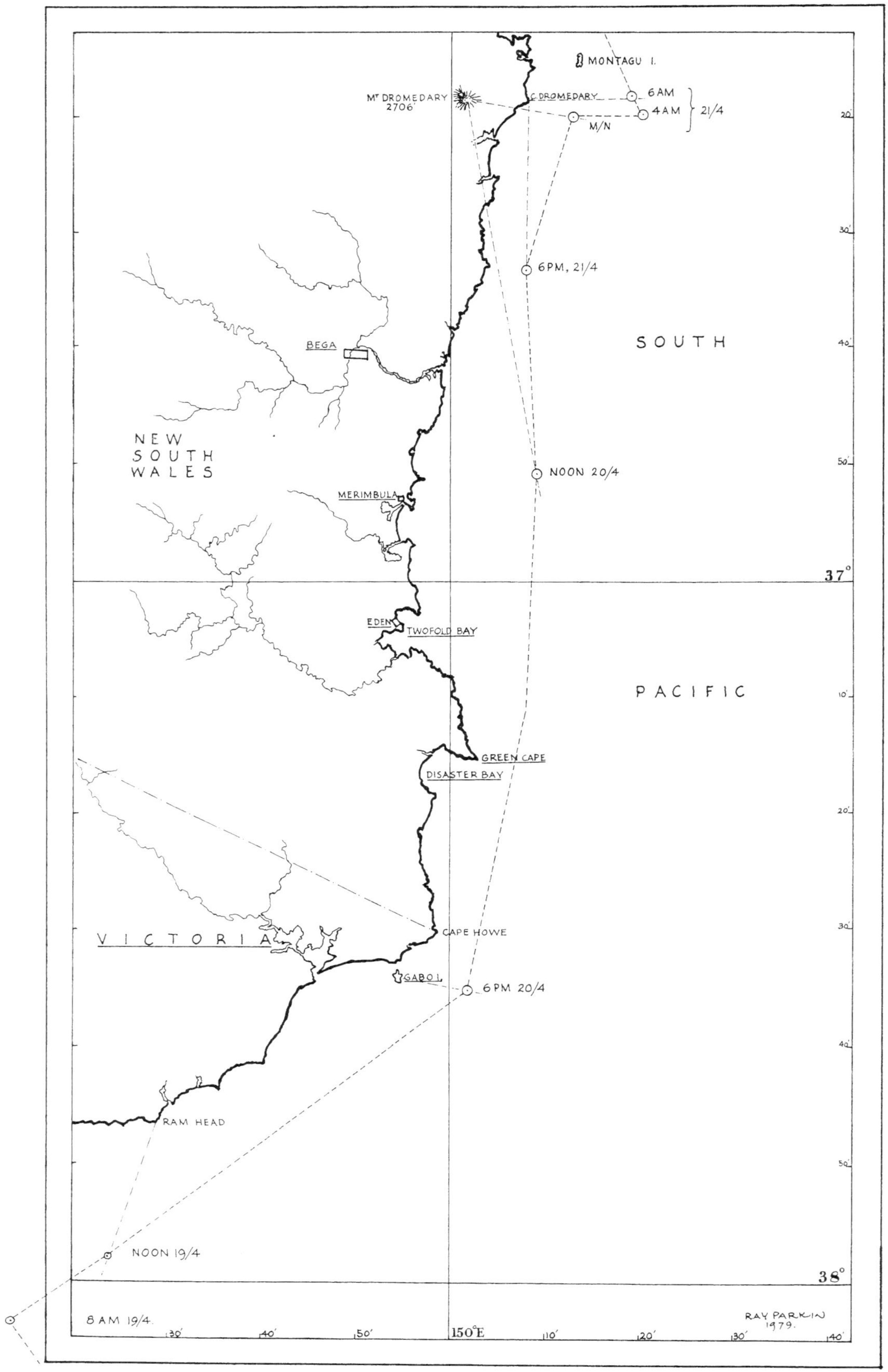

MONTAGU I.
Mt DROMEDARY
2706'
C. DROMEDARY
6AM
4AM
21/4
M/N
6PM, 21/4
SOUTH
BEGA
NEW
SOUTH
WALES
NOON 20/4
MERIMBULA
37°
EDEN
TWOFOLD BAY
PACIFIC
GREEN CAPE
DISASTER BAY
CAPE HOWE
VICTORIA
GABO I.
6 PM 20/4
RAM HEAD
NOON 19/4
38°
8 AM 19/4
RAY PARKIN
1979.
150°E

description of the trend of the land from it (north on one side and sw on the other) seems to describe the present Cape Howe. However, the name Gabo *is said, in the New South Wales Historical Records of 1893, to be an Aboriginal rendition of* Cape Howe. *The Captain had named the cape after Richard Earl Howe (1726–99) who was a Lord of the Admiralty when the ship left England.*

By noon on the 20th, when the ship's day ended, the ship had passed, without remarking, Green Cape at the north end of Disaster Bay, then Twofold Bay, and the noon position was just north of present-day Merimbula. In sight to the north was the peak of Mount Dromedary, at 2,708 feet.

SHIP'S LOG:

SATURDAY, APRIL 21ST, 1770

H.	K.	F.	Courses.	Winds.	Remarks, &c.
1	3	4	N.b.E.	S.	Mod't breezes and pleasant wea'r.
2	3	5	..	..	Saw a smoak on the shore.
3	3	6	..	..	
4	3	2	..	..	
5	3	4	North.	..	
6	3	4	..	..	The no'ermost land in sight No. Shorten'd sail and in 2nd reefs of the tops'ls. 44 fa'm water, fine brown sand.
7	2	4	N.N.E.	..	
8	1	7	..	..	Variation by severell azym'ths, 10° 42′ E.
9	2	2	..	..	Little wind and fair. Sounded 56 fa'm, coarse brown sand.
10	3	..	..	..	
11	3	4	..	..	Sounded 70 fa'm.
12	4	..	..	..	Haul'd up the foresail and bro't too. The high land set at noon W.b.N.
1	..	..	up E.S.E.	off Et.	Sounded 90 fa'm, do. ground.
2	..	..	..	..	
3	..	..	up S.E.	off E.S.E.	
4	..	..	..	..	65 ,, Made sail.
5	3	..	N.N.E.	S.S.W.	
6	4	5	..	..	Out all reefs and made all sail.
7	6	..	N.N.W.	..	Saw a remarkable peak, bearing N. —, called Pigeon-house Hill.
8	6	..	..	..	
9	6	..	..	..	Fresh breezes and fair.
10	5	..	..	..	
11	4	4	N.b.W.	S.	
12	5	..	..	..	The ext's of the land from N. 1° W. to S. 20° W. Shore dist. 3 or 4 leagues. Lat'd obs'd, 35° 51′ S.

COOK:

Winds southerly a gentle breeze and clear weather with which we coasted along shore to the northward. In the PM we saw a smoak of fire in several places a certain sign that the country is inhabited. At 6 oClock being about 2 or 3 leagues from the land we shortened sail and sounded and found 44 fathom water, a sandy bottom; stood under an easy sail until 12 oClock at which time we brought too untill 4 AM when we made sail again, having 90 fathom water 5 leagues from the land. At 6

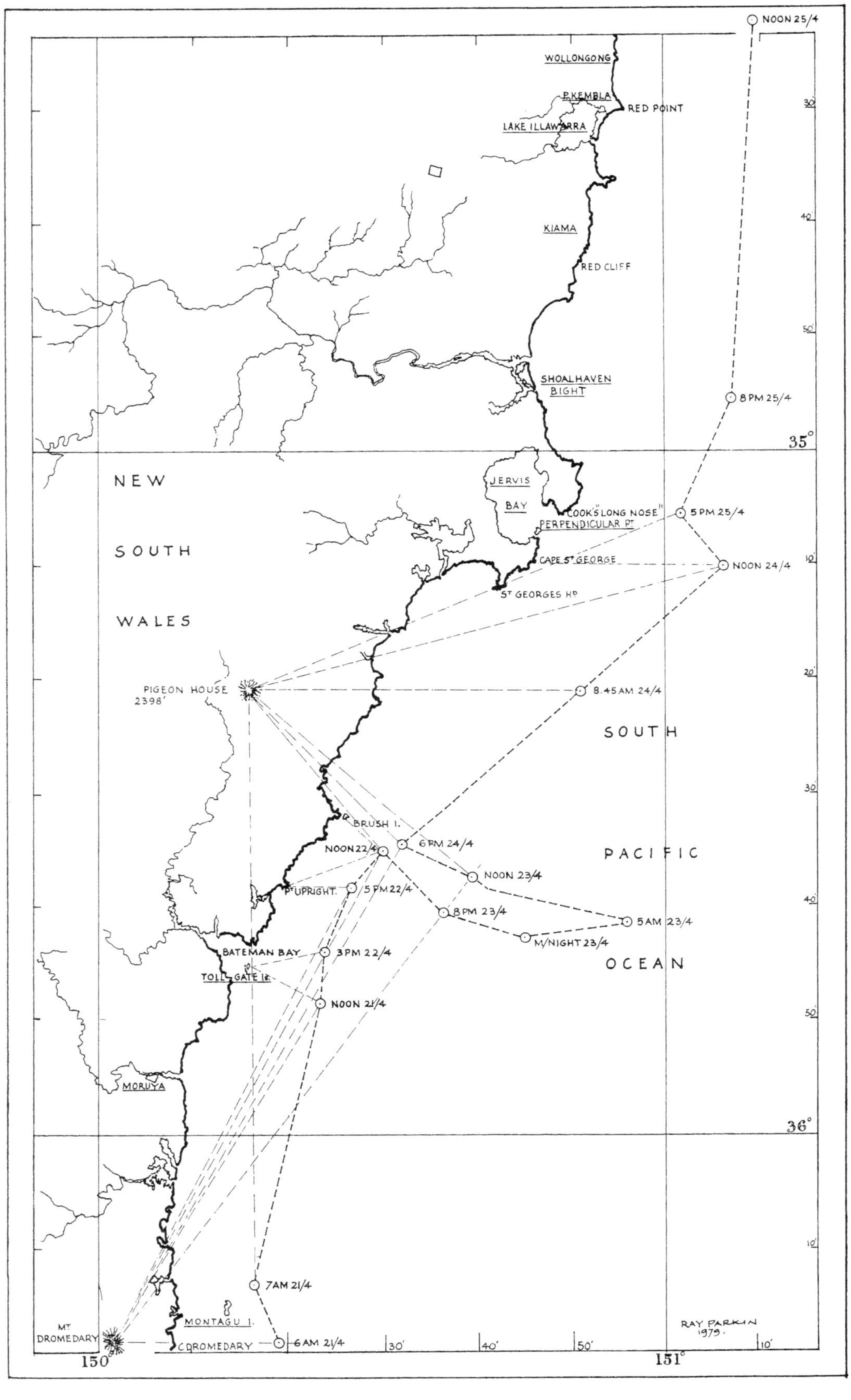
NOON 25/4
WOLLONGONG
P. KEMBLA
RED POINT
LAKE ILLAWARRA
KIAMA
RED CLIFF
SHOALHAVEN BIGHT
8 PM 25/4
35°
NEW SOUTH WALES
JERVIS BAY
COOK'S "LONG NOSE"
5 PM 25/4
PERPENDICULAR PT
CAPE ST GEORGE
NOON 24/4
ST GEORGES HD
PIGEON HOUSE 2398'
8.45 AM 24/4
SOUTH PACIFIC OCEAN
BRUSH I.
6 PM 24/4
NOON 22/4
NOON 23/4
PT UPRIGHT
5 PM 22/4
8 PM 23/4
5 AM 23/4
M/NIGHT 23/4
BATEMAN BAY
3 PM 22/4
TOLL GATE IS
NOON 21/4
MORUYA
36°
7 AM 21/4
MONTAGU I.
MT DROMEDARY
C DROMEDARY
6 AM 21/4
RAY PARKIN 1979.
150°
30'
40'
50'
151°
10'

MADE ALL SAIL (STUDDING SAILS EXCEPTED).

oClock we were abreast of a pretty high mountain laying near the shore which on account of its figure I called *Mount Dromedary* (Lat^{de} 36° 18′ S, Long^{de} 209° 55′ west). The shore underfoot of this mountain forms a point which I have called *Cape Dromedary* over which is a peaked hillick. At this time found the Variation to be 10° 42′ E. Between 10 and 11 oClock Mr Green and I took several observations of the Sun and Moon the mean result of which gave 209° 17′ West longitude from the Meridion of Greenwich. By observations made yesterday we were in the Longitude 210° 9′: –20′ gives 209° 49′ the Longitude of the ship today at noon per yesterdays observations, the mean of which and todays gives 209° 33′ W, by which I fix the Longitude of this coast. Our Latitude at noon was 35° 49′ S. Cape Dromedary bore S 30 W, dist 12 leagues. An open bay wherein lay three or 4 small islands bore NWbW dist 5 or 6 leagues, this bay seemed to be but very little sheltered from the sea winds and yet it is the only likely anchoring place I have yet seen upon the coast.

PICKERSGILL:
Running down along shore making high and seeming to be very fertile and rich being thickly cloathed with very tall trees which had a pleasant appearance. Saw a remarkable peaked hill with a tuft of tall trees on this resembling the top of a Pidgeon house from whence it is called Pidgeon House Hill.

PARKINSON:
On the 21st we had fine weather, and a brisk gale; the coast appeared much the same as it did the day before, excepting than it was rather lower. In the evening the land appeared very low and strait, stretching away to the NE and was well covered with

trees. We saw some clouds of smoke rising from them a good way up the country, but we found no harbour.

At noon the ship was abreast the South Head of Bateman Bay. Though the Captain has not mentioned it, he placed it on his chart naming it Bateman Bay after Nathanial Bateman who had been captain of Northumberland *when Cook had been serving in her as Master. Cape Dromedary bore* S *30° W, distant 12 leagues; Bateman Bay* NWbW.

SHIP'S LOG:

SUNDAY, APRIL 22ND, 1770

H.	K.	F.	Courses.	Winds.	Remarks, &c.
1	3	5	No.	So.	Mod. and fine pleas't weather. Saw a smoak on the shore.
2	4	..	..	..	
3	4	..	..	..	Two small islands, W.b.S. 2 leagues.
4	4	6	N.b.E.	..	
5	4	3	N.b.E. ½ E.	..	Ext's of the land from S. to N. 15°E. A remarkable bluff head W.b.S.
6	4	4	..	..	Shore dist't 2 leagues.
7	2	..	E.N.E.	..	In 2nd reefs and shorten'd sail. Sounded 31 fa'm, sandy ground.
8	2	..	..	..	
9	1	4	E.	S.b.E.	Sounded 53 fa'm, do ground.
10	1	2	..	..	,, 68 . Haul'd up the foresail. Saw a fire on shore
11	1	..	E.b.S.	..	
12	1	..	..	..	do. 70 , do. ground. Bro't too, her head off shore.
1	..	..	up S.b.E.	off S.E.	
2	..	..	..	..	Little wind and cloudy, with rain. Wore ship.
3	..	..	up W.	off N.W.b.W.	
4	..	..	..	..	73 fa'm. Stood in for the land.
5	2	..	W.N.W.	S.W.b.S.	
6	{2 1}	2	..	.	70 fa'm. Variations p'r azymuths, 9° 50′ E.
7	{2 2}	2	W.b.N.	..	
8	1	..	N.E.	..	The bluff head set last night S. 56° W. 3 leagues. Saw a ledge of breakers bearing N.N.E. These breakers lye off a low island. At 8 light breezes and cloudy, with a swell from the S.E.; shore dist't 4 or 5 miles. Saw severell Indians on the beach.
9	1	..	..	..	
10	1	4	..	..	
11	1	4	N.N.E.	S.S.W.	
12	1	4	..	..	At noon, lat obs'd, 35° 30′ S. { The so'm't ext't of the land called Mount Dromedary, S. 20 W. The no'most ext't N. 25 E. A remarkable peak nam'd Pidgeon-house Hill, N. 46 W. 59 fa'm wa'r, blue clay. Dist. off shore, 2½ leagues.

COOK:

In the PM had a gentle breeze at SbW with which we steered along shore NNE at the distance of about 3 leagues. Saw the smook of a fire in several places near the sea beach. At 5 oClock we were abreast of a point of land which on account of its perpendicular clifts I call'd *Point Upright* (Lat^{de} 35° 35′) it bore from us due west distance 2 leagues and in this situation we had 31 fathom water a sandy bottom. At 6 oClock falling little wind we hauled off ENE, at this time the northermost land in sight bore NNE ½ E. At midnight being in 70 fm water we brought too untill 4 AM at which time we made sail in for the land and at daylight found ourselves nearly in the same place we were at 5 oClock in the evening by which it was apparent we had drove about 3 leagues to the southward by a tide or current in the night, after this we steered along shore NNE having a gentle breeze at SW and were so near the shore as to distinguish several people upon the sea beach. They appeared to be of a very dark or black colour but whether it was the real colour of their skins or the clothes they might have on I know not. At noon we were by observation in the Latitude of 35° 27′ and long^{de} 209° 23′. Cape Dromedary bore S 28° W dist. 19 leagues. A remarkable peaked hill laying inland the top of which looked like a *Pidgeon house* occasioned my giving it that name, bore N 32° 30′ W and a small low island [Brush Island] laying close under the shore bore NW dist. 2 or 3 leagues. Variation of the compass 9° 50′ E. When we first discovered this island in the morning I was in hopes from its appearance that we should have found shelter for the ship behind it but when we came to approach it nearer I did not think there was even security for a boat to land, but this I believe I should have attempted had not the wind come on shore, after which I did not think it safe to send a boat from the ship as we had a large hollow sea from ye SE rowling in upon the land which beat everywhere very high upon the shore and this we have had ever since we came upon the coast. The land near the sea coast still continues of a moderate height forming alternately rocky points and sandy beaches, but inland betwixt Mount Dromedary and the Pidgeon house are several pretty high mountains two only of which was covered with trees and these lay behind Pidgeon House and are remarkably flat atop with steep rocky clifts all round them as far as we could see. [Probably Mount Budawang, 3,727 feet, and Currockbilly, 3,709 feet, with Pidgeon House, 2,398 feet.] The trees of this country hath all the appearance of being stout and lofty. For these two days the observed latitude has been 12 or 14 miles to the Southward of the ships account given by the Log which can be owing to nothing but a current setting to the Southward [the 2-knot East Australian Coast Current].

PICKERSGILL:

PM: Passed two small bays ye shore making in bluffs and little sandy bays. Very woody. In the morning stood in for the land & found we had drove to the s° ward against the wind. As we stood along shore we saw there 5 of the natives sitting near a fire. They appeared to be naked and very black which was all we could discern at that distance.

BANKS:

In the Even it became much flatter. Several smoaks were seen from whence we concluded it to be rather more populous; at night five fires. AM: The country hilly but rising in gentle slopes and well wooded. A hill was in sight which much resembled dove houses which are built four square with a dome at the top. In the morn we stood in for the land near enough to discern 5 people who appeared through our glasses to be enormously black: So far did the prejudices which we had built on Dampiers account influence us that we fancied we could see their colour when we could scarce distinguish whether or not they were men.—Since we have been on the coast we have not observed those large fires which we so frequently saw in the Islands and New Zealand made by the natives in order to clear the ground for cultivation; we thence concluded not much in favour of our future friends.—It has long been an observation among us that the air in the Southern hemisphere was much clearer than in our northern, these some days at least it has been remarkably so. A head land called Dromedaries Head, not remarkably high, had been seen at the dist. of 25 leagues and judged by nobody to be more than 6 or 8 from us; it was now in sight plain and our distance from it by the ships run was 23 leagues, yet the seamen acknowledge that tho they knew how far it was from them they could not think that it appeared more than 10 leagues off. The hill like a pigeon house was also seen at a very great distance; the little dome on top of it was first thought to be a rock standing up in the sea long before any other part was seen, and when we came up with it we found it to be several miles inland.

It seems that Banks had on board with him Dampier's New Voyage round the World *(1697), and* Voyage to New Holland *(1703) in which Dampier gives a very poor opinion of the Aborigines of this country.*

The ship had sailed at 4 knots until sunset, but during the following forenoon was making a bare 1 ½, making good just 25 miles northward for the twenty-four hours from the previous noon.

SHIP'S LOG:

MONDAY, APRIL 23RD, 1770

H.	K.	F.	Courses.	Winds.	Remarks, &c.
1	1	..	N.N.E.	E.	Lights airs and fair weather.
2	1	..	..	..	
3	1	..	..	..	
4	1	..	..	..	
5	..	{4 {4	N.N.W. S.E.	N.E. E.N.E.	Tack'd ship.
6	1	..	..	..	The Dromedary S. 18° W. The northern ext't of the land N. 4° E.
7	..	6	E.S.E.	variable.	
8	1	..	..	..	Sounded; had 74 fa'm water.
9	1	5	E.b.S.	N.E.b.N.	
10	2	..	E.N.E.	N.	
11	2	..	..	..	
12	2	..	..	..	do. 82
1	2	3	N.E.	N.N.W.	

H.	K.	F.	Courses.	Winds.	Remarks, &c.
2	2	4	..	..	
3	3	..	E.N.E.	N.	
4	3	..	N.E.b.E.	N.b.W.	Tack'd ship.
5	3	..	W.N.W.	N.	
6	3	..	..	..	
7	2	4	..	..	
8	2	2	..	..	
9	1	..	..	..	Tack'd ship. 74 fa'm water.
10	1	3	N.N.E.	N.W.	Light airs and pleas't weather. Shifted the main jeers end for end.
11	..	4	..	..	
12	..		..	..	At noon { Ext's of the land from N. 8 E. to S. 27 W. (the Dromedary). The Pidgeon house Hill N. 49 W. Dist't off shore, 6 leagues. Latit'de observ'd, 35° 36′ S.

COOK:

In the PM had a gentle breeze at east which in the night veered to NE and North. At ½ past 4 PM being about 5 miles from the land we tacked and stood off SE and East untill 4 AM at which time we tackd and stood in, being then about 9 or 10 leagues from the land. At 8 oClock it fell little wind and soon after calm. At noon we were by observation in the Latitude of 35° 38′ and about 6 leagues from the land.

BANKS:

Calm today, myself in small boat but saw few or no birds. Took with the dipping net *Cancer Erthropptamus, Medusa radiata, pelagica, Dagysa gemma, strumosa, cornuta, Holothuria obtusata, Phyllodoce Velella* and *Mimus volutator*. The ship too far from shore to see much of it; a larger fire was however seen than any we have seen before.

The Master today in conversation made a remark on the Variation of the Needle which struck me much, as to me it was new and appeard to throw much light on the Theory of that Phaenomenon. The Variation here is very small, he says: he has three times crossed the line of no variation and that at all times as well as this he has observed the Needle to be very unsteady, moving very easily and scarce at all fixing: this he shewed me: he also told me that in several places he has been in, the land had a very remarkable effect upon the variation, as in the place we were now in: at 1 or 2 leagues distant from the shore the variation was 2 degrees less than 8 leagues distance.

PARKINSON:

On the 22d the Coast made a good view, being flat, level and covered with verdure. The hills within were remarkably flat: we discovered 5 men upon them, through our glasses, who were quite naked. It is probable that they live upon the produce of the earth, as we did not see any canoes, and the coast seems unfavourable for fishing.

The ship, this day, went mostly at 1 knot, except from 10 PM until 8 AM, when she touched 2 and 3 knots. But at noon it was calm. At 10 AM the log reads, 'shifted the main jeers end for end.' To do this the main yard was temporarily suspended with the top chains while the jeers were overhauled. Jeers are the heavy tackles upon which the lower yards are hoisted and lowered. That part of the fall or rope which had been rove through the blocks, being constantly at work and so much more worn than the rest, was unrove. Then the other end, comparatively unworn, was rove in its place, thus giving the whole fall a double life. In Mr Banks's talk with Mr Molyneux, the Master, on the variation of the compass, the difference shown in differing places of 2 degrees was probably due to a local magnetic anomaly, a phenomenon which is well known today and usually shown on charts, although it could possibly have been due to the influence of the magnetism within the ship herself, which varies with the different directions of the ship's head. It was Matthew Flinders who eventually identified this and called it deviation. He demonstrated how it could be corrected for by placing before the compass a soft iron bar which is known today as the Flinders Bar.

The ship tacked three times these twenty-four hours: this movement brings the wind from one side of the ship to the other by bringing her head across the wind. This evolution calls for smooth handling of the helm, sheets and braces to avoid being caught in stays—a situation in which the ship is caught head to wind, being unable to pay off one way or the other. In such a situation the sails are caught aback, threatening the masts, with the ship gathering sternway and out of control. But the effectively handled ship will turn and require less searoom tacking than by wearing, which is going about stern to wind. Though the distance sailed this day was 40 miles, the noon position showed the ship to be but 2 miles southward and 8 miles eastward from noon of the previous day.

SHIP'S LOG:

TUESDAY, APRIL 24TH, 1770

H.	K.	F.	Courses.	Winds.	Remarks, &c.
1	..	..	..	..	Calm clear weather. Ship's head all round the compass.
2	..	..	..	..	
3	..	..	..	..	
4	1	..	N.	S.E.	Light airs.
5	..	..	..	..	Calm. Ship's head to the no'ward.
6	..	..	..	..	The extrem's of the land from N. 9° E. to S. 22° W., and Pidgeon-house Hill N. 49° W. 70 f'am water.
7	1	..	N.E.	N.N.W.	
8	1	..	..	..	Lights air and fair.
9	1	4	..	..	
10	1	4	..	..	
11	1	4	..	..	
12	1	4	..	..	Do. weather.

H.	K.	F.	Courses.	Winds.	Remarks, &c.
1	1	..	N.N.E.	W.N.W.	
2	1	4	..	..	
3	2	..	N.	..	
4	2	..	..	..	Moderate breezes and fair.
5	2	..	..	..	110 fa'm water.
6	2	..	..	..	Variation p'r amp'd, 7° 41' } E.
7	5	..	N.b.E.	N.W.b.W.	By sev'l azym'ths, 7° 54' } E.
8	3	6	..	..	A fresh breeze and fair wea'r. A swell from the eastward.
9	4	4	..	..	Employ'd repairing the old mainsail and working up junk.
10	4	4	N.N.E.	N.W.	
11	4	4	..	..	
12	4	4	N.E.b.N.	N.W.b.N.	At noon { A fresh breeze and remarkable clear wea'r. N. extreme of the land N.W.b.N. Pidgeon-house Hill S. 62° W. A bluff head, near which was two large smoaks N. 72° W. Latit'de obs'd, 35° 10' S.

COOK:

In the PM had variable light airs and calms until 6 oClock at which time a breeze sprung up at Nbw. At this time we had 70 fathom water being about 4 or 5 leagues from the land. The Pigeon house bearing N 40° West, Mount Dromedary S 30° West and the northermost land in sight N 19° East. Stood to the NE untill noon having a gentle breeze at NW at which time we tacked and stood to the westward being then by observation in Lat^{de} 35° 10' S and Long^{de} 208° 51' W. A point of land I named *Cape St George* we having discovered it on that Saints day, bore West distant 19 miles and the Pigeon House S 75° West, the Latitude and Longitude of which I found to be 35° 19' S and 209° 42' West. In the morning we found the Variation to be by Amp^{de} 7° 50' East and by several Azimuths 7° 54' East.

BANKS:

The wind was unfavourable all day and the ship too far from the land for much to be seen; 2 large fires however were seen and several smaller.

This day there was a swell coming in from the eastward. Though the winds were light to calm in the PM, by morning they were freshening and by noon the ship was making 4½ knots through the water. The mean course was N 39° 45' E, and the distance made good 36 miles. This morning the variation of the compass was obtained both by azimuth and amplitude. Variation of the compass is the extent to which the compass needle is deflected east or west from true north by the magnetic field of the earth, which varies from place to place. As the ship steers and takes bearings by magnetic compass, it is important that this variation be known to calculate 'true' *course and bearings.*

Variation by amplitude is obtained by observing the magnetic bearing of the sun, star or planet at the time of its rising or setting. Then, knowing the approximate latitude *of the ship and the heavenly body's declination, the observer can easily calculate its true bearing. The difference between the two is magnetic variation. Variation by azimuth is obtained by observing the magnetic bearing of a heavenly body when above the horizon; and its true bearing is calculated as before to obtain variation. Variation continually changes. Not only does it differ from place to place, but in the same place it will increase or decrease by a small amount annually. For instance, where the ship was on this day, the modern chart shows on the compass rose (right abreast of Cape St George): 'Var^{n} 13° 00' E (1994) increasing about 4' (E) annually'.*

But observations in Endeavour *still contained the unrecognised compass error of deviation. As has been mentioned, this was the discovery of Matthew Flinders. It seems fitting that he was, so to say, the professional grandson of James Cook—in that he received his early training, in what he was made to realise was an exacting discipline, from Captain William Bligh, who, as a Master with Cook, had been inculcated in, and inherited, a high tradition from Cook himself.*

Since this time, complete charts have been made for magnetic variation alone, clearly defining the lines of no variation mentioned by Mr Molyneux to Banks; the modern chart is generously supplied with compass roses showing both true and magnetic bearings, with full information on variation. The coasts are clearly marked, with orange blobs for the numerous lighthouses and other navigational aids; the sea is peppered with swarms of soundings. Latitudes and longitudes of all and any places are there at a glance.

What was happening during April 1770 was that a small group of men and a small ship were sailing over a blank space on the world map and observing the sea and shore in such a way, and with such understanding, as to be able to place it on that map with unprecedented accuracy, very much as it would still be placed more than two hundred years later, and having as their only reference points the Equator, and Greenwich, 13,000 miles away.

At noon the ship was just south of Jervis Bay, the future nursery of Australian Naval Officers, which would be criss-crossed innumerable times, day and night, by ships of the squadron exercising at then undreamed-of speeds, as the 1918 chart (illustrated, page 164) attests, with its scrubbed surface and peppering of divider prickings, each the considered mark of some concentrating navigator.

SHIP'S LOG:

WEDNESDAY, APRIL 25TH, 1770

H.	K.	F.	Courses.	Winds.	Remarks, &c.
1	3	4	W.S.W.	N.W.	Moderate breezes and fair weather.
2	3	4	..	..	
3	3	6	So.	W.S.W.	Tack'd ship.
4	4	..	N.N.W.	W.	Variation p'r azym'ths, 9° 15' Et.
5	4	2	No.	W.N.W.	Extremes of the land from N.N.W. to S.W. Pidgeon-house Hill S.W.b.W. ¼ W. Dist't off shore 6 or seven leagues. At 6 in 2nd reefs and shorten'd sail. 86 fa'm water. Lightning to the so'ward.

H.	K.	F.	Courses.	Winds.	Remarks, &c.
6	4	..	N. ½ E.	..	
7	3	..	N.N.W.	W.	
8	3	..	N.W.	W.S.W.	Squally weather. Close-reeft the tops'ls and handed the mainsail.
9	..	..	up N.W.b.W.	off N.N.W.	Bro't too her head inshore. 120 fa'm water, soft ground.
10	..	..	up W.	off N.W.b.W.	110
11	..	..	up W.N.W.	off N.W.b.N.	
12	..	..	..	..	100
1	..	..	up N.W.b.W.	off N.W.	
2	..	..	..	..	A strong breeze. Wore ship. 90
3	..	..	up S.E.b.S.	S.E.b.E.	Wore ship and made sail under the tops'ls.
4	3	3	No.	S.S.W.	
5	3	2	..	..	
6	3	3	N.b.W.	S.W.	The no'm't land N. ½ W. Out reefs and made all sail.
7	4	5	..	..	
8	4	4	..	..	Variation { pr. amplit'de, 9° 36'E. / pr. azym'ths, 9° 07' E. } Mean, 9° 21' E.
9	3	6	..	..	
10	3	3	..	S.S.W.	Sailm'rs employ'd on the mainsail. Armourers cleaning the arms. Seamen working up junk.
11	2	3	..	..	At noon { Mod. breezes and fair wea'r. Saw sev'l smoaks on shore, and pass'd large quantity of spawn. Ext's of the land from N. 8. E to S.17 W. Shore dist. 3 or 4 leag's. Latit'de obs., 34° 22' So. }
1	2	2	..	N.W.	

COOK:

In the PM had a fresh breeze at NW untill 3 oClock at which time it came to west and we tack'd and stood to the Northward. At 5 oClock being about 5 or 6 leagues from the land, the Pigeon House bearing WSW distant 9 leagues, sounded and had 86 fathom water. At 8 oClock being very squally with lightning we close reef'd the top-sails and brought too being then in 120 fathom water. At 3 AM, we made sail again to the northward having the advantage of a fresh gale at SW. At noon we were about 3 or 4 leagues from the land and in the Lat^{de} of 34° 22' and Longitude 208° 36' West. Course and distance sailed sence yesterday noon is NbE, 49 miles. In the course of this days run we saw the smook of fire in several places near the sea beach. About 2 leagues to the northward of Cape St George the shore seems to form a bay which appeared to be sheltered from the NE winds but as we had the wind it was not in my power to look into it and the appearance was not favourable enough to induce me to lose time in beating up to it. [Jervis Bay was so named in 1791, after Sir John Jervis, Earl of St Vincent.] The north point of this bay on account of its figure I named *Long Nose* Latitude 35° 6' S. 8 leagues to the northward of this is a point which I called *Red Point*, some part of the land about it appeared of that colour (Latitude 34° 29' Long^{de} 208° 49') a little way inland to the NW of this point is a round hill the top of which looks like the crown of a hatt. [Mount Kembla or Hat Hill, 1780 feet.]

BANKS:

At night a little lightning to the Southward. Large fires were lighted this morn about 10 O'Clock, we supposed that the gentlemen ashore had a plentiful breakfast to prepare. The country tho in general well enough clothed appeared in some places bare; it resembled in my imagination the back of a lean Cow, covered in general with long hair, but nevertheless where her scraggy hip bones have stuck out further than they ought accidental rubs and knocks have entirely bared them of their share of covering.

PARKINSON:

The weather was very fine, but we were often becalmed. The land appeared still flat, remarkably level and strait on the top. We saw several fires along the coast lit up one after another, which might have been designed as a signal to us.

The noon position at the end of this day placed the ship abreast of Bellambi Point, just south of Bulli, on which there is now a light. The fires that Mr Parkinson supposed to be a signal to the ship were most probably part of the very efficient telegraph of the Aborigines, advertising the presence of a ship on the coast. Mr Banks this day was full of levity and imagination.

SHIP'S LOG:

THURSDAY, APRIL 26TH, 1770

H.	K.	F.	Courses.	Winds.	Remarks, &c.
1	1	3	N.N.E.½ E.	N.W.	Light airs and fair weather.
2	1	3	N.E.b.N.	N.W.b.N.	
3	1	4	..	..	Sounded, 54 fa'm water.
4	1	3	..	..	
5	1	..	..	..	Variation by azym'ths, 8° 48′ Et.
6	..	..	Calm. Her head alround.		Ext's of the land from S. 20° W. to N. 5° E 48 fa'ms. In 1st reef tops'ls.
7, 8	..	..	H'd to the So'ward.		
9, 10	..	..	Her head at So. to W.S.W.		42 fa'm. Saw a fire on shore. 38 do.
11, 12	..	..	Head to the E'tward.		Calm and fair. 42 fa'm water.
1	..	..	..	..	
2	1	..	Et.	S.W.	A light breeze. 64 fa'm water.
3	2	4	N.E.b.N.	..	
4	2	..	..	..	
5	2	4	..	Wt.	
6	2	4	..	..	
	1	2	..	..	
7	1	2	N.b.E.	W.b.N.	
8	2	4	..	..	
9	2	..	..	..	Took the tent curtains to repair the old maintopsail.
10	1	4	..	..	Sailm'rs repairing the sails. Exercis'd the marines.
11	1	..	N.N.E.	N.W.	
12	..	5	..	..	At noon { Light airs and fine pleas't wea'r. Ext's of the land from S.28 W. to N.3 W. Shore dis't 5 or 6 leagues. Lat'd obs'd, 34° 10′ S.

COOK:

Clear serene weather. In the PM had a light breeze at NNW untill 5 oClock at which time it fell calm we being then about 3 or 4 leagues from the land and in 48 fathom water. Variation per Azimuth 8° 48′ East, the extremes of the land from NEbN to SWbS. Saw several smooks alongshore before dark and 2 or 3 times a fire in the night. We lay becalmed driving before the sea untill 1 oClock AM at which time we got a breeze from the land with which we steered NE being then in 38 fathom water. At Noon it fell little wind and Veered to NEbN, we being then in the latitude of 34° 10′ and Longitude 208° 27′ W and about 5 leagues from the land which extended from S 37° W to N ½ E. In this latitude are some white clifts which rise perpendicularly from the sea to a moderate height.

BANKS:

In the even it was calm. All the fires were put out about 5 O'Clock. Several brown patches were seen in the sea looking much as if dirt had been thrown into it, but upon nearer examination they proved to be myriads of small *dagysas*.

At noon this day the ship was abreast of Wattamolla, just south of Port Hacking.

SHIP'S LOG:

FRIDAY, APRIL 27TH, 1770

H.	K.	F.	Courses.	Winds.	Remarks, &c.
1	1	4	E.b.S.	N.E.b.N.	76 f'm. Little wind and clear weather.
2	1	6	..	..	
3	1	..	..	..	
	1	2	N.W.b.N.	..	Tack'd ship and in 1st reef topsails.
4	2	..	N.W. ½ N.	..	
5	2	..	..	..	
6	2	..	..	..	54 f'm. Tack'd ship. Ext's of the land from S. 26° W. to N. 16° E.
7	2	..	E.S.E. ½ E.	N.E.b.N.	
8	2	..	..	..	
9	2	..	E.b.S.	..	
10	2	..	..	..	
11	2	..	..	..	
12	2	..	Et.	N.N.E.	Tack'd ship.
1	1	..	W.N.W.	No.	
2	1	6	S.W.b.W.	N.W.b.W.	
3	2	4	W.b.S.	N.W.b.N.	
4	3	..	..	..	Tack'd ship.
5	2	3	N.N.E.	N.W.	
6	2	3	..	..	
7	1	..	N.E.b.N.	N.W.b.N.	Tack'd ship.
	1	4	W.S.W.	N.W.	
8	2	6	..	..	
9	2	7	..	..	
10	2	..	S.W.b.W.	N.W.b.W.	Little wind and fine clear weather.
11	2	2	W.b.S.	Variable.	
12	2	2	..	..	Lat'de observ'd, 34° 21′ So. Ext's of the land from S. 11° W. to N. 20° . Distance off shore, 4 or 5 miles.

COOK:

Variable light airs between NE and NW and clear pleasant weather. In the PM stood off-shore untill 2 oClock then tack'd and stood in untill 6 at which time we tack'd and stood off being then in 54 fathoms water and about 4 or 5 miles from the land, the extremes of which bore from S 28° W to N 25° 30′ East. At 12 oClock we tackd and stood in untill 4 AM then made a trip off until daylight, after which we stood in for the land; in all this time we lost ground owing a good deal to the Variableness of the winds, for at noon we were by observation in the latitude of 34° 31′, Red Point bearing S 27 W distant 3 leagues. In this situation we were about 4 or 5 miles from the land which extended from S 19° 30′ West to N 29° East.

BANKS:

The Countrey today again made in slopes to the sea covered with wood of a tolerable growth tho not so large as some we have seen. At noon we were very near it; one fire only was in sight. Some bodies of three feet long and half as broad floated very buoyant past the ship; they were supposed to be cuttle bones which indeed they a good deal resembled but for their enormous size.

PARKINSON:

On the 27th in the morning, the wind being against us, we stood off and on shore.

These winds drove the ship to the south at noon so that she was practically in the same latitude as two days before, but 8 miles further inshore, and between Bulli and Bellambi.

*Concerning the cuttle bones, Professor J.C. Beaglehole remarks that, according to Cotton (*South Australian Natural History, *1931), the largest and most common Australian sepia is* Amplisepia apama *(Gray). Cotton figures a cuttle bone from one of these measuring 280 × 100 mm, but a specimen exists in the British Museum which is no less than 460 × 150 mm.*

SHIP'S LOG:

SATURDAY, APRIL 28TH, 1770

H.	K.	F.	Courses.	Winds.	Remarks, &c.
1	1	4	W.N.W.	N.	Mod. breezes and fine pleas't wea'r.
	1	6	E.S.E.	N.E.	Tack'd ship. Bro't too and hoisted out the yawl.
2	..	..	up N.N.W.	off N.W.	Tack'd. Distant off shore 2 or 3 miles. The capt'n, Mr. Banks, &c., went away in the yawl. 17 fa'm water.
	1	2	N.W.b.N.	N.E.b.N.	
3	1	2	..	..	
	1	2	E. ½ S.	..	
4	2	4	N.W. ½ N.	..	
5	..	..	..	..	Tacked ship. The yawl return'd, the capt'n not being able to land for ye surf.
	..	..	Calm, her h'd e'd	..	Extent of the land from N.N.E. to S. Dis't off shore 4 or 5 miles. From 11 to 13 fa'm water.

H.	K.	F.	Courses.	Winds.	Remarks, &c.
6	1	5	E't.	W.S.W.	
7	1	..	N.E.	..	
8	1	..	..	..	27 fa'm.
9	1	4	E't.	..	32 fa'm.
10	1	4	..	..	
11	1	4	N.E.	..	
12	2	2	..	..	
1	2	..	N.N.E.	N.W.	
2	3	..	..	West.	
3	3	..	N.b.W.	S.W.	Sounded, 61 fa'm. Saw several fires along shore.
4	3	..	N.b.E.	..	Mod't and fair.
5	1	6	N.E.bN.	Variable.	Sounded, 58 fa'm. Out 1 reefs.
6	2	4	N.b.E.	W.N.W.	Saw a bay. Haul'd up for it. In 1 reefs.
7	2	5	N.b.W.	W.b.N.	
8	3	2	N.N.W.	West.	Tack'd ship. Sounded 38 fa'm.
9	3	..	S.S.W. ½ W.	W.b.N.	32 fa'm water. Hoisted out the pinnace, and sent ye
10	3	..	S.b.W. ½ W.	W.b.S.	master inshore to sound the entrance of the harbour.
11	{1	5	N.W. ½ W.	..	Tack'd ship.
	{1	3	W.N.W.	..	
12	..	..	..	..	Working to windward into the bay, bearing W.N.W. 2 miles.

COOK:

In the PM hoisted out the pinnace and yawl in order to attempt a landing but the pinnace took in water so fast that she was obliged to be hoisted in again to stop her leakes. At this time we saw several people a Shore four of whome were carrying a small boat or Canoe which we imagined they were going to put in the water in order to come off to us but in this we were mistaken. Being now above 2 miles from the

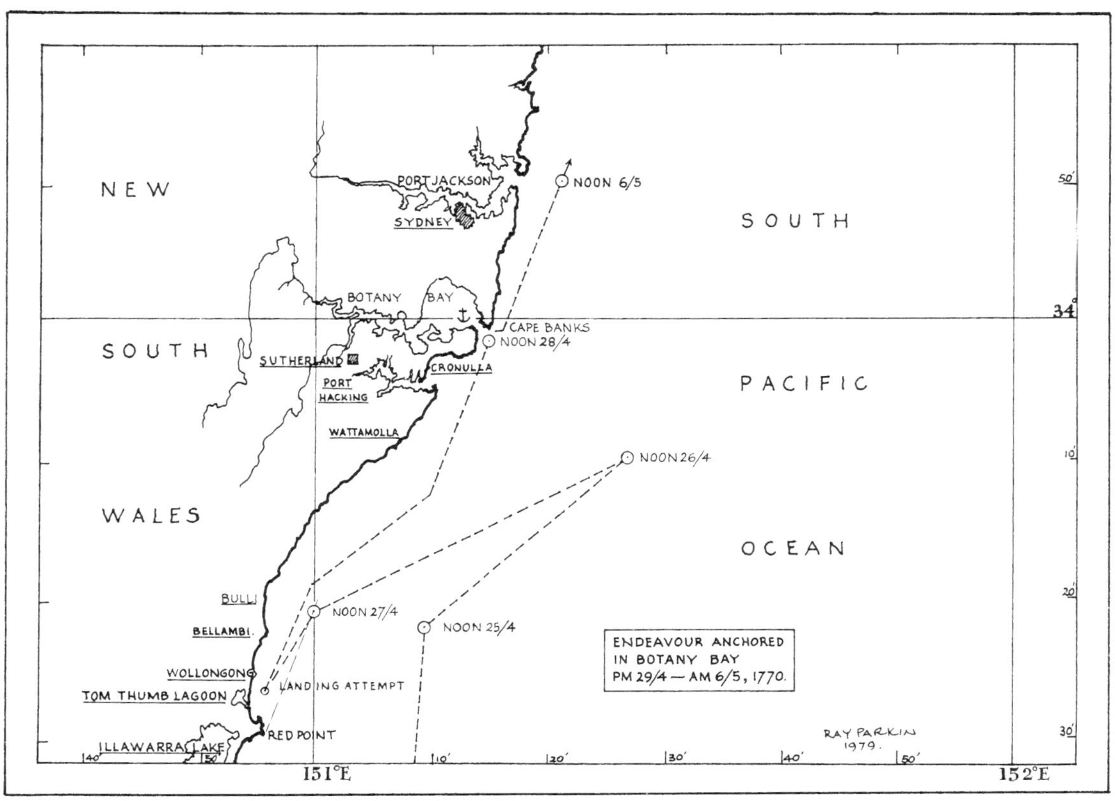

shore Mr Banks, Dr Solander, Tupia and my self put off in the yawl and pull'd in for the land to a place where we saw four or five of the natives who took to the woods as we approached the Shore, which disappointed us in the expectation we had of getting a near view of them if not to speak to them; but our disappointment was heighten'd when we found that we no where could effect a landing by reason of the great surff which beat every where upon the shore. We saw hauled up on the beach 3 or 4 small Canoes which appeared not much unlike the small ones of New Zeland, in the woods were several trees of the Palm kind and no under wood and this was all we were able to observe from the boat after which we returned to the Ship about 5 in the evening. At this time it fell calm and we were not above a mile and a half from the shore in 11 fathom of water and within some breakers that lay to the southward of us, but luckily a light breeze came from the land which carried us out of danger and with which we stood to the northward. At daylight in the morning we discovered a Bay which appeared to be tolerably well sheltered from all winds into which I resolved to go with the Ship and with this in view sent the Master in the Pinnace to sound the entrance while we kept turning up [to the wind] with the Ship having the wind right out. At noon the entrance bore NNW distance 1 mile.

PICKERSGILL:

PM: Standing off and on shore under an easy sail; the bay is covered well to ye southward by a low patch of red earth which looked like islands, and runs a good way into the sea. AM: At noon working into ye bay, depth of water 29 fathom; off ye points 1½ miles.

BANKS:

After dinner the Captn proposed to hoist out boats and attempt to land, which gave me no small satisfaction; it was done accordingly but the Pinnace on being lowered down into the water was found so leaky that it was impractical to attempt it. Four men were at this time observed walking briskly along shore, two of which carried on their shoulders a small canoe; they did not however attempt to put her in the water so we soon lost hopes of their tending to come off to us, a thought with which we had once flattered our selves. To see something of them however we resolved and the Yawl, a boat just capable of carrying the Cap^{tn}, Dr Solander, myself and 4 rowers was accordingly prepared. They sat upon the rocks expecting us but when we came within about a quarter of a mile they hastily ran away into the countrey; they appeared to us as well as we could judge at that distance exceedingly black. Near the place were four small canoes which they had left behind. The surf was too great to permit us with a single boat and that so small to attempt to land, so we were obliged to content ourselves with gazing from the boat at the productions of nature which we so much wished to enjoy a nearer acquaintance with. The trees were not very large and stood separate from each other without the least under wood; among them we could discern many cabbage trees but nothing else which we could call by name. In the course of the night fires were seen.

The ship continued to be driven south until she reached the bay just south of Wollongong towards Port Kembla. Regarding Pickersgill's entry, the Historical Records of New South Wales, 1893, tell us: 'This entry enables us to locate the spot where Cook attempted to land, with greater accuracy than has been possible heretofore. The "low patch of red earth which looks like islands and runs a great way into the sea" was evidently that which Cook named Red Point, not far from where Wollongong now stands; the land which had the appearance of a part of the main proving to be—as surmised by Pickersgill—islands. They are known as the Five Islands and near the entrance to Tom Thumb Lagoon (so named after Flinders' and Bass's boat) was where the attempt to land was made.'

The palms and cabbage trees which Cook and Banks remark upon were the great Cabbage Palm, Livistona australis, *which flourishes here and has given the name* Cabbage Tree *to one of the small towns nearby. Banks's entry for this day contains valuable evidence for the small size of the yawl.*

After the landing attempt failed a light breeze sprang up, enabling a northerly course to be resumed so that at noon the ship was just off what was eventually to become known as Botany Bay.

Chapter 4
Botany Bay

SHIP'S LOG:

SUNDAY, APRIL 29TH, 1770

Day and Month.	Winds.	Remarks, &c.
1770. Sunday, April 29	S.W. W.N.W. S.E. E't.	Little wind and and fair wea'r. ½-p't 1, came too with the b't bower in 6½ fa'm water. Sandy ground. Hoisted the boats out at 3. The captain, with Mr. Banks and Doctor Solland'r, went on shore. They were oppos'd in attempting to land by some of the natives, whom they were oblig'd to sting with small shots, which frighten'd them into the woods. In the evening the capt'n return'd, having found a watering-place. A.M.—A party of men on shore with the 1st lieut't for water. Veered away to ½ a cable on the b't b'r, and steady'd her with the streem anchor to the N.E. Ye captain and gentlemen away in the pinnace. Extremes of the mouth of the bay from E. to S.E. ½ E.; distance from the shore, ab't ¾ of a mile. The carp'r with his crew on shore wooding.

COOK:

In the PM winds southerly clear weather with which we stood into the bay and Anchor'd under the south shore about 2 mile within the entrance in 6 fathoms water, the south point bearing SE and the north point East. Saw as we came in on both points of the bay several of the natives and a few hutts, Men, women and children on the south shore abreast of the Ship, to which place I went in the boats in the hopes of speaking with them accompanied by Mr Banks, Dr Solander and Tupia; as we approached the shore they all made off except two Men who seemed resolved to oppose our landing. As soon as I saw this I ordered the boats to lay upon their oars in order to speake to them but this was to little purpose for neither us nor Tupia could understand one word they said. We then threw them some nails beeds &c[a] a shore which they took up and seemed not ill pleased in so much that I thought that they beckoned to us to come a shore; but in this we were mistaken, for as soon as we put the boat in they again came to oppose us upon which I fired a musket between

BANKSIAS AT BOTANY BAY, 1770. FIRST NOTED BY *ENDEAVOUR*'S NATURALISTS.

the two which had no effect other than to make them retire back where bundles of their darts lay, and one of them took up a large stone and threw at us which caused my fireing a second musquet load with small shott, and altho some of the shott struck the man yet it had no other effect than to make him lay hold of a shield or target to defend himself. Immediately after this we landed which we had no sooner done than they throw'd two darts at us, this obliged me to fire a third shott soon after which they both made off, but not in such haste but what we might have taken one, but Mr Banks being of the opinion that the darts were poisoned, made me cautious how I advanced into the woods. We found here a few small hutts made of the bark of trees in one of which were four or five small children with whom we left some strings of beeds &c[a]. A quantity of darts lay about the hutts these we took away with us. Three canoes lay upon the beach the worst I think I ever saw, they were about 12 or 14 feet long made of one piece of the bark of a tree drawn or tied up at each end and in the middle kept open by means of pieces of stick by way of Thwarts.

After searching for fresh water without success except a little in a small hole dug in the sand, we embarqued and went over to the north point of the bay where coming in we saw several people, but when we landed there was no body to be seen. We found here some fresh water which came trinkling down and stood in pools among the rocks; but as this was troublesome to come at I sent a party of men a shore in the morning abreast the ship to the place we first landed to dig holes in the sand by which means and a small stream sufficient to water the ship. The strings of beeds

&c[a] we had left with the children last night were found laying in the hutt this morning, probably the natives were afraid to take them away. After breakfast we sent some empty casks a shore and a party of men to cut wood and I went myself in the Pinnace to sound and explore the Bay, in the doing of which I saw several of the natives but they all fled at my approach. I landed in two places one of which the people had just left, as there were small fires and fresh mussels broiling upon them—here likewise lay vast heaps of the largest oyster shell I ever saw. [I like wise saw of the oysters themselves as I rowed over the shoals but being high-water I could not get any having nothing to take them up. (deleted)]

GREEN:
[landing] . . . but were opposed on the rocks and sandy beach by two Indians with 4-pronged wooden fish-gigs, tipped at the ends with four fish bones and fastened to y[e] wood with a gummy resinous substance. One of them under cover of a shield, approached the boat and threw his gig, and in return was wounded with small shot. They now fled and with them a woman and six or seven boys . . . the houses too (about five) were no more than angular kennels made by bending a piece of bark in the middle and resting either end on the ground, increasing the number of bark according to y[e] length required.

FORWOOD:
[opposed] by the two Indians on the shore with their spears in their hands ready to heave at the boat. Notwithstanding the Captain tried all means to persuade them to lay their weapons down by heaving them ashore presents but all to no purpose. At last finding nothing would do the Captain fired a load of small shot at them which so frightened them that they ran away into the woods.

BANKS:
The land this morning appeard Cliffy and barren without wood. An opening appearing like a harbour was seen and we stood directly in for it. A small smoak arising from a very barren place directed our glasses that way and we soon saw about 10 people, who in our approach left the fires and retired to a little eminence where they could conveniently see the ship; soon after this two canoes carrying 2 men each landed on the beach under them, the men hauld up their boats and went to their fellows on the hill. Our boat which had been sent ahead to sound [the pinnace] now approached the place and they all retired up the hill; we saw however that at the beach or landing place one man at least was hid among some rocks who never that we could see left that place. Our boat proceeded along shore and the Indians followed her at a distance. When she came back the officer who was in her [Molyneux] told me that in a cove a little within the harbour they came down to the beach and invited our people to land by many signs and words which he did not at all understand; all however were armed with long pikes and a wooden weapon made something like a small scymetar. During this time a few of the Indians who had not followed the boat

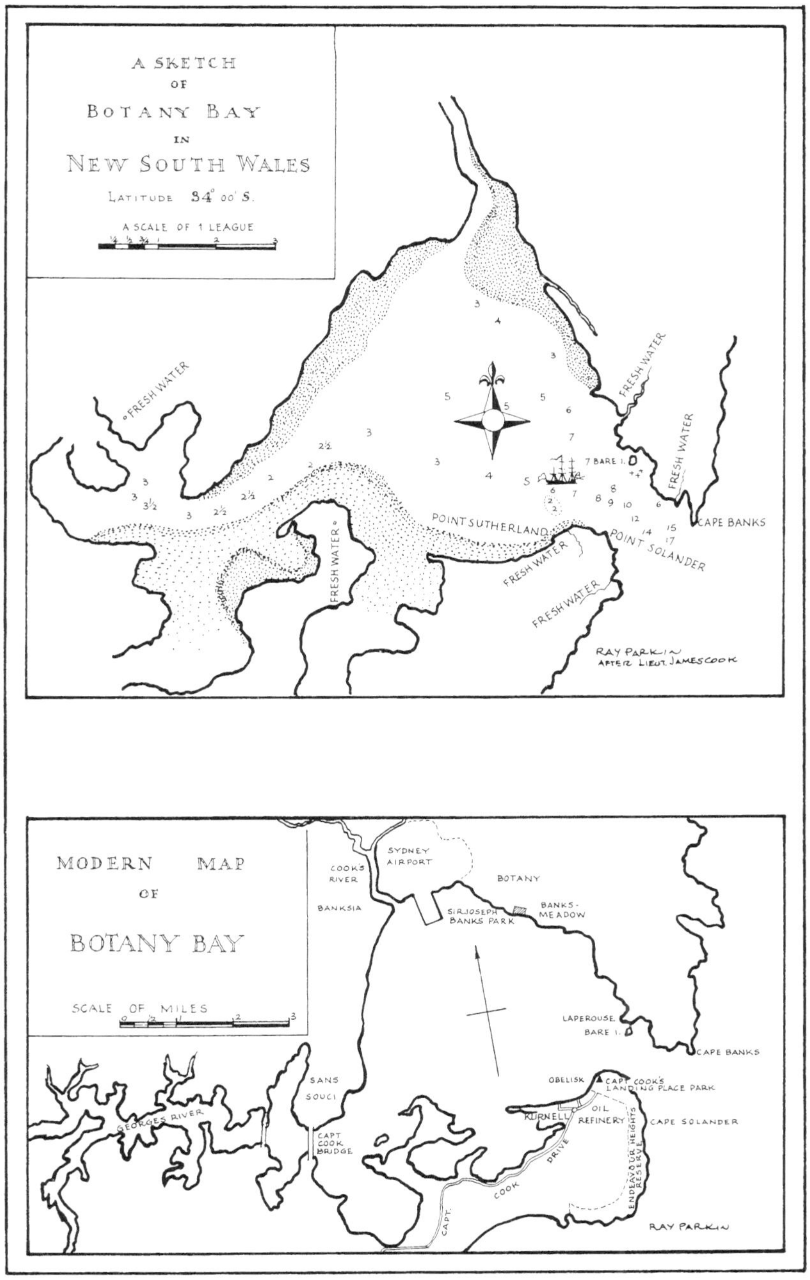

remained on the rocks opposite the ship, threatening and menacing with their pikes and swords—two in particular were painted with white, their faces seemingly dusted over with it, their bodies painted with broad strokes over their breasts and backs resembling much a soldiers cross belts, and their legs and thighs also with such like broad strokes drawn around them which imitated broad garters or bracelets. Each of these held in his hand a wooden weapon about 2½ feet long, much resembling a scymeter; the blades of these looked whitish some thought shining in so much that they were almost of the opinion that they were made of some kind of metal, but myself thought they were no more than wood smeared over with the same white pigment with which they paint their bodys. These two seemed to talk earnestly together, at times brandishing their crooked weapons at us in a token of defiance. By noon we were within the mouth of the inlet which appeared to be very good. Under the South head of it were four small canoes; in each of these was one man who held in his hand a long pole with which he struck fish, venturing with his little embarkation almost into the surf. These people seemed to be totally engaged in what they were about: the ship passed within a quarter of a mile of them and yet they scarce lifted their eyes from their employment; I was almost inclined to think that attentive to their business and deafened by the noise of the surf they neither saw nor heard her go past them. At 1 we came to an anchor abreast of a small village consisting of about 6 or 8 houses. Soon after this an old woman followed by three children came out of the wood; she carried several pieces of stick and the children also had their little burthens; when she came to the houses 3 more younger children came out of one of them to meet her. She often looked at the ship but expressed neither surprize nor concern. Soon after this she lighted a fire and the four canoes came in from fishing; the people landed, hauld up their boats and began to dress their dinner to all appearance totally unmoved at us, tho we were within a little more than ½ a mile of them. Of all these people we had seen so distinctly through our glasses we had not been able to observe the least signs of Cloathing: myself to the best of my judgement plainly discerned that the woman did not copy our mother Eve even in the figleaf.

After dinner the boats were manned and we set out from the ship intending to land at the place where we saw these people, hoping as they regarded the ships coming into the bay so little they would as little regard our landing. We were in this however mistaken, for as soon as we approached the rocks two of the men came down upon them, each armed with a lance about 10 feet long and a short stick he seemed to handle as if it was a machine [a throwing stick] to throw the lance. They called to us very loud in a harsh sounding language of which neither us nor Tupia understood a word, shaking their lances and menacing, in all appearance resolved to dispute our landing to the utmost tho they were but two and we 30 or 40 at least. In this manner we parlyed with them for about a quarter of an hour, they waving us to be gone, and we again signing that we wanted water and that we meant them no harm. They remained resolute so a musquet was fired over them, the effect of which was that the youngest of the two dropped a bundle of lances on the rock at the instant in which he heard the report; he however snatched them up again and both renewed their threats and opposition. A Musquet loaded with small shot was now fired at the eldest of the two who was about 40 yards from the boat; it struck him on the legs but he minded it very little so another was immediately fired at him; on this he ran up to the house about 100 yards distant and soon returned with a shield. In the meantime we had landed on the rock. He immediately threw a lance at us and the young man another which fell among the thickest of us but hurt nobody; two more musquets with small shot were then fired at them on which the eldest threw one more lance and then ran away as did the other. We went up to the houses, in one of which we found the children hid behind the shield and a piece of bark in one of the houses. We were conscious from the distance the people had been from us when we fired that the shot could have done them no material harm; we therefore resolved to leave the children on the spot without even opening their shelter. We therefore threw into the house to them some beads, ribbands, cloths &c. as presents and went away. We however thought it no improper measure to take away with us all the lances which we could find about the house, amounting in number to forty or fifty. These were of various lengths from 15 to 6 feet in length; both of those which were thrown at us and all we found except one had four prongs headed with very sharp fish bones, which were besmeared with a greenish coloured gum that at first gave me some suspicions of Poison. The people were blacker than any we had seen in the Voyage tho by no means negroes; their beards were thick and bushy and they were seen to have a redundancy of hair upon those parts where it commonly grows; the hair of their heads was bushy and thick but by no means woolley like that of a Negro; they were of a common size, lean and seemed active and nimble; their voices were coarse and strong. Upon examining the lances we had taken from them we found that most of them had been used in striking fish, at least we concluded so from sea weed that was found stuck in among the four prongs.—Having taken the resolution before mentioned we returned to the ship in order to get rid of our load of lances, and having done that went to that place at the mouth of the harbour where we had seen the people in the morn; here however we found nobody.—At night moving lights were seen in different parts of the bay such as we had been used to see in the Islands; from hence we supposed that the people here strike fish in the same manner. The fires (fishing fires as we supposed) were seen through the greatest part of the night. In the morn we went ashore at the houses, but found not the least good effect from our presents yesterday: no signs of people were to be seen, in the house in which the children were yesterday was left every individual thing we had thrown to them; Dr Solander and myself went a little way into the woods and found many plants but saw nothing like people. At noon all hands came aboard for dinner. The Indians, about 12 in number, as soon as they saw our boat put off came down to the houses. Close by these was our watering place at which

Aboriginal huts at Botany Bay, 1770 (after sketches by Parkinson).

stood our cask; they looked at them but did not touch them, their business was merely to take away two of the four boats which they had left at the houses; this they did and hauled the other two above high water mark, and then went away as they came.

PARKINSON:
On the 28th, we got into a fine bay, and some of our people went ashore on one side of it, where we saw some houses. On our approaching the shore, two men with different kinds of weapons, came out and made towards us. Their countenances bespoke displeasure; they threatened us, and discovered hostile intentions, often crying to us, Warra warra wai. We made signs to them to be peaceable, and threw them some trinkets; but they kept aloof, and dared us to come on shore. We attempted to frighten them by firing off a gun loaded with small shot; but attempted in vain. One of them repaired to a house immediately, and brought out a shield, of an oval figure, painted white in the middle, with two holes in it to see through, also a wooden sword, and then they advanced boldly, gathering up stones as they came along, which they threw at us. After we had landed they threw two of their lances at us; one of which fell between my feet. Our people fired again, and wounded one of them; at which they took the alarm and were very frantic and furious, shouting for assistance, calling Hala, hala, mae; that is (as we afterwards learned) Come hither; while their wives and children set up a most horrid howl. We endeavoured to pacify them, but to no purpose for they seemed implacable, and, at length, ran howling away, leaving their wives and children, who hid themselves in one of the huts behind a piece of bark. After looking about us a little while, we left some nails on the spot and embarked, taking with us their weapons; and then proceeded to the other side of the bay, where we had seen a number of people, as we came in, round a fire, some of whom were painted white, having a streak around their thighs, two below their knees, one like a sash over their shoulders, which ran diagonally downwards, and another across their foreheads. Both men and women were quite naked, very lean and rawboned; their complexion was dark, their hair black and frizzled, their heads unadorned, and the beards of the men bushy. Their canoes were made of one piece of bark, gathered at the two ends, and extended in the middle by two sticks. Their paddles were very small, two of which they used at one time; and we found a large lump of yellow gum in their gigs which seemed to be for striking fish. Some of their weapons had a kind of chisel fixed at their ends [throwing stick], but of what substance they were formed we could not learn.

Such was the first contact with the people of this coast. In making his descriptions Mr Banks was not unaware of those previous ones of Dampier, whom he had attentively been reading. There was some new quality about these people that had not been seen in other natives on the voyage. That they seemed not greatly impressed by the newcomers' material advantages was puzzling, when these had so readily been acknowledged by all others; but this was put down to a supposed ignorance rather than a perceptive discrimination. This tendency towards material values is implicit in some of the descriptions. Even the gentle Mr Parkinson, with his Quaker brotherliness toward all, does not entirely avoid it. But his keen artistic observations have left records otherwise unmade: of colours, shapes and sounds which are very just.

It was the Captain himself, though much constrained by the customs and traditions of his race, who did not presume to judge the customs or conduct of other peoples (except for immediate practical purposes), but was rather apt to see in them a completely different set of circumstances pertaining. He was sad and disturbed when forced to act upon the presumptions of his *race rather than of* theirs*—as he once said 'to prevent being knocked on the head'.*

On the actual landing, young Isaac Smith was the first to put his foot ashore. In later years, as an Admiral, together with Mrs Cook, his aunt, he liked to tell how the Captain had said to him as the boat beached, 'Isaac, you shall land first,' then Cook himself followed.

SHIP'S LOG:

MONDAY, APRIL 30TH, 1770

Day and Month.	Winds.	Remarks, &c.
Monday, April 30 . .	E.S.E. Variable. N.	Little wind and fine pleas't wea'r throughout these 24 hours. The first lieut't with a party watering. The carp'r with his crew wooding. On board employ'd in the holds; arm'rs at the forge; sailm'rs repairing the sails. P M.—Sent the yawl to haul the sean. She brought on board as much fish as run 3lb. a man throughout the ship's company.

COOK:

As soon as the wooders and waterers were come on board to dinner 10 or 12 of the natives came to the watering place and took away their canoes that lay there but did not offer to touch any one of our casks that had been left ashore, and in the afternoon 16 or 18 of them came boldly up within 100 yards of our people at the watering place and there made a stand. Mr Hicks who was the officer ashore did all in his power to entice them to him by offering them presents &c[a] but it was to no purpose, all they seem'd to want was for us to be gone. After staying a short time they went away. They were all armed with darts and wooden swords [throwing sticks], the darts have each four prongs and pointed with fish bones, those we have seen seem to be intended more for striking fish than offensive weapons neither are they poisoned as we at first thought. After I had returned from sounding the bay I went to a cove on the north side where in three or four hauls with the saine we caught above 300 pounds of weight of fish which I caused to be equally divided among the Ships Company. In the AM I went in the Pinnace to sound and explore the North side of the bay where I neither met with inhabitants or anything remarkable. Mr Green took the Suns Meridion Altitude a little within the south entrance of the bay which gave the Latitude 34° 0′ s.

BANKS:

In the Evening 15 of them armed came towards our waterers; they sent two before the rest, our people did the same; however they did not wait for a meeting but gently retired. Our boat was about this time loaded so everybody went off in her, and at the same time the Indians went away. Myself with the Cap^{tn} &c were in a sandy cove on the Northern side of the harbour, where we hauled the seine and caught many very fine fish, more than all hands could eat.

AM: Before daybreak this morn the Indians were at the houses abreast the ship: they were heard to shout much. At sunrise they were seen walking along the beach; we saw them go into the woods where they lighted fires about a mile from us. Our people went ashore as usual, Dr Solander and myself into the woods. The grass cutters [for the sheep and goat] were farthest from the body of the people; towards them came 14 or 15 Indians having in their hands sticks that shone (sayd the Sergeant of marines) [John Edgcumbee] like a musquet. The officer on seeing them gathered his people together: the hay cutters coming to the main body appeared like a flight so the Indians pursued them, however but a very short way, for they never came nearer than just to shout at each other, maybe a furlong.

The watering place was later to be called Kurnell, after the Aboriginal Kundel.

SHIP'S LOG:

TUESDAY, MAY 1ST, 1770

Day and Month.	Winds.	Remarks, &c.
Tuesday, May 1 . .	N.W. W.W.N.	Do. weather. All parties employ'd as yesterday. The yawl but little success in fishing. At 6 p.m. departed this life Forby Sutherland, seaman. A.M.—Sent the body on shore to be burried. Latit'de obs'd, 34° 06′ S.

COOK:

Gentle breezes northerly. In the PM ten of the natives again visited the watering place. I being on board at this time went immediately ashore but before I got there they were going away, I follow'd them alone and unarm'd some distance along the shore but they would not stop untill they got farther off than I choose to trust myself; those were armed in the same manner as those that came yesterday. In the evening I sent some hands to haul the saine but they caught but a very few fish. A little after sunrise I found the Variation to be 11° 3′ East. Last night Forby Sutherland seaman departed this life and in the AM his body was buried ashore at the watering place which occasioned my calling the south point of this bay after his name (*Point Sutherland*). This morning a party of us went ashore to some hutts not far from the watering place where some of the natives are daily seen, here we left several articles such as Cloth, Looking glasses, Combs, beeds, nails &c^{a}. After this we made an excursion into the country which we found diversified with woods, lawns and marshes; the woods are free from underwood of every kind and the trees are at such a distance from one another that the whole country or at least a great part of it might be cultivated without being oblig'd to cut down a single tree; we found the soil everywhere except in the marshes to be a light white sand and produceth a quantity of good grass which grows in little tufts about as big as one can hold in ones hand and pretty close to one another, in this manner the surface of the ground is coated in the woods between the trees. Dr Solander had a bad [or bare?] sight of a small animal something like a rabbit and we found the dung of an animal which must feed upon grass and which we judged could not be less than a deer [kangaroo?], we also saw the track of a dog or some such like animal [dingo?]. We met with some hutts and places where the natives had been and at our first setting out one of them was seen, the others I suppose had fled upon our approach. I saw some trees that had been cut down by the natives with some sort of blunt instrument and several trees that were barked the bark of which had been cut by the same instrument, in many of the trees, especially the palms, were steps cut about 3 or 4 feet asunder for the conveniency of climbing them. We found 2 sorts of Gum one sort of which is like Gum Dragon and is the same as I suppose Tasman took for gum lac, it is extracted from the largest trees in the woods [the Eucalypt].

PICKERSGILL:
At 6 PM Departed this life Forby Sutherland seaman, of consumption with which he had been afflicted ever since our departure from Streight le Maire.

WILKINSON:
Eleven or twelve Indians came down to the beach within a quarter of a mile of our people and behaved in a very insolent manner, the Captain endeavouring by every fair means to induce a friendship with them, but all to no purpose; we observed these people have not the least rag of clothing on them.

BANKS:
At night they came again in the same manner and acted over again the same half pursuit. Myself in the even landed on a small island on the Northern side of the bay [Bare Island] to search for shells; in going I saw six Indians on the main who shouted to us but ran away into the woods before the boat was within half a mile of them, although she did not even go towards them. AM: The Cap^{tn} Dr Solander, myself and some of the people, making in all 10 musquets, resolved to make an excursion into the country. We accordingly did so and walked till we compleatly tired ourselves, which was in the evening, seeing by the way only one Indian who ran away from us as soon as he saw us. The Soil wherever we saw it consisted of either swamps or light sandy soil on which grew very few species of trees, one of which was large yielding a gum much like *sanguis draconis* [dragon's blood], but every place was covered with vast quantities of grass. We saw many

Indian houses and places where they had slept on the grass without the least shelter; in these we left beads &c. We saw one quadruped the size of a Rabbit, my greyhound just got sight of him and instantly lamed himself against a stump which lay concealed in the long grass; we also saw the dung of a large animal that fed on grass which much resembled that of a Stag; also the footsteps of an animal clawed like a dog or wolf and as large as the latter; and of a small animal whose feet were like those of a polecat or weasel [native cat?]. The trees over our heads abounded very much with Loryquets and Cocatoos of which we shot several; Both of these sorts flew in flocks of several scores together.

Our Second Lieutenant [Gore] went in the boat drudging; after he had done he landed and sent the boat away, keeping with him a midshipman with whoom he set out to walk to the Waterers. In his way he was overtaken by 22 Indians who followed him often within 20 yards, parleying but never daring to attack him tho they were all armed with lances. After they had joined our people 2 or 4 more curious perhaps than prudent, went again towards these Indians who remained about ½ a mile from our watering place. When they came pretty near them they pretended to be afraid and ran from them; four of the Indians on this immediately threw their lances which went beyond our people, and by their account were thrown about 40 yards; on this they stopped and began to collect the lances, on which the Indians retired slowly. At this time the Cap^{tn} Dr Solander and myself came to the waterers; we immediately went toward the Indians; they went fast away; the Cap^{tn} Dr Solander and Tupia went towards them and every one else stayed behind; this however did not stop the Indians who walked leisurely away till our people were tired of following them. The accounts of every one who saw the Indians near today was exactly consonant with what had been observed on the first day of our landing: they were black but not negroes, hairy, naked &c. just as we had seen them.

PARKINSON:

On this day, Forbes Sutherland, a native of the Orkneys, who had departed this life, was carried on shore and decently interred. The natives often reconoitered us but we could not prevail on them to come near us or be social; for as soon as we advanced, they fled as nimbly as deer, excepting at one time, when they seemed determined to face us: then they came armed with spears, having their breasts painted white; but as soon as they saw our boat go off from the ship, they retreated. Constrained by hunger, they often came into the bay to fish; but they kept in the shallows, and as near as possible to the shore. In one of their houses, at the top of the bay, we had laid some nails, pieces of cloth and various trinkets; and though the natives had been there in our absence, yet they had not taken any of them.

The name the journal keepers were using at this time for the bay was Stingray Bay *or* Stingray Harbour.

Forby Sutherland, the poulterer who had plucked and dressed the many birds of all sorts that had been shot (especially by Mr Gore and Mr Banks), did not prepare the lorikeets and cockatoos that had been shot this day.

His name has since vanished from the place where the Captain put it on his plan of the harbour, replaced by the name Inscription Point. *However, this humble sailor is memorialised by the town and shire of Sutherland, some ten miles from where he was buried. Point Solander, the outer southern headland of the bay, has been shifted a mile or so south and become Cape Solander. Only Cape Banks, the northern headland, is unmoved.*

SHIP'S LOG:

WEDNESDAY, MAY 2ND, 1770

Day and Month.	Winds.	Remarks, &c.
Wednesday, May 2 . .	N.N.W. S. S.S.E.	The first p't, little wind and fair wea'r. P.M.—All parties employ'd as yesterday. Little success in fishing. In the nig't, light airs and dark cloudy wea'r, with thunder, lightning, and showers of rain. All hands employ'd scrubbing the ship's bottom and giving her a thorough clean within board. At 10, mod't and fair; sent the wooders and waterers on shore.

COOK:

Between 3 and 4 oClock in the PM we returned out of the Country and after dinner went ashore to the watering place where we had not been long before 17 or 18 natives appeared in sight. In the morning I had sent Mr Gore with a boat up to the head of the bay to dridge for oysters; in his return to the ship he and another person came by land and met with these people who followed him at a distance of 19 or 20 yards; when ever Mr Gore made a stand and fac'd them they stood also and notwithstanding they were all armed they never offered to attack him, but after he had parted from them and they were met by Dr Munkhouse and one or two more who upon making a sham retreat they throwed 3 darts after them, after which they began to retire. Dr Solander, I and Tupia made all haste we could after them but could neither by words nor actions prevail upon them to come near us. Mr Gore saw some up the bay who by signs invited him ashore which he prudently declined. In the AM had wind at SE with rain which prevented me from making an excursion up to the head of the bay as I intended. In the evening compleated our water and in the AM scrubbed the ship between wind and water.

HICKES:

At 5 PM about 17 Indians came to our party armed with lances & swords. Two of them advanced and talked much in an unknown tongue I believe the purport was either commanding us to go away or daring to single combat.

PICKERSGILL:
Scraped and cleaned the ships bottom.

WILKINSON:
All trades as yesterday.

BANKS:
The morn was rainy and we who had got already so many plants were well contented to find an excuse for staying onboard to examine them a little at least.

The puzzle of these people continued: the self-contained aloofness coupled with no overt hostility or belligerence; meagre and seemingly primitive, yet self-sufficient, and appearing without envy or greed.

SHIP'S LOG:

THURSDAY, MAY 3RD, 1770

Day and Month.	Winds.	Remarks, &c.
Thursday, May 3	S.E.b.S. W.S.W. Calm.	Mod. breezes and fair weather. P.M.—Wooders and waterers on shore. Completed our water, amounting to 80 tons. The captain and gentlemen a dist. up the country. Received on board a longboat load of wood. A.M.—The carpenter with his crew on shore. Loos'd sails to dry. Saw 12 cannoes fishing along shore.

COOK:
Winds at SE a gentle breeze and fair weather. In the PM I made a little excursion along the Sea Coast accompanied by Mr Banks and Dr Solander. At our first entering the woods we saw 3 of the natives who made off as soon as they saw us; more of them were seen by others of our people who likewise made off as soon as they found they were discovered. In the AM I went in the Pinnace to the head of the bay accompanied by Drs Solander and Munkhouse in order to examine the country and to try to form some connections with the natives: in our way thither we met with 10 or 12 of them fishing each in a small canoe who retired into shoal water upon our approach, others again we saw at the first place we landed at, who took to their canoes and fled before we came near them; after this we took water and went almost to the head of the inlet where we landed and travel'd some distance inland. We found the face of the country much the same as I have before described but the land much richer, for instead of sand I found in many places a deep black soil which we thought capable of producing any kind of grain, at present it produceth besides timber as fine meadow as was ever seen. However we found it all not like this, some few places were very rocky but this I believe to be uncommon; the stone is sandy and very proper for building &c^a^. After we had sufficiently exam-

BARK CANOES, BOTANY BAY, 1770 (AFTER PARKINSON'S CANOE SKETCHES).

ined this part we returned to the boat and seeing some smook and canoes at another part we went thither in hopes of meeting with the people but they made off as we approached. There were six canoes and six small fires near the shore and mussels roasting upon them and a few oysters laying near, from this we conjectured that there had been six people who had been out each in his own canoe picking up the shell fish and come ashore to eat them where each had made a fire to dress them by; we taisted of their cheer and left them in return strings of beeds &c[a]. Near to this place at the foot of a tree was a small well or spring of water. The day being now far spent we set out on our return to the ship.

BANKS:

In the afternoon however it cleared up and we returned to our old occupation of collecting, in which we had our usual good success Tupia who strayed from us in pursuit of Parrots, of which he shot several, told us on his return that he had seen nine Indians who ran away from him as soon as they perceived him.

AM: Our collection of plants has now grown so immensely large that it was necessary that some extraordinary care should be taken of them least they should spoil in the books. I therefore devoted this day to that business and carried all the drying paper, near 200 Quires of which the larger part was full, ashore and spreading them upon a sail in the sun kept them in this manner exposed the whole day, often turning them and sometimes turning the Quires, in which were plants, inside out. By this means they came on board at night in very good condition. During the time this was doing 11 canoes, in each of which was one Indian, came toward us. We soon saw that the people in them were employed in striking fish; they came within about ½ a mile of us intent on their own employments and not at all regarding us. Opposite the place where they were several of our people were shooting; one Indian may be prompted by curiosity landed, hauled up his canoe and went towards them; he stayed about a quarter of an hour and then launched his boat and went off, probably that time had been spent in watching behind trees to see what our people did. I could not find however that he was seen by any body. When the damp of Even made it necessary to send my plants and books onboard I made a small excursion in order to shoot anything I met with and found a large quantity of Quails, much resembling our English ones, of which I might have killed as many as I pleased had I given my time up to it, but my business was to kill variety and not too many individuals of one species.—The Cap^{tn} and Dr Solander employed the day in going in the pinnace into various parts of the harbour. They saw fires at several places and people who all ran away at their approach with the greatest precipitation, leaving behind the shell fish which they were cooking; of this our gentlemen took advantage, eating what they found and leaving beads ribbands &c in return. They also found trees which bore fruit of the Jambosa kind, much in colour and shape resembling cherries; of these they eat plentifully and brought home also abundance, which we eat with much pleasure tho they had little to recommend them but a light acid.

SHIP'S LOG:

FRIDAY, MAY 4TH, 1770

Day and Month.	Winds.	Remarks, &c.
Friday, May 4	Calm. N.E. Calm.	The afternoon calm. In the evening, light airs with fine pleas't weather. Wooders on shore. The captain and gentlemen examining the country. On board stowing away wood and clearing the ship for sea. A.M.—The wooders on shore. Little wind and cloudy weather. Served fish to all hands. N.B.—Low water, ½-p't 11 a.m.

COOK:

Employed as yesterday and fishing. Winds northerly, serene weather. Upon my return to the ship in the evening I found that none of the natives had apppeared near the watering place but about 20 of them had been fishing in their canoes at no great distance from us. In the AM as the wind would not permit us to sail I sent out some parties into the country to try to form some connections with the natives. One of the Midshipmen met with a very old woman and two small children; they were close to the water side where several more were in canoes gathering shell fish and he being alone was afraid to make any stay with the old people least he should be discovered by those in the canoes. He gave them a bird he had shott which they would not touch neither did they speak one word but seemed much frightened, they were quite naked even the woman had nothing to cover her nuditie. Dr Munkhouse and another man being in the woods not far from the watering place discovered six more natives who at first seemed to wait his coming but as he was going up to them he had a dart thrown at him out of a tree which narrowly escaped him, as soon as the fellow had thrown the dart he descended the tree and made off with him, all the rest and these were all that were met with during the course of this day.

FORWOOD:

Served 5 lb of fish per man which was caught by striking with grains; brought on board one stingray which weighed 280 lb weight.

PICKERSGILL:

The Captain and company away up the harbour this day; the Second Lieutenant [Mr Gore] and some of the petty officers went up the bay striking stingrays, of which were sufficient to serve all hands.

BOOTIE:

Ships draught of water forward 14 feet 1 inch; aft 14 feet. Variation per Azimuth 6° 42′ E.

BANKS:

Myself botanizing in the woods as usual, now quite void of fear as our neighbours have turned out such rank cowards. One of our midshipmen straggling by himself a long way from anyone else met by accident with a very old man and woman and some children; they were setting under a tree and neither party saw the other till they were close together. They shewed signs of fear but did not attempt to run away. He had nothing about him to give them but some parrots which he had shot: these they refused, withdrawing themselves from his hand when he offered them in token either of extreme fear or disgust. The people were very old and grey headed, the children young. The hair of the man was bushy about his head, his beard long and rough, the womans was cropped short round her head; they were both very dark coloured but not black nor was their hair woolly. He stayed however with them but a very short time, for seeing many canoes fishing at a small distance he feared that the people in there might observe him and come ashore to the assistance of the old people, who in all probability belonged to them. 17 canoes came fishing near our people in the same manner as yesterday only stayed rather longer, emboldened a little I suppose by having yesterday met with no kind of molestation. Myself in the afternoon ashore on the NW side of the bay, where we went a good away into the country which in this place is very sandy and resembles something our Moors in England, as no trees grow upon it but everything is covered with a thin brush of plants about as high as the knees. The hills are low and rise one above the other a long way into the country by a very gradual ascent, appearing in every respect like those we were upon. While we were employed in this walk the people hauled the seine upon a sandy beach and caught a great plenty of small fish. On our return to the ship we found also that our 2^{d} Lieutenant who had gone out striking had met with great success: he had observed that the large stingrays of which there are an abundance in the bay followed the flowing tide into shallow water; he therefore took the opportunity of flood and struck several in not more than 2 or 3 feet of water; one that was larger than the rest when his guts was taken out weighed 239 pounds. Our surgeon who strayed a long way from the people with one in his company, in coming out of a thicket observed 6 Indians standing about 50 yards from him; one of these gave a signal by a word pronounced loud, on which a lance was thrown out of the wood at him which however came not very near him. The 6 Indians seeing that it had not taken effect ran away in an instant, but on turning about towards the place from whence the lance came he saw a young lad, who undoubtedly had thrown it, come down from a tree where he had been stationed probably for that purpose; he descended however and ran away so quick that it was impossible even to attempt to pursue him.

'153':

The Captain &c examining the country. AM: Wooders on shore. Marked a tree in his Britannick Majestys name with the name of the ship, month and year.

The Captain's excursion to the head of the bay on Thursday took him to what was later to become Tom Ugly's Point in the Georges River.

Mr Forwood, the Gunner, mentions the striking of fish with the grains; Mr Pickersgill tells of the Second Lieutenant and some petty officers (of whom he was most probably one) striking stingrays; Mr Banks writes of how Mr Gore had followed the flooding tide into shallow water as he had observed the rays to do. This is typical of the initiative and keen observation of Gore. He was a natural hunter and his log seldom fails to note as something significant the particular birds that were about him at sea, whereas others do not. He took a leading part whenever food had to be shot for the ship. One feels certain that he had watched with a keen and comprehending interest the way of the Aborigine standing poised with his four-pronged fish spear in his frail bark canoe drifting in the shallows. Respecting their knowledge and experience, he did the same. The grains was an iron fish spear with a number of points half-barbed inwardly. The name grains *was derived from the old Norse* grein, *meaning division.*

Mr Banks was neither unkind nor inhumane, but he was affected by the unconscious and therefore unquestioned assumptions of his class and race. Courage to him had the positive connotation of assertiveness, born as he was of a civilisation which owed much of its character to the war and conquest upon which it was founded. One may well wonder what Mr Banks's feelings and trepidations would have been if he, like the natives, had found himself naked on this coast with only a wooden spear in his hand to get a living by. He appears not to have imagined that the conduct of this people towards the newcomers sprang from their experience of a world in which they had survived for longer than the whole span of western civilisation. They were perceptive enough to recognise a threat—possibly in a vague but sure way—as a profound and disastrous one, but they made only a token resistance, as if to communicate their real fears. Their ancient wisdom, quiet and unyielding in the face of a new force, and in such contrast to the undeniable and volatile belligerence of the Maori just encountered, was more than a little frightening.

BANKSIA SERRATA, BOTANY BAY, 1770 (AFTER A SKETCH BY PARKINSON).

Banks was collecting and drying botanical specimens for the expansion of European knowledge on the march. He would take back with him 'curiosities' to which would be given difficult and impressive names. He did not suspect that these people—whom he charitably pitied and thought of as 'ignorant savages'—were in traditional possession of the botanical secrets he so passionately sought. They had not the impressive nomenclature and classification in a foreign tongue but each *of these people possessed a deep knowledge of the natural world about them. Their empathy for the appearances and ways of life of things permeated their highly developed spiritual lives, giving to their daily living the substance and demonstrability of an old wisdom as well as ensuring their day-to-day domestic survival. Theirs was knowledge that was literally unforgettable because they had not one written word among them.*

This group of people at the landing site were of the Gwyeagal tribe who had been able to live on this small peninsula for some eight thousand years (three thousand years longer, according to one ecclesiastical authority, than the time since we had been tipped out of the Garden of Eden) and with little evidence of war, either against nature or their fellows, during that time. Such had been the mutual support practised between these people and their home that Banks and Solander could now find that home in pristine condition.

We now know so much about the later-knighted Joseph Banks; if only he had known as much about what the old black man and woman and children were talking about—and understood.

SHIP'S LOG:

SATURDAY, MAY 5TH, 1770

Day and Month.	Winds.	Remarks, &c.
Saturday, May 5	N. and N.W.	Light breezes and pleas't wea'r. P.M.—Employ'd wooding. Fill'd the empty water-casks. At 7 the yawl and pinnace return'd from fishing. Served 5 lb. p'r man to all hands. A.M.—Employ'd wooding and fishing. Ship's draught of water forw'd, 14ft. 1in.; aft, 14 feet. Variation by mean of a great many good azymuths, 6° 42′ E.

COOK:

In the PM I went with a party of men over to the North shore and while some of the hands were hauling the saine a party of us made an excursion of 3 or 4 miles into the country or rather along the sea Coast. We met with nothing remarkable, great part of the country for some distance in land from the sea Coast is mostly barren heath diversified with marshes and morasses. Upon our return to the boat we found they had caught a great number of small fish which the sailors call leather Jackets on account of their having a very thick skin, they are known in the West Indias. I had sent the yawl in the morning to fish for *sting rays* who returned in the evening with up to 4 hundred weight; one single one weighed 240 lb exclusive of the entrails. In the AM as the wind still continued northerly I sent the yawl again afishing and I went with a party of men into the country but met with nothing extraordinary.

CLERKE:

PM: Served 5 lb of fish to all hands. AM: Served 6 lb of fish per man.

PICKERSGILL:

Employed wooding and watering and striking stingerrays of which they caught 300 lb, one weighing 236 lb; served 5 lb per man and stopped ye sea provisions. Variation per azimuth 6° 42′ E. Stingerray Bay lies in Latitude 34° 6′ S and Longitude west from London 207° 43′; It is formed by two low points between which there is a passage of one mile, with 12 fathoms of water. On the eastern side lies a little island, and off the southern end of it is a shore where the sea sometimes breaks. After you are in the bay spreads and tends off to ye westward 7 or 8 miles, and then ends in two large lagoons. Off the shore lie large flats with only 7 or 8 feet of water. Upon them is a great quantity of stingerrays. The bay is very shoal but there is a channel which lies open to ye entrance with 5 and 6 fathoms water but after you are two miles within it it shoals too. The bay is about 4 miles wide and has a regular tide. The country is very rich and fertile and has a fine appearance, and we saw a large tree which grows alone and yields a gum like dragons blood: this we found in great quantities sticking to ye bark. The tree on which it grows is very large and spreads but does not grow straight or tall, besides we saw a wood which had a grain like oak and would be very durable if used for building [casuarina or sheoak?]. The leaves are like pine leaf. The soil is a light sandy black earth mixed but very shallow. Upon digging we found quantities of Oyster shells, which seemed to have been underground a great while. We also found a tree which bore a red berry the size of a cherry, but they grew only in one place. The inhabitants are so shy that we had no intercourse with them. They used to come down every evening armed with lances and wooden swords. They appeared very thin, and had their faces (and breasts) daubed over with something white. One day as the surgeon was walking in the woods which are all clear of underwood, he had a lance thrown at him out of a tree, but the man made off. This was all we saw of them except when they were fishing off their in their canoes, which are very small and made of bark; they carry one man who paddles with two small pieces of wood; they use them in striking fish on y[e] flats. Their houses are several pieces of bark set up one against another and open at one end, and are the worst I ever saw. The people have nothing to cover themselves, but go quite naked, men and women, and, in short, are the most wretched set I ever beheld or heard of.

FORWOOD:

Remarks on Sting Ray Bay, New Holland. This bay is in Latitude 34° 00′ s and Long, by several observations ashore and on board 109° 13′ [209°?] West of Greenwich. During our stay here we saw parties of Indians—but could not come near enough to make any kind of—with them but they always made signals for us to be gone. They go quite naked not having the least thing to cover their nakedness. They are very black and live entirely on fish. Their canoes are only bark of a tree stopt at each end and so light that one man may carry them. We saw no kind of boat although the Captain went some distance into the country. Their houses are very low and small and are only covered with bark of trees & some grass and the branches of trees.

BANKS:

As tomorrow was fixed for our sailing Dr Solander and myself were employed the whole day in collecting specimens of as many things as we possibly could to be examined at sea. The day was calm and the Mosquetos of which we have always had some more than usually troublesome. No Indians were seen by any one during the whole day. The 2nd Lieutenant went out striking and took several large Stingrays the biggest which weighed without his gutts 336 pounds.

PARKINSON:

This bay is in latitude 34° 6′, and makes a good harbour, being only two or three points open to the eastward; but the water in general is shallow; and it has several arms extending from it, which are also shallow. On these shallows we found a great number of rays, some shell fish, and a few sharks. The rays are of an enormous size: one of them which we caught weighed two hundred and thirty-nine pounds, and another three hundred and twenty-six. They tasted much like European rays, the viscera had an agreeable flavour, not unlike stewed turtle. These rays and shell fish are the natives chief food.

The country is very level and fertile; the soil, a kind of grey sand; when we arrived everything seemed in perfection. There is a variety of flowering shrubs; a tree that yields gum, and a species of palm [*Borafus flabellifer*] the berries of which are of two sorts; one small eaten by the hogs, and the other as large as a cherry, has a stone in it; it is of a pale crimson colour, and has the taste of sweet acid. We also found a species of Salvia Fortea.

We met with one quadruped on the island, which was about the size of a hare: we found also the skin of a snake, and saw a great number of birds of a beautiful plumage: among which were two sorts of parroquets, and a beautiful loriquet: we shot a few of them, which we made into a pie, and they ate very well. We also met with a black bird very much like our crow, and shot some of them too, which also tasted agreeably. From the number of curious plants we met with on shore, we called the bay Botany-Bay.

The Captain in his excursion along the sea coast north of the bay possibly got as far as what was later to be called the Long Bay Rifle Range, toward Maroubra. Pickersgill's mention of the oyster shell found on digging—evidence of time-buried middens—is an indication of the antiquity of the Aboriginal occupation here.

SHIP'S LOG:

SUNDAY, MAY 6TH, 1770

H.	K.	F.	Courses.	Winds.	Remarks, &c.
1	..	..	Low water.	Calm.	Pleas't wea'r. People employ'd on shore wooding and refreshing. The yawl return'd in the evening from fishing, having caught two skeat, whose weight was near 600 lb. Served 5 lb. of fish p'r man.
2	..	..	..	..	
3	..	..	..	Variable.	
4	..	..	..	..	
5	..	..	..	Easterly.	
6	..	..	..	..	
7	..	..	..	N.E.	High-water.
8	..	..	..	..	
9	..	..	..	Westerly.	
10	..	..	..	..	
11	..	..	..	..	
12	..	..	..	N.W.	Light airs and fair weather.
1	..	..	..	..	
2	..	..	..	..	
3	..	..	..	..	
4	..	..	..	..	
5	..	..	..	..	Hove up the b't b'r and hove ahead on the streem cable.
6	..	..	..	..	
7	..	..	..	..	Weighed and hoisted in the boats.

H.	K.	F.	Courses.	Winds.	Remarks, &c.
8	..	..	..	..	Made sail, the two heads of the bay in one W. ½ S.; nearest dis't 2 miles.
9	2	..	N.b.E. ½ E.	Westerly.	
10	2	..	N.	S.W.	Employ'd cleaning and clearing ship fore and aft. Set steering sails.
11	2	..	N.b.E.	..	
12	2	4	..	S.S.W.	At noon { The extr's of the land from N. 5° E. to S.b.W. ½ W., abrest of an open bay; dist. off the nearest shore, 2 or 3 miles. Lat'd. obs., 33° 47'.

COOK:

In the evening the yawl returned from fishing having caught two sting rays weighing near 600 pounds. The great quantity of New Plants &c[a] Mr Banks and Dr Solander collected in this place occasioned my giving it the name of *Botany Bay*. It is situated in the Latitude of 34° 0' s, Longitude 208° 37' West; it is capacious safe and commodious, it may be known by the land on the sea coast which is of a pretty even and moderate height, rather higher than it is farther inland with steep rocky clifts next the sea and looks like a long island lying close under the shore: the entrance of the harbour lies about the middle of this land, in coming from the Southward it is discovered before you are abreast of it which you cannot do in coming from the northward; the entrance is little more than a mile broad and lies in WNW. To sail into it keep the south shore on board untill within a small bare island [Bare Islet] which lies close under the north shore, being within that island the deepest water is on that side 7, 6 and five fathom a good way up. There is shoaled water a good way off from the south shore from the inner south point quite to the head of the harbour, but over towards the north and NW shore there is a channel of 12 or 14 feet water at low water 3 or 4 leagues up to a place where there is 3 & 4 fathom, but here I found but very little fresh water. We anchored near the south shore about a mile within the entrance for the conveniency of sailing with a southerly wind and the getting of fresh water, but I afterwards found a very fine stream of fresh water on the north shore in the first sandy cove within the island before which a ship might lay almost land locked and wood for fuel may be got every where: altho wood is here in great plenty yet there is very little variety, the largest trees are as large or larger than our oaks in England and grows a good deal like them and yields a reddish gum, the wood itself is heavy hard and black like Lignum Vitae; another sort that grows tall and straight something like pines, the wood of this is hard and ponderous and something of the nature of American live oaks; these two are all the timber trees I met with. There are a few sorts of Shrubs and Palm trees, and mangroves about the head of the harbour. The country is woody low and flat as far inland as we could see and I believe the soil is generally sandy, in the wood are a variety of very beautiful birds such as Cocatoos, Lorryquets, Parrots &c[a] and Crows exactly like those we have in England. Water fowl are no less plenty about the head of the harbour where there are large flats of sand and mud on which they seek their food, the most of these unknown to us, one sort especially which was black and white and as large as a goose but most like a pelican [a pelican]. On the sand and mud banks are oysters, mussels, cockles &c[a] which I believe are the chief support of the inhabitants, who go into the shoaled water with their little canoes and pick them out of the sand and mud with their hands and sometimes roast and eat them in the canoe, having often a fire for that purpose as I suppose, for I know of no other use it can be for. The natives do not appear to be numberous neither do they seem to live in large bodies but dispersed in small parties along by the water side; those I saw were about as tall as Europeans, of a very dark brown colour but not black nor had they woolly frizled hair, but black and lank like ours. No sort of cloathing or ornaments were ever seen by any of us upon any one of them or in or about their hutts, from which I conclude they never wear any. Some we saw that had their faces and bodies painted with a sort of white paint or pigment. Altho I said that shell fish is their chief support yet they catch other sorts of fish some of which we found roasting on the fire the first time we landed, some of these they strike with gigs and others they catch with hook and line; we have seen them strike fish with gigs & hooks and lines were found in their hutts. Sting rays I believe they do not eat because I never saw the least remains of one near any of their hutts or fire places [neither were any of their darts or offensive weapons armed with the sting of sting rays the use I think they would [have] applied them to did they make use of the fish, none of us ever saw any provisions laid up in store so that I believe that they depend upon the present day for their subsistence (deleted)]. However we could but know very little of their customs as we were never able to form any connections with them, they had not so much as touched the things we had left in their hutts on purpose for them to take away. [The arms we saw among them were darts, some of which were barbed with fish bones stuck on with gum, and wooden swords, their defensive weapon is a Target made of the bark of a gum tree. (deleted)] During our stay in this harbour I caused the English colours to be displayed ashore every day and an inscription to be cut in one of the trees near the watering place setting forth the Ships name, date &c[a]. Having seen everything this place afforded we at daylight in the morning weighed with a light breeze at NW and put to sea the wind soon after coming to the southward. We steered alongshore NNE and at noon we were by observation in the Latitude of 33 50′ S about 2 or 3 miles from the land and abreast of a bay or harbour wherein there appeared to be safe anchorage which I called *Port Jackson*. It lies 3 leagues to the northward of Botany Bay. I had almost forgot to mention that it is high water in this bay at the full and change of the moon about 8 oClock and rises and falls upon a perpendicular about 4 or 5 feet.

ROBERTS:

. . . served it [sting ray] to the ships company instead of salt provisions. It was very strong and made a great many of the Ships Company sick which eat of it.

PARKINSON:

Having got on board a good stock of hay for our sheep, on the 6th of May we weighed anchor and left the bay.

BANKS:

Went to sea this morn with a fair breeze of wind. The land we sailed past during the whole forenoon appeared broken and likely for harbours; in the afternoon again woody and pleasant. We dined today upon the sting-ray and his tripe: the fish itself was not quite as good as skate nor was it much inferior, the tripe everybody thought excellent. We had it with a dish of the leaves of *tetragonia cornuta* boiled, which eat as well as spinach or very near it.

Although the Captain has said, under this date, that he gave the name of Botany Bay *to this place, it was in fact a later substitution. Compare these two entries, the first from Cook's Log and the second from his Journal, which was later written up from the Log: 'The yawl returned from fishing having caught two sting rays, whose weight was near 600 lbs. The great quantity of these sort of fish found in this place occasioned my giving it the name of Stingrays Harbour.'* And the Journal entry: *'In the evening the yawl returned from fishing having caught two sting rays weighing near 600 pounds. The great quantity of New Plants &c[a] Mr Banks and Dr Solander collected in this place occasioned my giving it the name of* Botany Bay. *' This shows how neatly the substitution of this afterthought was made. Just when the change was made is not clear, but it was at least some time later, and, at first, it was not* Botany *but* Botanist *which, even in this entry, had been deleted for* Botany. *The logs and journals of this time are headed: Hickes, 'Sting-Rea Bay'; Forwood, 'Sting Ray Bay'; Pickersgill, 'Stingerray Bay'; Clerke, 'Sting Rea Bay; Wilkinson and Bootie, 'Stingray Bay'.*

Thus the Captain wanted the remembered thing to be the plants which had so delighted the naturalists. It is possible that, had he been aware of what the grey-headed old black man and woman were passing on to those children, he would have wished to commemorate it. He had written that this peninsula 'looks like a long island lying close under the shore': ten thousand years before, Kurnell had been just that, until the drifing sands of wind and sea joined it to Cronulla on the main. For eight thousand years these people, the Gwyeagal, had lived here. But after the arrival of the First Fleet they had, perforce, drifted north to Port Jackson in the early part of the nineteenth century to their final dissolution.

Even the peninsula itself was doomed. In 1815, a grant of seven hundred acres was made; by 1851, one man owned twelve thousand acres. Adding to the depredations of sheep and cattle grazing, timber-cutting rights were sold in the late 1860s. During the 1880s, the peninsula was declared the future industrial site for noxious trades—never to be un-declared. Its birthright was thus foresworn. By 1931, the land between Kurnell and Cronulla was reported to be 'a desolate waste of flat ground covered with scattered shells and the exposed roots of [once] large trees.'

Perhaps none would have been more sad over this unthinking vandalism, and the resultant passing of this shy simple people, and none have mourned with more inexpressible feeling, than James Cook. Though the term Botany Bay *does not memorialise these humble departed, it does stand as a wry and ironic monument to the present.*

Gone are the self-perpetuating and life-supporting woods of banksia and eucalypt ('the largest are as large as or larger than our oaks in England'). The dominant 'plant' now is a petro-chemical one: an artificial heart machine without which the pulse of the non-regenerative body of the new order sinks dangerously low, in an organism which takes but never replaces. What the botanists found delightful has been trampled; what the old Aborigine had to tell the children, all-knowingly disdained.

CHAPTER 5

PORT JACKSON TO SANDY CAPE

SHIP'S LOG:

MONDAY, MAY 7TH, 1770

H.	K.	F.	Courses.	Winds.	Remarks, &c.
1	2	..	N.E.b. ½ E.	S.S.W.	Little wind and fine pleas't wea'r.
2	2	..	..	..	
3	1	6	..	..	
4	1	5	..	..	Variation p'r sev'l azymuths, 8° 00′ E't.
5	1	6	..	..	½-past, the no'm't ext. of the land N.b.E. ½ E. Some broken land, like a bay, N. 48° W. Shore dist. 2½ leagues.
6	1	6	..	..	
7	1	5	..	..	
8	1	5	..	..	Do. weather; haul'd down the steering sails.
9	1	3	..	..	
10	1	3	..	..	Sounded 32 fa'm.
11	1	4	..	..	
12	1	4	..	.	33
1	1	4	..	W.S.W.	
2	1	6	N.b.E.	..	34
3	2	..	..	S.W.b.S.	
4	2	..	..	..	36
5	2	..	..	..	Variation by several setts of azymuths and four differant compasses, 7° 56′E.
6	2	..	..	..	Set steering sails.
7	1	6	..	..	
8	1	5	..	..	Lights airs and fair weather.
9	..	..	..	..	
10	..	..	..	..	Calm and clear weather.
11	..	..	..	..	Ship's head all round ye compass.
12	..	..	..	..	At noon, the northerm't ext. of the land N.b.E.; shore dist. 3 leagues. Lat'de obs'd, 33° 22′ S.

COOK:

Little wind and serene pleasant weather. In the PM found the Variation by several azimuths to be 8° East. At sunset the northermost land in sight bore N 26° E and some broken land that appeared to form a bay bore N 40° W distant 4 leagues. This bay I named *Broken Bay*, Latitude 33° 36′ South. We steered along shore NNE all night at the distance of about 3 leagues from the land having from 32 to 36 fathom, a hard sandy bottom. A little after sunrise I took several azimuths with four needles belonging to the Azimuth compass the mean result of which gave the variation 7° 56′ East. At noon we were by observation in the Latitude of 33° 22′ S and about 3 leagues from the land, the northermost part of which in sight bore N 19° East. Some pretty high land which projected out in three bluff points and occasioned my calling it Cape Three Points (Lat^{de} 33° 33′) bore SW distant 5 leagues. Longitude made from Botany Bay 0° 19′ East.

BANKS:
During last night a very large dew fell which wetted all our sails as completely as if they had been dipped overboard; for several days past our dews have been uncommonly large. Most part of the day was calm.

This twenty-four hours was light weather, during which the ship carried studding sails some hours after dark and set them again before sunrise. But she made only 1 ½ to 2 knots and, by 10 AM, was becalmed, with her head swinging through all points of the compass and, at noon, was south. The bay which the Captain named Broken Bay *was not the one so called today, which lies at the mouth of the Hawkesbury River, for this was passed, unremarked, during the hours of darkness. Cook's Broken Bay was only a few miles north of Port Jackson and near what is now known as the Narrabeen Lagoon. Matthew Flinders was the first to note the difference. Cape Three Points was about the northern head of the present Broken Bay. The ship made only 30 miles to the northward on this day.*

SHIP'S LOG:

TUESDAY, MAY 8TH, 1770

H.	K.	F.	Courses.	Winds.	Remarks, &c.
1	..	..	..	Calm.	Head S. Fine clear weather. Saw breakers inshore.
2	{ ..	..	..	..	Light airs.
	{ ..	2	S.E.b.E.	N.E.b.E.	
3	1	..	E.S.E.	N.E.	
4	1	..	E.b.S.	N.E.b.N.	Variation p'r azym'ths, 8° 25′ E.
5	{ ..	5	..	..	Tack'd. Sounded 28 fa'm. Sandy ground.
	{ ..	5	N.W.b.N.	..	
6	1	5	..	..	Do. In 1st reef topsails. Ext's off the land from S.W.b.S. to N.
7	1	6	E.	N.N.E.	
8	2	..	..	..	
9	2	..	E.b.S.	N.E.b.N.	Sounded 56 fa'm. Soft ground. Lost the deep-sea lead and 70 fa'm of line and two hand-leads endeavouring to clear it of the rudder.
10	2	4	..	..	
11	3	4	E.	N.N.E.	
12	3	6	..	..	Tack'd.

H.	K.	F.	Courses.	Winds.	Remarks, &c.
1	3	2	N.W.b.W.	N.b.E.	
2	2	6	W.b.N.	N.b.W.	
3	2	4	N.W.½ W.	N.N.E.	
4	2	4	..	..	
5	2	4	N.W.	..	
6	{1	..	..	..	Taken aback.
	..	..	..	Calm.	Her head all round Co.
7	1	4	N.	Variable.	Little wind and fine clear wea'r.
8	1	4	..	S.W.	
9	1	4	N.½ E.	..	
10	1	4	N.b.E.	..	
11	1	2	N.N.E.	Variable.	Light airs and fine wea'r.
12	1	..	..	..	At noon, ext's of the land from S. 27° W. to N. 10° ½ E.; shore dist. 5 miles; 29 fa'm water; soft g'd. Lat'de obs'd. 33° 24′ S.

FORWOOD:

Condemned the remainder of the Best Bower Cable for Junk.

BOOTIE:

AM: Mending sails and the longboat. Working in the holds.

WILKINSON:

Employed as occations [*sic*] required.

COOK:

Variable light winds and clear weather. In the PM saw some smooks upon the shore and in the evening found the Variation to be 8° 25′ East. At this time we were about 2 or 3 miles from the land and had 28 fathom water. Our situation at noon was nearly the same as yesterday having advanced not one step to the northward.

BANKS:

Very light breezes and weather sultry all day. We had lost ground yesterday so that the land was what we had seen before; upon it however we observed several fires upon it [*sic*]. At night a foul wind rose up much the same time and in much the same manner as yesterday.

During the afternoon, with calm and light winds, the ship made no more than 1 ½ knots, and that for no more than two hours. Studding sails were taken in when she tacked at 5 PM. At 6 PM, topsails were reefed for the night, and at 8 AM they were shaken out again. From noon to midnight the course made good had been EbS, 25 miles offshore. At midnight she tacked inshore again and at noon was about the same distance offshore as yesterday but two miles southward. At 6 AM, with the wind fluky, she was caught aback; that is, the wind caught her on the foreside of the sails, pressing them back against the masts. In rougher conditions this can be very serious in making the ship unmanageable and out of control. However, almost at once it fell calm and did not settle to the SW until 8 AM.

SHIP'S LOG:

WEDNESDAY, MAY 9TH, 1770

H.	K.	F.	Courses.	Winds.	Remarks, &c.
1 2	} . .	. .	Calm, h'd betw'n S. & E.		Fair weather.
3	. .	4	Et.	N.N.E.	Light airs.
4	. .	4	. .	. .	
5	2	. .	E.b.N.	N.b.E.	In 1st reef topsails, ext's of the land from N.b.E. to S.S.W.
6	2	4	Et.	N.N.E.	
7	3	4	E.b.S.	N.E.b.N.	
8	3	6	Et.	N.N.E.	Fresh breezes and fair wea'r; sounded in 70 fa'm.
9	3	5	. .	. .	
10	3	5	E.b.S.	N.E.b.N.	
11	3	4	Et.	N.N.E.	
12	3	3	. .	. .	Do. wea'r; sounded no ground at 150 fa'm line. Tack'd.
1	3	6	N.W.b.W.	N.b.E.	
2	2	6	W.N.W.	N.	
3	3	5	N.W.	N.N.E.	
4	3	6	. .	. .	Sounded 80 fa'm water.
5	3	3	W.N.W.	Variable	
6	2	5	W.	N.N.W.	
7	2	2	W.b.S.	N.W.b.N.	
8	1	. .	S.W.b.W.	Variable	Little wind and fair weather.
9	1	. .	E.b.N.	N.b.E.	
10	1	4	. .	. .	Carpenters repairing the longboat; sailmakers, the sails; people drawing yarns to make rope.
11	2	2	E.N.E.	N.	
12	2	. .	E.b.N.	N.b.E.	Ext's of the land from N.W.b.N. to S.W. ½ W., shore dist. 5 leagues. Lat'de obs'd, 33° 37′ S.

COOK:

Winds northerly most part a fresh breeze with which we stood off shore until 12 at midnight. At the distance of 5 leagues from the land had 70 fathom, at the distance of 6 leagues 80 fathoms which is the extent of the soundings for, at the distance of 10 leagues, we had no ground at 150 fathom. Stood inshore untill 8 oClock AM, and hardly fetched Cape Three Points. Having little wind at NWbN we tacked and stood off until noon at which time we tacked with the wind at NNE being then in the Latitude of 33° 37′ S. Cape Three Points bearing NWbW distant 4 leagues.

BANKS:

Wind continued foul and we turned to windward all day to no manner of purpose.

PARKINSON:

Having only moderate breezes from N & NE we made but little headway until the 9th.

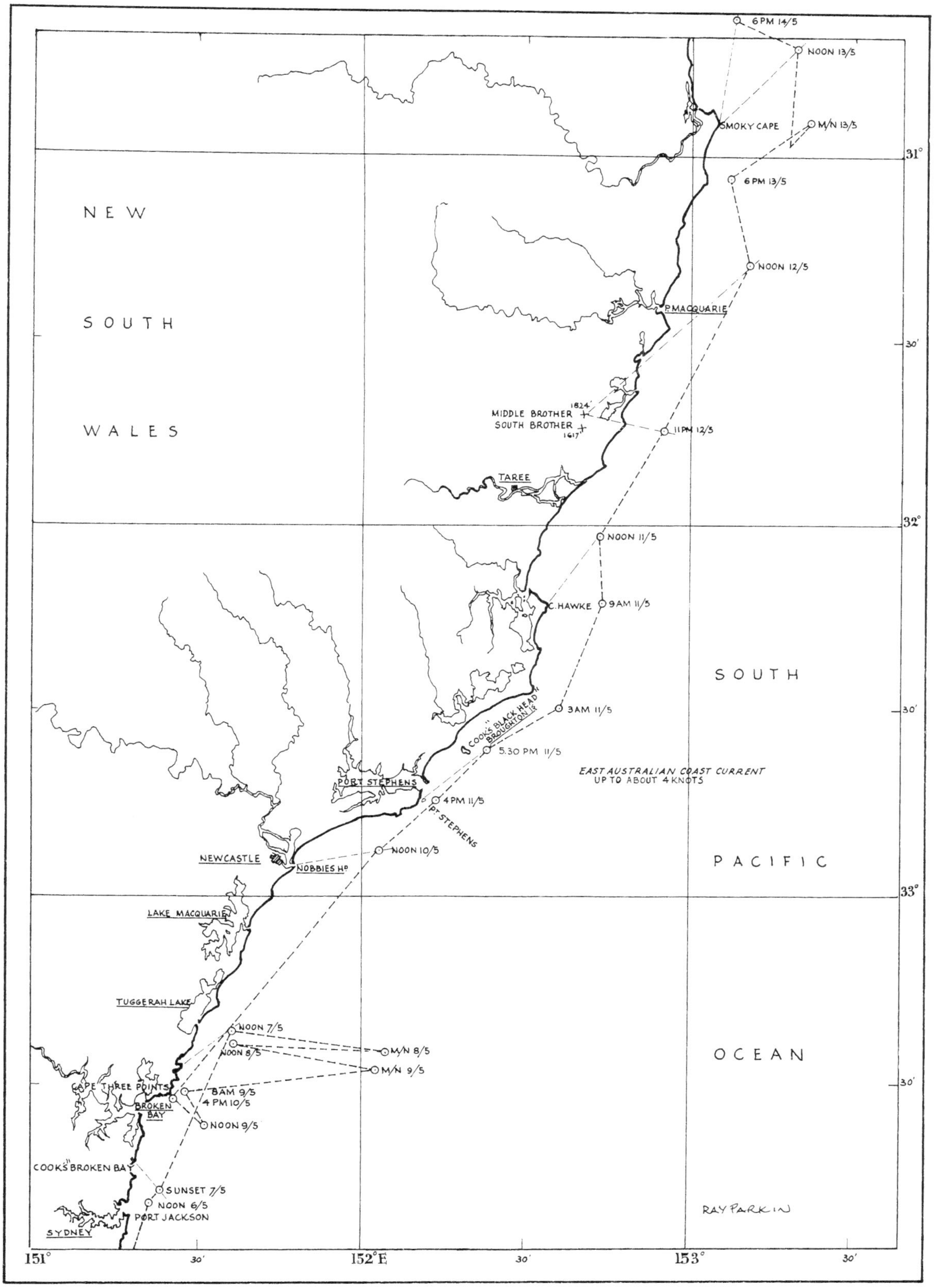
6 PM 14/5
NOON 13/5
SMOKY CAPE
M/N 13/5
31°
6 PM 13/5
NEW
SOUTH
WALES
NOON 12/5
P. MACQUARIE
30'
1824'
MIDDLE BROTHER
SOUTH BROTHER
1617'
11 PM 12/5
TAREE
32°
NOON 11/5
C. HAWKE
9 AM 11/5
SOUTH
3 AM 11/5
30'
COOK'S "BLACK HEAD"
BROUGHTON IS.
5.30 PM 11/5
EAST AUSTRALIAN COAST CURRENT
UP TO ABOUT 4 KNOTS
PORT STEPHENS
4 PM 11/5
PT. STEPHENS
NEWCASTLE
NOBBIES HD.
NOON 10/5
PACIFIC
33°
LAKE MACQUARIE
TUGGERAH LAKE
NOON 7/5
NOON 8/5
M/N 8/5
M/N 9/5
OCEAN
CAPE THREE POINTS
8 AM 9/5
4 PM 10/5
BROKEN BAY
NOON 9/5
30'
COOK'S "BROKEN BAY"
SUNSET 7/5
NOON 6/5
PORT JACKSON
SYDNEY
RAY PARKIN
151°
30'
152°E
30'
153°
30'

'153':

Carpenters repairing the longboat being very bad.

The pattern of sailing was similar to that of the previous day, but she lost more ground to the southward and, by this noon, was some 14 miles to the south, and a little west of the previous day at noon. Added to the normal leeway was the influence of the south-going East Australian Coast Current which is less constant at this time of the year but runs up to 2 knots and is strongest at about the 100-fathom line where the ship had been. The ship was now off the present Broken Bay and a little south of Barrenjoey Head some 12 miles off. A 'foul' wind does not indicate tempestuous weather, but simply means a wind of any strength that is opposed to the course the ship is endeavouring to take. A 'fair' wind favours it.

The league had been used as a measure of distance for several centuries, but it was for practical reasons, rather than mere archaic tradition, that it was retained. Just as the sea-mile was equal to one minute of latitude, the league represented three sea-miles as a measure of the average hourly run of a ship in average conditions, so that there was at once a time and distance component in it.

SHIP'S LOG:

THURSDAY, MAY 10TH, 1770

H.	K.	F.	Courses.	Winds.	Remarks, &c.
1	3	5	N.W.	N.N.E.	Mod. breezes and cloudy wea'r.
2	3	6	..	..	
3	3	4	N.W. ½ N.	N.E.b.N.	Tack'd. Dist. off shore ¼ of a mile. A bluff head N.N.E, and a small bay S.W.b.S. Sounded 23 fa'm.
4	2	..	..	..	
	1	..	E.	N.N.E.	
5	1	..	E.N.E.	Variable.	
6	1	..	..	..	The no'most ext. of the land N.b.E. ½ E.
7	2	..	N.E.b.E.	N.b.W.	
8	2	6	..	..	Modt. breezes and fair weather.
9	2	5	..	..	
10	2	6	N.E.	N.N.W.	
11	2	5	..	..	
12	2	6	N.E.b.N.	N.W.b.N.	
1	3	2	N.N.E.	N.W.	
2	4	..	N.b.W. ½ W.	Variable.	
3	3	6	N.N.W.	West.	
4	3	6	N.b.W.	W.b.N.	
5	4	..	..	..	
6	4	..	N.N.W.	West.	Saw the land, making like islands to the N.N.E. Out 1st reef tops'ls and set steering sails.
7	4	..	..	..	
8	5	..	N.b.E. ½ .E.	..	Mod. breezes and fine clear weather.
9	3	..	N.N.E.	..	
10	3	4	..	..	Carpenters, sailmakers, and seamen employ'd as before.
11	3	6	..	..	
12	3	2	N.E.	S.W.	Ext. of the land from N. 32° E. to S.W.b.S. Lat. obs'd, 32° 53' S.

COOK:

'CAME-TOO WITH THE SMALL BOWER . . . HOISTED OUT THE BOATS.'

In the PM had the wind at NEbN with which we stood inshore untill near four oClock when we tacked in 23 fathom water being about a mile from the land and as much to the southward of Cape Three points. In the night the wind veered to NW and West and in the morning to SW. Having the advantage of a light moon we made the best of our way northward. At noon we were by observation in the Latitude of 32° 53′ S, Long^{de} 208° 00′ West and about 2 leagues from the land, which extended from N 14° E to S 41° W. A small round rock or Island laying close under the land bore S 82° West distant 2 or 4 leagues. At sunrise in the morning found the Variation to be 8° East. In the Latitude of 33° 2′ S a little way inland is a remarkable hill that is shaped like the Crown of a hatt which we passed about 9 oClock in the forenoon.

BANKS:

Last night a heavy squall came off from the land which according to the seamans phrase 'Made all sneer again'; it payed for the trouble it gave us however by bringing a fair wind. In the morn the land appeared broken and likely for harbours; its face was very various, some parts being well wooded and others covered with bare sand.

PARKINSON:

In the evening of that day [ship's 10th] we saw two of the most beautiful rainbows my eyes ever beheld; the colours were strong, clear and lively; those of the inner one were so bright as to reflect its shadow on the water. They formed a complete semicircle; and the space between them was darker than the rest of the sky.

In the latitude of 32° 51′, on the 10th, the land appeared considerably higher, and more broken, very sandy and less fertile. We saw several clusters of islands; among which it is probable, there may be found some good harbours.

During this day the wind came fair and the course made good was N 21° E, 47 miles. They had advanced along the coast some 37 miles to the northward of the noon position on the 7th. The point on which the southerly noon bearing had been taken was what is now Nobbys Head at the entrance to Newcastle Harbour. To 'make all sneer again' was the expression used when a squall of wind was putting a critical strain upon the spars and rigging. In quoting this, one feels, Mr Banks was, to use another sailors' phrase, 'being a bit salty'.

SHIP'S LOG:

FRIDAY, MAY 11TH, 1770

H.	K.	F.	Courses.	Winds.	Soundings.	Remarks, &c.
					Fathoms.	
1	3	6	N.E.	S.W.b.S.	..	Fresh breezes and pleas't weather.
2	3	3	..	..	..	
3	4	..	N.E. ½ E.	..	..	Runing along shore, the land making broken and like several islands. Saw several smoaks on the shore. At 4, the no' extreeme of the land N. 29° E.
4	4	2	..	..	..	An opening, forming a bay, S.
5	4	4	..	..	..	86 W. ½ - p't 5, the ext. of the land from N. 27 E. to S.W. ½ W. A small high island abreast, N. 30 W., distance 2 or 3 miles. Sounded 27 fa'm.
6	4	4	..	..	..	
7	2	5	..	..	48	
8	2	..	..	Variable.	48	Haul'd down steering sail and in 1st reef topsails.
9	1	4	..	N.W.	..	Variati'n p'r amp'd, 8° 00′ E.
10	2	..	..	..	..	
11	2	..	N.N.E.	W.N.W.	..	
12	2	..	..	..	62	
1	2	..	..	..	60	
2	2	..	..	..	58	
3	2	5	N.b.E.	W.S.W.	58	
4	3	..	N. ½ E.	..	57	Modt. breezes and fair wea'r.
5	4	..	N.	..	..	
6	4	2	N. ½ W.	..	..	Variat'n p'r amplit'd and azymuths, 9° 10′ E. At 6, the ext's of the land from N. to S.W.b.W.; dist. off shore, 3 or 4 leagues.
7	4	2	..	..	..	
8	4	..	..	..	..	Made all sail.
9	4	3	N.	S.W.	..	
10	4	3	..	..	..	People employ'd as yesterday.
11	4	..	..	S.	..	
12	3	6	..	..	..	Ext's of land from N. 1° W. to S. 15½° W. A low p't, making like a small isl'd, N. 4E. Shore dist., 3 or 4 leagues. Lat'de obs'd, 32° 02′ S.

COOK:
Winds southerly all the day and in the night Westerly a gentle breeze and clear weather. At 4 PM past at the distance of 1 mile a low rocky point which I named *Point Stephens* (Lat^{de} 32° 45′) on the north side of this point is an inlet which I called *Port Stephens* (Lat^{de} 32° 40′, Long^{de} 207° 51′) that appeared to me from the mast-head to be sheltered from all winds. At the entrance lay three small islands two of which are a tolerable height and on the Main near the shore are some high round hills that make at a distance like Islands in passing this bay at a distance of about 2 or 3 miles from the shore our soundings were from 33 to 27 fathoms from which I conjectored that there must be sufficient water for shipping in the Bay. We saw several smooks a little way in the country rise up from the flat land, by this I did suppose that there were Lagoons which afforded subsistence for the natives such as shell fish &c^{a} for as yet we know nothing else they live on. At ½ past 5 the Northermost land in sight bore N 36° E and Point Stephens South-west distant 4 leagues. At this time we took in our studding sails and run under an easy sail all night until 4 oClock AM when we made all sail. Our soundings in the night was from 48 to 62 fathom at the distance of between 3 and 4 leagues from the land. At 8 oClock we were abreast of a high point of land which made in two hillocks, this point I called *Cape Hawke*: Lat^{de} 32° 14′ S, Long^{de} 207° 30′ West; it bore from us at this time west distant 8 miles and at the same time the northernmost land in sight bore N 6° E and appeared high like an island. At noon this land bore N 8° E and the northermost land in sight N 13° East and Cape Hawke S 37° West, Lat^{de} in p^{r} Observation 32° 2′ S, which was 12 miles to the southward of that given by the Logg, which I do suppose to be owing to a current setting that way. Course and distance sailed sence yesterday at Noon was first NEbE 27 miles, then N 10° E 37 miles. Long^{de} in 207° 20′ West. Variation per Morning Amplitude and Azimuths 9° 10′ East.

BANKS:
Fair wind continued. Land today trended more to the northward than it had done lately, looked broken and likely for inlets.

PARKINSON:
On the 11th, we passed high broken land, having several distinct peaks and hills, an extensive flat along the shore covered with pretty large trees, and a sandy beach. We saw also many [sea] snakes.

ROBERTS:
At 2 PM passed by several small islands and a fine harbour which lies around a bluff point and within the islands this harbour seemed very commodious and the country round it seemed very fertile.

The Captain's choice of names for Point and Port Stephens had at first been Point Kepple *and* Kepple Bay*; and for Cape Hawke,* Cape Morton. *However, he seems to* *have found a better use for these later on. The islands that lay at the entrance to Port Stephens are Cabbage Tree, Boondelabah and Little Islands. The 'small high island abreast' at 5.30 PM, mentioned in the Ship's Log, the Captain marked on his chart as* Black Head *and is now known as Broughton Island. The ship made a good 60 miles along the coast northwards on this day.*

SHIP'S LOG:

SATURDAY, MAY 12TH, 1770

H.	K.	F.	Courses.	Winds.	Soundings.	Remarks, &c.
					Fathoms.	
1	2	6	N.b.E. ½ E.	S.S.E.	..	Little wind and fair weather.
2	2	5	..	..	..	Several fires along shore.
3	3	..	..	..	..	
4	2	6	..	..	..	
5	3	2	N.N.E.	..	..	
6	3	..	..	..	..	Sounded 26 fa'm. Ye northerm't ext. of the land N. ½ E., 5 or 6 leagues. ½-past 6, had 23 fa'm water.
7	3	3	N.E.b.N.	..	..	Shorten'd sail and in 1st reef topsails. 30 fa'm; soft ground.
8	3	..	..	..	..	
9	{2	2	..	..	..	
	{1	4	N.N.E.	..	..	
10	3	..	..	..	..	
11	3	..	..	..	52	Northerm't of three remarkable hills, call'd the 3 Brothers, W.b.N.
12	3	..	..	..	..	Fresh breezes and cloudy.
1	3	..	..	..	58	Taken aback.
2	..	..	H'd round ye compass		..	Light airs and variable.
3	2	6	N.N.E.	Variable.	..	Little wind.
4	2	6	..	S.S.W.	67	Mod't breezes.
5	2	6	..	..	..	Out 1st reef tops'ls and made sail.
6	3	..	..	..	..	
7	3	4	N.	..	..	Open'd a cask of beef, No. 535, cont. 189 p.; short 1 piece, and of weight 82 pound.
8	3	4	..	S.b.W.	..	Also open'd a cask of pork, cont'ts 306 p.; short 2 p's, and of w't 5 ls.
9	{1	6	..	..	..	
	{1	4	N.b.W.	..	..	
10	2	4	..	..	..	Carpenters repairing the longboat, sailmakers on the sails, and people in the holds.
11	1	4	..	..	..	
12	1	3	..	..	..	At noon, little wind and fair wea'r. Ext's of the land from N. 20° W. to S.W.b.S. Lat'de obs., 31° 18′ S.

COOK:

Winds southerly and a gentle breeze. In the PM as we run along shore we saw several smooks a little way in land from the sea and upon the top of a hill which was the first we have seen upon elevated ground sence we have been on the coast. At sun set we were in 23 fathom water and about a League and a half from the land, the northermost part of which that we had in sight bore N 13° East and three remarkable large high hills lying contiguous to each other and not far from the shore bore NNW. As these hills bore some resemblance to each other we called them the *Three Brothers*, they lay in the latitude of 31° 40′ S and are of a sufficient height to be seen 14 or 16 Leagues. We steered NEbN all night having from 27 to 67 fathom water from

2 to 5 Leagues from the land. At day light we steered north for the northermost land we had in sight. At noon we were 4 leagues from the land and by observation in the Latitude of 31° 18′ S, which was 15 miles to the south[rd] of that given by the Log. Our course and distance made good sence yesterday noon was N 24° E 48 miles. Long[de] in 206° 58′ West. Several smooks seen a little way in land.

BANKS:
At sunset three remarkable hills were abreast the ship standing near the shore, of nearly equal size and shape; behind them the countrey rose in gradual slopes carrying a great shew of fertility. AM: Land much as yesterday, fertile but varying its appearance a good deal, generally however well clothed with good trees. This evening we finished drawing the plants got in the last harbour [Botany Bay], which had been kept fresh till this time by means of tin chests and wet cloths. In 14 days just, one draughtsman [Parkinson] has made 94 sketch drawings, so quick a hand has he acquired by use.

ROBERTS:
Opened a cask of Beef and Pork being bad the Ships Company was ordered to full allowance while it lasted.

Mr Banks pays a just tribute to Sydney Parkinson, his botanical draughtsman, for his industry and ability. It is to Parkinson almost alone that we are indebted for the visual records of the voyage, which he made with an objective vision somewhat rare at this time and on such occasions. Unfortunately he was dead before the ship got home and the vision was lost by the engravers, who presented to the public soul-destroying translations of it.

The shortage of 32 lb in the cask of beef was not all in the one piece that tallied short. Beef was cut into 4-lb pieces, so that the shortage would have been in the undercutting of other pieces as well. Pork was cut into 2-lb pieces and the shortage of 5 lbs was spread over 308 pieces, two of which were short.

On the modern chart only two of the Three Brothers are named: Middle Brother, 1,834 feet; and South Brother, 1,617 feet. Six miles north-east of Middle Brother is a third peak, presumably North Brother, 1,605 feet.

SHIP'S LOG:

SUNDAY, MAY 13TH, 1770

H.	K.	F.	Courses.	Winds.	Remarks, &c.
1	1	..	No.	So.	Light winds and clear weather.
2	1	..	..	..	
3	2	..	N.N.W.	N.E.	
4	2	2	..	..	
5	3	1	..	..	The no. ext. of the land N. ½ E. Tack'd. Sound'd 24 fa'm.
6	3	2	N.W.b.N.	N.E.b.N.	In 1-reef topsails.

H.	K.	F.	Courses.	Winds.	Remarks, &c.
7	3	..	E.b.N.	N.b.E.	
8	3	..	..	..	
9	4	..	E.N.E.	No.	
10	4	5	..	..	
11	4	6	N.E.b.N.	N.b.W.	
12	3	5	N.E.	N.N.W.	Tack'd. Sounded 118 fa'm.
1	5	3	W't	..	
2	3	..	S.W.b.W. ½ W.	Variable.	
3	{1	4	S.W.	..	
	1	..	N.b.W.	W.b.N.	
4	2	..	..	..	
5	2	4	N. ½ W.	..	
6	3	..	..	..	Fresh breezes and fair. Lightning to the S.E.
7	3	4	N.N.W.	West.	
8	3	..	..	..	Saw some porposes.
9	3	4	N.W.b.N.	W.b.S.	Variat'n p'r azym'th, 9° 26′ E.
10	3	..	..	..	
11	3	4	..	W.S.W.	At noon, ext's of the land from S. 24 W't to N. 22½ W't; a bluff head set for the No. ext. yesterday
12	4	2	N.N.W	..	at noon S. 36 W.; shore 3 or 4 lea's. Saw a smoak ashore. Lat'de observ'd, 30° 43′ So.

COOK:

In the PM stood in shore with the wind at NE untill 6 oClock at which time we tacked being about 3 or 4 Miles from the land and in 24 fathom water. Stood off shore with a fresh breeze at North and NNW untill Midnight then tacked being in 118 fathom water and 8 Leagues from the land. At 3 AM the wind veered to the westward and we tacked and stood to the northward. At noon we were by observation in the Latitude of 30° 43′ S and Long^{de} 206° 45′ West and about 3 or 4 leagues from the land, the northermost part of which bore from us N 13° West and a point or head-land on which were fires that caused a great quantity of smook which occasioned my giving it the name of *Smooky Cape,* bore SW distant 4 Leagues. It is moderately high land, over the pitch of the point is a round hillock within it two others much higher and larger and within them very low land. Latitude 30° 51′ S, Longitude 206° 54′ West. Besides the smook seen upon this Cape we saw more in several other places along the Coast. The observed latitude was only 5 miles to the southrd of the Log.

BANKS:

Wind off shore today, it let us however come in with the land. Many porpoises about the ship. At noon several fires about the shore one very large which I judged to be at least a league inland.

During the forenoon this day the ship was making 3 to 4 knots, and, at noon, was just east of present-day Nambucca Heads. Smooky (now 'Smoky') Cape has kept its name to this day.

SHIP'S LOG:

MONDAY, MAY 14TH, 1770

H.	K.	F.	Courses.	Winds.	Soundings.	Remarks, &c.
					Fathoms.	
1	1	..	N.b.W.	Variable.	..	Light airs and pleas't weather. Saw some smoaks ashore.
2	..	..	H'd all round ye Co.			..
3	..	4	E.b.N.	..	..	Serv'd slops to the ship's company.
	..	6	N.W.½ W.	Variable.	..	
4	2	2	N.W.½ N.	..	..	Variation by sev'l azym'th, 8° 13' E't.
5	2	6	N.N.W.	N.E.	..	½-p't, ext's of the land from S. 7 W. to N. 11 W.31 fa'm
6	3	..	N.W.	N.N.E.	..	water. Hard ground. Shore dist. 4 miles. ¼ pt., tack'd and sounded 30 fa'm.
7	2	4	N.E.b.N.	N.W.b.N.	..	Do. ground.
8	2	2	..	..	..	Mod. and fair wea'r. Sounded 30 fa'm, soft g'd.
9	2	2	S.W.b.W.	N.W.b.W.	..	
10	2	2	No.	W.N.W.	..	
11	1	6	..	W.b.N.	..	
12	1	4	..	..	26	Light airs and fair weather.
1	1	3	N.b.E.	..	26	
2	1	2	..	..	..	Do. weather, with thunder and lightning to the eastward.
3	1	2	..	W't	..	
4	1	2	..	..	21	
5	1	..	N.E.b.E.	Variable	..	
6	2	..	..	N.b.W.	..	The ext's of the land from S.b.W. to N.N.W.
7	3	..	..	..	..	
8	2	6	E.b.N.	Variable.	..	
9	2	4	N.N.E.	..	..	Squally, with thunder, lightning, and rain.
10	..	..	S's h'd all round.		..	At 11, fresh breezes and cloudy; out all reefs and set steering sails.
11	3	4	N.N.W.	S.b.W	..	At noon, So. ext. of the land (being the No. ext. the 12) bore S. 33 W.; distance off the nearest shore, 4
12	5	2	..	..	..	leagues. No. ext. N.N.W. Lat. obs., 30° 22' So.

COOK:

At 1 PM it fell calm and continued so about an hour when a breeze sprung up at NE with which we stood in shore untill 6 oClock when being in 30 fathom water and 3 or 4 miles from the land we tacked having the wind at NNW. At this time Smooky Cape bore S ¾ W distant about 5 Leagues and the northermost land in sight N ¼ E. At 8 oClock we made a trip in shore for an hour, after this the wind came Cross off shore with which we stood along shore to the northward having from 30 to 21 fathom water at the distance of 4 or 5 miles from the land. At 5 AM, the wind veered to the north and blowed a fresh breeze attended with squalls and dark clowdy weather. At 8 oClock it began thunder and rain which lasted about an hour and then fell calm which gave us an opportunity to sound and found 86 f^{m} water being about 4 or 5 leagues from the land. After this we got the wind southerly a fresh breeze and fair weather and we turned NbW for the northermost land in sight. At noon we were about 4 Leagues from the land and by observation in the Latitude of 30° 22' S, which was 9 miles to the southward of that given by the Log. Longitude in 206° 39' W, and the course and distance made good sence yesterday noon N 16° East 22 miles. Some

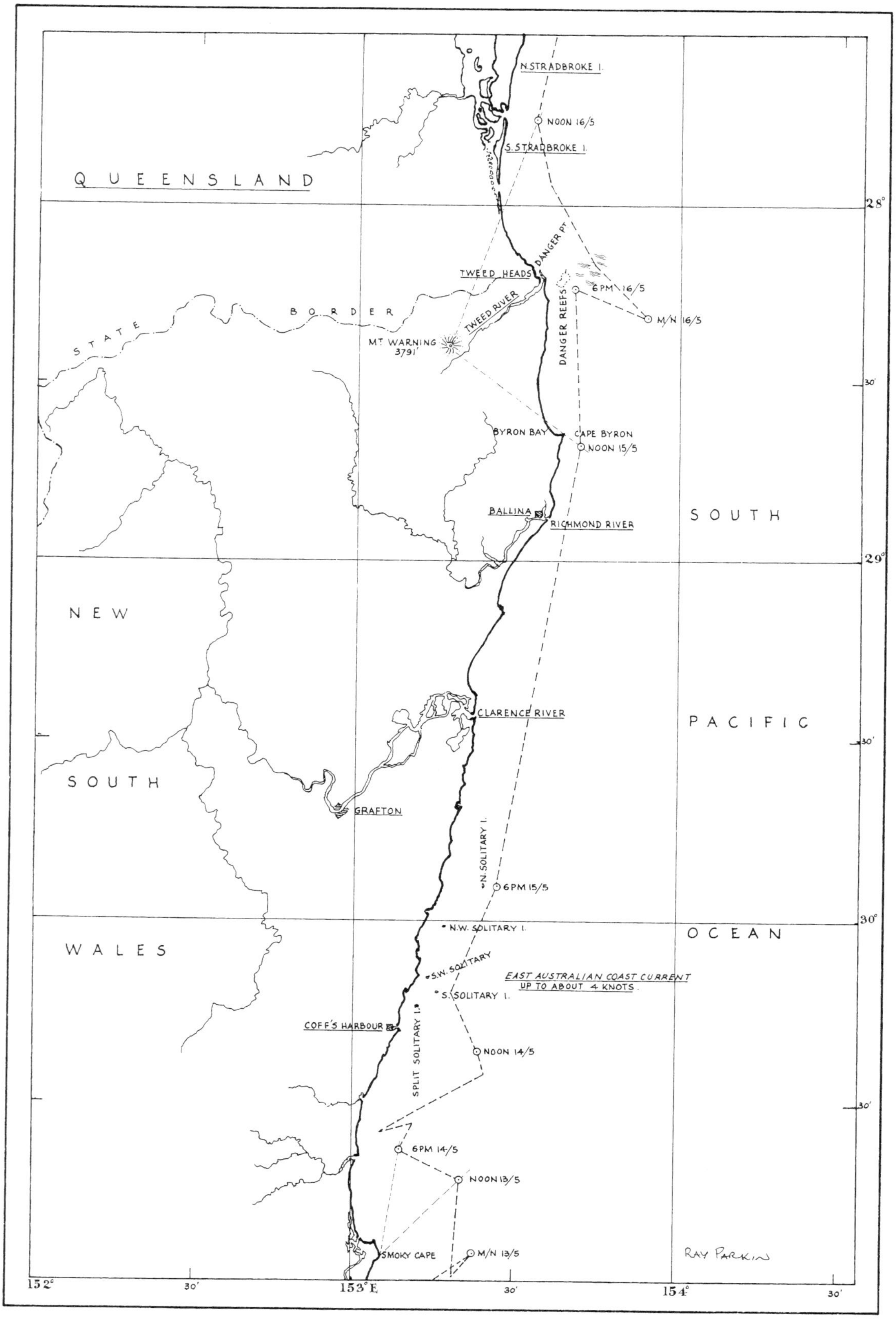
N.STRADBROKE I.
NOON 16/5
S.STRADBROKE I.
QUEENSLAND
28°
DANGER PT
TWEED HEADS
6PM 16/5
STATE BORDER
TWEED RIVER
M/N 16/5
MT WARNING 3791'
DANGER REEFS
30'
BYRON BAY
CAPE BYRON
NOON 15/5
BALLINA
RICHMOND RIVER
SOUTH
29°
NEW
CLARENCE RIVER
PACIFIC
30'
SOUTH
GRAFTON
N. SOLITARY I.
6PM 15/5
30°
N.W. SOLITARY I.
OCEAN
WALES
S.W. SOLITARY
EAST AUSTRALIAN COAST CURRENT
UP TO ABOUT 4 KNOTS
S. SOLITARY I.
COFF'S HARBOUR
SPLIT SOLITARY I.
NOON 14/5
30'
6PM 14/5
NOON 13/5
SMOKY CAPE
M/N 13/5
RAY PARKIN
152°
30'
153°E
30'
154°
30'

tolerable high land near the shore bore west. As I have not mentioned the aspect of the Country sence we left *Bottany Bay* I shall now describe it as it hath at different times appeared to us. As we have advanced to the north ward the land hath increased in height in so much that in this latitude it may be called hilly country but between this and Botany Bay it is diversified with an agreeable variety of hills ridges Vallies and large planes all clothed with wood which to all appearances is the same as I have before mentioned. As we could discover no visible alteration in the soil near the shore the land is in general low and sandy except the points which are rocky and over many of them are pretty high hills which at first rising out of the water appear like islands.

BANKS:

Innumerable shoals of fish about the ship in the afternoon and some birds of the Nectris kind [Shearwaters]. AM: For these three nights last much lightning has been seen to the Eastward. Early in the morning it was calm and some few fish were caught; after, the weather became squally.

PARKINSON:

On the 14th, in the latitude of 30° 22′, the land appeared high, and well covered with wood; but being 3 or 4 leagues from it we could not distinguish many particulars upon it, though we saw clouds of smoke arise from different parts of the country. The wind was very variable since our leaving the last bay, and we had some calms. The wind being mostly between N and E on this coast, blows very gently and then dies away to a stark calm; but this day we had a fresh breeze from the SW.

The journals of both Peter Briscoe and James Roberts, Banks's servants, end on this day. Noon on this day found the ship almost abreast of the present Coffs Harbour.

SHIP'S LOG:

TUESDAY, MAY 15TH, 1770

H.	K.	F.	Courses.	Winds.	Soundings.	Remarks, &c.
					Fathoms.	
1	5	..	N.N.W.	S.S.W.	..	Fresh breezes and fair wea'r.
2	5	2	..	..	..	Saw more land to the no'wards.
3	6	5	N.b.W.	..	..	Fresh gales and squally with flying showers of hail and rain. Haul'd down the steering sails; had some thunder.
4	3	..	..	..	..	
	3	4	N.b.E.	..	..	
5	7	..	N.b.E. ½ E.	..	..	In 1st reef fore-topsail. Several smoaks along shore.
6	5	2	N.b.W.	..	..	Handed the mizen topsail. ½-p't, close-reeft topsail. At 5, pass'd an island, distant from it about 3
7	5	2	..	..	..	miles. 33 fa'm water

H.	K.	F.	Courses.	Winds.	Soundings.	Remarks, &c.
8	4	. .	. .	W.S.W.	. .	Ext's of the land from N.N.W. to S.b.W. At 7, haul'd up the foresail; at 8, bro't too, main topsail to the mast.
9	} . .	. .	up N.W.	off N.N.W.	. .	
10	. .	. .	. .	. .	. .	Fill'd the main topsail, and sounded every half-hour.
11	3	. .	N.b.W.	. .	30, 32	
12	3	. .	. .	. .	32, 31	Fresh gales and fair wea'r. Soundings sandy ground.
1	3	3	. .	. .	32, 32	
2	3	. .	. .	. .	30, 26	
3	3	2	No.	. .	26, 25	
4	3	. .	. .	. .	25, 26	
5	3	3	. .	W.b.S.	. .	
6	4	6	. .	. .	26, 26	Out 1st and 2nd reef topsail, and made sail.
7	5	6	. .	. .	. .	
8	6	. .	. .	. .	25	Saw several natives ashore.
9	5	7	. .	. .	. .	
10	5	6	N.b.E.	. .	29	Out 3rd reef topsails. Sailmakers repairing the sails. Carpenters ab't the longboat. People drawing yarns to make rope.
11	5	5	No.	. .	. .	
12	5	6	N. ½ W.	S.S.W.	. .	At noon, ext's of the land from N. 28 W. to S. 2 W't, a bluff head abreast of the ship, N. 70 W't, about 1 league, 30 fa'm water. Fresh breezes and fine pleas't wea'r. Set steering sails. Saw sev'l smoaks. Latit'd obs'd, 28° 40' So.

COOK:

Fresh gales and SW, WSW and SSW. In the PM some heavy squalls attended with rain and hail which obliged us to close reef our topsails. Between 2 and 4 we had some small rocky islands between us and the land, the souther-most lies in Latitude 30° 10′ and the northermost in 29° 58′ and about 2 leagues or more from the land. We sounded and had 33 fathom water about 2 miles without this last island. At 8 oClock we brought too untill 10 at which time we made sail under topsails having the advantage of a moon. We steered along shore North and NbE keeping at the distance of about 3 Leagues from the land having from 30 to 25 fathom water. As soon as it was day-light we made all the sail we could having the advantage of a fresh gale and fine weather. At 9 oClock being about a League from the land we saw upon it people and smook in several places. At noon we were by observation in the latitude of 28° 39′ S and Longitude 206° 27′ Course and distance sailed sence yesterday noon North 6° 45′ East 104 miles. A tolerable high point of land bore NWbW distant 3 miles—this point I named *Cape Byron* (Latitude 28° 27′ 30″ S, Longde 206° 30′ West). It may be known by a remarkable sharp peaked Mountain lying inland NWbW from it. From this point the land trends N 13° W. Inland it is pretty high and hilly but near the shore it is low; to the southward of the point the land is low and tolerable level.

GREEN:

10 AM, made all sail. Three sets of observations by Clerke, Monkhouse, Saunders and self. The above observations have every advantage accepting the Moon being in her appogee. The country very pleasant to the eye; the beach sandy and

part low bluffs. The nearest shore west 3 or 4 miles. The Indians visible to the naked eye on shore.

BANKS:

PM: In the afternoon the land was rather more hilly than it has been. Several fires were seen and one high up upon a hill 6 or 7 miles at least from the beach.

AM: Wind continued fair, a brisk breeze. The land in the morning was high but before noon it became lower and was in general well wooded. Some people were seen, about 20, each of which carried upon his back a large bundle of something which we conjectured to be palm leaves for covering their houses; we observed them with glasses for near an hour during which time they walked upon the beach and then up a path up a gently sloping hill, behind which we lost sight of them. Not one was once observed to stop and look towards the ship; they pursued their way in all appearance intirely unmoved by the neighborhood of so remarkable an object as the ship must necessarily be to people who have never seen one. The Thermometer was at 60 which rather pinched us.

PARKINSON:

On the 15th we were in the Latitude of 28° 40′. The breeze continued brisk from the SW, the land appeared very uneven, and we saw a remarkable high peak with three points at the top: behind it were three other hills, with round tops, and the nearest land was well covered with wood. We saw six men, quite naked walking upon a strait, white sandy beach.

The names of the small rocky islands passed at sunset and later are not mentioned in any of the journals, but the Captain put them on his chart as the 'Solitary Islands'. This seems to show something of the personal feelings of the Captain for the mood of time and place: in the squally gathering gloom of that sunset these barren rocks stood alone and unmoved; perhaps identifying with them, he called them 'solitary'. Four of them are shown on the chart now: North and South Solitary, each with a warning light held about 190 feet above the sea; and the unlighted NW and SW Solitaries, closer inshore. In laying down Cape Byron (named after Commodore the Hon. John Byron, who took Dolphin *on her first circumnavigation of the world in 1764–66) Cook had marked the most easterly part of the continent. 'The remarkable sharp peaked Mountain lying NWbW from it', the Captain later called Mount Warning, whose peak is remarkably like that of the Matterhorn from this bearing.*

In the morning, when the reefs had been shaken out and all sail made, the ship was headed north with the wind at SSW. This was her best sailing point and she was making from 5½ to 6 knots which she held steadily until 5 PM of the next twenty-four hours. During the dark hours of the night she had passed, unknowingly, the Clarence River; and, during the forenoon, the mouth of the Richmond River upon which now stands the town of Ballina.

SHIP'S LOG:

WEDNESDAY, MAY 16TH, 1770

H.	K.	F.	Courses.	Winds.	Soundings.	Remarks, &c.
					Fathoms.	
1	5	6	N.b.W.	S.b.E.	..	Fresh breez's and fair.
2	5	7	..	..	..	Saw more land to the no'ward.
3	6	..	..	..	..	Unbent the mainsail and fore-topsail, and bent the old ones.
4	5	3	..	..	..	
5	5	4	N.N.W.	..	..	
	2	..	N.b.E.	..	..	Saw some breakers on the larboard bow; 20 f'm water; ½-p't 5, saw more breakers, bearing N.b.E.; 19 fa'm water;
6	1	2	E't.	..	..	haul'd off; the extremes of the land from N.W. to S., dist't
7	3	5	..	..	..	off shore 5 miles. In standing off had 25, 25, 25, 26, 27, 29,
8	3	4	..	..	..	30, 32, 34, 37, and 44 fa'ms, soft ground, at which time hove too under double-reef'd topsails, having fresh gales and cloudy wea'r, with a high swell from the southward.
9	..	..	up S.E.b.E.	off S.E.b.S.	..	
10	..	..	..	..	67 do. gd.	Wore ship; bro't too, her head inshore.
11	..	..	up W.S.W.	off W't	80 do. gd.	
12	..	..	..	..	76 do. gd.	
1	..	..	up W.b.S.	off W.b.N.	..	
2	..	..	..	..	52	
3	..	..	..	..	42	
4	..	..	..	..	42	
5	..	..	..	..	43	Do. made sail.
6	2	..	N.W.	S.b.W.	..	At 6, saw ye breakers on the larboard
	2	3	N.N.W.	..	..	bow; made more sail at 7; the breakers one with a remarkable high peak S.W., dist. from them 4 miles;
7	2	5	N.W.b.N.	..	..	clewed the fore-top-sail up to mend.
	2	5	N.W.	..	..	
8	5	5	.	..	..	Out 2nd reefs and set topgall't sails.
9	5	6	.	..	..	
10	5	4	N.W.b.N.	..	..	
11	5	..	N.N.W.	..	..	At noon, the ext's of land from S. 8 E. to N. 11 W., the peak S.12 W.; shore dist. 6 miles. Latit'de obs., 27° 46′ S.
12	4	5	No.	So.	..	

COOK:

Winds southerly a fresh gale with which we steered north along shore untill sun set at which time we discovered breakers ahead and on our larboard bow, being at this time in 20 fathom water and about 5 miles from the land. Hauled off East untill 8 oClock at which time we had run 8 miles and had increased our water to 44 fathoms. We then brought too with her head to the eastward and lay on this tack untill 5 oClock AM when we made sail. At daylight we were surprized at finding ourselves farther to the southward than we were in the evening and yet it had blowen strong southerly all night. We now saw the breakers again within us which we past at the distance of about 1 League, they lay in the Lat[de] of 28° 8′ & stretch off East two Leagues from a point under which is a small island, their situation may always be found by the peaked mountain before mentioned which bears SWbW from them and on this account I have named *Mount Warning*. It lies 7 or 8 Leagues inland in the latitude of 28° 22′ S, the land is high and hilly about it but it is conspicuous enough to be distinguished from everything else. The point off which these shoals lie I have named *Point Danger*. To the northward of it the land which is low trends NWbN but we soon found that it did not keep that direction long before it turned again to the northward. At noon we were about 2 Leagues from the land and by observation in the latitude of 27° 46′ S, which was 17 Miles to the southward of the Log. Longitude 206° 26′ W. Mount Warning bore S 20° West distant 14 Leagues, the northermost land in sight bore North. Our course and distance made good sence yesterday noon N 1° 45′ West 53 miles.

BANKS:
In the evening two small turtle were seen. At sun set a remarkable peaked hill was in sight 5 or 6 leagues off in the countrey, which about it was well wooded and looked beautiful as well as fertile. We were fortunate enough just at this time to descry breakers ahead lying in the very direction in which the ship sailed; on this we went upon a wind and after making sufficient offing brought too, but it blowed rather fresh and a great sea running made the night rather uncomfortable.

In the morn we were abreast of the hill and saw the breakers we last night escaped between us and the land. It still blew fresh; at noon we were abreast of some very low land which looked like an extensive plain in which we supposed there to be a lagoon, in the neighborhood of which were many fires.

PARKINSON:
On the 16th, we were in the Latitude of 27° 40′, and saw a vast tract of low land, with, here and there, a rising hill.

Point Danger is now the north point of Tweed Heads at the mouth of the Tweed River and on the present border between Queensland and New South Wales. Mount Warning is 15 miles in from the coast and 20 miles SW of Point Danger. It is from the SE that the peak bears a strong resemblance to the Matterhorn. However, the Point Danger to which the Captain refers is probably the one now called Fingal Head, on the south side of the river, because this is the point off which the breakers 'stretch off East two Leagues from a point under which is a small island', and from which 'the peaked mountain before mentioned bears SWbW from them'. During this forenoon the ship had sailed past the now-famous Gold Coast. By noon she was north of Southport and abreast of an opening called Jumpin Pin, between South and North Stradbroke Islands. Banks's observation of the 'low land which looked like an extensive plain in which we supposed there to be a Lagoon' was quite accurate. The ship was again under the influence of the East Australian Coast Current, being 17 miles to the southward of reckoning because of its southerly set. However, the influence is not consistent. To quote the chart caution, 'Northerly sets, however, are frequent throughout the year, particularly from June to August, with rates up to about 2 knots; and currents of similar strengths in other directions, including on-shore, are frequently experienced.'

It will be seen from this that the Captain had to deal not only with the observed or apparent, but also with the capricious, which he had to disentangle from fond speculation. How he was able to do this is apparent in the practical results of his work, remembering that, with no chart, he had only the surface of the sea, reluctant to reveal anything beneath. What he plotted on this previously blank space of the world map stands today alongside the sum total of modern chart-making, still evoking awe in those who know.

SHIP'S LOG:

THURSDAY, MAY 17TH, 1770

H.	K.	F.	Courses.	Winds.	Remarks, &c.
1	4	..	N.	S.	Fresh breezes and clear weather; unbent the foresail and mizen, and bent the old ones.
2	4	2	..	..	
3	4	3	..	..	
4	4	3	..	..	37 fam's
5	{2	2	.	..	
	{2	..	N.b.E.	S.b.E.	The no'most extreme of the land seen from the masthead N.b.W., the so'm't S. ½ W., a ledge of breakers N.W.b.W., a heavy swell from the S.S.W.;
6	3	4	..	..	at 6, had 45 fa'm wa'r; haul'd down steering sails, and in 1st reef main and mizen topsails.
7	2	2	..	..	52 fa'm.
8	2	..	..	..	52
9 } 10 }	..	..	up E.S.E.	off E.b.N.	48
11 } 12 }	..	..	up S.E.b.E.	off E.	54; mod. gales and fair wea'r; made sail and sounded every ½ hour; no ground at 50 fa'm
1	2	..	N.b.E.	S.b.W.	
2	2	..	..	..	
3	2	2	..	..	Bro't too and sounded, 86 fa'm.
4	3	..	..	..	Do. 104 do.
5	4	..	N.W.b.N.	..	Do. 135 do.
6	4	..	..	..	
7	{2	..	N.W.	..	
	{3	..	W.N.W	..	
8	5	6	..	..	
9	5	5	..	..	Carpenters employ'd, and seamen drawing yarns to make rope.
10	5	5	..	..	At noon { The extremes of the land from N. 16 W. to S.b.W. ¼
11	6	..	..	..	W.; a bluff head N. 53 W. 4 leagues; a fresh breeze and
12	6	..	N.W.	..	fair; several smoaks on shore; latit'de obs'd, 26° 28′ S.

COOK:

Winds southerly mostly a fresh breeze with which in the PM we streered along shore N ¾ E at the distance of about 2 Leagues off. Between 4 and 5 we discovered breakers on our larboard bow, our depth of water at this time was 37 fathom. At sunset the northermost land in sight bore NbW, the breakers NWbW distant 4 miles and the northermost land set at noon, which formed a point I named *Point Lookout* bore west distant 5 or 6 miles (Latitude 27° 6′). On the north side of this point the shore forms a wide open Bay which I have named *Morton Bay*, in the bottom of which the

Mt Tunbubudla
Mt Beerburrum 918'
Mt Tibrogargan 1,194'
Mt Ngungun 846'
Mt Coonowrin (Crookneck) 1,236'
Mt Beerwah 1,824'
Mt Coochin 771'

Glasshouse Mountains silhouetted by passing storm. From about the same bearing as seen by *Endeavour* in the forenoon of May 17th, 1770.

land is so low that I could but just see it from the topmast head. The breakers I have mentioned lies about 3 or 4 miles from Point Lookout. At this time we had a great sea from the southward which broke prodigious high upon them. Stood on NNE untill 8 oClock when being past the breakers and having deepened our water to 52 fathom we brought too untill 12 oClock and then made sail again to the NNE, at 4 in the AM we sounded and had 135 fathom. At daylight I found that we had in the night got much farther to the northward and from the shore than I expected from the course we had steered for we were at least 6 or 7 Leagues off and therefore hauled in to NWbW having the advantage of a fresh gale at SSW, the northermost land seen last night bore from us at this time SSW distant 6 Leagues. This Land I named *C. Morton* it being the N point of the Bay of the same name (Lat^{de} 26° 56′, Long^{d} 206° 28′). From C. Morton the Land trends away west farther than we could see for there is a small space where we could see no land; some on board was of the opinion that there is a river there because the sea looked paler than usual, upon sounding we found 34 fathom water a fine white sandy bottom, which alone is sufficient to change the apparent colour of the sea water without the assistance of Rivers. The land need only be as low here as it is in a thousand other places upon the coast to have made it impossible to have seen it at the distance we were off. Be this as it may it was a point that could not be cleared up as we had the wind, but should anyone be desirous of doing it that may come after me this place may always be found by three hills which lay to the northward of it in the Latitude of 26° 53′ S. These hills are but a little way inland and not far from each other, they are very remarkable on account of their singular form of elevation which very much resembles glass houses which occasioned my giving them that name, the northermost of the three is the highest and largest. There are likewise several other peaked hills inland to the northward of these but they are not so remarkable. At Noon we were by observation in the latitude of 26° 28′ S, which was 10 miles to the northward of the Log a circumstance that hath not happened sence we have been on the coast before. Our course and distance run sence yesterday noon was NbW 80 miles, which brought us to the Long^{de} of 206° 46′. At this time we were about 2 or 3 leagues from the land and in 24 fathom water. A low bluff point which was the south point of an open sandy bay bore N 62° W distant 3 leagues and the northermost point of land in sight bore N ¼ E. Several smooks seen today and some pretty far inland.

BANKS:

Continued to blow tho not so fresh as yesterday. Land trended much to the westward; about 10 we were abreast of a large bay the bottom of which was out of sight. The sea in this place suddenly changed from its usual transparency to a dirty clay colour, appearing as if charged with freshes, from whence I was led to conclude that the bottom of the bay might open into a large river. About it there were many smoaks especially on the northern side near some remarkable conical hills.

PARKINSON:

On the 17th, the land appeared higher, having many remarkable peaks; one of which was like a glass house: we also saw some smoke and the appearance of a large river; the water of which was a pale green colour. Latitude 26° 28′ S.

During the afternoon the ship had sailed the whole length of what is now North Stradbroke Island and at sunset was abreast of Point Lookout which is its north-east tip. The shallow bight formed by Moreton Island to the north of this the Captain named Morton Bay, which is not the present Moreton Bay (see page 228). Even the presently named Moreton Bay derives its spelling from a mistake in the published account of Cook's voyage; the bays were both named after Lord Morton, President of the Royal Society. By daylight the ship was north of this island at a point about opposite the present Caloundra Head and more than 20 miles offshore, with Cape Moreton SSW. The breakers mentioned off Point Lookout were probably those on Flat Rock just off the point. The bay which they could not see the bottom of and which Cook on his chart named Glasshouse Bay is now called Moreton Bay. There was a river at the bottom of it—the Brisbane River—upon which now stands the capital of Queensland, Brisbane. Cook mentions only three peaks of the Glasshouse Mountains. These were most probably, from the north: Mount Beerwah (1,824′); Mount Coonowrin (Crookneck) (1,236′); and Mount Tibrogargan (1,194′). But there are others, such as Tunbubudla, Ngungun, Beerburrum, Coochin—making in all 'ten steep cones of trachyte, a striking geological formation.' At noon, the low bluff point which bore N *62° W, 3 leagues, was the present Noosa Head, and the bay north of it Laguna Bay. The ship had run this day the length of what is now the Queensland tourist industry's centrepiece, the Sunshine Coast.*

SHIP'S LOG:

FRIDAY, MAY 18TH, 1770

H.	K.	F.	Courses.	Winds.	Soundings.	Remarks, &c.
					Fathoms.	
1	5	..	N.b.W.	S.	..	Mod. breezes and fair weather; lower'd down the main topsail and set the topmast shrouds up; ½-past 2, had 27 fa'm water, hard ground.
2	3	3	..	..	..	
3	2	6	..	..	..	
4	2	4	..	..	..	
5	3	..	..	..	32	
6	3	3	N.	..	..	The northermost land N.b.W., 2 or 3 leagues.
7	1	2	..	..	..	Variation by several azymuths, 8° 44′ S.
	1	2	N.b.E.	..	..	
8	2	..	..	..	31	
9	2	..	N.N.E.	..	..	
10	2	..	..	..	32	Bro't too, main topsail to the mast.
11, 12	..	..	up E.b.S.	off E.N.E.	32	Little wind.
1, 2	..	..	Do.	Do.	32	
3	1	..	N.N.W	S.S.W.	..	
4	1	2	..	..	32	The point set last night W.S.W.
5	2	..	N.W.	..	30	Out all reefs and made sail.
6	3	2	..	..	..	
7	4	3	N.N.W.	S.W.	..	
8	4	3	..	..	25	
9	3	2	..	..	22	Carpenter and seamen as yesterday.
10	1	6	..	..	..	
	1	6	N.	..	..	
11	2	..	..	..	24	At noon { Little wind and fair wea'r; ext's of the land from S. to N. 3 W.; dist. off shore, 2 or 3 leagues; lat'de obs'd, 25° 33′ S.
12	1	6	N.N.E.	..	..	

COOK:

In steering along shore at the distance of two leagues off our soundings was from 24 to 32 fathom a sandy bottom. At 6 oClock PM, the northern point of land set [at noon] bore N ¼ West distant 4 leagues. At 10 oClock it bore NWbW ½ W and as we had seen no land to the northward of it we brought too not knowing which way to steer, having at this time but little wind and continued so most part of the night. At 2 AM we made sail with the wind at SW and at daylight saw the land extending as far as N ¾ E. The point set last night bore SWbW distant 3 or 4 Leagues, I have named it [*Fiddle head* (deleted)] *Double Island Point* from its figure (Lat[de] 25° 58′ S, Long[de] 206° 48′ West). The land within this point is of a moderate and pretty equal height but the Point itself is of such an unequal height that it looks like two small islands laying under the land. It likewise may be known by the white clifts on the north side of it, here the land trends to the NW and forms a large open Bay [Wide Bay on the chart] in the bottom of which the land appeared to be very low, in so much that we

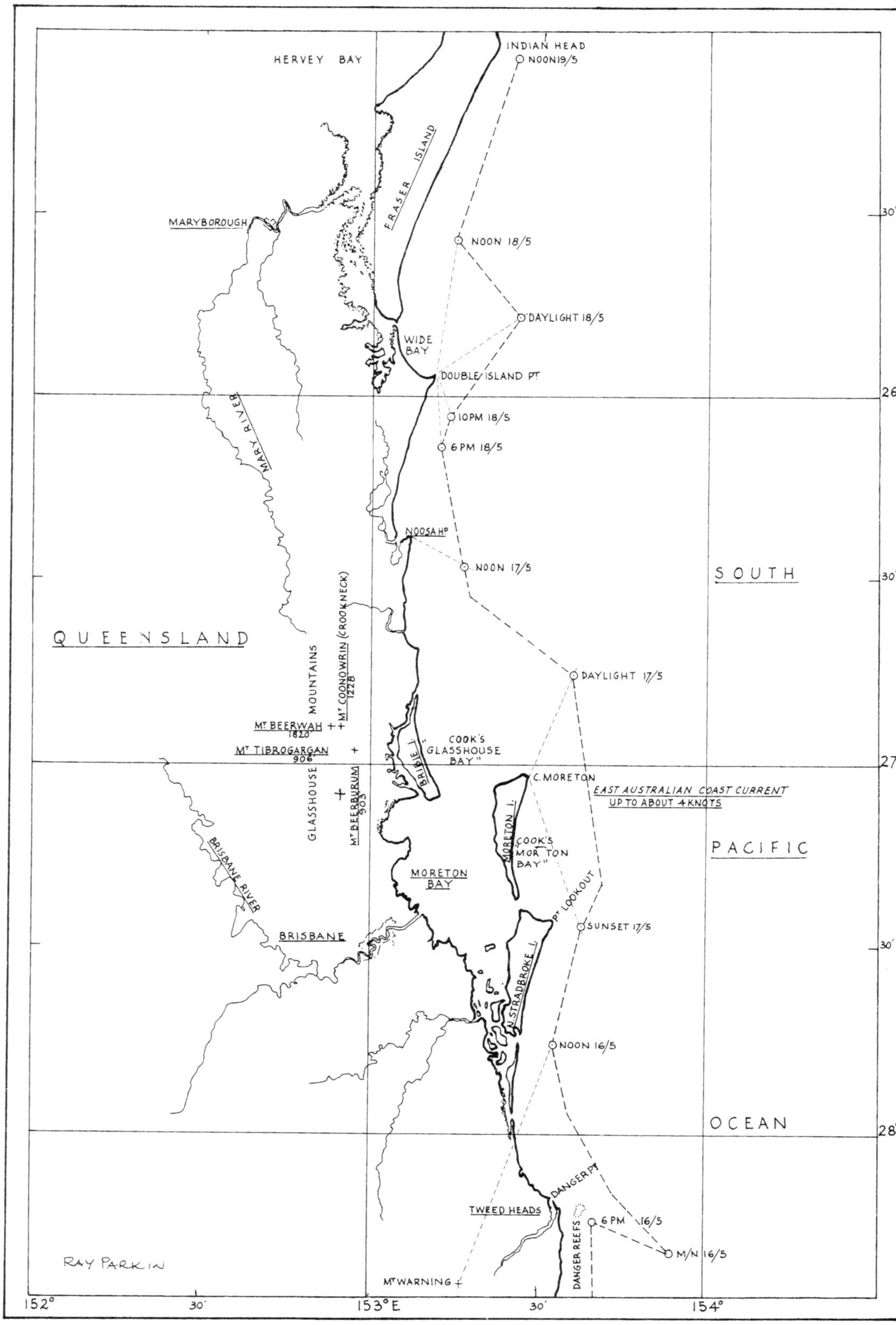

INDIAN HEAD
NOON 19/5
HERVEY BAY
FRASER ISLAND
MARYBOROUGH
NOON 18/5
DAYLIGHT 18/5
WIDE BAY
DOUBLE ISLAND PT
10 PM 18/5
6 PM 18/5
MARY RIVER
NOOSA HD
NOON 17/5
SOUTH
QUEENSLAND
MOUNTAINS
MT COONOWRIN (CROOKNECK) 1228
DAYLIGHT 17/5
MT BEERWAH 1820
MT TIBROGARGAN 906
COOK'S "GLASSHOUSE BAY"
BRIBIE I.
GLASSHOUSE
MT BEERBURUM 903
C. MORETON
EAST AUSTRALIAN COAST CURRENT
UP TO ABOUT 4 KNOTS
MORETON I.
COOK'S "MOR TON BAY"
PACIFIC
BRISBANE RIVER
MORETON BAY
PT LOOKOUT
SUNSET 17/5
BRISBANE
N. STRADBROKE I.
NOON 16/5
OCEAN
DANGER PT
TWEED HEADS
DANGER REEFS
6 PM 16/5
M/N 16/5
RAY PARKIN
MT WARNING
152°
30′
153°E
30′
154°
30′
26°
30′
27°
30′
28°

could but just see it from the deck; in crossing the mouth of this Bay our depth of water was from 30 to 22 fathom a white sandy bottom. At noon we were about 3 Leagues from the land and in the Latitude of 25° 34′ S, Long^de^ 206° 45′ West. Double Isl^d^ Point bore S ¾ W and the northermost land in sight N ¾ E. The land here abouts which is of a moderate height appears more barren than any we have yet seen on this coast and the soil more sandy, there being several large places where nothing else is to be seen; in other places the wood looks to be low and shrubby nor did we see any signs of inhabitants.

GREEN:
Observers, Clerke, Monkhouse and Self. Three sets. Very clear very good observation. A remarkable sugar loaf bore S 42° W. Another large one bore N 75° W and a bluff point not high N 45° W. There were at this time 8 sugar loafs or conical peeks one very high Frustrum of a cone & several odd hummocks. The inland part moderately high very even. The cones appeared next the shore & some behind just showing their apex. The beach mostly sandy in sight.

BANKS:
At sun set the land made in one bank over which nothing could be seen; it was very sandy and carried with it no signs of fertility. Land this morn very sandy. We could see through our glasses that the sands which lay in great patches of many acres each were moveable; some of them had been lately moved, for the trees which stood up in the middle of them were quite green, others of a longer standing had many stumps sticking out of them which had been trees killed by the sand heaping about their roots. Two water snakes swam by the ship; they were in all respects like land snakes and beautifully spotted except that they had broad flat tails which probably serve them instead of fins in swimming.

PARKINSON:
On the 18th in the Latitude 25° 36′, the land appeared to rise perpendicular of an unequal height, and looked like a wall along the coast, without having any breaks: which prevented us from seeing the back land; it was covered with great patches of white sand and stinted shrubs. The sea was full of a sort of orange coloured powder, like that we saw on the coast of Brazil. On this day we saw a water snake.

By daylight in the morning the ship was abreast of the break between Fraser Island and the main, and by noon, about one-third of the way along it northwards and off the Seventy-five Mile Beach. They were coasting one of the largest sand islands of the world, some 65 miles long and along whose sandy backbone were supported lakes with thick humus bottoms, preventing seepage and becoming the centres of a marvellous habitat for the ever-adaptable of nature. Its crest was between 600 and 785 feet, dropping to 284 at the northern end. Being rich in rutile, it was at one time the scene of a prolonged controversy between conservationists and miners, which has resulted in a stay of execution for the island.

SHIP'S LOG:

SATURDAY, MAY 19TH, 1770

H.	K.	F.	Courses.	Winds.	Soundings.	Remarks, &c.
					Fathoms.	
1	1	..	N.b.W.	Variable.	..	Light airs and clear weather.
2	..	..		Calm.	..	Her head north. Unbent the main topsail and bent the old one.
3	1	..	N.N.W.	N.E.	..	
4	1	..	..	..	..	Variat'n by azym'ths, 8° 36′ E.
5	..	..	Calm. Her head to ye S.E.		..	
6	} ..	..				The N. extreme of the land N. ½ W.
7			Head to the Eastward.		..	
8						
9	1	..	N.N.E. ½ E.	N.W.	..	Little wind and fair wea'r.
10	1	3	..	..	..	
11	1	2	..	..	25	
12	1	6	..	..	26	
1	2	..	N.N.E.	..	..	
2		6	N.b.E.	N.W.b.W.	27	
3	1	4	.	..	..	
4	1	4	..	..	27	
5	1	6	..	W.S.W.	..	
6	2	..	..	..	..	Mod't breezes and fair wea'r; set steering sails.
7	3	2	N. ½ E.	S.W.	.	Variation .. { By an amplit'd, 8° 23′ / ,, azym'th, 8° 20′ } East.
8	3	5	..	..	..	
9	3	3	N. ½ W.	..	..	
10	3	2	..	..	..	
11	{1	4	..	..	..	
	1	5	N.b.E.	..	Sand	
12	3	3	..	..	13½	Do. wea'r; extremes of the land at N. 31 W. to S 22 W.; shore dist. 5 m's; latitude obs'd, 25° 04′ S.

COOK:

In the PM had variable light airs and calms, in the night had a light breeze from the land which in the AM veered to SW and SSW. In the evening found the Variation to be 8° 36′ East and in the morning 8° 20′. As we had but little wind we kept on to the northward all night having from 23 to 27 fathom a fine sandy bottom at the distance of 2 or 3 Leagues from the land. At noon we were about 4 miles from it and by observation in the Latitude of 25° 4′ and in this situation had but 13 fathom water. The northermost land in sight bore N 21° W, distant 8 miles. Our course and distance sence yesterday noon was N 13° 15′ East 31 miles.

BANKS:

In the evening I went out in the small boat but saw few birds of three sorts, Men of War birds (*Pelecanus aquilus*) [the Lesser Frigate Bird], Boobies (*Pelicanus sula*) [probably the Brown Booby] and *Nectris munda* [possibly Audubon's Shearwater], of which last shot one, and took up two cuttle bones differing from European ones in nothing but having a small peg or prickle at one end. AM: Countrey as sandy and barren as ever. Two snakes were seen, a Man of War bird, and a small turtle.

SHIP'S LOG:

SUNDAY, MAY 20TH, 1770

H.	K.	F.	Courses.	Winds.	Soundings.	Remarks, &c.
					Fathoms.	
1	3	..	N.b.E.	S.b.W.	17	Mod. breezes and clear wea'r.
2	2	4	N.b.W.	..	20, 17	
3	2	4	..	..	17	
4	2	4	..	..	..	
5	2	..	..	Wt.	..	¼-past, the ext's of the land seen off deck from N. 42 W. to S. 7 W.
6	2	..	..	..	..	Land seen from the masthead, N.N.W. ½ W.; dist'ce off shore, 2 or 3 leagues.
7	1	4	..	..	..	Variation p'r severell azym'ths, 8° 45′ E't.
8	1	..	..	..	33	
9	..	6	..	..	..	
10	1	2	..	..	21, 23	
11	1	6	..	..	22, 21	
12	2	..	..	..	21, 22	
1	2	..	..	..	22, 24	
2	2	..	..	..	26, 27	
3	2	..	..	..	29, 30, 32	
4	{1	6	..	..	33	
	up	..	Wt.	off W.N.W.	34	
5	3	..	N.b.W.	S.W.	..	Fresh breezes and fair wea'r.
6	3	2	..	..	..	
7	{2	..	W.b.N.	..	..	Made all sail; saw ye land ending in a point bearing W.S.W.; haul'd up for it; saw a ledge of breakers running out from the land to N.W.
	1	..	W. ½ S.	..	18	
8	4	4	N.W.b.N.	..	17, 16, 15	
9	{..	2	..	..	14, 13, 13	The point S.W. and the end of the breakers N.W.b.N.; dist. off the nearest part of them 3 or 4 miles.
	2	2	N.E.	..	14, 15, 16	
					15, 14, 10	
10	4	4	N.W.	S.S.W.	from 10 to 7¼	
11	{2	2	N.W.b.N.	..	..	Mod. breezes and fair wea'r; ye ex' of the land from S. 7 E't to S. 4 W.; ye No. ext'n of ye reef, N.W. ½ W.
	2	2	N.b.W.	..	..	
12	3	..	N.N.W.	..	from 7 to 11	Lat'de obs'd, 24° 26′ S.

COOK:
Winds southerly gentle breezes. At 10 oClock in the PM we passed at the distance of 4 miles having 17 fathom water a black bluff head or point of land on which a number of natives were assembled which occasioned my naming it *Indian Head* (Lat^de 25 0′). NbW 4 miles from this head is another much like it [Waddy Point] from this last the land trends a little more to the westward and low and sandy next the sea, for what may be behind it we know not, if land it must be very low for we could see no part of it from the mast head. We saw people in other places besides the one I have mentioned, some smooks in the day and fires in the night. Having but little wind all night we kept on to the northward having from 17 to 34 fathom water from 4 miles to 4 leagues from the land, the northermost part of which bore from us at

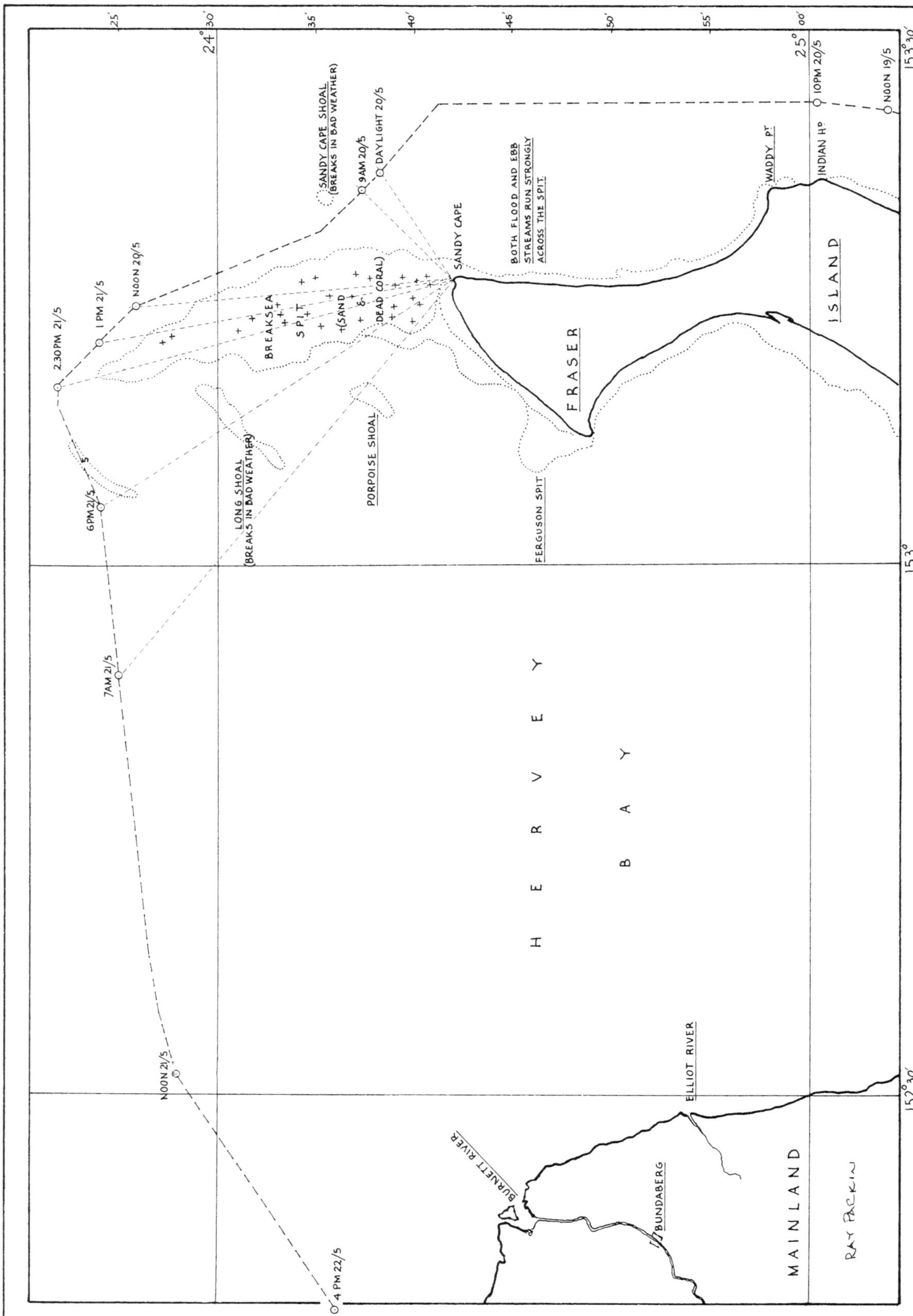
SANDY CAPE SHOAL
(BREAKS IN BAD WEATHER)
9AM 20/5
DAYLIGHT 20/5
NOON 20/5
1 PM 21/5
2.30PM 21/5
BREAKSEA SPIT
(SAND & DEAD CORAL)
SANDY CAPE
BOTH FLOOD AND EBB STREAMS RUN STRONGLY ACROSS THE SPIT.
WADDY PT
INDIAN Hd
10PM 20/5
NOON 19/5
FRASER
ISLAND
LONG SHOAL
(BREAKS IN BAD WEATHER)
PORPOISE SHOAL
FERGUSON SPIT
6PM 21/5
7AM 21/5
HERVEY BAY
ELLIOT RIVER
BURNETT RIVER
BUNDABERG
MAINLAND
NOON 21/5
4 PM 22/5
24° 30'
25° 00'
153° 30'
153°
152° 30'
25'
35'
40'
45'
50'
55'

daylight wsw and seemed to end in a point from which we discovered a reef stretching out to the northward as far as we could see, being at this time in 18 fathom water, for we had before it was light hauled our wind to the westward and this course we continued untill we had plainly discovered the breakers a long way on our lee bow which seemed to stretch quite home to the land. We then edged away NW and NNW and along the east side of the shoal from 2 to 1 mile off having regular even soundings from 13 to 7 fathom a fine sandy bottom. At Noon we were by observation in the latitude of 24° 26′ s, which was 13 miles to the northward of that given by the Log. The extreme point of the shoal we judged to bear about NW from us and the point of land above mentioned bore s ¾ w distant 20 miles, this point I have named *Sandy Cape* on account of two very large white patches of sand upon it. It is of a height sufficient to be seen 12 leagues in clear weather. (Lat^{de} 24° 46′, Long^{de} 206° 51′) from it the land trended away wsw and sw as far as we could see.

GREEN:
Observers: Clerke, Monkhouse and self. Three sets. Observations very good for anything I know.

BANKS:
At sun set the land appeared in a low bank to the sea over which nothing was seen, so that we imagined that it was very narrow and that some deep bay on the other side ran behind it.

At day break the land in sight terminated in a sandy cape behind which a deep bay ran in, across which we could not see; our usual good fortune now again assisted us, for we discovered breakers which we certainly had ran on had the ship in the night sailed 2 or 3 leagues farther than she did. This shoal extended a long way out from the land for we ran along it till 2 oClock and then passed over the tail of it in seven fathom water; the Sea was so clear that we could distinctly see the bottom and indeed it was 12 and 14 fathom deep, the colour of the sand might be seen from the mast head at a large distance. While we were upon the shoal innumerable large fish, Sharks, Dolphins &c. and one large Turtle were seen; a Grampus of middle size leaped with his whole body out of the water several times making a splash and foam in the sea as if a mountain had fallen into it.

PARKINSON:
On the 20th, in the forenoon, we were abreast of a point which seemed to be the last of the land to the north, and trended abruptly away to the south. From this point there runs a very large shoal, on several parts of which the water broke. We sailed alongside of it, and had from seventeen to nine fathoms water. Before night came on we got round it and kept our course westward, as we had seen the looming of the land in that quarter. The barren sandy land continued to this point, and was

uninhabited. We saw a large turtle, many sharks which would not take the bait, and several man of war birds. Latitude 24° 24′ s.

By noon this day the ship was almost abreast of the northern end of the shoal which the Captain was to name Break Sea Spit. She was indeed most fortunate to have had such fair winds, which made plain sailing possible in a place where other circumstances could have made it a death trap. Nevertheless the nicety with which Cook piloted the ship along this undelineated shoal makes the ship's track look more like that of a powered vessel using a modern chart. Banks, without the burden of responsibility or the insight of profounder knowledge of the realities, can pass it off as 'our usual good fortune', hinting at some lack of appreciation of the Captain's rare combination of art and skill in his profession.

CHAPTER 6

SANDY CAPE TO THIRSTY SOUND

SHIP'S LOG:

MONDAY, MAY 21ST, 1770

H.	K.	F.	Courses.	Winds.	Soundings.	Remarks, &c.
					Fathoms.	
1	2	6	N.W.	S.	. .	Mod'te breezes and fair weather. From noon to 2, soundings regular from 9½ to 11 fathom. At 2, sent the yaul to sound a place that had the appearance of being very shoal from the breaking of the water over it; they found from 5 to 7 fathoms. ½ - past 2, passed the tail of the shoal, sounding irregular from 6 to 9 fa'm. The point of land set at noon then bear'g S.14°E.
2	3	. .	W.N.W.	. .	. .	
3	{1 1	4} . .}	W. ½ N.	. .	19	
4	2	. .	W.S.W.½ W.	. .	20	
5	2	2	W.S.W.	. .	22	
6	2	2	. .	. .	. .	The land S.E.b.S. 7 or 8 leagues.
7	2	2	S.W.	S.S.E.	23	
8	1	4	. .	. .	24	
9	. .	. .	. .	. .	23	
10	. .	. .	. .	. .	23	Calm, head to ye So'ward.
11	. .	. .	. .	. .	23	
12	. .	. .	. .	. .	23	Fair weather.
1	. .	. .	. .	. .	23	
2	. .	. .	. .	. .	23	Head betw'n ye N. & E. Found a current setting S.-w'tly 1 k. 2 f. p. hour.
3	. .	. .	. .	. .	23	
4	2	. .	W.N.W.	Variable.	23	Light airs and smooth water.
5	2	. .	W.S.W.	S.	22	
6	2	4	S.W.b.W.	S.b.E.	26	Saw land from the masthead, S.E. ½ S.
7	3	. .	. .	. .	. .	
8	3	. .	. .	. .	21	
9	3	4	W.S.W.	S.	17½	More land to the W.S.W.
10	3	6	S.W.b. W. ½ W.	S.b.E.	16	Carpenters caulking the main deck.
11	3	7	. .	. .	14½	
12	3	4	. .	. .	{from 14 to 14½	At noon {Mod't breezes and fair wea'r. Ext's off the land from S.W. to N. 86 W. Shore dist. 7 or 8 leagues. Some smokes along shore. Lat. obs'd, 24° 28' S.

COOK:

In the PM we kept along the East side of the shoal untill 2 oClock when judging that there was water for us over I sent a boat ahead to sound and upon making the signal for more than 5 fathom we hauled our wind and stood over the tail of it in 6 fathom. At this time we were in the Latitude of 24° 22′ and *Sandy Cape* bore S ½ E distant 8 Leagues, but the direction of the shoal is nearest NNW and SSE. At the time we had 6 fathom the boat was not above a quarter of a Mile to the south[d] of us had little more than 5 fathom. From 6 fathom we had the next cast 13 and then 20 immediately as fast as the men could heave the lead, from this I did suppose that the west side of the shoal is pretty steep too whereas on the other side we had gradual shoaling from 13 to 7 fathom. This shoal I called *Break Sea Spit*, because we now had smooth water whereas upon the whole coast to the south[rd] of it we had always a high sea or swell from y[e] SE.

At 6 oClock the land of *Sandy Cape* extending from South 17° East distant 8 Leagues, depth of water 23 fathom, which depth we kept all night as we stood to the westward with light airs from the southward; but between 12 and 4 AM we had it calm after which a gentle breeze sprung up at south with which we still kept upon a wind to the westward. At 7 oClock we saw from the mast head the land and *Sandy Cape* bearing SE ½ E distant 12 or 13 Leagues. At 9 we discovered from y[e] mast head land to the westward and soon after saw smooks upon it; our depth of water now decreased to 17 fathom and by noon to 13, at which time we were by observation in the Latitude of 24° 28′, and about 7 Leagues from the land which extended from SbW to WNW. Longitude made from Sandy Cape 0° 45′ West.

For these few days past we have seen at times a sort of sea fowl we have no where seen before that I remember, they are of that sort called Boobies; before today we seldom saw more than 2 or 3 at a time and only when we were near the land. Last night a small flock of these birds passed the Ship and went away to the NW and this morning from half an hour before sun rise to half an hour after flights of them were continually coming from the NNW and flying to the SSE and not one was seen to fly in any other direction, from this we did suppose that there was a Lagoon, River or Inlet of shallow water to the southward of us [in y[e] Bottom of the deep Bay which I named Hervey's Bay in honour of y[e] Hon Hervey (inserted by Cook in the Admiralty copy of his journal)] where these birds resorted to in the day to feed and that not very far to the northward lay some island where they retired for the night.

BANKS:

At sun set a few Boobies flew past towards the NW. AM: Land seen only from the mast head. Innumerable Boobies for near 2 hours before and after sun rise flew by the ship coming from NNW and flying SSE, I suppose from some bird Island in the direction where they roosted last night. At 9 new land was in sight the other side of the bay which we left last night; as we approached it the depth of water gradually decreased to 9 fathom.

PARKINSON:

On the 21st, in the forenoon, discovered land again, extending a very great way and forming a curve. It was very flat, level and covered with trees, with a few hills within land.

Two views of the longboat under sail (based on Parkinson).

One needs to see this passage over the tail of Break Sea Spit on the modern chart to appreciate the skill and confidence with which the Captain could read and interpret the nature and form of the sea floor with nothing but the lead-line and the blank surface of the water which could reflect cloud shadow or reef almost identically, to startle the nervous or fool the unwary. This quality of discrimination was what put Cook at the top of his profession, especially in the realm of inshore surveys which demand this extra sense if the ship and the surveyor are to survive.

Although Cook reserved the name Labyrinth *for a smaller section between about 15° and 16° South latitude, the whole coast from this point to Cape York could have qualified for the description. For the next thousand miles, the chains would be constantly manned by the leadsmen as long as the ship was under way, the boats would be fully employed in sounding ahead of the ship and scouting hazards so numerous that one marvels at the quality of perseverance and endurance sustaining this nerve-racking work. Yet the logs and journals remain full of matter-of-fact understatement.*

The ship had crossed the tail of the Break Sea Spit within which the red-hulled Breaksea Light vessel is now moored. Modern vessels are warned to keep 6 miles to the northward of it. The Australia Pilot *further says,* 'Caution *should be exercised when approaching Breaksea Spit as both the flood and ebb streams set strongly across it.'*

By noon the ship was in a position a little over half-way across the opening of Hervey Bay at a point NW of the Burnett River and not 20 miles from it, and about EbN from Baffle Creek. Burnett River now supports Bundaberg, and the great bulk carriers now regularly load sugar at the modern bulk terminal at its mouth. Hervey Bay (which the Captain named after Augustus John Hervey (1724–99), later Third Earl of Bristol, a naval officer who became a Lord of the Admiralty the year Endeavour *returned), was well known and used by the Royal Australian Navy during the 1920s and 30s for gunnery and torpedo exercises, with the sailors recreating and swimming in the lagoons of Fraser Island.*

Flinders also noted the flight of the boobies and thought that they came from the Bunker Group, about 45 miles northward, to feed in Hervey Bay. Here the shallows of Great Sandy Strait between the southern half of Fraser Island and the mainland would seem ideal for these birds to feed, and the lagoon Cook 'did suppose' was close to the truth.

SHIP'S LOG:

TUESDAY, MAY 22ND, 1770

H.	K.	F.	Courses.	Winds.	Remarks, &c.
1	3	..	S.W.	S.S.E.	Mod'te breezes and clear wea'r. Regular soundings from 12 to 9 fa'm.
2	3	2	..	..	
3	3	..	S.W.b.S.	S.E.b.E.	
4	3	..	..	..	
5	2	2	W.N.W.	E.S.E.	From 9 to 7½ fa'm. Variat'n p'r amplitude, 8° 3′ E.
6	2	..	..	..	
7	1 1	..	N.W.b W.	..	From 7½ to 7 and 8 fa'm. At 8, came too with the bt. bower in 8 fa'm. Veer'd to ⅓ of a cable.
8	..	..	..	..	
9	..	..	..	..	
10	..	..	..	..	
11	..	..	..	..	
12	..	..	..	..	Ye water fell 2 foot slack water.
1	..	..	..	..	
2	..	..	..	..	
3	..	..	..	..	
4	..	..	..	..	Found the tide to rise 1 foot 11 inches.
5	..	..	..	..	½-p't, found it to rise one inch. Hove short. ½-p't, weighed and came to sail.
6	1	2	N.W.b.W.	S.	
7	2	4	..	..	
8	3	..	..	..	Soundings from the time we weighed from 8 to 9½ fa'm.
9	2	4	..	..	Out 1 reef the main topsails. Variat'n p'r azym'ths, 7° 50′ E.
10	2	2	..	..	Carp'rs caulking the main deck.
11	1 1	2 ..	W.N.W.½ W.	..	Soundings from 8 to ½-p't 10 from 8½ to 10 fa'm, from that time till noon from 10 to 11 fa'm.
12	2	..	..	..	At noon: Ext's of the land from N. 37° W. to S. 22° E. Shore dist. 2 miles. Lat'de obs'd, 24° 19′ S. Little wind and fair wea'r.

COOK:

In the PM had gentle breezes at SE with which we stood in for the land SW untill 4 oClock when being in the Latitude of 24° 36′ S and about 2 Leagues from the land in 9 fathom water we bore away along the shore NWbW. At the same time we could

Pinnace with jack: Have found safe anchorage. Ship answers with jack or ensign kept out if intending to anchor (boat based on Parkinson).

see the land extending to the South South East about 8 Leagues. Near the sea land is very low but in land are some moderately high hills and the whole appeared to be thickly cloathed with wood. In running along shore we shoalden our water from 9 to 7 fathom and at one time had but 6 fath^{m} which determined me to anchor for the night and accordingly at 8 oClock we came too in 8 fathom water a fine gravely bottom about 5 miles from the land. This evening we saw a water snake and two or three evenings ago one lay under the ships stern some time, this was about a yard and a half in length and was the first we had seen.

At 6 oClock in the AM we weighed with a gentle breeze southerly and steered NW ¼ W edgeing in for the land untill we got within 2 miles of it having from 7 to 11 fathom water, we then steered NNW as the land laid. At noon we were by observation in the Latitude 24° 19′ S, Longitude made from Sandy Cape 1° 14′ West.

BANKS:

At 4 in the evening the land appeared very low but covered with fine wood; on it were many very large smoaks several of which were seen before we could see the land itself. At night water still shoal, land low and well wooded, fertile to appearance as any thing we have seen upon this coast. At 8 came to an anchor till morn.

In the course of the night the tide rose very considerably. In the morn we got under sail again. The land as last night fertile and well wooded; at noon the land appeared much less fertile, near the beach it was sandy and we plainly saw with our glasses that it was covered with palm nut trees, *Pandanus Tectorius* which we had not seen since we left the Islands within the tropicks. Along shore we saw 2 men walking along who took no kind of notice of us.

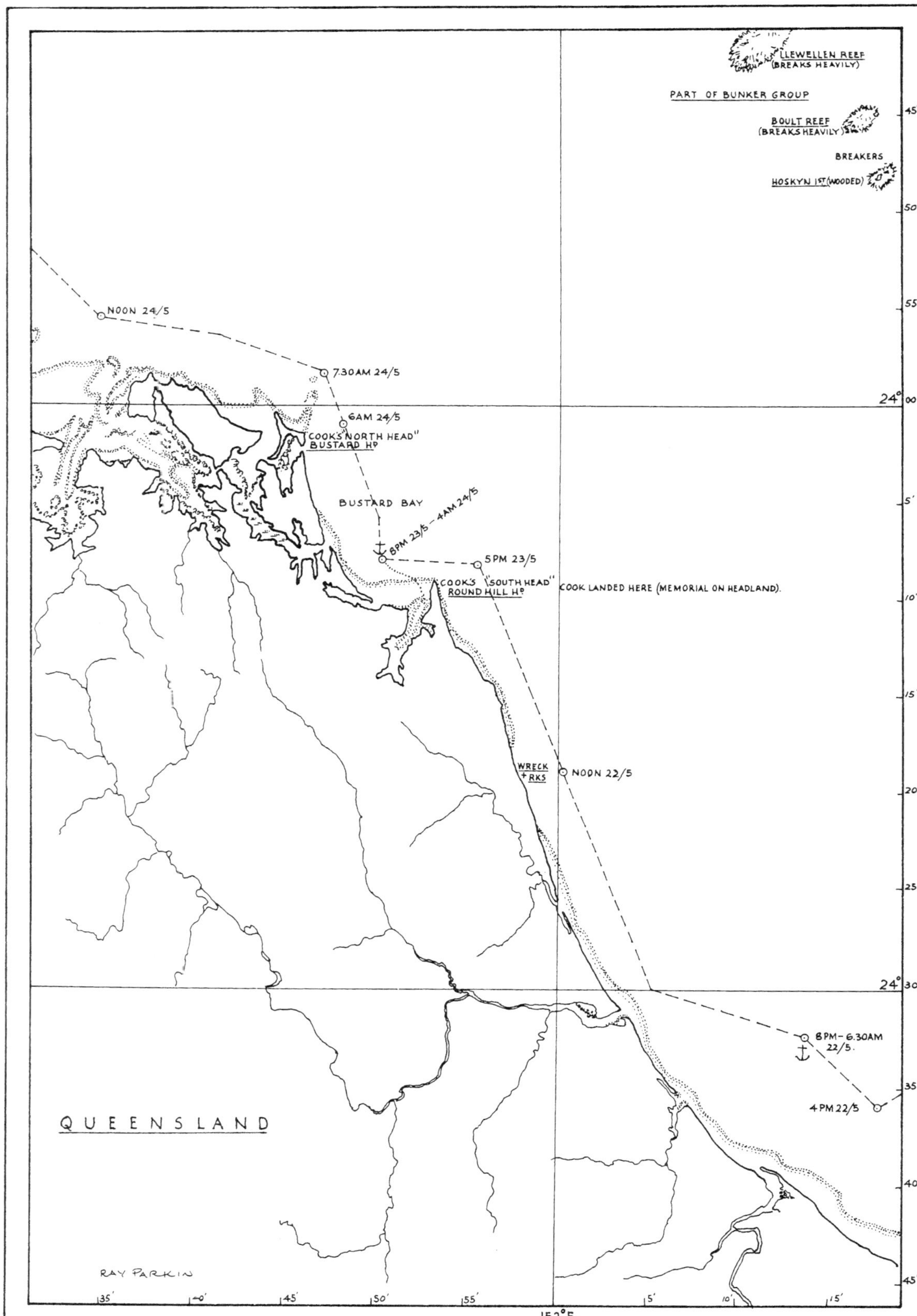
LLEWELLEN REEF (BREAKS HEAVILY)
PART OF BUNKER GROUP
BOULT REEF (BREAKS HEAVILY)
BREAKERS
HOSKYN IST (WOODED)
NOON 24/5
7.30AM 24/5
6AM 24/5
COOK'S "NORTH HEAD" BUSTARD Hd
BUSTARD BAY
8PM 23/5 – 4AM 24/5
5PM 23/5
COOK'S "SOUTH HEAD" ROUND HILL Hd
COOK LANDED HERE (MEMORIAL ON HEADLAND).
WRECK + RKS
NOON 22/5
8PM – 6.30AM 22/5.
4PM 22/5
QUEENSLAND
RAY PARKIN
45'
50'
55'
24° 00'
5'
10'
15'
20'
25'
24° 30'
35'
40'
45'
35'
40'
45'
50'
55'
5'
10'
15'
152°E.

PARKINSON:

We sailed along it [the shore] to look for a harbour to the NW. There was no appearance of land to the SW so that it is pretty probable that there is a river in that part. We found no current, and our course was very shallow, as we had from seven to twenty fathoms water at a Great distance from the land.

By noon the ship was some 30 miles WNW of her noon position of the previous day, having first made some southing getting inshore. Wreck Rocks is marked on the modern chart due west of this position. Both bower anchors were now at the cat-heads ready for letting go at any time, and the watch on deck was fully alert for any sail handling. The ship was in a state of efficient caution and readiness, which prevent panic or confusion. All hands knew their jobs and no order could come as a surprise, knowing their captain to be constantly vigilant beneath a calm and commanding exterior and a matter-of-fact competence.

SHIP'S LOG:

WEDNESDAY, MAY 23RD, 1770

H.	K.	F.	Courses.	Winds.	Remarks, &c.
1	2	4	N.N.W.	S.E.	Little wind and clear weather.
2	2	..	..	..	Soundings from 10¾ to 15 fa'm.
3	1	6	..	Variable.	½-p't, saw more land to the No ward.
4	..	6	..	..	
	1	6	N.W.b.W.	..	
5	1	2	W.N.W.	..	
	1	..	W.b.S.	S.b.W.	Open'd a large bay. Hoisted out the yaul and sent a m'te in her to sound for an anchoring-place.
6	2	..	..	..	Variation by an amplit'd, 8° 30′ easterly. ½-p't 5,
7	..	..	..	..	the ext's of the land from S.77 E. to N. 42 W. Soundings since, 4, 6, & 7 fa'm. Working into ye bay till 8, sounding 5 & 6 fa'm. At 8, anchor'd
8	..	..	..	..	with the b't bower in 5 fa'm water, and veered to ⅓ of a cable. Ext's of
9	..	..	..	..	the land from E. to N.W. ½ W. Shore dist. 1 league.
10	..	..	..	..	
11	..	..	..	..	
12	..	..	..	..	Found the tide to have ebb'd 3 feet since 9 o'clock.
1	..	..	..	..	
2	..	..	..	..	
3	..	..	..	..	Slack water. Ebb'd since 12, 1 foot & ½.
4	..	..	..	..	Tide had flow'd 10 inches.
5	..	..	..	S.	Fresh breezes and fair wea'r.
6	..	..	..	..	
7	..	..	..	..	Veer'd to ⅔ of a cable on the bt. bower.
8	..	..	..	..	
9	..	..	..	..	
10	..	..	..	..	The cap'tn and gentlemen away in the pinnace examining the country.
11	..	..	..	..	The 2nd lieut't in the yawl with a fishing party.
12	..	..	..	S.E.	Lat'de obs'd, 24° 04′ S.

COOK:
Continued our course along shore at the distance of about 2 Miles off 12 to 9, 8 and 7 fathom water untill 5 oClock at which time we were abreast of the South point of a large open bay where I intended to anchor, accordingly we hauled in close upon a wind and sent a boat ahead to sound. After making some trips [tacks] we anchored at 8 oClock in 5 fathom water a Sandy bottom. The south point of the Bay bore E ¾ South distance 2 miles, the north point NW ¼ N about 2 miles from the shore in the bottom of the bay.

Last night some time in the Middle watch a very extraordinary affair happened to Mr Orton my Clerk, he having been drinking in the Evening, some Malicious person or persons in the Ship took the advantage of his being drunk and cut off all the cloaths from off his back, not being satisfied with this they some time after went into his Cabbin and cut off part of his Ears as he lay asleep in his bed. The person whom he suspected to have done this was Mr Magra one of the Midshipmen, but this did not appear to me upon inquirey. However as I had been told Magra had once or twice before this in their drunken frolicks cut off his cloaths and had been heard to say (as I was told) that if it were not for the Law he would Murder him, these things considered induced me to think that Magra was not altogether innocent. I therefore, for the present dismissed him the quarter deck and suspended him from doing any duty in the Ship, he being one of those gentlemen, frequently found on board Kings Ships, that can very well be spared [Or to speak more plainer good for nothing (deleted)]. Besides it was necessary in me to show my immediate resentment againest the person on whome the suspicion fell least they should not have stopped here. With respect to Mr Orton he is not a man without faults, yet from all the inquirey I could make, it evidently appeared to me that so far from deserving such treatment he had not designedly injured any person in the Ship, so that I do and shall all ways look upon him as an injured man. Some reasons might however be given why this misfortune came upon him in which he himself was in some measure to blame, but this is only conjecture and would tend to fix it on some people in the Ship whom I would fain believe would hardly be guilty of such an action. I shall say nothing about it unless I shall hereafter discover the Offenders which I shall take every method in my power to do, for I look upon such proceedings as highly dangerous in such Voyages as this and the greatest insult that could be offered to my authority in this Ship, as I have always been ready to hear and redress every complaint that have been made against any Person in the Ship.

In the AM I went with a shore party of men in order to examine the Country accompanied by Mr Banks and the other gentlemen. We landed a little within the south point of the Bay where there is a channel leading into a large Lagoon [Round Hill Creek]. The first thing I did was to sound and examine this channel in which I found 3 fathom water untill I got about a mile up it, where I met with a shoal whereon there was little more than one fathom, being over this I had 3 fathom again. The entrance to this channel lies close to the South point of the Bay being formed on the East by the shore and on the West by a large spit of sand, it is about a quarter of a Mile broad and lies in sbw; here is room for a few ships to lay very secure and a small stream of fresh water. After this I made a little excursion into the woods while some hands made 3 or 4 hauls with the Sain but caught not above a dozen very small fish; by this time the flood was made and I embarqued in the boat in order to row up the Lagoon but in this I was hindered by meeting every where with shoal water. As yet we had seen no people but saw a great deal of smook up and on the west side of the Lagoon which was all too far off for us to go by land excepting one; this we went to and found 10 small fires in a very small compass and some cockle shells laying by them but the people were gone. On the windward or south side of one fire was stuck up a little bark about a foot and a half high and some few pieces lay about in other places; these we concluded were all the covering they had in the night and many of them I firmly believe have not this but sleep naked as they sleep in the open air. Tupia who was with us observed that they were *Taata Eno's* that is bad or poor people. The country is visibly worse than the last place we were at, the soil is dry and sandy and the woods are free of underwood of every kind. Here are some of the same sort of trees as we found in Botany Bay with a few other sorts; one sort which is by far the most numerous of any kind in the woods grows something like a birch [Scrub Ironbark or Grey Birch] the bark at first sight looks like birch bark but on examination I found it to be very different and so I believe is the wood, but this I could not examine as having no ax or any thing with me to cut down a tree. About the skirts of the Lagoon grows the true Mangrove such as are found in the West Indias and which we not having seen during the Voyage before, here is likewise a sort of Palm tree which grows on low barren and sandy places in the South Sea Islands [*Pandanus pendunculatus*]. All or most of the same sorts of land and water fowl as we saw at Botany Bay we saw here, besides these Black & White ducks, and Bustards such as we have in England one of which we killed that weighed 17½ pounds which occasioned my giving this place the name of *Bustard Bay* (Lat[d] 24° 4′, Long[d] 208° 22′). Here are plenty of small oysters sticking to the rocks, stones and Mangrove trees and some few other shell fish such as large mussels, Pearl oysters, Cockles &c[a]. I measured the perpendicular height of the last tide and found it to be 8 feet above low-water mark and from the time of low water today I found that it must be high water at the full and change of the Moon at 8 oClock.

BANKS:

At night we were working into a bay which seemed to be good anchorage, where we came to an anchor resolved to go ashore tomorrow and examine a little of the produce of the country.

AM: Wind blew fresh off the land so cold that our cloaks were very necessary in going ashore; as the ship lay a good way from the land we were some time before we got there; when landed however the sun recovered its influence and made it sufficiently hot, in the afternoon almost intolerably so. We landed near the mouth of a large lagoon which ran a good way into the countrey and sent out a strong tide; here we found a great variety of Plants, several however the same as those we ourselves had before seen in the Islands between the tropicks and others known to the natives of the East Indies, a sure mark that we were upon the point of leaving the Southern Temperate Zone and for the future we must expect to meet with plants &c. a part of which at least have been before seen by Europæans. The soil in general was very sandy and dry: tho it produced a large variety of plants yet it never was covered with thick verdure. Fresh water we saw none, but several swamps and bogs of salt water; in these and upon the sides of the lagoon grew many Mangrove trees in the branches of which were many nests of Ants, one sort of which were quite green. These when the branches were disturbed came out in large numbers and revenged themselves very sufficiently upon their disturbers, biting sharper than any I have felt in Europe. The mangroves had also another trap which most of us fell into, a small kind of Caterpiler, green beset with many hairs: these sat upon the leaves many together ranged by the side of each other like soldiers drawn up, 20 or 30 perhaps on one leaf; if these wrathfull militia were touched but ever so gently they did not fail to make the person offending them sensible of their anger, every hair in them stinging as much as nettles do but with a more accute tho less lasting smart. Upon the sides of the hills were many of the trees yielding gum like *Sanguis draconis*: they differed however from those seen in the last harbour in having their leaves longer and hanging down like those of a weeping willow, tho notwithstanding that I believe that they were of the same species. There was however much less gum upon them; only one tree that I saw had any gum upon it, contrary to all theory, which teached that the hotter a climate is the more gums exude. The same observation however held good in the plant yielding the Yellow gum, of which tho we saw vast numbers we did not see any that shewed signs of gum.

On the shoals and sandbanks near the shore of the bay were many large birds far larger than swans which we judged to be Pelicans, but they were so shy that we could not get within gun shot of them. On the shore were many birds, one species of Bustard, of which we shot a single bird as large as a good turkey. The sea seemed to abound with fish but unfortunately at the first hawl we tore our seine to pieces; on the mud banks under the mangrove trees were innumerable Oysters, Hammer Oysters and many more sorts among which were a large proportion of small Pearl oysters. Whether the sea in deeper water might abound with as great a proportion of full grown ones we had not the opportunity to examine, but if it did a pearl fishery here must turn out to immense advantage.

Those who stayed on board the ship saw about 20 of the natives, who came down abreast of the ship and stood on the beach for some time looking at her, after which they went into the woods; we on shore saw none. Many large fires were made at a distance from us where probably the people were. One small one was in our neighborhood, to this we went; it was burning when we came to it, but the people were gone; near it was left several vessels of bark which we conceived were intended for water buckets, several shells and fish bones, the remainder I suppose of their last meal. Near the fires, for there were 6 or 7 small ones, were as many pieces of soft bark about the length and breadth of a man: these we supposed to be their beds; on the windward side of the fires was a small shade about a foot high made of bark likewise. The whole was in a thicket of close trees, defended from the wind; whether it was really or not the place of their abode we can only guess. We saw no signs of a house or anything like the ruins of an old one, and from the ground being much trod we concluded that they had for some time remained in that place.

PARKINSON:

On the 22nd in the evening we anchored in an open road or bay, round the north cape of the great bay. As we sailed along, this day, the country appeared very barren and sandy, having only a few low shrubs. This day the captain's clerk had his ears cut off, and his cloaths also cut off his back. The captain and officers offered some time after, at Batavia, a reward of fifteen guineas, to any one who should discover the person or persons who cut off his ears, and fifteen gallons of arrack, to any one that should discover him or them who had cut off his cloaths.

On the 23rd, the captain and some others went on shore, and saw a few of the natives but could not get near them. We saw too, about twenty of them from the ship, who stood gazing at us upon the beach; also smoke arising out of the woods, which perhaps was only an artifice of theirs, to make us think that they were numerous. We observed nothing worthy of note on land, excepting a great variety of plants; one of which bore fruit like a small crab-apple having a large stone in it, the Eawharra of Otaheite, and the dung of some quadruped that fed on grass [Eaaawharra = *Pandanus-tectorius*]. We hauled the seine, and tore it in pieces, but caught no fish: though we saw great shoals of them in this bay, they would not take the bait. We found a nautilus pompilius, and some curious kind of hammer oysters; as also a number of porpoises. We shot a duck of beautiful plumage, with a white beak, black body, and white and green on the wings. We likewise shot another large bird, of the bustard kind, coloured black, white and brown, which weighed seventeen pounds. The hills seen in this bay, which was called Bustard Bay, appeared very barren, having nothing on them but a few diminutive shrubs; but we saw a large tract of low and flat land, that was covered with small wood, had several lagoons on it, and some of the kind of plants which grow on the island of Otaheite and in the East-Indies.

The Orton affair shows how great and unenviable the pressure placed upon a commander in such isolation. Faced with insufficient evidence upon which to take conclusive action, he is nevertheless obliged, for the safety and welfare of the ship, to take firm action that will have a salutary effect upon the general morale, and leave no doubt about the state of discipline in the ship. Magra offered Cook his only opportunity for this. But, having exercised his discipline, he did not remain adamant about it—an expedient may be one thing; but justice is another. On June 14th, a marginal note in the Captain's journal states, 'This day I restored Mr Magra to his Duty as I did not find him guilty of the crimes laid to his charge.' The affair was never cleared up and only the participants would ever know the truth. Parkinson notes in his journal at Batavia, 'One of our midshipmen ran away from us here, and it was suspected that he was the person who cut off Orton's ears.' This was Patrick Saunders who had also been disrated from midshipman to able seaman on the same day as Magra, though no mention of it is made by Cook, and no reason for it is given. It can only be surmised that there was at least suspected involvement, but no damning declarations, as in the case of Magra. By the muster list, Saunders was marked 'Run' as an able seaman, and not as a midshipman.

Cook's interpretation of Tupia's remark that the Aborigines here were 'Taata Eno's'*—'that is bad or poor people'—may not have been just what Tupia had in mind when he said it. Professor Beaglehole gives the note:* 'taata ino, *the mean or evil folk or* titi *of Tahiti, doomed as the victims of human sacrifice.' When Tupia saw the absolute primitive simplicity of the way of life of these people perhaps he saw, as an educated and politically involved priest, that they were but the destined sacrificial victims of any political and territorial ambition which righteously assumes that heaven is ever on the side of the greatest might—indeed, the doomed victims of human sacrifice.*

SHIP'S LOG:

THURSDAY, MAY 24TH, 1770

H.	K.	F.	Courses.	Winds.	Soundings.	Remarks &c.
					Fathoms.	
1	..	..	..	..	..	Light airs and fair wea'r. Hove in to ⅓ of a cable.
2	..	..	..	E.S.E.	..	
3	..	..	..	..	..	
4	..	..	..	..	..	The capt'n and 2nd lieut't returned, the latter in the yawl, who had met with no success in fishing.
5	..	..	..	..	..	
6	..	..	..	..	..	
7	..	..	..	..	..	
8	..	..	..	..	..	
9	..	..	..	..	..	
10	..	..	..	..	..	
11	..	..	..	..	..	
12	..	..	..	S.W.	..	Mod. breezes and fair wea'r.
1	..	..	..	..	..	
2	..	..	..	..	..	
3	..	..	..	S.E.	..	
4	..	..	..	..	..	½-p't, weighed and made sail out of the bay.
5	..	..	..	..		
	1	2	N.	..	from	
6	3	2	..	..	15	Saw a ledge of breakers laying off the N. ext's of the bay.
7	1	6	N.W.b W.	..	to	½-p't 7, run past them.
	1	6	N.N.W.	..	20	
8	2	..	..	..	20	
	2	..	W.b.N.			
9	3	2	..	..	19, 17	
10	2	6	..	..	17, 16	
11	2	3	..	..	16, 15	
12	2	..	..	..	14½	At noon, light breezes and pleas't wea'r. The W. point of the bay sail'd from S. 54 E., and the N. ext'm of the land N. 68 W. Dist. off the near't, 4 leagues. Lat'de obs'd, 23° 52′ S.

COOK:

In the PM I was employed ashore in the transactions before related. At 4 in the AM we weighed with a gentle breeze at south and made sail out of the Bay. In standing out our soundings were from 5 to 15 f^{m}, when in this last depth we were abreast of the north point and being daylight discovered breakers stretching out from it about NNE 2 or 3 miles. At the outermost part of them is a rock just above water, in passing these rocks at the distance of half a Mile we had from 15 to 20 fathom, being past them we hauled along shore WNW for the farthest land we had in sight. At noon we were by observation in the Latitude of 23° 52′ S, the north point of *Bustard Bay* bore S 62° East distant 10 miles and the northermost land in sight N 60° W. Long^{de} in 208° 37′ W, distant from the nearest shore 6 miles, in this situation we had 14 fathom water.

BANKS:

At daybreak we went to sea. The weather was fine; we however were too far from the land to distinguish any thing but that there were some fires upon it tho not many. At dinner we eat the Bustard we had shot yesterday, it turned out an excellent bird, far the best we all agreed that we have eat since we left England, and as it weighed 15 pounds our dinner was not only good but plentyfull.

PARKINSON:

On the 24th, in the morning, we weighed anchor, and left this bay. At noon, we were becalmed, and caught, with hook and line, several sorts of beautiful-coloured fishes. We saw some very large pelicans, which were near five feet high, and the tail of some quadruped, which we supposed to be a guanica. The latitude 23° 51′ the land tended away from the sandy point in the great bay to the north-west.

The Captain named the south point of Bustard Bay South Head*, and the north point* North Head*; but today South Head is called Round Hill Head, and North Head is called Bustard Head. On Round Hill Head there is now a monument to commemorate Cook's landing there. At noon the ship was about 3 miles east of where the light-buoy at the entrance to the South Channel to Gladstone now is, and almost in line with the present leading lights for the channel.*

SHIP'S LOG:

FRIDAY, MAY 25TH, 1770

H.	K.	F.	Courses.	Winds.	Soundings.	Remarks, &c.
					Fathoms.	
1	..	..	Calm, s's h'd	N.E.	15	Fine clear wea'r. Caught some fish of the snapper kind.
2	..	..	..	..	..	
3	..	..	..	..	..	
4	..	..	..	..	..	

H.	K.	F.	Courses.	Winds.	Soundings.	Remarks, &c.
5	..	..	..	..	..	½-p't, the exts. of the land from the masthead from N.W.b.W. to S.E.
6	1	4	N.W.	S.E.	14 } hard	
7	1	4	..	..	14½ } sand.	Light airs and clear.
8	2	..	..	..	14½	
9	2	..	..	..	15	
10	2	4	..	..	15	Bro't too.
11	..	..	up E't	off E.b.N.	15	
12	..	..	..	..	15¼	
1	..	..	..	..	16¾	Wore ship.
2	..	..	up W.S.W.	off W.b.S.	15	
3	..	..	..	..	14½	
4	..	..	..	..	14½	
5	..	..	..	..	14¾	Mod't and fair wea'r. Made sail.
6	2	..	N.W.	S.S.W.	15	
7	3	4	W.N.W.	..	16	At 7, a headland with one in a bluff, W.b.N.
8 {	2	..	..	..	17	
	1	6	W b.N.	..	17	
9	3	6	..	..	16, 15	Saw more land to the N.W., mak'g like high isl'ds.
10	2	..	W't	..	{ 14, 13, 12 12, 10, 9 }	Variat'n p'r amp'de and sev'l azym'ths, 7° 20' E't.
11	2	..	.	S.E.	8½, 7, 6¾	At 11, steering between the main and some rocky islands.
12	1	6	..	E't	7, 8, 8½, 9	At noon { The So'm't land in sight S. 66° E. An island abreast, N. 12° E., 2 or 3 m's. The No. extr. of the land (an isl'd) N.19 W't. The main dist. 5 miles. Lat'de obs'd, 23° 24' So.

COOK:

In the PM had it calm untill 5 oClock when a light breeze sprung up at SE and we steered NW as the land lay untill 10 oClock, then brought too having had all along 14 and 15 fathom water. At 5 in the AM made sail, at daylight the nothermost point of the Main bore N 70° West and soon after we saw more land making like Islands bearing NWbN. At 9 oClock we were abreast of a point distant from it 1 Mile, depth of water 14 fathom. I found this point to lay directly under the Tropick of *Capricorn* and for that reason I called it by that Name. Long^{de} 209° 0' West. It is of a moderate height and looks white and barren and may be known by some Islands which lays to the NW of it and some small rocks one League SE from it. On the west side of the Cape there appeared to be a Lagoon, on the two spits which formed the entrance were a great number of Pelicans at least so I call them. The most northermost land we could see bore from *C. Capricorn* N 24° West and appeared to be an Island, but the Main land trended WbN½N which course we steered having from 15 to 6 fathom and from 6 to 9 a hard sandy bottom. At noon our Latitude by observation was 23° 24' S, *C. Capricorn* bore S 60° East distant 2 Leagues, a small Island NbE 2 miles. In this situation had 9 f^{m} water at the distance of 4 miles from the Main land, which is here low and sandy next the Sea, except the points which are moderately high and rocky; in land the Country is hilly and affords but a very indifferent prospect.

BANKS:

In the evening it was calm and we caught some fish tho not many. Land in the morn rocky, varied here and there with reddish sand, but little wood was to be seen.

PARKINSON:
On the 25th, in the forenoon, we crossed the Tropic of Capricorn. The land appeared very desolate, being little else than sand and rocks, parcelled out into several islands and ragged points.

Cook's identification of Cape Capricorn was by 'some Islands which lays to the NW of it', being Hummocky Island and Ship and Fairway Rocks; and 'some small rocks one league SE from it' which was Rundle Island, now lighted. But the Captain did not name either of these features. Flinders later named Hummocky Island. From noon the ship had sailed along the seaward sides of Facing (which shelters the port of Gladstone) and Curtis Islands, and there was no way that Cook could have guessed at the narrow mangroved channel which separated them from the main. The lagoon west of Cape Capricorn is a mangrove swamp occupying almost all of the north coast of Curtis Island. At noon the ship was just off the delta and shoal mouth of the Fitzroy River. A few miles up this river, at the point of a rocky barrier in it, stands the town and port called Rockhampton. Noon bearings were on Cape Capricorn and Hummocky Island. Parkinson's description of the shoreline is most apt. It was Flinders in a more detailed survey who, in 1802, charted the channel between Curtis Island and the main running from Keppel Bay to Port Curtis, 'a channel of communication cutting off Cape Capricorn with a piece of land twenty-five miles in length, from the continent.'

SHIP'S LOG:

SATURDAY, MAY 26TH, 1770

H.	K.	F.	Courses.	Winds.	Soundings.	Remarks, &c.
					Fathoms.	
1	2	..	W.N.W.	E.S.E.	H'd sand. 9½, 10, 11	Light breezes and pleas't weather.
2	2	..	..	..	Soft g'd.12, 13, 14, 15	
3	1	..	..	..	Do. gd. 15, 14, 12, 10½	
4	1	..	..	..	Do. g'd. 10½, 11½, 12½	Calm and clear wea'r.
5	..	..	..	..	..	Variation p'r amplit'd and azym'ths, 7° 28′ E't.
6	..	..	..	..	..	Came too with the b't bower in 13 fat'm water, soft s'd. The isl'd pass'd at noon bearing E. 3 or 4 m's; the No. isl'ds N. b.W.4 leagues. Found the tide set as p'r column. At 11, it was high-water. Found the tide had flowed 6 feet 3 inches.
7	1		W't.	Flood.		
8	1	4	..		..	
9	..	..	..	..	..	
10	..	..	..	..	..	
11	..	..	..	..	..	
12	..	..	..	..	..	
1	..	..	..	Ebb		
2	1	6	E't.		..	Light breezes at S.W. Found the ebb as p'r column. At 4, found the water fallen 7 foot; ¼-past 5, was slack tide. Began to heave.
3	..	..	..			
4	..	..	..	..	..	

H.	K.	F.	Courses.	Winds.	Soundings.	Remarks, &c.
5	..	..	..	..	..	
6	..	..	..	..	..	Weighed and came to sail with a mod't breeze and clear wea'r.
7	3	4	W.N.W.	So.	13, 12, 12½, 14, 10	
8	4	..	..	..	10, 9½, 9, 7, 8, 7	At 11, upon shoaling our water to ¼ less 5, shorten'd sail, lower'd down the yawl, and sent a m'te in her to sound ahead.
9	4	..	N.W.	S.S.E.	7, 8, 8½, 6, 6½, 6	
10	4	..	N.W.b.N.	..	10, 9, 8, 6, 6½, 6	From 9 till 12, sailing betw'n some isl'ds and the m'n, each dist. 4 m's. Sound'gs as p'r column.
11	{1	6	..	..	6½, 6,	
	1	5	N.N.W.½ W	..	6½, 6¼, 6, 6, 5½, 5½ 5¼, 5, 5	
12	{1	1	..	..	5½, 5½,	At noon { A remarkable peak N. 25 W't, the No'm'st land in sight N. b.W.½ W., shore dist. 4 miles. Lat'de obs'd, 23° 06′ So.
	1	2	..	..	5¼, 5, 5½, 6, 7, 8, 7 6½, ¼, 7, 6, 5½, 4, 5, 7, 4½	

COOK:

In the PM had a light breeze at ESE with which we stood NW untill 4 oClock when it fell calm and soon after we anchored in 12 fathom water, *Cape Capricorn* bearing S 54° East distant 4 leagues, having the main land and islands in a manner all round us. In the night we found the tide to rise near 7 feet and the flood to set to the westward and Ebb to the Eastward, which is the very reverse to what we found it when at Anchor to the Eastward of Bustard Bay. At 6 in the AM we weighed with the wind at South a gentle breeze and stood away to the NW between the outermost rainge of Islands and the main land, leaving several small islands between us and the latter, which we passed close by. Our soundings was a little irregular from 12 to 4 fathom which caused me to send a boat ahead to sound. At Noon we were about 3 miles from the Main and about the same distance from the Islands without us, our Latitude by observation was 23° 7′ S and Longitude made from *Cape Capricorn* 18 miles west. The main land in this latitude is tolerable high and mountainous and the Islands which lay off it are the most of them pretty high and of a small circuit and have more the appearance of barrenness than fertility. We saw smooks a good way inland which makes me think that there must be a River, Lagoon or Inlet into the country and we passed two places that had the appearance of such this morning, but our depth of water at that time was too little to haul in for them where I might expect to meet with less.

BANKS:

In the evening it was calm, some few fish were caught. At night perceiving the tide to run very strong we anchored. No fires were seen the whole day.

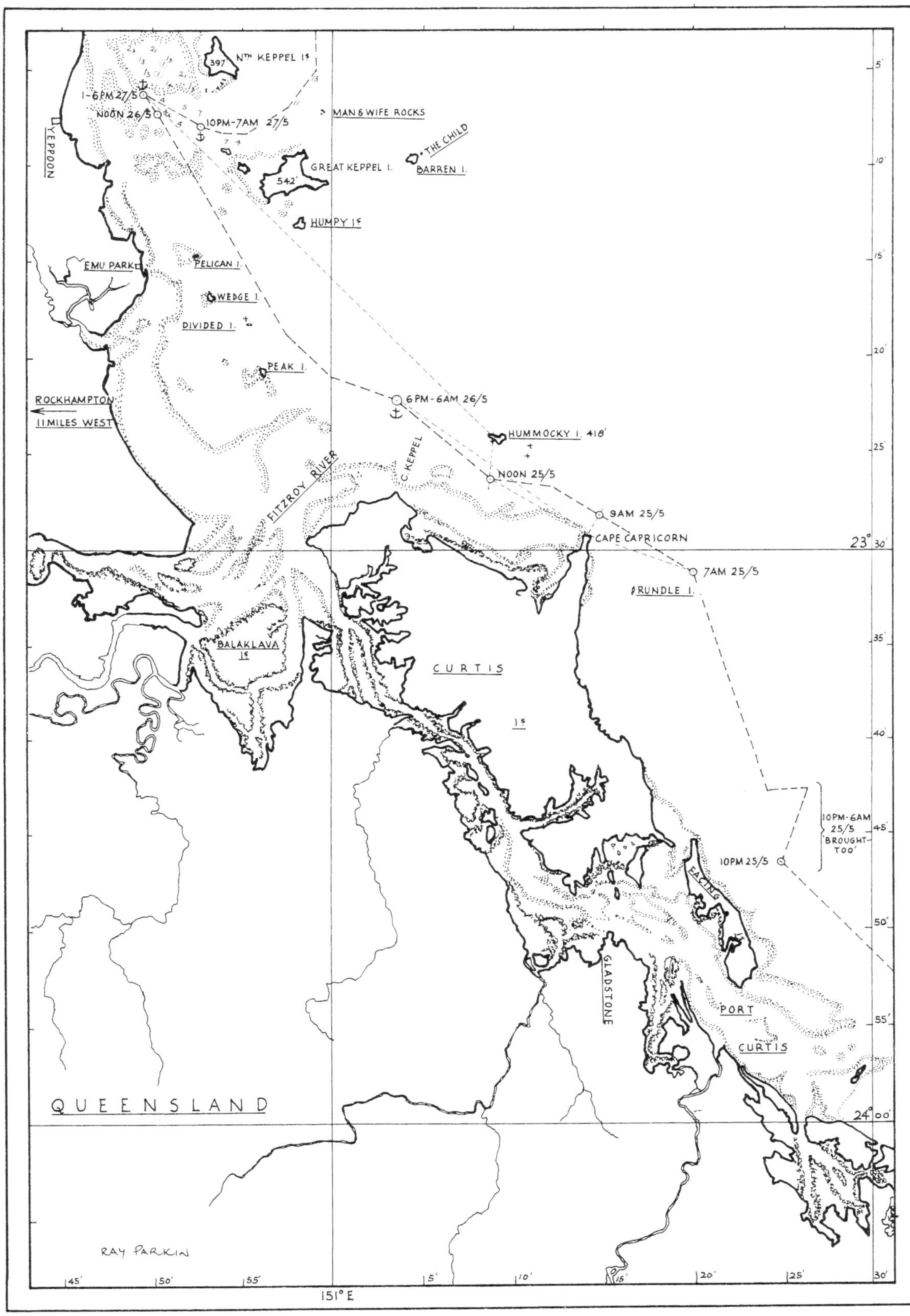
NTH KEPPEL IS
397'
1-6PM 27/5
NOON 26/5
10PM-7AM 27/5
MAN & WIFE ROCKS
THE CHILD
YEPPOON
GREAT KEPPEL I.
542'
BARREN I.
HUMPY IS
EMU PARK
PELICAN I.
WEDGE I.
DIVIDED I.
PEAK I.
ROCKHAMPTON
11 MILES WEST
6PM-6AM 26/5
HUMMOCKY I. 418'
C. KEPPEL
NOON 25/5
FITZROY RIVER
9AM 25/5
CAPE CAPRICORN
23° 30'
7AM 25/5
RUNDLE I.
BALAKLAVA IS
CURTIS
IS
10PM-6AM 25/5 'BROUGHT-TOO'
10PM 25/5
FACING
GLADSTONE
PORT
CURTIS
QUEENSLAND
24° 00'
RAY PARKIN
151° E

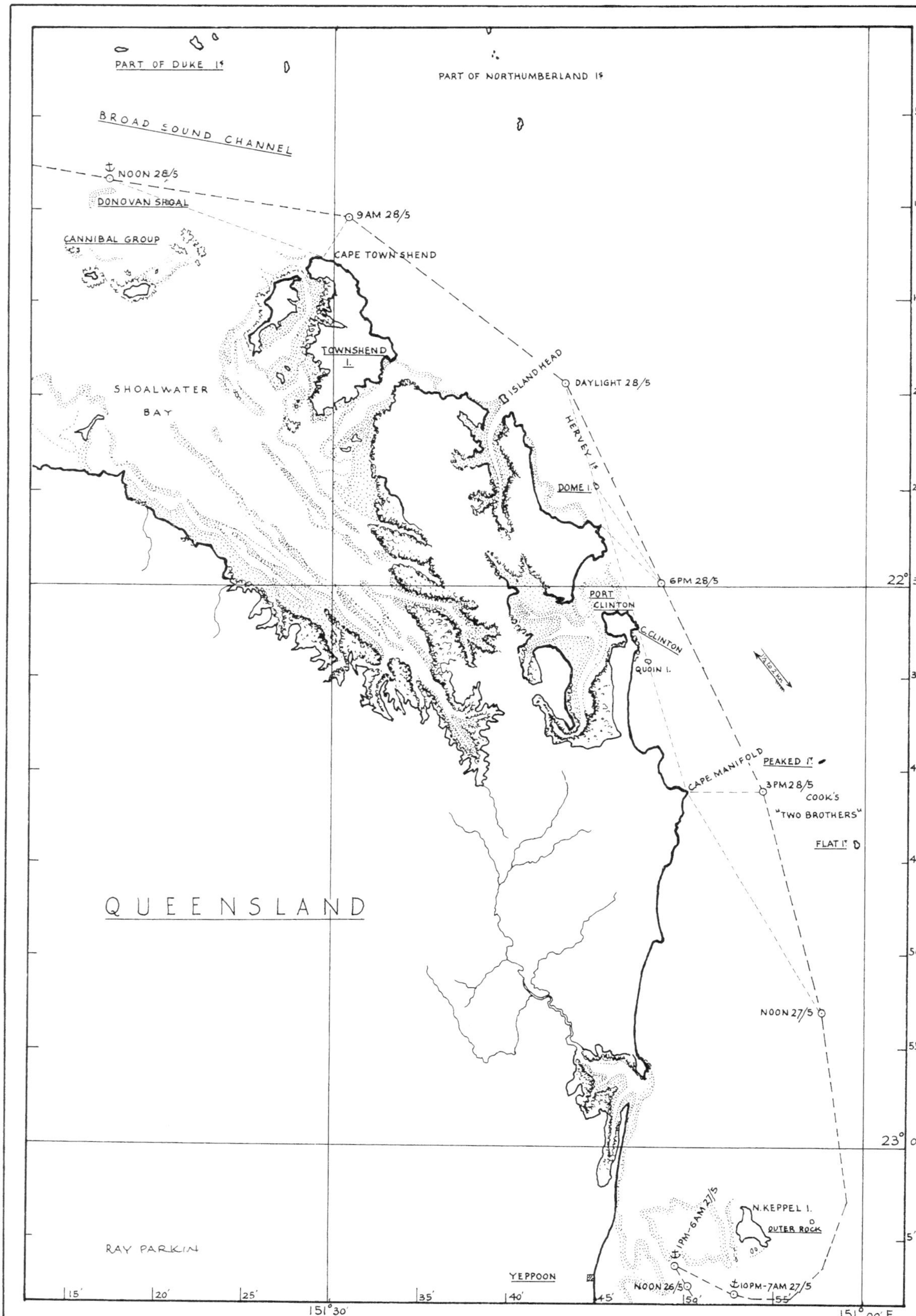
PART OF DUKE Is
PART OF NORTHUMBERLAND Is
BROAD SOUND CHANNEL
NOON 28/5
DONOVAN SHOAL
9AM 28/5
CANNIBAL GROUP
CAPE TOWNSHEND
TOWNSHEND I.
ISLAND HEAD
DAYLIGHT 28/5
SHOALWATER BAY
HERVEY Is
DOME I.
6PM 28/5
PORT CLINTON
C. CLINTON
QUOIN I.
CAPE MANIFOLD
PEAKED Is
3PM 28/5
COOK'S "TWO BROTHERS"
FLAT Is
QUEENSLAND
NOON 27/5
N. KEPPEL I.
OUTER ROCK
RAY PARKIN
YEPPOON
NOON 26/5
10PM-7AM 27/5
5'
10'
15'
20'
25'
22° 30'
35'
40'
45'
50'
55'
23° 00'
151°30'
151° 00' E

We examined the orange juice and brandy which had been sent on board as prepared by Dr Hulmes directions. [See Hulme's letter, p. 254.] It had never been moved from the cag [keg] in which it came on board. About ½ of it had been used or leaked out; the remainder was covered with a whitish mother but otherwise not damaged at all either to taste or sight when it came out of the cag, but when put into a bottle in 3 or 4 days it became ropey and good for nothing. On this we resolved to have it evaporated immediately to a strong essence and put up in bottles immediately.

AM: Standing into a channel with land on both sides of us and water very shoal, many rocky islets, main very rocky and barren; at 1 the water became so shallow that we came to an anchor.

PARKINSON:

On the 26th, we got among a parcel of Islands, to get clear of which we proposed going by a passage to the north-west which was next to the main . . .

By 6 PM, when the ship anchored north of Cape Keppel, she was off the channel leading into the Fitzroy River; she had made only 6 miles to the WNW since noon. Cook's surmise regarding the low lying parts about its lower reaches were correct, though it was based on his observation of the smokes which indicated to him the cooking fires of the Aborigines who, he thought, mainly got their living from the produce of shallow water. The tide flow he observed was to and from these shallows. From the time of weighing anchor the following morning he was soon in very shoal water and the leadsmen had no rest. The small islands between the ship and the main on his larboard hand were: Peak, Divided, Wedge and Pelican Islands, after which he had the Keppel Isles to seaward on his starboard hand. Unknowingly the Captain was sailing right into a cul-de-sac. Though the entry for the day is short, conditions called for the utmost attention and reading of signs in a way that had to be almost wholly intuitive. The Captain had to anticipate because he had only his anchors to bring him up, which they could not do in an instant, especially as he was sailing to leeward. He could not steer or carry way in any direction he liked, but was constantly constricted by the wind and tide. One should always remember this when looking at his track on a modern chart, for it is so easy to imagine that he possessed such a chart and was piloting a powered vessel. He had nothing on paper, he had the land he could see; but what was most important of all, and upon which his survival depended, was completely invisible and unknown, hidden beneath the obscuring surface of the sea. The tallow-armed leads could tell him the nature of the bottom, and the marked line the water he had under him, chanted by the singing voices of the leadsmen in the chains. But what was ahead (apart from what he could learn from the boats when they were sent ahead) was, at best, a calculated guess. It is no trite phrase to say that danger was always imminent. It takes a special sort of man to be able to live with this responsibility, day and night for months on end. It takes a devotion to one's calling not cheaply bought.

At noon the ship was 4 miles east of the present small town of Yeppoon, and between North and Great Keppel Islands, and standing right on to the shoals which block the passage between North Keppel and the mainland.

Dr Hulme's letter, referred to by Banks this day, is worth quoting in relation to the scurvy problems:

Sir,

The vessels containing the orange and lemon juice which were sent to you by order of Dr. Fothergill were to be marked, that you might know their contents. But least, in the hurry of sending them, that circumstance should have been neglected, I will take the liberty to explain them. N° 1. The Case contains six gallons of Lemon-juice evaporated down to less than two gallons. N° 2. The large Cask contains seven gallons of Orange-juice and one of Brandy. N° 3. The small Cask contains five Quarts of Lemon-juice and one of Brandy.—When you come to make use of the juice which is in the Casks, do not open the bunghole but draw it off at the end of the Cask, by means of a wooden-cock, and make a vent-hole at the top of the Cask, with a peg in it, and always observe this method when you draw off your Juice which you keep in Casks. You may find the proper directions for the preservation of the juice in Casks, in the Proposal for preventing the Scurvy, p. 67, 82, 83. It would not be amiss, then, if you were to take out with you several wooden Cocks, *least any should be lost or broken: and perhaps 2 or 3 strong iron-bound Casks, holding ten Gallons a piece might be very useful for taking-in a quantity of orange, lemon or lime Juice, when you touch at any place abroad where those Fruits grow; for the directions on this head see the Proposal p. 82.—Besides the Juices, I would recommend to you carry out a quantity of Molasses, and two or three pounds of the best Chio and Strasburgh Turpentine, in order to brew Beer with, for your daily drink, when your water becomes bad. The rules for brewing this kind of Beer you will find in the Appendix to the Proposal. In this case you will want Yeast, and the manner of preserving this at sea you may also meet with in the Appendix p.103. So small a quantity of Molasses as two Gallons, or two Gallons and an half are said to be sufficient for making a hogshead of tolerably good Beer. And this method of brewing Beer at sea, will be peculiarly useful in case you should have stinking water on board; for I find by Experience that the smell of stinking water will be entirely destroyed by the process of fermentation. I sincerely wish you and your companions a most prosperous Voyage, and a safe return to old England, loaded with all the honours you so justly deserve; and am,*

Sir,
Your most humble servant
N. Hulme.
Hatton-Garden,
Aug[t] 1[t] 1768.

SHIP'S LOG:

SUNDAY, MAY 27TH, 1770

H.	K.	F.	Courses.	Winds.	Soundings.	Remarks, &c.
					Fathoms.	
1	1	4	N.N.W.	S.S.E.	4¾, 4½, 4, 3¾, 3½	Little wind and fair wea'r. Came too with the b't bow'r in 3½ fa'm water. Sent the pinnace and yawl to the no'-ward to sound the passage. In the evening they return'd. The master reported the passage a bad one.
2	..	..	..	..		
3	..	..	..	..	..	
4	..	..	..	..	..	
5	..	..	..	..	..	
6	..	..	..	..	..	Weigh'd and made sail. Light airs and fair wea'r. The pinnace and yawl on the bows sounding.
7	1	3	S.E. ½ S.	E.N.E.	3½, 4, 4½, 4¾, 5	
8	1	2	..	..	5¼, 5½, 5¾	
9	1	2	..	..	6, 6¼, 6¾	
10	..	3	..	..	..	
	..	..	..	..	6, 5½, 6½	Came too with the b't b'r in 6½ fa'm, and veer'd to ¼ of a cable.
11	..	..	..	Southerly.	..	Light airs.
12	..	..	..	.	..	
1	..	..	..	..	..	
2	..	..	..	..	..	
3	..	..	..	..	..	
4	..	..	..	..	..	
5	..	..	..	..	..	
6	..	..	..	..	..	
7	1	..	E.b.S.	S.b.E.	4, 4,	Mod. breezes and fair wea'r. Weighed and made sail, the pinnace and yawl, with the ma'r and a m'te, sounding for a passage to the eastward between the islands. At 10, running between the islands. The yawl and pinnace return'd. Hoisted them in and set ye steering sails. The outerm't island S.E.3 or 4 m's. 13 fa'm water at ½ 11.
	1	3	E't	..	4½, 5, 5, 5, 6, 6, 5½	
8	1	5	E.N.E.	..	5½, 6, 6	
	1	6	N.E.b.E.	..	6½, 7, 7½	
9	3	4	N.E.	..	8, 8, 8½, 9, 10, 11, 12, 13	
10	1	4	..	..	12, 12½,	
	1	..	No.	..	11, 12, 13, 13, 13, 13	
11	3	6	..	..	14, 15, 15½	At noon: No g'd with the hand-line. The No ext. of the land N.32 W. Two small islands, the one No., the other N.12° E. Shore distant 4 leagu's. Lat'd obs'd, 22° 53' So.
12	4	2	..	..	15	

COOK:

We had not stood on to the northward quite an hour before we fell into 3 fathom water, upon which I anchored and sent away the Master with two boats to sound the channel which lay to leeward between the northermost Island and the mainland, which appeared to me pretty broad; but I suspected it was shoal and so it was found, for the Master reported to me on his return that he found in many places only 2½ fathoms, and where we lay at anchor we had only 16 feet which was not more than 2 feet more than the Ship drawed. In the evening the wind veered to ENE which gave us an opportunity to stretch 3 or 4 miles back the way we came before the wind shifted to the south and obliged us again to anchor in 6 fathom. At 5 oClock in the AM I sent away the Master with two boats to search for a passage out between the Islands while we got the Ship under sail. As soon as it was light the Signal was made by the boats of their having found a passage upon which we followed with the Ship. After we got out into deep water we hoisted the boats and made sail to the northward as the land lay, soundings 9 to 15 fathoms, having still some small islands without us. At noon we were about 2 Leagues from the main land by observation in the Latitude of 22° 53′ S, Longitude made from *Cape Capricorn* 20 miles west. At this time the northermost point of land we had in sight bore NNW distant 10 miles, this point I named *Cape Manyfold* from the number of high hills over it. Latitude 22° 43′ S. It lies N 26° West distant 17⅓ Leagues from *C. Capricorn*, between them the shore forms a large bay which I called *Keppel Bay* and the Islands which lay off it are known by the same name. In this bay is good anchorage where there is a sufficient depth of water. What refreshments it may afford for shipping I know not, we caught no fish here notwithstanding we were at anchor. It can hardly be doubted but what it affords fresh water in several places as both main land and Islands are inhabited; we saw smooks by day and fires in the night upon the main and people upon one of the islands.

BANKS:

Standing into a channel with the land on both sides of us and water very shoal, many rocky islets, the mainland very rocky and barren; at 1 the water became so shallow that we came to an anchor. While the ships boats were employed in sounding round about her, myself in my small boat went a shooting and killed several boobies and a kind of white bird called by the seamen Egg Bird, *Sterna* . . . [Crested Tern]. Before I went out we tried in the Cabbin to fish with hook and line but the water was too shoal (3 f^{hm}) for any fish. This want was however in some degree supplied by Crabs of which vast numbers were on the ground who readily took our baits, and sometimes held them so fast with their claws that they suffered themselves to be hawled into the ship. They were of 2 sorts, *Cancer pelagicus* Linn. and another much like the former but not so beautifull. The first was ornamented with the finest ultramarine blew conceivable with which all his claws and every joint was deeply tinged; the under part of him was of a lovely white, shining as if glazed and perfectly resembling the white of old China; the other had a little of the ultramarine on his Joints and toes and on his back 3 very remarkable brown spots [*Portunus sanguinolentus* Herbst]. 2 fires were seen upon an Island, and those who went to sound in the boats saw people upon an Island also who called to them and seemed very desirous that they should land.—In examining a fig which we had found at our last going ashore, we found in the fruit of it a Cynips, very like if not exactly the same species with the *Cynips sycomori* Linn. [possibly a Moreton Bay Fig] described by Haselquist in his *Iter Palestinum*; strong proof of the fact that figgs must be impregnated by means of Insects, tho indeed that fact wanted not any additional proofs.

The boats who sounded yesterday [in the PM] having brought back word that there was no passage ahead of the Ship, we were obliged to return, which we did and soon fell in with the main land again which was barren to appearance; on it we saw some smoaks. We passed by many islands.

PARKINSON:

. . . but finding our water shoal very much, we sent some men in a boat ahead of us, to sound, and came into three and two and a half fathom water. They returned with an account that there was hardly water enough; so we tacked about and stood out. The next morning we had a fine breeze and went through a passage to the north-east, between two islands: in this sound the tide fell thirteen feet. Our people, who went off in the boat, saw many of the natives on one of the islands, and they hallooed to them: they were of the same sort as those we had seen before. On the land round about, we saw both high and low ridges, with some peaks: part of it was well covered; though there appeared some large patches of white sand. Latitude 22° 52′.

It was fortunate that the offshore wind came that evening though ever so lightly, yet the Captain did not miss the opportunity to make the most skilful use of it. In the four hours, with the boats ahead, the ship made her way to the SE and into deeper water between North and Great Keppel Isles, no more than four miles, but so vital to the ship. In the morning, with the boats ahead and with careful shiphandling, the ship made her way EbS, E, NEbE, NE and then North, which took her round North Keppel inside Man and Wife Rocks and clear of Outer Rock. With the ship's head north and the wind at sbE, she set steering sails and made 3 ½ to 4 knots with a light wind. All this seems deceptively simple on paper and after the event. It leaves unstated what could *have happened: when one is there, this is where adventure lies and adrenalin flows.*

The noon bearings this day were taken by the Captain on two islands which were kept on the starboard hand and called by him the Two Brothers. The northern one is now Peaked Islet, and the southern one Flat Islet. A third bearing was taken on Cape Manyfold still bearing that name.

Augustus Keppel (1725–86) had been around the world as a junior officer in Centurion *in 1740–44, with Lord Anson. He became a captain at nineteen, and was made a peer and appointed First Lord of the Admiralty in 1782.*

SHIP'S LOG:

MONDAY, MAY 28TH, 1770

H.	K.	F.	Courses.	Winds.	Soundings.	Remarks, &c.
					Fathoms.	
1	3	. .	N.b.W.	S.E.b.S.	20. soft g'd	Mod't breezes and pleas't weather.
2	3	4	. .	. .	22	
3	3	6	N.N.W.	S.S.E.	25	Pass'd between two small islands and the main.

H.	K.	F.	Courses.	Winds.	Soundings.	Remarks, &c.
4	3	7	. .	. .	22	
5	4	. .	. .	. .	23	½-p't, the No. ext'm of the main N. 6 W. The outer island of the No. end N. 39° E't. The S. ext'm S. ½ E. An isl'd off it S. 45 E't. At 6, in 1st and 2nd reef maintopsail and 2nd reef foretopsail, and handed the mains'l and mizentops'l and shorten'd sail.
6	4	2	. .	. .	25	
7	. .	. .	up N.E.b.E.	off N.E.b.N.	28	
8	. .	. .	. .	. .	30	
9	. .	. .	up N.E.b.E.	off N.E.	. .	
10	. .	. .	. .	. .	32	Bro't too under the two topsails, m'ntopsail to the mast.
11	. .	. .	. .	. .	. .	
12	. .	. .	. .	. .	34	Wore ship.
1	. .	. .	up S.b.W.	off S.W.b.S.	. .	
2	. .	. .	.	. .	32	
3	. .	. .	.	. .	. .	
4	. .	. .	.	. .	32	
5	. .	. .	. .	. .	30	½-p't 5, made sail. Fresh breezes and cloudy wea'r.
6	{ . .	. .	. .	. .	30	
	2	. .	W.N.W.	S.E.	. .	
7	5	2	. .	. .	30	½-p't 8, pass'd by a headland and alter'd the course, steering between some islands. Sent a m'te in the yawl ahead to sound.
8	5	6	. .	. .	24	
9	{ 2	3	. .	So.	. .	
	1	. .	W.S.W.	. .	22, 19, 17	
10	{ 2	. .	. .	. .	. .	
	1	. .	E.S.E.	. .	17, 19, 17, 10	
11	5	2	W't	E.S.E.	10 to 14, 13 and 12	At noon { Shoaling our water to 7 fa'm, and the yawl making a signal for still shoaler water, at the same time, seeing the water break close ahead, hove in stays and let go the b't b'r, veer'd to ½ a cable, and then had 3¼ fa'm. Found the tide to set from the E.S.E. and to rise fast. The No. ext'm of the main in sight N. 88 W't. Several islands to the no'w'd and so'ward; dis't from the nearest 2 or 3 m's. The yawl return'd.
12	3	. .	.	. .	12, 10, 9, 7	

COOK:

Winds at SSE a fresh breeze. At 3 oClock in the PM we passed *Cape Manifold* from which the land trends NNW, the land of this cape is tolerable high and riseth in hills directly from the Sea; It may be known by three Islands laying off it, one near the shore and the other two 8 miles out at sea, the one of these is low and flat and the other high and round. At 6 oClock we shortened sail and brought too, the northermost part of the main we had in sight bore NW and some islands laying off it bore N 31° West. Our soundings sence noon were from 20 to 25 fathoms and in the night 30 and 34 fathom. At daylight in the morning we made sail. *Cape Manifold* bearing SbE distant 8 Leagues and the Islands set last night in the same direction distant from us 4 Miles; the farthest point of the main bore N 67° W distant 22 miles, but we could see several Islands to the northward of this direction. At 9 oClock we were abreast of the above point which I named *Cape Townshend* (Latitude 22° 13′, Long^{de} 209° 48′ West); the land of this Cape is of a moderate and pretty even height and is more barren than woody. Several Islands lay to the northward of it 4 or 5 League out to sea, to the SE the shore forms a bay in the bottom of which there appeared to be an inlet or harbour. To the westward of the Cape the land trends SW½S and there forms a very large bay which turns away to the eastward and probably communicates with the inlet above mentioned and by that means makes the land of the Cape an Island. As soon as we got round this Cape we hauled our wind to the westward in order to get within the Islands which lay scattered upon and down this bay in great numbers and extend out to sea as far as we could see from the mast head, how much farther will hardly be in my power to determine, they are as various both in their height and circuit as they are numerous. We had not stood long upon a wind before we met with shoal water and was obliged to tack at once to avoid it, after which I sent a boat ahead and we bore away WbN leaving many small Islands, Rocks & shoals between us and the Main and a number of larger Islands without us. Soundings from 14 to 17 fathom sandy bottom. A little before noon the boat made a Signal for Shoal water, upon this we hauled close upon a wind to the Eastward but it suddenly fell into 3½ fathom water, upon which we immediately let go an anchor and brought the ship up with all sails standing and had then 4 fathom coarse sandy bottom; we found here a strong tide setting to the NWbW ½ W at the rate of between 2 and 3 miles an hour which was what carried us so quickly upon the Shoal. Our Latitude by observation was 22° 8′ S. *Cape Townshend* bore East 16° South distant 13 miles and the westernmost part of the main in sight W ¾ N, having a number of Islands in sight all round us.

BANKS:
In the Eve the breeze was stronger than usual with cloudy weather. This morn at daybreak the water appeared much discoloured as if we had passed by some place where a river ran into the sea; the land itself was high and abounded with hills. Soon after we came round a point into a bay in which there were a multitude of Islands. We stood into the middle of them, a boat was sent ahead to sound and made a signal for a shoal, on which the ship came too but before the anchor went she had less than 3 fathom water; the boats now sounded all round her and found she was on the shoalest part, on which the anchor was got up and we stood on.

PARKINSON:
On the 28th, resolving to keep the main close aboard, which continued tending away to the west, we got into another cluster of islands; where we were much alarmed, having but three fathoms water on a sudden, in a rippling tide: we put about, and hoisted out the boats to seek for deeper water.

At 3 PM, as the ship came abreast of Cape Manyfold, Peaked Islet, the northern of the Two Brothers, bore ENE; the southern, Flat Islet, SE; while the third and inshore island mentioned by the Captain, Quoin Island, bore NNW. At 6 PM, she was abreast of the present Port Clinton, and at daylight abreast of Island Head, which was noted on the chart but not in the Journal. The islands offshore, passed in the night, were charted as Hervey Isles, and still shown as covering all the islands from Cape Clinton to Island Head. By 9 AM, she was abreast of Cape Townshend, which, as Cook suspected, was on an island that bears the same name. Flinders found that it was separated from the main by Strong Tide Passage and called it Townshend Island, having Shoal Water Bay to the west. The ship turned west into what is now Broad Sound Channel. The sudden encounter with shoal water at noon plainly tells the kind of navigation the ship was engaged in, and the nerve required in the man who commanded her, and the competence of the ship's company who virtually became his limbs reacting to his quick decision. The nervous reaction between Captain, crew and ship was sympathetic as if within a whole: with a singleness of purpose and method. The Captain acknowledges this in his unstinting praise of the conduct of the men to the Admiralty at the end of the voyage. In this demanding situation, which kept them all stretched, the men could feel pride and satisfaction that was self-fulfilling: a rare reward.

The 'very large bay' to the west of Cape Townshend, Cook put on his chart as Shoal Water Bay, with its limits indeterminate. The groups of islands so prolific to the northward he named Northumberland Isles, as they are today. The shoal so dramatically encountered is now known as the Donavan Shoal.

SHIP'S LOG:

TUESDAY, MAY 29TH, 1770

H.	K.	F.	Courses.	Winds.	Soundings.	Remarks, &c.
					Fathoms.	
1	..	..	..	..	..	Mod. gales and cloudy weather, with drizling rain. Sent a mate in the yawl to sound.
2	..	..	..	..	..	
3	2	6	W.	E.S.E.	5, 6, 7, 9, 10, 11	Weighed and came to sail; the yawl ahead.
4	4	..	..	..	12, 14, 14	
5	3	7	..	..	12, 11, 10	
6	2	..	..	..	10, 9¾, 9¾	Came too with the b't bower in 9¾ f'ms water, and veered to ye ½ cable service. An opening in the main, which has much the appearance of a harbour, W.b.S. about a league.
	1	4	W.S.W. ½ W.	..	9, 9½, 9¾	
7	..	..	..	..	..	
8	..	..	..	..	..	
9	..	..	..	..	..	
10	..	..	..	..	..	Little wind and cloudy, with small rain.
11	..	..	..	..	..	
12	..	..	..	..	..	
1	..	..	..	..	..	
2	1	6	W.N.W., tide run.	..	..	
3	..	..	..	..	..	Slack water; found the tide had flow'd 14 feet.
4	..	..	..	S.S.E.	..	Fresh gales and cloudy weather.
5	..	..	..	..	..	The master and mate, in the pinnace and yawl, sounding the oppening set last night.
6	..	..	..	..	9¾, 10, 10 9, 7, 7	At 6, weighed and stood towards it.
7	..	..	..	..	7, 7, 6, 5, 5	
8	..	..	..	..	6, 7, 6, 5, 6	Anchor'd with the b't bower in 5 fa'm water, and veer'd to ⅓ of a cable. Extremes of the mouth of the harbour at N. 75° E. to N. 33° E., shore dis't ¼ of a mile. An island open with the harbour's mouth N. 40 E.
9	..	..	..	..	..	
10	..	..	..	..	..	¼-p't 10, slack water.
11	..	..	..	..	..	The captain, in the pinnace, and the master, in the yawl, examining the harbour.
12	..	..	S.E.	.	..	Moderate breezes and pleas't wea'r.

COOK:

Fresh gales between SSE and ESE Hazy weather with some showers of rain in the PM. Having sounded about the Ship and found that there was sufficient water for her over the shoal we at 3 oClock weighed and came to sail and stood to the westward as the land lay having first sent a boat ahead to sound. At 6 oClock we Anchored in 10 fathom water a sandy bottom about 2 miles from the Main land, the westernmost part of which bore WNW having still a number of Islands in sight a long way without us. At 5 oClock in the AM I sent away the Master with two boats to sound the entrance of an inlet which bore from us west about one League, into which I intended to go with the Ship to wait a few days until the moon increased and in the meantime to examine the country. By such time as we had got the Ship under sail the boats made a signal for Anchorage upon which we stood in with the Ship and anchored in 5 fathom water about a League within the entrance to the inlet, which we judged to be a river running a good way inland. As I observed the tides to flow and Ebb something considerable I had some thoughts of laying the Ship ashore to clean her bottom. With this in view both the Master and I went to look for a convenient place for that purpose and at the same time to look for fresh water, not one drop of which we could find, but met in several places where a ship might be laid ashore with safety.

BANKS:

Weather was hazey; at night anchored.

Early this morn we got up our anchor and stood in for an opening in which by 9 oClock we came to an anchor. We saw in coming in no signs of people. After breakfast we went ashore and found several plants which we had not seen before; among them however were still more East Indian plants than in the last harbour. One kind of grass which we had also seen there was very troublesome to us: its sharp seeds were bearded backwards and whenever they stuck into our clothes were by these beards pushed forward until they got into our flesh: this grass was so plentifull that it was hardly possible to avoid it and with the Musketos that were likewise innumerable made walking almost intolerable. We were not however to be repulsed but proceeded into the countrey. The gum trees were like those in the last bay both in leaf and producing a very small proportion of gum; on the branches of them and other trees were large ants nests made of Clay as big as a bushel, something like those described by S[r] Hans Sloanes Hist of Jamaica Voll II, p. 221, t. 258, but not so smooth: the ants also were small and had whitish abdomens. In another species of tree *Xanthoxiloidesmite*, a small sort of black ants had bored all the twigs and lived in quantities in the hollow part where the pith should be, the tree nevertheless flourishing, bearing leaves and flowers as freely and as well as upon others that were sound. Insects in general were plentifull, Butterflies especially: of one sort of these much like *P. Similis* Linn. the air was full for the space of 3 or 4 acres crowded with them to a wonderful degree: the eye could not be turned in any direction without seeing millions and yet every branch and twig was almost covered with those that sat still: of these we took as many as we chose, knocking them down with our caps or anything that came to hand. On the leaves of the gum tree we found a Pupa or Chrysalis which shone almost all over as bright as if it had been silvered over with the most burnished silver and perfectly resembled silver; it was brought on board and the next day came out into a butterfly of a velvet black changeable to blue, his wings both upper and under marked near the edges with many light brimstone coloured spots, those of his under wings being indented deeply at each end [*Euploea sylvester*]. We saw no fresh water but several swamps of salt water overgrown with mangroves; in these we found some species of shells, among the *Trochus perspectivus* Linn. Here was also a very singular Phaenomenon in a small fish of which there was a great abundance [Mud-skipper or Walking Goby]. It was about the size of a minnow in England and had two breast finns very strong. We often found him in places quite dry and where may be he had been left by the tide: upon seeing us he immediately fled from us leaping as nimbly as a frog by the help of his breast finns: nor did he seem to prefer water to land for if seen in the water he often leapd out and proceeded on dry land, and when the water was filled with small stones standing above its surface would leap from stone to stone rather than go into the water; in this manner I observed several pass over puddles of water and proceed on the other side leaping as before.

PARKINSON:

On the 29th, in the morning, we passed into a bay, which appears to be an entrance into some river, by the strong tide that runs into the channel, which fell twelve feet in six hours. The Captain intended to ground the ship here in order to clean her bottom; but . . .

Bootie's Journal for this day is headed: 'At anchor in Labyrinth Harbour'. *This suggests that this may have been the first choice of name for the place. It may also suggest that the labyrinthine nature of the navigation they were pursuing was a figure that came to the Captain's mind to describe more adequately its extraordinary character.*

From noon to 6 PM, when the ship anchored, no more than 9 miles were made. The entrance to this place was scarcely a mile across and was very little wider within. Its only recommendation could be the great rise and fall of the tide for the possibility of beaching the ship to scrape and bream her bottom, and the opportunity to refill her water.

SHIP'S LOG:

WEDNESDAY, MAY 30TH, 1770

Day and Month.	Winds.	Remarks, &c.
1770. Wednesd'y, May 30th . .	E.S.E E. S.E.	Fresh breezes and clear wea'r. At 4 the master return'd, being then high-water. At 5 a.m. the capt. went on shore to survey the harbour, and at 8 a.m. he proceeded up the river. Carpenters empl'd caulking the quick-work. Lat'de obs'd, 22° 7' S.

COOK:

In the PM I went again in search of fresh water but had no better success than before, wherefore I gave over all thoughts of laying the Ship a shore being resolved on spending as little time as possible in a place that was likely to afford us no form of refreshment, but as I observed from the hills the Inlet to run a good way inland I thought this a good time to penetrate into the Country to see a little of the inland parts. Accordingly I prepared for making that excursion in the morning, but the first thing I did was to get upon a pretty high hill which is at the NW entrance of the inlet before sunrise in order to take a view of the Sea coast and the Islands &c[a] that lay off it, and to take their bearings having the Azimuth compass with me for that purpose, the needle of which differed from its true position something very considerable even above 30° in some places more and in others less for I tried it in several. I found it differ from itself above 2 points [a point = 11 ¼ degrees] in the space of 14 feet, the loose stones that lay upon the ground had no effect upon the needle, I therefore concluded that it must be owing to the Iron ore in the hill, visible signs of which appeared not only here but in several places. As soon as I had done here I proceeded up the inlet. I set out with the first of the flood and long before high water got above 8 Leagues up it, its breadth thus far was from 2 to 5 miles upon a SWbS direction, but here it spread every way and formed a large lake which communicated with the Sea to the NW; I not only saw the Sea in this direction but found the tide of flood coming Strong from the NW. I likewise observed an arm of this lake extending to the eastward and it is not at all improbable but that it communicates with the sea in the bottom of the bay which lies to the westward of *C. Townshend*. On the south side of the lake is a ridge of pretty high hills which I was desireous of going upon, but as the day was far spent and high water I was afraid of being bewildered among the shoals in the night, which promised to be none of the best being already rainy dirty weather, and therefore I made the best of my way to the Ship. In this little excursion I saw only two people and those at a distance, but we have met with several fire places and seen smooks at a distance. This Inlet which I have named *Thirsty Sound* by reason we could find no fresh water lies in the Latitude of 22° 05′ S and Longitude 210° 24′ West. It may be known by a group of small Islands laying under the shore from 2 to 5 leagues NW from it, there is likewise another Group of Islands laying right before it 3 and 4 Leagues out to Sea.

Over each of the points that form the entrance is a pretty high round hill, that on the NW is a peninsula surrounded by the Sea at high-water, the distance from one to the other is about two mile bold to both shores. Here is a good anchorage in 7, 6, 5 & 4 fathom water and very convenient places for laying the Ship ashore where at Spring tides the tides doth not rise less than 16 or 18 feet and flows at full and change of the Moon about 11 oClock. We met with no fresh water or any other kind of refreshment whatever, we saw two turtle but caught none nor no sort of fish or wild fowl except a few small land birds. Here the same sort of water fowl as we saw in *Botany Bay* and like them so Shy that it is hardly possible to get within shott of them. No signs of fertility is to be seen upon the land, the soil of the uplands is mostly hard reddish clay and produceth several sorts of trees as we have seen before and some others and clear of all under wood. All the low lands are mostly over run with Mangroves and at spring tides over flowed by the Sea, and I believe in the rainy seasons here are large land floods as we saw in may places gullies which seemed to have been made to torrents of water coming from the adjacent hills, besides there are other visible signs of the water having been a considerable height above the common spring tides. Dr Solander and I was upon a rising ground up the Inlet which we thought had at one time or another been over flowed by the sea, and if so great part of the Country must at that time be laid under water. Up in the lakes or Lagoons I suppose are shell fish on which the few natives subsist. We found oysters sticking to most of the rocks upon the shore which were so small as not to be worth picking off.

BANKS:

In the afternoon we went ashore on the opposite side of the bay: the productions were much like those on the side we were on in the morn, but if anything the soil was rather better. In neither morning nor evening were there any traces of inhabitants ever having been where we were, except here and there trees had burnt down. AM: Went ashore in the same place as yesterday. In attempting to penetrate farther into the country it was necessary to pass a swamp covered with mangrove trees; this we attempted chearfully tho the mud under them was midleg deep, yet before we got half way over we heartily [repented of] our undertaking: so entangled were the arched branches of those trees that we were continually stooping and often slipping off from their slimey roots on which we stepped; we resolved however not to retreat and in about an hour accomplished our walk of about ¼ of a mile. Beyond this we found a place where there had been 4 small fires; near them were fish bones, shells &c. that had there been roasted, and grass laid together upon which 4 or 5 people had slept as I guessed about a fortnight before. Several of our people went ashore on liberty, one of these saw a small pool of standing water which he judged to contain about a ton. Our second Lieutenant also saw a little laying at the bottom of a gully near which were the tracks of a large animal of the deer or Guanicoe kind; he who had been in Port Desire on the coast of South America seemed inclined to think them the latter. Some Bustards were also seen but none of them shot; Great Plenty however of the Beautiful Loriquets seen in the last but one anchorage place were seen and killed. The 2nd Lieutenant and one man more who were in very different places Declared that they heard the voices of Indians near them, but neither saw the people. The country in general appeared barren and very sandy; most of the trees were gum trees but they seemed not inclined to yield their gum, I saw only one tree which did. It was most probably destitute of fresh water, probably that was the reason so few inhabitants were seen: it seemed to be subject to a severe rainy season, so at least we judged by the deep gullys which we saw had been plainly washed down from hills of small height.

Whether the sea was more fruitfull than the land we had not an opportunity to try. It did not seem to promise much as we with our hooks and lines could catch nothing, nor were there any quantity of Oysters on the shore. The tide rose very much, how high was not measured, but I think I may venture to guess not less at spring tides than 18 or twenty feet, perhaps much more.

The Captn and Dr Solander went today to examine the bottom of the inlet which appeared to go very far inland; they found it to increase in its width the farther they went into it, and concluded from that and some other circumstances that it was a channel which went through to the sea again. They saw two men who followed the boat along shore a good way but the tide running briskly in their favour they did not chuse to stop for them; at a distance from them far up the inlet they saw a large smoak. At night they returned having found neither fresh water nor any other refreshment, it was resolved to leave this place tomorrow morn.

PARKINSON:

On the 31st, we left this bay, not being able to find any fresh water, or any kind of provisions, even fish. The bay is open to the north; it is very large and deep and capable of containing a navy to anchor. There were many creeks, that seemed to end in a lagoon; but the Captain could not determine whether the inlet, that led into the country, was a river. The country about the bay is but indifferently cloathed; the trees are small; and the soil on the hills is very stoney and bare of grass under the trees. That part of the shore, which I saw, seemed to be a rock composed of broken stones, cemented together with mud. On our first view of this coast, we conceived the most pleasing hopes, but were unhappily disappointed. We saw only two of the Indians, but the marks of many more, and the footsteps of an animal that had a cloven hoof. We also saw many of the yam trees, the greater part having been stripped of the bark and several sorts of ants, some of which build their nests of earth against the side of a tree, while others make them of leaves, glued together and hung upon the branches.

More and more the voyagers were discovering the uncompromising nature of this last continent, inhabited only by adaptive and enduring species evolved uniquely over millions of years; born of itself in a triumph of emerging indefeasible life among the dry, red oxide agglomerates of hills parched for months on end. Having put itself above this patient struggle, having, as it prided itself, eaten of the fruit of the tree of knowledge, humankind had come to dream of Nature as its slave and was disappointed by a lack of the ready-made that would serve its needs. The Captain and the ship's company had been shackled to this idea; but, unlike the majority of urban humankind, were here getting a glimpse of the ultimate reality of life. It is the measure of us humans that we can be self-centredly disappointed while yet in the midst of incredible natural triumph. The impartiality of nature is too much for us; instead, we attempt to live with arbitrary human law, inevitably partial to the law-maker alone, without circumventing the fact that one man's meat is another's poison. Cook seems to have had some intuitions on the disparity between the two systems—sensitive and close as he now was to the original one.

The entrance to Thirsty Sound is between the NW *point of Shoalwater Bay, Arthur Point; and the eastern tip of Quail Island, Pier Head. Long Island lies to the west of Quail Island and is separated from it by a mangrove-fringed north-south channel; together these two islands form the north-eastern shore of the sound which issues out from mangrove swamps and shoals into Broad Sound. A peninsula of the mainland separates Broad Sound and Shoalwater Bay. Thirsty Sound, virtually connecting the two, is flanked on both sides by extensive mangrove swamps up to three thousand yards wide. The Captain was able to traverse this to the westward on the flood tide and return on the ebb. From his estimation of the breadth of the sound it would suggest that, for the past two hundred years, the mangroves have steadily invaded the shoalwater along its edges. The island that was 'open with the harbours mouth* N 40° E' *was Marble Island, the* SE *one of the Duke Islands which, in turn with several other groups, make up the Northumberland Isles. The Captain named Thirsty Sound, Long Island and Broad Sound. The north head of the sound, on the end of a spit running offshore and almost cut off at high tide, he called Pier Head, as it is known today.*

Cook climbed the 378-foot-high hill on Quail Island to take bearings of the coast and islands before sunrise, when visibility is generally better, and possibly to avoid hampering glare and glittering water from the low sun. The erratic behaviour of the compass seems unexplainable; later Flinders went there to look for an answer but did not encounter the same variations. 'But,' he wrote, 'it is to be observed that he [Cook] used a ship's azimuth compass, probably not raised further from the ground than placed on a stone, whereas my theodolite stood upon legs, more than four feet high . . . I did not find, any more than Captain Cook, that a piece of stone applied to the theodolite drew the needle at all out of its direction.'

The footprints of the quadruped were probably those of a kangaroo or wallaby, yet to become known to the European world. From Banks we get another glimpse of John Gore (second lieutenant) the hunter and fisher, and observer of natural life. From Gore himself we have nothing because, after December 7th, 1769, the rest of his journal is missing.

Chapter 7
Thirsty Sound to Trinity Bay

SHIP'S LOG:

THURSDAY, MAY 31ST, 1770

H.	K.	F.	Courses.	Winds.	Soundings.	Remarks, &c.
					Fathoms.	
..	..	..	..	S.E.b.E.	..	Fresh breezes and cloudy wea'r. P.M., had some small rain. At 6 p.m. the captain return'd, having been 8 leagues up
				E.S E.		the river or lagoon. Clear'd ship for sea. At 6 a.m. weighed
				S.E.b.E.		and came to sail. At 8 a.m. the river's mouth bore S.S.W., distance 5 miles; depth of water, 10 fa'm.
9	3	5	N.W.	S.	10, 10, 10	
10	2	..	..	..	$9\frac{3}{4}$, $9\frac{1}{2}$	Fresh breezes and cloudy weather.
	2	2	N.W. b. W	S.S.E.	..	
11	4	2	..	..	$9\frac{1}{4}$, 9	Pass'd by some rocks. Sent the pinnace ahead to sound a passage between some islands.
12	4	..	W.	..	$9\frac{1}{4}$, $9\frac{1}{2}$	At noon, do. wea'r; the port sail'd from S. 40 E. No. ext'm of the main N.E. b. W. The nearest island S.S.W. 5 miles. Lat'de obs'd, 21° 53′ S. The pinnace ahead sounding. Saw several more islands to the N.W.

COOK:

Winds southerly and SE dark hazey weather with rain in the PM. Finding no inducement to stay longer in this place we at 6 in the AM weighed and put to Sea and stood to the NW having the advantage of a fresh breeze at SSE. We kept without the group of Islands which lay in shore & to the NW of *Thirsty Sound*, as there appeared to be no safe passage between them and the main; at the same time we had a number of Islands without us extending out to sea as far as we could see. As we run in this direction our depth of water was 10, 8 and 9 fathom. At noon the NW point of *Thirsty Sound* which I have named Pier Head bore S 36° E, distant 5 Leagues, the East point of the other inlet, which communicates with the former as I have before mentioned, bore sbw distant 2½ Leagues, the group of Islands above mentioned laying between us and the point; the farthest part of the Main in sight on the other side of the Inlet bore NW. Our Latitude by observation was 21° 53′ S.

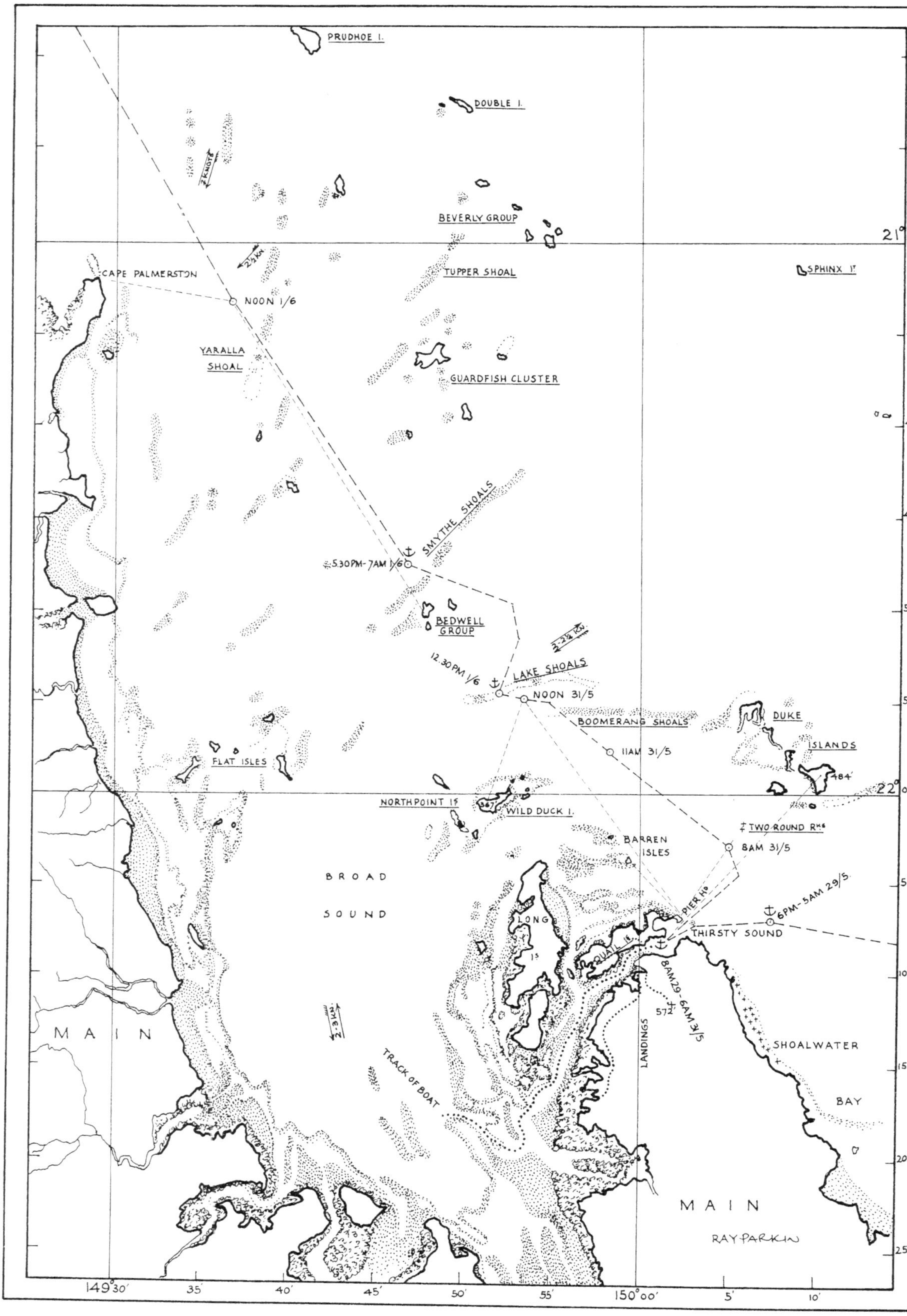
PRUDHOE I.
DOUBLE I.
BEVERLY GROUP
21° 30'
TUPPER SHOAL
SPHINX I^T
CAPE PALMERSTON
NOON 1/6
YARALLA
SHOAL
GUARDFISH CLUSTER
SMYTHE SHOALS
5.30PM-7AM 1/6
BEDWELL
GROUP
12.30PM 1/6
LAKE SHOALS
NOON 31/5
BOOMERANG SHOALS
DUKE
ISLANDS
11AM 31/5
FLAT ISLES
22° 00'
NORTHPOINT IS
WILD DUCK I.
TWO ROUND R^KS
BARREN
ISLES
8AM 31/5
BROAD
SOUND
LONG
PIER Hd
6PM-5AM 29/5
THIRSTY SOUND
8AM 29-6AM 31/5
LANDINGS
MAIN
TRACK OF BOAT
SHOALWATER
BAY
MAIN
RAY PARKIN
149°30'
35'
40'
45'
50'
55'
150°00'
5'
10'

BANKS:
Went out this morn, the weather misty and rainy and fresh breezes. As we found by experience that many sands and shoals lay off the coast a boat was sent ahead.

On departing Thirsty Sound the ship steered NNE until well clear, then NW until within a mile or two of Two Round Rocks which lie SW of Duke Islands. She then altered course to NWbW. At 11 AM, as she passed some rocks, the Duke Islands lay on the starboard quarter, and North Point Islands abeam to larboard, Wild Duck being the nearest and largest of them. Just before noon the ship unknowingly had passed over the tail of the Boomerang Shoal and shortly after she altered course to the west. Noon bearings were taken on Pier Head and Wild Duck Island. The Captain remarked, 'We kept without the Group of Islands which lay inshore & to the NW of Thirsty Sound.' These were made up of three contiguous groups—Barren Isles, North Point Isles and, inshore, the Flat Isles—making a chain across the mouth of Broad Sound. As well as these islands, the whole area is liberally strewn with reefs, shoals and rocks lying at lethal depths. This situation was to continue for the next two degrees of latitude, at least until the ship was clear of Whitsunday Passage, so that everybody was on a 'split yarn' for any emergency. (The split yarn is the way some things are secured so that, when suddenly required, they may swiftly be broken adrift rather than being untied, making for a state of instant readiness.)

SHIP'S LOG:

FRIDAY, JUNE 1ST, 1770

H.	K.	F.	Courses.	Winds.	Soundings.	Remarks, &c.
					Fathoms.	
1	..	..	Wt.	S.E.	9, 7, 5, 3	Fresh breezes and thick cloudy wea'r, with rain. ½-p't 12, shoaling our water suddingly to 5 fa'm, and the
2	..	..	..	..	..	signal being made in the pinnace for shoal water, let go the b't bower in 3 fa'm, sandy ground.
3		2	N.E.	..	4, 5, 6, 7, 8	½-past 3, weighed; the pinnace ahead. Stretch'd into the offing.
4		3	..	..	..	½-past 4, bore up for a passage between some islands.
	2	4	N.N.E.	..	9, 10, 11, 12	
5	1	6	..	..	..	
	2	4	N.b.W.	..	13, 13, 12⅓	¼-past 5, saw some rocks ahead; ½ p't, came too under the lee of an island, it bearing S.E. 1¼ miles; veered to ½ a
6	2	..	W.N.W.	..	14, 14, 15, 15½, 16	cable. At 6 it was high water, then had 16½ fa'm, gravel and shells.
7	..	..	..	..	..	
8	..	..	..	..	..	
9	..	..	..	..	..	
10	..	..	..	..	..	
11	..	..	..	..	..	
12	..	..	..	..	..	
1	..	..	..	..	..	
2	..	..	..	..	..	
3	..	..	..	Southerly.	..	

H.	K.	F.	Courses.	Winds.	Soundings.	Remarks, &c.
4	..	..	..	..	..	
5	..	..	..	..	..	
6	..	..	..	..	..	Weighed and came to sail between the islands, having the tide of ebb against us. At 9 saw the main as far as W.N.W. At 11 shoal'd our water. Hove too, and sent the yawl to the N.W. to sound.
7	1	..	N.W. ½ W.	S.S.E.	16, 15, 14, 13	
8	4	..	..	..	12, 11, 10, 9½	
9	2	..	..	..	10, 11, 12, 11	
	2	..	N.W.	..	10½, 11, 9¾, 10½, 12, 13, 12	
10	4	..	..	..	12, 9, 10½, 9¾, 10½, 10, 9½, 10, 11½	
11	4	..	N.W.b.W.	S.E.	11½, 11, 10, 11¾, 11, 10½, 9, 8¼, 8½, 9.	At noon, fresh breezes and fair wea'r. Made sail after the boat. The N.W. ext'm of ye main N. 71 W. Island sail'd from S. 32 E. Sailing between a great number of islands and the main. Dist. from the nearest island 3 or 4 miles. Lat'd obs'd, 21° 30′ S.
12	..	..	up S.b.W. ½ W.	off S.W.b.W	10, 9, 8, 7, 5, 7	

COOK:

At ½ an hour after noon upon the boat, which we had ahead sounding, makeing the Signal for Shoal water* we hauled our wind to the NE having at that time 7 fathom, the next cast 5 and then 3 upon which we let go an Anchor and brought the Ship up. The NW point of *Thirsty Sound* or *Pier Head* bore SE distant 6 leagues, being midway between the Islands which lies off the East point of the western inlet [North Point Island] and three small islands laying directly without them [Bedwell Group], it being now the first of the flood which we found set NWbW ½ W. After sounding about the shoal on which we found not quite 3 fathom [Lake Shoals] but without it deep water, we got under sail and hauled round the three Islands just mentioned and came too an anchor under the lee of them in 15 fathom water, having at this time dark hazey weather which continued until 7 oClock AM; at which time we got again under sail and stood to the NW with a fresh breeze at SSE and fair weather, having the main land in sight and a number of Islands all round us some of which lay out at sea as far as we could see. The western inlet before mentioned known in the chart by the name of *Broad Sound* we now had all open. It is at least 9 or 10 Leagues wide at the Entrance with several Islands laying in and before it and I believe shoals also, for we had very irregular soundings from 10 to 5 and 4 fathom. At noon we were by observation in the Latitude of 21 29′ S and Longitude made from *Cape Townshend* 59′ West. A point of land which forms the NW entrance into Broad Sound bore from us at this time West by North distance 3

*See illustration page 428.

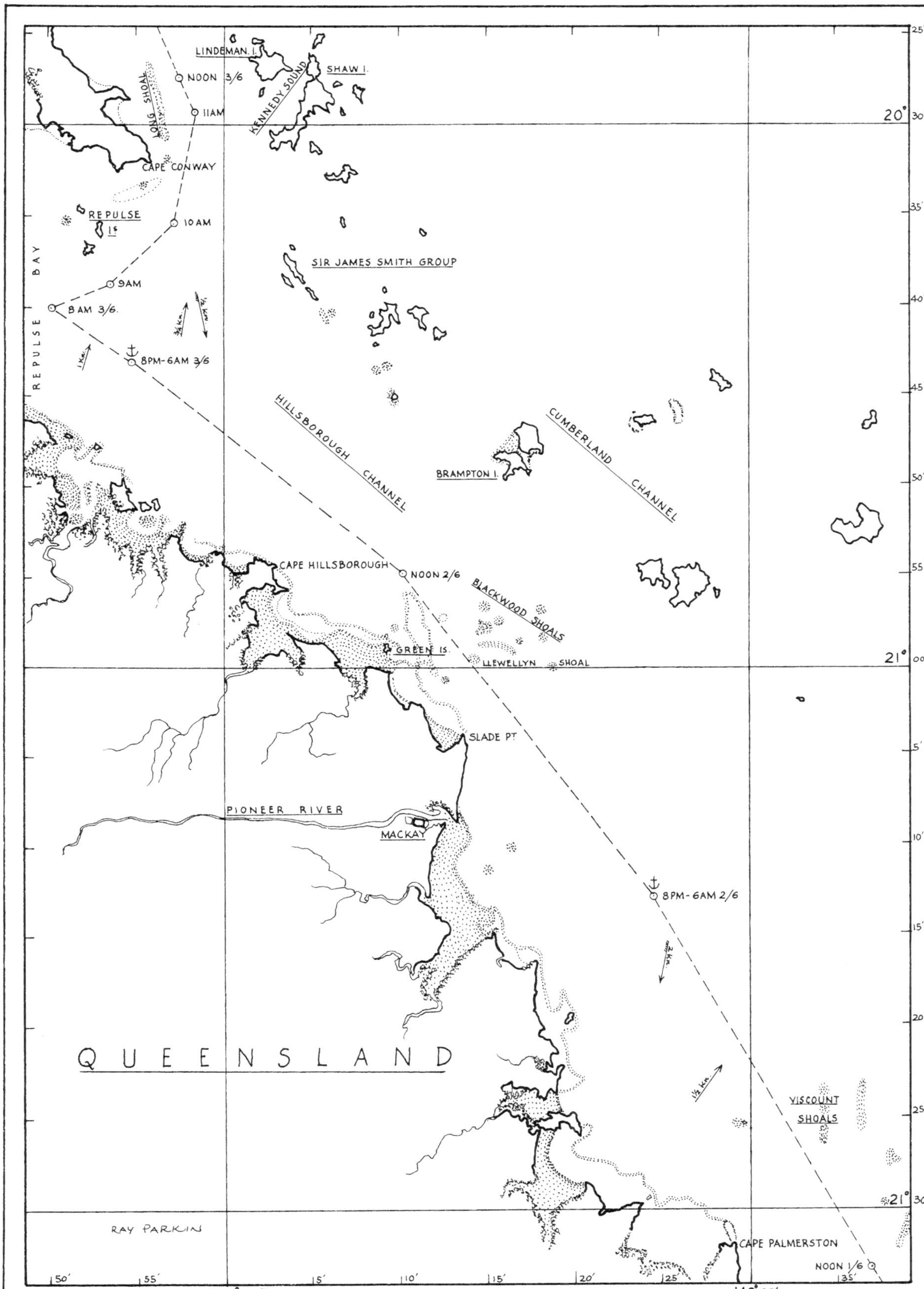
LINDEMAN I.
SHAW I.
KENNEDY SOUND
LONG SHOAL
NOON 3/6
11AM
CAPE CONWAY
REPULSE Is
10AM
REPULSE BAY
SIR JAMES SMITH GROUP
9AM
8AM 3/6.
8PM-6AM 3/6
HILLSBOROUGH CHANNEL
CUMBERLAND CHANNEL
BRAMPTON I.
CAPE HILLSBOROUGH
NOON 2/6
BLACKWOOD SHOALS
GREEN IS.
LLEWELLYN SHOAL
SLADE PT
PIONEER RIVER
MACKAY
8PM-6AM 2/6
QUEENSLAND
VISCOUNT SHOALS
RAY PARKIN
CAPE PALMERSTON
NOON 1/6
149°00' E.
149°30'
20°30'
21°00'
21°30'

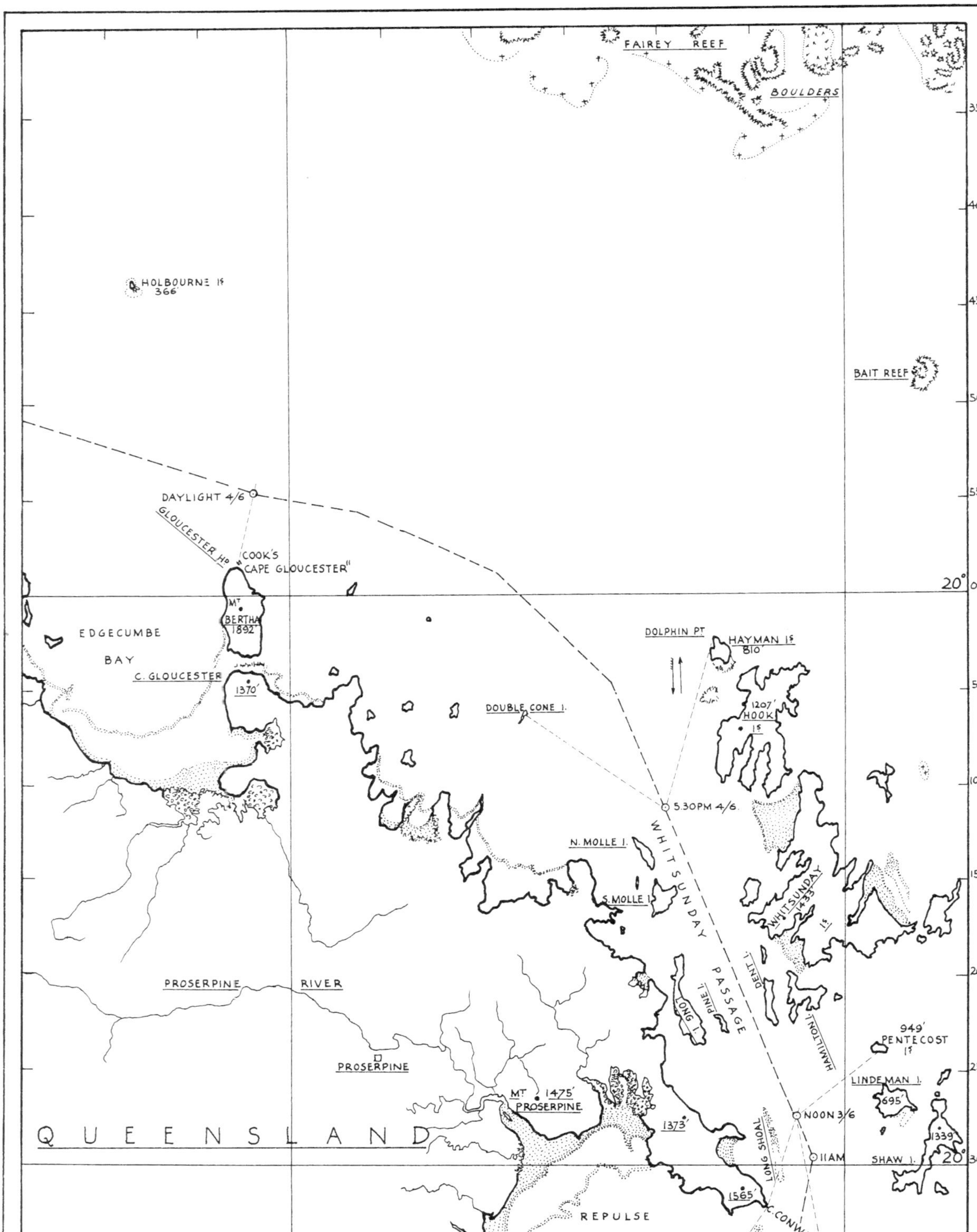
FAIREY REEF
BOULDERS
HOLBOURNE Is 366
BAIT REEF
DAYLIGHT 4/6
GLOUCESTER Hd
COOK'S "CAPE GLOUCESTER"
Mt BERTHA 1892'
EDGECUMBE BAY
C. GLOUCESTER
1370'
DOLPHIN PT
HAYMAN Is 810'
1207' HOOK Is
DOUBLE CONE I.
5.30PM 4/6
N. MOLLE I.
S. MOLLE I.
WHITSUNDAY PASSAGE
WHITSUNDAY 1433' Is
LONG I.
PINE I.
DENT I.
HAMILTON I.
PROSERPINE RIVER
PROSERPINE
Mt 1475' PROSERPINE
949' PENTECOST Is
LINDEMAN I.
695'
1339'
NOON 3/6
11AM
SHAW I.
QUEENSLAND
1373'
LONG SHOAL
1565'
C. CONWAY
REPULSE BAY
REPULSE Is
10AM
9AM
8AM 3/6.
ANCHOR Is
35'
40'
45'
50'
55'
20° 00'
5'
10'
15'
20'
25'
20° 30'
35'
40'
20'
25'
148° 30'
35'
40'
45'
50'
55'
149° E.
5'

Leagues. This point I have named *Cape Palmerston* (Latitude 21° 27′ Long[de] 210° 57′). Between this cape and Cape Townshend lies the *Bay of Inlets*, so named from the number of Inlets Creeks &c[a] in it.

BANKS:
At noon she [the pinnace] made a signal for shoal water on which we came to an anchor; the boats sounded and found a passage on which we proceeded and at night came to an anchor under the shelter of an Island, in the midst of innumerable islands, rocks and shoals. In the night it rained and at times blew strong not so much to our satisfaction who were in a situation not very desirable, as if our anchor should come home or cable break we had nothing to expect but going ashore on some one or other of the shoals which lay round us. The night passed however without the least accident, and at daylight in the morn the anchor was got up and we proceeded, in hopes of getting out of our Archipelago. By noon we got in with the main land which made hilly and barren; on it were some smoaks.

PARKINSON:
From a hill, at the entrance into the bay [Thirsty Sound], we had thirty islands in view. Through this labyrinth of Islands we passed with some difficulty, on account of the number of shoals we met with; one of which we should have been upon, had not the men in the boat given us timely notice. We were encouraged to attempt a passage through them, from an expectation, we had formed, of finding one to the north side of the land.

Again the term labyrinth *is being used, this time by Parkinson. Mr Banks, too, this day was well aware of the dangers they faced; but the rest of the journal keepers simply state the bare facts. When one looks at their situation on a modern chart one sees that Mr Banks's anxiety was well justified. Rear-Admiral Sir William J.L. Wharton, K.C.B., F.R.S. and Hydrographer to the Royal Navy (1884–1904), has remarked of this time: 'A look at a modern chart causes amazement that Cook managed to keep his ship off the ground, as the whole sea in his track is strewed with dangers.' As well, there was always the distinct possibility that, once the ground had taken hold of the ship, it would never let go. Yet, to the thoughtful and even mildly perceptive reader, the bare statements of the log-keepers are still more chillingly descriptive than any over-dramatisation ever could be. When the boat gave the signal for shoal water the ship brought up with only 4 feet of water under her keel. This was on Lake Shoals which lay completely athwart the course, and being thus cut almost in the middle. The ship had been steering a course inshore to leeward of the Bedwell Group of islands which were then on the starboard bow. They are five bare-topped islands, rocks and shoals. Having got soundings the ship weighed anchor and hauled out to windward and skirted to the east of them. At 5.30 rocks were sighted ahead, and in this area night sailing was out of the question, so the anchor was let go, since they had passed (unbeknown to the crew) through a narrow gap in the Smythe Shoals and anchored in the lee of these. After weighing again at 7 AM, the ship steered NW with rocks and islands on both sides. At noon Cape Palmerston bore WbN 9 miles on the larboard bow. Shortly before this, without remarking it, she had crossed the 3-fathom Yaralla Shoal which lay right across the course. Cape Palmerston was named after Henry Temple, Second Viscount Palmerston (1739–1802), a politician, member of the Board of Trade in 1765, and a Lord of the Admiralty 1766–77. All the coast between Cape Palmerston and Cape Townshend the Captain called the Bay of Inlets, which included Broad Sound and Shoal Water Bay. It is no longer on the charts.*

SHIP'S LOG:

SATURDAY, JUNE 2ND, 1770

H.	K.	F.	Courses.	Winds.	Soundings.	Remarks, &c.
					Fathoms.	
1	1	6	W.b.N.	S.S.E.	7, 6, 6, 6, 6	Mod. breezes and cloudy; the yaul ahead.
	1	4	N.W.b.W.	..	7, 8, 9, 9½	
2	1	..	N.W.	..	9, 8, 7, 6, 5	
	1	..				
3	3	3	..	..	5½, 6, 7, 8, 9 9, 9½, 9, 9	
4	3	4	..	..	9, 8, 10, 9½	
5	3	..	..	..	9, 10, 9½, 9	Made a signal for the yawl.
6	2	4	N.W.b.N.	..	9, 9, 9, 10	The No. ext'e of the land making like an isl'd N. 45 W.; some land making like islands N. 18 W.; same time hoisted the yawl up.
7	2	6	..	..	11, 10½, 9¾, 10, 11	
8	2	5	..	..	11, 11¼, 11¼, 11	Came too with the b't bower in 11 fa'm water and veered to the ½ cable.
9	..	..	..	..	..	
10	..	..	..	..	..	Found a slow motion of a tide setting to the Westward.
11	..	..	..	..	..	
12	..	..	..	..	..	
1	..	..	..	..	..	Slack water.
2	..	..	..	..	..	½-p't 2, the ship tended and rode ahead of her cable; found the tide had rizen 2 feet.
3	..	..	..	..	..	
4	..	..	..	..	..	
5	..	..	..	..	..	Began to heave, the tide rizen 9 feet.
6	..	..	..	..	..	Weighed, and came to sail; tide rizen 11 feet, and set strong from ye W.N.W.
7	3	4	N.N.W.	S.b.E.	11, 11½, 12, 12	Variation p'r amplit'd, 6° 45′ E't.
8	3	4	..	..	12½, 12, 11½, 10½, 10	
9	3	4	..	..	10, 10½, 11, 11¼, 11	Set steering sails.

H.	K.	F.	Courses.	Winds.	Soundings.	Remarks, &c.
10	3	3	N.W.b.N.	..	10, 10, 9½, 10, 9	Saw more land to the N.-W't.
11	3	3	N.W't	..	9, 7, 6, 6, 6, 5¼ 4¾, 5, 7, 9, 8	The ground so uneven that the yaul was sent ahead to sound.
12	2	..	..	..	8, 7, 5, 4½, 5 6, 6½, 7½, 8, 8	At noon, ext'm's of the land from N. 66° W't to S. 27° E.; the ext of a number of isl'ds from N. 51½ W. to E.; dist. off the nearest shore, 2 leagues; saw an opening on the main, bearing N. 86 W. Lat'd obs'd, 20° 56' So.

COOK:

Winds at SSE and SE a gentle breeze, with which we stood to the NW and NWbN as the land lay under an easy sail, having a boat ahead sounding; our soundings were at first very irregular from 9 to 4 fathoms, but afterwards regular from 9 to 11 fathom. At 8 oClock being about 2 Leagues from the main land we anchored in 11 fathom sandy bottom. Soon after this we found a slow motion of the tide to the westward. At 1 oClock it was slack or low water and at ½ past 2 oClock the ship tended to the eastward and rode so untill 6 at which time the tide had risen 11 feet, we now got under sail and stood away NNW as the land lay. From observations made on the tides last night it is plain that the flood comes from the NW, whereas yesterday and for several days before we found it to come from the SE. This is neither the first or second time we have observed the same thing and in my opinion easy accounted for but I shall do this in another place. At sun rise we found the Variation to be 6° 45' East. In steering along shore between the Islands and the Main at the distance of 2 Leagues from the latter and 3 or 4 from the former, our soundings were regular from 12 to 9 fathom but about 11 oClock we were again embarrassed by shoal water but got clear without letting go an anchor, we had at one time not quite 3 fathom. At noon we were about 2 Leagues from the Main land and about 4 from the Islands without us; our latitude by observation was 20° 56', Longitude made from *Cape Palmerston* 16' West. A pretty high promontory which I named *Cape Hillsborough* bore W½N distant 7 Miles. The main land here is pretty much diversified with Mountains, Hills Plains and Vallies and seems to be tolerably cloathed with wood and Verdure. The Islands which lay parallel with the coast and from 5 to 8 or 9 Leagues off are of various extent both for height and circuit; hardly any exceeds 5 Leagues in circuit and many again are very small, besides this chain of Islands which lay at a distance from the coast there are other small ones laying under the land. Some few smooks were seen on the Mainland.

BANKS:

In the evening the weather settled and fine and we sailed along shore; at night came to an anchor.

Tupia complained this evening of swelled gums; he had it seems his mouth sore for near a fortnight, but not knowing what cause it proceeded from did not complain. The Surgeon immediately put him upon taking extract of lemons in all his drink.

AM: Sailing along ashore with fine weather, the countrey hilly and ill wooded. Some islands still in sight ahead of us. At noon the irregularity of the soundings made it necessary to send a boat ahead again.

PARKINSON:

On the 2[d] of June, we were in the latitude of 20° 56′, and still among islands, through which we were obliged to steer with great caution, keeping a boat out ahead, and coming-to every night: we yet so narrowly escaped a bank, the soundings were so unequal. The land appeared very high, and much broken, but had an indifferent aspect, and seemed to be thinly inhabited.

From noon to 8 PM, the ship sailed through what is now known as Coaster Channel, which is sometimes used by coastal vessels with a local knowledge, coming north out of Broad Sound. It lies between Sandy, Stony, Torch, Yaralla and Viscount Shoals on the east side and the mainland to the west. During the following forenoon the ship was well within the ten-fathom line, and for the latter part fairly among the Blackwood Shoals with Green Island a few miles to larboard. At noon, with Cape Hillsborough W ½ N about 8 miles, Brampton Island was on the starboard beam to the NE. Cape Hillsborough was named after Wills Hill, First Viscount Hillsborough (1718–93) who was from 1763 to 1765 President of the Board of Trade and Foreign Plantations, and from 1768 to 1772 Secretary of State for the Colonies. On the chart, the Captain named a cape Point Slade, which lay some 7 miles SE of Green Island. Sir Thomas Slade was one of the members of the Navy Board, Surveyor of the Navy 1755–71, and builder of the Victory *1759–65. Here the ship was entering the Hillsborough Channel which leads to Whitsunday Passage. The present town of Mackay is just south of Slade Point, at the mouth of the Pioneer River.*

The fact that studding sails were set in this situation says something of the efficiency of the crew in sail-handling and the Captain's recognition of it. It calls for 'kite-flying' the sails out of the tops and from on deck to distant yardarms, and sheeting them home to slender booms extended from those yardarms so that they will set handsomely without fouling the maze of other gear in going up or coming down. It is an evolution in which each sailor has to be completely familiar, not only with what he himself is doing but also with co-ordinating with what others are doing at some distance from him. It calls for a special sort of proprioceptive sense of the ship and one's shipmates, acting like an anatomical whole. Textbook knowledge is not sufficient. The real test may come in an emergency—for example, if the ship has to be suddenly brought into the wind to get the way off her. Then the steering sails would have to be doused without an hurrah's-nest of sheets, halyards and downhauls, or twisted sails and broken booms—and this at the same time as the helm went down and the yards braced up. Cook was not a reckless man, therefore we can only conclude that he knew the capabilities of his men.

SHIP'S LOG:

SUNDAY, JUNE 3RD, 1770

H.	K.	F.	Courses.	Winds.	Soundings.	Remarks, &c.
					Fathoms.	
1	2	..	N.W.b.W.	S.E.	9, 9½, 10	Mod. breezes and pleas't weather.
2	2	..	..	..	9¾, 9, 9	The boat ahead.
3	2	3	..	..	9½, 10, 9	
4	3	..	..	..	9¼, 9, 9½	Steering for an opening.
5	2	6	..	..	9½, 9, 9	½-p't, made a signal for the boat.
6	2	2	..	..	9¼, 9¾, 10	Hoisted the boat up.
7	2	..	..	..	9½, 10, 10	
8	2	..	..	..	10, 10, 10	Came too with the bt. bower and veer'd to ½ a cable.
9	..	..	..	..	..	
10	..	..	..	..	..	Found the tide set to the No'ward.
11	..	..	..	..	..	
12	..	..	..	..	..	Found the tide fallen 7½ feet.
1	..	..	..	..	..	
2	..	..	..	..	..	Slack water; found the tide fallen 9 feet.
3	..	..	..	..	..	
4	..	..	..	..	..	
5	..	..	..	..	..	Found the tide come from the No'ward, and tide rizen 3 feet; weighed and made sail.
6	1	..	N.W.b.W.	E.b.S.	10, 10, 10	
7	3	..	..	..	9½, 9¼, 9	Variat'n p'r amp', 6° 57′ E.
8	3	..	N.W. b. W. ½ W.	..	8½, 8¼, 8¼	Found the opening mention'd last night had low land run across it. Haul'd up for the islands.
9	3	4	E.N.E.	..	8½, 9, 9½	
10	3	6	N.E.	..	9¾, 11, 13	Saw another opening, bearing N.b.E.
11	{1	4	..	..	13, 13	So. extreme of the main, S. 23 E. 7 leagues.
	1	4	N.b.E.	..	20, 22	So. extreme of the opening or (streights) from S. 50 W't to S. 44 E.
12	3	..	N.N.W.	..	23, 20	No. extreme of do. from N. 17 W. to N. 32½ W.; an island with a remarkable peak, N.E.; sailing mid-channel; dist't from each shore, 4½ miles. Lat'd obs'd, 20° 26′ So'.

COOK:

Winds between SbE and SE a gentle breeze and clear weather. In the PM we steered along shore NW½W at the distance of 2 Leagues from the Main having 9 and 10 fathoms regular soundings. At sun set the farthest point of the main land that we could distinguish as such bore N° 48 West; to the northward of this lay some high land which I took to be an island the NW point of which bore N 41° West, but as I was not sure that there was a passage this way we at 8 oClock came too an anchor in 10 fathom muddy bottom. Two hours after this we had a tide setting to the northward and at 2 oClock it had fallen 9 feet sence the time we anchored. After this the tide begun to rise and the flood came from the northward which was from the islands out at Sea and plainly indicated that there was no passage to the NW. But as this did not appear at daylight when we got under sail we stood away to the NW untill 8 oClock, at this time we discovered low land quite across what we took for an opening between the main and the Islands which proved to be a Bay about 5 or 6 Leagues deep. Upon this we hauled our wind to the Eastward round the north point of the Bay which bore from us at this time NEbN distant 4 Leagues. From this point we found the main land trend away NbW ½ W and a strait or passage between it and a large Island or Islands laying in a parallel direction without, which passage we stood into having the tide of Ebb in our favour. At noon we were just within the entrance and by observation in the Lat[de] of 20° 26′ S. *Cape Hillsborough* bore SbE distant 10 Leagues and the North point of the Bay before mentioned bore S 19° West distant 4 miles. This point I have named *Cape Conway* (Lat[de] 20° 30′, Long[de] 211° 28′) and the Bay *Repulse Bay* which is formed by these two capes. The greatest and least depth of water we found in it was 13 and 8 fathom, everywhere safe anchorage, and I believe that was it properly examined there would be found some good harbours in it especially on the north side within *Cape Conway*, for just within this Cape lay two or three small islands which alone would shelter that side of the bay from the SE and Southerly winds which seem to be the prevailing or trade winds. Among the many Islands that lay upon this coast there is one more remarkable than the rest being of small [circuit] very high and peaked and lies 10 miles from *Cape Conway* at the south end of the passage above mentioned.

BANKS:

In the evening the countrey was moderately hilly and seemed green and pleasant; one smoak was seen upon it. At night we anchored. At day break the anchor was weighed and we stood along shore till we found ourselves in a bay off the outermost point of which were the islands seen yesterday; by 8 it was resolved to stand out again through the passage which was seen between them and the Main which was acccordingly done. The countrey within the bay, especially on the innermost side, was well wooded, looked fertile and pleasant.

PARKINSON:

On the 3[d], in the morning, we had land on every quarter, excepting at South-east, and stood to North-west, where there appeared to be an opening, which carried us into a strait, in which we found deep water.

After leaving the Blackwood Shoals off Cape Hillsborough the ship steered north-westerly with regular soundings until anchoring at 8 PM. The high land taken to be an island to the NW was Mount Proserpine (1,475 feet), and the heights of Cape Conway (1,565 feet) were ESE of it. At this time to the eastward of the ship lay the Sir James Smith Group of islands, a part of the long chain of the Cumberland Isles. This group has individual islands appropriately named: Silversmith, Coppersmith, Blacksmith, Hammer, Anchor, Ladysmith, Locksmith, Goldsmith and Tinsmith Islands. Weighing at 6 AM, the ship sailed NW towards Repulse Bay until Cape Conway and the outer Repulse Island were on the starboard beam, when the low mangrove shore to the west of Proserpine River was seen. Course was then altered to ENE which brought the ship close upon the wind with the yards braced hard upon the backstays taking her clear of the Repulse Islands. At 9 AM, she eased away to NE until 10 AM, when she turned to NbE until 11 AM, when the ship was fairly into the mouth of Whitsunday Passage, having Kennedy Sound, between Shaw and Lindeman Islands, due east. With the wind on her starboard quarter, she then turned NNW straight up the middle of the passage. At Noon Cape Conway was on the larboard quarter, and the remarkable (as the Captain noted) Pentecost Island some 5 miles on the starboard bow. When seen from this bearing, as a powder-blue silhouette on the straight horizon, this island is a giant version of the couchant lions at the foot of Nelson's Column in Trafalgar Square, with full mane and front paws extended. Its summit is 949 feet above the sea. Cape Conway was named after Henry Seymour Conway (1721–95). From 1765 to 1768 he was Secretary of State, and was made a field marshal in 1793.

SHIP'S LOG:

MONDAY, JUNE 4TH, 1770

H.	K.	F.	Courses.	Winds.	Soundings.	Remarks, &c.
					Fathoms.	
1	3	2	N.N.W.	N.E.	24	Mod. breezes and pleas't wea'r; running between the main and a chain of islands, dist' from the main 1 and from the the isl'ds 2 mile; saw several albecores; saw 2 of the natives and a cannoe with an outrigger, the largest was ever seen on the coast. ½-p't 5, the n'm't ext's of the streights in sight from N. 57° 30'W. to N. 15° E.; the southermost from S. 32 E. to S. 21 E. A small island, N. 55 W. Distance from the nearest shore, 4 or 5 miles.
2	3	2	..	..	25	
3	3	2	..	..	23	
4	3	..	..	..	20	
5	3	..	N.W.b.N.	..	21	
6	2	4	..	..	24	
7	2	7	N.W.	..	23	
8	2	6	N.W.b.W.	..	22	
9	2	2	N.W.	..	21	
10	2	..	..	..	21	
11	1	6	..	..	22, 20	
12	1	6	..	..	19, 22	
1	2	..	..	..	22, 23	
2	2	..	..	..	23	
3	2	4	W.N.W.	..	..	
4	3	..	W.b.N.	..	23	Do, weather; bro't too.
5	..	..	up S.W.	off W't	20	Made sail.
6	2	2	W.N.W.	..	22	Extremes of the land from E.b.N. to W.
7	4	..	W.	..	19, 17	
8	3	7	..	..	16½	
9	3	5	..	..	16	
10	3	4	W.b.S.	..	15, 14½	
11	3	3	W.b.N.	S.E.b.E.	14½, 14½	
12	3	2	..	..	14½, 14¾	At noon { Ext's of the land from S. 69 E. to N. 76 W. An isl'd N. 56½ E. Dist'ce off shore, 3 leagues. } Lat'de obs'd, 19° 48' S.

COOK:

Winds at SE and SSE a gentle breeze and clear weather. In the PM steered through the passage which we found from 3 to 6 or 7 miles broad and 8 or 9 Leagues in length NbW½E and SbE½E. It is formed by the main on the west and by islands on the east one of which is at least 5 Leagues in length. Our depth of water in running through was between 25 and 20 fathom every where good anchorage. Indeed the whole passage is one continued safe harbour, besides a number of small Bays and Coves on each side where ships might lay as it were in a Bason, at least so they appeared to me for I did not wait to examine them as having been in Port so lately and being unwilling to lose the benefit of a light Moon. The land on both the Main and the Islands especially on the former is tolerable high and distinguished by Hills and Vallies which are diversified with woods and Lawns that looked green and pleasant. On a sandy beach upon one of the Islands we saw two people and a canoe with an outrigger that appeared to be both larger and differently built to any we have seen upon the coast. At 6 oClock we were nearly the length of the north end of the passage the NWermost point of the Main in sight bore N 54° West and the north end of the Islands NNE having an open sea between these two points. This passage I have named *Whitsunday's Passage*, as it was discovered on the Day the Church commemorates that Festival and the Islands which form it *Cumberland Isles* in honour of His Roy^{l} Highness the Duke of Cumberland. We kept under an easy sail and the lead going all night having 21, 22 and 23 f^{m} at the distance of 3 Leagues from the Land. At daylight in the morning we were abreast of the point above mentioned which is a lofty promontory that I named *Cape Gloucester* (Latitude 19° 57′ S, Long^{de} 211° 54′ W); it may be known by an Island which lies out at sea NbW ½ W 5 or 6 Leagues from it, this I called *Holburn Isle*. There are also Islands laying under the land between it and *Whitsundays Passage*; on the west side of the Cape the land trends away SW and SSW and forms a deep bay, the land in the bottom of this bay I could but just see from the Mast head, it is very low and is a Continuation of the same low land as is at the bottom of *Repulse Bay*. Without waiting to look into this bay which I called *Edgcumbe Bay* we continued our course to the westward for the westermost land we had in sight, which bore from us WbN ½ N and appeared very high. At noon we were about 3 Leagues from the land and by observation in the Latitude of 19° 47′ S, Cape Gloucester bearing S 63° East, distant 7½ leagues.

BANKS:
After dinner standing among Islands which were very barren, rising high and steep from the sea; on one of these we saw with our glasses 2 men and a woman and a small canoe fitted with an outrigger which made us hope that the people were something improved as their boat was far preferable to the bark canoes of Stingrays Bay. Hills in the morn were high and steep but they soon fell into very low land to all appearance barren. The water now began to be discoloured and an appearance of Islands was seen ahead which made us look out for more shoals.

PARKINSON:
The strait lies almost north and south; is about 7 leagues long, and one and a half broad. On the west of it lies the main, and on the east, a row of islands which extends a considerable way to the south. The land on both sides looked much

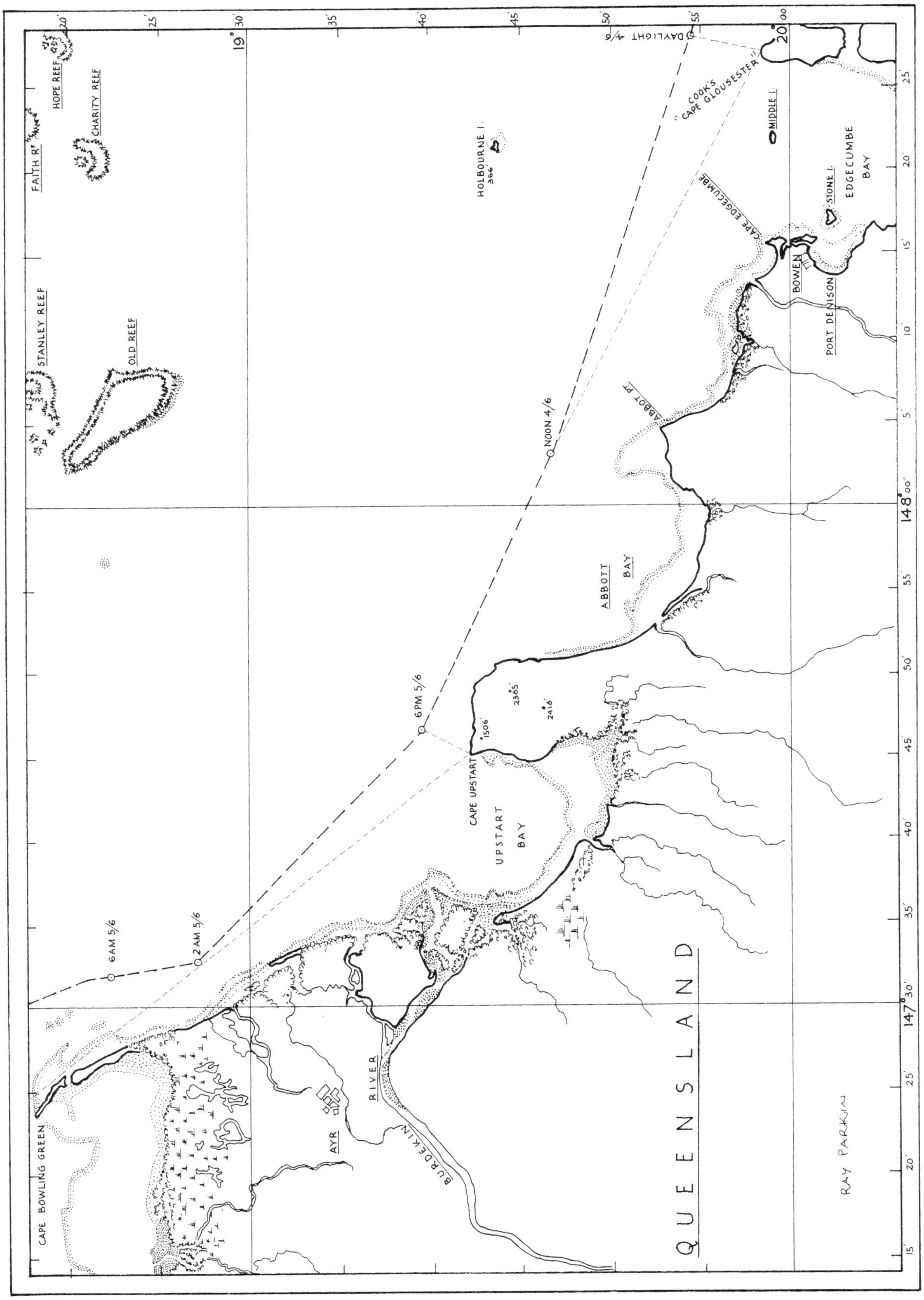
QUEENSLAND
CAPE BOWLING GREEN
AYR
BURDEKIN RIVER
UPSTART BAY
CAPE UPSTART
ABBOTT BAY
ABBOT PT
CAPE EDGECUMBE
EDGECUMBE BAY
BOWEN
PORT DENISON
STONE I.
MIDDLE I.
HOLBOURNE I.
COOK'S CAPE GLOUSESTER
DAYLIGHT 4/6
NOON 4/6
6PM 5/6
2AM 5/6
6AM 5/6
FAITH RF
HOPE REEF
CHARITY REEF
STANLEY REEF
OLD REEF
19°30'
20°00'
147°30'
148°00'
RAY PARKIN

better than that which we had seen before being high, abounding in trees and not sandy. We discovered 3 persons through our glasses, and a canoe with an outrigger like those of Otaheite. In the evening we had almost got out of the straits, the islands failing and the main tending more to the west. On the 4th [AM], we cleared the straits and islands and got into open sea. The land upon the coast was full of very high hills, whose bowels are probably rich in ore, but their surface is poor indeed, being more barren and full of stones, than any land we had seen. We had clear and pleasant weather, and the land still tended away to the west. Latitude 19° 48′.

The afternoon of this date was the Ship's Monday, but in Civil Time it was still Sunday; this is how Whitsunday Passage got its name on a Monday. From noon to 6 PM, the ship had passed what are now famous tourist playgrounds served by facilities that were beyond the wildest fantasy of the time. It was the first sighting by Europeans. Pine and Long Islands were left a few miles on the larboard hand, with Dent and Hamilton Islands on the starboard hand, immediately picking up the largest of the group, Whitsunday, on the same side. When halfway along this island, the three Molle Islands lay to larboard. By 5.30 PM, the ship was in mid-channel a little north of North Molle and abreast the foot of Hook Island, with Dolphin Point on Hayman Island, marking the end of the whole Cumberland Island chain, just in sight on the starboard bow. On the larboard bow, Double Cone Island marked the western end of the passage. What appeared to be open sea was dead ahead. But that 'open sea' was still within the close-knit chain of the Great Barrier Reef. The Captain did not name one of these Whitsunday Islands, but grouped them in with the Cumberland Isles.

It should be remembered that Cook was limited by both time and the state of his provisions. He was not attempting in any sense really to chart this coast. His was but a first running survey, limning in as accurately as opportunity and conditions allowed. The latitudes and longitudes given in his journal are by no means the final ones he fixed upon: for he was constantly reworking his material with a thoroughness that would have defeated lesser men. His reputation rests in this fact. Yet it is certain that nothing as accurate, nor as thorough, had ever been achieved in a first discovery by anyone before. Certainly new means and new aids had been made available by this time, but the man to use them to their full potential did not arrive until the advent of James Cook. Cook set new standards which made previous ones henceforth unacceptable. Yet, on this voyage, he achieved these exemplary standards without the chronometer. Vice-Admiral Sir John Edgell, K.B.E., C.B., F.R.S., Hydrographer to the Navy 1932–45, in his Sea Surveys, *compares Cook's chart from Cape Palmerston to Holburn Isle with a modern Admiralty chart of about the same scale, upon which it could almost be precisely superimposed. Be it remembered that the one was the work of a single man passing by, while the other is the collective work of many men over a long period, backed up by the developing technology of nearly two hundred years. As well, to compare Cook's Queen Charlotte Sound in New Zealand, or his Tahiti Island, with modern charts is to wonder if he perchance had a helicopter and aerial photography! The key, perhaps, is in some genius of an inner vision intuitively applied: mere professionalism could not have been enough.*

As the ship cleared Whitsunday Passage and turned westwards its occupants were still unaware of the Barrier Reef that was steadily closing in with the coast with every degree of lower latitude they made, to squeeze them finally into the ultimate labyrinth. But, for the time, the ship had reasonably open sailing so that under an easy sail, leadsmen in the chains giving regular soundings and the clear light of the moon, the ship sailed all night giving the land a reasonable berth. At daylight the ship was abreast a high point which the Captain called Cape Gloucester, after William Henry, Duke of Gloucester and Edinburgh (1743–1805), the second younger brother of George III. This point is now called Gloucester Head and is the outer tip of Gloucester Island with its Mount Bertha (1,892 feet), which is separated from the present Cape Gloucester on the mainland by Gloucester Passage. Holburn Isle is 15 miles approximately NNW *of the Cape, as the Captain called it. During the forenoon, the ship passed, about 7 miles off, the opening of Edgecumbe Bay, which is bounded on the west of Cape Edgecumbe. Just within this cape is Port Denison which is where the pier of the Port of Bowen is. This was once a sugar port, but the bulk-handling ports of Mackay and Townsville have made it redundant.*

At noon, the ship was just north of Abbot Point with her Cape Gloucester almost astern to larboard, and Holburn Isle on the starboard quarter. She was 6 miles offshore.

SHIP'S LOG:

TUESDAY, JUNE 5TH, 1770

H.	K.	F.	Courses.	Winds.	Soundings.	Remarks, &c.
					Fathoms.	
1	1	4	W.b.N.	E.b.S.	16	Mod. breezes and fair wea'r. Carpenters employ'd repairing the pinnace, and seamen making oacham.
	1	4	W.N.W.	..	16, 16	
2	2	6	..	..	16½, 16	
3	3	2	..	..	16	
4	3	4	..	..	15¾, 15	
5	3	4	..	..	15, 17	
6	3	2	..	..	16½	Saw high land, bearing W.b.N.
7	2	6	..	..	16	
8	2	4	..	..	15½, 15	Abreast of some high barren land.
9	2	6	..	..	14½	
10	2	6	..	..	14, 13, 11½	
11	2	3	..	..	11, 10, 10	
12	2	2	..	..	11¼, 9, 8, 7	Do. weather.
1	2	2	..	..	9, 8½, 7	Upon shoaling our water to 7 fa'm, haul'd from the land.
2	2	3	N.W.bW.	..	8, 8¼	
3	2	4	N.	Et.	9, 9, 9, 9	
4	2	3	N.b.W.	..	9¼, 9, 8½, 8¼	
5	1	..	..	..	..	Variat'n p'r amplit'd, 5° 27′ E't.
	1	2	N. ½ W.	..	8, 7½, 7	
6	1	2	..	..	..	Saw land extending as far as W.N.W.
7	2	2	N.N.W.	..	8, 8, 7½	
8	2	2	..	S.S.E.	8, 7½, 7, 6¾, 6¾	Little wind and fair weather, set steering sails.

H.	K.	F.	Courses.	Winds.	Soundings.	Remarks, &c.
9	2	3	N.W.b.N.	. .	7, 9, 9, 10 11, 12	
10	2	4	. .	S.E.b.S.	14, 14	
11	1	. .	. .	. .	. .	
	2	. .	W.N.W.	. .	14½, 14	
12	3	. .	. .	. .	14, 15	Ext's of the land from N. 44 E. to N. 84 W., shore dis. 4 leag's. Lat. obs'd, 19° 12'.

COOK:

Winds between South and East a very gentle breeze and serene weather. At 6 oClock we were abreast of the western point of land above mentioned (distant from it 3 miles) which I have named *Cape Upstart* because being surrounded by low land, it starts or riseth up singly at the first making of it (Latitude 19° 39′ Long[de] 212° 32′ W) it lies west-north-west 14 Leagues from *Cape Gloucester* and is of a height sufficient to be seen 12 Leagues, but is not so much of a promontory as it appears to be because on each side of it near the sea is very low land which is not to be seen unless you are pretty well in with the shore. Inland are some tolerable high hills or Mountains which like the Cape afford but a very barren prospect. Having passed this Cape we continued standing to the west-north-west as the land lay under an easy sail, having from 16 to 10 fathom water, untill 2 oClock in the AM when we fell into 7 fathom, upon which we hauled our wind to the northward judging ourselves to be very near the land as so we found, for at daylight we were little more than 2 Leagues off; what deceived us was the lowness of the land which is but very little higher than the surface of the sea but in this low country were some hills. At noon we were in 15 fathom water and about 4 Leagues from the land—our Latitude by observation was 19° 12′ S, *Cape Upstart* bore S 38° 30′ East distant 12 leagues; course and distance sailed sence yesterday noon N 48 45 [W], 53 miles. At and before noon some very large smooks were seen rise up out of the lowland. At sun rise I found the Variation to be 5° 35′ Easterly. At sunset last night the same needle gave near 9°, this being close under *Cape Upstart* I judged that it was owing to Iron ore or other magnetical matter lodged in the earth.

BANKS:

At noon one smoak was seen behind some hills inland. At night we passed pretty near a headland which appeared miserably rocky and barren. Much sea weed with very fine leaves passed by the ship all day. AM: Land near the sea very low and flat behind which hills rose: in the countrey very little appearance of fertility however either on one or the other: at noon a large fire was seen. Several Cuttle bones and 2 sea snakes swam past the ship.

The highest point on the peninsula of Cape Upstart is 2,416 feet, with two others 2,365 and 1,506. Beyond this is Upstart Bay into which the Burdekin River empties itself. Here the whole coast is low and mangrove-fringed. This which lured the ship closer than expected and was avoided by hauling the wind and working around a low point which the Captain placed on his chart as Cape Bowling Green. The present-day chart carries the caution: 'As the banks in the vicinity of C. Bowling Green are constantly shifting due to strong and irregular tidal streams, great caution should be exercised in this area.' At noon, this cape was on the same bearing between the ship and Cape Upstart. To the west of it is the mangrove-swamp shore line of Bowling Green Bay. The ship did not make above 3 ½ knots during this twenty-four hours. According to Australia Pilot, *vol. III (sixth edition, 1973), there are no recorded anomalies at Cape Upstart or Magnetic Head. Perhaps what Cook observed was the effect of the then-unknown 'deviation'; that is, the effect of magnetism within the ship.*

SHIP'S LOG:

WEDNESDAY, JUNE 6TH, 1770

H.	K.	F.	Courses.	Winds.	Soundings.	Remarks, &c.
					Fathoms.	
1	2	2	W.N.W.	E.S.E.	14	Little wind and pleas't wea'r. Carpenters and seamen as yest'd.
2	2	..	..	..	14	
3	2	..	..	..	13	
4	1	6	..	..	14	
5	1	7	..	..	13½	Ext's of the main from W. to S.E., a hummock appearing like an island,
6	1	4	W.b.N.	..	13	N.W.b.W.; haul'd down steering sails.
7	1	4	..	..	14, 14½	
8	1	4	..	..	14½, 14¾	
9	1	2	..	..	14	
10	1	..	..	..	14, 14	
11	1	..	..	..	14	
12	1	..	..	..	14	
1	..	4	..	..	13½	
2, 3, 4	..	..	..	..	13¼, 13	Calm, h'd to the Westward.
5	..	4	W.b.N.	..	13	Light airs. Variat'n, 5° 31' E't.
6	1	3	..	..	14	Set steering sails.
7	1	4	..	..	15	
8	1	6	..	..	14½, 13½	Little wind and fair wea'r.
9	1	6	..	..	13½	
10	1	6	W.N.W.	..	13¾	
11	1	4	..	..	13½, 14	
12	1	4	..	..	14½	At noon, extremes of the land from N. 49 W. to S. 28 E., dist. 5 m's. Lat. obs., 19° 00' S.

COOK:

Light airs at ESE with which we steered WNW as the land now lay, depth of water 12 & 14 fathoms. At noon we were by observation in the Latitude of 19° 1', Longitude made from Cape Gloucester 1° 30' West, course and distance sailed sence yesterday noon WNW, 28 miles. In this situation we had the mouth of a Bay all open extending from S½E to SW½S distant 2 Leagues. This bay which I named *Cleveland Bay* appeared to be about 5 or 6 miles in extent every way; the east point I named

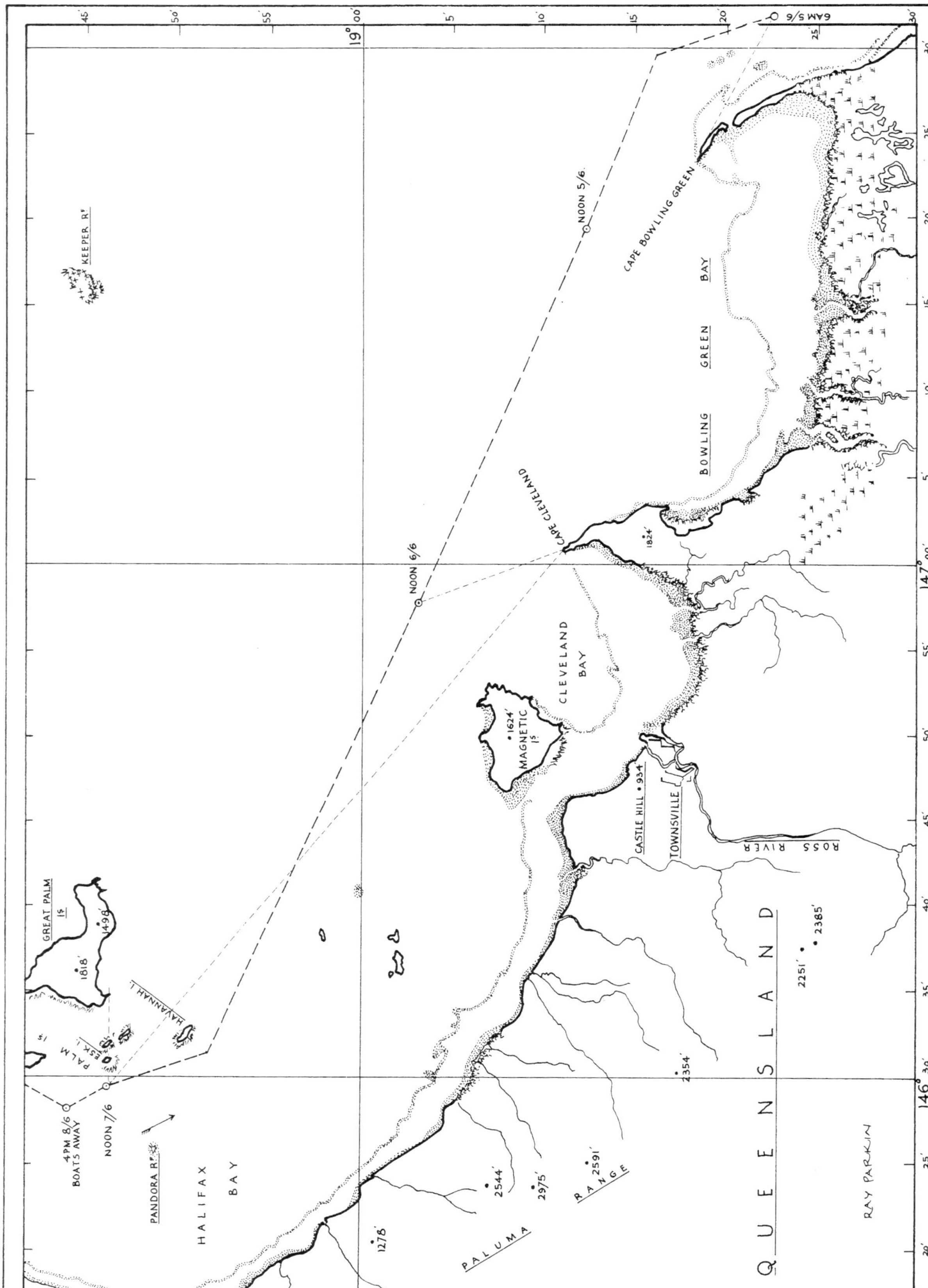
KEEPER R^f
NOON 5/6
6AM 5/6
CAPE BOWLING GREEN
BOWLING GREEN BAY
CAPE CLEVELAND
NOON 6/6
CLEVELAND BAY
MAGNETIC I^S
1624'
1824'
CASTLE HILL • 934
TOWNSVILLE
ROSS RIVER
GREAT PALM I^S
1498'
1818'
HAVANNAH I.
PALM I^S
NOON 7/6
4PM 8/6 BOATS AWAY
PANDORA R^f
HALIFAX BAY
QUEENSLAND
PALUMA RANGE
2591'
2544'
2975'
1278'
2354'
2251'
2385'
RAY PARKIN
19° 00'
146° 30'
147° 00'

Cape Cleveland and the west *Magnetical Head* or *Isle* as it had much the appearance of an island and the compass would not travis [traverse] well when near it. They are both tolerable high and so is the mainland within them and the whole appeared to have been most rugged, rocky and barrenest Surface of any we have yet seen. However it is not without inhabitants as we saw smooks in several places in the bottom of the bay. The northermost land we had in sight at this time bore NW, this we took to be an island for we could not trace the main land farther than WbN. [Notwithstanding we have been long in soundings, have had it frequently calm and been often at an anchor we have caught no fish worth mentioning sence we left Sting-Ray Harbour. (deleted)]

BANKS:

In the evening the thermometer was at 74 and the air felt to us much hottter than we have felt it on the coast before. Many clouds of a thin scum lay floating upon the water the same as we have before seen of Rio de Janeiro; some few flying fish also. AM: Land made in barren rocky capes; one in particular which we were abreast of in the morn appeared much like Cape Roxent; at noon 3 fires upon it. Many cuttle bones, some sea weed and 2 or 3 sea snakes were seen.

Cleveland Bay and Cape were probably named after John Cleveland, secretary to the Admiralty 1751–63. It is here, on the Ross River, that Townsville, one of the principal ports of North Queensland, now stands. Magnetical Head was at first called Barren Head and is on the present Magnetic Island. It reminded Mr Banks of 'Cape Roxent' which is Cabo da Rocca, just NW of Lisbon, and, according to Fielding in the eighteenth century, 'commonly called the rock of Lisbon'.

The unchanged 'Sting-Ray Harbour' continues to remind us of the first choice of name for Botany Bay. The island bearing NW at noon was Great Palm Island (1,818 feet), then distant about 25 miles.

SHIP'S LOG:

THURSDAY, JUNE 7TH, 1770

H.	K.	F.	Courses.	Winds.	Soundings.	Remarks, &c.
					Fathoms.	
1	1	..	W.N.W.	S.E.	13	Light airs, inclinable to calms.
2	1	..	..	..	14	
3	1	..	..	E.	15	
4	1	..	..	..	14, 15	
5	1	2	..	..	14	Variation by an amplitude, 5° 26′ E.; ½-p't, ext's of the main from N. 83 W. to S. 40 E.; an island from N. 41 W. to N. 55 W.; nearest shore, 4 or 5 m's.
6 {	..	5	N.N.W.	..	14	
	..	4	W.N.W.	..	14¼	
7	1	4	..	..	14	
8	1	..	..	..	14½	
9	1	..	..	..	14½	
10	1	2	..	..	14	
11	1	4	..	..	13¾	

H.	K.	F.	Courses.	Winds.	Soundings.	Remarks, &c.
12	1	6	. .	. .	14	
1	1	4	W.N.W. ½ W.	. .	14	
2	1	4	. .	. .	13½	
3	1	4	. .	S.S.W.	14	
4	1	6	. .	. .	12¾	
5	2	6	W. ½ N.	. .	13	Variat'n by an amplitude, 5° 00′ E.
6	3	. .	. .	. .	13½	Ext. of the land from N. 21 E. to S. 70 E.
7	2	7	W.	. .	13	Carpenters and seamen employ'd as before.
8	2	6	W.b.N.	. .	13	Punish'd Tho. Dunster, marine, with a dozen lashes for theft.
9	2	6	W.N.W.	. .	11½, 11	At 10, running between a chain of islands and the main.
10	2	6	N.W.	. .	14¾, 14½	Saw some large cannoes and several Indians.
11	{1	3	. .	. .	11, 11¾	
	1	3	N.N.W.	. .	11½, 11	
12	2	3	. .	. .	11¼, 11¼	At noon, sailing between some islands and the main; ext's of the main from S. 57 E. to N. 24 W.; dist'ce from it, 3 or 4 leagues. Ext. of the islands from N. 3½ W. to N. 42 E.; nearest dist'ce, 3 or 4 miles. Saw a number of smokes ashore. Lat'de obs'd, 18° 48′S. Light airs and fair wea'r; steering for an opening between the isl'ds and the main.

COOK:

Lights airs between South and East with which we steered WNW, keeping the Main land onboard the outermost part of which at sun set bore from us WbN, but without this lay high land which we took to be Islands. At daylight in the morning we were the length of the eastern part of this land which we found to consist of a group of Islands laying about 5 Leagues from the Main we being at this time between the two; we continued advancing slowly to the NW untill noon at which time we were by observation in the Latitude of 18° 49′, and about 5 Leagues from the Main land, the NW part of which bore from us Nbw½w the Island extending from North to East, distant off the nearest 2 Miles; *Cape Cleveland* bore S 50° East distant 18 Leagues. Our soundings in the course of this days sail were from 14 to 11 fathom.

BANKS:

In the evening it fell quite calm and I went out in the small boat and shot *nectris nugax* but saw nothing remarkable on the water; the weather most sultry hot in an open boat. AM: Sailing between the Main and Islands. The Main rose steep from the water rocky and barren [Paluma Range, at the back of Halifax Bay]. Just about sunrise a shoal of fish about the size and much like flounders but perfectly white went by the ship. At noon the Islands had mended their appearance and people were seen on them; the Main as barren as ever with several fires upon it, one vastly large.

PARKINSON:

On the 7th, we were between a parcel of islands and the main. The main land looked very barren and dreary; the hills upon it looked like a heap of rubbish on which nothing was to be seen, excepting a few low bushes; but the islands made a

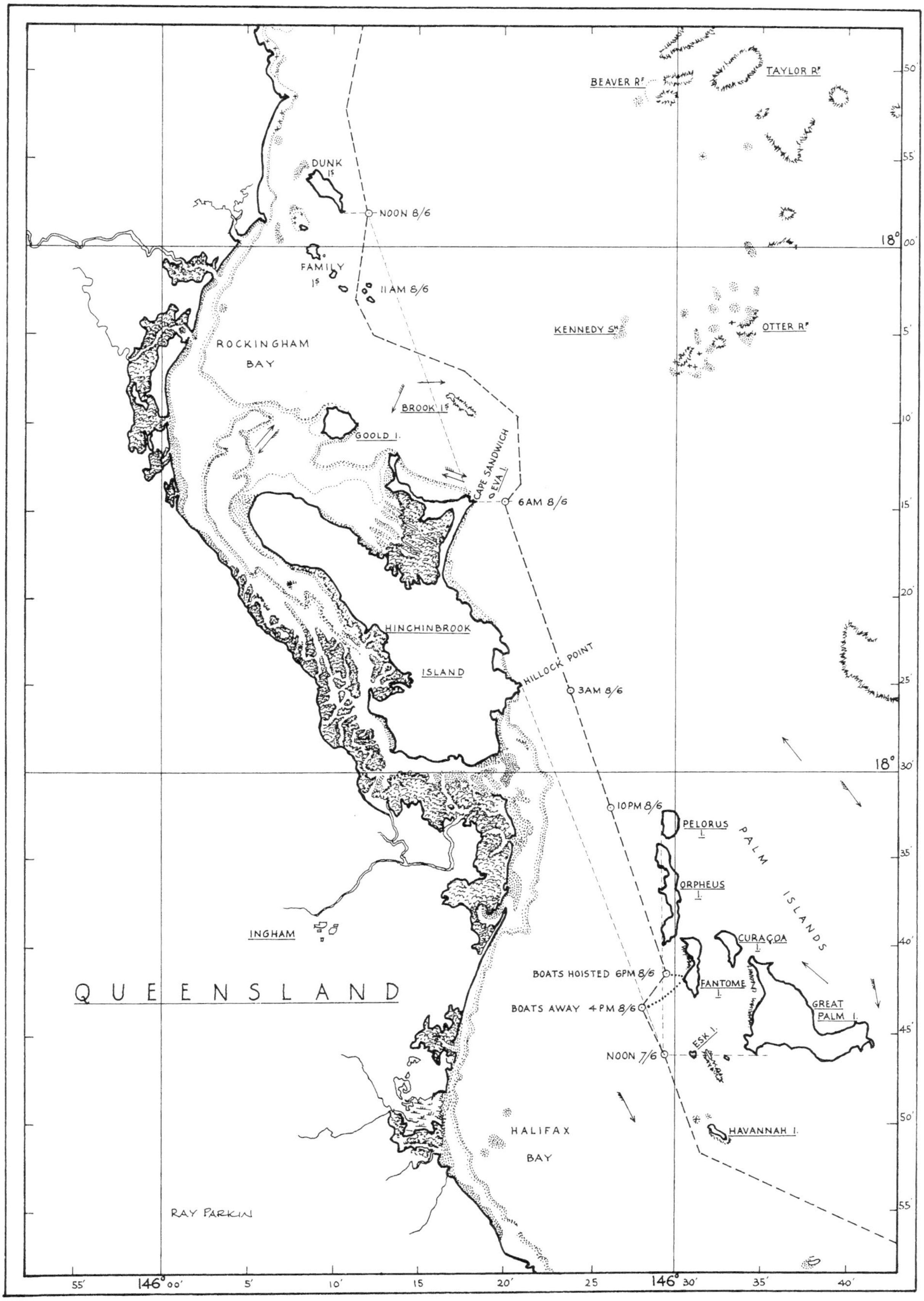
BEAVER Rf
TAYLOR Rf
DUNK Is
NOON 8/6
FAMILY Is
11 AM 8/6
ROCKINGHAM BAY
KENNEDY Sh
OTTER Rf
BROOK Is
GOOLD I.
CAPE SANDWICH
EVA I.
6 AM 8/6
HINCHINBROOK ISLAND
HILLOCK POINT
3 AM 8/6
10 PM 8/6
PELORUS I.
PALM ISLANDS
ORPHEUS I.
INGHAM
CURAÇOA I.
BOATS HOISTED 6 PM 8/6
FANTOME I.
QUEENSLAND
BOATS AWAY 4 PM 8/6
GREAT PALM I.
ESK I.
NOON 7/6
HALIFAX BAY
HAVANNAH I.
RAY PARKIN
18° 00'
18° 30'
146° 00'
146° 30'

better appearance. We saw a few people in canoes striking fish, some smoke on the main, and some palm trees. Latitude 18° 48′ s.

The winds were very light this day and the ship remained under way all night on a north-westerly course, having regular soundings. At 11 AM, being off a small island, now known as Havannah Island, which is the southernmost of the Palm Islands, a passage was sighted between the group and the mainland, and course was altered to NNW. At noon, the ship was abreast Esk Island, one of a small group some 3 miles to the westward of Great Palm Isle and in line with its southern shore. The ship had made only 30 miles since the previous noon.

Only the Ship's Log makes mention of the punishment of Thomas Dunster, the marine. There was no drama: he had been caught, and took his punishment as a routine—sorry, no doubt, but not traumatised.

SHIP'S LOG:

FRIDAY, JUNE 8TH, 1770

H.	K.	F.	Courses.	Winds.	Soundings.	Remarks, &c.
					Fathoms.	
1	1	..	N.N.W.	S.S.E.	13, 12	Light airs, inclinable to calms.
2	1	..	..	..	10	Running between a chain of islands and
3	1	..	..	..	8½	the main. Several smokes and several of
4	1	2	..	..	10	the natives and cannoes along shore.
5	1	4	N.E.	..	10½	The 1st lieutenant went on shore with the yaul and jolly-boat to the island; at 6 she return'd. Hoisted in the boats.
6	1	6	..	..	10	The no'most p't of the main N. 30 W. ½-p't 6, made
7	..	..	up N.E.b.E.	of N.N.E.	11	sail. Nearest shore dist. ½ a mile.
	1	..	N.b.W ½ W.	..	12	
8	2	2	..	..	13	
9	2	2	..	..	13, 14	
10	2	2	..	..	16, 16	
11	2	..	..	..	16, 15½	
12	2	4	..	S.S.E.	14, 14	Little wind and fair weather.
1	2	4	..	S.S.W.	15	
2	3	..	N.W.	..	14½	Haul'd up for the appearance of an opening.
3	2	6	..	..	14, 13	Saw low lan' across. Bore away.
4	2	4	N.N.W.	..	12, 11	
5	2	5	N.b.W.	..	11, 12	Haul'd up for an opening between an island and ye main. At daylight saw some breakers in the passage. Bore away and
6	..	..	up S.W.	off W.S.W.	..	stood round the island.
	1	3	N.E.	..	13, 14	
7	3	4	N.W. b. W.	..	15, 14, 12	Open'd cask of beef, N. 542; contents short 12 p.
8	3	6	W.N.W.	..	11, 10, 9	Do a cask of pork, compleat.
9	4	..	..	S.S.E.	9, 8, 7½	
10	3	5	N.N.W.	..	7, 7, 7½	
11	3	4	N.	..	8, 9, 10, 11	At 11, steering between some islands, dist't from each ¾ of a mile. Saw sev'l Indians.
12	3	2	N.b.E.	..	11½, 12, 11½	At noon, ext's of the land from S.S.E. to N. An island, distance 1½ miles. Lat'de obs'd, 18° 00′ S.

COOK:

Winds at SSE and South, first part light airs and the reminder a gentle breeze. In the PM we saw several large smooks on the main, some people, canoes and as we thought Cocoa-nutt trees upon one of the Islands, and as a few of these nutts would have been acceptable to us at this time I sent Lieutt Hicks a shore with whom went Mr Banks and Dr Solander to see what was to be got, and in the mean time we kept standing in for the Island with the Ship. At 7 oClock they returned on board having met with nothing worth observing, the trees we saw were a small kind of Cabbage Palms; they heard some of the natives as they were putting off from the shore but saw none. After the boats were hoisted in we stood away NbW for the northermost land we had in sight which we were abreast of at 3 oClock in the Morning having passed all the islands 3 or 4 hours before; this point I have named *Point Hillick* [Point Hillock on Cook's chart] on account of its figure. The land of this point is tolerable high and may be known by a round hillick or rock that appears to be detached from the point but I believe it joins it. Between this Cape and *Iron Head* [*Cape Cleveland* (substituted, then removed)] the shore forms a large bay which I named *Rockingham Bay* [*Halifax Bay*, finally, on the chart], before it lay the group of islands before mentioned and some others near the shore. These Islands shelter the bay in a manner from all winds, in which is good anchorage, the land near the shore in the bottom of this Bay is very low and woody, but a little way back in the country is a continued ridge of high land which appeared to be barren and rocky [Paluma Range]. Having passed *Point Hillick* we continued standing to the NNW as the land trended having the advantage of a light moon. At 6 oClock in the AM we were abreast of a point of land which lies NbW ½ W 11 miles from *Point Hillick*, the land between them is very high and of a craggy barren surface; this point I named *Cape Sandwich* to honour the Earl of that name. It may not only be known by the high craggy land over it but by a small island which lies East one mile from it and some others about two Leagues to the northward of it. From *Cape Sandwich* the land trends west and afterwards north and forms a fine large bay which I called *Halifax Bay* [*Rockingham Bay*, finally, on the chart]; it is well sheltered and affords good anchorage, at least so it appeared to me, for having hitherto met with so little encouragement by going ashore that I would not wait to land or examine it further, but continued ranging along shore to the northward for a parcel of small islands laying off the northern point of the Bay, and finding a channel of a mile broad between the three outermost and those nearer the shore we pushed through. While we did this we saw on one of the nearest Islands a number of natives collected together who seemed to look very attentively upon the Ship, they were quite naked and of a very dark colour with short hair. At Noon we were by observation in the Latitude of 17° 59′ and abreast the north point of *Halifax [Rockingham] Bay* which bore west from us 2 miles. This boundary of the Bay is formed by a tolerable high Island known on the Chart by the name of *Dunk Isle*, it lays so near the shore as not to be distinguished from it unless you are well in with the land. At this time we were in the Longitude of 213° 57′ W, *Cape Sandwich* bore SbE ½ E distant 19 miles and the northermost land in sight N ½ W. Our depth of Water in the course of this days sail was not more than 16 nor less than 7 fathom.

BANKS:

After dinner an appearance very much like Cocoa nut trees tempted us to hoist out a boat and go ashore, where we found our supposed Cocoa nut trees to be no more than bad Cabbage Trees. The countrey about them was very stony and barren and it was almost dark when we got ashore; we made a shift however to gather 14 or 15 new plants after which we repaired to our boats, but scarce were they put off from the shore when an Indian came very near it and shouted to us very loud; it was so dark that we could not see him, we however turned towards the shore by way of seeing what he wanted with us, but he I suppose ran away or hid himself immediately for we could not get a sight of him. AM: Still sailing between the Main and Islands; the former rocky and high looked rather less barren than usual and by the number of fires seemed to be better peopled. In the morn we passed within ¼ of a mile of a small islet or rock on which we saw with our glasses about 30 men women and children standing all together and looking attentively at us, the first people we have seen shew any signs of curiosity at the sight of the ship.

PARKINSON:

On the 8th, the main land appeared still higher, and very barren. We discovered several islands that looked like so many heaps of rubbish, which had lain long enough to have a few weeds and bushes grow on them. On one of them, which is not more than two miles in circumference, we saw a company of the natives, entirely naked and of a dark complexion, standing quite still, and beholding the ship with astonishment. At night we saw a fire, which yielded a very grateful odour, not unlike that produced by burning the wood of gum benjamin.

Mr Parkinson's description was probably the first record of a smell that would be one of the most nostalgic to the senses of future Australians. As the familiar smell of a mother's breast comforts the infant, so this burning eucalyptus was the smell that would bind many thousands of pioneers to their new country in a tough–tender relationship.

By 4 PM on this day the ship was but 4 miles further on, making only 1 knot in the light SSE breeze. At the sight of the palms, the yawl and the jolly boat (Mr Banks's cockleshell) were lowered. Mr Hickes and Mr Banks went in the yawl, while Dr Solander and the Surgeon were in the jolly boat. The cabbage palms were a disappointment. While the boats were away, the ship worked to within half a mile of the beach of what is now called Fantome Island and it was after sunset when the boats were hoisted in again. It must have been with some rueful humour that the Captain named these islands Palm. It would be small consolation to Mr Banks to know that coconuts flourish on lofty palms there today. Under way again and at 10 PM, the ship was abreast of Pelorus Island, the northernmost of the group. By 3 AM, she was abreast of Point Hillock, off which is a round rock. By 6 AM, *in the coming light, Cape Sandwich was abeam. In naming this cape, the Captain demonstrated a nice piece of imagery: he described the nearby country as 'very high and of a craggy barren surface', then called the cape Sandwich in 'honour of the earl of that name'. According to others' descriptions of the Earl, 'his face was ugly but his personality was charming.'*

The ship hauled offshore to avoid Eva Island off this cape, and skirted the islands mentioned 'about two leagues to the northward of it', which are a small group on a common shoal, now called Brook Islands and carrying a group flashing light. Passing these a mile or so distant, she hauled WNW *into Rockingham Bay. In the journal there is some confusion between this and Halifax Bay. On the Captain's chart, however, they are marked as on the chart today. George Montague Dunk was Second Earl of Halifax 1716–71, a president of the Board of Trade, First Lord of the Admiralty 1762, and Secretary of State 1763–5. Charles Watson-Wentworth was Second Marquis of Rockingham 1730–82. John Montagu was Fourth Earl of Sandwich 1718–92 and First Lord of the Admiralty from 1771.*

Point Hillock and Cape Sandwich are not on the mainland but on what is now Hinchinbrook Island, separated from the main by a mangrove swamp and a very narrow channel invisible from seaward. Appropriately, Hinchinbrook was the Huntingdonshire home of the Earl of Sandwich.

They sighted a channel between a small parcel of islands to the north and the ship steered towards it. They saw, as Mr Banks tells, 'about 30 men women and children standing all together'. Again the Captain's own style of imagery is at work: earls and marquises forgotten, he calls these the Family Isles. Then, altering to NbE, *by noon the ship was abreast of the southern point of the lumpy island which was called Dunk Island. During these twenty-four hours the ship made some 50 miles of northing.*

On this day the only known surviving portion of the log of Charles Clerke, Master's Mate, ends. It was to this man, on the death of Captain Cook in February 1779, that the command of the expedition of the Third Voyage fell. While in ill health, with great devotion to duty, he doggedly persisted with the original aims of the expedition. But he finally had to turn back after his ships, Resolution *and* Discovery, *met an impenetrable barrier of ice beyond Bering Strait. The last words he ever wrote were: '. . . for this Sea is now so Choak'd with Ice that a passage I fear is totally out of the question.' On the 22nd of August, only six months after his Captain, he too died, off the coast of Kamchatka. The expedition was then brought home by John Gore, reaching the Thames in October 1780.*

SHIP'S LOG:

SATURDAY, JUNE 9TH, 1770

H.	K.	F.	Courses.	Winds.	Soundings.	Remarks, &c.
					Fathoms.	
1	3	..	N.W.b.N.	S.E.	12	Mod'te breezes and pleas't weather.
2	2	7	N.b.W.	..	11, 10	
3	3	..	N.b.E.	..	11	
4	3	2	..	..	12, 13	

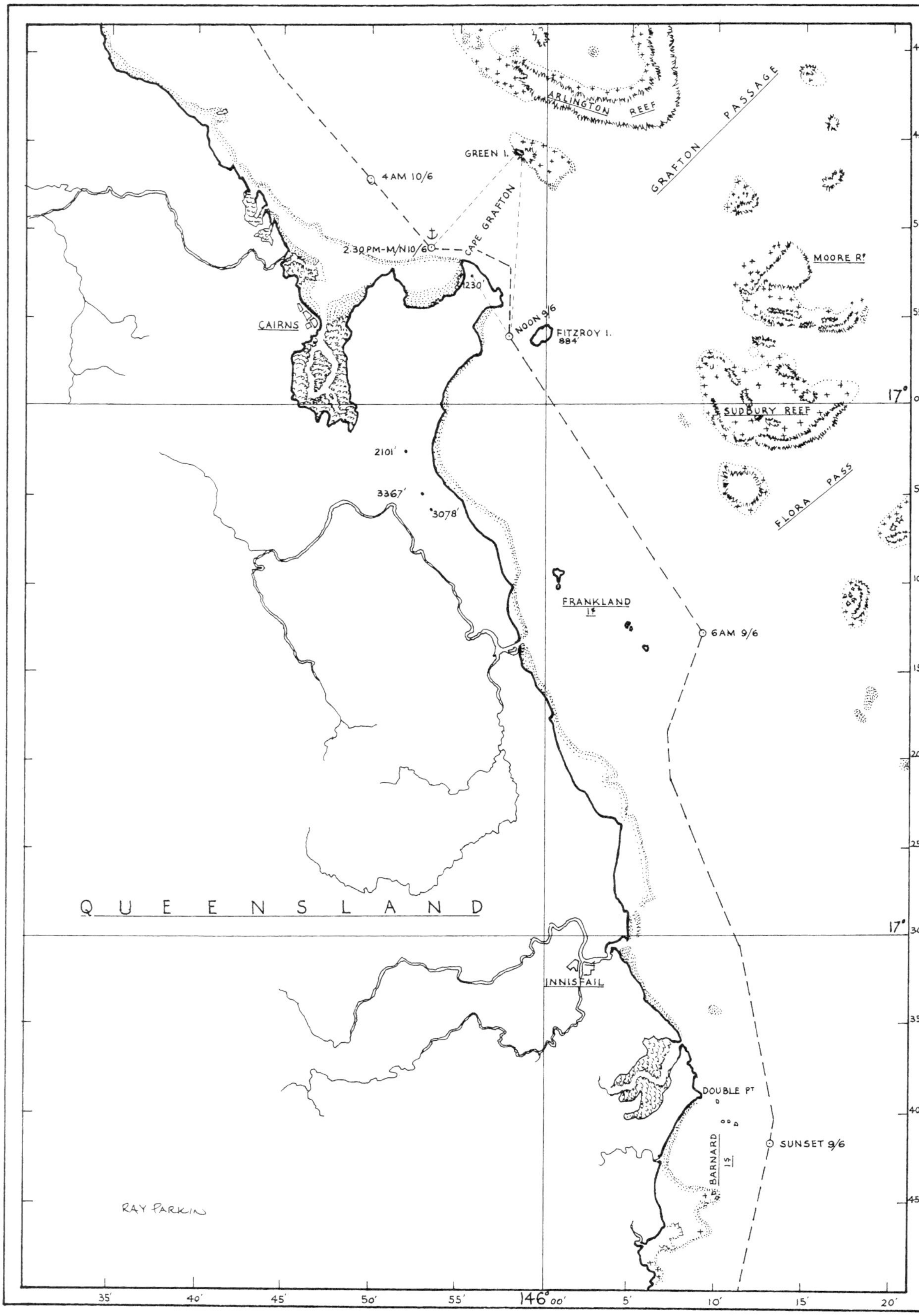
ARLINGTON REEF
GRAFTON PASSAGE
GREEN I.
4 AM 10/6
CAPE GRAFTON
2.30 PM-M/N 10/6
1230'
MOORE Rf
CAIRNS
NOON 9/6
FITZROY I.
884'
SUDBURY REEF
2101'
3367'
3078'
FLORA PASS
FRANKLAND Is
6AM 9/6
QUEENSLAND
INNISFAIL
DOUBLE Pt
BARNARD Is
SUNSET 9/6
RAY PARKIN
146° 00'
17° 00'
17° 30'

H.	K.	F.	Courses.	Winds.	Soundings.	Remarks, &c.
5	3	..	..	..	14, 14½	
6	2	6	..	..	14¾, 14½	The no'm't extreme of the land N. 30° W., 4 or 5 leagues.
7	3	..	N.b.W.	..	14	
8	3	..	..	..	14	Saw several fires along shore.
9	2	4	..	..	14	
10	2	5	N.N.W.	..	14	
11	2	4	..	..	14	
12	2	4	..	..	14¼	
1	2	3	..	..	15	
2	2	2	..	..	14	
3	1	6	N.	..	13½, 13¼	
4	1	4	N.½.E.	..	14	
5	1	4	N.b.E.	S.b.W.	14½	
6	{1	..	..	..	..	Set steering sails, the no'most extreme of the land N.N.W.
	1	..	N.N.W.	..	14, 14½	
7	3	5	N.W. b. N.	..	14½	Variation by an amp'd, 4° 53' E.
8	3	7	..	..	15	
9	4	..	..	..	14	
10	3	6	..	..	14	Saw a smoak ashore.
11	3	3	N.W.½N.	S.S.E.	15	
12	{1	6	N.W.b.N.	..	..	At noon, ext's of the main from S. 15 E. to N. 32 W., an isl'd N. 3 W. Sailing between an island and the main, each dist. one mile. Lat. obs'd, 16° 55' S.
	1	6	N.b.W.	S.S.E.	17, 20	

COOK:
Winds between South and SE a gentle breeze and clear weather: with which we steered NbW as the land lay, the northern extreme of which at sun set bore N 25° West. We kept our course under an easy sail all night having from 12 to 15 fathom water at the distance of about 3 or 4 Leagues from the land. At 6 oClock in the AM we were abreast of some small Islands which we called *Frankland Isles* that lay about 2 Leagues from the main land the northern point of which bore NbW ½ W but this we afterwards found to be an Island tolerable high and about 4 miles in circuit. It lies about 2 miles from the point on the main between which we went with the Ship and were in the middle of the channel at noon and by observation in the Latitude of 16° 55′, where we had 20 fathom water. The point of land we were now abreast off I called *Cape Grafton* (Lat^{de} 16° 55′ S, Long^{de} 214° 11′ West) it is tolerable high land and so is the whole coast for 20 leagues to the southward and hath a very rocky surface which is thinly covered with wood. In the night we saw several fires along shore and a little before noon some people.

BANKS:
Countrey much the same as it was, hills near the sea high, looked at a distance not unlike Mo[o]res or heaths in England but when you came nearer them they were covered with small trees; some few flatts and valleys looked tolerably fertile. At noon a fire and some people were seen.

Passing Dunk Island the ship followed the coast, keeping outside the Barnard Islands. At sunset, North Barnard Island and Double Point were almost in line NW. *This point, not named in Cook's journal, was put on the chart as Double Point, as it stands today. At 3* AM, *course was altered to North, then* NbE, *to pass outside the* Frankland Islands, *named after Sir Thomas Frankland (1717?–84) who saw service in the West Indies and was later a rear-admiral and finally an admiral. Having cleared these, course was altered to* NWbN *to a point midway between Fitzroy Island and the coast. By noon the ship was in midchannel there. The Captain named the cape Cape Grafton and the island Fitzroy Isle. Possibly his Cape was the easternmost point of the peninsula, but the present Cape Grafton is the northernmost. Augustus Henry Fitzroy was the Third Duke of Grafton 1735–1811 and Secretary of the State in Rockingham's administration.*

SHIP'S LOG:

SUNDAY, JUNE 10TH, 1770

H.	K.	F.	Courses.	Winds.	Soundings.	Remarks, &c.
					Fathoms.	
1	3	4	N.W.	N.E.	10½, 10, 9, 8, 7, 6	Fresh breezes and clear wea'r. ½-p't 1, shorten'd sail and stood in for a bay. Sent a m'te in the yawl to sound ahead. ½-p't 2, came too with the b't bower in 4¼ fa'm water. Extremes of the bay from S. 79 E. to S. 78 W. A low island in the offing, N. 30 E. Shore distance, 2½ m. The captain went on shore in ye pinnace.
2	1	4	..	..	..	
	2	..	W.S.W.	..	5, 4, 3½	
3	1	4	W.	..	3¾, 4, 4¼	
	..	..	..	..	..	
4	..	..	..	..	..	
5	..	..	..	..	..	
6	..	..	..	..	..	
7	..	..	..	..	..	
8	..	..	..	..	..	
9	..	..	..	..	..	
10	..	..	..	..	..	
11	..	..	..	..	..	
12	..	..	..	..	..	Light airs and cloudy weather; weighed and made sail out of the bay.
1	..	..	..	S.b.E.	4½, ½, 5	
2	..	..	..	Variable.	5¾, 6, 6	Had several showers of rain.
3	..	..	..	..	7, 8, 9	
4	..	..	..	..	10, 10½	Mod. breezes and fair wea'r. Ye place sail'd from S.E., 3 miles.
5	3	..	N.W.	S.b.E.	11, 12	
6	4	4	N.W. ½ W.	..	12, 13	Extremes of the land from S.E. to N. 27 W.
7	2	2	..	..	..	
	2	..	N.W.b.N.	..	13	
8	3	2	..	..	13	
9	3	2	..	..	13	
10	3	4	..	..	13¼	Pass'd some low sandy islands.
11	2	..	..	..	..	
	1	6	N.	..	14, 14½, 15	
12	2	..	..	..	15, 14¾	At noon, ext. of the land from N. 25 W. to S. 37½ E. Lat'de obs'd, 16° 20′ S.; the nearest of the main N. 66 W., 7 or 8 miles.
	2	..	N.N.W.	..	14¾	

COOK:

After hauling round Cape Grafton we found the land trend away NWbW. Three miles to the westward of the Cape is a Bay wherein we anchored about 2 miles from the shore in 4 fathom water an owsey bottom. The east point of the bay bore S 74° East, the west point S 83° West and a low green woody Island laying in the offing bore N 35° East. This Island lies NbE ½ E distant 3 or 4 Leagues from *Cape Grafton* and is known in the chart by the name of *Green Island*. As soon as the Ship was brought to an anchor I went ashore accompanied by Mr Banks and Dr Solander, the first thing I did was to look for fresh water and with that view rowed out towards the Cape because the bottom of the Bay was low mangrove land and little probability of meeting with any there, but the way I went I found two small streams which were difficult to get at on account of the surff and rocks upon the shore. As we came round the Cape we saw in a sandy cove a small stream of water run over the beach, but here I did not go in the boat because I found that it would not be easy to land. We hardly advanced anything into the country, it being here hilly which were steep and rocky and we had not time to visit the low lands and therefore met with nothing remarkable. My intention was to have stayed at least one day to have looked into the country had we met with fresh water convenient or any other refreshment, but as we did not I thought it would be only spending time and losing so much of a light moon to little purpose, and therefore at 12 oClock at night we weighed and stood away to the NW, having at this time but little wind attended with showers of rain. At 4 oClock the breeze freshened at SbE with fair weather. We continued steering NNW ½ W as the land lay having 10, 12 and 14 fathom at a distance of 3 Leagues from the land. At 10 oClock we hauled off north in order to get without a small low Island which lay about 2 Leagues from the Main; it being about high water at the time we passed it the greater part of it lay under water. About 3 Leagues to the north-westward of this Island close under the main land is a nother Island tolerable high which bore from us at noon N 55° West distant 7 or 8 miles, we being at this time in the Latitude of 16° 20′ S. Cape Grafton bore S 29° East distant 40 miles and the northermost point of land in sight N 20° W, and in this situation had 15 fathom water. The shore between *Cape Grafton* and the above northern point forms a large but not very deep Bay which I named *Trinity Bay* after the day on which it was discovered, the north point *Cape Tribulation* because here began all our troubles. Latitude 16° 6′ S, Long^{de} 214° 39′ W.

BANKS:

After dinner came to an anchor and went ashore, but saw no people. The countrey was hilly and very stoney affording nothing but fresh water, at least that we found, except a few plants that we had not before met with. At night our people caught a few small fish with their hooks and lines. AM: Just without us as we lay at anchor was a small sandy Island laying upon a large coral shoal, much resembling the low Islands to the eastward of us but the first we had met with in this part of the

South Sea. Early in the morn we weighed and sailed as usual with a fine breeze along shore, the Countrey hilly and stoney.

At 2.30 PM, the ship anchored in what is now Mission Bay, on the edge of an area that is marked for spoil dumping. This is immediately to the eastward of the inlet that is the entrance to the large town of Cairns. From the Captain's anchor bearings it does not appear that he considered the east point of Mission Bay as his Cape Grafton. The western point of this bay is now called False Cape. Green Island is today visited by many tourists who view the undersea life through a glass-bottomed boat. The Captain had landed just under the present Cape Grafton. The low islets, passed at 11 AM, are now known as Low Islets, lying 8 miles NE of Port Douglas. The island remarked upon as north-west of this group is Snapper Island, lying SEbS of Cape Kimberley. The Captain's Trinity Bay embraces the whole of the shallow bight between Cape Grafton and Cape Tribulation; but the present Trinity Bay is only that more defined bight between Cape Kimberley and Island Point, at Port Douglas. Cairns Harbour and Mission Bay have supplanted the southern half of the original.

Green Island was the first visual contact with the Great Barrier Reef, showing its inner edge. The ship had sailed north into the narrowing wedge of safe water. Mr Banks had noted the difference in character of this island, but this was no adequate warning.

CHAPTER 8

ENDEAVOUR REEF

In the welter of activity that was now to take place any reader might become lost in confusion. All the more crucial, then, to consider the evidence of each eye witness as it is presented, that the whole might knit sensibly together as each new morsel is added.

SHIP'S LOG:

MONDAY, JUNE 11TH, 1770

H.	K.	F.	Courses.	Winds.	Soundings.	Remarks, &c.
					Fathoms.	
1	3	6	N.N.W.	E.S.E.	14, 14, 14. H'd s'd.	Mod. breezes and fair wea'r. Sailing along shore; dist'ce off, 3 or 4 leagues.
2	3	6	..	..	15, 16, 15	
3	3	7	..	..	14, 13, 12	Saw two low sandy keys bearing N.E., dist. 4 or 5 leagues.
4	4	6	No.	..	Sandy clay. 13, 14, 10	Cloudy wea'r and smooth water.
5	5	..	N.b.W.	..	14, 14½	Saw some rocks above water, bearing N.b.W. 2 or 3 leagues.
6	4	5	..	..	14, 14, 14	Shorten'd sail in 2nd reef and haul'd off shore.
7	2	4	N.E.b.E.	S.E.b.E.	15, 16, 17	
8	2	4	..	..	20, 20, 21	Mod. breezes and clear wea'r.
9	2	2	..	..	Rocks. 21, 20, 21, 13, 10, 9, 8	Pass'd over a bed of rocks, sound's as p'r column.
10	2	..	E.N.E.	S.E.	Sandy. 9,11 12, 15	Shoal'd the water from 20 to 17 fa'm, and standing on a cable's length further the ship struck on some rocks. Clew'd all up and hoisted out the boats, sounded round the
11	{1	6	..	..	17, 17, 21, 20	ship and found she was upon the edge of a bank of coral which lay to the N.W. of her.
	..	..	..	..	17. Clay.	Carried out the streem anchor with two hawsers to the
12	..	..	..	..	..	southward. Hove tort meantime. Got down t'gall't yards,
1	..	..	..	..	..	struck yards and topmasts. The ship still forcing into
2	..	..	..	..	..	shoaler water upon the bank and striking hard, carried out
3	..	..	..	..	..	the coasting anchor and cable to the S.W.
4	..	..	..	..	..	Hove tort on the coasting cable and employ'd all hands in
5	..	..	..	..	..	clearing ship. Hove hoops, staves, empty casks, and oil-jars
6	..	..	..	..	..	overboard, as well to lighten her as to clear away for heavyer articles. Meantime carried out the spare stream anchor to the S.W. and hove tort on't.

H.	K.	F.	Courses.	Winds.	Soundings.	Remarks, &c.
7	..	..	..	..	..	Started 30 tons of water, hove some of the boatswain's and carpenter's condemn'd stores overboard, got the stone and iron ballast out of the hold, with a large quantity of firewood, and hove them all overboard. At 8, found the ship had sprung a leak. Cutt off the heels of the two spare topmasts to clear the foremast pumps. Got 3 pumps to work, the 4th being chok'd. Meantime carried out the b't b'r anchor and cable to ye westward, and hove the 6 carriage guns that was upon deck overboard.
8	..	..	..	..	..	
9	..	..	..	..	..	
10	..	..	..	..	..	
11	..	..	..	..	..	
12	..	..	..	..	..	At noon, light airs and fair weather. The ship now lays with three streaks heel to starboard. Lat'd observ'd, 15° 45' So.

[Green, Bootie, Wilkinson, Pickersgill, Forwood, Hickes, 'M.S. 3' and '153' all agree with the Ship's Log, but Pickersgill adds a few details.]

PICKERSGILL:
. . . at 1 AM, Sent a small boat to sound round the ship and found she was on the edge of a bank of coral lying NW of her . . . at 8 AM, found the ship strained and had sprung a leak.

COOK:
Wind at ESE with which we steered along shore Nbw at the distance of 3 or 4 leagues off having 14 to 10 & 12 fathom water. Saw two small Islands in the offing which lay in the Latitude of 16° 0' S, and about 6 or 7 Leagues from the Main. At 6 oClock the northermost land in sight bore Nbw ½ W and two low woody Islands which some took to be rocks above water bore N ½ W. At this time we shortened sail and hauled off shore ENE and NEbE close upon a wind. My intention was to stretch off all night as well to avoid the dangers we saw ahead of as to see if any Islands lay in the offing as we now began to draw near the latitude of those discovered by Quiros which some Geographers, for what reason I know not, have thought proper to tack to this land, having the advantage of a fine breeze of wind and a clear moon-light night. In standing off from 6 to near 9 oClock we deepened our water from 14 to 21 fathom when all at once we fell into 12, 10 and 8 fathom. At this time I had everybody at their stations to put about and come too an anchor but in this I was not so fortunate for meeting again with deep water I thought there could be no danger in standing on. Before 10 oClock we had 20 and 21 Fathom and continued in that depth untill a few minutes before 11 and before the man at the lead could heave another cast the Ship Struck and stuck fast. Immediately upon all this we took in all our sails and hoisted out the boats and sounded round the Ship, and found that we had got upon the SE edge of a reef of coral rocks having in some places round the Ship 3 and 4 fathom and in other places not quite so many feet, and about a ships length from us on our starboard side (the ship laying with her head to the NE) were 8, 10 and 12 fathom. As soon as the long boat was out we struck yards and top-masts and carried out the stream anchor upon the starboard bow, got the coasting

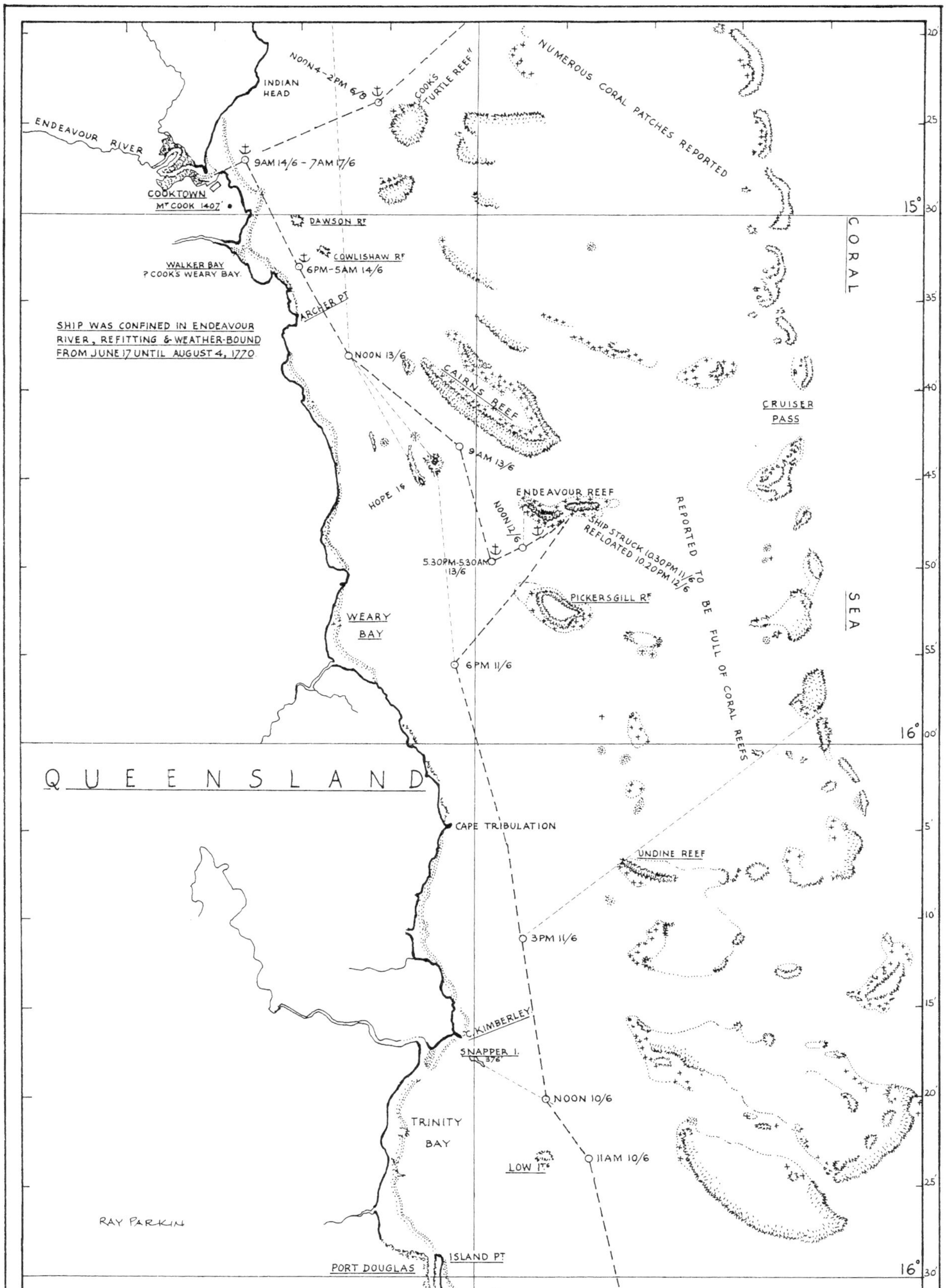

ENDEAVOUR RIVER
INDIAN HEAD
NOON 4-2PM 6/8
COOKS "TURTLE REEF"
NUMEROUS CORAL PATCHES REPORTED
9AM 14/6 - 7AM 17/6
COOKTOWN
Mt COOK 1407'
DAWSON Rf
COWLISHAW Rf
6PM-5AM 14/6
WALKER BAY
? COOK'S WEARY BAY
ARCHER PT
SHIP WAS CONFINED IN ENDEAVOUR RIVER, REFITTING & WEATHER-BOUND FROM JUNE 17 UNTIL AUGUST 4, 1770
NOON 13/6
CAIRNS REEF
9AM 13/6
HOPE Is
ENDEAVOUR REEF
NOON 12/6
SHIP STRUCK 10.30PM 11/6
REFLOATED 10.20PM 12/6
5.30PM-5.30AM 13/6
REPORTED TO BE FULL OF CORAL REEFS
PICKERSGILL Rf
WEARY BAY
6PM 11/6
CRUISER PASS
CORAL
SEA
QUEENSLAND
CAPE TRIBULATION
UNDINE REEF
3PM 11/6
C. KIMBERLEY
SNAPPER I.
376'
NOON 10/6
TRINITY BAY
LOW Is
11AM 10/6
RAY PARKIN
ISLAND PT
PORT DOUGLAS
15°
16°
16° 30'
145°
10'
15'
20'
25'
35'
40'
45'
50'

anchor and cable into the boat and were going to carry it out the same way; but upon my sounding the second time round the ship I found the most water astern, and therefore had this anchor carried out upon the starboard quarter and hove upon it a very great strain which was to no purpose the Ship being quite fast, upon which we went to work to lighten her as fast as possible which seemed to be the only means we had left to get her off as we went ashore about the top of high-water. We not only started water but throwed over board our guns Iron and stone ballast Casks, Hoops staves oyle jars decayed stores &C[a], many of these last articles lay in the way at coming at heavyer. All this time the Ship made little or no water. At 11 oClock in the AM being High water as we thought we tryed to heave her off without success, she not being afloat by a foot or more notwithstanding by this time we had thrown overboard 40 or 50 Tun weight; as this was not found sufficient we continued to lighten her by every method we could think of. As the tide fell the Ship began to make water as much as two pumps could free. At noon she lay with 3 or 4 strakes heel to starboard. Latitude observed 15° 45′ South.

BANKS:

At night fall rocks and sholes were seen ahead, on which the ship was put upon a wind off shore. While we were at supper she went over a bank of 7 or 8 fathom water which she came upon very suddenly; this we concluded to be the tail of the Sholes we had seen at sunset and therefore went to bed in perfect security, but scarce were we warm in our beds when we were called up with the alarming news of the ship being fast ashore upon a rock, which she in a few moments convinced us of by beating very violently against the rocks. Our situation became now greatly alarming: we had stood off shore 3 hours and a half with a pleasant breeze so that we could not be very near it: we were little less than certain that we were upon sunken coral rocks, the most dreadful of all others on account of their sharp points and grinding quality which cut through a ships bottom almost immediately. The officers however behaved with inimitable coolness void of all hurry and confusion; a boat was got out in which the Master went and after sounding round the ship found that she had ran over a rock and consequently had shole water all round her. All this time she continued to beat very much so that we could hardly keep our legs upon the Quarter Deck; by the light of the moon we could see her sheathing boards &c. floating thick around her; about 12, her false keel came away. In the mean time all kind of preparations were making for carrying out anchors, but by reason of the time it took to hoist out our boats &c. the tide ebbed so much that we found it impossible to attempt to get her off till next high water, if she would hold together so long; and now we found to add to our misfortune that we had got ashore at the top of high water and as the night tides generally rise higher than the day ones we had little hopes of getting off ever then. For our Comfort however the ship as the tide ebbed settled to the rocks and did not beat near so much as she had done; a rock however under her starboard bow kept grating her bottom and making a noise very plainly to be heard in the fore store rooms; this we doubted not would make a hole in her bottom, we only hoped that it might not let in more water than we could clear with our pumps.

In this situation the day broke upon us and showed us the land about 8 leagues off as we judged; nearer than that was no Island or place on which we could set foot. It however brought with it a decrease of wind and soon after that a flat calm, the most fortunate circumstance that could Possibly attend people in our circumstances. The tide we found had fallen 2 feet and still continued to fall; Anchors were however got out and laid ready for heaving as soon as the tide should rise but to our great surprize we could not observe it to rise in the least. Orders were now given for lightning the ship which was began by starting our water and pumping it up; the ballast was then got up and thrown overboard, as well as 6 of our guns (all that we had upon deck). All this time the seamen worked with surprizing chearfullness and alacrity; no grumbling or growling was to be heard throughout the ship, no not even an oath (tho the ship in general was as well furnished with them as most in his majesties service.)

PARKINSON:

On the 10th [Ship's PM, 11th], we continued our course to the north-west; and about nine o'clock in the morning [evening] we sailed down a reef of coral rocks. Our water shoaled very soon, from twenty-one to eight fathoms; which alarmed us very much: every countenance expressed surprize, and every heart felt some trepidation. About eleven, the ship struck upon the rocks and remained immoveable. We were, at this period, many thousand leagues from our native land, (which we had left upwards of two years,) and on a barbarous coast, where, if the ship had been wrecked, and we had escaped the perils of the sea, we should have fallen into the rapacious hands of savages. Agitated and surprized as we were, we attempted every apparent eligible method to escape, if possible, from the brink of destruction. The sails were immediately handed, the boats launched, the yards and topmasts struck, and an anchor carried out to the southward; the ship striking hard, another anchor was dispatched to the south-west. Night came on [a strange confusion here by Parkinson] which providentially was moonlight; and we weathered it out as patiently as possible, considering the dreadful suspense we were in.

On the 11th, early in the morning, we lightened ship, by throwing over-board our ballast, fire wood, some of our stores, our water casks, all our water, and six of our great guns; and set the pumps at work, at which every man on board assisted, the Captain, Mr Banks and all the officers, not excepted; relieving one another every quarter of an hour. About noon, the ship heaved much on one side; upon which five anchors were carried out, and dropt at different parts; while all hands on board plied the pumps incessantly, hoping to have heaved her off the rock, but hoping in vain.

When we threw the guns overboard, we fixed buoys to them, intending, if we escaped, to have heaved them up again; but on attempting it we found it was impracticable.

This was the situation thus far at noon, the end of the ship's day. One may read over the summary of events swiftly, but thirteen hours of continuous and vigorous action had gone by, six of them in the dark.

Two things had struck Mr Banks, upon which, as a landsman, he remarks. Knowing how he himself was alarmed, but 'the officers however behaved with inimitable coolness void of all hurry and confusion.' He was also surprised by the seamen themselves. What he may have thought the topsy-turvydom of sailor psychology was in fact just the sailors' simple way. It may seem obligatory to many that, in times of dire peril, one appeals to a Higher Power. Though the sailor may not be entirely averse to this idea, he intuitively goes to the heart of the matter, convinced that a prayer of words may be a waste of vital time: so action is his prayer. Not one wasted word, forgoing even the luxury of habitual oaths, as Mr Banks bears witness: 'All this time the seamen worked with surprizing chearfullness and alacrity; no grumbling or growling was to be heard throughout the ship, no not even an oath'. At such times as these, the sailor will seldom die in a despair of supine supplication.

Should the Captain be censured for sailing on that night? With hindsight it is very easy to think he should. Later, Dalrymple (himself disaffected because he thought that he should have been in command of this expedition) accused the Captain of rash navigation in coral waters. Certainly the ship was in conditions where coral grew, but so far there had been nothing to suggest that the unique mass of coral that was encircling her, hitherto completely unsuspected and unknown, was the largest in the world. Green Island had been the first visible sign, but, even from that sighting, who was to know that it was part of a 2,500-mile densely packed chain of reefs mostly submerged at high water? Yet from noon on the 10th, they had been sailing with its inner limits five miles and less in their offing—the offing which may normally be considered a safe refuge for a wind-dependent ship sailing along an unknown lee shore which is a constant hazard. By 6 PM, this day, the ship had advanced some 25 miles from noon, and Cape Tribulation was 10 miles astern, with the Hope Islands being sighted ahead in the gathering darkness as breakers. This strongly suggested offshore shoals near the coast and gave a convincing reason to go close upon a wind to seaward. There was nothing to suggest that these were in fact the inner limits of hazard, and not the outer. So the Captain decided to haul the ship offshore for the night and brought her within six points of the wind on the starboard tack. Both chains were kept continually manned as they had been for near a thousand miles. The two leadsmen kept singing, with the long drawn-out, penetrating call of their De-e-e-e-ps *and* Ma-a-a-a-arks *being plainly heard on the quarterdeck. But the whole ship listened to these liturgical chants, with every man interpreting the vital implications in simple numbers. For two hours the calls had been from fourteen to an encouraging twenty-one fathoms; but, about 9 o'clock, there was sudden apprehension with the call of* De-e-e-ep Eight! *Almost at once, being all the time on a split yarn, all were at their stations for bringing her up and letting go an anchor. But then, two calls later,* De-e-e-e-p Twelve! *Then* Ma-a-a-a-rk Fifteen!

The ship had just passed over the western tail of Pickersgill Reef, missing its lethal edge and outlying bomies by less than a mile. At sunset the second reef had been put in the topsails and, under an easy sail, had reduced speed from 4 ½ knots to just 2. It was clear moonlight and all hands were in a state of readiness.

The Captain had a secondary intention in stretching off the coast for the night, which fitted well enough into the evasive action he was taking to avoid shoals. In this latitude, the Captain thought that there was just a possibility that he might strike those elusive islands Quiros had discovered in 1606, when he had sailed from Peru. Elusive because, in Quiros's time, though calculation of latitude had been reasonable, that of longitude was made almost entirely from a deduced reckoning from the 'error-abounding log', as Herman Melville called even the log of his day. Apart from the deficiencies of the log, there were the unknowns of tides and currents, leeway, and so on. So inexact was the calculation for longitude known to be that the only chance of a rediscovery, or even coming up with a well-known place, was to sail down its latitude. The Captain was aware of this and that there was only a chance possibility of finding these islands 'which some Geographers, for what reason I know not, have thought proper to tack to this land.' This made the east coast of New Holland, from Van Diemen's Land out to the Solomons and back to Torres Strait, look not unlike the breast of a pouter pigeon on their maps. But Cook was not a man to neglect a possibility out of hand.

It would seem that the very logic and probability of the situation conspired against him. Who could have guessed that the only safe passage here was against all probability, as indicated by his previous experience. Not long before, in the cul-de-sac at Keppel Isles, he had had to seek a passage to seaward to find deeper water. Yet the fact is that, just here, the only safe passage lay between the Hope Islands and the main, barely a mile and a half offshore. This is the one that is used now, but only after a century of surveying, beacon laying and coast lighting, with modern charts and sailing directions and powered vessels. But Endeavour *was sailing almost at ninety degrees to this course, out to the impenetrable shelf of the Barrier Reef.*

The leadsmen leaned well out from the chains at the foot of the fore-lower rigging at an angle of sixty degrees, hanging in their breast ropes which ran back under their arms to the shrouds above and behind them, each continually recovering and coiling the dripping line as soon as his call was made. Then, with the coil in his inboard hand, and a slack bight of the line to the other which held the 14-pound lead on the end of a fathom or so, he would begin a pendulum movement with it.

The ship was sailing smoothly under double-reefed topsails with scarcely a heel; at two knots there was the steady splashing of the ripple of the bow-wave being pushed aside by the bluff hull, making a pale green fire of phosphorescence as it went. On the larboard side the bright moon laid a silver carpet to the horizon on an otherwise inky sea which gave not an inkling of what lay beneath. The moon's brilliance lit the air like a gossamer, subtly veiling the blackness of space and paling the stars in its wake. At the zenith, away from this influence, the indigo sky was riddled with the ice-blue brilliance of stars of all magnitude. All within this horizon seemed unshakeably constant.

The pendulum swing of the lead was almost level with the leadsman's shoulder and, at the end of its backward swing, he stooped slightly and began to accelerate the lead on its forward swing. Just as it came above shoulder level in front of him, he pulled his clenched fist sharply to his shoulder, speeding the lead as it went up and over. As it passed overhead, he allowed his arm to extend smoothly behind him so that, on this extended radius, he increased the speed of it more as it came forward. Once more overhead and, as it came forward, at about 45° to the sea, he opened his hand and let the lead take the turns off his hand and the rest of the line with it on its way to the bottom. He quickly gathered in the slack as the ship came ahead so that by the time it was underfoot he had the 'feel' of the bottom with no slack in the line. He noted that the red rag rove into the line was just at the surface. By the M-a-a-rk Seven-t-e-e-en! *He faced aft to haul in the line again for the next cast, but, before he could do so, the ship suddenly brought-up, all-standing, with a tremendous surge that shook all on their feet and set them grabbing for support. The rigging gave a great drawn-out grumbling creak as the whip of the masts suddenly strained at every point, while spars and blocks rattled in their constraint.*

The ship had struck Endeavour Reef, which lay unseen at the top, almost, of high water, and right athwart her course. She had struck it almost in the middle of its 4-mile length. Fortunately she had grounded not on the main shelf but on a bomie outcrop a little from it, though this was not apparent at the time. The reef is steep-to, having 13, 16 and 21 fathoms right up to it.

Action was immediate and reflexive in all the men. Courses and topsails were at once clewed up to stop her driving further. One watch began clearing away the main-stay and yardarm tackles to hoist out the boats. The others went aloft to make the sails fast to the yards, swiftly passing the sennit gaskets to leave only the triangular ears of the clews free with their tacks and sheets. This was done not in a moment but with a deliberateness devoid of panic, in the best possible time.

The 10-foot yawl was fleeted from its stowage on the quarterdeck to the main deck, hooked on to the falls and hoisted out first. With a boatkeeper holding her alongside she was soon manned and the Master went in her to sound round the ship. Hoisting boats out in this manner takes time, and boat davits were not yet known. The pinnace and long boat were next in the water to lay out the small anchors, as a first measure, to hold or haul off the ship. The stream and coasting (which was the kedge) anchors were laid out to starboard and astern with 6-inch hawsers which were brought to the capstan and windlass and hove upon with all the strain that could be brought to bear, but to no effect. These anchors were small enough to allow them to be put into a boat, carried out, then hove over the side. The lighter pinnace could manage this well enough, but the bower anchors were a job for the long boat.

Once the boats were in the water, all spare hands were turned to striking the yards and topmasts. This is a complicated enough job even in daylight, without the pressure of an emergency. There is a great deal of standing and running rigging that has to be unrove or part-unrove and stopped securely with spunyard just where it will be required when it has to be set up again. But now it had to be done by the deceptive light of the moon whose white highlights and black shadows make tricky the judging of distance aloft. This is important to men who are working together but separated by as much as 80 feet between those aloft and those on deck tending, who see each other only through a maze of interlacing rope.

First, the topgallant yards were sent down from the fore and main. The men worked aloft in the dark over a black sea without yet knowing what damage the ship had taken below the water. As the ship bumped heavily from time to time on the coral beneath her, it made the men on deck stagger, but, for the men aloft it was magnified into a dangerous whip of the masts which, without warning, could well shake a man off his perch if his grab for support was not quick or precise enough. But as long as a sailor has a job to do, habit has trained him to give his attention to it and develops in him unconscious reflexes for his preservation. The same experience makes him vitally aware of the folly and dangers of overanxiety. The men in Endeavour *knew a discipline that had nothing in common with being made marionettes on a parade ground. They took for granted what had surprised the more erudite Mr Banks. It was not that the men were insensitive to real danger. They knew quite well when they saw the sheathing boards floating alongside, having been beaten off the bottom of the ship, what was threatening them; but, because they could assess it, they did not let their imaginations run away with them. When part of the false keel surfaced alongside, they knew that this six-inch piece of timber had taken the first shock that may well have saved the main keel from more serious damage: and this was the very purpose for which it had been put there. There was gravity and urgency in the situation, they well knew, but efficient deliberation was the only way out. The 'surprizing chearfullness and alacrity' that Joseph Banks observed was simply that of men presented with one of those rare occasions in life in which they were being extended to the limits of their capabilities, the outcome of which was how well they would be able to live with themselves afterwards.*

Though the logs say only, 'Struck yards and topmasts', the topgallants had to be brought down first. Men went aloft on the fore and main to get the topgallant yards ready for sending down from their slings 80 feet above the deck. The main t'gallant yard was 31′ 8″ long, and the fore 28′ 9″, heavy with sails or gear. The tye or halliard of the yard was cast off and bent to the jack-block which was then hoisted up and the toprope rove through it, upon which the yard was lowered. The sheets, bowlines, buntlines and clewlines were cast off the yard and fastened to the crosstrees out of the way. Then the toprope was made fast to the bunt or centre of the yard, with a fisherman's bend, and the bight taken out halfway to the quarter of the yard and seized so that the yard would go down end-on. The parral, which holds the yard to the mast, was cast off, allowing the yard to cant until it was up-and-down, being eased into this position by the weather lift. With the yard in this position, and one man standing on the crosstrees and another in the topmast rigging, each unrigged the braces and lifted them to his hand. Fixing a traveller or hoop about the weather topmast backstay and seizing it to the bunt of the yard, those tending the toprope below lowered it to the deck. This way the yard was controlled—even in bad weather at sea, where this evolution was mostly done.

The same process was then repeated for the considerably larger topsail yards. The main was 41′ 1″ long and 10 ½″ thick; the fore, 36′ by 9″. The former weighed close on 1,000 pounds, and the latter 700 pounds, both without their large sails and gear. The total weight of the masts and spars of Endeavour *was around 12 ½ tons, without rigging or fittings, which would have been at least half again. With the jarring bumps of the ship on the reef, and the shock loading from it, which normally doubles the inert load, being brought on the hull and rigging, this reduction of top hamper was imperative to preserve the ship, and this was why it was taking precedence.*

It is on nights such as this one, in tropic waters, that the stars come nearer, being brighter and clearer. As the men worked in the dark aloft they could hear the voices of those in the boats reflected clearly up to them from the flat sounding board of the water's surface. Voices, the wooden rattle of oars, splashes and thumps as hawsers were being handled, occasional calls from boat to ship or ship to boat—all of these kept the men in the rigging comfortably aware of the general situation as they worked.

When the topsail yards were on deck and stowed clear out of the way, the lower yards were lowered. These, the fore and the main, were respectively 44′ 2″, weighing about 1,320 pounds without gear, and 47′ 10″. These could be lowered to the deck on their jears, which were twofold purchases with 12″ blocks and 3″ rope falls of some 68 fathoms long. The lower yards were lowered square across the ship, and left secured to the lower shrouds to keep them clear of the deck.

Once the yards were down, the topgallant masts had to be struck and brought on deck. For this they had to be completely unrigged. The sheets, bowlines, buntlines and clewlines, lifts, braces, shrouds, backstays, forestays, staysail halliards and so on were all cast off and had to be coiled and stopped in the topmast crosstrees where they would be to hand when the mast was sent up again. The topgallant masts had to be stripped so that they would pass down through the topmast cap and between the trestle- and crosstrees on the foreside of the topmast. For lowering, the toprope was rove from one side of the cap of the topmast passing close-down through a diagonal sheave in the heel of the topgallant mast, then up to the cap on the other side, through the top-block there, and down to the deck from whence it was manned. As the men hauled, the weight of the mast was taken off the square fid which passed through its heel, and on which it normally rested across the trestletrees. When this fid was withdrawn, the mast was free to be lowered in the bight of the toprope as the men checked away on it. Those aloft controlled its head until it was safely on deck.

After the topgallants were down, the work of dismantling the topmasts, so that they could be housed, began. The foretopmast was 38′ 4″ by 12″, the main was 40′ 7″ by 12″ and a little heavier. These carried a great deal more rigging then the topgallants, having four pairs of shrouds, and these nearly twice as thick; the crosstrees, with all the topgallant gear coiled up and stopped in them, now had all that of the topsail yard as well. These were lowered in the same way as the topgallants, but not brought right down on deck. They were left 'housed'—that is, hanging in the bight of their topropes with the crosstrees close-down on the lower caps and their heels lashed close to the foreside of the lower masts. Thus, the topmast shrouds had not been cast off, but hung in bights from the tops where their lower ends were normally secured.

By this time it was after 3 AM. The moon was lower and had moved westwards towards the main: as remote and unconcerned with the struggling ship as could be imagined, coldly striking a few experimental sparks of lunar light off the ripples made on the water by the toiling men. But equally, it might be said, the men paid no attention to the westering moon, as they worked among this familiar tangle of rigging as single-mindedly as spiders in a web.

Dismantling had taken precedence over the laying out of the anchors, and it was 4 o'clock before the second anchor had been laid out and the strain hove upon it. The ship was still being bumped heavily on the reef by the breathing sea. It was hoped that the straining hawsers would relieve this. The long boat was brought under the bows and the spare stream anchor passed down into her with a six-inch hawser. She laid this anchor out astern and pulled back to the ship, paying out the hawser as she came, and passed the end of it up inboard as she came alongside. This was brought to the capstan on the quarterdeck and hove to a strain. The ship now had three small anchors, with their flukes biting deep into the bottom on taut cables, holding her from driving further on.

As she had gone on near the top of high water, the Captain knew the only hope of getting her off was to lighten her by every means at his disposal. The hatches were opened up, the stay-tackles were brought over them, and all spare hands began getting out what they could; much inconsequential stuff was thrown out as it was cleared away from the heavier articles they were trying to come at. There was a considerable amount of firewood as well as the loose bits of broken stowage. The iron and stone ballast was not easy to get to. Most of it was stowed in the bread room, which was right aft in the run. It had been placed there by the Captain in an endeavour to get the ship trimmed by the stern. The last attempt at this, totally successful, was with extra stone ballast taken on in Queen Charlotte Sound, New Zealand. This could be reached only through a small hatch a bare 3 feet square, in the lobby outside the officers' cabins on the lower deck. The headroom under the beams here was not 5 feet, while the hold was 10 feet deep. All of this ballast had to be manhandled up into the lobby. Once there, it was taken, by lamplight, right aft and jettisoned out through the two square raft ports in the stern. The ship had originally taken in 8 tons of iron ballast and, later, a further 56 pigs of it. A pig of iron was 56 pounds, or half a hundredweight. Two hundred years after the iron ballast had been thus jettisoned, a recovery expedition found it 'in one tidy heap cemented together by iron oxide'. Ten tons of it were brought to the surface, together with a quantity of the stone ballast. It was located just 85 feet away from the cannon. To get out this amount of weight in such a constricted working space had taken some considerable hard work and time.

It was, by this time, daylight. At 7 AM, the fresh water was 'started'—that is, it was pumped or siphoned out of the cask into the bilges where it found its way along the limbers into the pump well, from whence it was pumped over the side. The pipes and butts in which it was stowed each held half a ton; and the hogsheads, a quarter of a ton. The ton was reckoned at 252 gallons. The ship had started thirty tons.

But still more deadweight had to be got rid of, and the six carriage guns, the four-pounders, which were on the main deck abreast the fore and main hatches, were hove over the side. Each of these guns weighed 11 ½ hundredweight. By knocking out the forelock of the cap square, which held the gun to its carriage by its trunnion, the guns were released. Eight men passed four capstan bars under each gun and, from either side, lifted it free. They carried it to the 'lee' or downward side which was to starboard and there the inboard men raised their bars and tilted the gun so that it slid out over the side like a corpse committed to its standing grave. It had to clear the bulging tumblehome of the ship's side which here was some three feet beyond the line of the gunwale on deck. The carriages, too, were hove over.

Thus far the ship had made no appreciable amount of water overnight, but, at 8 AM, the water was found to increase. The pumps were cleared away and the brakes shipped. But before this could be done with the two foremost ones, the heels of the two spare topmasts had to be cut off to clear a way, for the after gallows on which they were lashed to the booms was only 3 feet above the quarterdeck, just before the two foremost pumps, forward of the main mast. There was no time to unlash and restow these 40-foot spars, so their heels were cut off, and the pump brakes shipped. Of the four pumps, only three could be made to suck. The fourth was choked. Each of these pump shafts was made of a single elm tree, bored through the centre of its whole 23-foot length by hand augers. Each went right to the bottom of the ship and sucked from the pump well by the keel. The men were now working the pumps continuously in fifteen-minute spells, with no one excused, not even Mr Banks—or the Captain.

The Captain estimated that he had got rid of some 40 or 50 tons of deadweight. Preparations were now being made, as the forenoon wore on, for the laying out of the bower anchors to be ready to heave the ship off at the next high water if possible. These, too, with their cables, would take several more tons out of the ship. In the second sounding round the ship, by the light of day in the forenoon, the master reported: 'Sounded round the ship with a staff and found we had no more water on the starboard side than 7 feet; 8 feet on the larboard bow; and, on the starboard side from the chess-tree [about halfway between the fore and main masts] aft, water enough, as there was from the aft part of the main channel aft on the larboard side.' The 'channels' were the platforms on the ship's side to which the lower rigging was secured—the 'chains' from which the leadsmen hove the lead.

By noon, on a falling tide, the ship had come to rest, partially supported by the reef where she had struck and remained fast. She was heeled three or four strakes (planks) to starboard. The strakes at the waterline were those of the main wale which was made up of four, each 7 ½ inches broad. This would, on calculation, give her an eight-degree list, quite noticeable to those on board shifting weights. Her head lay to the NE.

Everybody there well knew that the boats could not possibly hold all the people. In the eighteenth century, boats were supplied solely for the work they had to do, and their life-saving capacity was never considered. The nearest place to the ship where the men could have stood with dry feet was on the small cays of the Hope Islands, eight miles away.

SHIP'S LOG:

TUESDAY, JUNE 12TH, 1770

H.	Remarks, &c.
1 2 3 4	These 24 hours light airs and fair wea'r. Employ'd at the pumps and clearing ship. Carried out the small bower anchor to the westward Lash'd blocks on both bower cables, reeved hawsers and hove tort on all the 5 anchors. At 4 it was low water, which we could perceive by the rocks about the ship and part of the bank being dry. The rise and fall does not exceed 3 or 4 feet.
5 6 7 8	Found the tide began to rise. Hove a fresh strain and made use of every method that our situation would admit off to heave the ship off. Found the leak did not gain on the three pumps.
9 10 11 12	½-p't 9, the ship righted, and at 10 hove her afloat. Veered away on the stream cable and small bower and bro't the b't bower and coasting anchors ahead in 15 fa'm water, muddy ground. Found it impossible to save the small bower, so cut it away at a whole cable.
1	Sent the longboat to weigh the streem anchor. Purchas'd the anchor, but lost the cable amongst the rocks.
2	People employ'd at the pumps and shifting the coasting cable and spare stream hawser from the quarter forward.
3	The leak gain'd on the pumps these 4 hours. Had 3 feet 9 inches in the hold.
4	
5	Sent the longboat to weight the spare streem anchor and run it out to ye S.E. for to warp the ship to windward.
6	Hove tort on ye warp, hove up the b't bower and coasting anchors, and got up the foretopm't and foreyards.
7	The pumps gain'd on the leak these 4 hours.
8	
9 10 11	Warp'd head. Some hands employ'd sewing hair, wool, and oacham into a low steering sail to fother the ship. At 11, weigh'd and came to sail with a light air at E.S.E. Sent the pinnace ahead to tow, and a small boat to lye on the edge of the bank.
12	At noon the dry bank bore No., distance 1½ miles. Got up maintopm'st and main yards.

COOK:

Fortunately we had little wind and fine weather and a smooth sea all these 24 hours which in the PM gave us an opportunity to carry out the two bower Anchors, the one on the starboard quarter and the other right a stern. Got blocks and tackles upon the cables and brought the falls in abaft and hove taught. By this time it was 5 oClock in the PM, the tide we observed now begun to rise and the leak increased upon us which obliged us to set the 3rd pump to work as we should have done the 4th also, but could not make it work. At 9 oClock the Ship righted and the leak gained upon the Pumps considerably. This was an alarming and I may say terrible Circumstance and threatened immediate destruction to us as soon as the Ship was afloat. However I resolved to risk all and heave her off in case it was practical and accordingly turned as many hands to the Capstan and Windlass as could be spared from the Pumps and about 20′ past 10 oClock the Ship floated and we hove her off into deep water having at this time 3 feet 9 inches water in the hold. This done I sent the long boat to take up the stream anchor—got the anchor but lost the Cable among the rocks, after this turned all hands to the Pumps the leak increasing upon us. A Mistake soon after happened which for the first time caused fear to operate upon every man in the Ship. The man which attended the well took y[e] depth of water above the ceiling he being relieved by another who did not know in what manner the former had sounded, took the depth of water from the outside plank, the difference being 16 or 18 inches and made it appear that the leak had gained this upon the Pumps in a short time, this mistake was no sooner cleared up than it acted upon every man like a charm; they redoubled their vigour in so much that before 8 oClock in the morning they gained considerably upon the leak. We now hove up the best bower but found it impossible to save the small bower so cut it away at a whole cable. Got up the fore topmast and foreyard, warped the Ship to the SE and at 11 got under sail and stood in for the land with a light breeze at ESE, some hands employed sowing ockam wool &c[a] into a lower studding sail to fother the Ship, others employed at the Pumps which still gained upon the leak.

BANKS:
About one the water was fallen so low that the Pinnace touched ground as he lay under the ships bows ready to take an anchor, after this the tide began to rise and as soon as it rose the ship worked violently upon the rocks so that by 2 she began to make water and increased very fast. At night the tide almost floated her but she made water so fast that three pumps hard worked could but just keep her clear and the 4th absolutely refused to deliver a drop of water. Now in my own opinion I entirely gave up the ship and packing up what I thought I might save prepared myself for the worst.

The most critical part of our distress now approached: the ship was almost afloat and everything ready to get her into deep water but she leaked so fast that with all our pumps we could just keep her free: if (as was probable) she should make more water when we hauled off she must sink and we well knew that our boats were not capable of carrying us all ashore, so that some, probably the most of us, must be drowned: a better fate maybe than those would have who should get ashore without arms to defend themselves from the Indians or provide themselves with food, on a countrey where we had not the least reason to hope for subsistance had they even every convenience to take it such as netts &c, so barren had we always found it; and had they even met with good usage from the natives and food to support them, debarred from a hope of ever again seeing their native countrey or conversing with any but the most uncivilized savages perhaps in the world.

Endeavour fast on Endeavour Reef, June 12th, 1770. 'Smooth sea . . . which gave us the opportunity to carry out the two bower anchors.'

A dreadful time now approached and the anziety in every bodys countenance was visible enough: the Capstan and Windlace were manned and they began to heave: fear of death now stared us in the face; hopes we had none but of being able to keep the ship afloat till we could run her ashore on some part of the main where out of her materials we might build a vessel large enough to carry us to the East Indies. At 10 o'Clock she floated and was in a few minutes hawled into deep water where to our great satisfaction she made no more water than she had done, which was indeed full as much as we could manage tho no one there was in the ship but who willingly exerted his utmost strength.

The people who had been 24 hours at exceeding hard work now began to flag; myself unused to labour was much fatigued and had laid down to take a little rest, was awakened about 12 with the alarming news of the ships [sic] having gained so much upon the Pumps that she had four feet water in her hold; add to this that the wind blew off the land a regular land breeze so that all hopes of running her ashore were totally cut off. This however acted upon everybody like a charm; rest was no more thought of but the pumps went with unwearied vigour till the water was all out which was done in a much shorter time than was expected, and upon examination it was found that she never had half so much water in her as was thought, the Carpenter having made a mistake in sounding the pumps. We now began again to have some hopes and talk of getting the ship into some harbour as we could spare hands from the pumps to get up our anchors; one Bower however we cut away but got the other and three small anchors far more valuable to us than the Bowers, as we were obliged to warp her to windward that we might take advantage of the sea breeze to run in shore.

PARKINSON:
At four o'clock in the afternoon it was low water, and the ship, in several places, grounded on the rock. Between nine and ten the tide rose four feet, and the ship righted again; and, about ten, after some attempts to clear her, she providentially got off. This desirable event gave us spirits; which, however, proved but the transient gleam of sun-shine, in a tempestuous day; for they were soon depressed again, by observing that the water increased in the hold, faster than we could throw it out; and we expected, every minute, that the ship would sink, or that we should be obliged to run her again upon the rocks.

PICKERSGILL:
PM . . . . carried out the Small bower anchor and cable WNW; lashed blocks on both (Bower) cables; reeved a 5″ hawser and hove taut on y[e] capstan; and brought y[e] coasting cable to y[e] windlass. At 3 PM, hove on all five anchors . . . at ½ past, the ship began to right. At ½ past 10 hove her afloat . . . 1 AM, the people these 4 hours employed at the pumps and shifting the coasting cable and spare stream hawser from y[e] quarter to the bow . . . at 8 AM, hove taut on the coasting anchor and the best bower . . .

In full daylight the sun was glancing off the ripples made by people toiling on a calm sea. There was a curious quality in those brilliant flashes of reflected morning sun which could strike across the face with palpable warmth.

With the falling tide, the brown reef exposed its dorsal vertebrae, whale-like, while still concealing its full limits which now so tantalised the voyagers. Would it keep hold of them, or let them go?

The reflections of Joseph Banks tell something of the very real possibilities in their situation, and which he thought, perhaps, that the sailors were disregarding. He was much more apprehensive of the bumping of the ship than they appeared to be; yet perhaps they were assessing it more clinically, without the magnification of an imagination only part-knowing. In Mr Banks's soliloquy there seems to be some echo of Richard Walter's account of Lord Anson's Voyage Round the World, 1740–44*, a copy of which was onboard* Endeavour*. He would appear to be identifying with the experience at Tinian when* Centurion *dragged her anchors into deep water and was blown offshore, with her anchors and cables up-and-down. This marooned Anson and many of the crew on shore with him. They at once began building themselves a boat, assuming that* Centurion*, badly thus undermanned, and those men sickly, would be lost or unable to recover the land. In the event it was a full nineteen days before they did, and then they had to be assisted to anchor by those from the shore.*

Even so, the speculations of Mr Banks were not all that insubstantial; the men, working hard at the pumps in short strenuous shifts, and the water appearing to gain, gave them some substance.

But there was still heavy work to be done before the ship had a chance of hauling off. This may be called the story of the anchors, and demonstrates the vital part that they play in the survival of a ship. As well, there is a curious twist to this particular story that took a full two centuries to unravel, due to variations concerning the placing of the anchors in entries by the Captain, the Ship's Log, John Bootie, Richard Pickersgill, Stephen Forwood, Zachary Hickes, Francis Wilkinson and, probably, Robert Molyneux (in 'Anonymous 153'). So that it is well to try to follow these events as graphically as possible. And it is important, for an appreciation of the work that had to be done, to remember the comparatively small size of the boats doing the work.

The smaller anchors were the first laid out. In this the pinnace, which was a lighter and finer boat than the long boat, was able to assist. These anchors were the stream, and kedge (which was the smaller). But either of these could be used as a coasting anchor, and used for anchoring the ship in light conditions to save the heavy work of weighing the bowers. Otherwise they were normally used to carry out astern, when the bower was down, with a hawser to prevent the ship swinging in a restricted roadstead. They could also be used to carry ahead of the ship on which she could haul herself to gain an offing in calm conditions. This was called kedging or warping.

The boats backed, stern-first, under the bows to receive the anchors. The long boat took in the stream anchor and the two six-inch hawsers which were coiled down in the stern sheets of the boat as they were passed down. Being on the starboard side she worked in the moon-shadow. Each hawser was 120 fathoms long, so that she could lay the anchor well out from the ship. Having buoyed and dropped the anchor, the boat's crew pulled back to the ship, paying the hawser out over the stern as they came, having to pull a strong steady stroke to keep headway against its drag. Once alongside, the end was passed inboard and brought to the capstan and hove taut to a strain. The Captain says that this was carried out on the starboard bow, while all others say that it was on the quarter. From the master in the yawl sounding, it became certain that the deeper water lay astern, so the pinnace with the coasting anchor pulled out to the starboard quarter where she let it go, bringing the end of its hawser back to the ship. Here it, too, was brought to the capstan and hove to a strain to prevent the ship driving on further. While the pinnace had been under the bow, she had touched bottom in one spot. Later, the long boat took out the spare stream anchor to the SW, which was right astern, again being hove taut to a strain. Thus at noon, the end of the ship's day, the ship remained fast with three small anchors holding her from further driving-on.

The sea was calm with a vague somnolent breathing that rippled on the revealed remnants of the restraining reef. From the chesstree amidships forward, the ship had shallow water that would not support her and she was hard-down on the rasping coral which, heeling her eight degrees to starboard, gave her the appearance of a wreck, with *her yards and topmasts down. Forward, there was only 7, 8, and 9 feet of water. This was the position at noon, when the twenty-four hours of the ship's Tuesday, 12th began.*

The calm weather permitted the bower anchors to be laid out. This was the first time the long boat had been called upon for this heavy job. An 18′ 6″ boat with a 7′ beam had to carry an anchor that was 12′ 9″ long and 7′ 6″ across, from the bill of one fluke to the other, each 2′ broad. But making it much more awkward was the heavy oaken stock, 15″ square in the centre and 13′ 6″ long. At 58 pounds per cubic foot, this alone weighed some 7 cwt 3 qr. At the top of the shank of the anchor was the 2′-diameter ring, 2″ thick and heavily 'puddened' over with old rope, and having the 13 ½″ cable fastened to it with a massive inside clench, well seized.

The bower anchor had been lowered to the water from the projecting cathead on the bow. Hung on the large hook of the cat-tackle, it was sunk enough for the flukes of the anchor to clear the bottom of the long boat as she backed up to it. From the after lifting ring in the sternpost of the boat, a strop was passed round the shank of the anchor, below the stock, then back through its own part with a well-tallowed wooden fid thrust into the bight to hold it. The anchor was then lowered away handsomely until this strop took the weight, then the cat-tackle was unhooked. The boat now had some 25 hundredweight of anchor hanging on its transom at the stern. The buoy and buoy rope were sent down, and some of the heavy cable coiled into the stern sheets—enough to allow the anchor to fall freely to the bottom and bite well when let go. The rudder was unshipped, and a steering oar got out over the stern. This was necessary so that the coxswain could hold the boat on course against the drag of the cable being payed out from the ship.

The eight men gave way together on the oars, rising off their thwarts and straining the oars into a bow with cracking shoulders, their feet hard against the stretchers, lifting their chests to throw more weight on: making a taut straining bridge of knotted muscle. This was the only means of getting way on such a heavily laden boat deep in the water. Each stroke had to be just as strenuous as this, or the boat would be dragged back. The blades of the oars made strong sucking sounds as they were pulled through the water, straining against the sluggishness of the boat. There was the solid clump of the looms of the oars against the thole pins, as they snapped straight leaving the water at the end of each stroke. The men knew from experience that nothing less than a dogged, mulish effort would get them where they had to go, and settled down to a job that had to be done. When in position, finally, the buoy was streamed over the side, the slack cable cleared, and the toggle pulled from the strop on which the anchor hung. The end of the strop flew aft, releasing the anchor, which plunged to the bottom. At a signal from the boat, the ship began to heave in on the cable, bringing it to a strain. Then this same procedure was repeated with the other bower.

The best bower, which was stowed on the starboard side, was laid out on the starboard quarter; while the small bower, stowed on the larboard side, was laid out right astern. Though called the small bower, this anchor was the same weight as both the best and the sheet anchors. The Captain gives this disposition of the anchors in both his log and journal. All other logs state that these bowers were laid out to the west-ward. *From this it would appear that the Captain was wrong. Yet, if we look at the situation a little closer, to take the anchors to the westward would have meant taking the best bower athwart hawse, on quite a foul lead across the stem of the ship, to its opposite side. Again, it would be into very doubtful water, and most likely to run foul of the western part of the reef which lay, from where the ship struck, a little south of west. Nor does this tally with the way the ship finally came off. This point does not seem to have bothered posterity, and indeed it may be unimportant. But it was a point that did become important, for some, two hundred years afterwards, and the results should be of interest to the historian in showing how to deal with evidence.*

In 1886, the Working Men's Progress Association of Cooktown, where Endeavour *had been laid ashore, proposed a memorial to Captain Cook, and it was hoped to recover the cannons to surround that memorial. A £300 reward was offered for their recovery. A search was made that year and the next, but with no success. Again, in 1966, 1967 and 1968 there was no success either. But in 1969 the Philadelphia Academy of Natural Sciences mounted an expedition under Dr Virgil Kauffman, using the sophisticated magnetometer which he had developed. They located and recovered four of the guns and some of the iron ballast, but a time limit allowed no more. The last two guns were raised by Mr Vince Vlasoff, a Cairns charter launch owner who had worked with the Americans. By one of those strange coincidences of history, the last gun came to the surface on 14 February 1969: this was the 190th anniversary of Captain Cook's death.*

*The significance of this in relation to the anchors was that it pinpointed just where the ship had grounded, and made the search for the lost small bower more feasible. Vince Vlasoff and David Hume discussed this possibility with a group of others and formed the Captain Cook's Anchor Expedition. Curiously, they became convinced that they should have to search for this anchor to the westward of the cannon dump. David Hume writes, 'We decided that we should accept the log [journal] written by Captain Cook. From the log it was apparent that the little [*sic*] bower anchor should be to the west of the cannon dump.' Yet nowhere in the Captain's log or journal, holograph or transcript, can I find any such inference. However, the expedition squared off an area of search to the west, over which a magnetometer was to be towed astern of a 12-foot aluminium boat. Markers were left at the cannon dump, and 700 feet to the west and south-west, and buoys were laid to give 40-foot intervals. As the magnetometer was being towed about 100 feet astern of the boat to avoid interference, wide 180-degree turns had to be made at the end of each run. It was during one of these wide sweeps that an anomaly was detected on the bottom, 260 feet SSW of the cannon dump. This lucky chance finally proved to be the lost small bower. It lay in about 45 feet, or 7½ fathoms, of water. But there was still doubt: 'We were concerned however that it was not in the area which Captain Cook's log had indicated the little bower had been dropped.' Neither the log nor the journal says which bower was dropped on which side, but it is reasonable to suppose that the small bower was the one laid out* *astern, while the best would have been on the starboard quarter, the side on which it was stowed—especially remembering the heavy labour involved. But, as this was the only anchor lost, such must have been the case. With the odds of probability 7 to 1 against the Captain's placing of the anchors, time, in this case at least, proved him right.*

Thus in the Afternoon Watch of the 12th, all five anchors were laid out ready for an attempt to haul the ship off at high water. Blocks were lashed to both bower cables so that, with one end of a five-inch hawser fastened to a timberhead in the ship, it was taken out, rove through the sheave of the block on the cable, and brought back to the windlass or capstan. This doubled the purchase or power that could be brought to bear on these cables. With the windlass and capstan thus fully occupied, the hawsers from the small anchors had tackles clapped on them with selvagee strops, and their hauling parts led inboard to be manned directly by some of the hands. A twofold tackle could just about treble the power brought on its hauling part.

At 9 PM*, the ship righted on the rising tide and began to work, the coral audibly chewing at her planking with dreadful possibilities. As the leak began to gain on the pumps, the Captain was confronted by a grave decision which he does not dramatise when he writes, 'This was an alarming and I may say terrible Circumstance and threatened immediate destruction to us as soon as the Ship was afloat. However I resolved to risk all and heave her off in case it was practical'. There were only three pumps that could be got to work: these could throw out only so much water, while the leaks had an unknown capacity to let in so much water. The result was a mathematical certainty, to be known only by the acid test. If ever a word was justly used, it was by Mr Banks: 'the* anxiety *in every bodys countenance was visible enough'. The pumps were fully manned and every ounce brought to bear on the anchors, and she was hove into deep water at about 10.20 at night. She had been twenty-three hours on the reef.*

Now, the small bower and spare stream cables were veered away, and the best bower and coasting cables hove in, which swung the ship to starboard, bringing her up on the best bower and coasting anchors, with her head SE*. The ship had attempted to weigh the small bower but could not break it out of apparently foul ground. It was cut away to a full cable. The long boat was sent to weigh the stream anchor, now on the ship's larboard quarter. For this procedure the long boat was fitted with a windlass beneath the midship thwart. The hawsers of this anchor had fouled amid the rocks so that it had to be weighed by the buoy rope secured to its crown. This made it easier to break the fluke out of the bottom by applying an up-and-down pull. The buoy rope was brought to the boat's windlass, being led into the boat over a midship roller in the transom. The windlass was fitted with pawls to check it from running back, and was worked with short handspikes much like the ship's. Once the anchor was clear of the bottom, and the tangled hawser cut away, the boat made its way back to the ship where the anchor was taken inboard. At the same time as this, the spare stream and coasting cables were fleeted forward from aft, and led inboard so that the ship now rode to these anchors. All of this work had been carried out in the dark at the end of more than twenty-four hours' unremitting work. But there was not* *yet time to rest and the men were not in the best state to face a climax which rose up suddenly with a misunderstanding.*

The pump well is that part of the ship into which the bilges drain and from which the pumps suck. The ship's bottom here is made by the floor timbers, or ribs, which cross the keel and on the outside of which is fastened the bottom plank, the skin of the ship. On top of these timbers is the inside plank, known as the ceiling because it is a roof, so to speak, on the floor timbers, taking a fish-eye view. The height between the bottom plank and this ceiling was, as the Captain observed, 16 to 18 inches. When the carpenter sounds the well, he lowers his marked plumbline into it, and, depending on how he does this, the plumbline rests on either the ceiling or the bottom plank, but he will always use the same datum. In this case the relieving Carpenter's Mate had taken his sounding from the bottom plank while the carpenter had taken his from the ceiling. And so it seemed that the hold was rapidly flooding.

At 5 AM, with the coming light of day, the long boat was sent to weigh the spare stream anchor and carry it out to windward—that is, to the SE. By 6 AM, this had been done, and the ship hauled herself to the best bower and weighed it, after which she weighed the coasting anchor. She warped to windward on the spare stream anchor and rode to it until she was ready to make sail and get under way. The fore-topmast was got up again and the lower yard hoisted, and the topsail yard crossed and all the running and standing rigging set up again. At 11 AM, the fore-topsail was loosed, the anchor weighed and the ship was under way, having gained enough offing by warping to clear the SW edge of the reef, on which the yawl lay as a marker. This part of the reef was, by noon, 1 ½ miles due north of the ship.

Under fore-topsail, fore course, jib and mizen the ship was steering about SWbW to get well clear of the reef. At first the pinnace was towing in the light airs. The main-topmast and yards were being got up again and the sails set as the ship began her new day.

SHIP'S LOG:

WEDNESDAY, JUNE 13TH, 1770

H.	K.	F.	Courses.	Winds.	Soundings.	Remarks, &c.
					Fathoms.	
1	1	..	S.W.	E.S.E.	White sand. 15, 15, 15	Light airs and fair wea'r. Standing off the shoal and in for the main; it being suspected that she suffered most on the starboard bow, fother'd her there, and presently after the leak decreas'd so much as to keep clear with one pump with ease.
2	1	..	S.S.W.	..	16, 16, 16	
3	1	..	W.S.W.	S.E.	16, 16½	
4	1	..	W.	..	16½, 17	
5	1	..	W.b.N.	..	17, 17½	½-p't, came too with the coasting anchor.
6	..	4	..	..	..	
7	..	..	..	..	..	
8	..	..	..	..	..	Found the ship made 15 inches water p'r hour.
9	..	..	..	..	..	
10	..	..	..	..	..	
11	..	..	..	..	..	
12	..	..	..	S.W.	..	Mod. breezes off the land and fair wea'r.

H.	K.	F.	Courses.	Winds.	Soundings.	Remarks, &c.
1	..	..	..	..	..	
2	..	..	..	..	..	
3	..	..	..	S.S.W.	..	
4	..	..	..	..	..	Mod. and fair.
5	..	..	..	..	..	½-p't, weighed and came to sail.
6	..	6	N.W.b.W.	..	17, 17	
7	1	4	..	S.S.E.	16, 16	Sent the pinnace ahead to sound.
8	2	..	..	..	15, 15	
9	2	5	N.W. ½ N.	..	14, 14	Pass'd two small low isl'ds, the main dist'ce 4 leagues.
10	2	5	N.W. ½ W.	..	13, 13	Got up topgall't yards.
11	2	5	N.W. ½ W.	..	12, 12	
12	2	4	..	..	11½, 11½	At noon, ext. of the main from S. 16 E. to N. 14 W't. Ye two isl'ds from S. 35° 30′ E. to S. 47 E. Some land mak'g like isl'ds N. 8° 30′ W. Shore d. 2 or 3 l's. Lat'd obs'd, 15° 37′ So.

COOK:

In the PM had light airs with which we kept edging in for the land, got up the main topmast and main yard and having got the sail ready for fothering the ship we put it under the starboard fore chains where we suspected the ship had suffered most and soon after the leak decreased so as to be kept clear with one pump with ease, this fortunate circumstance gave new life to every one on board. It is much easier to conceive than to describe the satisfaction felt by every body on this occation, but a few minutes before our utmost wishes were to get hold of some place upon the main or an Island to run the ship ashore where out of her materials we might build a vessel to carry us to the East Indias; no sooner were we made sensible that the outward application to the ships bottom had taken effect than the field of every mans hopes inlarged so that we now thought of nothing but ranging along shore in search of a harbour where we could repair the damages we had sustained. In justice to the Ships Company I must say that no men ever behaved better than they have done on this occasion animated by the behaviour of every gentleman on board, every man seemed to have a just sense of the danger we were in and exercised himself to the utmost.

The Ledge of rocks or Shoal we have been upon lies in the Lat^{de} of 15° 45′ and about 6 or 7 Leagues from the Main land, but thus is not the only shoal that lay upon that part of the coast especially to the northward, and one which we now saw to the southward, the tail of which we passed over when we had uneven soundings two hours before we struck; a part of this shoal is always above water and looks to be white sand [Pickersgill Reef]. Part of the one we were upon drys at low water and in that place consists of sand and stones but every where else coral rocks. At 6 oClock we anchored in 17 fathom water about 5 or 6 leagues from the land and one from the land and one from the shoal. At this time the ship made about 15 inches water per hour. At 6 oClock in the AM we weighed and stood to the NW edging in for the land having a gentle breeze at SSE. At 9 oClock we past close without two small low islands laying in the Latitude of 15° 41′ and about 4 leagues from the Main. I have named them *Hope Islands* because we were always in hopes of being able to reach these

Islands. At noon we were about 3 Leagues from the land and in the Latitude of 15° 37′ South, the northermost part of the main in sight bore N 3° W and the above islands extending from S 30° E to South 40° E, in this situation had 12 fathoms water and several sandbanks without us. The leak now decreaseth but for fear it should break out again we got the sail ready filled for fothering. The manner it is done is thus, we mix ockam & wool together (but ockam alone would do) and chop it up small and then stick [stitch] it loosely by handfulls all over the sail and throw over it sheeps dung or other filth. Horse dung for this purpose is the best. The sail thus prepared is hauled under the Ships bottom by ropes and if the place of the leak is uncertain it must be hauled from one part of her bottom to a nother untill the place is found where it takes effect; while the Sail is under the ship the ockam &c[a] is washed off and part of it carried along with the water into the leak and in part stops up the hole. Mr Munkhouse one of my Midshipmen was once in a merchant ship which sprung a leak and made 48 inches water per hour by this means was brought home from Virginia to London with only her proper crew, to him I gave the direction of this who executed it very much to my satisfaction.

BANKS:

One of our midshipmen now proposed an expedient which no one else in the ship had seen practised, tho all had heard of it by the name of fothering the ship, by the means of which he said he had come home from America in a ship which made more water than we did; nay so sure was the master of that ship of his expedient that he took her out of harbour knowing how much water she made and trusting entirely to it. He was immediately set to work with 4 or 5 assistant to prepare his fother which he did thus. He took a lower studding sail and having mixt together a large quantity of Oakum chopt fine and wool he sticked it down upon the sail as loosely as possible in small bundles each about as big as his fist, these were ranged in rows 3 or 4 inches from each other; this was to be sunk under the ship and the theory of it was this, where ever the leak was must be a great suction which would probably catch hold of one or other of these lumps of Oakum and wool and drawing it in either partly or intirely stop up the hole. While this work was going on the water rather gained on those who were pumping which made all hands impatient for the tryal. In the afternoon the ship was got under way with a gentle breeze of wind and stood in for the land; as soon as the fother was finished and applied by fastening ropes to each corner, then sinking the sail under the ship and with these ropes drawing it as far backwards as we could; in about ½ an hour to our great surprize the ship was pumped dry and upon letting the pumps stand she was found to make very little water, so much beyond our most sanguine Expectations had this singular expedient succeeded. At night came to an anchor, the fother still keeping her almost clear so that we were in an instant raised from almost dispondency to the greatest hopes: we were now almost too sanguine talking of nothing but getting her to some harbour where we might lay her ashore and repair her, or if we could not find such a place we little doubted to the East Indies.

During the whole time of this distress I must say for the credit of our people that I believe that every man exerted his utmost for the preservation of the ship, contrary to what I have universally heard to be the behaviour of sea men who have commonly as soon as a ship is in a desperate situation began to plunder and refuse all command. This was no doubt owing to the cool and steady conduct of the officers, who during the whole time never give an order which did not shew them to be perfectly composed and unmoved by the circumstances howsoever they might appear.

One pump and that not half worked kept the ship clear all night. In the morn we weighed with a fine breeze of wind and steered along shore among innumerable shoals, the boats keeping ahead and examining every appearance of a harbour which presented itself; nothing however was met with which could possibly suit our situation, bad as it was, so at night came to an anchor.

PARKINSON:

In the midst of these gloomy prospects and alarming apprehensions, we found means to stop the leak, by a method suggested to us by an officer who had in a former voyage made use of it with success; we sewed a great quantity of hair and oakum into a large piece of canvas, which we let down by two ropes, one on each side of the bow of the ship; in making way she sucked this under, close to her bottom; and when it reached the leak, it was forced by the intruding water, and obstructed its passage so much that we kept it under with a single pump. Providentially too at this instant a breeze sprang up and we steered toward the land, the boats going before, in quest of a harbour which they also happily found, at about two or three leagues distance.

With the ship under way once more, masts and yards hoisted again and sail set, and with the fothered sail over the side—effective beyond all hopes—the need for unremitting action and labour was eased. Food and drink had been snatched in passing. With all that behind them, an intense relief was felt throughout the ship. The terrible apprehensions, which were not wild imaginings but practical probabilities, had received not much more than a nod of recognition as action had been applied to immediate survival.

The principle of fothering the hull to stop the inflow of water was retained in the Navy until as recently as World War II. The spare sail evolved into a specially fitted square of stout N° 1 double canvas, strongly surrounded by a bolt rope fitted with iron cringles. It became known as a Collision Mat. Instead of oakum and wool, one side of the mat was heavily 'thrummed' with tufted rope yarn which made a thick, coarse, furred surface to be forced against the jagged hole in the hull by the water pressure, thus tending to seal it. It was hauled under the ship by a chain bottom-line, permanently rove under the ship. It was lowered, diamond-wise and kept taut by fore-and-afters. It proved its utility, especially in war time, particularly in small ships.

When the Captain gave this job to Jonathan Munkhouse it showed that he was prepared to delegate authority to the capable, unrestrained by any over-anxiousness. This implied respect, and trust in another's ability nurtured loyalty and reliability which had been the keynote in the whole ship's company during this stressful occasion. The Captain led in more ways than by simply making decisions and giving orders.

By 5 PM, on the afternoon of the 13th, the ship was only a few miles south and west of her noon position when she anchored for the night. At 5.30 in the morning she weighed, and, at 9 o'clock, had just passed the northern of the Hope Islands, clearing it by about 1 ½ miles to the eastward. She then altered course to NW ½ W. This took her, unknowingly, parallel to the 8-mile-long Cairns Reef only a mile or so to starboard.

At noon, the ship was past the northern end of this reef, with Archer Point 3 ½ miles ahead, as she drew in with the land. At this point she was crossing what is now the recommended Inner Route, which lies almost due north–south, past Cape Bedford, from this position. The peninsula upon which Cape Bedford stands, more than twenty miles away, appeared only like islands. The boats were still searching for a suitable place to lay the ship ashore.

Chapter 9
Endeavour River: June

SHIP'S LOG:

THURSDAY, JUNE 14TH, 1770

H.	K.	F.	Courses.	Winds.	Soundings.	Remarks, &c.
					Fathoms.	
1	2	2	N.W.	S.E.b.E.	12, 11	Mod. breezes and fair wea'r. Pinnace ahead sounding.
2	2	2	N.W.b.N.	..	10, 9, 8, 7	
3	1	2	N.W.	..	7, 7, 6½, 6	Saw an opening that had the appearance of a harbour, bearing W.S.W. 4 or 5 miles. Stood off with the ship, whilst the master and m'te in the pinnace and yawl went to sound it. At 6, bro't too with a spare anchor (which is now us'd as a small bower, having lost the other, as remark'd) in 5½ fa'm. Ext't of the land from No. to S.S.E., the opening S.W.b.W. 3 or 4 m's. The boats upon sounding found this harbour but inconvenient for the ship. Ye pinnace run along shore, and at 8 return'd and reported a very good harbour 2 or 3 leag's to the No'ward.
	1	6	N.W. ½ W.	..	5½, 5, 5	
4	..	..	..	..	4½, 5, 5	
5	..	..	..	..	5½, 6, 6, 5, 4, 3½, 4	
6	..	..	..	..	4, 5, 6, 5½	
7	..	..	..	..	..	
8	..	..	..	..	..	
9	..	..	..	..	..	
10	..	..	..	..	..	
11	..	..	..	..	..	
12	..	..	..	..	..	
1	..	..	..	..	..	
2	..	..	..	..	..	
3	..	..	..	..	..	
4	..	..	..	..	..	Fresh breezes and fair wea'r.
5	..	..	..	S.E.	5½, 6, 6	Weighed and made sail. Pinnace and yawl ahead sounding. Irregular muddy g'd. At 9 came too with the b't bower in 4 fa'm and veered to ⅓ of a cable. Ext's of the land from N. 20 E. to S. 28° E. Last anchoring-place, S. 25 E., 7 miles. Mouth of the harbour S. 63 W., 1½ miles. A shoal N. 49 E., 2 miles.
6	..	..	..	..	7, 8, 6, 7	
7	..	..	..	..	6, 5, 4, 3½, 3, 7, 6½, 6	
8	..	..	..	..	5, 5½, 6	
9	..	..	..	..	5, 5½, 5	
10	..	..	..	..	4½, 4	
11	..	..	..	..	..	
12	..	..	..	..	..	At noon, a fresh trade and fair wea'r. The capt'n and master went inshore in the pinnace and yawl to buoy ye chan'l into the river. Carp'rs employ'd repair'g ye bad pump. Lat. obs'd, 15° 26' So.

COOK:

In the PM had a gentle breeze at SEbE. Sent the Master with two boats as well to sound ahead of the ship as to look out for a harbour where we could repair our defects and put the Ship into a proper trim both of which she now very much wanted.—At 3 oClock saw an opening that had the appearance of a harbour. Stood off and on while the boats were examining it who found that there was not sufficient depth of water for the Ship. By this time it was almost sun set and seeing many shoals about us we anchored in 4 fathom water about 2 miles from the shore and the Mainland extending from N½E to SbE½E. At 8 oClock the pinnace in which was one of the Mates returned on board and reported that they had found a good harbour about 2 Leagues to leeward. In consequence of this information we at 6 in the AM weighed and run down to it, first sending two boats ahead to lay upon the Shoals that lay in our way and notwithstanding this precaution we were once in 3 fathom water with the Ship; having passed these shoals the boats were sent to lay in the channel leading in to the harbour. By this time it began to blow in so much that the ship would not work having missed stays twice, and being entangled among shoals I was afraid of being drove to leeward before the boats could place themselves, and therefore Anchor'd in 4 fathom about a mile from the shore and then made a signal for the boats to come onboard, after which I went myself and buoy'd the Channel which I found very narrow and the harbour much smaller than I had been told but very convenient for our purpose. At noon Latitude observed 15° 26′ South. [Marginal note: This day I restor'd Mr Magra to his Duty as I did not find him guilty of the crimes laid to his charge.]

BANKS:

The pinnace [. . .] which had gone far ahead was not returned, nor did she until nine O'clock, when she reported that she had found just the place we wanted, in which the tide rose sufficiently and there was every natural convenience that could be wished for in laying the ship ashore or heaving her down. This was too much to be believed by our most sanguine wishes: we however hoped that the place might do for us if not so much as we had been told yet something to better our situation, as yet but precarious, having nothing but a lock of Wool between us and destruction.

AM: Very fresh sea breeze. A boat was sent ahead to shew us the way into the harbour, but by some mistake of signals we were obliged to come to an anchor again off the mouth of it without going in, where it soon blew too fresh for us to Weigh. We now began to consider our good fortune; had it blown as fresh the day before yesterday or before that we could never have got off but must inevitably have been dashed to pieces on the rocks. The Captn and myself went ashore to view the Harbour and found it indeed beyond our most sanguine wishes: it was the mouth of a river the entrance of which was to be sure narrow enough and shallow, but when once in the ship might be moored afloat so near the shore that by a stage from her to it all her Cargo might be got out and in again in a very short time; in this same place she might be hove down with all ease, but the beach gave signs of the tides rising in the springs 6 or 7 feet which was more than enough to do our business without that trouble. The meeting with so many natural advantages in a harbour so near us at the very time of our misfortune appeared almost providential; we had not in the voyage before seen a place so well suited for our purpose as this was, and certainly had no right to expect the tide to rise so high here that did not rise half so much at the place where we struck, only 8 leagues from this place; we therefore returned onboard in high spirits and raised the spirits of our friends on board as much as our own by bringing them the welcome news of approaching security.

PARKINSON:

On the 14th of June, we dropped anchor in the mouth of it; but the entrance was so narrow, that we were obliged to place buoys all the way, to steer by. While we lay on the rock, it was calm; and from the time we left it, till this day, it blew gently; but now it began to blow hard which prevented us from getting into the bay until the 18th; when we reached the desired haven, though not without some danger, the ship having several times touched ground.

From noon to 6 PM, the ship had made only some 6 miles north-westerly. Shoals and reefs were evident ahead and on the bow, and, with the sun dropping behind the hills on the main, the ship was anchored for the night. The pinnace returned by starlight at 8 PM, reporting that she had found a likely place for the ship either to heave down or to be laid ashore. Heaving down would require the ship to be laid close alongside the shore so that heavy purchases could be taken from the heads of the lower masts to some secure anchorage in the ground, to heave her over on her side and expose the bottom.

The appearance of a harbour that had proved unsuitable earlier was probably the present Walker Bay.

At daylight, when the ship weighed and ran towards this last-found harbour with a following wind at SE, the boats were sent to lie on some shoals to seaward. These were probably those now known as the Cowlishaw and Dawson reefs and today wearing beacons. But having left these on the starboard hand, the ship unpleasantly ran across a 3-fathom patch more than a mile offshore. This would have been part of the Blackbird Patches running offshore NE of Mount Cook. As the wind began to freshen it became difficult to work the ship into the narrow channel. Twice she missed stays—that is, in attempting to tack, she did not get across the wind, but hung in irons without being able to pay off either way, and making dangerous leeway, even stern-way, meantime. It is to be remembered that the ship was now badly out of trim as a result of all the weight that had been jettisoned to save her. She would not answer her helm as well, and her shallower draught added to her windage on the hull and also her leeway. In this unfavourable situation at 9 AM, the ship anchored about a mile and a half off the entrance. The Captain was concerned that, if she did not, she might well be driven to leeward and not be able to recover the harbour, with the seemingly prevailing wind at SE.

SHIP'S LOG:

FRIDAY, JUNE 15TH, 1770

Day and Month.	Winds.	Remarks, &c.
1770. Friday, June 15	S.E. E.S.E. S.E.	A fresh trade and cloudy wea'r; in the night had some showers of rain. P.M.—Got down topgall't yards. Unbent the mainsail and some of the small sails. At 8 veered away to 2/3ds of a cable. A.M.—Got in ye jibboom and spritsail yard. Condem'd the fore topgall't sail and converted p't of it to parsling for the bad pump. Condem'd the topgall't bowline for woulding it. Some hands employ'd splicing the hawsers that were cut amongst the rocks the 11th and 12th inst. Saw a smoke ashore.

COOK:

A fresh gale at SE and Clowdy weather attended with showers of rain in the night. As it blowed too fresh to break the Ship loose to run into the harbour we got down the topgallant yards, unbent the mainsail and some of the small sails, got down the fore topgallant Mast and the Jibb boom and spritsail yard in, intending to lighten the ship forward as much as possible in order to lay her ashore to come at the leak.

HICKES:

Condemned the fore topgallant sail and converted part of it for parcelling the bad pump and woolded it with ye topgallant bowlines . . . our leak keeps one pump jogging.

BANKS:

It blew [. . .] too fresh to night for us to attempt to weigh the anchor, I even think as fresh as it has ever done since we have been upon the Coast. AM: Blew all day as fresh as it did yesterday. We thought much of our good fortune in having fair weather upon the rocks when upon the Brink of such a gale. Our people were now however pretty well recovered from their fatigues having had plenty of rest, as the ship since she was Fothered has not made more water than one pump half worked will keep clear.

Here Banks gives some hint of the reaction and relief of the whole ship's company, and the extent to which they had expended themselves in the concerted and resolute actions to save the ship. Considered as a succession of seamanship drills, it was exemplary; having been carried out, as much of it was, in the hours of darkness, with real dangers imminent, could only make this more so.

The 'parcelling' of the bad pump-shaft was the bandaging it about with strips of the old topgallant sail, well tarred. The 'woolding' of it was the close binding of it at intervals with the topgallant bowlines which were of 1-inch rope. Woolding is the binding of a mast or spar with rope to reinforce it.

SHIP'S LOG:

SATURDAY, JUNE 16TH, 1770

Day and Month.	Winds.	Remarks, &c.
Saturday, June 16 ..	S.E. S.E.b.S S.E.b.S	Fresh gales and cloudy with passing showers of rain. At 6 a.m. the weather was a little more mod't. Hove ahead, but the gale increasing veer'd away as before.

COOK:

Strong gales at SE and Clowdy hazey weather with showers of rain. At 6 oClock in the AM it moderated a little and we hove short intending to get under sail, but was obliged to desist and veer away again. Some people were seen ashore today.

BANKS:

At night we observed a fire ashore near where we were to lay, which made us hope that the necessary length of our stay would give us an opportunity of being acquainted with the Indians who made it.

In the morn it was a little more moderate and we attempted to weigh but were soon obliged to vere away all that we had got, the wind freshening upon us so much. Fires were made upon the hills and we saw 4 Indians through our glasses who went away along shore, in going along which they had made two more fires for what purpose we could not guess. Tupia whose bad gums were very soon followed by livid spots on his legs and every symptom of inveterate scurvy, notwithstanding acid, bark and every medicine our Surgeon could give him, became now extreemly ill; Mr Green the astronomer was also in a poor way, which made everybody in the Cabbin very desireous of getting ashore and impatient at our tedious delays.

This incidence of scurvy as mentioned by Mr Banks is curious. It demonstrates that the disease was very imperfectly understood, even in this ship, in which—according to some popular opinion—the problem was once and for all solved. The ship carried the inspissated orange juice and sauerkraut, among other things. But this orange juice had been subjected to heat in its concentration, so that much of the volatile, and then-unknown, vitamin C had been lost. By this strange perversity of fate, Cook, from close observation of its efficacy, at the end of the voyage reported unfavourably on this orange juice he had carried. Later, on the basis of his observations on its doubtful value, he advised against it on the grounds of unnecessary expense. This significantly influenced the delay of its final introduction until 1795—and then it was the equally effective lemon juice—forty years after the publication of Dr Lind's treatise. Nevertheless the cure was onboard in the hands of Banks himself. He had tried it and found it immediately effective. This was the juice he had preserved in brandy. It seems curious that he did not give any to his own man, Tupia.

Banks's unexplained fires were probably part of the Aboriginal telegraph, making known the presence of the ship on the coast.

SHIP'S LOG:

SUNDAY, JUNE 17TH, 1770

Day and Month.	Winds.	Remarks, &c.
Sunday, June 17 ..	S.E. and S.E.b.S.	First and middle p't, do wea'r; the latt'r, fresh breezes and fair. At 7 a.m. weighed and came to sail. At 8 she struck on the bar. At 9 she back'd off; soon after, comming to near the weather shore, she grounded. Carried out the stream anchor. Hove tort, and turn'd all hands too to get the booms and spars over the side for a raft; same time got down the fore yard, fore topm'st, and fore topsail yard upon the raft. Low water at 11 o'clock.

COOK:

Most part strong gales at SE with some heavy showers of rain in the PM. At 6 in the AM being pretty moderate we weighed and run in to the harbour in doing of which we run the Ship ashore twice, the first time she went off without any trouble but the second time she stuck fast, but this was of no consequence any farther than giving us a little trouble and was no more than what I expected as we had the wind. While the Ship lay fast we got down the fore yard, fore topmast, booms &c[a] overboard and made a raft of them alongside.

BANKS:

Weather a little less rough than it was. Weighed and brought the ship in but in doing it ran her twice ashore by the narrowness of the channel; the second time she lay until the tide lifted her off. In the meantime Dr Solander and myself began our Plant gathering.

SHIP'S LOG:

MONDAY, JUNE 18TH, 1770

Day and Month.	Winds.	Remarks, &c.
Monday, June 18 ..	S.E. S.E.b.E. S.E.b.S.	The first and middle part, fresh gales and cloudy with rain; latter, fresh breezes and fair. At 1 p.m. got the ship off and warp'd her alongside of a steep beech, on the N. side the river, having two hawsers out fast to ye trees, the bower on the starboard bow in the stream, and the stream anchor run out from the starboard quarter. Got the anchors and cables on shore and all the hawsers. A.M.—Made a stage from the ship to the shore. Landed the empty water-casks and all the dry provisions. Errected two tents—one for the provision and store, the other for the sick. Landed the carpenter's stores. Sent a boat to haul the saen; they return'd at noon without success.

COOK:

Fresh gales and clowdy with showers of rain. At 1 PM the Ship floated and we warped her into the Harbour and moored her alongside of a Steep beach on the south side. Got the anchors and cables and All the Hawsers [six hawsers: Wilkinson] ashore. In the AM made a stage from the Ship to the shore; erected two tents one for

ALONGSIDE AT ENDEAVOUR RIVER. LANDING THE SPARE ANCHOR.

the Sick and the other for the Stores and Provisions; landed all the empty casks and part of the Provisions; and sent a boat to haul the sene who returned without success.

HICKES:
Moored in Charco Harbour.

BANKS:
In the Evening the ship was moored within 20 feet of the shore afloat and before night much lumber was got out of her. AM: A stage was built from the ship which much facilitated our undertakings. Myself walking in the countrey saw old frames of Indian houses and places where they had dressed shellfish in the same manner as the Islanders, but no signs that they had been at the place for six months at least. The countrey in general was sandy between the hills and barren made walking very easy; Musquetos there were some but few a piece of good fortune in a place we were likely to remain for some time. Tupia who had employed himself since we were here in angling and had lived entirely on what he had caught was surprizingly recovered.

Poor Mr Green still very ill. Weather blowing hard with showers; had we not got in yesterday we certainly could not today.

PARKINSON:

Soon after we arrived in the bay, we laid the ship on a steep bank, on the side of a river; set up tents ashore, unloaded her, carried all the cargo and provisions into them, and there lodged and accommodated our sick.

The stage to the shore was made of spars and planks securely lashed together. The distance between the ship and shore was only two-thirds' the width of the ship herself. Movement of the ship was prevented by the cables and hawsers stretched out from her four quarters, on both bows and quarters.

Concerning 'Charco Harbour', Hickes's log for this period is so headed. The Historical Records of New South Wales, 1893, has the following note: 'Charco Harbour, now Endeavour River. See Pickersgill 18 July states that the natives were often heard to mention the word Charco. *There is no allusion to this either in the published or unpublished accounts by Cook; but there can be little doubt that this was generally regarded by the discoverers, as the native name of the place.' But Banks, on July 14th, records: 'They almost continually made use of the word* Chircau, *which we conceived to be a term of Admiration as they still used it when ever they saw any thing new.'* Yir-ke *was an expression of surprise.*

SHIP'S LOG:

TUESDAY, JUNE 19TH, 1770

Day and Month.	Winds.	Remarks, &c.
Tuesday, June 19 ..	S.E.b.S.	Fresh breezes and cloudy, with frequent showers of heavy rain. P.M.—Employ'd landing the provisions and stores. Sent all the sails, that is unbent, on shore. A.M.—Got the 4 guns out of the main hold and mounted them on the quarter-deck. Got a spare bower and anchor and anchor-stock ashore. Also landed the remaining part of the store and ballast.

COOK:

Fresh gales at SE and clowdy weather with frequent showers of rain. In the PM landed all the provisions and part of the stores; got the sick ashore which amounted at this time to 8 or 9 afflicted with different disorders but none very dangerously ill. This afternoon I went upon one of the highest hills over the harbour from which I had a perfect view of the inlet or River and adjacent country which afforded a very indifferent prospect, the low lands near the river is all over run with mangroves among which the salt water flows every tide and the high land appeared to be barren and stoney. In the AM got the 4 remaining guns out of the hold and Mounted them on the quarter deck. Got a spare anchor and anchor stock a shore and the remaining part of the stores and ballast that were in the hold. Set up the Smiths forge and set the Armourer and his mate to work to make nails &c[a] to repair the ship.

WILKINSON:
Latitude Observed 15° 26′ South [1′ 15″ north of actual].
Longitude Observed 214 15′ West [30′ too far east].

BANKS:
Went over the Water today to spy the land which there was sand hills. On them I saw some Indian houses which seemed to have been inhabited since those on this side, tho not very lately. There were vast flocks of Pigeons and crows; of the former which were very beautiful we shot several; the latter exactly like those in England were so shy that we could not come near them by any means. The inlet or river in which we lay ran very far into the country, keeping its course over flat land overgrown with Mangroves; the Countrey inland however was sufficiently hilly.

SHIP'S LOG:

WEDNESDAY, JUNE 20TH, 1770

Day and Month.	Winds.	Remarks, &c.
Wednesday, June 20 . .	S.E.b.S.	Do. wea'r P.M.—Got most of the ground tier of butts out, many of which were quite rotten and would not bear the rolling. Got most of the boatsw'n's and carp'r's stores ashore. A.M.—Got a spare anchor ashore and a spare windlass, the remaining part of the ground tier, two spare caps, and sundry other spare stores.

COOK:
[Journal] Winds at SE a fresh breeze, fore and middle parts rainy, the latter fair. This day got out all the officers stores and the ground tier of water having now nothing in the fore and main hold but the coals and a little ballast.

[Log] In the AM had fair weather, got all the ground tier of water out, wood &c[a] and landed the Gunners stores [and powder (Forwood)].

BANKS:
Evening hard rain. AM: Weather cleared up so we began to gather and dry plants of which we had hopes of as many as we could muster during our stay. Observed that in many parts of the inlet were large quantities of Pumice stones which lay a good way above the high water mark. Probably carried there by freshes or extraordinary high tides as they certainly came from the sea.

Most probably the pumice had drifted across the Coral Sea from vulcanite Vanuatu, some 1,200 miles. The ground tier of water butts had been undisturbed since the ship

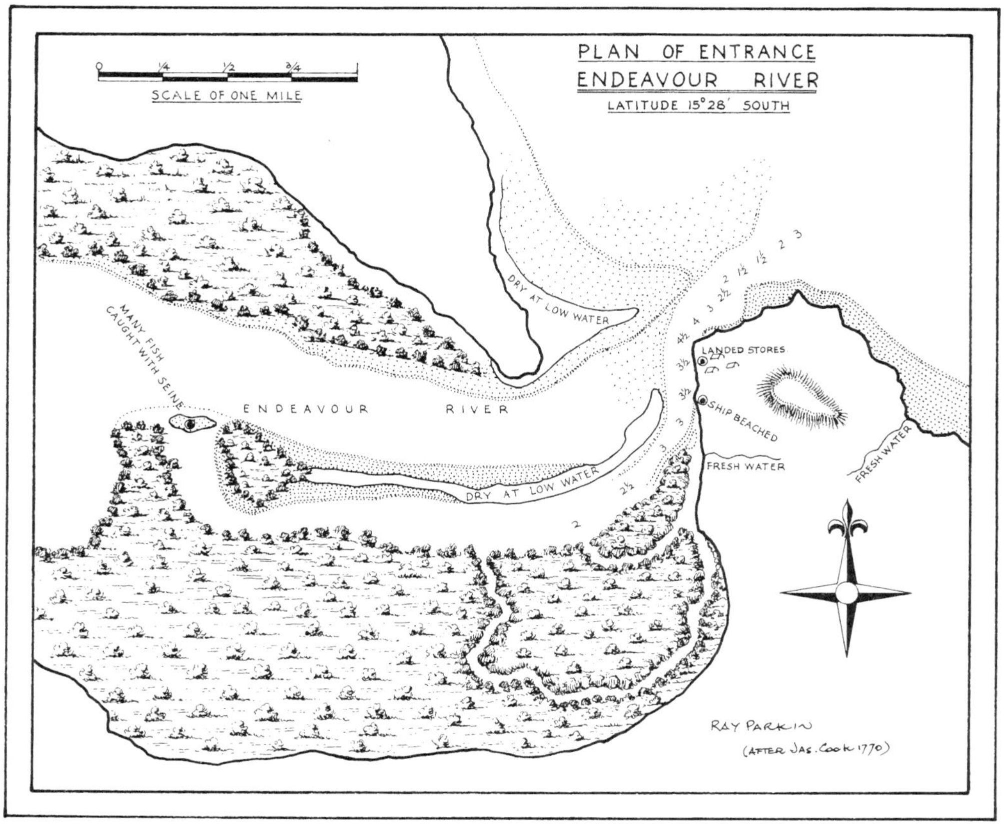

left England. With the chafe of the ship's movement and the damp at the bottom of the hold, with its limited ventilation, it is small wonder that their condition was as it was.

SHIP'S LOG:

THURSDAY, JUNE 21ST, 1770

Day and Month.	Winds.	Remarks, &c.
1770. Thursday, June 21 . .	S.E. S.E.b.S.	Mod. breezes and fine wea'r. Employ'd clearing ship and making ready for hauling the ship ashore. In triming the coals aft heard the leak making its way by the flooring ends two feet abaft the foremast. A.M.—Employ'd getting the coals ashore. The surgeon went up the river to get beans for the sick. Boil'd wheat for the ship's company's breakfast.

COOK:

In the PM landed the Powder, got out the stone ballast wood &c^{a} which brought the ships draught of water to 8^{f} 10^{i} forward and 13 feet abaft; this I thought by trimming the coals aft would be sufficient as I find the tides will rise and fall upon a perpendicular 8 feet at spring tides, but after the coals was trimmed away from over the leak we could hear the water come gushing in a little abaft the foremast and about 3 feet from her keel; this determined me to clear the hold entirely. Accordingly very early in the morning we went to work to get out the Coals which was employment for all hands.

BANKS:

Before night the ship was lightened and we observed with great pleasure that the springs which were now beginning to lift rose as high as we could wish. AM: Fine clear weather: began today to lay Plants in sand.

SHIP'S LOG:

FRIDAY, JUNE 22ND, 1770

Day and Month.	Winds.	Remarks, &c.
Friday, June 22	S.E. S.E.b.E. S.E.b.S.	Fresh breezes and fair wea'r. P.M.—Employ'd landing the coals. The gunner got his powder and all his other stores ashore. At 4 cast loose and warp'd up the river a cable's length to the bank where the ship is appointed to lie for stopping the leak. At 8 it was high water; hove her close ashore. Draught of water forward 7 feet 9 inches, aft 11 feet 6 inches, her bow being close up to the mangrove trees and her stern in 3½ fa'm. At 2 a.m. the tide left the ship dry forward. Examin'd the leak, and 4 feet of the plank cut thro' by the rocks. Found a piece of the rock sticking in her bottom and several other streaks much damag'd. Also found much sheathing off the larboard bow, and sundry other damages. At 10 the carpenters begun to work on her, it being two hours ebb. Some hands employ'd making a well and clearing the watering-place. Unbent the main tops'l to mend. Sent the longboat to take up the stream anchor, the ship being fast to the shore by the messenger. Had a 6-in. hawser to the spare stream anchor out in the river for a sternfast.

COOK:

Winds at SE fair weather. At 4 in the PM having got out most of the coals, cast loose the moorings and warped the Ship a little higher up the harbour to a place I had pitched upon to lay a Shore for stopping the leak, her draught of water forward 7 feet 9 inches and abaft 13 feet 6 inches [all other logs say 11 feet 6 inches]. At 8 being high water hauled her bow close ashore but kept her stern afloat because I was afraid of neeping [neaping], and yet it was necessary to lay the whole of her as near the ground as possible. At 2 oClock in the AM the tide left her which gave us an opportunity to examine the leak which we found to be at her floor heads a little before the starboard fore chains. Here the rocks had made their way thro' four planks quite to and even into the timbers and wounded three more. The manner these planks were damaged or cut out as I might say is hardly credible, scarce a splinter was to be seen but the whole was cut away as if it had been done by the hands of Man with a blunt edge tool. Fortunately for us the timbers in this place were very close, other ways it would have been impossible to have saved the Ship and even as it was it appeared extraordinary that she made no more water than she did. A large piece of Coral rock (as large as a man's fist) was sticking in one hold and several pieces of the fothering, small stones, sand &c[a] had made its way in and lodged

H.M. BARK *ENDEAVOUR'S* ANCHORS ASHORE, JUNE 22ND TO 23RD, 1770.

between the timbers which had stopped the water from forcing its way in in great quantities. Part of the sheathing was gone from under the larboard bow, part of the false keel was gone and the remainder in such a shattered condition that we should be much better off was it all gone also; her fore foot and some part of her main keel was also damaged but not materially, what damage she may have received abaft we could not see but believe not so much as the Ship makes but little water while the tide keeps below the leak forward. At 9 oClock the Carpenters went to work upon the Ship while the Smiths were busy making bolts nails &c[a].

WILKINSON:
Unbent the main topsail and sent it on shore to mend.

BANKS:
By night the ship was quite clear and in the nights tide (which we had constantly observed to be much higher than the days) we hauled her ashore. In the morn I saw her leak which was very large: in the middle was a hole large enough to have sunk a ship with twice our pumps but here providence had most visibly worked in our favour, for it was in great measure plugged up by a stone which was as big as a

mans fist: round the edges of this stone had all the water come in which had so near over come us, and here we found the wool and oakum or fothering which had relieved us in so unsuspected a manner. The effects of the Coral rock upon her bottom is difficult to describe but more to believe; it had cut through her plank and deep into one of her timbers, smoothing the gashes still before it so that the whole might easily be imagined to be cut with an axe. Myself employed all day in laying in plants. The people who were sent to the other side of the water to shoot Pigeons saw an animal as large as a greyhound, of a mouse colour and very swift; they also saw Indian houses and a brook of fresh water.

PARKINSON:

On the 22[d] we examined the ship's bottom, and found a large hole, through the planks and into the hold, which had a piece of coral-rock, half a yard square, sticking into it: the same rock therefore, that endangered us, yielded us the principal means of our redemption; for, had not this fragment intruded into the leak, in all probability the ship would have sunk.

We lost no time, but immediately set about repairing the ship's bottom, and in a few days made it sound again.

The point at which the ship had taken the damage was well forward, before the foremast. 'Fortunately for us the timbers in this place were very close . . .' This was so, because the square timbers of the ship cease at the foremast, and from thence to the stem of the ship are the cant frames, which radiate around the curve of the bow. This radiation brings their heels close together like the spokes of a wheel to the hub. They are also reinforced by a considerable amount of deadwood internally, to which these half-frames are bolted. The outside plank at this point is 3″ thick and the sheathing over it would have been about ⅞″. The false keel was 6″ deep, fastened to the bottom of the main keel. It had undoubtedly prevented more serious damage to the main keel, which was its reason for being.

The Captain was anxious that the ship should not be 'neaped'. This meant that if the spring tides passed, the lesser neap tides would not be sufficient to lift the ship off, and he would have to wait another two weeks for the next springs.

Mr Banks has this day recorded what seems to be the first European sighting of the kangaroo.

SHIP'S LOG:

SATURDAY, JUNE 23RD, 1770

Day and Month.	Winds.	Remarks, &c.
Saturd., June 23 . .	S.E. to E.S.E.	Fresh breezes and fair wea'r. Carpenters employ'd shifting the damag'd plank. Seamen scraping the ship's bottom. A.M.—Carried out the spare streem anchor astern ready to heave off by. Carpenters employ'd sheathing the new plank. Clear'd ship between decks. Sent a boat to haul the saen; at noon they returned with success. Sa lm'rs on the old main topsail.

COOK:

Winds south easterly a fresh gale and fair weather. Carpenters employed shifting the damaged planks as long as the tide would permit them to work. At low water in the PM we examined the ships bottom under the starboard side she being dry as far aft as the after part of the fore chains, we could not find that she had received any other damage on this side but what has been mentioned. In the Morning I sent three men into the country to shoot pigeons as some few of these birds had been seen flying about, in the evening they returned with about half a dozen; one of the men saw an animal something less than a grey hound, it was of a Mouse colour very slender made and swift of foot. In the AM I sent a boat to haul the saine who returned at noon having made three hauls and caught only three fish (which were given to the sick), and yet we see plenty jumping about in the harbour but can find no method of catching them.

BANKS:

The people who went over the river saw the animal again and described him in much the same manner as yesterday.

SHIP'S LOG:

SUNDAY, JUNE 24TH, 1770

Day and Month.	Winds.	Remarks, &c.
Sunday, June 24 ..	S.E.b.E. and E.S.E.	Strong breezes and fair wea'r. P.M.—The carpenters finished the starboard side. Sent a boat to haul the saen. People employ'd triming everything over for heeling ship the other way. At 6 the fishing-boat return'd without any fish. At 9 haul'd the ship a little off and heel'd her to starboard. A.M.—The carpenters employ'd on the sheathing of the larboard bow.

COOK:

Winds and weather as yesterday. In the PM the Carpenters finished the starboard side and at 9 oClock heeled the Ship the other way and hauled her off about 2 feet for fear of neeping. In the AM they went to work upon repairing the sheathing under the larboard bow where we found two planks cut half thro' (about 6 strakes from the keel). Early in the morning I sent a party of men into the Country under the direction of Mr Gore to seek for refreshments, they returned about noon with a few palm cabbages and a bunch or two of wild plantains, these last were smaller than any I had ever seen and the pulp full of small stones otherwise they were well taisted. I saw myself this morning a little way from the Ship one of the animals before spoke of, it was of a light mouse colour and the full size of a greyhound and shaped in every respect like one, with a long tail which it carried like a grey hound, in short I could have taken it for a wild dog, but for its walking or running in which it jumped like a hare or deer; another of them was seen today by some of our people who saw the first, they describe him as having very small legs and the print of a foot like that of a goat, but this I could not see myself because the ground the one I saw was upon was too hard and the length of the grass hindered my seeing its legs.

BANKS:
Gathering plants and hearing descriptions of the animal which is now seen by everybody. A seaman who had been out in the woods brought home the description of an animal he had seen composed in so Seamanlike a stile that I cannot help mentioning it: it was (says he) about as large and much like a one gallon cagg [keg], as black as the Devil and had 2 horns on its head, it went but slowly but I dared not touch it.

This last animal was probably a fruit bat or a flying fox—possibly Gould's Fruit-bat, which is very black.

The heel of the ship while she lay thus careened ashore was some 17 degrees. Life within it at the time was made much more awkward by needing to traverse decks at such an angle. At meal times all eating and drinking vessels were so tilted unless held in the hand and of course the food had to be carried from the galley to the messes—not to mention the adaptive art of the cook in preparing it. But, thanks to the swinging hammock, all slept comfortably enough. One of the virtues of this ship, which the Captain commented on, was that 'She is a good Roader and Careens easy and without the least danger.' However, though putting up with this necessary inconvenience, most on board indulged in traditional therapeutic grumbling, not devoid of humour, and all were glad when she was back on an even keel. Mr Banks had expressed his dislike of this situation on previous occasions when the ship had been heeled to scrub between wind and water.

The re-sheathing of the ship was of the most importance, almost as much as that of the damaged plank. Its object was to retard the attack of the teredo worm especially. The ship had already seen the disastrous effects of this worm at Tahiti when both solid oaken anchor stocks had been so destroyed in a couple of months, as well as the unpainted bottom of the long boat. It was this fact, equally with the main plank damage, which gave the Captain real anxiety, operating as he was in the tropical home of this destructive worm.

SHIP'S LOG:

MONDAY, JUNE 25TH, 1770

Day and Month.	Winds.	Remarks, &c.
Monday, June 25 . .	E.S.E.	Do. wea'r. P.M.—Carpenters employ'd as before. Sent a boat over the river for some beans and parcelain for the sick. A.M.—A party went on shore to fill water.

COOK:

At low water in the PM while the Carpenters were busy repairing the sheating and plank under the larboard bow I got people to go under the ships bottom to examine all her larboard side, she only being dry forward, but abaft were 9 feet water. They found part of the sheathing off abreast the mainmast about her floor heads and part of one plank a little damaged. There were three people who went down who all agreed in the same story, the Master was one who was positive that she had received no material damage besides the loss of the sheathing. This alone will be sufficient to let the worm into her bottom which may prove of bad consequence; however we must run all risk for I know of no other method to remedy this but by heaving her down which would be a work of immense labour & time, if not impractical in our present situation.

The Carpenters continued hard at work under her bottom untill put off by the tide in the evening, and the morning tide did not ebb out far enough for them to work, for we have only one tolerable low and high tide in 24 hours. In the AM a party of men were employed in overhauling the rigging.

BANKS:

In gathering plants today I myself had the good fortune to see the beast so much talked of, tho but imperfectly; he was not only like a grey hound in size and running but had a long tail, as long as any grey hounds; what to liken him to I could not tell, nothing certainly that I have seen at all resembles him.

SHIP'S LOG:

TUESDAY, JUNE 26TH, 1770

Day and Month.	Winds.	Remarks, &c.
Tuesday, June 26 ..	E.S.E.	Do. wea'r. P.M.—The carpenters finished their work on the larboard bow. Some hands employ'd filling water. A.M.—Employ'd filling water and getting casks under the ship's bottom to float her off the next flood.

COOK:

Fair weather winds at S, a fresh gale. At low-water in the PM the Carpenters finished under the larboard bow and every other place the tide would permit them to come at. Lashed some casks under the Ships bows in order to help float her at High-water in the night Attempted to heave her off but could not, she not being afloat partly owing to some of the casks not holding that were lashed under her. In the AM employed getting more Casks ready for the same purpose; But I am much afraid that we shall not be able to float her now the tides are taking off.

BANKS:
Since the ship has been hauled ashore the water that has come into her has of course all gone backwards and my plants which were for safety stowed in the bread room were this day found under water; nobody had warned me of this danger which had never once entered into my head; the mischief was however now done so I set to work to remedy it to the best of my power. The day was scarce long enough to get them all shifted &c: many were saved but some intirely lost and spoiled.

The water the ship had made had drained aft to the Bread Room because the ship was so down by the stern, especially at low water, and thus not within reach of the pumps.

With the passing of the present spring tides, the ship was about to be 'neaped' after all.

SHIP'S LOG:

WEDNESDAY, JUNE 27TH, 1770

Day and Month.	Winds.	Remarks, &c.
1770. Wedns., June 27	E.S.E. and S.E.	Fresh breezes and fair wea'r P.M.—Employ'd watering. Got 19 ton of cask under and the ship redy for high water. Carp'rs employ'd caulking. At 4 carried the other streem anchor out astern. High water ¾ p't 11; hove a great strain upon both anchors, but the tide did not rise near so high as last night. At daylight got a considerable weight of sundry articles from aft, forward, to ease the ship. A party of men filling water, another party overhauling the rigging, some hands landing the casks from under the ship, having lost hopes of getting her afloat till next spring tides. The carpenters empl. fitting stocks to the spare anchors.

COOK:
Winds at SE a fresh breeze and clowdy weather. In the PM lashed 38 empty butts under the ships bottom in order to float her off which proved ineffectual and therefore gave over all hopes of getting her off untill the next spring tides. At daylight got a considerable weight of sundry articles from aft forward to ease the ship. The Armourers at work at the forge repairing Iron work &c[a], Carpenters caulking the Ship and stocking one of the spare anchors, seamen employed filling water and over hauling the rigging; I went in the pinnace up the harbour and made several hauls with the Sain but caught only between 20 and 30 lb of fish which were given to the sick and such as were weak and ailing.

BANKS:
Some of the gentlemen who had been out in the woods yesterday brought home some leaves of a plant which I took to be *Arum Esculentum*, the same I believe as is

called Coccos in the West Indies. In consequence of this I went to the place and found plenty; on tryal however the roots were found to be too acrid to be eat, the leaves however when boiled were little inferior to spinage. In the same place grew plenty of Cabbage trees, a kind of wild plantain whose fruit was so full of stones [hard round black seeds] that it was scarce eatable, another fruit about as large as a small golden pippin but flattter, of a deep purple colour; these when gathered off from the tree were very hard and disagreeable but after being kept a few days became soft and tasted much like indifferent Damsons.

During the time the ship spent ashore here, the after end lost its support on the falling tides, while the forward part remained supported and unmoving. This was causing the ship to hog at low water as the after part sagged, tending to bend the keel downwards and bring a critical strain on all the ship's fastenings. By shifting some weight forward, the Captain was endeavouring to relieve her of some of that strain.

Though there was plenty for the men to do, they must have relished those all-night-ins, *which the harbour routine would allow to all except the few watch-keepers.*

SHIP'S LOG:

THURSDAY, JUNE 28TH, 1770

Day and Month.	Winds.	Remarks, &c.
Thursday, June 28 . .	S.E.	Do. weather. Employ'd rigging and watering. Carp'rs as before. Coopers on the casks.

COOK:
Fresh breezes and cloudy; all hands employed as yesterday.

PICKERSGILL:
Riggers, Carpenters, Armourer, Coopers and waterers at work in their respective employments.

BANKS:
Tupia by Roasting his Coccos very much in his oven made them lose intirely their acridity; the roots were so small that we did not think them at all an object for the ship so resolved to content ourselves with the greens which are called in the West Indies Indian Kale. I went with the seamen to shew them the place and they gathered a large quantity. Saw one tree and the only one notched in the same manner as those in Botany Bay. We have ever since we have been here observed the nests of a kind of ants much like White Ants in the East Indies but to us perfectly harmless; they [the ant hills] were always pyramidical, from a few inches to 6 feet in height and very much resembled stones which I have seen in English Druidical monuments.

Today we met with a large number of them of all sizes ranged in a small open space which had a very pretty effect; Dr Solander compared them to the Rune Stones on the Plains of Upsal in Sweden, myself to all the smaller Druidical monuments I had seen.

SHIP'S LOG:

FRIDAY, JUNE 29TH, 1770 to and

Day and Month.	Winds.	Remarks, &c.
Friday, June 29	S.E. and E.S.E.	Do. weather. Employ'd wholly as before. P.M.—The captain went on shore at night attending an observation of Jupiter's satilites. Sent a boat to haul the saen, who returned with 154 lb. of fish.

COOK:

Winds and weather as yesterday and the employment of the people the same. Lieutenant Gore having been 4 or 5 miles in the Country where he met with nothing remarkable, he saw the foot steps of Men and likewise those of 3 or 4 sorts of wild beasts but saw neither man nor beast; some others of our people who were out yesterday on the north side of the River met with a place where the natives had just been, as there were fires still burning but they saw nobody nor have we seen one since we have been in Port. In these excursions we found some wild Yamms or Coccos growing in the swampy grounds and this afternoon I sent a party of men to gather some, the tops we found made good greens and eat exceeding well when boiled but the roots were so Acrid that few besides myself could eat them. This night Mr Green and I observed an Emersion of Jupiters first satellite which happened at $2^h\ 58'\ 53''$ in the AM, the same Emersion happened at Greenwich according to calculation on the 30th at $5^h\ 17'\ 43''$ in the PM; the difference is $14^h\ 18'\ 50''$ equal to $214^\circ\ 42'\ 30''$ of Longitude, and the Latitude is $15^\circ\ 26'$ South. In the AM sent some hands with a boat up the River to haul the sain while the rest were employed about the rigging and sundry other duties.

PICKERSGILL:

The Captain ashore all night attending some observations.

BANKS:

One of our Midshipmen an American who was out shooting today saw a Wolf, perfectly he say'd like those he had seen in America; he shot at it but did not kill it. The seine was hauled today for the first time [?] and 150 lb of Fish caught in it.

The American midshipman was James Maria Magra (later Matra) whom the Captain had restored to duty on the 14th, when he found him not guilty of charges in relation to Orton's ears. Possibly it was a dingo he had shot at.

This day we get another glimpse of Mr Gore as the man of initiative and hunting; also one of the Captain with the bitter Taro root, determined to eat almost anything to test its value. This was possibly part of his intuitive approach to the problem of scurvy, somehow sensing that a healthy omnivorousness would do much more than theory. We also see Mr Green, undoubtedly still ill, yet doggedly carrying on with his job of painstaking astronomical observation with the Captain. Cook the Scientist emerges here too. Captain Matthew Flinders was to write later: 'This voyage of Captain Cook, whether considered in the extent of his discoveries and the accuracy with which they were traced, or in the labour of his scientific associates, far surpassed all that had gone before.' In further comments on Cook's accuracy he writes: 'Timekeepers were in their infancy in 1768, when Captain Cook sailed upon his first voyage and he was not furnished with them; his longitude was therefore regulated only by occasional observations of lunar distances and some few of Jupiter's satellites, which even in the present improved state of instruments and tables require to be connected by the time keepers before satisfactory conclusions can be drawn. Errors of greater or less magnitude were thence unavoidable.'

Cook had no chronometer, but he had a watch for observations. Nevertheless, he still had to set this watch to his local time by his own observations to the accuracy of one second, *in itself no small task. Then, with Green, he had to observe the emersion of Jupiter's first satellite as accurately as he could. Finally, by long calculations, he had to compare that moment with a simultaneous one in Greenwich some 12,000 miles away, while the platform on which he stood was not yet on the world's map.*

He deduced his longitude to be 214° 42′ 30″ West of Greenwich, or 145° 17′ 30″ East. And, with all his limitations, he had placed himself less than 2 ½ miles east of his actual position. In this amazing result, the error need not have been all Cook's, for it is now known that there were some errors in the Nautical Almanac *from which he had to work. Assuming the almanac to have been correct, the Captain's combined error from (a) the calculation of local time and (b) the emersion of Jupiter's First Satellite from that planet and its conversion into difference of longitude between himself and Greenwich was only 2 ½ minutes of angle or 10 seconds of time. Yet, when Cook was twelve years of age, men were still sailing down a latitude to find a place: so little could the calculations for longitude be relied upon.*

As an aside, while the Captain seems to have been fully occupied with the fate and working of the ship and the welfare of the men under him, he was also making detailed observations on the tides, a summary of which he later published in the Philosophical Transactions.

SHIP'S LOG:

SATURDAY, JUNE 30TH, 1770

Day and Month.	Winds.	Remarks, &c.
Saturday, June 30 ..	S.E.b.S. to S.E.b.E.	First and latter p't, fresh breezes and cloudy wea'r; middle part, light airs with some rain. Employ'd as before. The fishing-boat returned, having caught 254 lb. A.M.—Sent a boat fishing. Carp'rs employ'd cutting firewood.

COOK:

Moderate breezes at SE and clear serene weather. In the PM the Boat [long boat] returned from hauling the sain having caught as many fish as came to a pound and a half a man. In the AM I sent her again to haul the sain and some hands to gather greens while others were employed about the rigging &c^{a} &c^{a}. I likewise sent some of the young gentlemen to take a Plan of the harbour and went myself upon the hill which is over the south point to take a view of the Sea, at this time it was low water and I saw what gave me no small uneasiness which were a number of sand banks or shoals laying all along the coast; the innermost lay about 3 or 4 miles from the shore and the outermost extended off to sea as far as I could see with my glass, some just appeared above water. The only hopes I have of getting clear of them is to the northward where there seems to be a passage for as the winds blow constantly from the SE we shall find it difficult if not impractical to return back to the southward.

BANKS:

The second lieutenant saw two animals like dogs but smaller, they ran like hares and were of a straw colour. Sein caught 213 lb of Fish.

Here, on Grassy Hill, observing the mass of shoals confronting him, realising the virtual impossibility of ever working back to windward, the way he had come, against the prevailing SE *wind, remembering that he had not dared to leave the chains unmanned for the past thousand miles, the Captain was facing alone the to-be-or-not-to-be of his and the whole ship's future. 'We have sailed 360 Leagues without ever having a man out of the chains heaving the lead when the Ship was under way, a circumstance I dare say never happened to any ship before and yet here it was absolutely necessary.' This must have been a strong thought in his mind, and which he later committed to paper. This was the burden being placed squarely on the man and not the professional, though in him they seemed inseparable. It was the man who held tenaciously to the coast he had discovered, allowing the professional to complete the task in a situation such as many other professionals had abandoned in the past. Yet, with all this acheivement, he generously gives credit to the quality of the ship herself for making it possible for him to do so.*

CHAPTER 10
ENDEAVOUR RIVER: JULY

SHIP'S LOG:

SUNDAY, JULY 1ST, 1770

Day and Month.	Winds.	Remarks, &c.
Sunday, July 1	S.E. W.S.W. S.E. b. S.	First and middle p't , fresh breezes and fair wea'r; middle p't, light breezes and cloudy. P.M.—Employ'd wholly as before. A boat employ'd fishing, with much the same success. A.M.—A man from every mess fishing. The rest of the ship's company ashore to refresh.

COOK:
Gentle breezes at SE and clowdy weather with some gentle showers in the morning. In the PM the People returned from hauling the Sain having caught as much fish as came to 2½ pound a man, no one on board having more than another, the few greens we got I caused to be boiled among the Pease and makes a very good mess, which together with the fish is a great refreshment to the People. In the AM a party of men (one from each mess) went again afishing and all the rest I gave leave to go into the Country knowing that there was no danger from the natives. Today at noon the Thermometer in the shade ris to 87° which is two or three degrees higher than it has been on any day before, in this place.

BANKS:
Being Sunday, all hands were ashore on liberty, many animals were seen by them. The Indians had a fire about a league off up the river. Our second Lieutenant found the husk of a cocoa nut full of barnacles cast up on the beach; probably it had come from some island to windward, from Terra del Espirito Santo [New Hebrides] possibly as we are now in its latitude.

The ship was now finished and tomorrow being the highest spring tide it was intended to haul her off, so we began to think how we should get out of this place, where so lately to get only in was our utmost ambition. We had observed in coming in innumerable shoals and sands all round us, so we went upon a high hill to see what passage to the sea might be open. When we came there the Prospect was indeed melancholy: the sea every where full of innumerable shoals, some above and some under water, and no prospect of any streight passage out. To return as we came was impossible, the trade wind blew directly in our teeth; most dangerous then our navigation must be among unknown dangers. How soon might we again be reduced to the misfortune we had lately escaped! Escaped indeed we had not until we were in an open sea.

The Captain is confirming his conviction that, on all voyages such as this, it is essential for all provisions to be equally shared, irrespective of rank or rating. As well, it demonstrates an equal conviction that each individual is a person in his own right, and that the imposition of discipline was no more than the sensible regulation of relations between people in given situations, but which should never cancel the basic rights of a person. One feels, too, in this man the humanity of an equable temperament always controlling the fervour of the professional to keep ambition within its proper bounds.

SHIP'S LOG:

MONDAY, JULY 2ND, 1770

Day and Month.	Winds.	Remarks, &c.
Monday, July 2	S.S.E. W.S.W. S.E.	Do. wea'r. P.M.—People employ'd fishing and refreshing. A.M.—The master, in the pinnace, went to the eastward to find a passage between the reefs. People employ'd on the rigging. Carpenters and cooper as before.

COOK:

D° weather. In the PM the fishing party caught as much fish as came to 2 pound a man, those that were in the Country met with nothing new. Early in the AM I sent the Master in the Pinnace out of the Harbour to Sound about the shoals in the offing and to look for a channel to the northward. At this time we had a breeze of wind from the land which continued till about 9 oClock, what makes me mention this is because it is the first land breeze we have had since we have been in this River. At low-water lashed some empty Casks inder the Ships bows being in some hopes of floating her the next high-water and sent some hands afishing while other were employed refitting the Ship.

BANKS:

A great dew, which is the first we have had, and a land breeze in the morn the first likewise. The Wild Plantain trees, tho their fruit does not serve for food, are to us of a most material benefit; we make baskets of their stalks (a thing we learned from the Islanders) in which our plants which would not otherwise keep home remain fresh for 2 or 3 days; indeed in a hot climate it is hardly practicable to go without such baskets which we call by the Island name of *Papa Mya*. Our plants dry better in paper books than in sand, with this precaution, that one person is intirely employed in attending them who shifts them all once a day, exposes the Quires in which they are to the greatest heat of the sun and at night covers them most carefully up from any damps, always careful not to bring them out too soon in a morning or leave them too late in the evening.

SHIP'S LOG:

TUESDAY, JULY 3RD, 1770

Day and Month.	Winds.	Remarks, &c.
Tuesday, July 3	S.E.b.S. and S.E.	Fresh breezes and fair wea'r. P.M.—The carpenters employ'd repairing the longboat. Lash'd cask under the ship in order to get her off, if possible, next high water. At 6 hove a strain to no purpose. A.M.— Sent the boat fishing as usual. A party of men having been out all night in quest of some beasts that we have seen frequently, return'd without success. At noon the master return'd, having found a passage; they also bro't on board a quantity of cockles, large clams and other shell-fish, with which the reefs abound. Served them out to all hands. The boat employ'd fishing, with much the same success.

COOK:

Winds at SE, fore and middle parts a gentle breeze, the remainder a fresh gale. In the evening the fishing party returned having got as much fish as came to 2 lb a man; at high-water attempted to heave the Ship off but did not succeed. At noon the Master returned and reported that he had found a passage out to sea between the shoals which passage lies out ENE or EbN from the Rivers mouth, he found these shoals to consist of coral rocks; he landed upon one which dries at low-water where we found very large cockles and a variety of other shell fish a quantity of which he brought away with him. He told me that he was 5 leagues out at sea having at that distance off 21 fathom water and judged himself to be without all the shoals, which I very much doubted; after this he came in shore and stood to the northward where he met with a number of shoals laying a little distance from the shore, about 9 oClock in the evening he landed in a bay about 3 leagues to the northward of this place where he disturbed some of the natives whome he supposed to be at supper; they all fled upon his approach and left some fresh Sea Eggs and a fire ready lighted behind them, but there was neither house nor hut near.

Altho these shoals lay within sight of the coast and abound very much with shell fish and other small fish which are to be caught at low-water in holes in the rocks, yet the natives never visit them for if they did we must have seen these large shells on shore about their fire places, the reason I do suppose is that they have no boats that they dare venture so far out to sea in.

BANKS:

The tide rose not so high as was expected so the ship would not come off.

AM: The pinnace which had been sent out yesterday in search of a Passage returned today, having found a way by which she passed most of the shoals that we could see but not all. This passage was also to windward of us so that we could only hope to get there by a land breeze, of which we have had but one since we lay in this place, so this discovery added little comfort to our situation. He had in his return landed on a dry reef where he found vast plenty of shell fish so that the boat was compleatly loaded, chiefly with a large kind of cockles (*Chama Gigas*). One of which was more than 2 men could eat. Many were indeed larger; the Cockswain of the boat [Samuel Evans, Quartermaster] a little man declared that he saw on the reef a dead shell of one so large that he got into it and it fairly held him.

Mr Banks's interpretation of Molyneux's report seems to have been quite different from the Captain's. In his view from Grassy Hill, Cook had made a lively appreciation of his general situation and was sceptical of the Master's report that he thought himself outside the reefs at five leagues off. In fact, here, the outer edge of the Barrier Reef is ten leagues offshore.

SHIP'S LOG:

WEDNESDAY, JULY 4TH, 1770

Day and Month.	Winds.	Remarks, &c.
1770. Wedn'sd., July 4 ..	S.E.	Strong gales and fair wea'r. P.M.—Employ'd wholly as before. At 7 p.m. hove the ship afloat, and landed the spars and empty casks that was under her bottom. A.M.—Employ'd triming ship to bring her on an even keel. Got the fore-top mast up, fore yard and fore-tops'l yard across. Shifted the provisions and stores from the after hold, forward.

COOK:

Strong gales at SE and fair weather. In the PM the fishing party returned with the usual success. At High-water hove the Ship afloat. In the AM employed trimming her upon an even keel intending to lay her ashore once more to try to come at her bottom under the larboard Main chains.

BANKS:

At night the ship floated and was hauled off; an Allegator was seen swimming along side of her for some time. As I was crossing the harbour in my small boat we saw many sholes of Gar fish leaping high out of the water, some of which leaped into the boat and were taken. The ship has been a good deal strained by laying so long as she has done with her head aground and her stern afloat; so much so that she has sprung a plank between decks abreast the main chains.

Of concern to the Captain was not so much this leak of which Mr Banks speaks. He was still not sure of the damage to the ship further aft than they had been able to examine. He wanted, if possible, to make a further survey and perhaps effect some more repairs. The ship, trimmed and with her fore topmast up and yards again crossed, was looking more like her old self, wanting only her topgallants and jib boom.

SHIP'S LOG:

THURSDAY, JULY 5TH, 1770

Day and Month.	Winds.	Remarks, &c.
Thursday, July 5 ..	S.E. and E.S.E.	Strong breezes and fair wea'r. P.M.—Examin'd the bank on the south side ye river, and shifted the streem anchors in order to heave her on at high water. In the meantime employ'd shifting everything in order to bring her on an even keel. ½-p't 8, hove on the bank to examin the ship under the main chains on the larboard side, where we know the sheathing board was beat off on the rocks. Attended her at 2 a.m. (being low water), but the tide did not fall above 5 feet. At daylight got a purchase from the b. b'r anchor in readiness to heave the ship off. Some hands employ'd ab't the rigging.

COOK:
Strong breezes at SE and fair weather. In the PM warped the Ship over and at high-water laid her ashore on the sandbank on the south side of the river for I was afraid to lay her broad side to the shore where she lay before because the ground lies with too great a descent and she already hath received some damage by laying there these last neap tides, at least she still makes water.

BANKS:
At night she was laid ashore again in order if possible to examine if she had got any damage near that place. AM: Went to the other side of the harbour and walked along a sandy beach open to the trade wind. Here I found innumerable fruits, many of Plants I had not seen in this countrey; among them were some Cocoa nuts that had been opened (as Tupia told us) by a kind of crab, called by the Dutch *Beurs Krabbe (Cancer Latro)* that feeds upon them. All these fruits were incrusted with sea productions and many of them covered with Barnacles, a sure sign that they have come far by sea, and as the trade wind blows almost right on shore they must

have come from some other country—probably that discovered by Quiros and called Terra del Espirito Santo [New Hebrides] as the latitudes according to his own account agree pretty well.

Tupia, who parted from us and walked away a shooting, on his return told us that he had seen 2 people digging in the ground for some kind of roots; on seeing him they ran away with great precipitation.

PARKINSON:

On the 4th [ship's 5th] of July the ship was carried over to the other side of the river and examined thoroughly; but, being found in good condition, she was soon placed in her former station; where she was loaded, and properly fitted to proceed on the voyage.

The bank on which the ship was laid was a few hundred yards offshore NW *of where the ship had been previously beached, and nearer to that side than the other. It was a long narrow shoal, dry at low water, which curved back upstream from the entrance. It was on the seaward end that the ship was beached, off which a three-fathom channel lay between it and their shore.*

The discreet conduct of the Aborigines whom Tupia had encountered, and which was so consonant with the general conduct of nature here, shows the significant courage of these people whom Mr Banks had previously assumed to be cowards.

SHIP'S LOG:

FRIDAY, JULY 6TH, 1770

Day and Month.	Winds.	Remarks, &c.
Friday, July 6	E.S.E. S.E	P.M.—Do wea'r. At 2, low water, had 4 feet under the ship. One of the carp'rs examin'd her and found three streaks of the sheathing gone, about 7 or 8 feet in length; found, also, the main plank a little chaff'd. This account agreed perfectly well with the report of master and several others who have been under the ship. Bent the coasting cable to a bower anchor at the tents to assist in heaving off at high water. Hove off the bank and hove alongside the bank, where we clear'd ship. A.M.—Got a stage made from the ship to the shore. Got on board 8 tons of water for the ground tier of the after hold. Got the provisions out off the main hold into the after hold. Some hands employ'd about the rigging.

COOK:

[Journal] D° weather. At low water in the PM had hardly 4 feet of water under the ship yet could not repair the sheathing that was beat off, the place being all under water. One of the Carpenters crew, a man I could trust [George Nowell?] went down and examined it and found three streaks of the sheathing gone about 7 or 8 feet long and the Main plank a little rubbed: this account agrees with the report of the

Master and others that were under her bottom before. The Carpenter [John Satterly] who I look upon to be well skilled in his profession and a good judge of these matters was of the opinion that this was of little consequence, and as I found that it would be difficult if not impractical for us to get under her bottom to repair it I resolved to spend no more time about it. Accordingly at High-water hove her off and Moored her alongside the beach where the stores &c[a] lay and in the AM got everything in readiness for taking them on board, and at the same time got on board 8 tuns of water and stowed in the ground tier in the after hold. In the morning Mr Banks and Lieut[t] Gore with three men in a small boat went up the River with a view to stay 2 or 3 days to try to kill some of the animals we have so often seen about this place.

[Log] AM: Carpenters caulking the ships sides.

GREEN:
Fixed a stage to the shore from the bends.

The stage being fixed this time from the 'bends', as Green says, meant that the end at the ship's side was slung on lanyards at a level of about the main wale, near the waterline: the bends *being that part of the ship's side at the floor-heads where it curves or bends upwards. This may have overcome some of the 'up-hill' carrying of the stores from shore to ship. But, once at the ship's side, they would either have to be hoisted on board or parbuckled up the side, some ten or eleven feet to the rail.*

As it was not practical to have repaired the underwater damage aft, and for the peace of mind of all in the ship, it was just as well that they were satisfied with these reports. The revelation of their real position was not finally made clear until November 9th, at Onrust Island, Batavia, when the ship was hove-down. The Captain's entry for that day reads: 'In the PM Hove the Larboard side of the Ship Keel out and found her bottom to be in a far worse condition than we expected, the False Keel was gone to within 20 feet of the stern post, the Main Keel wounded in many places very considerably, a great quantity of Sheathing off, several planks much damaged especially under the Main channell near the Keel, where two planks and a half near 6 feet in length were within ⅛ of a Inch of being cut through, and here the worms had made their way quite into the Timbers, so that it was a Matter of Surprise to every one who saw her bottom how we had kept her above water; and yet in this condition we had saild some hundreds of Leagues in as dangerous a Navigation as is in any part of the world, happy in being ignorant of the continual danger we were in.'

On 13 November, the starboard side was hove keel-out and found 'very little damage'd and was therefore soon done with.' They were indeed fortunate that the worm had not done more damage, for, by the time the ship got to Batavia, she had been four months thus exposed in tropical waters, which are the ideal conditions for the activity of the worm—a month longer than had seen the complete destruction of both oaken bower anchor stocks at Tahiti.

With the Captain's decision made, the way was now clear for the ship to be got ready for sea again.

SHIP'S LOG:

SATURDAY, JULY 7TH, 1770

Day and Month.	Winds.	Remarks, &c.
Saturday, July 7 ..	S.E. Variable. S.b.E.	First and latter p't, mod't breezes and fair; middle, light airs. P.M.—Employ'd in the after hold. A.M.—Got the coals in; cleared the spirit-room to receive them, and stow'd the spirits in the after hold. Got the spare anchor in and sundry other spare stores. Stow'd the iron ballast belonging to the main hold on the larboard side in the pump-well.

COOK:

[Journal] Fresh breezes at SE and fair weather. Employed getting on board Coals Ballast &c[a] and caulking the Ship, a work that could not be done while she lay aground [because of the seams working with the tides]. The Armourer and his mate are still at work at the forge making and repairing sundry articles in the Iron way.

[Log] PM: Some hands hauling the saen who had but bad success. Employed stowing the after hold with water and provisions.

SHIP'S LOG:

SUNDAY, JULY 8TH, 1770

Day and Month.	Winds.	Remarks, &c.
Sunday, July 8	S.E.b.E. and E.S.E.	P.M.—Light breezes and fair wea'r. Employ'd getting on board stores. Open'd a cask of beef, 1 piece short, and a cask of pork, 1 piece short. A.M.— Fresh breezes and fair. The master went out to examine the se'ward passage thro' the reefs. Sent a boat fishing and clean'd ship fore and aft.

COOK:

Gentle breezes at SE and clear weather. I sent the Master in a boat out to sea to sound again about the shoals because the account he had given of the Channell before mentioned was to me by no means satisfactory, likewise some hands to haul the sain who caught near 80 pound of fish, the rest of the people I gave leave to go into the country.

BANKS:

[Mr Banks and Mr Gore set out in the AM of the 6th, as mentioned in the logs; but no mention is made, except by Banks himself and Cook, of their return, which was at 4 pm of the ship's 9th.]

6th. Set out today with the second lieutenant resolved to go a good way up the river and see if the countrey inland differed from that near the shore. We went for about 3 leagues among mangroves, then we got into the countrey which differed very little from what we had seen. From hence we proceeded up the river which contracted itself much and lost most of its mangroves; the banks were steep and covered with trees of a beautiful verdure particularly what is called in the West Indies Mohoe or Bark tree (*Hibiscus tiliaceus*); the land within was generally low, covered with thick long grass, and seemed to promise great fertility were these people to plant and improve it. In the course of the day Tupia saw a Wolf, so at least I guess by his description [dingo?], and we saw 3 of the animals of this countrey but could not get one; also a kind of Batts as large as a Partridge but these also we were not lucky enough to get. At night we took our lodgins close to the banks of the river and made a fire, but the Musquetos, whose peaceful dominions it seems we had invaded, spared no pains to molest us as much as was in their power: they followed us into the very smoak, nay almost into the fire, which hot as the climate was we could better bear the heat of than their intolerable stings.

Between the hardness of our beds, the heat of the fire and the stings of these indefatigable insects the night was not spent so agreeably but that day was earnestly wished for by all of us; at last [7th] it came and with its first dawn we set out in search of Game. We walked many miles over the flats and saw 4 of the animals, two of which my greyhound fairly chased, but they beat him owing to the length and thickness of the grass which prevented him from running while they at every bound leapt over the tops of it. We observed much to our surprize that instead of going on all fours this animal went only on two legs, making vast bounds as the Jerbua (*Mus Jaculus*) does. We returned about noon and pursued our course up the river, which soon contracted itself to a fresh water brook where however the tide rose pretty considerably; towards evening it was so shallow being almost low water that we were obliged to get out of the boat and drag her, so finding a convenient place for sleeping in we resolved to go no further. Before our things were got out of the boat we observed a smoak about a furlong from us: we did not doubt at all that the natives, who we had so long had a curiosity to see well, were there so three of us went immediately towards it hoping that the smallness of our numbers would induce them not to be afraid of us; when we came to the place however they were gone probably upon having discovered us before we saw them. The fire was an old tree of touchwood; their houses were there, and the branches of trees broken down with which the children had been playing not yet withered; their footsteps also upon the sand below the high tide mark proved that they had very lately been there; near their oven, in which victuals had been dressed since morn, were shells of a kind of Clam and roots of a wild Yam which had been cooked in it. Thus we were disappointed of the only good chance we have had of seeing the people since we came here by their unaccountable timidity, and Night soon coming on we repaired to our quarters, which was upon a broad sand bank under the shade of a bush where we hoped the Musquitos would not trouble us. Our beds of plantain leaves spread on the sand as soft as a mattrass, our Cloaks for bedcloths and grass pillows, but above all the intire absence of Musquetos made me and I believe all of us sleep without intermission; had the Indians came they certainly would have caught us all Napping but that was the least of our thoughts.

The land about this place was not so fertile as lower down, the hills rose almost immediately from the river and were barren, stoney and sandy much like those near the ship. The river near us abounded much in fish who at sun set leaped about in the water much as trouts do in Europe but we had no kind of tackle to take them with. [8th] At day light in the Morn the tide serving we set out for the ship. In our passage down we met with several flocks of Whistling Ducks of which we shot some; we saw also an Allegator of about 7 feet long come out of the mangroves and crawl into the water. By 4 oClock we arrived at the ship where we heard that the Indians had been near them but had not come to them; yesterday they had made a fire about a mile and a half off and this morn two had appeared on the beach opposite the ship.

SHIP'S LOG:

MONDAY, JULY 9TH, 1770

Day and Month.	Winds.	Remarks, &c.
1770. Monday, July 9	S.E. to E.S.E.	Mod. breezes and fair wea'r. P.M.—The master return'd, having been 7 leagues out sounding without being able to bring in a satisfactory account of the passage. In coming in over the nearest reef he met with a number of turtle; struck 3; w't between 8 and 900 lb. On board, employ'd taking the ground tier. The sain has less success than latily. A.M.— Two boats went out in quest of turtle. Serv'd turtle to all hands.

COOK:

Gentle breezes in the day at SE and in the night calm. In the PM Mr Gore and Mr Banks returned having met with nothing remarkable, they were about 3 or 4 leagues up in the country without finding hardly any variation either in soil or produce. In the evening the Master returned having been seven leagues out at sea and at that distance off saw shoals without him and was of the opinion that there was no getting out to sea that way. In his return he touched upon one of the shoals the same as he was upon the first time he was out, here he saw a great number of turtle three of which he caught weighing 791 pounds. This occasioned my sending him out again this morning provided with proper gear for striking them he having before nothing but a boat hook. Carpenters Smiths and Coopers at their respective employments and the seamen employed in getting on board stone ballast. This day all hands feasted on turtle for the first time.

WILKINSON:

AM: The Master and self went out to the reef in quest of turtle.

BANKS:

At night the pinnace which had been sent in search of a passage to leeward returned, she had been unsuccessful in her main errand. Shoals innumerable she had met with, upon one of them was lucky enough to see a turtle which was pursued and many more were seen, so many that three were taken only with a boat hook. The promise of such plenty of good provisions made our situation appear less dreadfull; were we obliged to wait here for another season of the year when the winds might alter we could do it without fear of wanting Provisions: this put everybody in vast spirits.

Here Banks brings to the surface an anxiety that must have been on everybody's mind, yet which is only obliquely, if at all, referred to in the logs. Working to windward against the prevailing south-easters, they well knew, was out of the question, even in clear water in which to make substantial tacks. The Captain had already recognised that in these constricted shoal-strewn waters, short of a reversal of the seasonal wind, it was hopeless. Therefore if no passage to the north could be found they would have to face a protracted period of delay when, already, the state of the provisions was critical. The ship had been absent from England now for two years all but a month, most of which had been spent at sea. She had been under considerable stress of weather on the coast of South America, in the Forties approaching New Zealand, and particularly during her six months charting and circumnavigating the two islands. So that, at this present time, she had to work on this challenging coast with worn and deteriorated gear: with sails and rigging that had to be nursed by the sailmakers and riggers with a vigilance that involved everybody onboard.

The Captain, on leaving New Zealand, had decided to sail this way, estimating his provisions sufficient for six months at two-thirds' allowance. With this threat of a prolonged and uncertain delay, serious doubts must have occupied his mind.

SHIP'S LOG:

TUESDAY, JULY 10TH, 1770

Day and Month.	Winds.	Remarks, &c.
Tuesday, July 10 ..	Variable. Et'ly.	Mod. and fair. Employ'd in the hold and on the rigging. P.M.—One boat return'd from the reef without success. A.M.—Sent a boat to the reef.

COOK:

Winds and weather as yesterday. Employed hoisting on board and stowing away the ground tier of water. In the PM saw seven or eight of the natives on the South [opposite] side of the River and two of them came down upon the sandy point opposite the Ship but as soon as I put off in a boat in order to speak with them they run away as fast as they could. At 11 oClock Mr Banks who had gone out to sea with Mr Molineux the Master, return in his own small boat and gave but a very bad account of the turtle catchers. At the time he left them which was about 6 oClock they had not got one nor were they likely to get any, and yet the Master was so obstinate that he would not return; which obliged me to send Mr Gore out in the yawl this morning to order the boat and the people in, in case they could not be employed there to some advantage.

In the AM, 4 of the natives came down to the sandy spit on the north side of the harbour having along with them a small wooden Canoe with outriggers in which they seemed to be employed in striking fish &c[a]. Some were for going over in a boat to them but this I would not suffer but let them alone without seeming to take any notice of them, at length two came in the Canoe so near the Ship as to take some things we throwed them, after this they went away and brought over the other two and came again along side nearer than they had done before and took such trifles as we gave them. After this they landed close to the Ship and all 4 went ashore carrying their arms with them, but Tupia soon prevailed upon them to lay down their arms and come and set down by him, after which more of us went to them, made them again some presents and stayed by them until dinner time, when we made them understand that we were going to eat and asked them by signs to go with us, but they declined and as soon as we left they went away in their canoe. One of these men was something above middle age, the other three were young, none of them above 5½ feet high and all their limbs proportionally small; they were wholly naked their skins the colour of wood soot or a dark chocolate and this seemed to be their natural colour, their hair was black, lank and cropped short and neither wooly nor frizled nor did they want for their fore teeth, as Dampier has mentioned those did he saw on the western side of this Country. Some parts of their bodies has been painted with red and one of them had his upper lip and breast painted with streaks of white which he called *Carbanda*; their features were far from being disagreeable, the Voices were soft and tunable and they could easily repeat many words after us, but neither us nor Tupia could understand one word they said.

In the AM, opened and aired some casks of bread, part of which we found but in bad condition, and yet, bad as it is, we shall be obliged to eat it.

BANKS:

Myself went turtling in hopes to have loaded our long boat, but by a most unaccountable conduct of the officer not one turtle was taken. I however went ashore upon the reef, saw the large Cockles and gathered many shells and sea productions. At night returned with my small boat leaving the large one upon the reef who I was sure would catch no turtle.

AM: Four Indians appeared on the opposite shore; they had with them a canoe made of wood with an outrigger in which two of them embarked and came towards the ship but stopped at a distance of a long Musquest shot, talking much and very loud to us. We hollowed to them and waving made them all the signs we could to come nearer; by degrees they ventured almost insensibly nearer and nearer untill they were, quite alongside, often holding their lances as if to shew us that if we used them ill they had weapons and would return our attack. Cloth, Nails, Paper &c &c. was given to them all which they took and put into the canoe without shewing the least signs of satisfaction: at last a small fish was by accident thrown to them on which they expressed the greatest joy imaginable, and instantly putting off from the ship made signs that they should bring over their comrades, which they very soon did and all four landed near us, each carrying in his hand 2 Lances and his stick to throw them with. Tupia went towards them; they stood all in a row in the attitude of throwing their lances; he made them signs that they should lay them down and come forward without them; this they immediately did and sat down with him on the ground. We then came up to them and made them presents of Beads, Cloth &c. which they took and soon became very easy, only jealous if any one attempted to go between them and their arms. At dinner time we made signs to them to come with us and eat but they refused; we left them and they going into their canoe paddled back to where they came from.

SHIP'S LOG:

WEDNESDAY, JULY 11TH, 1770

Day and Month.	Winds.	Remarks, &c.
Wedn'sd., July 11 ..	Easterly.	Do. wea'r. Employ'd wholly as before. P.M.—Both boats returned with only one turtle and a load of clams. Serv'd the clams to the ship's company.

COOK:

Gentle land and sea breezes. Employed airing the bread, stowing away water, stores &c[a]. In the night Mr Gore and the Master returned with the long boat and brought with them one turtle and a few shell fish, the Yawl Mr Gore left upon the reef with six men to endeavour to strike more turtle. In the morning four of the natives made us another short visit, 3 of them had been with us the preceeding day and the other was a stranger. One of these men had a hole through the Bridge [septum?] of his nose in which he stuck a piece of bone as thick as my finger, seeing this we examined all their noses and found that they all had holes for the same purpose, they had likewise holes in their ears but no ornaments hanging to them, they had bracelets upon their arms made of hair and like hoops of small cord they sometimes must wear a kind of fillet about their heads for one of them had applied some part of an old shirt I had given them to this use.

BANKS:

Indians came over again today, 2 that were with us yesterday and two new ones who our old acquaintance introduced to us by their names, one of which was Yaparico. Tho we did not yesterday observe it they all had the Septum or inner part of the nose bored through with a very large hole, in which one of them had stuck the bone of a bird as thick as a mans finger and 5 or 6 inches long, an ornament no doubt tho to us it appeared rather an uncouth one. They brought with them a fish which they gave to us in return I suppose for the fish we had given them yesterday. Their stay was but short for some of our gentlemen being rather too curious in examining their canoe they went directly to it and pushing it off went away without saying a word.

SHIP'S LOG:

THURSDAY, JULY 12TH, 1770

Day and Month.	Winds.	Remarks, &c.
Thursday, July 12 ..	Variable.	Do. weather. Employ'd stowing the hold and rigging the ship with all expedition. A quantity of our bread being spoil'd by wet, some hands employ'd cleaning and drying it. The yawl bro't on board a turtle and a skeat.

WILKINSON:

I brought on board in the yawl two turtle and a large skate. At 4 am went out on the yawl to the reef.

COOK:

Winds and weather as yesterday and the employment of the people the same. At 2 oClock in the AM the Yawl came on board with three turtle and a large skeat and as there was a probability of succeeding in this kind of fishery I sent her out again after breakfast. About this time 5 of the natives came over and stayed with us all the forenoon, there were 7 in the whole 5 men a woman and a boy, these two last stayed on the point of sand on the other side of the River about 200 yards from us, we could very clearly see with our glasses that the woman was as naked as ever she was born, even those parts which I allways before now thought nature would have taught a woman to conceal were uncovered.

BANKS:

At night the boat which had been sent to the reef for turtle came home and brought 3.

Indians came again today and ventured down to Tupias tent, where they were so well pleased with their reception that three staid while the fourth went with the Canoe to fetch two new ones; they introduced their strangers (which they always made a point of doing) by name and had some fish given them. They received it with indifference, signed to our people to cook it for them, which was done, and they ate part and gave the rest to my Bitch. They stayed most part of the morning but never ventured above 20 yards from their canoe. The ribbands by which we had tied medals round their necks the first day we saw them were covered in smoak; I suppose they lay much in the smoak to keep off the Musquetos. They are a very small people, in general about 5 feet 6 in height and very slender; one we measured 5 feet 2 and another 5 feet 9, but he was far taller than any of his fellows; I do not know by what deception we were to a man of the opinion, when we saw them run on the sand about ¼ of a mile from us, that they were taller and larger than we were. Their colour nearest to that of chocolate, not that their skins were so dark but the smoak and dirt with which they were all cased over, which I suppose served them instead of Cloths, made them of that colour. Their hair was straight in some and curled in others; they always wore it cropped close round their heads; it was of the same consistence with our hair, by no means wooly or curled like that of Negroes. Their eyes were in many lively and their teeth even and good; of them they had compleat setts, by no means wanting two of their fore teeth as Dampiers New Hollanders did. They were all of them clean limn'd, active and nimble. Cloaths they had none, not the least rag, those parts which nature willingly conceals being exposed to view compleatly uncovered; yet when they stood still they would often or almost allways with their hand or something they held in it hide them in some measure at least, seemingly doing that as if by instinct. They painted themselves with white and red, the first in lines and bars on different parts of their bodies, the other in large patches. Their ornaments were few: necklaces prettyly enough made of shells, bracelets worn round the upper part of their arms, consisting of strings lapped round with other strings as what we call gymp in England, a string no thicker than a packthread tied around their bodies which was sometimes made of human hair, a piece of bark tied over their forehead, and the preposterous bone in their noses which I have before mentioned were all that we observed. One indeed had one of his ears bored, the hole being big enough to put a thumb through, but this was peculiar to that one man and him I never saw wear in it any ornament. Their language was totally different from that of the Islanders; it sounded more like English in its degree of harshness tho it could not be called harsh neither. They almost continually made use of the word *Chircau,* which we conceived to be a term of Admiration as they still used it when ever they saw any thing new; also Cherr, tut tut tut tut tut, which probably have the same signification. Their canoe was not above 10 feet long and very narrow built with an outrigger fitted much like those at the Islands only far inferior; they in shallow waters set her on with poles, in deep paddled her with paddles about 4 feet long; she just carried 4 people so that the 6 who visited us today were obliged to make 2 embarkations. Their lances were much like those we had seen at Botany Bay, only they were all of them single pointed with the stings of sting-rays and bearded [barbed] with two or three beards of the same, which made them indeed a terrible weapon; the board or stick with which they flung them was also made in a neater manner. After having staid with us the greater part of the morning they went away as they came. While they staid 2 more and a young woman made their appearance on the Beach; she was to the utmost that we could see with our glasses as naked as the men.

Both the Captain and Mr Banks were being as objective as they could in observing the Aborigines and they made no moral judgements, yet phrases they habitually used demonstrate the constrictions of the culture to which they were bound, and give, in cameo, a revealing contrast between two cultures.

'. . . the woman was as naked as ever she was born, even those parts which I allways before now thought nature would have taught a woman to conceal were uncovered.'

THREE VIEWS OF THE YAWL UNDER SAIL (AFTER PARKINSON).

Cook was no prude. Yet, wide and disinterested though his observations generally were, he was reflexively tied to the popular cosmogony of his time. It was a world that began with Genesis and which was professedly occupied subduing Nature with a conviction of 'original sin'.

But on this day, in the brilliant tropical sunshine, on a golden sandspit laid flat upon sparkling blue water, and a bare two hundred yards away, stood a woman and a boy with copper highlights glancing from their bare dark skins, beneath a clear canopy of cerulean blue—perfect strangers to original sin. And though they were so seemingly close and real to the observers, they were as distant as the prehistory of Genesis. They were children of that distant time in which humans saw every mark upon the earth as a pristine print made by some great ancestral spirit, to be carefully nurtured from generation to generation in myth, commemorating great Mother Earth. The world, as it was, was their cathederal and altar. They *had not left Eden.*

There was a vast chasm between these two states of existence.

SHIP'S LOG:

FRIDAY, JULY 13TH, 1770

Day and Month.	Winds.	Remarks, &c.
Friday, July 13 . .	do.	Light breezes and hazy. Employ'd wholly as before. Got on board all the provisions. The yawl bro't on board a turtle and skeat.

WILKINSON:
At 11 pm the yawl returned with two turtle and one skate. AM: Sent the Yawl to the reef. [Wilkinson was probably the Mate in charge of this boat.]

COOK:
[Journal] Gentle breezes from the SE in the day and Calm or light airs from the land at night. Employed taking on board water stores &c[a]. At noon the yawl returned with one turtle and a large sting-ray.

[Log] In the PM got the bread aired, amounting to 27 butts or 81[c] 0[q] 0[lb], five hundred and sixty pound of which was so bad that it could not be eat and about the same quantity very much damaged, which I believe was owing to the casks being wet when the ship was a shore on the rocks. In the AM got on board our anchor and most of our water.

BANKS:
Two Indians came in their canoe to the ship, staid but a very short time and then went along shore striking fish. Our boat returned from the reef with one turtle and one large sting ray.

SHIP'S LOG:

SATURDAY, JULY 14TH, 1770

Day and Month.	Winds.	Remarks, &c.
Saturday, July 14 ..	Easterly and S.E.	Light breezes and fair wea'r. Got a quantity of stone ballast into the bread-room to trim ship. Some hands employ'd on the rigging and stowing the hold. This day an animal was shot, w't about 28lb. gross.

COOK:
Gentle breezes at SE and hazey weather. In the PM compleated our water got on board all the bread and part of the Boatswains stores; in the evening sent the turtlers out again. In the AM employed getting on board stone ballast and airing the spare sails. Mr Gore being out in the country shott one of the animals before spoke of, it was a small one of the sort weighing only 28 pound clear of entrails. The head neck and shoulders of this animal was very small in proportion to the other parts; the tail was nearly as long as the body, thick next to the rump and tapering towards the end; the fore legs were 8 inches long and the hind 22, its progression is by hopping or jumping 7 or 8 feet at each hop upon its hind legs only, for in this it makes no use of the fore, which seem only to be designed for scratching in the ground &c[a]. Excepting the head and ears which I thought was something like a Hare's, it bears no sort of resemblance to any European animal I ever saw; it is said to bear much resemblance to the Gerbua excepting in size, the Gerbua being no larger than a common rat.

PICKERSGILL:

This day we shot a wild beast, whose weight was 28 lb; its head was like a hares, with very small forequarters and fore legs not above ⅓ as long as the hind ones, three paws [toes?] and very different; it runs or rather jumps, on its hind legs at a great rate and is generally seen sitting on large stones or rocks, and its tail is twice as long as ye whole body, and thick in proportion.

BANKS:

Our second lieutenant who was a shooting today had the good fortune to kill the animal that had so long been the subject of our speculations. To compare it to any European animal would be impossible as it has not the least resemblance to any one I have seen. Its fore legs are extremely short and of no use to it in walking, its hind again as disproportionally long; with these it hops 7 or 8 feet at each hop in the same manner as the Gerbua, to which animal indeed it bears much resemblance except in size, this being in weight 38 lb and the Gerbua no larger than a common rat. [Banks called this animal, in his running heading for the day, 'kill Kanguru', from what he had heard the Aborigines call it.]

SHIP'S LOG:

SUNDAY, JULY 15TH, 1770

Day and Month.	Winds.	Remarks, &c.
Sunday, July 15	Variable. E.N.E. East.	Light breezes and hazy. P.M.—Employ'd as before. A.M.—Another boat went out to ye shoals. A boat employ'd with the saen. Clean'd ship fore and aft, and the remainder of the day is a holliday.

COOK:

Gentle breezes at SE and East. In the PM got on board the spare sails and sundry other articles. In the AM as the people did not work upon the Ship one of the petty officers was desireous of going out to catch turtle; I let him have the pinnace for that purpose and sent the long boat to haul the Sain who caught about 60 pounds of fish. Today we dined of the animal shot yesterday & thought it excellent food.

BANKS:

The beast which was killed yesterday was today dressed for our dinners and proved excellent meat.

With the work of the ship now pretty well in hand, there is, this day, the relaxed routine of a Sunday, in harbour. The AM, the latter part, is Sunday, proper, as is the ship's Monday, PM. Thus in the logs we find Civil Sunday, spread over two dates. In the forenoon before and after breakfast the ship was cleaned above and below decks fore-and-aft. After which all hands, excepting watch-keepers and dutymen, secure for the day to be 'at their own disposal'. One of the Petty Officers, probably Pickersgill, Master's Mate (for Wilkinson was already out on the reef in the yawl), got the Captain's permission to take away the pinnace, turtling with his own crew. This was for sport and not as a duty, illustrating how effectively the sailor, so engrossed in his calling, can make work into play. It was quite possible that they would return with no more than the proverbial 'wet arse and no fish', but for them it would be a day well spent, and they would sleep well. The yawl, being already out, had caught the imagination of the others. The long boat took the seine net to a favourite spot about two miles upstream and hauled for fish on a shoal patch between a mangrove point and an island just off it. All of this with the robustness of men and the minds of children on a picnic. Others wandered about the shore and country with an inquisitiveness natural to those who live amid the wonders of the deep, and who, as part of their lives, come to walk on exotic shores to savour, with a simple unconsciousness, the essential fabric of all life, transcending the narrower concepts held within their own native shores. A new-found but ancient land so different could, on this calm and peaceful Sunday, with its comforting space-limiting haze, reach deep into such an idly wandering fossicker. On these days, these men were not the sailors Dr Johnson had pictured.

SHIP'S LOG:

MONDAY, JULY 16TH, 1770

Day and Month.	Winds.	Remarks, &c.
Monday, July 16	N.E. Calm. Variable.	First p't, moderate breezes and fair; middle p't, a close fog; latter, light breezes and clear. P.M.—The yawl arriv'd with 4 turtle and 1 skeat, and set out for the reef immediately. A.M.—Got on board some of the spare spars, put a topsail yard between decks and a spare cable in the hold. Serv'd fish to the people.

WILKINSON:

At 10 pm returned in the yawl [self] with four large turtle and one skate. At 3 am, went out in the yawl to the reef.

COOK:

Fore and latter parts gentle breezes at ENE, in the night had light airs and calm. In the evening the yawl came in with 4 turtle and a large sting-ray and soon after went out again, but the pinnace did not return as I expected. In the AM employed getting on board the Cables. At the same time I went upon one of the high hills on the north side of the river from which I had an extensive view of the inland country which consisted of hills and vallies and large planes agreeably diversified with woods and lawns.

BANKS:

In the evening the Boat [yawl] returned from the reef bringing 4 turtles, so that we may now be said to swim in plenty. Our turtles are certainly far preferable to any I have eat in England, which must proceed from their being eat fresh from the sea before they have wasted their fat, or by unnatural food which is given them in tubs where they are kept given themselves a fat of not so delicious flavour as it is in their wild state. Most of those we have caught have been Green turtle from 2 to 300 lb weight: these when killed were always found to be full of Turtle Grass (a kind of Conferva I believe); two only were Loggerheads which were but indifferent meat; in their stomachs were nothing but shells.

As the ship was now nearly ready for her departure Dr Solander and myself employed ourselves in winding up our Botanical Bottoms [*'to wind up one's bottom'* = an idiom for finishing a job in hand] examining what we wanted and making up our complement of specimens of as many species as possible.

Turtle Reef, where the boats were turtling, was just about ten miles ENE *of the mouth of Endeavour River. The yawl and her crew were seeming to spend most of their time there; coming in, it would appear, for water and provisions only, and a little sleep. When she returned this night at 10 pm, with four turtle and a large stingray, the little ten-foot boat must have been down almost to her gunwales, and it would not have taken much lop on the water to have kept one hand busy with a bailer. Most of the passage out and back would be made under the small spritsail and foresail. The pinnace laid on the reef all night in spite of the Captain expecting her back. One suspects that Pickersgill wanted to justify himself against the yawl's catch. But the yawl seems to have been the more successful all round; perhaps she was more manœuvrable. In his enthusiasm Wilkinson was probably spurred on by his initial success and an ambition to keep his title.* Endeavour's *Turtle Reef is now known as Boulder Reef from the large boulders on its eastern and south-eastern sides. The natural seamanship of these men is glimpsed by their being at home in small boats for extended periods, which is not particularly remarked upon.*

'One of the high hills on the north side of the river' upon which the Captain went to get a view of the country inland was possibly either Mount Saunders (934') or Mount Millman (1,216'), a mile adjacent to each other and about three miles north of the ship.

The stowing of the spare cable in the hold would have given extra room to the men on the mess decks.

SHIP'S LOG:

TUESDAY, JULY 17TH, 1770

Day and Month.	Winds.	Remarks, &c.
Tuesday, July 17 ..	N.E. S.E.	P.M.—Mod. breez's and fair wea'r. Got the b't bower cable in its place. Got all the firewood on board. The pinnace arrived with 3 turtle. A.M.—Fresh breezes and cloudy. Employ'd setting up the lower rigging and getting on board the officer's stores.

WILKINSON:
The pinnace returned with 3 turtle, two of which she received from the yawl.

COOK:
Wind at SE a fresh breeze. People employed as yesterday and setting up the rigging. In the evening the pinnace returned with three turtle, two of which the yawl caught and sent in. At 7^h 41′ 17″ PM observed the first Satellite of Jupiter to Emerge; the same Emersion happened at Greenwich at 10^h 00′ 52″ in the AM, the difference is 14^h 19′ 35″ = to 214° 53′ 45″ of Longitude. The observation made on the 29th of last month gave 214° 42′ 30″, the mean is 214° 48′ 7½″ which this place is west of Greenwich. [This places Cook's position about 3′ to the westward of actual.]

BANKS:
The Boat brought 3 Turtle again today, one of which was a male which was easy to be distinguised from the female by the vast size of his tail, which was four times longer and thicker than hers; in every other respect they were exactly alike. One of our people on board the ship who had been a turtler in the West Indies told me that they never sent a male turtle home to England from thence because they wasted in keeping much more than the females, which we found to be true.

AM: Tupia who was over the water by himself saw 3 Indians who gave him a kind of longish roots as thick as a mans finger and of a very good taste. On his return the Cap^{tn} Dr Solander and myself went over in hopes to see them and renew our connections; we met with four in a canoe who soon after came ashore and came to us without any signs of fear. After receiving the beads &c that we had given them they went away; we attempted to follow them hoping that they would lead us to their fellows where we might have an opportunity of seeing their Women; they however by signs made us understand that they did not desire our company.

The yawl was still holding her turtle-catching title; and her coxswain, Wilkinson, may well have been the West Indian turtler of whom Mr Banks spoke. This would explain his success and enthusiasm.

SHIP'S LOG:

WEDNESDAY, JULY 18TH, 1770

Day and Month.	Winds.	Remarks, &c.
1770. Wednesday, July 18 ..	E't.	Fresh breezes and fair wea'r. P.M.—The master went to the no'ward to look for a passage. Hove the ship into the streem a little more to prevent her taking the ground. Employ'd about the rigging. Got on board the sails. Bent the maintop sail and topgall't sails. A.M.—Struck the tents. Got them and the armourer's forge on board. Employ'd getting everything on board. Bent the mainsail and got on board a turn of water for present expence. Some Indians about the ship.

WILKINSON:
PM. The yawl returned with three turtle.

PICKERSGILL:
Some Indians came to the ship, who seemed very inoffensive and tractable. They were of a very small stature, and quite naked and black. They had got y[e] lances, but did not seem fond of toys &c. Their voices is very shrill and they were often heard to mention the word "charco".

COOK:
Winds at ESE a gentle breeze. In the PM I sent the Master and one of the mates in the pinnace to the northward to look for a channell that way clear of shoals. Mr Banks Dr Solander and myself took a turn into the woods on the other side of the water where we met with five of the natives and altho we had not seen any of them before they came to us without showing the least signs of fear, two of these wore necklaces made of shells which they seemed to value as they would not part with them. In the evening the yawl came in with three turtle and early in the AM she went out again. About 8 oClock we were visited by several of the natives who now became more familiar than ever. Soon after this Mr Banks and I went over to the north side of the river and travelled six or 8 miles along shore to the northward, where we ascended a high hill from whence we had an extensive view of the Sea Coast to leeward; [which] afforded us a melancholy prospect of the difficultys we are to encounter, for in what ever direction we turned our eyes Shoals innumerable were to be seen. After this we returned to the Ship without meeting with anything remarkable and found several of the natives on board; at this time we had 12 turtle upon our decks which they took more notice of than any thing else in the Ship, as I was told by the officers for their curiosity was satisfied before I got on board and they went away soon after. Got on board the Booms &c[a].

BANKS:
Indians were over with us today and seemed to have lost all fear of us and became quite familiar; one of them at our desire threw his lance which was about 8 feet in length—it flew with a degree of swiftness and steadyness that really surprised me, never being above 4 feet from the ground and stuck deep in at a distance of 50 paces. After this they ventured on board the ship and soon became our very good friends, so that the Cap[tn] and me left them to the care of those who staid on board and went to a high hill about six miles from the ship; here we overlooked a great deal of the sea to Leeward which afforded a melancholy prospect of the difficulties we were to encounter when we came out of our present harbour: in which ever direction we turned our eyes shoals innumerable were to be seen and no such thing as any passage to sea but through the winding channels between them, dangerous to the last degree.

The high hill that the Captain, Mr Banks and Dr Solander climbed for their dismal view was Rocky Mount (1,807′), about a mile inland from Indian Head which was just six miles north of the ship. Here the Captain was confronted with a full realisation of his situation. The absolute unpredictability of what lay beneath the surface of such a close population of 'innumerable' shoals was enough to daunt the most intrepid navigator with any sense of reality. The greatest skill would need good fortune as an ever-present ally. Chance and caution, boldness and discretion, would have to go hand in hand, and intuition be their pilot. The feelings within must have been profound, for Cook was still Lieutenant (not Captain) Cook on his first testing voyage of discovery yet to be completed. His inner feelings he did not reveal to those under him; but he did not conceal the plain facts of the hazards from them either. Cook knew that to be trusted as a commander one must give trust to others. Noblesse oblige *works as powerfully with the lowly sailor as with his 'betters'. The Great Barrier Reef, though innocently neutral, became like a gauntlet thrown down before him.*

SHIP'S LOG:

THURSDAY, JULY 19TH, 1770

Day and Month.	Winds.	Remarks, &c.
Thursday, July 19 ..	S.S.E. to E.b.N.	Do. Wea'r. P.M.—Employ'd getting everything from the shore. A.M.—Scrap'd and grees'd the top and topgall't masts. Several Indians on board the ship. About 9 they went on shore and fired all the country round about us. Mr. Bankes' markee was with difficulty sav'd from the flame by being hastily pull'd down. They continued to increase the fire, notwith standing our signs to the contrary. The captain wounded one of them with small shot, which effectually dispers'd them. In ab't 2 hours' time they return'd without there arms, and seemingly verry good friends.

COOK:

Gentle breezes and fair weather. Employed getting everything in readiness for sea. In the AM we were visited by 10 or 11 of the natives, the most of them came from the other side of the river where we saw six or seven more the most of them women and like the men quite naked; those that came onboard were very desirous of having some of our turtle and took the liberty to haul two to the gangway to put over the side, being disappointed in this they grew a little troublesome and were for throwing everything over board they could lay their hands upon; as we had no victuals dressed at this time I offered them some bread to eat, which they rejected with scorn as I believe they would have done anything else excepting turtle. Soon after this they all went ashore, Mr Banks my self and five or six of our people being a shore at the same time; immediately upon their landing one of them took a handful of dry grass and lighted it at a fire we had ashore, and before we well knowed what he was going about he made a large circuit round about us and set fire to the grass in this way and in an Instant the whole place was in flames, luckily at this time we had hardly anything ashore besides the forge and a sow and a litter of young pigs one of which was scorched to death in the fire. As soon as they had done all this they all went to a place where some of our people were washing and where all our nets and a good deal of our linen were laid out to dry, here with the greatest obstinacy they set fire to the grass which I and some others who were present could not prevent, untill I was obliged to fire a musquet loaded with small shott at one of the ring leaders which sent them off. As we were apprised of this last attempt of theirs we got the fire out before it got a head, but the first spread like wild fire in the woods and grass. Notwithstanding my firing, in which one must have been a little hurt because we saw a few drops of blood on some of the linen he had gone over, they did not go far from us for soon after we heard their voices in the woods; upon which Mr Banks and I and 3 or 4 more went to look for them and very soon met them coming towards us. As they had each 4 or 5 darts a piece and not knowing their intention we seized upon six or seven of the first darts we met with, this alarmed them so much that they all made off and we followed them for near half a mile and then set down and called to them and they stopped also; after some little unintelligible conversation had passed they lay down their darts and came to us in a very friendly manner; we now returned the darts we had taken from them which reconciled every thing. There were 4 strangers among them we had not seen before and these were introduced to us by name by the others; the man which we supposed to have been struck by the small shott was gone off but he could not be much hurt as he was at a great distance when I fired. They all came along with us abreast of the Ship where they stayed a short time and then went away, and soon after set the woods on fire about a mile and a half and two miles from us. In the PM the Carpenters finished caulking the outside of the ship.

PICKERSGILL:

. . . They went ashore at 9 oClock and set fire to all the country around us, which burst with such rapidity that we with difficulty preserved Mr Banks's Marquee, which was up and obliged to be pulled down; the Indians continued to make more fires, notwithstanding our signs to the contrary, we were obliged to fire and wound one of them, after which they dispersed, we having first taken their arms from them, which they afterwards came for in a very submissive manner and got them; this accident so trivial as it may seem, if it had happened 12 hours sooner would have ruined us, for all our powder was ashore and nobody could have saved it besides the tents &c.

BANKS:

Ten Indians visited us today and brought with them a larger quantity of lances than they had ever done before, these they laid up in a tree leaving a man and a boy to take care of them and came on board the ship. They soon let us know their errand which was by some means or other to get one of our turtles of which we had 8 or 9 laying upon the decks. They first by signs asked for one and on being refused shewed great marks of resentment; one who had asked me on my refusal stamping his foot pushed me from him with a countenance full of disdain and applyed to some one else; as however they met with no encouragement in this they laid hold of a turtle and hauled him towards the side of the ship where their canoe lay. It however was soon taken from them and replaced. They nevertheless repeated the experiment 2 or 3 times and after meeting with so many repulses all in an instant leapt into their canoe and went ashore where I had got before them just ready to set out plant gathering; they seized their arms in an instant, and taking fire from under a pitch kettle which was boiling they began to set fire to the grass to windward of a few things we had left ashore with surprising dexterity and quickness; the grass which was 4 or 5 feet high and dry as stubble burnt with vast fury. A tent of mine which had been put up for Tupia when he was sick was the only thing of any consequence in the way of it so I leapt into a boat to fetch some people from the ship in order to save it, and quickly returning hauled it down to the beach Just time enough. The Cap^tn^ in the meantime followed the Indians to prevent their burning our linnen and the Seine which lay on the grass just where they had gone. He had no musquet with him so soon returned to fetch one for no threats or signs would make them desist. Mine was ashore and another loaded with shot, so we ran as fast as possible toward them and came just time enough to save the Seine by firing at an Indian who had already fired the grass in two places just to windward of it; on the shot striking him, tho he was a full 40 yards from the Cap^tn^ who fired, he dropped his fire and ran nimbly to his comrades who all ran off pretty fast. The Cap^tn^ then loaded his musquet with ball and fired it into the mangroves abreast of where they ran to shew them that they were not yet out of our reach, they ran on quickening their pace on hearing the ball and we soon lost sight of them; we then returned to the Seine where the people who were ashore had got the fire under. We now thought that we were freed from these troublesome people but we soon heard their voices returning on which, anxious for some people who were washing that way, we ran towards them; on seeing us with our musquets they again retired leisurely after an old man had ventured quite to us and said something which we could not understand. We followed for near a mile, then meeting with some rocks from whence we might observe their motions we sat down and they did so too about 100 yards from us. The little old man now came forward to us carrying a lance without a point. He halted several times and as he stood employed himself collecting moisture from under his arm pit with his finger which he every time drew through his mouth. We beckoned him to come: he then spoke to the others who all laid their lances against a tree and leaving them came forwards likewise and soon came quite to us. They had with them it seems 3 strangers who wanted to see the ship but the man who was shot at and the boy were gone, so our troop now consisted of 11. The strangers were presented to us by name and we gave them such trinkets as we had about us; then we all proceeded towards the ship, they making signs as they came along that they would not set fire to the grass again and we distributing musquet balls among them and by our signs explaining their effect. When they came abreast of the ship they sat down but could not be prevailed upon to come on board, so after a little while we left them to their contemplations; they stayed about 2 hours and then departed.

We had great reason to thank our good fortune that this accident happened so late in our stay, not a week before this our powder which was put ashore when we first came in had been taken on board, and that very morning only the store tent and that in which the sick had lived were got on board. I had little idea of the fury with which the grass burnt in this hot climate, nor of the difficulty of extinguishing it when once lighted: this accident will however be sufficient warning for us if ever we should again pitch tents in such a hot climate to burn everything round us before we begin.

There is no reference in any of the logs to when the gunpowder specifically was restowed in the ship, except in this mention by Pickersgill of the lucky escape from the fire. However, in the AM of the 17th the ship was taking onboard warrant officers' stores, which would have included the gunner's stores. So that the good fortune was by a narrower margin than Mr Banks indicates.

This incident also draws attention to the livestock which, after all this time, was still alive in the ship and whose welfare must have been the responsibility of some bucolic seamen to whom, by this time, they must have become more pets and mascots than prospective food. If there was a sow and litter, there must also have been a boar. This was an English sow and boar, for the Tahitian pigs they had picked up began to die of cold as they had approached latitude 40° South, en route to New Zealand. They had long since been eaten. There was also the goat and the sheep kept in the pen on the poop under the tiller platform. These had supplied the wool for the fothering, as well as their droppings.

There is also a glimpse of the personal hygeine of the ship's company, with the men at the washing place and their linen laid out to dry. One method used in this ship for washing clothes was to fasten them to a line and tow them overboard, using the whole ocean as a washing machine. Some, thus towing, had been stolen by Maori off the coast of New Zealand in one of a number of incidents there.

This day the topmasts and topgallant masts were being scraped and greased. They were being stripped of previously accumulated dried grease and dirt, then being payed afresh with tallow. The fat from the beef and pork cooked in the galley is the cook's perks which he keeps in his slush pot, but he is obliged to share this perquisite with the boatswain for just this use. The reason for greasing the masts in this way is so that the yards will slide freely when being hoisted or lowered. These yards, topsail and topgallants are always lowered when furled; they are hoisted only to spread the sails, thus helping to keep the centre of gravity lower and to relieve the masts of unnecessary strain. The yard is fully hoisted only when the sail is fully set with all reefs shaken out. As each reef is put in, the yard is lowered that much.

In an emergency, if the yard should stick and not come down when the halliards are let go, there may be serious damage, even dismasting. The yard is held to the mast and travels on parrals, *which are loops of ropes encircling the mast and made fast to the yard. They are rove through large round wooden beads which give a ball-bearing effect for the movement of the yard up and down the mast. These beads are known as* trucks. *So the importance of this greasing becomes apparent.*

From the time when Endeavour *was refloated, the rigging party had been overhauling everything aloft with the greatest of care. For over two years now, this rigging had been constantly exposed to extremes of weather, to constant wear and persistent strain, not to mention natural deterioration. The stocks of replacement had become ever more scarce, and extemporisation more necessary. Already the tents and the spritsail-topsail had been cannibalised to the topgallants; a main topsail had been reduced by having the head cut off at the first reef band; some staysails had been taken to replace others more used; rope was having to be made from junk; sailmaker's twine was scarce; and the sails worn thin. This would test the sailor and his craft, as well as the ship herself.*

It was with a full realisation of this internal situation that the Captain had looked out over that daunting labyrinth of reef and shoal laid out so graphically before him from the top of Rocky Mount. From this, perhaps, one may understand more the real emotion implied in his later praise of both the ship and the men, in a man of so little outward show.

SHIP'S LOG:

FRIDAY, JULY 20TH, 1770

Day and Month.	Winds.	Remarks, &c.
Friday, July 20	East'y.	Weather as yesterday. P.M.—Employ'd birthing the ship in the river. At midnight the master return'd and reported that there was no passage to the no'ward. A.M.—The capt. and master went out on the bar to sound and place the Rec'd on board water for pres't use.

COOK:

[Journal] Fresh breezes at SE and fair weather. In the PM got everything on board the ship, new birthed her and let her swing with the tide. In the night the Master returned with the pinnace and reported that there was no safe passage for the Ship to the northward. At low-water in the AM I went and sounded and buoyed the bar, being now ready to put to sea the first opportunity.

[Log] In the PM took down the forge.

BANKS:

Yesterday evening the ship was hauled off the shore ready for her departure. In the night by some unlucky accident she tailed ashore during the Ebb, and as the tide settled brought much strain on her rudder as alarmed all greatly; the Tiller which was in most danger beat hard under some strong sheep pens which had been built in a platform over it; as the tide settled still more it came to the point whether the tiller or platform would break, for one must, which the platform fortunately did and made us at once easy. No Indians came near us but all the hills about us for many miles were on fire and at night made the most beautiful appearance imaginable. The pinnace returned which had been sent to Leeward in search of a passage: the officer in her had met with nothing but shoals and not the least likelihood of a passage that way, no very comfortable situation. Our ship it is true was now repaired: Leaky she was from the strains she had got but the water she made was trifling. We were ready to sail with the first wind but where to go?—to windward was impossible, to leeward was a Labyrinth of Shoals, so that how soon we might have the ship to repair again or lose her quite no one could tell. Encounter the difficulty however we must and since our Bargain was a bad one make the Best of it. At night the yawl returned with one turtle in her: it had blown so much since she had been out that she with difficulty took even that, for as all our turtle had been taken by chasing moderate weather was absolutely necessary.

Mr Banks was only stating soberly the predicament in which all onboard knowingly found themselves. It was with memory of this and similar situations that Cook later wrote, absolutely without hyperbole, 'In justice to the Officers and the whole crew I must say that they have gone through the fatigues and dangers of the whole voyage with that chearfullness and allertness that will always do honour to the British Seamen.' And Admiralty had 'great satisfaction in the account he gives . . .'

SHIP'S LOG:

SATURDAY, JULY 21ST, 1770

Day and Month.	Winds.	Remarks, &c.
Saturday, July 21 . .	E.b.N. to E.b.S.	First and latter part, fresh breezes and cloudy; middle, mod. and fair. P.M.—Sent the pinnace to haul the saen. In the evening the yawl and pinnace return'd, the pinnace with fish for all hands, and the yawl with one turtle, which they caught in the net. A.M.—The wind blue so strong that the turtlers could not get out to the reef, nor the ship could not stir from her moorings. Sent the boatswain ashore with materials to make rope. Fill'd the empty water-cask. Some hands employ'd making brooms.

COOK:

Strong breezes at SE and clowdy weather. In the PM sent a boat to haul the sain which returned with as much fish as came to 1 ¾ lb a man. The yawl returned with one turtle which was caught in the nett for it blew too hard for the boat to strike any. In the morning I sent her out again but she was obliged to return not being able to get to windward. Carpenters employed in repairing the boats and overhauling the pumps and as the wind would not permit us to sail I sent the Boatswain with some hands ashore making rope and a petty officer and two men to gather greens for the Ships Company.

WILKINSON:
In the evening [I] returned in the yawl with one turtle which we caught in the net and the wind blew so fresh that we could not give chase to any. At 5 am I set out to the reef in the yawl, at half past 6 am we returned, the wind was so strong.

BANKS:
No signs of the Indians today nor indeed any thing else worthy of note.

All brooms in the ship had to be made by the people themselves. It was part of the boatswain's duties to see to this and to select the most suitable bushes from ashore wherever they were. And today he was ashore with a party making rope from the knotted yarns of junk that the people had from time to time knotted into lengths of over a hundred fathoms. For this he had to set up his warping frames with the winches to which were hooked the yarns to be twisted into strands. The frames had to be set 600 feet apart, with clear ground between them. The firing of the grass by the Aborigines had simplified this.

The sag of the yarn between the ends was held clear of the ground by stakes at intervals. The three sets or bundles of yarn which made the three strands of the rope were now twisted by the winches in an anticlockwise direction so that the tension in the strand 'locked' with that of the yarn, which was clockwise. When these had been laid to a sufficient 'hardness' in a way that had to be quite even along the whole length, they were ready to be brought together as one rope. At one end, then, the three strands were fastened to one hook of the winch, while at the other end they remained on three separate hooks as before. By being twisted in opposite directions the three strands began to come together around each other in a clockwise direction against the anticlockwise tension of the strands. This point of combination was controlled by a cone-like 'top' which led the strands to a true centre and which was mounted on a sledge that moved along as the laying progressed. This movement happened in such a way that all was kept even and compact according to the requirements of the rope: that is, either 'soft-laid' or 'hard-laid'. Like all simple processes, the best results came only from experience and practice, requiring more than can ever be put into books.

SHIP'S LOG:

SUNDAY, JULY 22ND, 1770

Day and Month.	Winds.	Remarks, &c.
Sunday, July 22	E't. and S.E.	Fresh breezes and fair weather for the most p't. In the p.m. had light winds and some rain. Boatswain employ'd making rope. In the evening he brought on board 100 fa'm of 3-inch. The pinnace haul'd the saen with pretty good success. A.M.—Employ'd as before. Sent a party of men for greens. High water at 9 o'clock. Served fish to the people, and sent the yawl to the reef.

WILKINSON:
Served turtle to one third of the ships company [one watch?].

COOK:
Fresh breezes at SE and ESE. Employed as yesterday. In the AM as the wind would not permit us to sail I sent the yawl out to catch turtle; in opening one today we found sticking thro both shoulder bones a wooden harpoon or turtle peg 15 inches long bearded at the end such as we have seen among the natives, this proves to a demonstration that they strike turtle, I suppose at the time they come ashore to lay their eggs for they certainly have no boat fit to do this at sea or that will carry a turtle and this harpoon must have been a good while in as the wound was quite healed up.

BANKS:
The turtle that was killed this morn had an Indian turtle peg in it which seemed to have laid there a long time. It was in the breast across the fore fins, having entered the soft part near the finns but the wound it made in going in was entirely grown up; the peg itself was about 8 inches in length and as thick as a mans little finger. One of our people who had been sent out to gather Indian Kale straying from his party met with three Indians, two men and a boy, he came upon them as they sat down among some long grass on a sudden before he was aware of it. At first he was much afraid and offered them his knife, the only thing he had which he thought might be acceptable to them; they took it and after handing it from one to another returned it to him. They kept him about half an hour behaving most civilly to him, only satisfying their curiosity in examining his body, which done they made signs that he might go away which he did very well pleased. They had hanging on a tree by them, he said, a quarter of a wild animal and a cocatoo; but how they had been clever enough to take these animals is almost beyond my conception, as both of them are most shy especially the Cocatoos.

With the wind now often easterly, the ship was weatherbound within the bar of the river, and so it would be for a further twelve days. But the Captain did not spend this time impatiently pacing the quarterdeck, looking anxiously to windward. When not making observation, he was busy with the consolidation and co-ordination of the vast amount of data he had previously collected. His journal is only the tip of the iceberg of his work. But he, himself, was anything but an icicle. Cook found young Isaac Smith, 16, a rated able seaman, of great assistance to him in the making of his plans, surveys and drawings. Cook was quick to recognise ability in another and ready with a helping hand. Molyneux, the Master, was only 22, and Pickersgill, a Mate, 19, were also assistants. Mr Green also taught much to the 'young gentlemen' of this ship that was far beyond the general standard of the time. In this ship was beginning the practice of making common the then-esoteric art of the mariner by simply demonstrating that it was possible. Molyneux had young Isaac Manley under his wing as a servant, receiving instruction nevertheless in things nautical. Possibly also Pickersgill had a winger to assist him and be assisted. Such tutelage was the basis of all sea training then and tended to be an educator of the whole person. It was also a reciprocal thing, for the paternal and unselfish in the teacher was no less fulfilled than the pupil was informed; and in both cases the best tradition was maintained, to be handed on. This was a tradition embraced equally on the mess decks and in the great cabin.

SHIP'S LOG:

MONDAY, JULY 23RD, 1770

Day and Month.	Winds.	Remarks, &c.
Monday, July 23	S.E.	Strong breezes and fair wea'r. Employ'd making rope. Pinnace with the saen with little success.

PICKERSGILL:
Strong gales and fair; making rope; no fish.

COOK:
Fresh breezes in the SE quarter which so long as it continues will confine us in port. Yesterday in the AM I sent some people into the country to gather greens, one of which straggled from the rest and met with four natives by a fire on which they were broiling a fowl and the hind leg of one of the animals before spoke of, he had the prescience of mind not to run from them (being unarmed) least they should pursue him, but went and sit down by them and after he had sit a little while and they felt his hands and other parts of his body they suffered him to go away without offering the least insult, and perceiving that he did not go right for the Ship they directed him which way he should go. Carpenters employed caulking the quick work. Seamen employed making rope and sundry other duties.

BANKS:
In botanizing today on the other side of the river we accidentally found the greatest part of the cloathes which had been given to the Indians left all in a heap together, doubtless as lumber not worth carriage. May be had we looked farther we should have found our other trinkets, for they seemed to set no value upon anything we had except our turtle, which of all things we were least able to spare them.

The 'quick work' which the carpenters were caulking was the top part of the ship's side above the channel wale. It is so called because it does not require the same sort of fastening or working to secure it as do the more substantial parts of the hull.

Primitive though the Aborigine was supposed to be, he was far less impressed by the opulence and 'wonders' of western humanity than were the practically civilised people of Tahiti and New Zealand. It would seem that, as yet, he had not lost that pristine individuality and independence of possessing all that is necessary within one's skin.

SHIP'S LOG:

TUESDAY, JULY 24TH, 1770

Day and Month.	Winds.	Remarks, &c.
Tuesday, July 24 . .	S.E. and E.S.E.	Do. wea'r. Employ'd as before. A.M.—Struck the topgallant mast to fix new backstays.

COOK:
[Journal] Winds and weather continues the same. Employed making rope, caulking the ship . . .

[Log] . . . and in fishing but in this had little success.

BANKS:
The blowing weather which had hindered us from getting out several days still lasted, not at all to our satisfaction who had not one wish to remain longer in this place, which we had pretty well exhausted even of its natural history. The Dr and me were obliged to go very far for any thing new; today we went several miles to a high hill where after sweating and broiling among the woods till night we were obliged to return almost empty. But the most vexatious accident imaginable befell us likewise: travelling in a deep valley, the sides of which were steep almost as a wall but covered with trees and plenty of brush wood, we found marking nuts (*anacardium orientale*) laying on the ground, and desirous as we were to find the tree on which they had grown, a thing I believe no European Botanist has seen, we were not with all our pains able to find it; so after cutting down 4 or 5 trees and spending much time were obliged to give over our hopes.

Those long lengths of rope the boatswain had been making found immediate use as topgallant backstays, demonstrating again the exhausted state of the rigging and the resourceful extemporisation of Endeavour*'s company.*

SHIP'S LOG:

WEDNESDAY, JULY 25TH, 1770

Day and Month.	Winds.	Remarks, &c.
1770. Wednesday, July 25 . .	S.E. to E.S.E.	Strong breezes and fair wea'r. This day the boatswain made two grapnell ropes for the pinnace and longboat. P.M.— Haul'd the saen and got fish enough for the sick. A.M.— The yawl return'd from the reef without success, as it has blown a fresh gale ever since they went out. Boil'd cabbage in the ship's company's pease.

WILKINSON:
I returned in the yawl from the reef without success as it has blown a fresh gale for several days past; boiled mountain cabbage in the pease.

COOK:
Fresh gales at SE and fair weather. In the evening the yawl came in having not been able to strike one turtle on account of the blowing weather nor can we catch much fish with the sain in the harbour.

BOOTIE:
This day the Boatswain made two grappling ropes for the boats . . . boiled cabbage (of the cabbage tree) in the pease.

BANKS:
The captain who was up the river today found the canoe belonging to our friends the Indians, which it seems that they had left tied to some mangroves within a mile of the ship; themselves we could see by their fires were 5 or 6 miles off from us directly inland.

The boats' anchors were called grapnels and generally had four prongs or flukes which did not need a stock to ensure biting. The ropes for these would be of 2 ½–3-inch circumference, and of considerable length.

SHIP'S LOG:

THURSDAY, JULY 26TH, 1770

Day and Month.	Winds.	Remarks, &c.
Thursday, July 26 . .	S.E.b.E. and E.S.E. E.S.E.	Do. wea'r. People employ'd working up junk to make rope. Sent a party of men for greens and cabbage. Served turtle to the ship's company. Haul'd the saen as usual.

COOK:
Wind and weather as yesterday. Such people as can be spared from the necessary duties of the Ship are employed fishing and gathering greens and other refreshments.

BANKS:
In botanizing today I had the good fortune to take an animal of the Opossum (Didelphis) tribes; it was a female and with it I took two young ones. It was not unlike that remarkable one which De Buffon has described by the name of Phalanger as an American animal; it was however not the same for De Buffon is certainly wrong

in asserting that this tribe is peculiar to America; and in all probability, as Pallas has said in his *Zoologia*, the Phalanger itself is a native of the East Indies, as my animal and that agree in the extraordinary conformation of their feet in which particular they differ from all others.

It was the heart of the Cabbage Palm top that was being boiled. By sending the spare hands fishing and collecting greens, the Captain was not only supplementing their low provisions but also providing them with recreation and recuperation, so valuable between sea-time.

SHIP'S LOG:

FRIDAY, JULY 27TH, 1770

Day and Month.	Winds.	Remarks, &c.
Friday, July 27	S.E. S.E.b.E.	Fresh gales and cloudy. Fill'd the empty water-casks. A party of men making brooms, cutting of wood, and a party of men hauling the saen. A.M.—Mr. Gore shot a beast, w't 80lb.

PICKERSGILL:
AM: Shot another of them beasts which weighed 80 lb.

COOK:
Very fresh gales at SEbs and fair weather. In the AM caught in the sain as much fish as come to ¾ lb a man and Mr Gore shott one of the animals before spoke of which weighed 80 lb and 54 exclusive of the entrails, skin and head, this was as large as most we have seen. Carpenters still at work caulking the Ship, a party of men hauling the sain, another cutting and making brooms, another wooding and watering.

BANKS:
This day was dedicated to hunting the wild animal. We saw several and had the good fortune to kill a very large one which weighed 84 lb.

GREEN:
Observers, Munkhouse, Forwood & self: 3 setts.

It would seem that Mr Gore was the most experienced hunter in the ship; he was certainly the most successful. The specimen has since been thought to have been a Wallaroo. This day Mr Green made another three sets of observations assisted by Midshipman Munkhouse and Gunner Forwood.

The carpenters still on the caulking would be making their characteristic staccato of caulking mallets on the heads of steel chisels, their sporadic rhythm of plink-

plonking xylophonics ringing out notes not unlike those of the Australian bellbirds in the bush. During working hours this became like the pulse of the ship herself, penetrating her whole frame.

SHIP'S LOG:

SATURDAY, JULY 28TH, 1770

Day and Month.	Winds.	Remarks, &c.
Saturday, July 28 . .	S.E. S.E.b.E. Calm.	Fore the most part do. wea'r. Employ'd cutting wood, hauling the saen, and making oacham. Continued to serve turtle every meat-day.

FORWOOD:
Served turtle on meat days in lieu of beef and pork to the ships company.

COOK:
Winds and weather as above without the least variation the whole 24 hours. The carpenters finished caulking the ship.

BANKS:
Botanizing with no kind of success. The plants were now entirely compleated and nothing new to be found, so that sailing is all we wish for if only the wind would but allow us. Dined today upon the animal, who eat but ill, he was I suppose too old. His fault however was an uncommon one, the total want of flavour, for he was certainly the most insipid meat I eat.

The hands making oakum were replenishing the stock used by the carpenters in caulking the ship. The meat days were Sunday, Tuesday, Thursday and Saturday, when they got turtle instead.

SHIP'S LOG:

SUNDAY, JULY 29TH, 1770

Day and Month.	Winds.	Remarks, &c.
Sunday, July 29	W.S.W. S.E. S.S.E. N.E.	P.M. do. wea'r. Employ'd as before . At ½-p't 5 a.m. had a light air off the land. Hove up and got the boats ahead to tow. Sent a boat on the bar to sound. She return'd immediately, and inform'd us that there was only 13 ft. water upon the bar. Came too and sent the yawl out to reef. Draught of water forward, 13 feet 6; aft, 13 feet 7 inches.

COOK:
Winds at SE a fresh breeze until 5 am at which time it fell calm and soon after had a light breeze from the land; upon this I sent a boat to see what water was upon the bar

(it being two hours of ebb) and hove up the anchor in order to put to sea, but upon the return of the boat came too as there was only 13 feet of water upon the bar which was 6 inches less water than the ship drawed. After this I sent the yawl to look for turtle as those we had got before were nearly all expended; about 6 oClock the sea breeze set in again which put an end to our sailing this day after I sent the pinnace to haul the sain who returned with only 20 pounds of fish.

BANKS:
Went out again in search of the animals: our success today was not however quite as good as the last time, we saw few and killed one very small one which weighed no more than 8½ lb. My greyhound took him with ease tho the old ones were much too nimble for him.

The ship, finally stored, wooded and watered, was now trimmed one inch by the stern. They had not always been able to get her thus trimmed by the stern. Her ideal trim, in the Captain's opinion, was three or four inches by the stern.

Mr Banks's dog must have caught a mere 'joey' who had not had time to take refuge in its mother's pouch.

SHIP'S LOG:

MONDAY, JULY 30TH, 1770

Day and Month.	Winds.	Remarks, &c.
Monday, July 30	E.S.E. S.E. S.S.E.	First part, strong breezes and fair wea'r; middle and latter, fresh breezes and cloudy, hazy, rainy wea'r. P.M.—The pinnace return'd, having caught only 25lb. of fish, which was serv'd to the sick. At 3 a.m. the master went out on the bar, and found it impossiable for the ship to get out. People employ'd scraping the decks. Carp'rs finish caulking.

PICKERSGILL:
Tended the bar, not water for us to get out.

COOK:
Winds at SE a fresh gale and fair weather in the PM, the remainder hazey with rain but the winds tho moderate kept in the SE quarter.

BANKS:
Ever since the ship was hawled off for sailing we have had blowing weather till to day, when it changed to little wind and rain which gave us some hopes; in the evening however the wind returned to its old bias.

The deck scraping which employed the hands (mentioned in the log) was the scraping off of the surplus pitch after the carpenters, with long-lipped ladles, had payed the hot pitch into the new-caulked seams between the planks. It had to be scraped back to deck-level, leaving a clean plank separated by the black pitch. As it is scraped the brittle pitch flies in small fragments and dust so that the forearms of the men develop a thick black powdered fuzz on their hairiness as they progress. Then there is the sweeping up, the washing down, and, finally, the holystoning until the last trace of the pitch is out of the grain of the decks.

SHIP'S LOG:

TUESDAY, JULY 31ST, 1770

Day and Month.	Winds.	Remarks, &c.
Tuesday, July 31 . .	S.S.E. S.E. E.S.E.	First and latter p't, strong breezes and cloudy; the middle, strong breezes, with squalls of wind and rain. Attended the tide on the bar, but found it impossiable to get out, the wind blowing so fresh at S.E. Caught 125lb of fish with the saen.

COOK:

[Journal] Fresh gales at SE and hazey with rain all the PM and most part of the night. At 2 oClock in the AM I had thoughts of trying to warp the ship out of the harbour but upon my going first out in a boat I found it blowed too fresh for such an attempt.

[Log] At 2 oClock in the AM we were going to unmoor in order to warp the ship out of the harbour, but upon my going out first in a boat I found it blow too fresh wind, and therefore lay fast. Some hands employed fishing &c[a].

HICKES:

Moored in Charco Harbour . . . to squally to cross the bar.

PICKERSGILL:

Water on the bar, but too much wind.

WILKINSON:

Dr Solander returned with the yawl with 265 lb of skate; the weather has been so exceedingly bad that it has been impossible to give chase to turtle; the pinnace caught 125 lb of fish with the seine.

BANKS:

Morning cloudy and boisterous enough.

Wilkinson, the turtle hunter, would also have been in the yawl with Dr Solander, and in charge of it.

Chapter 11
Departure

SHIP'S LOG:

WEDNESDAY, AUGUST 1ST, 1770

Day and Month.	Winds.	Remarks, &c.
1770. Wednesday, August 1 . .	S.E. E.S.E. S.E.	Do. wea'r. P M.—Employ'd picking oacham. A.M.— Attended on the bar as usual to no purpose. We have been waiting here since 20 ult. for a land wind to sail or a calm to warp out, neither of which circumstances have happen'd at a proper time of tide. At 7, the ship being moor'd to near the shore, weighed and warp'd further into the streem. Loos'd sails to dry. The carpenters employed repairing the yawl and examining the starboard pumps. In the p.m. the return'd with 265lb. of skeat. They inform'd us that weather has been exceeding bad on the reef.

COOK:

[Journal] Strong gales from the SE with squalls attended with rain. In the PM the yawl came in with two rays which together weighed 265 lb, it blowed too hard all the time they were out for striking turtle. Carpenters employed in overhauling the pumps all of which we find in a state of decay, and this the carpenter says is owing to the sap having been left on which in time has decayed the sound wood. One of them is quite useless and was so rotten when hoisted up as to drop to pieces, however I cannot complain of a leaky ship for the most water she makes is not quite an Inch an hour.

[Log] In the PM the yawl came in with a sting ray and a whip ray, together which weighed 265 lb. Some hands employed fishing with the sain with very little success.

WILKINSON:

AM: The Master attended the bar as usual to no purpose.

BANKS:
Even clear with less wind which supplyed hopes at least for tomorrow. During the night it blew hard as ever; the day was rainy with less wind but still not moderate enough for our undertakings.

The state of the pumps was yet another hazard to haunt them. Staunch though the ship had proved herself to be, she was not indestructible and, to survive, she would need those intangible streaks of good fortune—whether from the gods themselves or merely from the blind workings of Chance. This was not dramatised, but brought to the men's awareness by the circumstances.

SHIP'S LOG:

THURSDAY, AUGUST 2ND, 1770

Day and Month.	Winds.	Remarks, &c.
Thursday, August 2 ..	S.E.	Strong breezes and cloudy; in the night had heavy rain. People employ'd making oacham and hauling the saen.

COOK:
Winds and weather as yesterday or rather more stormy. We have now no success in the sain fishing hardly getting above 20 or 30 pound a day.

HICKES:
Moored in Charco Harbour. Employed picking oakum and mending the seine.

BANKS:
Moderate and very rainy; great hopes that the rain is a pressage of approaching weather.

SHIP'S LOG:

FRIDAY, AUGUST 3RD, 1770

Day and Month.	Winds.	Remarks, &c.
Friday, August 3 ..	S.E. E.S.E. S.E.b.E.	Strong breezes and cloudy in the first and middle p'ts; latter, moderate and fair. At 7 a.m. weighed and attempted to warp out, but the ship tailing on the bank on the No. side, a fresh breeze coming on, and the ebb tide made, hove her over to the So. side and came too with the b't bower in 3½ fa'm, 1½ cable's length to the eastward of the last anchoring-place. Carried the top-chains ashore to make fast to the rocks, and the messenger to make fast to the top-chains, with which moor'd ship as before.

COOK:
Strong breezes and hazey untill 6 oClock in the AM when it moderated and we

unmoored, hove up the anchor and began to warp out, but the ship tailing on the sand on the north side of the river, the tide of Ebb making out and a fresh breeze setting in we were obliged to desist and moor the ship again just within the barr.

BANKS:
In the morn our people were dubious about trying to get out and I believe delayed it rather too long. At last however they began and warped ahead but desisted from their attempts after having run the ship twice ashore.

Here Banks is being rather a 'bulwark critic'—one who leans on the bulwarks with advice while others do the job. It perhaps reflects his impatience to be away rather than his judgement. On this day the known portion of Francis Wilkinson's log ends: 'the Master's Mate so occupied with turtling.'

SHIP'S LOG:

SATURDAY, AUGUST 4TH, 1770

Day and Month.	Winds.	Remarks, &c.
Saturday, August 4 . .	S.E. S.S.E. Westerly. S.E.	P.M.—Mod. and fair wea'r. Sent a boat to haul the saen. The capt'n and master went out on the bar. At 4 carried the coasting anchor without the bar ready for the first opportunity to warp out by. At 6 the fishing boat return'd with little success. A.M.—Do. wea'r. At 3 laid a warp over the bar. At 5 weigh'd and warp'd ahead. At 6 was over the bar. Run a warp to the coasting cable. At 8 weighed the coasting anchor and made sail into the offing, having a light land breeze. At 10 had a moderate sea-breeze. Stood close on a wind, steering E.N.E. Sounding from 3½ to 15 fa'm. The pinnace ahead sounding. Sent the yawl to the Turtle Reef. At noon came too with the b't bower in 15 fa'm, good ground. Harbour, sail'd from W.S.W. 4½ leagues, the turtle shoal E't 1 mile.

COOK:
In the PM having pretty moderate weather I ordered the Coasting anchor and cable to be laid without the barr to be ready to warp out by, that we might not lose the least opportunity that might offer, for laying in Port spends time to no purpose, consumes our provisions of which we are very short in many articles, and we have yet a long passage to make to the East Indies through an unknown and perhaps dangerous sea; these circumstances considered makes me very anxious of getting to sea. The wind continued moderate all night and at 5 oClock in the morning when it fell calm, gave us an opportunity to warp out. About 7 we got under sail having a light air from the land which soon died away and was suceeded by the sea breeze from SEbE with which we stood off to sea EbN, having the pinnace ahead sounding. The yawl I sent to the Turtle bank to take up the net that was left there but as the wind freshened we got there before her, and a little after noon anchored in 15 fathom water a sandy bottom; for I did not think it safe to run in among the shoals untill I had well

viewed them at low-water from the mast-head, that I might be better able to judge which way to steer for as yet I had not resolved whether I should beat back to the Southward round all the shoals or seek a passage out to the Eastward or to the North[rd], all of which appeared equally difficult and dangerous. When at anchor, the harbour sailed from bore S 70° West distant 4 or 5 Leagues; the northward point of the mainland we had in sight which I named *Cape Bedford* (Lat[de] 15° 15′ S, Longitude 214° 45′ W) bore N 20′ West distant 3½ Leagues, but we could see land to the NE of this Cape which made like two high islands, the Turtle bank bore East distant 1 mile. Latitude by observation 15° 23′ S, our depth of water standing off from the land was from 3½ to 15 fathom.

BANKS:
Fine calm morn. Began early and warped the ship out, after which we sailed right out till we came to the turtle reef where our turtlers took one turtle. Myself got some few shell but saw many beautiful sea insects &c. At night our people who fished caught an abundance of sharks.

PARKINSON:
On the 4th of August, in the morning, we weighed anchor, left the harbour and steered NE till we were near the Turtle Reefs; there we anchored again, and sent the boats on shore, which returned with a turtle, a large skate, and a great number of clams, a sort of cockle, some of them very large.

COOK:
I shall now give a short description of the harbour or River we have been in which I have named after the Ship *Endeavour River*.

It is only a small bar Harbour or Creek which runs winding 3 or 4 Leagues inland, at the head of which is a small fresh water brook as I was told for I was not so high myself; but there is not water for shipping above a mile within the bar, and this is on the north [south?] side where the bank is so steep for near a quarter of a mile that ships may lay a float at low water so near the shore as to reach it with a stage, and it is extreamly convenient for heaving a ship down; and this is all this river hath to recommend it especially for large shipping, for there is no more than 9 or 10 feet water upon the bar at low-water and 17 or 18 at high, the tide rising and falling about 9 feet at spring tides and is high water on the days of new and full moon between 9 and 10 oClock. Besides this part of the coast is so barricaded with shoals as to make this harbour still more difficult of access. The safest way I know of to come at it is from the southward keeping the main land close on board all the way, its situation may always be found by the Latitude which hath been before mentioned. Over the south point is some high land but the north point is formed by a low sandy beach which extends about 3 miles to the northward then the land is again high. The refreshments we got there were chiefly turtle, but as we had to go 5 leagues out to sea for them and had much blowing weather we were not over stocked with this article, however what with these and the fish we caught in the sain we had not much reason to complain considering the country we were in. Whatever refreshment we got that would bear division I caused to be equally divided amongest the whole compney generally by weight, the meanest person in the ship had an equal share with myself or any one on board, and this method every commander of a ship on such a voyage as this ought ever to observe. We found in several places on the sandy beaches and sand hills near the sea Purslain and beans which grows on a creeping kind of vine, the first we found very good when boiled and the latter not to be despised and were at first very serviceable to the sick, but the best greens we found here was the Tarra or Cocco tops called in the West Indies Indian Kale, which grows in most boggy places, these eat as well or better than spinnage; the roots for want of being transplanted and properly cultivated were not so good yet we could have dispenced with them could we have got them in any tolerable plenty, but having a good way to go for them it took up too much time and too many hands to gather both root and branch: the few Cabbage Palms we found here were in general small and yielded so little Cabbage that they were not worth the looking after and this was the case with most of the fruits &c[a] we found in the woods. Besides the animal which I have before mentioned called by the natives *Kangooroo* or *Kanguru*, here are Wolves, Possums, an animal like a rat, and snakes both of the venomous and other sorts. Tame animals here are none except dogs and of these we never saw but one who frequently came about our tents to pick up the bones &c[a]. The Kanguru are in the greatest number for we seldom went into the country without seeing some. The land fowls we met with here which are far from being numerous were Crow, Kites, Hawks, Cockadores of two sorts the one white and the other brown, very beautiful Lorryquets of two or three sorts, Pidgions, Doves and a few other sorts of small birds. The sea or water fowl are Herns, Whistling Ducks, which perch and I believe roost in trees, Curlews &c[a] and not many of these neither. Some of our gentlemen who were in the country heard and saw wild geese in the night.

The country as far as I could see is diversified with Hills and Plains and these with woods and lawns. The soil of the hills is hard dry and very stoney yet it produceth a thin coarse grass and some wood; the soil of the plains and vallies is sandy and in some places Clay and in many parts very rocky and stoney as well as the hills, but in general the land is pretty well cloathed with long grass, wood shrubs &c[a]. The whole country abounds with an immence number of Aunt [*sic*] hills some of which are 6 or 8 feet high and more than double that in circuit. Here are but few sorts of trees besides the Gum tree which is the most numerous and is the same as we found on the southern part of the coast, only here they do not grow near so large. On each side of the river all the way up it are Mangroves which extend in some places a mile from its banks. The country in general is not badly watered there being several fine rivulets at no great distance from one another, but none so near the place where we lay, at least not in the Dry season which is at this time, however we were very well supplied with water by springs which were not far off.

PARKINSON:

[Description of the place]

During the time we staid here, we picked up a great many natural curiosities from the reef we struck upon, consisting of a variety of curious shells, most of which were entirely new to Mr Banks and Dr Solander. We also met with many new species of fish, Madrepores and other curious corals; seaweed and other beautiful marine productions.

On shore we were not less successful. Of vegetables, we found Clycine rosea, which yields a sort of bean purslain, that eats very well, boiled; Cicas circinalis, the kernels of which, roasted, tasted like parched pease; but it made some of our people sick, who ate of it; of this fruit that made a kind of sago in the East-Indies: we cut down many of them for the cabbage, which is very good food. We also found a black purple fruit, with a kernel in it which had a flat sweet taste; two sorts of fruit like pears, having stony sides, somewhat like the Guava, and of a very indifferent taste; a small-leaved plant, that smelt like lemon and orange peel, and made an agreeable substitute for tea; the E peea, Taro E owhaee, and E peepee, of Otaheite: also wild Plaintain, like the Meiya of Otaheite which is very full of seed, and has hardly any pulp; a sort of fig-tree that bears the fruit on the main stem, which tastes very insipid; the Etee and Eroa, of which the natives of Otaheite make their best lines; many gum trees, and a great number of other plants among which was the beautiful Nymphea with blue and white petala.

Of birds we found grey pigeons, with red beaks and reddish brown crests which ate very well; two sorts of small doves; two sorts of beautiful parroquets; a very uncommon hawk, pied black and white; several other sorts of hawks; large black cockatoos, with scarlet and orange coloured feathers on their tails, and some white spots between the beak and ear, as well as one on each wing; the goat-sucker or churn owl; merops or bee-eaters; large bats; a small bird with wattles of deep orange red; a bird like a Tetrao, having wattles of a fine ultramarine colour, whose beak and legs were black; an owl having the iris of its eyes gold colour, the pupil of them dark blue; a large black and white gull, with a bright yellow beak, on the gibbous part of which was a spot of scarlet; the corners of its mouth and the irides of the eyes, were of a bright scarlet colour; the legs and feet a greenish yellow: a black-bird of the oyster-cracker genus, with a bright red beak, except toward the point where it was yellow; the iris of its eyes scarlet and the irides of them bright orange; the feet and legs of a pale red colour: a large olive coloured bird of the loxia genus, having the iris of its eyes of a gall-stone colour, and the pupils of them black: a black and white shag, the iris of whose eyes was of a fine dark-green colour, the pupils black; the skin which surrounded the eyes was of a verditer-green colour; the beak pale grey; on each side of which was a bare yellow spot; the feet were black: a large pigeon, the iris of the eyes of which was a blood colour, the pupils of them black; their irides of a carmine colour; its legs and feet pale red. The last two were taken in a bay called Tasmano Bay. The black and white hawk before mentioned, had the iris of its eyes very broad of a rich scarlet colour, inclining to orange; the beak was black, the cera dirty grey-yellow; the feet were of a gold or deep buff colour, like king's-yellow. Besides these we saw many other curious birds.

Of quadrupeds there are goats, wolves, a small red animal about the size of a squirrel; a spotted one of the viverra kind; and an animal of a kind nearly approaching the mus genus, about the size of a grey-hound, that had a head like a fawn's; lips and ears which it throws back, like a hare's; on the upper jaw fix large teeth; on the under one two only; with a short small neck, near to which are the fore feet, which have five toes each, and five hooked claws; the hinder legs are long, especially from the last joint, which, from the callosity below it, seems as if it lies flat on the ground when the animal descends any declevity; and each foot had four long toes, two of them behind, placed a great way back, the inner one of which has two claws; the two other toes were in the middle, and resembled a hoof, but one of them was much larger than the other. The tail, which is carried like a grey-hound's, was almost as long as the body and tapered gradually to the end. The chief bulk of this animal is behind; the belly being the largest, and the back rising towards the posteriors. The whole body is covered with short ash-coloured hair; and the flesh of it tasted like a hare's, but has a more agreeable flavour.

Mr Banks found in the woods an Opossum (This creature has a membraneous bag near the stomach in which it conceals and carries its young when it is apprehensive of danger), with two young ones sucking at her breasts.

There were many alligators on the coast, some of them very large, and we frequently saw them swimming round the ship.

We found several sorts of snakes, ants, and a small culex or fly, which is no bigger than a grain of sand; the bite or sting of which is venomous, and caused protuberances on the skin which itched violently.

Of fish, we found many different sorts, and a variety of beautiful shell-fish; among them three sorts of oysters; some were found in lagoons; some adhering to the mangroves; and others along the shore: large cavalhe, or scomber; large mullets, some flat-fish, a great number of small scombri; and skate or ray-fish; one of which, that we caught, was curiously marked with polygons finely coloured; and another was of an orbicular figure, with blue grey-coloured back, and white belly, which tasted like veal; some other parts like beef; and the entrails as agreeable as turtle. We also caught turtles of a bright green colour, some of which weighed near four hundred pounds. On opening a turtle that we caught we found part of a wooden lance in it, which had gone in by the breast before the calapee.

The natives who were naked, though of a diminutive size, ran very swiftly, and were merry and facetious. Their bones were so small that I could more than span their ancles; and their arms too, above the elbow joint. The tallest we saw measured but five feet nine inches, though their slimness made them appear taller, most of them were about five feet five inches; and were painted with red and white in various figures. The colour of their skin was like that of wood-soot. They had flattish noses, moderate-sized mouths, regular well-set teeth, tinged with yellow.

Most of them had cut off their hair from their heads; but some of them wore their hair, which was curled and bushy, and their beards frizzled. On their breasts and hips were corresponding marks like ridges, or seams, raised above the rest of the flesh, which looked like cicatrices of ill-healed wounds. Some of them were painted with red streaks across the body, and others streaked over the face with white, which they called Carbanda. Some of them had a small hair-rope about their loins, and one about an arm, made of human hair. They also had a bag that hung by their necks, which they carried shellfish in. Their noses had holes bored in them, through which they drew a piece of white bone about three or five inches long, and two round. One of them had his ears bored in a like manner and pieces of bone hung in them. Some of them had necklaces made of oval piece of bright shells, which lay imbricated over one another, and linked together by two strings. The women, who did not approach nearer to us than the opposite shore, had feathers stuck on the crown of their heads, fastened, as we were informed, to a piece of gum.

They had lances and levers, very neatly made of reddish wood; and had two pieces of bone, joined together with pitch, that stood out at the end of them. To polish their lances they made use of the ficus ridola, which served the purpose of a rasp. Their canoes were made out of the trunks of trees; had an outrigger; and eight outriggers on which they laid their lances. Their paddles were long in the blade. To throw the water out of their canoes, they used a large shell called the Persian-crown.

Their language was not harsh [. . .] and they articulated their words very distinctly, though in speaking they made great motion with their lips, and uttered their words vociferously, especially when they meant to shew their dissent or disapprobation. When they were pleased, and would manifest approbation, they said *Hee*, with a long flexion of the voice, in a high shrill tone. They often said Tut, tut many times together, but we knew not what they meant by it, unless it was meant to express astonishment. At the end of this Tut, they sometimes added Urr, and often whistled when they were surprized.

As a mark of dissent, they said Aipa, several times, and this was the only word we could distinguish, to accord with the Otaheitean language.

On our arrival, the natives shewed themselves, on the land opposite us, by degrees; and after having thrown them some fish, they ventured to approach us in a canoe; landed by us; laid down their lances, and came forward to meet us, shewing signs of amity as they came along; but they were so much abashed at first, that they took but little notice of us, or anything about us, though they did not seem to be apprehensive of danger. We made them some presents, which they accepted, but did not shew much fondness for them. They became at length more free when only three of us were present, and made signs for us to take off some of our garments, which we did accordingly. They viewed them with surprize; but they seemed to have no idea of cloaths; nor did they express a desire for any; and a shirt which we gave them, was found later torn into rags.

The natives shewed great antipathy to our tame birds, and attempted to throw one over-board; and a little before we left the land, they set fire to the grass round the spot where we pitched our tent; but luckily for us, most of our things were on board, or they would in all probability, have been consumed, as the fire burnt very fiercely, and had like to have destroyed a litter of pigs, and some other things. We shot one of them who ran up the hill with a fire-brand, and wounded him. Several of them came to us afterwards, and made peace with us.

They seem to live mostly on shell-fish, the remains of which we frequently saw about their fires, which they procure by twirling a piece of wood in a hole, made in another piece, till it is lit up into a flame.

Some of our people, in a pinnace, went in search of a passage to go out of the bay, and landed on a coral reef, where they met with a great number of shells; and, among the rest, the sponsylus, a large sort of trochus, or top-shell, with which they loaded the boat.

The Aborigines had a good ear. Here Parkinson remarks that 'they articulated their words very distinctly, though in speaking made great motion with their lips.' Previously it had been remarked that they also had great facility for repeating words and phrases of the Europeans. Later observers found that some of the Aborigines on the northern coast were able to speak some Chinese as a result of brief contacts.

Cook has been smugly accused, by some, of merely paying lip-service to the cult of the Noble Savage; suggesting, presumably, that he had no original thoughts of his own outside his profession.

*What he wrote, a little later (**see page 449**), was not a contribution to the school of the Noble Savage, but rather a clear and revealing statement about his own culture. Compassionate towards the Aborigines it certainly was; but, more importantly, it was a penetrating evaluation of his own civilisation, which would seem to grow more pertinent with the passing years. It was not mawkish sentimentality, but a manifesto of Cook the Man. Because it contains some vital truth it may well be considered subversive in some quarters, two hundred years after it was written.*

Little is more humbling to a thoughtful person than to be faced with an individual—man, animal, or plant—which needs nothing outside its skin to achieve the survival of its species. This is the very heart of the origin of species—an exquisite eugenics. One feels that Cook, long before Darwin or Wallace, was writing directly to this point, especially in his reference to 'superfluities'.

CHAPTER 12
ESCAPE TO SEA

SHIP'S LOG:

SUNDAY, AUGUST 5TH, 1770

Day and Month.	Winds.	Remarks, &c.
Sunday, August 5 ..	S.E. and S.E.b.S.	P.M.—Moderate breezes and fair wea'r. Sent the boats on the reefs for clams and turtle. In the evening they return'd with 1 large turtle and one large stingray and clams for all hands on board. Employ'd clearing the ship fore-and-aft and stowing our small anchors. A.M.—Sent two boats on the reef, but it blowing fresh they soon return'd, with only one turtle. ½-p't 9, high water. At 10 hoisted the longboat and yawl up. ½-p't began to heave, but she drove long before we could come near ye anchor. Veer'd away again as before. Lat'd obs'd, 15° 24' So. Caught a No. of shirks.

COOK:

[Journal] In the PM a gentle breeze at SE and clear weather. As I did not intend to weigh untill the morning I sent all the boats to the reef to get what turtle and shell fish they could. At low-water from the mast head I took a view of the shoals and could see several laying without this one, a part of several of them appearing above water, but as it appears pretty clear of shoals to the NE of the turtle reef, I came to a resolution to stretch out that way close upon a wind, because if we found no passage we could always return back the way we went, In the evening the boats returned with one turtle and a sting-ray and as many large clams as came to one and a half pounds a man, in each of these clams were about two pounds of meat, added to this we caught in the night several sharks. Early in the morning I sent the pinnace and yawl to the reef as I did not intend to weigh untill half Ebb at which time the shoals began to appear, before 8 oClock it came on to blow and I made a signal for the boats to come onboard which they did and brought with them one turtle. We afterwards began to heave, but the wind freshening obliged us to bear away again and lay fast.

[Log] We lay fast untill noon as it blowed too fresh to break the ship loose.

The ship now lay anchored in the lee of Turtle (Boulder) Reef, just west of its northern edge. She had come there close-hauled to within 6 points of the wind, as close as she would lay. Endeavour River lay WSW *almost 10 miles. From the masthead the Captain could see clear deep water to the* NE *for a full 10 miles, beyond which the odd dry spots were visible on Lark and Pullen Reefs. He was confined, both to windward and to leeward, by reefs and shoals. Therefore his decision to attempt a passage to windward was sound, because, if impractical, he had a fair wind to return on. The nature of his difficulty he clearly saw; the extent of it he was not sure of. That it may prove impossible was possible; but he had one simple rule (habit, reflex, practice), which was to keep on with all the experience, patience, skill and attention he could bring to bear.*

SHIP'S LOG:

MONDAY, AUGUST 6TH, 1770

Day and Month.	Winds.	Remarks, &c.
1770. Monday, August 6 . .	S.E.b.E. S.E. S.E.b.E. S.E. S.E.b.S. S.E.	P.M.—Fresh breezes and cloudy weather. At 2 weighed and came to sail. Steered out N.E. b. E. 8 miles. Passing by the lee end of the Turtle Reef had 14¼ and 14½ fa'm. Dist. off, 1¼ miles. The pinnace ahead sounding. At ½-p't 4 had run the above distance. The pinnace made the signell for shoal water. Same time saw a small sandy island on a shoal, bearing NE.b.N. 3 or 4 miles. Saw breakers ahead and on the weather bow. Tack'd ship. Stood off and on making short trips, the pinnace sounding on the shoal nearest us. At ½-p't 5 she came on board and inform'd us that there was not above 6 foot water on some part of the shoal. Came too with the b't bower in 20 fa'm water, brown clay. Veer'd to a whole cable. Served hoocks and lines to the ship's company A.M.—Strong breezes and a head sea. People employ'd on sundry necessary dutys. Lat. obs. 15° 16′ So.

COOK:

Winds at SE. At 2 oClock in the PM it fell pretty moderate and we got under sail and stood out upon a wind NEbE having the Turtle Reef to windward, having the pinnace ahead sounding. We had not stood out long before we discovered shoals ahead on both bows. At ½ past 4 oClock having run off 8 miles the pinnace made a signal for shoal water in a place where we little expected it, upon this we tacked and stood off and on while the pinnace stretched farther to the Eastward, but as night was approaching I thought it safest to anchor which we accordingly did in 20 fathom water muddy bottom. *Endeavour River* bore S 52° West, *Cape Bedford* WbN ½ N distant 5 Leagues, the northermost land in sight which made like an island North, and a shoal a small sandy part of which appeared above water bore NE distant 2 or 3 miles [Swinger Reef]. In standing off from Turtle Reef to this place our soundings were from 14 to 20 fathoms, but where the pinnace was about a mile farther to the ENE were no more than 4 or 5 feet water rocky ground, and yet this did not appear to us in the Ship. In the morning we had a strong gale from the SE, that instead of

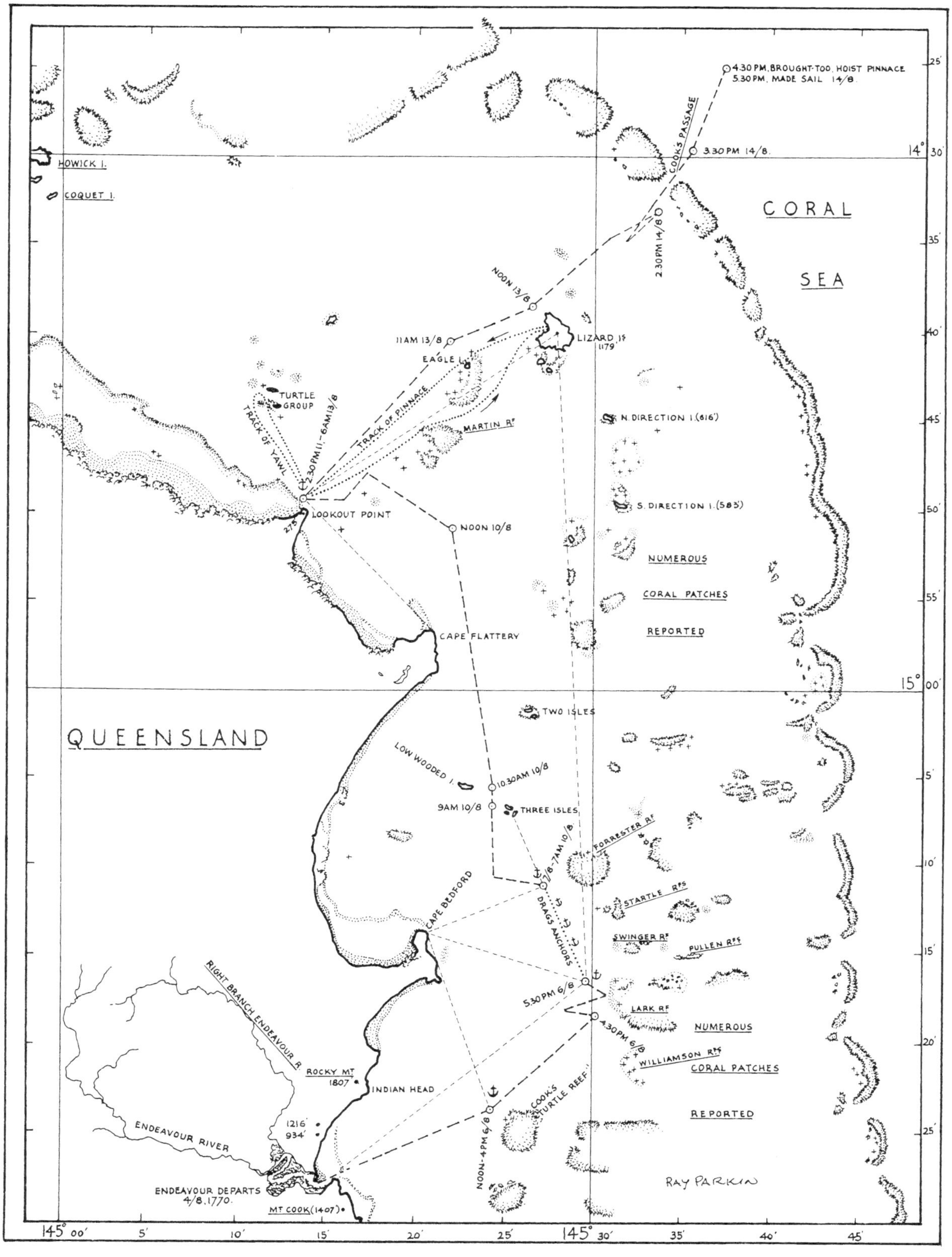

4.30 PM. BROUGHT-TOO. HOIST PINNACE
5.30 PM. MADE SAIL 14/8.
COOKS PASSAGE
3.30 PM 14/8.
2.30 PM 14/8
HOWICK I.
COQUET I.
CORAL
SEA
NOON 13/8
11AM 13/8
LIZARD IS
1179'
EAGLE I.
TURTLE GROUP
TRACK OF YAWL
TRACK OF PINNACE
2.30PM 11 - 6AM 13/8
MARTIN Rf
N. DIRECTION I. (616')
S. DIRECTION I. (583')
LOOKOUT POINT
NOON 10/8
NUMEROUS
CORAL PATCHES
REPORTED
CAPE FLATTERY
QUEENSLAND
TWO ISLES
LOW WOODED I.
10.30AM 10/8
9AM 10/8
THREE ISLES
FORRESTER Rf
STARTLE Rfs
SWINGER Rf
PULLEN Rfs
CAPE BEDFORD
DRAGS ANCHORS
5.30 PM 6/8
LARK Rf
4.30 PM 6/8
WILLIAMSON Rfs
RIGHT BRANCH ENDEAVOUR R.
ROCKY MT
1807
INDIAN HEAD
1216'
934'
ENDEAVOUR RIVER
ENDEAVOUR DEPARTS
4/8.1770.
MT COOK (1407)
NOON-4PM 6/8
COOKS TURTLE REEF
RAY PARKIN
14° 30'
15° 00'
145° 00'
145° 30'

weighing as we intended we were obliged to bear away more cable and strike topgallant yards.

BANKS:
At 2 we weighed, resolved to stand out as well as we could among the shoals, but before night were stopped by another shoal which lay directly across our way. AM: Blew so fresh that we could not move but lay still all day, not without anxiety least the anchor should not hold.

PARKINSON:
We could not weigh anchor until the afternoon, and then we stood out to the NE but, meeting with several shoals, we were obliged to cast anchor again. As the wind blew fresh we were detained until the 10th.

The ship had encountered the scattered collection of shoals and rocks here making up the Williamson, Lark, Swinger, Startle and Forrester Reefs and had anchored about a mile and a half to leeward of the NW edge of Lark Reef, with South Cape Bedford some 8 miles almost due west. With the rising wind, the ship was about to face one of those impartial acts of nature.

SHIP'S LOG:

TUESDAY, AUGUST 7TH, 1770

Day and Month.	Winds.	Remarks, &c.
Tuesday, August 7 . .	S.E.b.S. S.S.E.	P.M.—Strong breezes and cloudy. Got down topgall't yards. Veered away a whole cable. Kept a good lookout to see for a passage between the shoals, it being low w'r about 4 o'clock. Could not see any opening, so that we are at a loss how to proceed when the weather grows moderate. At 11 found she drove. Veer'd away to a cable and ⅓d on the b't b'r. A.M.—The ship continued to drive. Let go the small bower and veer'd away and bro't it to bear at ¾ of a cable. Got the sheet and coasting anchors over the side. Got down to gall't mast and struck yards and topmasts. At noon, strong gales and cloudy. The No. ext't of the main seen from the harbour bore S. 55° W., dist 4½ leagues. No observation.

COOK:
[Journal] Strong gales at SE, SEbs & SSE with clowdy weather. At low-water in the PM I and several of the officers kept a lookout at the mast head to see for a passage between the shoals, but we could see nothing but breakers all the way round from South round by the East as far as NW, extending out to sea as far as we could see, it did not appear to be one continued shoal but several laying detached from each other, on the Eastermost that we could see the sea broke very high which made me judge it to be the outermost, for on many of those within, the sea did not break high attall; and from about half flood to half ebb they are not to be seen, which makes the sailing among them the more dangerous and requires great care & circumspection, for like all other shoals or reefs of Coral Rocks they are quite steep too; altho the

H.M. BARK *ENDEAVOUR* DRAGGING HER ANCHORS. 'AUGUST 7TH, 1770: MADE ALL SNUG, AFTER THIS SHE RID FAST . . . BREAKERS NOT FAR TO LEEWARD WHICH MADE OUR SITUATION NONE OF THE BEST.'—COOK

most of these shoals consists of Coral Rocks yet part of some of them is sand, the Turtle Reef and some others have a small patch of sand generally at the north end that is only covered at high-water. These generally discover themselves before we come near them. Altho I speak of this as Turtle Reef yet it is not to be doubted that there are turtle upon most of them as well as this one. After having well viewed our situation from the mast head I saw that we were surrounded on every side with Shoals and no such thing as a passage to sea but through the winding channels between them, dangerous to the highest degree in so much that I was quite at a loss which way to steer when the weather would permit us to get under sail; for to beat back to the SE the way we came as the Master would have had me done would be an endless piece of work, as the winds blow now constantly strong from that quarter without hardly any intermission—on the other hand if we do not find a passage to the north^{d} we shall have to come [back] at last. At 11 oClock the ship drove and obliged us to bear away to a cable and one third which brought her up again, but in the morning the gale increasing she drove again. This made us let go the Small Bower anchor and to bear away a whole cable on it and two on the other, and even after this she still kept driving slowly untill we had got down topgallant masts, struck yards and topmasts close down [including lower yards] and made all snug that she rid fast, *Cape Bedford* bearing WSW distant 3½ leagues. In this situation we had shoals to the Eastward of us extending from SEbS to NNW, distant from the nearest part of them about two miles.

[Log] Made all snug. After this she rid fast; but least she should start again we got the Sheet and Coasting anchors over the side ready for letting go for there were breakers not far to leeward which made our situation none of the best.

BANKS:

During last night the gale had freshened much and in the morn we found that we had drove about a league. Fortunately no shoal had in that distance taken us up but one was in sight astern [the ship was driving stern-first] and the ship drove fast towards it, on this another anchor was let go and much cable veered out but even this would not stop her. Our prospect was now more melancholy than ever: the shoal was plainly to be seen and the ship still driving gently towards it, the sea running at the same time which would make it impossible ever to get off it should we be unfortunate enough to get on. Yards and topmasts were therefore got down and every thing done which could be thought of to make the ship snug, without any effect: she still drove and the shoal we dreaded came nearer and nearer to us. The sheet anchor our last resource was now thought of and prepared, but fortunately before we were drove to making use of that expedient the ship stopped and held fast, to our great joy. During the time of its blowing yesterday and today we became certain that between us and the open sea was a ledge of rocks or reef just the same as we had seen at the Islands [Pacific], no very agreeable discovery, for should that at any time join in with the main land we must wait for another season when different winds from the present ones prevailed; in which case we must infallibly be short of provisions or, if the turtle should fail us, salt provisions without bread was all we had to trust to.

This day demonstrates the sort of difficulties that this navigation presents, with clear implications of the resolution required to face them. The Captain's appreciation from the masthead was just as we would see it on the chart today. He correctly deduced that the cause of high breakers seen some fifteen miles to the eastward was the Pacific swell exploding on the sheer wall of the outer reef. He would have guessed its power but could not have foreseen, that before the month was out, he would be at the mercy of that power in what was, perhaps, the most horrendous situation of his life.

But there were possibilities enough in the present. The ship was beginning to drag her anchor. The 2-foot triangle of the anchor fluke, on its 4-foot arm, was being dragged through the brown clay of the bottom like a plough and the cumbersome 14-foot oaken stock ahead of it levelled all in its path, as the ship pitched in the shouting shove of the unrelenting wind to stretch the heavy 13 ½-inch cable as if testing its 55-ton breaking strain. Another cable was bent to the one already at work and half of this veered away also. So that, now, there was 180 feet of cable trying to hold the ship from driving further to leeward toward the reefs waiting there. For a time it did hold. But, by daylight, the wind further increased and the small bower was let go, and both cables veered away until the small bower had a whole cable out and took hold, with the best bower at two cables, almost 1,500 feet. This almost brought her up, but bearings taken showed her to be still slowly going to leeward. The next step was to release some of the wind's hold on her. Topgallant and topsail yards were brought down, followed by the topgallant masts. The topmasts were lowered and housed close to the lower masts, and the fore and main loweryards lowered almost to the deck. This seemed to check her, but, as a further precaution, the sheet anchor was broken out of its stowage in the starboard fore-chains by the fish tackle suspended in the foretop, and fleeted forward for the cat tackle to be hooked on to bring it to the cathead ready for letting go. The sheet cable was taken out through the spare hawsehole and bent to the ring of the anchor. The smaller coasting anchor was also got ready, but this could be manhandled. The three main anchors were all approximately of the same weight, despite their names and popular opinion. The best bower was perhaps the most used, possibly from a prevailing opinion on the Law of Storms, and this being on the starboard side. The small bower was on the larboard side. The sheet anchor was stowed on the starboard side abaft the best and was to back up the others if needed. In Endeavour *it was not ever let go.*

Banks gives a fair assessment of the hazards confronting them, with more time to reflect and less to do than the seamen who habitually record only the action and seldom the drama. For them it was a two-way bet: what will be will be—but not if I can help it.

Mr Banks said that, in the night, the ship had driven one league; but, before the ship was finally brought up, she had driven a full two leagues. Had the wind had no east in it, and been south instead, the ship would have undoubtedly been driven on to Startle or Forrester Reefs. If she had scraped past Startle then the solid round lump of Forrester Reef stretched two miles across her path, a mile or so beyond, as she drove stern-first. Had there been any west in the wind she would have been taken into a whole complex of reefs with as much chance as a fly in a web.

It will be apparent that the Captain was not one to exaggerate or dramatise when he was constrained to write in his log (in which was recorded his immediate reaction) '. . . for there were breakers not far to leeward which made our situation none of the best.' Yet even this understatement he did not include in the journal later. This had been one of those touch-and-go situations saved only by a streak of fortune tipping the scales if enough skill and good management went with it.

SHIP'S LOG:

WEDNESDAY, AUGUST 8TH, 1770

Day and Month.	Winds.	Remarks, &c.
Wednesday, August 8 . .	S.b.E. S.S.E.	Strong gales and cloudy, with a head sea. The ship rides a great strain. People employ'd making sennit for various uses. In the a.m. more moderate. Lat'd obs'd, 15° 10′ So.

COOK:

Strong gales at SSE all this day in so much that I durst not get up the yards and topmasts.

PICKERSGILL:
Strong gales and cloudy with a great head sea. The ship was now drove near 2 leagues, and the breakers are 2 miles to leeward; [the Ship] rides a great strain.

BANKS:
The night Dark as pitch passed over not without much anxiety: whether our anchors held or not we could not tell and maybe might when we least thought of it be on the very brink of destruction. Daylight however releivd us and shewed us that the anchors had held and also brought us more moderate weather.

With the night so dark, no bearings could be taken by the anchor watch. Only a lead resting on the bottom might give an indication, though difficult with the movement of the ship pitching into a head sea and surging up to her retracting straining cables in the troughs or the lulls of wind. While waiting for the outcome, the seamen were preparing for another day spent making sennit for reef-points, gaskets, ropebands, etc. to keep pace with the relentless wear and failing parts used to the bitter end.

SHIP'S LOG:

THURSDAY, AUGUST 9TH, 1770

Day and Month.	Winds.	Remarks, &c.
Thursday, August 9 ..	S.E. S.S.E.	Do. wea'r. P.M.—Got up the topmasts. A.M.—Hove ahead on both cables and put the service on afresh.

COOK:
[Journal] In the PM the weather being somewhat moderater we got up the topmasts but kept the lower yards down. At 6 oClock in the morning we began to heave thinking to get under sail, but it blowed so fresh with the head sea that we could hardly heave the Ship ahead and at last was obliged to desist.

[Log] . . . but it blowed so fresh that with all out strength we could hardly heave ahead, and at last was obliged to lay fast.

PICKERSGILL:
Ship rides though there is a prodigious great sea, the breakers all round us; very high and no signs of a passage out to sea tho clear in Shore. Swayed up topmasts and yards.

Though the conditions were so wild, the ship was behaving admirably and the Captain might well report that 'She is a good roader.' She rode thus to a great strain with the heavy dripping cables stretching like harp-strings and scattering a fine globular spray of squeezed-out salt water as they vibrated with the excruciating rise of the ship to a shouldering sea. At such moments the turns of the cables on the cable bitts, and the deck stoppers, gave sharp, hard cracks and grunts like desperate members of a hard-pressed tug-o-war team digging in their toes. This movement, and the surge of the ship forward again towards the anchors, as she fell into the next passing trough, drawn by the recovery of the elastic cables, caused great strain and wear where the cables bore on the hawseholes in the bow. Here the cables had been serviced over with old rope to take the chafe and this was almost now frayed through. Though the men heaved with all their strength on their bars, the windlass could hardly gain a fathom, but enough was gained to allow a new service to be put on the cables again and resettled in the hawsehole. To say this was an arduous task barely conveys the sweat, struggle and skill, not to mention the supportive grunted curses, that went into it. Though the topmasts were hoisted again, the heavy fore and main loweryards were kept down. The boisterousness of the scene was added to by the wildness of the turbulent surrounding waters with half-tide reefs and shoals being over-run by racing broken water fleeing across them, chased by the noisy wind.

SHIP'S LOG:

FRIDAY, AUGUST 10TH, 1770

H.	K.	F.	Courses.	Winds.	Remarks, &c.
1	..	..	..	S.S.E.	Fresh breezes and cloudy. People employ'd making sennit and oacham.
2	..	..	..	..	
3	..	..	..	..	More mod't. Hove up the small bower anchor
4	..	..	..	..	
5	..	..	..	..	Hove in the long service of the b't bower.
6	..	..	..	..	
7	..	..	..	..	
8	..	..	..	..	Strong breezes and cloudy.
9	..	..	..	..	
10	..	..	..	..	
11	..	..	..	..	
12	..	..	..	..	A fresh gale and hazy.
1	..	..	..	..	
2	..	..	..	..	
3	..	..	..	..	More mod't. Got up the lower yards.
4	..	..	..	..	
5	..	..	..	..	Hove into the short service.
6	..	..	..	..	
7	..	..	..	..	Weighed and made sail inshore, with the pinnace ahead sounding. Sounded from 9 to 12½ fa'm regular. At 8 bore away for some small islands to the northward of where the master had been sounding. At 9 pass'd the three small islands, dis't from them ¼ of a mile, the No. head seen from the harbour bearing S. b. W. 4 leagues. Saw some islands to the northward. Shap'd a course between the islands and the main. ½-p't 10, pass'd a sm. low island. Depth of water, 17 f'm.
8	..	..	Sounding, 12½ fa'm.		
9	..	..	Do.		
10	4	..	N.b.W.	S.E.b.S.	
11	2	..	No.	..	
	2	..	N.N.W.	..	
12	3	2	N.W.	..	At noon, fresh breezes and cloudy hazy wea'r. Unbent the sheet and coasting cables; got the sheat anchor upon the gunwale. The No. ext's of the main, N. 78 W., 7 miles. Ext's of 6 isl'ds (3 of which are high and 3 small and low), from S. 56° E. to N. 22° E Nearest dist., 7 or 8 miles. Lat'd obs'd, 14° 51' So. Depth of water, 14 fa'm.

COOK:

[Journal] Fresh gales at SSE and SEbS. In the PM the wind fell so as we got up the small bower Anchor and hove to a whole cable on the best bower. At 3 oClock in the morning we got up the lower yards and at 7 weighed and stood in for the land (intending to seek a passage alongshore to the northward) having a boat ahead sounding, depth of water as we run in from 19 to 12 fathom: after standing in an hour we edged away for 3 small islands that lay NNE½E 3 Leagues from *Cape Bedford*, to these islands the Master had been in the pinnace when the Ship was in port. At 9 oClock we were abreast of them and between them and the main having another low Island between us and the latter which lies WNW, 4 miles from Three Islands, in this channel had 14 fathom water: the northermost point of the Main we had in sight bore from us NNW½W distant 2 Leagues. Four or 5 leagues to the NE of this head land appeared three high islands with some smaller ones near them, and shoals and reefs without us we could see extending to the northward as far as these islands: we directed our course between them and the above headland leaving a small island to the eastward of us which lies NbE 4 miles from the Three Islands having all the while a boat ahead sounding. At noon we were got betwixt the headland and the 3 High Islands distant from the former 2, and from the latter 4 leagues, our Latitude by observation was 14° 51′ S. We now judged ourselves to be clear of all danger having as we thought a clear open sea before us, but this we soon found otherwise and occasioned my calling the headland above mentioned *Cape Flattery* (Lat^{de} 14° 55′ S, Long^{de} 214° 43′ West) [Actual: 14° 57′ S, 145° 21′ E. (Cook's long. = 145° 17′ E)]. It is a lofty promontory making in two hills next the sea and a third behind them with low sandy land on each side, but it is better known by the Three high Islands out at sea, the northermost of which is the largest and lies from the Cape NNE distant 5 leagues. From this Cape the mainland trends away NW & NWbW.

[Log] Got up topgallant masts.

BANKS:

Night and morning still more moderate so that one anchor was got up and we had great hopes of sailing on the next morn.

AM: Fine weather so the anchor was got up and we sailed down to leeward, convinced that we could not get out the way we had tried before and hoping there might be a passage that way: in these hopes we were encouraged by the sight of some high islands where we hoped the shoals would end. By 12 we were among these and fancied that the grand or outer reef ended on one of them so were all in high spirits.

By coming inshore again, the Captain was, in fact, following closely what is now the recommended ships' track and, at 10.30 AM, when abreast of Low Wooded Island, was crossing it obliquely. Notwithstanding his preoccupation with finding a passage out of this labyrinth, his observations were as accurate and professional as if he had been in a sheltered laboratory. His fixing of Cape Flattery, which he later amended to 14° 56′ S, was only 1 mile north of its actual position, and 4 miles west. In the meantime the ship was completely rerigged with topgallant masts up and all yards crossed. As well, the men had been busy in the boats and in ship handling, yet they were also occupied with the continual refitting and overhauling of gear, the demands of which became ever more pressing so that failure and serious accident could be precluded by anticipation. Sydney Parkinson wrote of the recent incident: 'The wind blowing hard from the SSE we drove and at length were obliged to let go two anchors and rode by the first with near two hundred fathoms of cable.'

SHIP'S LOG:

SATURDAY, AUGUST 11TH, 1770

H.	K.	F.	Courses.	Winds.	Soundings.	Remarks, &c.
					Fathoms. Soft blue clay.	
1	4	. .	W.N.W.	S.E.b.S.	14, 13, 13	Fresh breezes and cloudy hazy wea'r. Saw low land and breakers to the N.W't. Hau'ld in shore, the weather not permitting us to run further to leeward. ½-p't 2 anchor'd in ¼ less 5 fa'm with the b't bower and veer'd to ½ a cable, the No. ext's, set at noon, bearing S. 37° E. one mile, the No.-Est and largest of the 6 isl'ds bearing N. 43 E't.— leagues. Unbent the fore topsail to mend, and got up topgall't masts. The capt'n and gentlemen went on shore in the pinnace. Saw a smoke ashore. At 5 the captain had got upon the highest hill hereabouts in order to see the coast further to the No'ward.
2	3	4	S.W.	S.S.E.	12, 11, 10	
3	1	4	West.	. .	9, 8, 7, 6, 5	
	. .	. .	. .	. .	. .	
4	. .	. .	. .	. .	. .	
5	. .	. .	. .	. .	.	
6	. .	. .	. .	. .	. .	
7	. .	. .	. .	. .	. .	
8	. .	. .	. .	. .	. .	
9	. .	. .	. .	. .	. .	
10	. .	. .	. .	. .	. .	
11	. .	. .	. .	. .	. .	
12	. .	. .	. .	. .	. .	
1	. .	. .	. .	. .	. .	
2	. .	. .	. .	. .	. .	
3	. .	. .	. .	. .	. .	
4	. .	. .	. .	. .	. .	The master went on shore for the same purpose, but the weather was so hazy that his acc't was of no consequence. The captain, in the pinnace, went to the east-ward to take a view from one of the high islands, and the master was sent in the yawl to leward to sound the passage between some islands and the main. Serv'd the last of the turtle to the ship's company.
5	. .	. .	. .	. .	. .	
6	. .	. .	. .	. .	. .	
7	. .	. .	. .	. .	. .	
8	. .	. .	. .	. .	. .	
9	. .	. .	. .	. .	. .	
10	. .	. .	. .	. .	. .	
12	. .	. .	. .	. .	. .	

BOOTIE:

Served out the last turtle but one. [Also M.S. 3, Green and Forwood.]

FORWOOD:

7 AM, the Captain and Mr Banks in the pinnace, took 3 days provisions with them and went to look for a passage. Noon, People picking oacham.

COOK:
Fresh breezes at SSE and SEbs with which we steered alongshore NWbW untill one oClock when a Petty Officer at the masthead called out that he saw land ahead extending quite round to the islands without us and a large reef between us and them. Upon this I went to the masthead myself, the Reef I saw very plain which was now so far to windward that we could not weather it, but what he took for the main land ahead were only small islands, for such they appeared to me but before I had well got from the masthead the Master and some others went up, who all asserted that it was a continuation of the main land, and to make it still more alarming they said that they saw breakers in a manner all round us. We immediately hauled upon a wind in for the land and made a signal for the boat which was ahead sounding to come on board, but as she was well to leeward we were obliged to edge away to take her up, and soon after came too an anchor under a point of the Main in ¼ less 5 fathom about a mile from the shore, Cape Flattery bearing SE distant 3½ Leagues. After this I landed and went upon the point which is pretty high, from which I had a view of the sea-coast which trended away NWbW 8 or 10 leagues which was as far as I could see, the weather not being very clear. I likewise saw 9 or 10 small low islands and some shoals laying off the coast and some large shoals between the main and the three high islands without, which I was now well assured were islands and not part of the main land as some had taken them to be. Excepting *Cape Flattery* and the point I am now upon, which I have named *Point Lookout*, the main land next the sea to the northward of *Cape Bedford* is low and chequered with white sand and green bushes &c[a] for 10 or 12 miles inland, beyond which is high lands. To the northward of *Point Lookout* the shore appeared to be shoaled and flat some distance off, which was no good sign of meeting with a channel in with the land as we have hitherto done. We saw the foot steps of people upon the sand and smook and fire up in the country, and in the evening returned on board where I came to the resolution to visit one of the high islands in the offing in my boat, as they lay at least 5 leagues out to sea and seemed to be of such height that from the top of one of them I hoped to see and find a passage out to sea clear of shoals: accordingly in the morning I set out in the pinnace for the northermost and largest of the three accompanied by Mr Banks, at the same time I sent the Master in the Yawl to leeward to sound between the low islands and the main. In my way to the Island I passed over a large reef of coral rocks and sand which lies about two leagues from the island [Martin Reef]. I left another to leeward which lays about 3 miles from the island; on the north part of this is a low sandy isle with trees upon it [Eagle Reef and Eagle Islet]. On the reef we passed over in the boat we saw several turtle and chased one or two, but caught none it blowing too hard and I had no time to spare being otherways employed. I did not reach the island untill half an hour after one oClock in the PM of [see continuation on the 12th.]

BANKS:
But about dinner time the people at the mast head saw as they thought land all round

us, on which we immediately came to an anchor resolved to go ashore and from the hills examine whether it was so or not.

The point we went upon was sandy and very barren so it afforded very few plants or anything else worth our observation. The sand itself indeed with which the whole country in a manner was covered was infinitely fine and white, but till a glass house was built here that would turn to no account. We had the satisfaction however to see that what was taken for land round us proved only a number of islands: to one very high one about 5 leagues from the land the Captain resolved to go in the boat tomorrow in order to see whether the grand reef had really left us or not.

AM: As proposed yesterday the Captain went today to the island, which proved 5 leagues off from the ship, I went with him. In going out we passed over two very large shoals on which we saw great plenty of turtle but we had too much wind to strike any. [continued on the 12th.]

The pinnace of course sailed out to Lizard Island, with her two-masted settee rig. All boats moved under sail whenever possible. They could be rigged, masts and all, by efficient crews in a very few minutes, almost as quickly as one could dress. The change from oars to sail was one in which competitive crews took a pride. The sailor was always making games of his work, with an enthusiasm that bred unthinking efficiency. For him there was no overtime or extra pay; but he could, and did, take for himself a bonus in exhilarating job satisfaction because of his good native sense; and he was childlike enough to make it work.

SHIP'S LOG:

SUNDAY, AUGUST 12TH, 1770

Day and Month.	Winds.	Remarks, &c.
1770. Sunday, August 12 . .	S.S.E. and S.E.	Fresh breezes and fair wea'r. People employ'd cleaning ship fore and aft and mak'g oacham. At noon the yawl return'd, having found from 5 to 7 fa'm in the passage between the low islands and the main. Lat'd obs'd, 14° 48' So.

COOK:

Sunday, 12th . . . when I immediately went upon the highest hill on the island where to my mortification I discovered a reef of rocks laying about 2 or 3 leagues without the island, extending in a line NW and SE farther than I could see on which the sea broke very high. This however gave me hopes that they were the outermost shoals, as I did not doubt but what I should be able to get without them for there appeared to be several breaks or Partitions in the reef and deep water between it and the islands. I stayed upon this hill till near sun set but the weather continued so hazey all the time that I could not see above 4 or 5 leagues round me, so that I came down much disappointed in the prospect I expected to have had, but being in hopes that the morning might prove clearer and give me a better view of the shoals. With this in view I stayed all night upon the island, and at 3 in the morning sent the Pinnace with one of the Mates I had with me to sound between the island and the reefs and to examine one of the breaks or channels, and in the meantime I went upon the hill where I arrived by sun rise but I found it much hazier than in the evening. About noon the pinnace returned having been out as far as the reef and found from 15 to 28 fathom water. It blowed so hard that they durst not venture into one of the channels which the mate said seemed to him very narrow but this did not discourage me for I thought from the place he was at he must have seen it at a great disadvantage. Before I quit this island I shall describe it. It lies as I have before observed about 5 leagues from the main, it is above 8 miles in circuit and of a height to be seen 10 or 12 leagues; it is mostly high land very rocky and barren except on the NW side where there are some sandy bays and low land, which last is covered with thin long grass Trees &c[a] the same as upon the main. Here is also fresh water in two places the one is at a running stream the water a little brackish where I tasted it which was close to the sea, the other is a pool close behind the sandy beach of good sweet water, as I dare say the other is a little way from the sea beach. The only Land-animals we saw here were Lizards and these seemed to be pretty plenty which occasioned my naming the Island *Lizard Island*. The inhabitants of the Main visit this Island at some seasons of the year for we saw the ruins of several of their hutts and heaps of shells &c[a]. SE 4 or 5 miles from this island lay the other two high islands [North Direction (616′), and South Direction (583′)] which are very small compared to this, and near them lay three other yet smaller and lower islands [Rocky Islets (150′)] and several shoals or reefs especially to the SE. There is however a clear passage from *Cape Flattery* to these islands and even quite out to the outer reefs leaving the above islands to the SE and Lizard Island to the NW.

BANKS:

The island itself was high; we ascended the hill and when we were at the top saw plainly the Grand Reef still extending itself parallel with the shore at about the distance of 2 or 3 leagues from us or 8 from the main; through it were several channels exactly similar to those we had seen in the Islands. Through one of these we determined to go which seemed most easy: to ascertain however the practicability of it we resolved to stay upon the island all night and at day break in the morn send the boat to sound one of them, which was accordingly done. We slept under the shade of a bush that grew on the beach very comfortably.

AM: Great part of yesterday and all this morn till the boat returned I employed in searching the island. On it I found some few plants which I had not before seen; the island itself was small and barren; on it was however one small tract of woodland which abounded very much with large lizards some of which I took. Distant as this isle was from the main, the Indians had been here in their poor embarkations, sure sign that some part of the year must have very settled fine weather; we saw 7 or 8 frames of their huts and vast piles of shells the fish of which had I suppose been their food. All the houses were built upon the tops of eminences exposed entirely to the SE, contrary to those of the main which are commonly placed under the shelter of some bushes or hill side to break off the wind. The officer who went in the boat returned with an account that the sea broke vastly high upon the reef and the swell was so great in the opening that he could not go in to sound. This was sufficient to assure us of a safe passage out, so we got into the boat to return to the ship in high spirits, thinking our danger now at an end as we had a passage open to us to the main sea.

At the present there are only small lizards on Lizard Island, some skinks and perhaps a gecko. But Mr Banks's mention of large lizards there suggests that perhaps the island may then have supported the monitor Varanus semirex *Kinghorn which is now confined to Coquet Island, twenty or so miles* NW *of where the ship was then anchored, which is part of the Howick Group.*

SHIP'S LOG:

MONDAY, AUGUST 13TH, 1770

Day and Month.	Winds.	Remarks, &c.
Monday, August 13 ..	S.E.'t.	Do. wea'r. A 7 p.m. the captain return'd, having had a view of the large outer reef to the eastward. Sent a boat with a m'te to examin the channell he had seen from an island through the reef, but the boat return'd with out effecting it. At 6 a.m. weighd and came to sail. Stood out to the eastward, and made several boards, while the pinnace proceeded sounding. Had not more then 15 nor less than 8 fa'm water. At 11 pass'd to the northward of two reefs; distance off a small sandy island on one of them, 1½ miles. At noon the northermost of the 6 islands bore S.E. 1 mile; the place sail'd from, S. 43 W.; distance, 5 leagues. Depth of water, 14 fa'm. Took the pinnace in tow. Lat'd observ'd, 14° 38′ So.

COOK:

At 2 oClock in the PM we left Lizard Island in order to return to the Ship and in our way landed upon a low sandy isle mentioned in coming out. We found on this island a great number of birds the most of them sea fowl, except Eagles, we like wise saw some turtle shells but caught none for the reasons before assigned. We found that some of the Natives resort to this island as we saw several turtle shells piled one upon another. After leaving *Eagle Island* we stood SW directly for the Ship, sounding all the way, had not less that 14 fathom. I found the same depth of water between Lizard and Eagle Island. After we got on board the Master informed me that he had been down to the islands I had directed him to go which he judged to lay about 3 leagues from the Main, he found 10, 12 & 14 fathom water without them and 7 between them and the main, this last channel was narrow because from the [main] run off flat above 2 leagues. He found upon the islands piles of turtle shells and some fins that were so fresh that both he and the boats crew eat of them, this shewed me that the Natives must have been there lately.

After well considering what I had seen myself and the report of the Master, who was of the opinion that the passage to leeward would prove dangerous; this I was pretty well convinced of myself that by keeping in with the main land we should be in continual danger besides the risk we should run of being locked in within the Main and the reef at last and have to return back to seek a passage out, an accident of this kind or any other that might happen to the Ship would infallibly lose our passage to the East Indias this season and might prove the ruin of the Voyage, as we now have little more than 3 months provisions on board and that short allowance in many articles. These reasons had the same weight with all the officers, I therefore resolved to weigh in the morning and endeavour to quit the coast altogether untill we could approach it with less danger: with this in view we got under sail at daylight and stood out NE for the NW end of Lizard Island, leaving Eagle Island to windward of us and some other islands and shoals to leeward having the pinnace ahead sounding, in this channel we had from 9 to 14 fathom. At noon the NW end of Lizard Island bore ESE distant one mile, Lat^{de} observed 14° 38′ S, depth of water 14 fathom.—We now took the pinnace in tow knowing that there was no danger till we got out to the reefs without the island.

BANKS:

PM: In our return we went ashore on a low island where we shot many birds; on it was an Eagles nest [sea eagle] the young ones of which we killed, and another built on the ground by I know not what bird, of a most enormous magnitude—it was in circumference 26 feet and in height 2 feet 8 inches built of sticks; the only bird I have seen in this country capable of building such a nest seems to be the Pelecan. The Indians have been here likewise and lived upon turtle, as we could plainly see by the heaps of Callipashes [carapace] which were piled up in several parts of the island. Our Master who had been sent to leeward to examine that Passage went ashore upon a low island where he slept. Here he saw vast plenty of turtle shells, and so great plenty had the Indians had when there that they had hung up the finns with the meat left on them in the trees, where the sun had dried them so well that our seamen eat them heartily. He also saw spots of clear grass which had lately been dug up; they were about 7 feet long and shaped like a grave, for which indeed he took them.

SHIP'S LOG:

TUESDAY, AUGUST 14TH, 1770

H.	K.	F.	Courses.	Winds.	Remarks, &c.
1	..	..	..	..	A fresh trade and fair wea'r. Standing for ye reef. At 2 tack'd ship. The
2	..	..	..	..	master went away in the pinnace to sound the channel in ye reef the
3 {	..	..	..	..	captain had discover'd from the island. ½-p't 2 he made the signall for
	1	..	N.E. b. E.	S.E.b.S.	having water enough for the ship. Tack'd, and stood out. At 3 the
4	3	..	E.N.E. ½ E.	..	master came on board and reported he had 25 fa'm water close to the
					southermost side of the reef; ½ p't, the opening in one with the high is
5 {	1	4	..	..	land, at noon, S. 39° W. Distance from the island, 3 or 4 leagues; from
	..	..	up E't	off	the reef, 2 miles. Could get no ground with 100 fa'm of line. ½-p't 4,
				N.E.b.E.	bro't too, and hoisted in the pinnace and secur'd the anchors. ½-p't 5,

H.	K.	F.	Courses.	Winds.	Remarks, &c.
6	..	..	..	..	made sail again. At 6 the island pass'd at noon, S.W.b.S. At 7 close-reef'd the fore and main and handed the mizen topsails. At 8 wore ship.
	2	..	E.N.E.	S.E.	
7	4	6	..	..	
8	3	4	E.b.N.	S.E.b.S.	
9	2	4	S.S.W. ½ W.	S.E.	
10	3	..	..	..	Wore ship.
11	2	5	E.b.N.	S.E.b.S.	
12	2	4	..	..	
1	2	6	S.S.W.	S.E.	
2	2	6	..	..	Wore ship.
3	3	..	E.N.E.	..	
4	3	2	..	..	Wore ship.
5	3	..	S.SW.	..	
6	1	6	..	..	
	2	..	N.N.W.	..	Out all reefs topsails and bore away. The island pass'd yesterday at noon S. ¾ W't 9 leagues.
7	5	..	..	..	
8	5	3	..	..	Swayed the topgall't yards.
9	5	5	..	..	
10	5	..	N.W.	..	Set steering sails.
11	5	..	..	..	
12	5	..	..	..	A fresh trade and fair wea'r. Lat'd obs'd, 13° 45′ So.

GREEN:

[Mr Green took 3 sets of observations for longitude assisted by Charles Clerke, Master's Mate, Patrick Saunders, a midshipman but classed as A.B. from 23/5/70 on the ship's books] But indifferent arising from the troublesome observations among the ropes. For the first time these three months we were this day out of sight of land to our no small satisfaction.

COOK:

Winds at SE a steady fresh gale. By 2 oClock we just fetched to windward of one of the channels in the outer reef I had seen from the island, we now tacked and made a short trip to the SW while the Master in the pinnace examined the channel, he soon made the signal for the Ship to follow which we accordingly did and in a short time got safe out, we had no sooner got without the breakers than we had no ground with 150 fathom of line and found a well growen sea rowling in from the SE, certain signs that neither land nor shoals were in our neighborhood in that direction, which made me quite easy at being freed from fears of shoals &c[a]—after having been entangled among them more or less ever since the 26th of May, in which time we have sailed 360 leagues without ever having a man out of the chains heaving the lead when the Ship was under way, a circumstance that I dare say never happened to any ship before and yet here was absolutely necessary. It was with great regret I was obliged to quit this Coast unexplored to its northern extremity which I think we were not far off, for I firmly believe that it doth not join to *New Guinea*, however this I hope to clear up being resolved to get in with the land again as soon as I can do it with safety and the reasons I have before assigned will I presume be thought sufficient for my having left it this time.

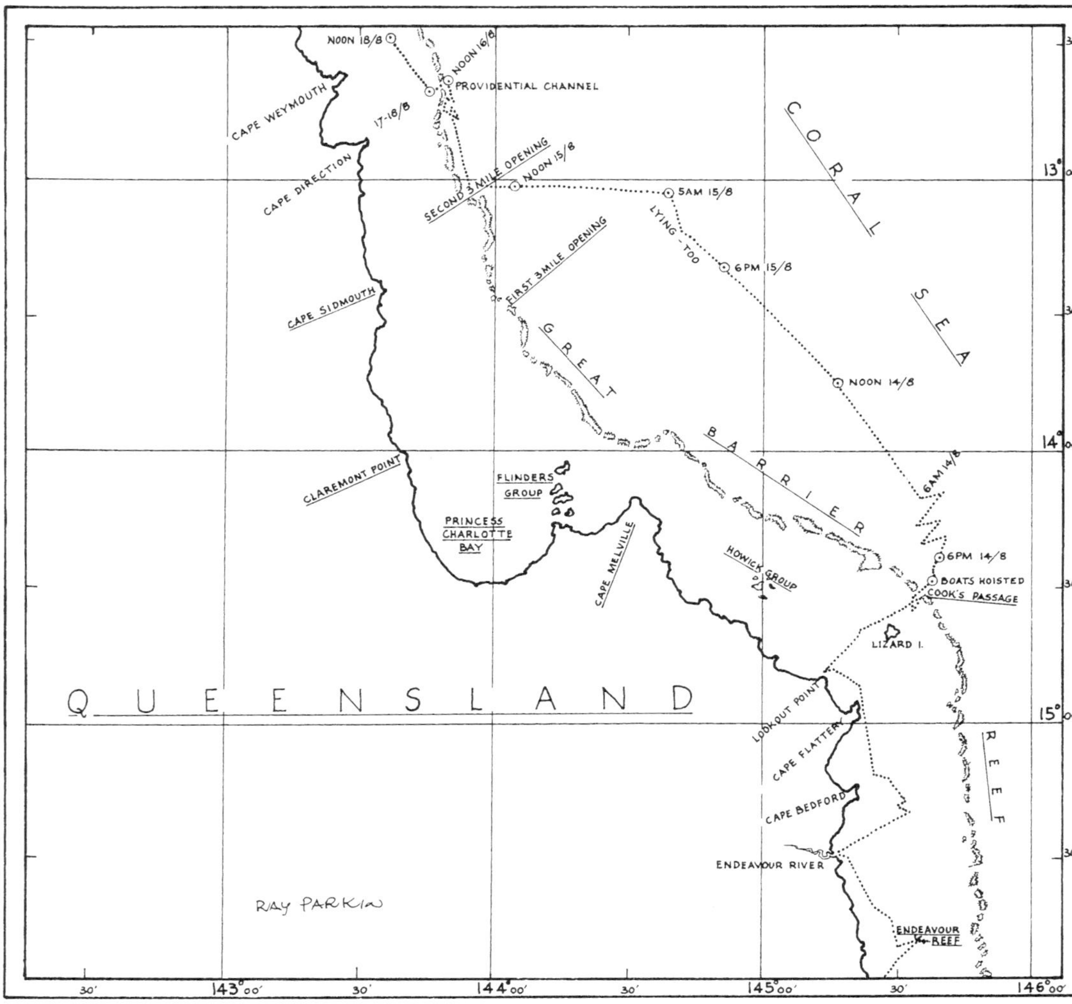

The Passage or Channel we now came out [Cook's Passage] lies in the latitude of 14° 32′, it may always be found by three high islands within it which I have called the *Islands of Direction* because by them a safe passage may be found, even by strangers, in within the reef and quite in to the Main; the channel lies from Lizard Island NE ½ N distant 3 leagues and is about one third of a mile broad and not more in length. Lizard Island which is the northermost and largest of the three affords snug anchorage under the NW side, fresh water and wood for fuel and the low islands and shoals which lay between it and the Main abound I am well assured, with Turtle and other fish which may be caught at all seasons of the year except in such blusterous weather as we have lately had; these things considered, there is perhaps not a better place on this whole coast for a ship to refresh at than this island. I forgot to mention in its proper place that not only on these islands but in several places on the sea beach in and about Endeavour River we found bamboos, Cocoa-nutts, the seeds of plants, and pummick [pumice] stones which were not the produce of this country from all the discoveries we have been able to make in it. It is reasonable to suppose that they are the produce of some country lying to the eastward and brought here by the easterly trade winds. The islands discovered by *Quiros* called

Escape to sea: wind, SE; course, NW; set steering sails.

by him Austrialia del Espiritu Santo lays on this parallel but how far to the east is hard to say, most charts place them as them as far to the west as any part of this coast. The published account of the Voyage which we must depend upon untill we have better authority places his discoveries about 22° to the east of the coast of New Holland.

[Variant version] 'The islands discovered by *Quiros* lies in this parallel but how far to the Eastward its hard to say, for altho' we found in most Charts his discoveries placed as far to the west as this country yet from the Acco[t] of his Voyage compared with what we ourselves have seen we are Morally certain that he was never upon any part of this Coast.'

As soon as we were without the reef we brought too and hoisted in the boats, then stood off and on upon a wind all night as I did not care to run to leeward untill we had a whole day before us. We now began to find that the Ship had received more damage than we imagined and soon felt the effect of the high rowling sea had upon her by increasing her leaks considerably so that it was as much as one pump could keep free continually at work; this however was looked upon as trifling to the danger we had lately made our escape from.

[Variant version] 'As soon as we had got without the Reefs, we Shortened sail & hoisted in the Pinnace and Longboat, which last we had hung alongside & then stretched off ENE close upon a wind as I did not care to stand to the Northward until we had a whole day before us for which reason we kept making short boards all night, the large hollow sea we have not got into acquaints us with a Circumstance we did not know before, which is that the Ship hath received more Damage than we were aware of or could perceive when in smooth water for now she makes as much water as one Pump will free, kept constantly at work.'

At daylight in the morning Lizard Island bore S 15° W distant 10 leagues, we now made sail and stood away NNW ½ W and at 9 oClock NW ½ N, having the advantage of a fresh gale at SE. At noon we were by observation in the latitude of 13° 46′ S, having at this time no land in sight.

BANKS:

Ship stood out for the opening we had seen in the reef and about 2 O'Clock passed it. It was about ½ a mile wide. As soon as the ship was well without it we had no ground with 100 fathom of line so became in an instant quite easy, being once more in the main ocean and consequently freed from all our fears of shoals &c.

For the first time these three months we were this day out of sight of land to our no small satisfaction: that very ocean that had formerly been looked upon with terror by (maybe) all of us was now the Asylum we had long wished for and at last found. Satisfaction was clearly painted in every mans face: the day was fine and the trade wind brisk before which we steered to the Northward; the well grown waves which followed the ship, sure sign of no land being in our neighborhood, we were contemplating with the greatest satisfaction, notwithstanding we plainly felt the effect of the blows they gave to our crazy ship, increasing her leaks considerably so that she now made 9 inches water every hour. This however we looked upon as a light evil in comparison to those we had so lately made our escape from.

This day's entries are evidence of the continual strain all had been under in their long, minute-to-minute involvement with the crowded complex of the Great Barrier Reef, large areas of which to this day are marked on the chart 'unexamined' and 'numerous coral patches reported'. They had no chart and were in fact making the first one as they edged along that tentative track. It was as risky as any razor's edge, and made almost impassable, not by mere potential dangers but by present physical ones. They had to read the chameleon surface of the sea with chasing cloud-shadows and reefs impersonating one another in a way that made identification almost a throw of the dice. Every bit of long-acquired conditioning experience converted into unconscious intuition or hunch was called for—stretching nerves to snapping point while keeping action effectively matter-of-fact. Here was the test of deep knowledge beyond the reach of words, and found only in action. Mere good fortune could not possibly have brought them through all of this: for good fortune gives only so many chances, and here were more than fortune could take care of. Only those involved could fully appreciate the true anxiety; yet much had passed by even these in the intensity of engagement demanding positive action.

Cook's Passage, about a mile long and three-quarters wide, is narrow enough for a sailing ship like Endeavour, *with the wind and tide placing close limits on her. But, with the wind steady on her starboard beam and entering the channel on its windward side, she was able to make a direct passage without having to go too close upon the wind. However, when within its walls at low tide and watching the dark powerful surge of the ocean swell guttering along either side, boiling as it goes, it carries some air of threat, and seems not much more than a biscuit-toss across. To try for the first time a channel in which hazards and obstructions follow no logic is never a carefree experience.*

Immediately outside the reef is 120 fathoms, 3 ½ miles off is 1,000 fathoms. They felt relieved at this vast amount of water under their keel. Here they felt safety. Yet this was to be the very thing that was to bring them to the brink of violent and total destruction.

Chapter 13

The Breadth of One Wave

SHIP'S LOG:

WEDNESDAY, AUGUST 15TH, 1770

H.	K.	F.	Courses.	Winds.	Remarks, &c.
1	5	6	N.W.	S.E.	A fresh trade and clear pleasant wea'r; carp'rs employ'd repairing the pinnace.
2	5	6	..	..	
3	5	6	..	..	
4	5	6	..	..	
5	5	6	..	..	
6	5	6	..	..	
7	..	..	up N.E.b.E.	off N.E.b.N.	Close-reef'd the topsails; handed the mizen topsail, and bro't too. Main topsail to the mast; sounded no ground with 100 fa'm of line.
8	..	..	..	..	
9	..	..	..	..	
10	..	..	up N.E. ½ E.	off N.N.E.	
11	..	..	..	..	
12	..	..	..	..	Do. weather.
1	..	..	up N.E.b.E.	off N.E.b.N.	
2	..	..	..	..	
3	..	..	..	..	
4	..	..	..	..	Wore ship.
5	..	..	up S.S.W.	off S.W.	
6 {	..	..	..	..	
	1	5	West	S.E.	Out all reefs and made sail.
7	4	2	..	..	Set steering sails.
8	4	7	..	..	
9	5	..	..	..	Got the hawsers up to air and clean'd ship below.
10	5	..	..	..	
11	4	..	..	..	Fresh breezes and pleasant weather.
12	4	4	..	..	Lat'd obs'd, 13° 1' 30" So.

GREEN:

Observers, Clerke, Munkhouse & self. 3 setts. Very distinct.

Error Quadrant O's altitude +4.

COOK:
Fresh trade at SE and clear weather. At 6 oClock in the evening shortened sail and brought too with her head to the NE. At 6 oClock in the AM made sail and steered west in order to make the land being fearful of over shooting the passage supposing there to be one between this land and New Guinea. At noon we had no land in sight, but our latitude by observation was 13° 2′ South, longitude 216° 0′ West which was 1° 23′ West of Lizard Island.

BANKS:
Fine weather and moderate trade. The Cap^{tn} fearfull of going too far from the land, least he should miss an opportunity of examining whether or not the passage which is layed down in some charts between New Holland and New Guinea really existed or not, steered the ship west right in for the land; about 12 O'Clock it was seen from the mast Head.

SHIP'S LOG:

THURSDAY, AUGUST 16TH, 1770

H.	K.	F.	Courses.	Winds.	Remarks, &c.
1	4	..	W't	E.S.E.	Mod. breezes and fair wea'r; saw the land making high, bearing W.S.W.; at 2 saw more land making like islands; at 3 saw a reef of rocks between us and the shore; at 5 found the reef extended to the northward and southward as far as we could extinguish anything; haul'd off and made all sail; kept a good look out all night to leeward, being douptful of our weathering the reef; sounded frequently, but had no ground with 140 fa'ms of line.
2	3	7	..	..	
3	3		..	..	
4	3	4	..	..	
5	3	5	..	..	
6	2	..	..	..	
	1	3	N.N.E.	E't	
7	3	..	N.b.E.	E.b.N.	
8	3	..	..	..	
9	3	2	..	..	At 12 tack'd ship, and at 1 a.m., it falling calm. At 4 heard and saw breakers on the bow close too; lower'd down the yawl, sent her ahead to tow off; meantime employ'd getting the longboat out; the ship all this time nearing the reef fast by means of a flood tide and S.E. swell. The pinnace, having suffered much in service on this coast, was now under repair; however, the carp'rs fasten'd on an upper streak, and she, with the rest of the boats, was all ahead towing at ¾ p't 5, at which time the ship was within 40 yards of the breakers, and no ground with 120 fa'm of line. Notwithstanding the ship might have been said was with the swell of the surf, the boats and a light air of wind run her out ½ a cable's length from present danger. Soon after saw an opening in the reef; sent a m'te to examine it. A signell being made from the boat for anchoring, and no hopes of clearing the reef, steered, or rather tow'd, for the opening, but meeting with a strong ebb tide, and the mate returning without a satisfactory account, tow'd off again, and by the help of the ebb got clear of another point of the reef further to the No'ward; same time saw a point of a reef bearing N.E.b.N.
10	3	3	..	..	
11	3	..	..	..	
12	3	..	..	..	
1	2	..	S.S.E	E't	
2	..	..	Calm, s's head	S.S.E.	
3	..	..	..	..	
4	..	..	..	..	
5	..	..	..	..	
6	..	..	..	..	
7	..	..	..	..	
8	..	..	..	..	
9	..	..	..	..	
10	..	..	..	..	
11	..	..	..	..	Calm and clear wea'r.
12	..	..	..	..	Low water, reef dist. ½ mile, and small hopes of getting clear. Lat'd obs'd, 12° 37′ So.

HICKES [and 5 other logs]:
At 5 am, the ship was within 40 yards of the breakers.

PICKERSGILL:
Pinnace . . . the Carpenters put on a board to keep out ye water. After this, notwithstanding the ship might be said to be within her own length of the breakers, nay once within the swell, yet by the activity of the men who saw immediate destruction before themselves and the help of the boats and sweeps she ran a little off from that impending danger; saw an opening in the reef, examined it with a small boat . . . by noon we got ½ a mile off ye reef. This is the narrowest escape we ever had, and had it not been for the help of providence we must inevitably have perished, for the ship must have sunk alongside the rocks which were as steep as a wall there and would have been no hopes of saving a single life in so great a surf.

GREEN:
[During this, Green, assisted by Clerke, Master's Mate, and Stephen Forwood, Gunner, were taking 3 sets of observations] These observations very good, the limbs very distinct, a good horizon. We were about 100 yards from the reef where we expected the ship to strike every minute, it being calm and no soundings, the swell heaving us right on.

'153':
The pinnace having suffered much on this coast was now under repair on the booms, however the Carpenter got on a temporary upper strake and she with all the other boats was towing by ¾ past 5.

COOK:
By one oClock in the PM or before we saw high land from ye masthead bearing WSW and at 2 oClock saw more land to the NW of the former making in hills like islands but we judged it to be a continuation of the Main land. An hour after this we saw breakers between us and the land extending to the Southward farther than we could see, but we thought we saw them terminate to the Northward abreast of us, this however proved only an opening for soon after we saw the Reef or breakers extend away to the northward as far as we could see, upon this we hauled upon a wind which was now at ESE. We hardly trimmed our sails before the wind came to EbN which was right upon the reef and of course made our weathering of the reef very doubtful, the northermost of it that we could see at sunset bore from us NbE distant about 2 or 3 leagues. However this being the best tack to clear it we kept standing to the northward with all sail we could set untill 12 oClock at night when fearing to stand too far up this tack we tacked and stood to the southward having run 6 leagues north since sun set. We had not stood above 2 miles SSE before it fell quite calm, we both sounded now and several times in the night but had no ground with 140 fathoms of line. A little after 4 oClock the roaring Surf was plainly heard and at day break the

vast foaming breakers were too plainly to be seen not a mile from us towards which we found the Ship was carried by the waves surprisingly fast. We had at this time not an air of wind and the depth of water was unfathomable so that there was not a possibility of Anchoring, in this distressed situation we had nothing but Providence and the small assistance our boats could give us to trust to; the pinnace was under repair and could not immediately be hoisted out, the Yawl was put into the water and the long boat hoisted out and both sent ahead to tow the Ship round which together with the help of our sweeps abaft got the Ships head round to the northward which seemed to be the only way to keep her off the reef or at least to delay time, and the carpenters having patched up the pinnace she was sent ahead likewise. By this time it was 6 oClock and we were not above 80 or 100 yards from the breakers, the same sea that washed the sides of the Ship rose in a breaker prodigiously high the very next time it did rise so that between us and destruction was only a dismal valley the breadth of one wave and even now no ground could be felt with 120 fathoms. The Pinnace by this time was patched up and hoisted out and sent ahead to tow; still we had hardly any hopes of saving the Ship and full as little our lives as we were full 10 leagues from the nearest land and the boats not sufficient to carry the whole of us, yet in this truly terrible situation not one man ceased to do his utmost and that with as much calmness as if no danger had been near. All the dangers we had escaped were little in comparison of being thrown upon this reef where the Ship must be dashed to pieces in a moment. A reef as is here spoke of is scarcely known in Europe, it is a wall of coral rock rising almost perpendicular out of the unfathomable ocean, always overflown at high-water generally 7 or 8 feet and dry in places at low-water; the largest waves of the vast Ocean meeting with so sudden a resistance make a most terrible surf breaking mountains high especially as in our case when the general trade wind blows directly upon it. At this critical juncture when all our endeavours seemed too little, a small air of wind sprung up, but so small that at any other time in a Calm we should not have observed it, with this and the assistance of our boats we could observe the Ship to move off from the reef in a slanting direction, but in less than 10 minutes we had as flat a calm as ever when our fears were again renewed for as yet we were not above 200 yards from the breakers. Soon after our friendly breeze visited us again and lasted about as long as before. A small opening was now seen in the Reef about a quarter of a mile from us which I sent one of the mates to examine, its breadth was not more than the length of the Ship but within was smooth water, into this place it was resolved to push her if possible having no other probable Views to save her, for we were still in the very jaws of destruction and it was a doubt whether or no we could reach this opening, however we soon got off it when to our surprise we found the Tide of Ebb gushing out like a mill stream so that it was impossible to get in; however we took all the advantage possible of it and it carried us out about ¼ of a mile from the breakers & was a great help to us in clearing another point of the Reef a little to the northward of us, but it was too narrow for us to keep in long; however what with the help of the ebb and our boats (which had very little effect upon the Ship against the swell) we by noon had got an offing of one and a half or two miles, yet we could hardly flatter ourselves with hopes of getting clear even if the breeze should spring up as we were by this time embayed by the Reef, and the Ship in spite of our endeavours driving before the Sea into the bight, the Ebb had been in our favour and we had reason to suppose that the flood which was now making would be against us, the only hopes we had was another opening we saw about a mile to the West ward of us which I sent Lieutenant Hicks in the small boat to examine & the NE part of the Reef being a detached shoal & not joined to the Main Reef which last trended away North for there appeared to us to be a Passage between the two, which we hoped to get through in case a breeze sprung up in our favour but this we had no prospect of. Latitude observed 12° 37′ S, the Main land in sight distant about 10 leagues.

BANKS:
About 12 O'Clock it [the land] was seen from the mast head; about one the Reef laying without it in just the same manner as when we had left it. He [the Captain] stood on however resolving to stand off at night after having taken a nearer view, but just at night fall found himself in a manner embayed in the reef so that it was a moot point whether or not he should weather it on either tack; we stood however to the northward and at dark it was concluded that we would go clear of everything we could see. The night however was not the most agreeable: all the dangers we had escaped were little in comparison of being thrown upon this reef if that should be our lot. A reef such as the one I now speak of is a thing scarcely known in Europe or indeed any where but in these seas; it is a wall of Coral Rock rising almost perpendicularly out of the unfathomable ocean, always overflown at high water commonly 7 or 8 feet, and generally bare at low water; the large waves of the vast ocean meeting with so sudden a resistance make here a most terrible surf breaking mountain high, especially when as in our case the general trade wind blows directly upon it.

At three O'Clock this morn it dropt calm on a sudden which did not at all better our situation: we judged ourselves not more than 4 or 5 leagues from the reef, maybe much less, and the swell of the sea which drove right upon it carried the ship towards it fast. We tried the lead often in hopes to find ground that we might anchor but in vain; before 5 the roaring of the surf was plainly heard and as the day broke the vast foaming billows were plainly to be seen scarce a mile from us and towards which we found the ship carried by the waves surprisingly fast, so that by 6 o'Clock we were within a cables length of them, driving on as fast as ever and still no ground with 100 fathom of line. Every method had been taken since we first saw our danger to get the boats out in hopes that they might tow us off but it was not yet accomplished; the Pinnace had had a plank stripped off her for repair and the longboat under the booms was lashed and fastened so well from our supposed security that she was not yet got out. Two large oars or sweeps were got out at the stern ports to pull the ships head round the other way in hopes this might delay till the boats were out. All this while we were approaching and came I believe before this could be effected within 40 yards of the breakers; the same sea that washed the side of the ship rose in a breaker enormously high the very next time it did rise so between us and it was only a dismal valley the breadth of one wave; even now the lead was hove 3 or 4 lines fastened together but no ground could be felt with above 150 fathom. Now our case was truly desperate, no man I believe but who gave himself entirely over, a speedy death was all we had to hope for and that from the vastness of the breakers which must quickly dash the ship all to pieces was scarce to be doubted. Other hopes we had none; the boats were in the ship and must be dashed to pieces with her and the nearest dry land was 8 or 10 leagues distant. We did not however cease our endeavours to get out the long boat which was by this time almost accomplished. At this critical juncture, at this I must say terrible moment, when all assistance seemed too little to save even our miserable lives, a small air of wind sprang up, so that at any other time in a calm we should not have observed it. We however plainly saw that it instantly checked our progress; every sail was therefore put in a proper direction to catch it and we just observed the ship to move in a slaunting direction off from the breakers. This at least gave us time and redoubling our efforts we at last got out the long boat and manning her sent her ahead. The ship still moved but little off but in less than 10 minutes our little breeze died away into as flat a calm as ever. Now was our anziety again renewed: innumerable small pieces of paper &c were thrown over the ships side to find whither the boats really moved her ahead or not so little did she move that it remained almost every other time a matter of dispute. Our little friendly breeze now visited us again and lasted about as long as before, thrusting us possibly 100 yards farther from the breakers: we were still however in the very jaws of destruction. A small opening had been seen in the reef about a furlong from us, its breadth was scarce the length of the ship, into this it was resolved to push her if possible. Within was no surf, therefore we might save our lives: the doubt was only whether we could get the ship so far: our little breeze however a third time visited us and pushed us almost there. The fear of Death is bitter: the prospect we saw before us of saving our lives tho at the expence of everything we had made my heart set much lighter on its throne, and I suppose there were none but what felt the same sensations. At length we arrived off the mouth of the wished for opening and found to our surprize what had with the little breeze been the real cause of our Escape, a thing that we had not before dreamt of. The tide of flood it was that had hurried us so unaccountably fast toward the reef, in the near neighborhood of which we had arrived just at high water, consequently its ceasing to drive us any farther gave us the opportunity we had of getting off. Now however the tide of Ebb made strong and gushed out of our little opening like a mill stream, so that it was impossible to get in; of this stream however we took the advantage as much as possible and it carried us out near a quarter of a mile from the reef. We well knew that we were to take all the advantage possible of the Ebb so continued towing with all our might and with all our boats, the pinnace being now repaired, till we had got an offing of 1½ or 2 miles.

By this time the tide began to turn and our suspence began again: as we had gained a little while the ebb was in our favour we had some reason to imagine that the flood would hurry us back upon the reef in spite of our utmost endeavours. It was still as calm as ever so no likelyhood of any wind today; indeed had wind sprung up we could only have searched for another opening, for we were so embayed by the reef that with the general trade wind it was impossible to get out. Another opening was however seen ahead and the 1st Lieutenant went away in the small boat to examine it.

PARKINSON:

About noon we saw the land again in latitude 13° s also a continuation of the reef which ran alongside of it. In the evening, standing right in for the land, we were alarmed by suddenly discovering that the reef extended to leeward of us, upon which we hauled in our wind and crouded all the sail we could, that we might be able to weather the farthest point of it. The wind was easterly this day, more moderate, and the swell of the sea less.

At the dawn of day, we had the reef under our lee, about a mile distance, which alarmed us much. When it was quite light, we saw breakers all round us excepting to windward, where we came in. The wind failing us about midnight, we tacked about, being afraid to stand any farther; and the wind's still failing was the cause that we drove on the reef, which we now neared apace. In this dilemma, we first hoisted out our small boats (the long boat being stowed, and the pinnace repairing) to tow her off, and got a pair of sweeps rigged out of the gun-room ports, to turn her head about. A slight puff of wind gave us some hopes of effecting it; but that failing, we approached so near the breakers, that there was but one heave of the swell between them and the ship. However, with our pulling, the alteration of the tide, and another slight puff of wind, we cleared her a little more from the reef, and stood to where we saw a break in the reef to leeward, there we hoped, at least, to find ground to anchor upon; but, when we got to the entrance of it, we were driven off by a ripple of the tide that set us out with great force; which, however, proved very providential, as we afterward found that there were rocks in the passage, and that it was not a proper break. We then stood to windward, intending either to get out as we came in, or a little further down to leeward, where the reef seemed detached; but, perceiving, soon after, the tops of some rocks in the passage, we declined attempting it. The wind again dying away, we were at a loss what to do for the best; but, at last, determined on sending some of our people in the boat to examine the appearance of another break still farther to leeward.

There can be no doubt that this situation was horrendous, in the sense of being hair-raising. In his account of it the Captain shows his nature, not merely as an objective observer, but as one involved, on whose perception and understanding of a wide range of factors depended effective and prompt decisions. Those vital slants of faint breeze were in themselves no handouts of salvation from providence—they had to be recognised, caught on the wing, and used. He found 'our friendly breeze visited us again', and he used it with all the camaraderie of an intuitive pantheist welcoming providence, which was an essence distilled from his sea experience that allowed him to be effective to the end. It did not preclude subjective reflections, but was not emasculated by them.

There are those who think that this description was practically copied from Banks, as if Cook had the capacity neither for original thought nor for the expression of it. It is far more likely that the reverse is true. Cook's narrative flows out of knowledge, perception and the experience of action for which he had the responsibility. His reflections are pertinent to a recognised reality. He was a trained observer of experience, and his job was to be able to transmit those observations to others with accuracy, as is shown here.

On the other hand, Banks was a young man beginning. He was, at this stage, less perceptive and more impressionable; passages are sometimes, in matters he is not familiar with, a little garbled; there is embellishment and sentences calculated to create suspense, which is quite understandable in a young man who has decided that his *Grand Tour shall not be of Europe, but of the world. There is more histrionic consciousness in Banks's version. This is not surprising, nor did Banks make any secret of this aspect of his tour, and fully confessed it on the death of Alexander Buchan, his landscape artist, in Tahiti. Banks's account here seems admirably designed to 'entertain my friends in England with scenes . . .' and is none the less readable because of it.*

From 6 PM, the ship had the threatening reef and exploding surf under her lee. She was close upon a wind, an easterly, steering NNE, but, because of the SE swell setting her to leeward, she was barely making north. This kept her close and parallel to her danger all night, with ears stretched for its doomlike sound. At about 10 PM, they were passing the small entrance off the southern end of Bligh Reef, through which Captain Bligh was to take his castaways in the Bounty's *23-foot boat and bring them to Restoration Island in 1789. (He gave it this name because that day was the anniversary of the Restoration of Charles the Second and 'we were restored to fresh life and strength'.) By midnight the ship had made some 15 miles of northing when she tacked to the SSE, not wishing to go further into the unknown. But, at 1 am, it fell calm, and the SE swell began to carry the ship NW. By 4 AM they had the booming roar of the surf close under their lee—heralding what would seem to them the inevitable end. By a quarter to six, all boats, including Mr Banks's small one, were in the water and towing, and, with the aid of the sweeps out of the stern ports, endeavouring to get her head round. It was now that there was only that 'dismal valley the breadth of one wave' between the ship and destruction. Then came that small breath of flukey air, which they skilfully caught by efficient sail-handling, to postpone the still apparently certain end a little longer.*

Their attempt at the opening when they were swept out by the mill race of the ebb tide was a providential frustration; for, as Parkinson remarks, that opening had teeth. But again swift reaction and skill were able to use this narrow stream to gain a further offing in a way which seemed to have escaped Banks's appreciation, just as he was more impressionable than objective about the hoisting-out of the boats. By this manœuvre they were able to scrape by the next point of the reef. But, by noon, they were still embayed by the NE *trend of the reef, and there seemed little hope.*

This was no hit-and-run affair, quickly over. For eighteen hours they had been facing constant threat with certain death as the most logical probability, with not one circumstance likely to alter. It was the acid test, not of spectacular courage, but of the men's real integrity. Without wind, being set in by the SE *swell, the vessel and the men were helpless. Their destruction was even less than the breadth of one wave away—it was that hair's breadth of the stretched nerve that was held by this integrity. This was exemplified by Mr Green and his assistants taking observations, with the ship seemingly about to be destroyed, and all they said about it was: Lat*[de] *Obs*[d] *12° 37′ s.*

SHIP'S LOG:

FRIDAY, AUGUST 17TH, 1770

Day and Month.	Winds.	Remarks, &c.
1770. Friday, August 17 . .	Calm.	Calm and light airs with clear wea'r.
	E.S.E. E't'y.	An opening being discover'd in the bend of the reef, Lieutenant Hicks went to examin it; at 2 he return'd with a favourable account of it. Nothing but danger appearing on all sides, it was resolv'd to attempt this passage to secure the ship till there was wind and opportunity to command her; accordingly, tow'd short round, steer'd W. b. S. 2 miles to the mouth of the oppening, and S.W.b.W. ½ W. 2 miles thro' the opening, having a rapid flood tide setting in; had variable soundings from 13 to 30 fa'm, mostly foul ground.
	E.b.N.	½-past 3, had a steady light breeze at east; all this time the boats ahead.
		½-p't 4, came too with the b't bower in 19 fa'm water, old corral and shells, veer'd to ⅓'d of a cable; the opening bearing N.E.b.E. ½ E. 2½ miles. Found the flood tide here to set strong from the E.N.E.
		A.M.—The carp'rs employ'd in the pinnace; sent the rest of the boats on the reef to get shell-fish or turtle, if possiable.
		Variation by amplit'de and sev'l azym'ths, 4° 09′ E't.
		Lat'd observ'd, 12° 38′ So.

PICKERSGILL:

. . . Even if a breeze came, as y[e] trade blows, we should have beat upon it [the Reef].

BOOTIE:

. . .accordingly towed her (with the assistance of the sweeps out the Gun Room ports which had been working occasionally since 6 o'clock) short round and stood wbs 2 miles to the mouth of the opening . . . all this time the boats ahead towing and 2 sounding.

COOK:

While Mr Hicks was examining the opening we struggled hard with the flood sometimes gaining a little and at other times losing. At 2 oClock Mr Hicks returned with a favourable account of the opening upon which it was immediately and unanimously resolved to try to secure the Ship in it which we did not in the least doubt of, as the flood tide was now made & set strong in & the swell set right in for it even supposing it continues calm, indeed it required very little consideration for this seemed to be the only probable means which Providence had Pointed out to us to save the Ship together with our Selves. We therefore towed the Ship round for the opening & soon after a light air sprung up at ENE which with the help of our boats and the flood tide we soon entered the opening and was hurried through in a short time by a rapid tide like a Mill race which kept us from driving against either side, though the channel was not more than a quarter of a mile broad, we had however two boats ahead to direct us through, our depth of water in the channel was from 30 to 7 fathom very irregular soundings and foul ground until we had got quite within the reef where we anchored in 19 fathom a Corally & Shelly bottom.

It is but a few days ago that I rejoiced at having got without the Reef, but that joy was nothing when Compared to what I now felt at being safe at anchor within it, happy once more to encounter those shoals which but two days ago our utmost wishes were crowned by getting clear of, such are the Vicissitudes attending this kind of service and must always attend unknown Navigation where one steers wholly in the dark without any manner of Guide whatever.

Was it not for the pleasure which naturally results to a man from being the first discoverer, even was it nothing more than sands and shoals, this service would be insupportable especially in far distant parts, like this, short of provisions and almost every other necessary. The world would hardly admit of an excuse for a man leaving a Coast unexplored he has once discovered, if dangers are his excuse he is then charged with *Timorousness* and want of Perseverance and at once pronounced the unfittest man in the world to be employed as a discoverer; if on the other hand he boldly encounters all the dangers and obstacles he meets and is unfortunate enough not to succeed he is then charged with *Temerity* and want of conduct. The former of these aspersions cannot with Justice be laid to my charge and if I am fortunate enough to surmount all the dangers we may meet the latter will never be brought in question. I own I have engaged more among the Islands and shoals upon this coast than may be thought with prudence I ought to have done with a single Ship and every other thing considered, but if I had not we should not have been able to give any better account of one half of it than if we had never seen it, that is we should not have been able to say whether it consisted of main land or Islands and as to its produce, we must have been totally ignorant of as being inseparable with the other & in this case it would have been far more satisfaction to me never to have discovered it, but it is time I should have done with this subject which at best is but disagreeable & which I was led into on reflecting on our late Danger.

I now came to a fixed resolution to keep the Main land on board in our route to the northward let the consequence be what it will, indeed now it was not advisable to go without the reef, for by it we might be carried so far from the coast as to not be able to determine whether or no New Guinea joins or makes part of this land. This doubtful point I had from my first coming upon the Coast determined if possible to clear up, but as I had lately experienced the inconveniency of a boat under repair I intend to lay fast with the Ship tomorrow to have the Pinnace repaired and as I had no employment for the other boats I sent them all out in the morning to the reef to get such refreshments as they could find. Found the Variation by the Amp^{d} and Azth to be 4° 9′ East. At noon Latitude observed 12° 38′ s, Longitude in 216° 45′ w. The channel we came in by which I have named *Providential Channel* bore ENE distant 10 or 12 miles being about 8 or 9 leagues from the Main land which extended from N 66° w to swbs. On the Main land within us was a pretty high promontory which I called *Cape Weymouth*, on the north side of this Cape is a Bay of the same name (Lat^{de} 12° 42′, Longitude 217° 15′ w.)

Here Cook gives a great insight into himself and his motivation. The recent dangers had been sufficient stimulus to bring this about—which is at once a measure of these dangers themselves. It shows clearly his commitment. By thus standing outside *himself and attempting an impartial self-evaluation, he is at once fulfilling that which is most central* within. *While this intrinsic integrity springs very much from the natural character of the man, it has also been reinforced by a tradition of the sea in which the ship externalises selfishness into self-fulfillment through a Common Good. We see that Cook's decisions are made not loftily and coldly but with the doubts and feelings common to all—yet made resolute by responsibility and tradition.*

The sweeps rigged out of the stern raft ports played a big part in the handling of the ship during this trying time, because for the greater part of the period the ship did not carry steerage-way so that the rudder was useless. The sweeps were the only method whereby her head could be brought round. And these were assisted by the boats. When entering Providential Channel, and being taken in hand by the fast-flowing flood tide and with so light a wind, she could not have been under command of the rudder. The sweeps and the boats would have kept her from swinging broadside and becoming unmanageable in the narrow passage. But it took skill to do. The measure of the strain that had been upon them all is best realised by the utter relief they all record. The vital part played by the boats in all this should not be lightly passed over.

BANKS:

At 2 however the Lieutenant arrived with news that the opening was very narrow: in it was good anchorage and a passage quite in free from shoals. The ships head was immediately put towards it and with the tide she towed fast so that by three we entered and were hurried in by a stream almost like a mill race, which kept us even from a fear of the sides tho it was not above ¼ of a mile in breadth. By 4 we came to an anchor once more happy to encounter those shoals which but two days before we thought ourselves supreamly happy to have escaped from. How little do men know what is for their real advantage: two days [ago] our utmost wishes were crowned by getting without the reef and today we were made again happy by getting within it.

PARKINSON:
A light breeze springing up from the east, we resolved to push in there, though the passage was but narrow, which we happily accomplished, being assisted by the tide; and we anchored between the reef and the shore in fifteen fathoms water; though, at the very edge of the reefs, we had no sounding at one hundred and fifty-five fathoms. At our first entrance into this place we had very unequal soundings; sometimes finding no bottom; and one fathom farther finding it with twenty fathoms of line. This, we apprehended, was occasioned by the coral rocks which rise up almost perpendicular. Latitude 12° 36′.

In the morning we sent some men in the boat to the reef for turtles and clams, but they returned without any of the former, and with but very few clams, though they were of a large size.

The reefs were covered with a numberless variety of beautiful corallines of all colours and figures, having here and there interstices of very white sand. These made a pleasing appearance under water, which was smooth on the inside of the reef, while it broke all along the outside, and may be aptly compared to a grove of shrubs growing under water. Numbers of beautiful coloured fishes made their residence among these rocks, and may be caught by hand on the high part of the reef at low water. There are also crabs, molusca of various sorts, and a great variety of curious shell-fish, which adhere to the old dead coral that forms the reef.

BANKS:
As we are now safe at anchor it was resolved to send boats upon the nearest shoal to search for shell fish, turtle or whatever else they could get. They accordingly went and Dr Solander and myself accompanied them in my small boat. In our way we met with two water snakes, one 5 the other 6 feet long; we took them both; they much resembled land snakes only their tails were flatted sideways, I suppose for the convenience of swimming, and were not venomous. The shoal we went upon was the very reef we had so near been lost upon yesterday, now no longer terrible to us; it afforded little provision for the ship, no turtle, only 300 lb of Great cockles, some were however of an immense size. We had in the way of curiosity much better success, meeting with many curious fish and molusca besides corals of many species, all alive, among which was the *Tubipora musica*. I have often lamented that we had not time to make proper observations upon this curious tribe of animals but we were so entirely taken up with the more conspicuous links of the chain of creation as fish, plants, birds &c &c that it was impossible.

The 'Chain of Creation' was a general theory of life before the advent of that of Evolution.

Chapter 14
Keeping the Main on Board

SHIP'S LOG:

SATURDAY, AUGUST 18TH, 1770

H.	K.	F.	Courses.	Winds.	Soundings.	Remarks, &c.
					Fathoms.	
1	..	..	..	N.E.	..	Mod. breezes and clear pleas't wea'r; at 1 low water; look'd well out for shoals; at 4 the boats return'd with 270 lb. of fish. Employ'd as occasions required. Carpenters on the the pinnace.
2	..	..	..	..	..	
3	..	..	..	..	..	
4	..	..	..	E.N.E.	..	
5	..	..	..	..	..	
6	..	..	...	..	..	
7	..	..	..	..	..	
8	..	..	..	..	..	Do. wea'r.
9	..	..	..	..	..	
10	..	..	..	..	..	
11	..	..	..	..	..	
12	..	..	..	E't	..	Do. wea'r.
1	..	..	..	..	..	
2	..	..	..	..	..	
3	..	..	..	..	..	
4	..	..	..	..	..	
5	..	..	..	..	..	Began to heave ahead.
6	..	..	..	..	..	Weighed and came to sail, the yawl ahead; an opening in the land bore S. 44 W. 5 ½ leagues; saw an island and 2 rocks N.W.b.N. Mod. breezes and smooth water; outer island ahead N.W 5 or 6 leagues; a sandy island on a small reef E.S.E. ½ E. Outer or no'most land of the main N. 78 W. 5 or 6 leagues. Saw a reef inshore bearing S.W.; yawl ahead sound'g.
7	2	6	N.W.b.W.	S.E.	16, 14, 10, 12, 14	
8	3	..	..	..	13, 12, 10, 15	
9	2	6	..	E.S.E.	17, 18, 18, 20	
10	{1	..	N.N.W.	..	24, 26, 27	
	1	..	N.W. ½ W.	..	23, 20, 17, 18	
11	2	2	..	..	10, 15, 22, 27 22, 19, 17, 16	
12	2	..	N.W. ½ N.	..	17, 19, 22, 27	Lat'd obs'd., 12° 28′ So.

BOOTIE:

At 8 AM, an opening S 44° W 5 ½ leagues [Lloyd Bay].

COOK:

Gentle breezes at East and ESE. At 4 oClock in the PM the boats returned from the reef with about 240 pounds of meat of shell fish mostly cockles, some of which are as large as 2 men can move and contain about 20 lbs of good meat. At 6 oClock in the morning we got under sail and stood away to the NW having two boats ahead to direct us, our soundings very irregular from 10 to 27 fathoms varying 5 or 6 fathoms almost every cast of the lead. A little before noon we passed a low small Sandy Isle which we left on our starboard side at a distance of two miles, Mr Banks landed upon it and shot several small birds, called Noddys. At noon our latitude was 12° 28′, being about 4 or 5 leagues from the main which extended from sbw to N 71° West and some small islands extending from N 40° W. Between us and the main were several shoals and some without us, besides the main or outer reef seen from the mast head away to the NE.

BANKS:
Weighed and stood along shore with a gentle breeze, the main still 7 or 8 leagues from us.

PARKINSON:
On the 18th, we weighed anchor, and stood along shore on the inside of the reef, thinking that would be the best way of finding the passage between New-Guinea and this land; we met with a great many shoals and reefs and came to at night. We kept along shore until the 21st.

As the ship got under way and headed NW, she was in reasonable water within the outer reef, but there were many shoals and reefs between her and the land. The irregular soundings showed the unpredictability of the bottom, even for a cable's length ahead. Only with reliable lookouts at the masthead (generally the Mates, if not the Captain or other officers), and the boats diligently sounding ahead, could the ship proceed with any measure of safety. This called for the skill and concentration of every man on board. By noon she was approaching the SE corner of the very extensive Eel Reef with another detached reef on her starboard bow. She was entering an area which is still very vague on the modern chart and marked across with 'Numerous detached reefs in this area'. The present recommended track is inshore of these major reefs, which spread from her then position to the NW for some 25 miles.

It is difficult from this distance in time to appreciate fully the skill and resolution that took them through these hazardous waters, that allowed them not a moment's lapse. Leadsmen manning both chains, continually calling their deeps *and* marks, *the boats ahead also anxiously searching the unseen and unknown beneath them, the masthead lookouts earnestly trying to separate cloud-shadow from reef-shadow on the glittering sea surface, the intent helmsman and watchful officer of the watch, the hands on the forecastle with both anchors ready for instant letting go, and the hands about the deck on a split-yarn ready for swift co-ordinated sail-handling or any other procedure that might be called for. This was no pretend situation; all had so recently learned the breadth of one wave. The ship was advancing at two to three knots with a sensible caution.*

SHIP'S LOG:

SUNDAY, AUGUST 19TH, 1770

H.	K.	F.	Courses.	Winds.	Soundings.	Remarks, &c.
					Fathoms.	
1	2	..	N.W.b.N.	S.E.b.E.	17¼, 17	Light breezes and fair weather; a boat ahead sounding; saw a
2	1	4	N.	..	19	sandy isl'd on a shoal extending 2 or 3 miles each way.
3	1	6	N.b.E.	..	no g'd with	½-past 2, haul'd up to weather the shoal. ½-past 3, had 8
					h'd line	fa'm water, rocky ground; haul'd off and deepen'd the
	..	6	N.E.b.N.	..	17, 16, 17	water, and soon after bore up again. The course and
4	2	4	N.	E.S.E.	15, 16, 18	dist'ce upon each course varry'd to avoid danger,
5	3	..	Steering between N. and		22, 18, 17	that 'tis impossiable to be sufficiently particular in the
6	2	6	W. round some shoals			log to make it of real use. At 4 haul'd round the shoal
			.		15	mention'd, and at 6 pass'd a flatt shoal to the eastward of
7	1	6	W.b.S.	E.	17	us, in form of a horseshoe, dist'ce from it ¾ of a mile.
	..	..	..	..	20	½-p't 6, came too with the b't bower in 13 fa'm, loose
8	..	..	Bearings at anchor; the			coral. Having seen several appearances of shoals round us,
9	..	..	island which bore N.W.			try'd the tide, and found it to sett west 1 k. 2 fa'm p'r hour,
10	..	..	at noon now bears			it being allmost now high-water.
			W.b.S. 2 or 3 m's.			
11	..	..	..	..	..	
12	..	..	..	..	..	
1	..	..	..	..	..	
2	..	..	..	..	..	
3	..	..	..	..	..	
4	..	..	..	..	..	
5	..	..	..	..	..	½-past 6 a.m., weighed with a fresh breeze and cloudy, the
6	..	..	..	..	..	wind at east; sent the yawl ahead; soon after, as p'r signell
7	..	..	..	..	..	from the yawl, haul'd up and pass'd to the eastward of
	1	4	N.W.b.N.	East.	8, 10, 11	a small shoal; soon after saw a considerable large flat shoal,
8	3	..	From N.N.E. to N.W.		13, 17	extending a great way to the easteward. ½-p't 8, got the
			lay too.			pinnace out, and sent her ahead; the yaul making the best
9	2	..	N.W.b.W.	..	22, 27	of her way between the shoals and the main; follow'd
10	4	2	W.N.W.	..	19, 22	with the ship. ½-past 11, haul'd round the N.E. p't of
11	2	4	N.W.b.W.	..	30, 19	the shoal to weather an island ahead, which being
	2	..	N.N.W.	..	19, 17	accomplish'd at noon, and the boats out of the stations, lay
12	4	..	N.W.b.N.	..	16, 19, 15,	too for them, being now in the middle of shoals.
			N.N.E.		14¼	At noon. Isl'd already mention'd yesterday at noon S. 35° E. 6
						legg's; the nearest island S.S.E. 2 miles; the N. ext's of ye
						main (a low point) N.W., 4 miles. Lat. obs'd, 12° 0' S.

PICKERSGILL:

So that we were obliged to keep a very good look out, a boat ahead and an easy sail . . . Tide set at 10 fathoms per hour.

BOOTIE:

At 6 PM, passed a crescent shaped reef east of us ¾ of a mile. At ½ past 6 came to anchor. Islands NW at noon, wbs.2 or 3 miles. Tide set west 10 furlongs per hour.

COOK:

Gentle breezes at SEbE and clear weather. At 2 oClock in the PM as we were steering NWbN saw a large shoal right ahead extending 3 or 4 points [34 to 45 degrees] on each bow, upon which we hauled up NNE and NEbN in order to get round the north point of it which we reached by 4 oClock and then edged away to the westward and run between the north end of this shoal and another which lays 2 miles to the northward of it, having a boat all the time ahead of the Ship sounding, our depth of water was very irregular from 22 to 8 fathoms. At ½ past 6 oClock we anchored in 13 fathom, the northermost of the small islands mentioned at noon bore W ½ S distant 3 miles; these islands, which are known in the chart by the name of *Forbes's Isles*, lay about 5 leagues from the main which here forms a moderately high point which we called *Bolt Head*, from which the land trends more westerly and is all low sandy land but to the southward it is high and hilly even near the sea. At 6 oClock in the AM we got again under sail and directed our course for an island which lay but a little way from the main and bore from us at this time N 40° W distant 5 leagues, but we were interrupted in our course by meeting with shoals; but by the help of two boats ahead and a good look out at the mast head we got at last into a fair channel which led us down to the island, having a very large shoal on our starboard side, and several smaller ones betwixt us and the main land; in this channel we had from 20 to 30 fathom water. Between 11 and 12 oClock we hauled round the NE side of the island leaving it between us and the main from which it is distant 7 or 8 miles. This island is about a league in circuit and of a moderate height and is inhabited [now Haggerstone Island]; to the NW of it are several small low islands and keys which lay not far from the main, and to the northward and eastward lay several other islands and shoals so that we were now encompassed on every side by one or other, but so much does great danger swallow up lesser ones that those once so dreaded shoals were now looked at with less concern. The boats being out of their stations we brought too to wait for them. At noon our latitude by observation was 12° 0′ S, longitude in 217° 25′ West, depth of water 14 fathoms. Course and distance sailed reduced to a straight line sence noon yesterday is N 29° West 32 miles. The main land within the above islands forms a point which I call *Cape Grenville* (Lat^{de} 11° 58′, Long^{d} 217° 38′); between this cape and Bolt Head is a bay which I named *Temple Bay*. E ½ N 9 leagues from Cape Granville lay some tolerable high islands which I called *Sr Charles Hardys Isles*, those which lay off the Cape I named *Cockburns Isles*.

BANKS:

In the even many shoals ahead; we were however fortunate enough to find our way through them and at night anchored under an island. The tide ran here immensely strong which we looked upon as a good omen: so strong a stream must in all probability have an outlet by which we could get out either on the South or North side of New Guinea. The smoothness of the water however plainly indicated that the reef was between us and the ocean.

AM: Weighed anchor and steered as yesterday with a fresh trade wind. All the morn we were much entangled with shoals, but so much do great dangers swallow up lesser ones that these once so much dreaded shoals were now looked at with much less concern than formerly.

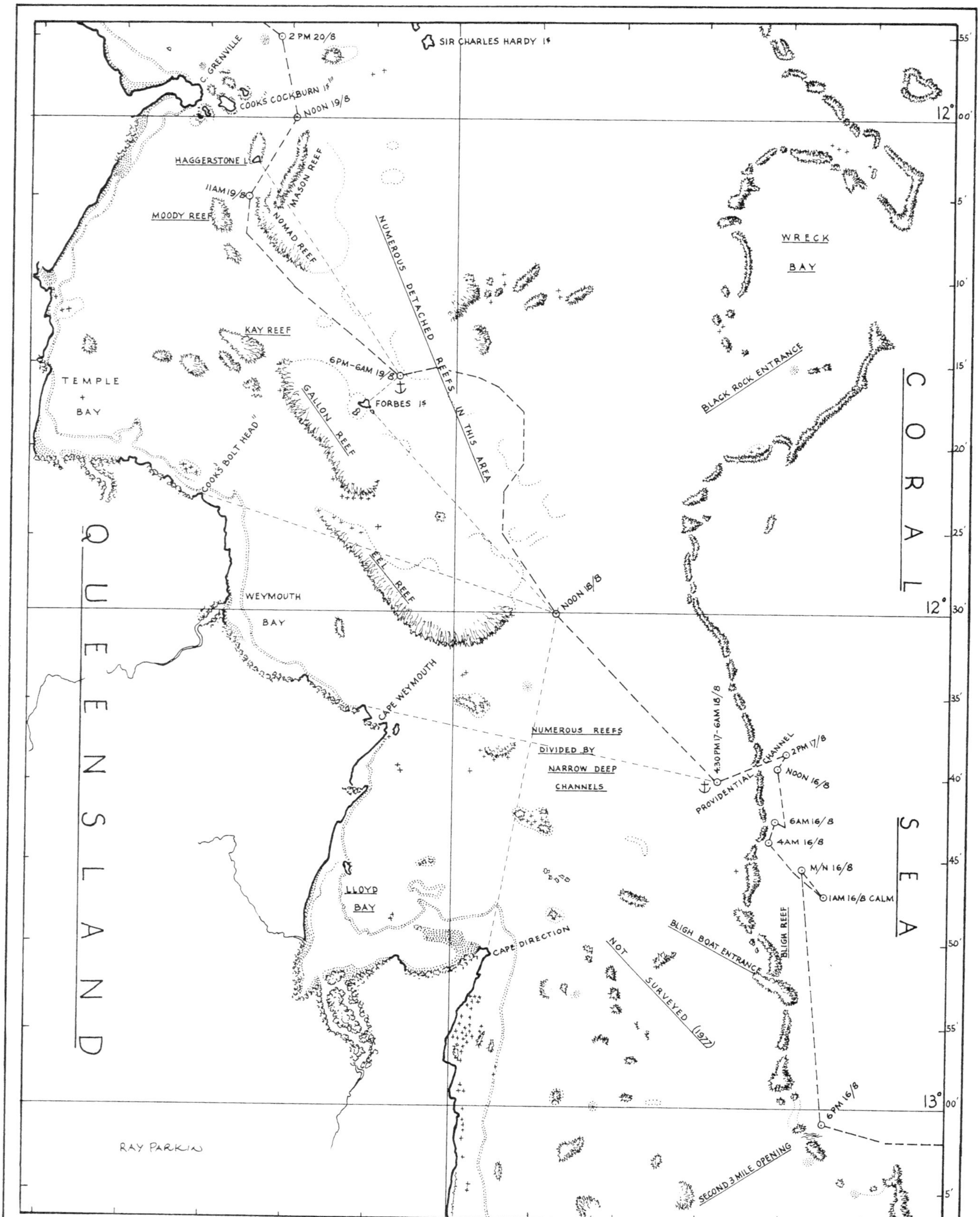
SIR CHARLES HARDY Is
2 PM 20/8
C. GRENVILLE
COOKS' COCKBURN Isles
NOON 19/8
HAGGERSTONE I.
MASON REEF
11AM 19/8
MOODY REEF
NOMAD REEF
NUMEROUS DETACHED REEFS IN THIS AREA
WRECK BAY
KAY REEF
6PM–6AM 19/8
FORBES Is
GALLON REEF
TEMPLE BAY
COOKS' BOLT HEAD
BLACK ROCK ENTRANCE
CORAL
SEA
QUEENSLAND
EEL REEF
WEYMOUTH BAY
NOON 18/8
CAPE WEYMOUTH
NUMEROUS REEFS DIVIDED BY NARROW DEEP CHANNELS
4.30 PM 17–6AM 18/8
PROVIDENTIAL CHANNEL
2PM 17/8
NOON 16/8
6AM 16/8
4AM 16/8
M/N 16/8
1AM 16/8 CALM
LLOYD BAY
CAPE DIRECTION
NOT SURVEYED (1977)
BLIGH BOAT ENTRANCE
BLIGH REEF
6PM 16/8
SECOND 3 MILE OPENING
RAY PARKIN
12° 00'
12° 30'
13° 00'
143° 30' E

This was a day on which all their attention and skill were required to keep the ship clear of the haphazard bottom. All afternoon they threaded their way northwards through a wide field of detached reefs and shoals in a manner too tortuous to be recorded accurately in the log. This instance reveals some of the qualities of the ship herself, who, too often, has been looked upon as an unhandsome and clumsy thing. They were to the east of, and separated from, the now-recommended channel by Eel, Fison, Gallon and Kay Reefs which extend NW/SE for twenty-five miles, and amongst still-unnamed and uncharted ones. Circling gradually to the westward they brought up at anchor just two miles east, and a little north of Forbes Is. Here they remained overnight. In the morning a course was laid for an island in sight to the NW, but the large mass of Nomad Reef soon barred a direct course. It was left to the eastward on their starboard hand and they entered a deep channel, which was only 1 ½ miles wide, with Laurel and Moody Reefs on their larboard hand. At 11 AM, with the steered-for island now ahead, they altered to starboard and passed it on the weather side which was to the eastward. At noon, in latitude 12° 00′ S, they were encircled by obstructions. Westwards was Cape Grenville with its off-lying Cockburns (now Home) Islands; south was Mason Reef at sou'west was Haggerstone Island, just passed, with its outlying reef at its northern end; north-east was Sir Charles Hardys Isles with reefs between it and them; to the north was the extensive Cockburn Reef. So the ship waited for the boats to take up station ahead again.

As for the features named by the Captain this day, he noted, but did not name, Haggerstone Island. On Cape Grenville, Professor Beaglehole gives us the lively note: 'The tactless, obstinate, honest, high- though narrow-minded George Grenville (1712–70), whose statesmanship in relation to the colonies has been so much decried, nevertheless deserved well of sailors, principally for the act which, when treasurer of the navy, he forced through (1758) providing for the speedy and punctual payment of seamen's wages—though not with any long effect.' The Captain had reported to him on returning from Newfoundland after his 1763 surveying season, when he was then First Lord 1762–63.

Forbes Islands were named after the Hon. John Forbes (1714–96), second son of the Third Earl of Granard, who rose to rank of Admiral of the Fleet 1781, and was a Lord of the Admiralty 1756–63, General of Marines 1763, and a commissioner of longitude 1768.

The Cockburn Isles was named after Admiral George Cockburn (?–1770), Comptroller of the Navy from 1755 to his death, and a commissioner of longitude. Cook's 'Cockburn Isles' are now called the Home Islands. Six of these islands now bear the names of some of Endeavour's *company: Orton, Gore, Hicks, Perry, Harvey and Clerke. The name* Cockburn Islands *has been transferred to those which lay on Cockburn Reef: among them are Bootie, Manley, Magra, Saunders Islands, and Forwood Reef and Buchan Rock. Temple Bay was probably named after Henry Temple, Second Viscount Palmerston (1739–1802), who was on the Board of Trade*

ENSIGN FROM PEAK OF SHIP: KEEP PACE OR GO AHEAD OF SHIP. FLAG HOISTED FROM BOAT: YOU ARE STANDING INTO DANGER — KEPT OUT UNTIL SHIP STEERS FROM IT (BOAT BASED ON PARKINSON SKETCH).

in 1765, and a Lord of the Admiralty 1766–77. The southern point of this bay Cook named Bolt Head (possibly, after Bolt Head on the Devonshire coast). It is possibly what is now 1st Stony Point, but certainly not the present Bolt Head, more than 10 miles NW.

The entries of Bootie and Pickersgill this day throw interesting light upon a technical point. The columns of the logs of this period, in which was shown the speed of the ship, were headed 'Knots' and 'Fathoms'. It would be difficult to know what the relation was between the knot and fathom in a speed/distance way. There could be considerable difference in the distance between the knots on the log lines of various ships, even at different periods in the same ship. One practice was to shorten the distance between knots so that one would not be ahead of one's reckoning, and thus anticipate a known danger before one actually ran into it. On earth measurements of the eighteenth century, when the nautical mile was reckoned at 6,120 feet (the present 6,080 feet), the division on the line for a half-minute glass would have been 51 feet. Pickersgill had entered in his log, early in the voyage, that the distance between knots on* Endeavour*'s log line was 49 feet. But, with today's information, Bootie and Pickersgill demonstrate that the actual difference of distances between knots is immaterial to the number of fathoms in a knot. The Ship's Log says the tide ran at 1 knot 2 fathoms; Pickersgill, at 10 fathoms; Bootie, 10 furlongs. Together, this clearly shows that this fathom (which represents a speed,* not a *distance) is 1/8 of a knot, or 1/8 of a mile per hour.*

The Captain was now quite conscious that he was approaching the resolution of one of his prime objectives, for which reason he had clung so tenaciously to this difficult

*Cook at one point writes the distance as 50 feet.

coast. Soon he would know whether or no New Guinea and New Holland were joined, for Torres, and the Portuguese, had not unduly advertised his findings. Cook was determined on an answer to the doubt.

SHIP'S LOG:

MONDAY, AUGUST 20TH, 1770

H.	K.	F.	Courses.	Winds.	Soundings.	Remarks, &c.
					Fathoms.	
1	..	..	..	..	..	Mod. breezes and hazy wea'r; lying too for the boats; ½-past, made sail, one being in her station and other on board.
	1	4	N.b.W.	E.S.E	..	
2	3	3	..	..	No g'd at 16	
3	2	..	N.W.b.N.	..	..	Sailing after a boat between a shoal and the main.
	1	6	N.W.b.W.	..	..	Pass'd 3 small islands.
4	3	6	..	..	22	
5	3	4	..	..	22	
6	2	..	..	..	..	Saw some low islands ahead.
	1	6	N.W. ½ N.	..	..	The low islands W.N.W., dist. 2 leagues.
7	3	..	N.W.	..	22, 20, 18, 16	Came too with the b. b'r in 16 fa'm, the low isl'ds bearing S.S.E., 1½ miles; made the signell for the boats.
8						Found the tide to sett N.W., 1 knot p'r hour.
9						
10						
11						
12						
1	..	..	..	..	..	Slack water.
2						
3						
4						
5						
6						Mod. breezes and fair weather.
7	3	2	N.N.W.	E. b. S.	16, 15, 14, 15	Weighed and came to sail; the pinnace ahead.
8	2	..	..	..	..	
	1	6	N. ½ W.	..	15	Haul'd up to clear a shoal to leeward.
9	4	..	N.N.E.	..	..	
10	2	..	S.W.b.W.	..	..	Saw shoals from W't to N.E., to leeward of which there seem'd to be a passage; made the pinnace signell; sent her to sound the pasage and the yawl on the reefs; bore up for the lee passage ½-past 10, lay too for the yaul; at 11 made sail.
	1	..	N.W.	..	No g'd at 16	
11	2	..	N.b.W. ½ W.	..	..	
	..	..	up N.E. off N.N.E.	..	18	At noon, a small isl'd one with the No. p't of the main N. 40 W.; isl'd dis't 7 or 8 miles; pass'd 2 sandy isl'ds, dist'ce 2 miles. Lat'd. obs'd, 11° 23' S.
12	4	6	N. ½ E.	..	..	

COOK:

Fresh breezes at ESE. About one oClock the pinnace having got ahead and the yawl we took in tow, we filled [the sails] and steered NbW for some small islands we had in that direction; after approaching them a little nearer we found them joined or connected together by a large reef [the Cockburn Reef]; upon this we edged away NW and left them a-starboard steering between them and the islands laying off the main, having a fair and clear passage, depth of water from 15 to 23 fathom. At 4 oClock we discovered some low islands and rocks bearing WNW, which we stood directly for. At half past 6 oClock we anchored on the NE side of the northermost in 16 fathom water distant from the island one mile. The isles lay NW 4 leagues from C. Granville,

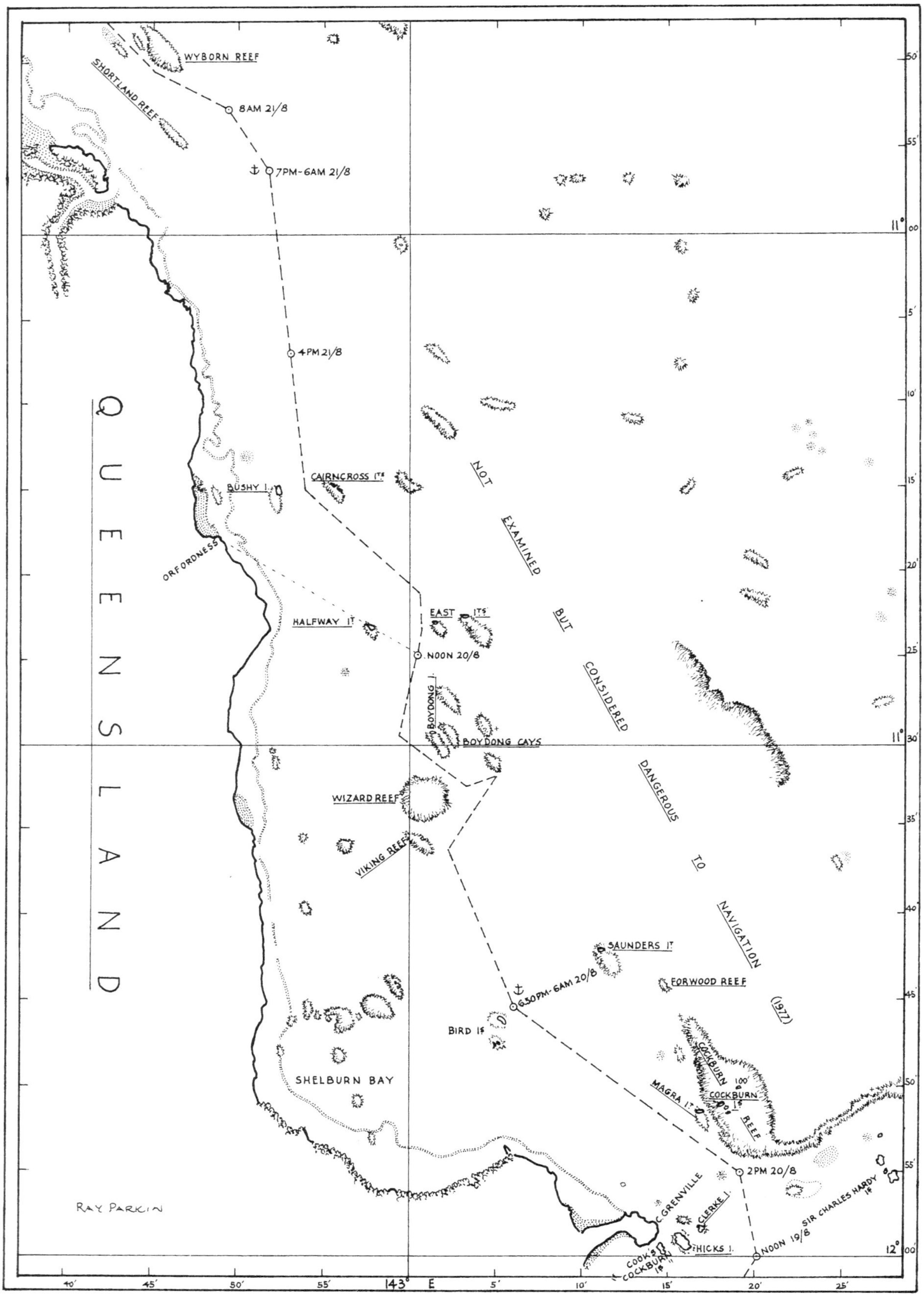
WYBORN REEF
SHORTLAND REEF
8AM 21/8
7PM-6AM 21/8
4PM 21/8
QUEENSLAND
CAIRNCROSS ITS
BUSHY I.
ORFORDNESS
HALFWAY IT
EAST ITS
NOON 20/8
BOYDONG I.
BOYDONG CAYS
WIZARD REEF
VIKING REEF
NOT EXAMINED BUT CONSIDERED DANGEROUS TO NAVIGATION (1977)
SAUNDERS IT
FORWOOD REEF
6.30PM-6AM 20/8
BIRD IS
COCKBURN
COCKBURN IS
REEF
MAGRA IT
SHELBURN BAY
2PM 20/8
C. GRENVILLE
CLERKE I.
HICKS I.
NOON 19/8
SIR CHARLES HARDY IS
COOK'S COCKBURN IS
RAY PARKIN
143° E
11° 00
11° 30
12° 00

on these islands we saw a good many birds which occasioned my calling them *Bird Isles*. Before and at sun set we could see the main land which appeared all very low and sandy extending as far northward as NWbN, and some shoals, keys and low sandy isles away to the NE of us.

At 6 oClock in the morning we got under sail again with a fresh breeze at east and stood away NNW for some low islands we saw in that direction; but we had not stood long upon this course before we were obliged to haul close upon a wind in order to weather a shoal which we discovered on our larboard bow [Viking and Wizard Reefs] 2 miles ahead, having at the same time others to the eastward of us [a still blank area on the chart, considered dangerous to navigation]. By such time as we weathered the shoal to leeward we had brought the islands well on our lee-bow, but seeing some shoals spit off from them and some rocks on our starboard bow which we did not discover untill we were very near them [Boydong], made me afraid to go to windward of the islands, wherefore we brought too and made a signal for the pinnace which was ahead to come on board; which done I sent her to leeward of the islands with orders to keep along the edge of the shoal which spitted off from the south side of the southermost island. The yawl I sent to run over the shoal to look for turtle and appointed them a signal to make in case they saw many, if not she was to meet us on the other side of the island [Boydong Island]. As soon as the pinnace had got a proper distance from us we wore and stood after her and run to leeward of the island where we took the yawl in tow, she having seen only one small turtle and therefore made no stay upon the shoal. Upon this island which is only a small spot of sand with some trees upon it, we saw a good many hutts or habitations of the natives which we supposed comes over from the main to these islands (from which they are distant about 5 leagues) to catch turtle at the time these animals come ashore to lay their eggs. Having got the yawl in tow we stood away after the pinnace NNE and NbE to two other low islands, having two shoals which we could see without us [East Islets] and one between us and the main [Halfway Islet]. At noon we were about 4 leagues from the main land which we could see extending to the northward as far as NWbN all low flat and sandy; our latitude by observation was 11° 23′ S, longitude in 217° 46′ West, and course and distance sailed sence yesterday at noon North 22° West, 40 miles. Soundings from 14 to 23 fathom, but these are best seen on the chart as likewise the islands, shoals &ca which are too numerous to be mentioned singly.

BANKS:

At noon we passed along a large shoal on which the boats which were ahead saw many turtle but it blew too fresh to catch them. We are now tolerably near the main, which appeared low and barren and often interspersed with large patches of very white sand spoke of before. On a small island which we passed very near to were 5 natives, two of whom carried their lances in their hands; they came down upon a point and looked at the ship for a little while and then retired.

AM: Steering along shore as usual among many shoals, luffing up for some and bearing away for others. We are now pretty well experienced in their appearances so as to be seldom deceived and easily to know asunder a bottom coloured by white sand from a coral rock, the former of which, tho generally in 12 or 14 fathom water, some time ago gave us much trouble. The reef was still supposed to be without us from the smoothness of our water. The mainland appeared very low and sandy and had many fires upon it, more than we had usually observed. We passed during the day many low sandy islands every one of which stood upon a large shoal; we have constantly found the best passage to lie near the main, and the farther that you go near the reef the more numerous are the shoals.

This day saw them sailing from Cape Grenville to Bird Island, a little east of the now-recommended track, but they were fairly on it when anchored that night off Bird Island. The next morning they were again to the eastward of it and the Viking and Wizard Reefs, when they turned NW *to run under the lee of the Boydong Cays. On passing Boydong Islet they turned north to run between Halfway Isle to larboard and the East Islets to starboard. At noon, a point on the main which the Captain named Orfordness, and Halfway Islet, were in line* NW. *The outer reef east of Cape Grenville is some 35 miles out, and there trends north, and opens out from the coast considerably. Cook was right to suspect that if he had stayed outside the reef he would have lost the coast. The search for turtle reminds us of the shortage of provisions, especially if there should prove to be no passage between New Holland and New Guinea.*

SHIP'S LOG:

TUESDAY, AUGUST 21ST, 1770

H.	K.	F.	Courses.	Winds.	Soundings.	Remarks, &c.
					Fathoms.	
1	2	..	N.b.E.	..	..	Mod. breezes and clear wea'r; the pinnace, with a m'te, ahead sounding. At 1 bro't too, m'n topsail to the mast; $\frac{1}{2}$-past, made sail; pass'd by several sandy flats.
	2	..	N.	S.E.b.E.	17, noground	
2	..	..	..	..	..	
	2	4	N.W.b.N.	..	$16\frac{1}{4}$	
3	4	2	N.N.W.	..	$16\frac{1}{4}$	
4	4	2	N.b.W.	..	16	
5	4	2	N.W.b.N.	..	17, 18, 17, 16	
6	2	4	N.W.b.N.	..	15, 14, 13	High land seen from the masthead, N.W. b. N.
	2	2	N.b.W.	...	13	
7	3	..	..	..	13, 14, 13	Bro't too with the b't bower in 13 fa'm.
8	..	..	..	..	..	
9	..	..	..	..	..	
10	..	..	..	..	..	
11	..	..	..	..	..	
12	..	..	..	..	..	
1	..	..	..	..	..	
2	..	..	..	..	..	
3	..	..	..	..	..	
4	..	..	..	..	..	
5	..	..	..	..	..	
6	..	..	..	..	..	Weighed and made sail; yawl ahead sounding.
7	3	4	N.N.W.	E.b.S.	13, 14, 15	Variat'n p'r amp'd, 3° 05′ E't; by an azym'th, 3° 08′ E't'ly.

H.	K.	F.	Courses.	Winds.	Soundings.	Remarks, &c.
					reg'r	Bro't too, m'n tops'l to the mast, and made a signell for the boat.
8	3	3	..	..	13 to 15 rg'r	At 9 bore away, and made sail; boat ahead.
9	..	..	up S. ½ E.	off S.b.W.	..	At 11 bro't too, m'n tops'l to ye mast, and sent the long boat and yawl to sound a passage between an isl'd and
10	3	..	from W.S.W.	to N.W.	13, 12, 11, 10½	the main. ½-p't, made sail.
						At noon, a mod. breeze and pleas't wea'r; steering between
11	3	..	N.W.	..	10, 11, 12, 12½	some isl'ds and ye main; ext's of the isl'd from N. 3 E to to E.; nearest dist. 2 or 3 miles; saw the land making high,
12	{ ..	..	up N.E.	off N.E.b.N.	..	and sev'l openings making it appear like a number of
	{ 2	..	W.N.W.	E.S.E.	13, 13½, 14	islands, some of which are at a great dist'ce. This land bore from N. to S., round by the W.; gave the boats fresh orders, and bore up for an opening. Lat. obs'd, 10° 36′ S.

COOK:

Winds at Ebs and ESE a fresh breeze. By one oClock we had run nearly the length of the southermost of the two islands before mentioned, and finding that we could not well go to windward of them without carrying us too far from the Main land, we bore up and run to leeward where we found a fair open passage. This done we steered Nbw in a parallel direction with the main land leaving a small island [Bushy Island] between us and it, and some low sandy isles and shoals [Cairncross Islets] without us, all of which we lost sight of by 4 oClock neither did we see any more before the sun went down at which time the farthest part of the main bore NNW ½ W. Soon after this we anchored in 13 fathom soft ground about 5 league from the land where we lay untill daylight when we got under sail again, having first sent the yawl ahead to sound. We steered NNW by compass for the northermost land in sight. Variation 3° 6′ East. Seeing no danger in our way we took the yawl in tow and made all sail we could untill 8 oClock, at which time we discovered shoals ahead and on our larboard bow [South Ledge and Wyborn Reefs] and saw that the northermost land, which we had taken to be part of the main, was an island or islands between which and the main there appeared to be a good passage, through which we might pass by running to leeward of the shoals on our larboard bow [Wyborn] which was now pretty near us; upon which we wore and brought too and sent away the pinnace and yawl to direct us clear of the shoals and then stood after them. After having got round the SE point of the shoal we steered NW along the SW or inside of it keeping a good lookout at the mast head, having another shoal on our larboard side, but we found a good channel of a mile broad between them wherein were from 10 to 14 fathom water. At 11 oClock being nearly the length of the above islands mentioned and designing to pass between them and the main, the yawl being thrown astern by falling in upon part of the reef she could not get over, we brought the ship too and sent away the long-boat (which we had astern and rigged) to keep in-shore upon our larboard bow and the pinnace on the starboard; for though there appeared to be nothing in the passage yet I thought it necessary to take this method because we had a strong flood which carried us on end very fast, and it did not want much of high-water. As soon as the boats were ahead we stood after them and got through by noon, at which time we were in the Latitude of 10° 36′ 30″ S. The nearest part of the main, and which we soon after found to be the northermost, bore west a little southerly distant 3 or 4 miles, the islands which formed the passage before mentioned extending from North to N 75° E[t], distant 2 or 3 miles. At the same time we saw islands at a good distance off extending from NbW to WNW and behind them another chain of high land which we likewise judged to be islands, the main land we thought extended as far as N 71° West but this we found to be islands [Horn Island]. The point of the main which forms one side of the passage before mentioned and which is the northern promontory of this country I have named *Cape York* in honour of his late Royal Highness the Duke of York. It lies in the longitude of 218° 24′ W, the north point in y[e] Lat[de] of 10° 37′4 S. [10° 42′ (correction by Cook)] & the East point in 10° 41′ S. The land over and to the southward of this point is rather low and very flat as far inland as the eye could reach and looks barren to the southward of the Cape, the shore forms a large open bay which I called *New Castle Bay* wherein are some small low islands and shoals and all the land about is very low flat and sandy. The land of the northern part of the Cape is rather more hilly and the shore forms some small bays wherein there appeared to be good anchorage, and the vallies appeared to be tolerably well cloathed with wood; close to the east point of the Cape are three small islands and a ledge of rocks spitting off from them, there is also an island laying close to the north point [Ebora Is]. The other islands before spoke of forming the passage lay about 4 miles without these; only two of them are of any extent, the southermost is the largest and much higher than any part of the main land [Mount Adolphus, 490′]. On the NW side of this island seemed to be a good anchorage and vallies that to all appearance would afford both wood and fresh water. These islands are known in the chart by the name of *York Isles*. To the southward and SE of them, and even to the eastward and northward are several low islands, rocks and shoals; our depth of water in sailing between them and the main was 12, 13 & 14 fathoms.

BANKS:

In the evening we observed the shoals to decrease in number but we were still in smooth water. AM: Running along shore with charming moderate weather, as indeed we have had ever since our second entering of the reef. We observed both last night and this morn that the main looked very narrow, so we began to look out for the passage we expected to find between New Holland and New Guinea, at noon one was seen very narrow but appearing to widen: we resolved to try it so stood in.

From noon the ship sailed northwards and, by 1 o'clock, she was passing between Halfway Islet, on her larboard hand to the west, and East Islets on her starboard hand. Shortly after this she altered course north-westerly to pass between Bushy Island, inshore, and Cairncross Islets, to seaward. Both of these lay on extensive coral shelves. Until anchoring at 7 PM, six separate courses were steered, all northerly with more or less westing in them. Just before anchoring, the 495-foot peak of Mount Adolphus, the highest point of the Adolphus Islands (Cook's York Isles) bore NWbN. *The distance run by the log was 28 miles since noon.*

On weighing in the morning, the ship steered for Mount Adolphus, at first thought to be part of the mainland; but, by 8 AM, *it was seen to be an island among others. About this time shoals were sighted ahead, probably South Ledge, and another on the larboard bow, almost certainly Wyborn Reef. Beyond these shoals there appeared to be a good passage between the mainland and the islands.*

There could be some doubt as to the actual track of Endeavour *from here to her noon position. On the chart, the obvious one would seem to be to windward of Wyborn Reef, then* NW *between this and South Ledge, altering a little more westerly to pass through the present Adolphus Channel. This is the recommended track today.*

Of course, the Captain had no chart or other information other than what his eyes and experience told him, and the soundings passed on to him by the leadsmen in the chains, and the boats ahead, whose view was intimate but restricted, and their horizon only a mile or so away because of their closeness to the surface. However, this close view complemented that of the masthead lookouts. And it would appear from the logs and journals that the above was not the track he, in fact, took. Two sentences written very clearly seem to preclude this possibility.

The ship had made a bare 7 miles NNW *from her overnight anchorage when, at 8* AM, *she brought to, with the main topsail to the mast, and made a signal for the boats to come onboard for new instruction. This was because the shoals had been sighted in their way, one ahead and the other under his lee bow, which gave Cook the option of either weathering the latter (quite practical as he had the wind just then at* EbS*) or running to leeward of it. It was at this time, also, that he saw the possibility of a passage between the islands and the main, and his appreciation was '. . . there appeared to be a good passage, through which we might pass by* running to leeward of the shoals on our larboard bow which was now pretty near us' *(not his emphasis). The ship followed the boats, clearing the* SE *point of the reef and steering* NW along the SW or inside of it. *The Wyborn Reef runs* NW/SE, *whereas South Ledge runs* E/W. *Furthermore, a good lookout was kept at the masthead who reported 'having another shoal on our larboard side'. There is such a one, just west of Wyborn, which now carries a radar reflecting beacon. It is not likely that it was the Shortland Reef they had run to leeward of; for, at 8 o'clock, that appears to have been on their larboard beam. 'But we found a channel of a mile broad between them', which is a reasonable spot estimate* SW *of Wyborn; whereas the narrowest part* SW *of South Ledge is almost 4 miles.*

But a pretty good fix can be made of the noon position this day, at the intersection of three clear bearings given. The western extremity of Adolphus Islands lay due north; the eastern extremity lay N 75° E; *and Cape York bore 'west a little southerly 3 or 4 mile.' This places the ship a little* SW *of the recommended channel and uncomfortably close to the unseen Mid Rock and Quetta Rock which, it is most probable, she passed south of as she turned west. The Quetta Rock was 'discovered' by S.S.* Quetta *on the night in February 1890 when she tore open her bottom on it and sank with great loss of life.*

Looking now, with hindsight, at the ship's passage through that narrow channel under the lee of Wyborn Reef, as shown on the present-day chart, one can more readily appreciate the skill and co-operation between ship and boats in the avoidance of hazards. Yet this had been almost the daily norm over the whole 14½ degrees of latitude that had been so tortuously traversed through an uncharted, and unknown, sea of reefs, more complex and extensive than probably anywhere else in the world.

SHIP'S LOG:

WEDNESDAY, AUGUST 22ND, 1770

H.	K.	F.	Courses.	Winds.	Soundings.	Remarks, &c.
					Fathoms.	
1	3	4	W.b.S.	E.b.S.	14, 13, 12	Mod. and clear wea'r; saw a number of smoaks along shore. At 1 lay too for the yawl; pinnace and longboat sounding. ½-p't 2, made sail and steer'd for a passage between some islands and the main. At 3 fired a gun, and made the signell for the boats to sound the next passage to the no'ward of the abovemention'd. ¾-p't 3, was in the passage; dist'ce from east shore, ¾ of a mile; saw several Indians, who follow'd us shouting. At 4 fired a gun, and made the signell for the boats; came too with the b't bower, in 6¾ fa'm, good ground; veer'd to ½ a cable. Ex't of the land on the east side, N. 56 E, an island to S.W., the main on the west side from N. 8° E. to S. 73° W., 8 miles; dist'ce from the eastern shore, one mile. The pinnace and yawl, with the capt'n and gentlemen, went on shore to examin the country, and view the coast from one of the hills; soon after saw some turtle. It was high-water when we came too; the tide of ebb set from the S.W., 3 k. 2 f'r. p'r hour. At 6 posession was taken of this country in his Majesty's name and under his coulours; fired several volleys of small arms on the occasion, and cheer'd 3 times, which was answer'd from the ship.
2	..	..	up 5½ E.	off W.b.S.	11, 10½, 10	
3	{ .. / 2	.. / ..	} W.S.W.	..	9, 8, 7½	
4	4	2	from W.S.W.	to S.W	{ 7, 6½, 6 / 5½, 4¾, 5, 6	
5	..	..	½-p't 4, slack tide.		6¾	
6	..	..	..	..	..	
7	..	..	..	..	..	
8	..	..	..	..	..	
9	..	..	..	..	..	
10	..	..	..	..	...	
11	..	..	..	..	..	
12	..	..	..	..	..	
1	..	..	..	..	..	
2	..	..	..	..	..	
3	..	..	..	..	..	
4	..	..	..	..	..	
5	..	..	..	..	..	
6	..	..	..	..	..	
7	..	..	..	..	..	
8	..	..	..	..	..	
9	..	..	..	..	..	
10	..	..	..	..	..	
11	2	4	S.W.	..	{ 7½, 8, 9, 9¾, 8, 7, 6, 5, 4¾	Slack water; weighed and made sail, the pinnace ahead.
12	2	4	S.W.b.W.	N.b.E.	9, 8, 7, 9	At noon, mod. and fair wea'r; N. ext'me of ye main S. 40 W.; the w't ext'm of the streight on the No' side N. 68 W.; dist'ce off shore, 2 or 3 miles. Lat. obs'd, 10° 45' S.

BOOTIE:

The Captain &c with marines armed in the pinnace and yawl went on shore . . .

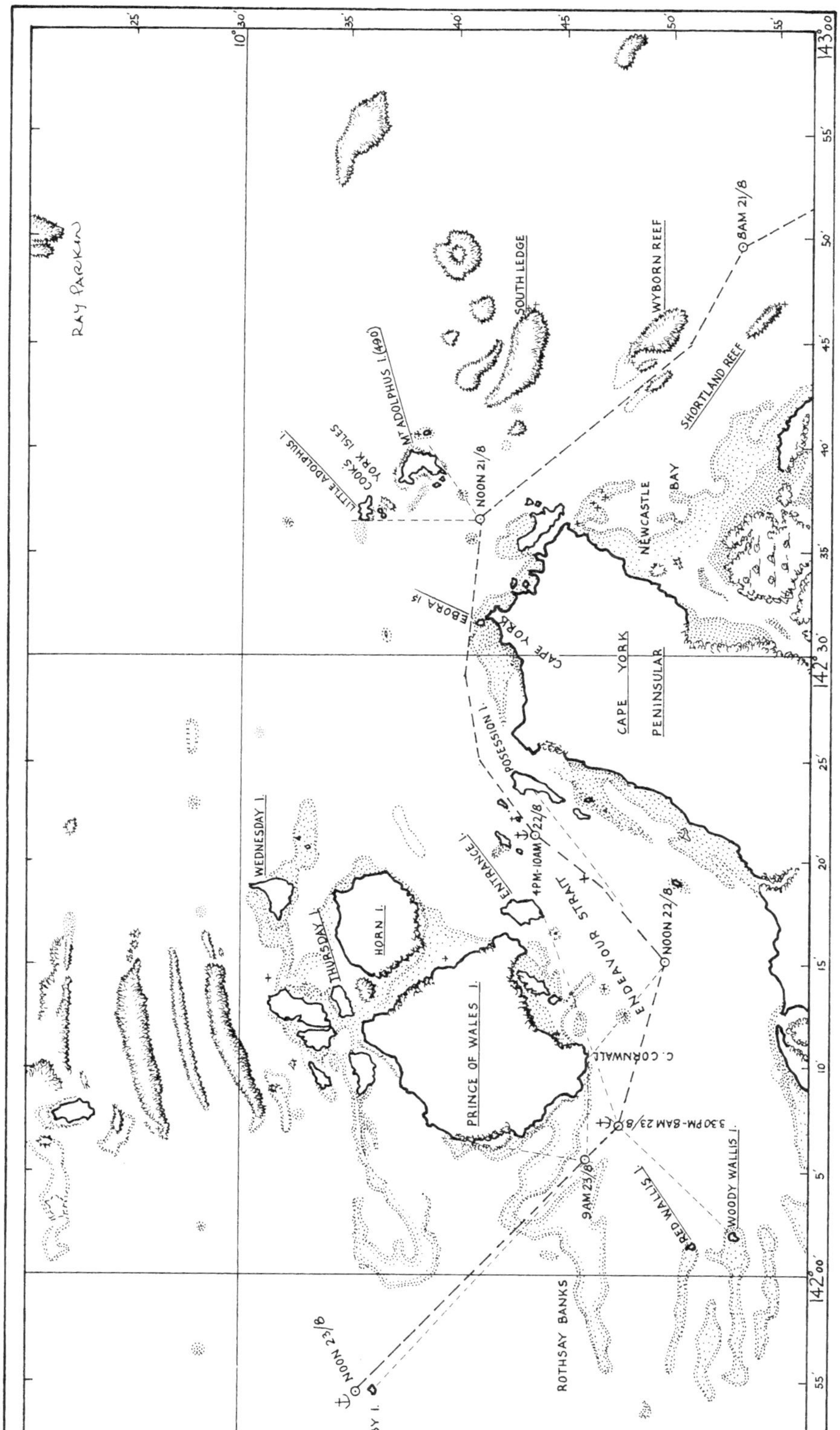
RAY PARKIN
BOOBY I.
NOON 23/8
ROTHSAY BANKS
9AM 23/8
330PM-8AM 23/8
RED WALLIS I.
WOODY WALLIS I.
C. CORNWALL
PRINCE OF WALES I.
HORN I.
THURSDAY I.
WEDNESDAY I.
ENTRANCE I.
4PM-10AM 22/8
NOON 22/8
ENDEAVOUR STRAIT
POSESSION I.
CAPE YORK
CAPE YORK PENINSULAR
EBORA Is
NOON 21/8
LITTLE ADOLPHUS I.
COOKS YORK ISLES
Mt ADOLPHUS I (490)
SOUTH LEDGE
WYBORN REEF
8AM 21/8
SHORTLAND REEF
NEWCASTLE BAY
10°30'
142°00'
142°30'
143°00'

FORWOOD:
At 6 PM, posession was taken of this country in His Majesty's name, and this announcement from the shore by volleys and answered from on board with colours flying and concluding with three cheers.

HICKES:
The Captain went on shore, hoisted y[e] colours and took posession of y[e] country for y[e] king, fired several volleys and cheered three times which was answered from y[e] ship.

'153':
At 6 possession was taken by hoisting a Jack on shore . . .

BANKS:
In passing through [Endeavour Strait], for it was not much more than a mile in length before it widened very much, we saw 10 Indians standing on a hill; 9 were armed with lances as we had been used to see them, the tenth had a bow and arrows; 2 had also large ornaments of mother of pearl shell hung round their necks. After the ship has passed 3 followed her, one of whom was the bow man. We soon came abreast, from whence we concluded we might have a much better view than from our mast head, so the anchor was dropped and we prepared ourselves to go ashore to examine whether the place we stood into was a bay or a passage; for as we sailed right before the trade wind we might find difficulty in getting out should it prove to be the former. The 3 Indians placed themselves upon the beach opposite to us as if resolved either to oppose or assist our landing; when however we came about Musquet shot from them they all walked leisurely away. The hill we were upon was by much the most barren we had been upon; it however gave us the satisfaction of seeing a streight, at least as far as we could see, without any obstruction. In the even a strong tide made us almost certain.

In the morn 3 or 4 women appeared upon the beach gathering shell fish: we looked with our glasses and to us they appeared as they always did more naked than our mother Eve. The ebb ran out so strong that we could not weigh until near noon.

PARKINSON:
We stood between two of these islands, to the west, and found a very strong tide, which carried us along briskly, and gave us hopes that this was a passage between New Holland and New Guinea. At length we came to, and the pinnace was sent on shore to a spot where we saw some of the natives stand gazing at us; but when the boat's company landed, they immediately fled. The captain, and some others, went up to the top of a hill, and, seeing a clear passage, they hoisted a jack, and fired a volley, which was answered by the marines below, and the marines by three vollies from the ship, and three cheers from the main shrouds. The natives were armed with lances, and one of them had a bow in his hand. In other respects they were much like

the people we saw last, being quite naked, and of a dark colour. This land was more rocky, and less sandy than we had lately seen, but still very barren; though the flats, indeed, were covered with many verdant trees. We also discovered very high land at a great distance to the NE which we took for the land of New Guinea.

We were obliged to keep a constant look-out while we passed between the reef and the land, as it was full of shoals, reefs, sandy keys, and small islands; and had we not come in again [from outside the reef], we should not have found a passage.

COOK:

Gentle breezes at Ebs and clear weather. We had not stood above 3 or 4 miles alongshore to the westward before we discovered the land ahead to be islands detached by several channels from the Main land; upon this we brought too to wait for the yawl and called the other boats on board, after giving them proper instructions sent them away again to lead us through the channel next the main, and as soon as the yawl was on board made sail with the Ship after them; soon after we discovered rocks and shoals in this channel, upon which I made the signal for the boats to lead through the next channel to the northward laying between the islands, which they accordingly did we following with the Ship, and had not less than 5 fathom water and this in the narrowest part of the channel which was about a mile and a half broad from island to island. At 4 oClock we anchored about a mile and a half or 2 miles within the entrance in 6½ fathom clear ground distant from the islands on each side of us one mile, the main extending away to the SW, the farthest point of which that we could see bore from us S 48° West, and the south-wester-most point of the islands on the NW side of the passage bore S 76° West. Between these two points we could see no land so that we were in great hopes that we had at last found a passage into the Indian Seas, but in order to be better informed I landed with a party of men accompanied by Mr Banks and Dr Solander upon the island which lies at the SE point of the passage. Before and after we anchored we saw a number of people on this island armed in the same manner as all the others we have seen, except one man who had a bow and a bundle of arrows, the first we have seen upon this coast. From the appearance of these people we expected that they would have opposed our landing but as we approached the shore they all made off and left us in peaceable posession of as much of the island as served our purpose. After landing I went upon the highest hill which however was of no great height, yet not less than twice or thrice the height of the ships mast heads, but I could see from it no land between SW and WSW so that I did not doubt but what there was a passage. I could see plainly that the lands laying to the NW of this passage were composed of a number of islands of various extent both for height and circuit, ranged one behind the other as far to the northward and westward as I could see, which was not less than 12 or 14 leagues. Having satisfied myself of the great probability of a passage, thro' which I intended to go with the Ship, and therefore may land no more upon this eastern coast of *New Holland*, and on the western side I can make no new discovery the honour of which belongs to the Dutch Navigators [and as such they may lay Claim to it as their property (deleted)]; but the eastern coast from the latitude of 38° South down to this place I am confident was never seen or visited by any European before [and therefore by the same rule belongs to Great Britton (deleted)] us, and notwithstanding I had in the name of His Majesty taken posession of several places upon this coast, I now once more hoisted the English colours in the name of His Majesty King George the Third took posession of the whole eastern coast from the above latitude down to this place by the name of *New South Wales*, together with all the Bays, Harbours, Rivers and Islands situate upon the said coast, after which we fired three Volleys of small arms which were answered by a like number from the Ship. This done we set out for the Ship but were some time getting on board on account of a very rapid ebb tide which set NE out of the passage. Ever since we came among the shoals this last time we have found a moderate tide, the flood setting to the NW and the ebb to the SE. At this place it is high-water at the full and change of the moon about 1 or 2 oClock and riseth and falls upon a perpendicular about 10 or 12 feet. We saw on all adjacent lands and islands a great number of smooks, a certain sign that they are inhabited, and we have daily seen smooks on every part of the coast we have lately been upon.

Between 7 and 8 oClock in the morning we saw several naked people, all or most of them women, down upon the beach picking up shells &c[a], they had not a single rag of any kind of cloathing upon them and both these and those we saw yesterday were in every respect the same sort of people we have seen every where upon the Coast; two or three of the men we saw yesterday had on pretty large breast plates which we suppose were made of Pearl Oysters Shells, this was a thing as well as the Bow and Arrows we had not seen before.

At low-water which happened about 10 oClock we got under sail and stood to the SW with a light breeze at East which afterwards veered to NbE, having the pinnace ahead, depth of water from 6 to 10 fathom except in one place where we passed over a bank of 5 fathom. At noon, *Posession Island* at the SE entrance of the passage bore N 53° East distant 4 leagues, the western extreme of the main land now in sight bore S 43° West distant 4 or 5 leagues, all being exceeding low. The SW point on the largest island on the NW side of the passage bore N 71° West distant 8 miles this point I named *Cape Cornwell* [C. Cornwall] (Lat. 10° 43′ S, Long. 219° 0′[3]) and some low islands laying about the middle of the passage which I called *Wallice's Isles* bore WbS ½ S distant about 2 leagues [Red Wallis and Woody Wallis Islands], our latitude by observation was 10° 46′ South.

It appears that Cook did not name this coast New South Wales just at this time, for the entry here has been put in over an erasure. The transcript in the Mitchell Library simply has 'New Wales'. No other log or journal mentions New South Wales. It has even been suggested that this name originated with Hawkesworth's editing and publication of the Endeavour Voyage, *which was taking place while Cook was on his second voyage. This suggestion was made in the Historical Records of New South Wales, 1893.*

The existence of the holograph journal, from which the present was originally taken, was not known to Dr Arnold Wood (the historian) then, nor had it been available to Hawkesworth most probably. But the words 'by the name of New South Wales' appear to be in Cook's own handwriting, whatever the controversy. It does however appear to have been a name that was decided upon some time after this date.

Chapter 15
L'envoi

SHIP'S LOG:

THURSDAY, AUGUST 23RD, 1770

Light airs and fair weather. 1 pm, the pinnace made a signell for shoal water. Sent the yawl ahead. ½ past 3, both boats making a signell for shoal water, came too with the Best Bower in 6¾ fathoms water sandy ground. A small island NW ½ W 6 miles. Two small islands N 16° W 3½ miles. The northermost land in sight an island N ½ E 7 or 8 miles. Variation per an Amplitude 2° 54′ E. Midnight. Calm. 8 am, Wind south. Light airs and fair weather. Weighed and made sail. Pinnace ahead. 9 am, passed over bar, soundings as per column (7,8,6,5,4,3,3,4,4,6,7.) At noon, moderate breezes and pleasant weather. Brought too under a small island. The Captain and gentlemen went on shore in the yawl. Distance off shore ¼ of a mile. No part of the main in sight. Latitude observed 10° 32′ S.

'153':
The Captain and gentlemen went on shore and landed on it. It being covered with birds dung and a quantity of Boobies & a number of piles of stones.

BOOTIE:
The Captain returned having shot several Boobies.

HICKES:
The Captain went ashore shooting.

PARKINSON:
On the 23d, we had light breezes from the N. and S.W. with some calms, and we were

certain of being in a strait, which seemed to be not very remote from the river Van Speult in Carpentaria; the land to the north being made up of a cluster of islands. We found shallow water all through this strait, which we named Endeavour Straits; and went over a bar that had only three fathoms and a half water. About noon, we saw a small island covered with birds-dung of a white colour, and some of our people went off in a boat, and shot a score of birds called Boobies.

BANKS:
We had the wind variable from N to W, the first time since we got the trade. Before we had proceeded far we met with a shoal which made us come to an anchor.

In the morn calm: at 9 however a small breeze sprang up on which we weighed and sailed through a channel which had been found during the calm. At noon we were abreast of an island which was white with the dung of birds; as we had little wind the ship was brought too, we went ashore on it and shot bobies [probably the Brown Booby] till our ammunition was quite expended. I myself botanized and found some plants which I had not seen before. After we came on board the winds were variable and soon after calm and very hot. Water still continued very shoal but the swell, which ran larger than any we had met with within the reef, gave us great hopes.

COOK:
In the PM had little wind and variable with which and the Tide of Flood we kept advancing to the WNW, depth of water 8, 7, 6, and 5 fathom. At half an hour past one oClock the pinnace which was ahead made a signal for shoal water upon which we tacked and sent away the yawl to sound also, and then tacked again and stood after them with the Ship: two hours after this they both at once made the signal for having shoal water, and it being now near high water I was afraid to stand on for fear of running aground at that time of the Tide, and therefore came too an anchor in a ¼ less 7 fathom sandy ground *Wallice's Islands* [Wallis] bore SBW ½ W distant 5 or 6 miles, the islands to the northward extending from S 73° East to N 10° E, and a small island just in sight bearing NW ½ W [Booby]; here we found the flood tide to set to the westward and the Ebb the contrary. After we had come to an anchor I sent away the Master with the long boat to sound, who upon his return in the evening reported that there was a bank stretching north and south upon which there were 3 fathom water and beyond it 7 fathom. We had it calm all night and untill 9 oClock in the morning, at which time we weighed with a light breeze at SSE and steered NWbW for the small island above mentioned having first sent the boats ahead to sound, depth of water 8, 7, 6, 5, 4, and 3 fathom when upon the bank, it now being the last quarter of Ebb. At this time the most northermost island we had in sight bore N 9° East, *Cape Cornwell* bore East distant 3 leagues, and *Wallace's Isles* S 3° East distant 3 leagues; this bank, at least so much as we sounded, extends north and south, how far I cannot say, its breadth however is not more than a quarter or at most half a mile; being over the bank we deepened our water to ¼ less 7 fathom which depth we

carried all the way to the small island ahead, which we reached by noon at which time it bore south distant near half a mile, depth of water 5 fathom, the most northermost land we had in sight (being part of the same chain of islands we have had to the northward of us since we entered the passage) bore N 71° East; Latitude in by observation 10° 33′ S. Longitude in 219° 22′ W. In this situation we had no part of the main land in sight. Being now near the island and having little wind Mr Banks and I landed upon it and found it to be mostly barren rock frequented by such birds as Boobies, a few of which we shott and occasioned my giving it the name of *Booby Island*. I made but a very short stay at this island before I returned to the Ship. In the meantime the wind had got to SW and altho it blowed but very faint yet it was accompanied with a swell from the same quarter; this together with concurring circumstances left me no room to doubt but we were got to the westward of *Carpentaria* or the northern extremity of *New-Holland* and now had an open sea to the westward which gave me no small satisfaction not only because the dangers and fatigues of the Voyage was drawing near to an end, but by being able to prove that New-Holland and New-Guinea are two separate lands or islands, which untill this day hath been a doubtful point with Geographers. The NE entrance of this passage or strait lies in the latitude of 10° 37′ S and in the Longitude of 218° 36′ West from the Meridian of Greenwich. It is formed by the Main or northern extremity of New-Holland on the SE and by a congeries of islands to the NW which I named *Prince of Wales's Islands*. It is very probable that these islands extend quite to New-Guinea, they are of various extent both for height and circuit and many of them seemed to be indifferently cloathed with wood &c[a] and from the smooks we saw some if not all of them must be inhabited. It is also very probable that among these Islands are as good if not better passages than the one we have come through, although one need hardly wish for a better was the access to it from the eastward less dangerous, but this difficulty will remain untill some better way is found out than the one we came, which no doubt may be done was it ever to become an object to be looked for; the northern extent of the main or outer reef which limits or bounds the shoals to the eastward seems to be the only thing wanting to clear up this point, and this was a thing I had neither time nor inclination to go about, having been already sufficiently harrassed with dangers without going to look for more.

This passage, which I have named *Endeavours Straight* after the name of the Ship, is in length NE and SW 10 Leagues and about 5 Leagues broad, except at the NE entrance where it is only 2 miles broad by reason of several small islands which lay there, one of which called *Posession Island* is of a moderate height and circuit; this we left between us and the main, passing between it and two small islands which lay NW 2 miles from it. There are also two small low islands called *Wallice's Isles* laying in the middle of the SW entrance which we left to the southward. The depth of water we found in the Straight was from 4 to 9 fathom every where good anchorage; only about 2 Leagues to the northward of Wallice's Islands is a bank whereon is not more than three fathom at low-water [Rothsay Banks] but probably there might be found more was it sought for. I have not been particular in describing this

Strait no more than I have been in pointing out the respective situations of the islands shoals &c[a] on the eastern coast of *New Wales*. For these I refer to the chart, where they are delineated with all the accuracy that the circumstances would admit of; with respect to the shoals that lay upon this coast I must observe for the benefit of those who may come after me, that I do not believe that one half of them are laid down in my chart, for it would be absurd to suppose that we could see or find them all, and the same thing may in some measure be said of the islands especially between the latitudes of 20° & 22°, where we saw islands out at sea as far as we could distinguish anything. However take the chart in general and I believe it will be found to contain as few errors as most Sea Charts which have not under gone a thorough correction, the latitude and longitude of all or most of the principal headlands, bays &c[a] may be relied on, for we seldom failed of getting an observation every day to correct our latitude by, and the observations for settling the longitude were no less numberous and made as often as the Sun and Moon came in play, so that it was impossible for any material error to creep into our reckoning in the intermediate times. In justice to Mr Green I must say that he was indefatigable in making and calculating these observations which other wise must have taken up a great deal of my time, which I could not at all times very well spare. Not only this but by his instructions several of the Petty Officers can make and calculate these observations almost as well as himself it is only by such means that this method of finding the Longitude at sea can be put into universal practice—a method that we have generally found may be depended upon to within half a degree; which is a degree of accuracy more than sufficient for all Nautical purposes. Would Sea Officers once apply themselves to the making and calculating of these observations they would not find them so very difficult as they at first imagine, especially with the assistance of the Nautical Almanac and Astronomical Ephemeris, by the help of which the calculations for finding the longitude takes but little more time than that of an Azimuth for finding the Variation of the Compass; but unless the Ephemeris is published for some time to come more than either one or two years it can never be of general use in long voyages, and in short voyages it is not so much wanting without it the calculations are laborious and discouraging to beginners and such as are not well versed in these kind of calculations.

It will be noticed that Cook here alludes to the East Coast simply as New Wales. *With his establishing the fact of a strait between New Holland and New Guinea he had achieved one of his major objectives in deciding to come this way home from New Zealand. This was to his 'no small satisfaction', and was the virtual climax of the voyage. The data had been collected, but its utilisation largely depended upon the application and quiet genius of Lieutenant James Cook.*

And so, finally, to Cook's summary of the entire voyage . . . A view prevails on the last paragraph of this summary that perhaps only in a fair-copied set piece could come the 'nonsense' about the happiness, tranquility and simplicity of the inhabitants of

New Holland (which, supposedly, Cook got from conversation with Banks). Such a view would appear to deny Cook any depth of personal perception, though it is manifest enough in many of his passages. Paradoxically, it would seem that, by thus perceiving a little deeper, Cook was over the heads of those who would assess him. To think that Cook would write merely for effect and affectation is to misunderstand his nature. He was the Plain Man, to be taken at face value.

On the 24th, Endeavour *departed Booby Island.*

THE CAPTAIN SUMMARISES:

In the course of this Journal I have at different times made mention of the appearance or aspect of the face of this Country, the nature of the soil, its produce &c[a]. By the first it will appear that to the southward of 33° or 34° the land in general is low and level with very few hills or mountains, further to the northward it may in some places be called hilly, but hardly any where can it be called a Mountainous Country, for the hills and mountains put together take up but a small part of the surface in comparison to what the Planes and Vallies do which intersect and divide these Hills and Mountains: It is indifferently well watered, even in the dry Seasons, with small Brooks and springs, but no great rivers, unless it be in the wet Season when the low lands and Vallies near the sea I do suppose are mostly laid under water; the small brooks may then become large Rivers but this can only happen within the Tropick. It was only in *Thirsty Sound* where we could find no fresh water, excepting one small pool or two which Mr Gore saw in the woods, which no doubt was owing to the country being there very much intersected with salt creeks and Mangrove land.

The low land by the sea and even as far in land as we were, is for the most part friable, loose, sandy soil; yet indifferently fertile and cloathed with woods, long grass, shrubs, plants &c[a]. The mountains or hills are chequered with woods and lawns. Some of the hills are wholly covered with flourishing trees; others but thinly, and the few that are on them are small and the spots of lawns or Savannahs are rocky and barren, especially to the northward where the country did not afford or produce near the vegetation it does to the southward, nor were the trees in the woods half so tall and stout.

The woods do not produce any great variety of trees, there are only 2 or 3 sorts that can be called timber; the largest is the Gum Tree which growes all over the country, the wood of this tree is too hard and ponderous for most common uses. The tree which resembles our Pines, I saw no where in perfection but in Botany Bay, this wood as I have before observed is some thing of the same nature as America Live Oak; in short most of the large trees in this country are of a hard and ponderous nature and could not be applied to many purposes. Here are several sorts of the Palm kind, Mangroves and several other sorts of small trees and shrubs quite unknown to me besides a great variety of plants hitherto unknown, but these things are wholly out of my way to describe, nor will this be any loss since not only plants but everything that can be of use to the Learn'd World will be very accurately described by Mr Banks and Dr Solander. The land naturally produces hardly anything fit for man to eat and the Natives know nothing of cultivation. There are indeed found growing wild in the woods a few sorts of fruits (the most of them unknown to us) which when ripe do not eat a miss, one sort especially which we called Apples, being about the size of a Crab-Apple, it is black and pulpy when ripe, and tastes like a Damson, it hath a large stone or kernel and grows on trees or shrubs.

In the Northern parts of the country as about *Endeavour River*, and probably in many other places, the boggy or watery lands produce Taara or Cocos which when properly cultivated are very good roots, without which they are hardly eatable, the tops however make very good greens.

Land animals are scarce, and so far as we know confined to a very few species; all that we saw I have before mentioned, the sort that is in the greatest plenty is the Kangooroo, or Kanguru so called by the natives; we saw a good many of them about Endeavour River, but killed only three which we found very good eating. Here are like wise Batts, Lizards, Snakes, Scorpions, Centumpees &c[a] but not in any plenty. Tame animals they have none but dogs, and of these we saw but one and therefore must be very scarce, probably they eat them faster than they breed them, we should not have seen this one had he not made us frequent visits while we lay in Endeavour River [dingo?].

The land Fowles are Bustards, Eagles, Hawks, Crows such as we have in England, Cockatoes of two sorts, white and brown, very beautiful birds of the Parrot kind such as Lorryquets &c[a], Pidgeons Doves, Quales, and several sorts of smaller birds. The Sea and Water fowls are Herons, Boobies, Nodies, Gulls, Curlews, Ducks, Pelicans &c[a] and when Mr Banks and Mr Gore were in the country at the head of Endeavour River they saw and heard in the night great numbers of Geese. The sea is indifferently well stocked with fish of various sorts, such as Sharks, Dog-fish, Rock-fish, Mullets, Breams, Cavallies, Mackerel, Old Wives, Leather-Jackets, Five-fingers, Sting-Rays, Whip-rays &c[a]—all excellent in their kind. The Shell-fish are Oysters of 3 or 4 sorts, viz Rock Oysters and Mangrove Oysters which are small, Pearl Oysters, and Mud Oysters, these last are the best and largest I ever saw; Cockles and Clams of several sorts, many of these that are found upon the Reefs are of a Prodigious size; Craw-fish, Crabs, Musles, and a variety of other sorts. Here are also among and upon the shoals and reefs great numbers of the finest Green Turtle in the world and in the rivers and salt creeks are some Aligators.

The natives of this country are of a middle stature straight bodied and slender limbed, their skins the colour of wood soot or of a dark chocolate, their hair mostly black, some lank and others curled, they all wear it cropped short, their beards which are generally black they likewise crop short or singe off. Their features are far from being disagreeable and their voices are soft and tunable. They go quite naked both men and women without any manner of cloathing whatever, even the women do not so much as cover their privities. Altho none of us were ever very near any of their women, one gentleman excepted, yet we are all as well satisfied of this as if we had lived among them. Notwithstanding we had several interviews with the men while we lay at Endeavour River, yet whether through jealousy or disregard they never brought any of their women along with them to the Ship, but always left them on the opposite side of the river where we had frequent opportunities of viewing them through our glasses. They wear as ornaments Necklaces made of shells, Bracelets or hoops about their arms, made mostly of hair twisted and made like a cord hoop, these they wear tight about the upper parts of their arms, and some have girdles made on the same manner. The men wear a bone about 3 or 4 inches long and a fingers thick, run through the Bridge [septum] of the nose, which the seamen called a sprit sail yard; they like wise have holes in their ears for Ear-rings but we never saw them wear any, neither are all the other ornaments wore in common for we have seen as many without as with them. Some of those we saw on Posession Island wore Breast Plates which we supposed were made of Mother of Pearl shells. Many of them paint their bodies and faces with a sort of white paste or pigment, this they apply differint ways each according to his fancy. Their offensive weapons are Darts, some are only pointed at one end others are barbed, some with wood others with the stings of Rays and some with Sharks teeth &c[a], these last are stuck fast on with gum. They throw the dart with only one hand, in the doing of which they make use of a piece of wood about 3 feet long made thin like the blade of a Cutlass, with a little hook at one end to take hold of the end of the Dart, and at the other end is fixed a thin piece of bone about 3 or 4 inches long; the use of this is, I believe, to keep the dart steady and to make it quit the hand in a proper direction; by the help of these throwing sticks, as we call them, they will hit a Mark at the distance of 40 or 50 yards, with almost, if not as much certainty as we can do with a Musquet, and more so than with a ball. These throwing sticks we at first took for wooden swords, and perhaps on some occasions they may use them as such, that is when all their darts are expended, be this as it may they never travel without them and their darts, not altogether for fear of enemies but for killing of game &c[a] as I shall shew hereafter. Their defensive weapons are Shields made of wood but these we never saw used but once in Botany Bay. I do not look upon them to be warlike People, on the contrary I think them to be a timorous and inoffensive People, no ways inclinable to cruelty, as appeared from their behaviour to one of our people in Endeavour River which I have before mentioned. Neither are they very numerous, they live in small parties along by the Sea Coast, the banks of lakes, rivers creeks &c[a]. They seem to have no fixed habitation but move about from place to place like wild beasts in search of food, and I believe depend wholly upon the success of the present day for their subsistence. They have wooden fish gigs with 2, 3 or 4 prongs each very ingeniously made with which they strike fish; we have also seen them strike both fish and birds with their darts. With these they like wise kill other Animals; they have also wooden harpoons for striking turtle, but of these I believe they got but few, except at the season they come ashore to lay. In short these people live wholly by fishing and hunting, but mostly the former, for we never saw an inch of Cultivated land in the whole Country; they know however the use of Taara and sometimes eat them. We do not know that they eat any thing raw but roast or broil all they eat on slow small fires.

Their Houses are mean small hovels not much bigger than an oven, made of pieces of Sticks, Bark, Grass &c[a], and even these are seldom used but in the wet seasons for in the dry times we know that they as often sleep in the open air as any where else. We have seen many of their sleeping places where there has been only some branches, or pieces of bark ris about a foot from the ground on the windward side. Their Canoes are as mean as can be conceived, especially to the Southward where all we saw were made of one piece of bark of trees, about 12 or 14 feet long, drawn or tied together at one end as I have before made mention. These Canoes will not carry above 2 people, in general there is never more than one in them, but bad as they are they do very well for the purpose they apply them to, better than if they were larger, for as they draw but little water they go in them upon the Mud banks and pick up shell fish &c[a] without going out of the canoe. The few canoes we saw to the Northward were made of a log of wood hollowed out, about 14 feet long and very narrow with out-riggers, these will carry 4 people. During our whole stay in Endeavour River we saw but one canoe and had great reason to think that the few people that resided about this place had no more; this one served them to cross the River and to go fishing in &c[a]. They attend the shoals and flatts one where or another every day at low-water to gather shell fish or what ever they can find to eat, and have each a little bag ['Dilly' bag] to put what they get in: this bag is made of net work. They have not the least knowledge of iron or any other metal that we know of; their working tools must be made of stone, bone and shells, those made of the former are very bad if I may judge from one of their Adzes I have seen.

Bad and mean as their canoes are they at certain seasons of the year, so far as we know, go in them to the most distant islands which lay upon the coast, for we never landed upon one but what we saw signs of people having been there before. We were surprised to find houses &c[a] upon Lizard Island which lies 5 leagues from the neareast part of the Main, a distance we before thought that they could not have gone in their Canoes.

The Coast of this Country, at least as much of it as lays to the Northward of 25° of Latitude, abounds with a great number of fine Bays and Harbours, which are sheltered from all winds. But the Country itself so far as we know doth not produce one thing that can become an article in trade to invite Europeans to fix a settlement upon it. However this Eastern side is not that barren and Miserable Country that *Dampier* and others have described the western side to be. We are to consider that we see this country in the pure state of Nature, the industry of Man has had nothing to do with

BEFORE THE WIND, WITH STUDDING SAILS AND DRIVER SET.

any part of it and yet we find all such things as nature hath bestowed upon it in a flourishing state. In this Extensive country it can never be doubted but what most sorts of grain, fruits, roots &c[a] of every kind would flourish here were they once brought hither planted and cultivated by the hand of industry, and here are provender for more cattle at all seasons of the year than ever can be brought in to this Country.

When one considers the proximity of this Country with New-Guiney, New-Britain and several other islands which produce Cocoa-Nutts and many other fruits proper for the Support of Man, it seems strange that they should not long ago have been transplanted here; by its not being done it should seem that the Natives of this Country have no Commerce with their neighbors the New-Guineans, it is very probable that they are a different people and speak a different Language; for the advantage of such as want to clear up this point I shall add a short Vocabulary of a few words in the New-Holland Language which we learnt when in Endeavour River.

English.	*New Holland.*
The head	Whageegee
" Hair of the head	Meul
" Eyes	Morye or More
" Ears	Melea

" Lips	Yembe or Jembi
" Teeth	Mulere or Moile
" Chin	Jacal
" Beard	Waller
" Tongue	Unjar
" Nose	Bonjoo
" Navel	Toolpoor or Julpr
" Penis	Kereil or Kerrial
" Scrotum	Coonal or Kunnol
" Arms	Aco or Acol
" Hands	Mangal
" Thumb	Eboorbalga
" Fore, Middle & Ring Fing[rs]	Egalbaiga
" Little finger	Nakil or Eboornakill
" Thighs	Coman
" Knees	Ponga
" Legs	Peigoorgo
" Feet	Edamal
" Nails	Kolke or Kulke
A Stone	Walba
Sand	Joowal, Yowall or Joralba
A Rope or Line	Goorgo or Gurka
Fire	Maianang or Meanang
The Sun	Gallan or Gallan
" Sky	Kere or Kearre
A Father	Dunjo
A Son	Jumurre
A Man	Bamma or Bámá
A Dog	Cotta or Kota
A Lorryquet	Perpere or Peer-pier
A Cocatoo	Wanda
Male Turtle	Poenja or Poinga
Female "	Mamingo
A great Cocle	Moenjo or Moingo
Cocoa Yamms	Maracotn
A Canoe	Maragan

From what I have said of the Natives of New-Holland they may appear to some to be the most wretched people upon Earth, but in reality they are far more happier than we Europeans; Being wholly unacquainted not only with the superfluous but the necessary Conveniences so sought after in Europe, they are happy in not knowing the use of them. They live in a Tranquillity which is not disturbed by the Inequality of Condition: the Earth and Sea of their own accord furnishes them with all things necessary for life, they Covert not Magnificient Houses, Household-stuff &c[a], they live in a warm and fine Climate and enjoy very wholesome Air, so that they have little need of Clothing and this they seem to be fully sencible of, for many to whome we gave Cloth &c[a] to, left it carelessly upon the Sea beach and in the woods as a thing they had no manner of use for. In short they seemed to set no Value upon any thing we gave them, nor would they ever part with any thing of their own for any one article we could offer them; this in my opinion argues that they think themselves provided with all the necessarys of Life and that they have no superfluities.

Thus, this compassionate man, who was able to sense in the native people something of his own innate feelings, took his departure from this ancient and somnolent land, leaving its children to continue their Dreaming a little longer.

NOTES TO PART I

NMM = National Maritime Museum, Greenwich, London
ADM./Adm. = Admiralty
PRO = Public Records Office, Surrey, United Kingdom
BL = British Library, London
op. cit. = in the work quoted above
loc. cit. = as quoted above

PREFACE

1 Beaglehole, *Cook*, vol. I, p. 399

INTRODUCTION

1 Knight, pp. 292–302
2 NMM ADM. 3814b, 1768
3 NMM ADM. 3819 and 3819a
4 PRO Adm. 106/3315, 22597
5 The ships surveyed were: *Valentine*; *Earl of Pembroke* (commissioned two months later as *Endeavour*); *Ann* and *Elizabeth*.
6 Beaglehole, vol. I
7 R. M. (Max) Crawford, one of the most influential teachers of Australian history, was professor of history at the University of Melbourne from 1937 to 1971.
8 Letter to author, 6 December 1969.
9 Assisted by a Special Purposes Grant from the Literature Board of the Australia Council.
10 Pepys's reforming era.
11 Chapelle, p. 40
12 BL Add. MS 9345, folios 15v, 16v, 50 and 57
13 BL Add. MS 9345
14 BL Add. MS 9345, folios 21, 21v, 23v and 24
15 PRO Adm. 95/94
16 Beaglehole, *Cook*, vol. I, p. 95
17 Beaglehole, *Banks*, vol. I, p. 281
18 op. cit., p. 283
19 Beaglehole, *Banks*, vol. II, p. 79
20 op. cit., pp. 105–6
21 Villiers, pp. 161 and 177
22 Beaglehole, *Cook*, vol. I, p. 620
23 Beaglehole, *Banks*, vol. II, p. 141
24 'Woolwich Yard, 16 October 1771, Bark Endeavour', National Maritime Museum. Plan reg. no.: 3819; ship or subject: Endeavour; press mark: box 54

Chapter 1: The Sailor and His Environment

1 Beaglehole, *Cook*, vol. I, p. 3
2 Rope is measured by its circumference.
3 A fathom equals six feet.
4 Philip Carteret, her captain, leaves no doubt about the seriousness of being deprived of two things: junk and a forge. iI was only the calibre of Carteret the man that averted disaster and gave us something inspiring in terms of seamanship, not to mention guts and uncommon understanding of his men.
5 Falconer (US edn), p. 620
6 Beaglehole, *Cook*, vol. I, p. 521
7 Rees, p. 117
8 Beaglehole, *Cook*, vol. 1, p. 375
9 'Swinging the lead' is something different: skulking or dodging work, implied by idly swinging the lead instead of heaving it and getting a sounding.
10 Runciman, pp. 83–4
11 *Endeavour*'s log line was knotted every 49 feet (15 metres). See Gore's log, 26 August 1768: 'The Length of each ordinary Knott of our normal log Line 49 feet and The Glass 29 seconds of Time.'

Chapter 2: The Captain

1 Badger, p. 13
2 op. cit., pp. 27 and 28
3 In 1771, the nautical mile was reckoned at 6,120 feet; it is now 6,080 feet.
4 Forbes, p. 6. Mayer's italics.
5 op. cit., p. v
6 Taylor, p. 1
7 Beaglehole, *Cook*, vol. I, p. 392
8 op. cit., p. 501
9 op. cit., p. 392
10 Taylor, pp. 1–2
11 Metropolitan Toronto Library Board, Canada. An edited version of this letter is quoted in Badger, pp. 3–4.
12 Taken out of commission, crew discharged.
13 Colville to Cleveland, 30 December 1762, Adm. 1/482, quoted in Beaglehole, *Cook*, vol. I, p. 59
14 Beaglehole, *Cook*, vol. I, p. 74
15 op. cit., p. 79
16 op. cit., p. 80

Chapter 3: The Ship

1 Quoted in Knight, p. 293
2 Quoted in Knight, pp. 296–7
3 Falconer (UK edn), pp. 14 and 18
4 Beaglehole, *Cook*, vol. II, p. 280
5 Beaglehole, *Cook*, vol. I, p. 608
6 op. cit., p. 636
7 Ships on independent voyages always wore the red ensign.
8 The goat in *Endeavour* had already made a complete voyage around the world in *Dolphin* with Captain Wallis, as shipmate of several of the men sailing again with her now. She had spent just ninety days ashore before being drafted back to sea again in this ship. But at the completion of this voyage she was to be honourably retired to English pastures for the rest of her life.
9 See Parkinson.
10 It was from its form when well lashed up that the hammock took its nickname, when I was young, of 'banana bedstead'.
11 A phrase used by Nelson in a letter.
12 It is worth noting that *Endeavour* stowed only stone and iron ballast, and not any shingle, which can become very foul. There is one recorded case of an admiral's body being buried in the shingle of a ship-of-the-line to be brought home for burial ashore. But *Endeavour*'s bilges were comparatively sweet.

CHAPTER 4: SCURVY AND PROVISIONS

1 See extract from John Knyveton, page 86.
2 *Encyclopaedia Britannica*, pp. 106–7
3 Smith, p. 96
4 Knyveton, p. 71
5 Knyveton, p. 112
6 Quoted by Knyveton, pp. 116–17
7 Scott, R.F., *Voyage of the Discovery*, London, 1905, quoted in *Problems of Medicine at Sea*, p. 24
8 Knyveton, p. 115
9 Lind, J.A., *A Treatise on Scurvy*, ed. C.P. Stewart & D. Guthrie, Edinburgh, 1953, quoted in *Problems of Medicine at Sea*, p. 23
10 *Problems of Medicine at Sea*, p. 22
11 Beaglehole, *Cook*, vol. I, p. 610
12 op. cit., p. 612
13 loc. cit.
14 loc. cit.
15 loc. cit.
16 Beaglehole, *Cook*, vol. I, p. 614
17 op. cit., p. 619
18 op. cit., p. 615
19 loc. cit. It is to be remembered that Cook was ship's purser as well as commander.
20 Beaglehole, *Cook*, vol. I, pp. 622–3
21 op. cit., p. 623
22 op. cit., p. 613
23 Falconer (US edn), p. 359
24 loc. cit.
25 Knyveton, p. 38
26 Beaglehole, *Banks*, vol. I, pp. 393–4
27 This describes not sauerkraut but Banks's own pickled cabbage.
28 Beaglehole, *Banks*, vol. I, pp. 248–9
29 Beaglehole, *Banks*, vol. I, p. 471

CHAPTER 5: THE SHIP'S COMPANY

1 Beaglehole, *Cook*, vol. I, p. cxxix
2 op. cit., p. 637
3 Beaglehole, *Cook*, vol. IV, p. 21
4 Beaglehole, *Cook*, vol. I, p. xxxv
5 Dan. C Solander to Carl Linnaeus, 1 December 1768; this translation published in E. Duyker and Per Tingbrand (eds & trans.), *Daniel Solander: Collected Correspondence 1753–1782*, Miegunyah/Melbourne University Press, Melbourne, 1996
6 The source of this passage is uncertain. It is believed to have been quoted in Beaglehole, J.C. (ed.), *The Journals of Captain James Cook on His Voyages of Discovery*, vol. II: *The Voyage of* Resolution, Cambridge University Press for the Hakluyt Society, London.
7 Beaglehole, *Cook*, vol. I, p. 74
8 op. cit., p. 366
9 op. cit., p. 635
10 op. cit., p. 501
11 op. cit., p. 637
12 Stanbury, p. 356
13 Quoted by Captain Robert FitzRoy in Stanbury, p. 39

CHAPTER 6: FROM MISFORTUNE, AND BY THEIR SINS

1 Beaglehole, *Cook*, vol. I, p. 7
2 Beaglehole, *Banks*, vol. I, pp. 220–2
3 op. cit., p. 222
4 loc. cit.
5 PRO Adm. 51/4546/152
6 Beaglehole, *Cook*, vol. I, p. 67
7 Beaglehole, *Banks*, vol. I, pp. 242–3

8 Beaglehole, *Cook*, vol. I, p. 81
9 Beaglehole, *Banks*, vol. I, pp. 257–8
10 Beaglehole, *Cook*, vol. I, pp. 159–60
11 PRO Adm. 51/4546/147–8
12 Beaglehole, *Banks*, vol. I, pp. 288–9
13 Falconer (US edn), pp. 666–75
14 Beaglehole, *Banks*, vol. I, p. 277
15 PRO Adm. 51/4547/149–50
16 For the 21st: Beaglehole, *Cook*, vol. I, p. 558; for the 28th: op. cit., p. 559
17 Knyveton, p. 19
18 op. cit., pp. 23–4
19 op. cit., pp. 42–3
20 Quoted by Captain Robert FitzRoy in Stanbury, pp. 39–40
21 Beaglehole, *Banks*, vol. I, pp. 266–7
22 Beaglehole, *Cook*, vol. I, p. 554
23 op. cit., p. 98
24 op. cit., p. 114
25 op. cit., pp. 562–3
26 Parkinson, p. 35
27 Beaglehole, *Cook*, vol. I, p. 563
28 op. cit., pp. 114–15
29 Beaglehole, *Banks*, vol. I, pp. 310–11
30 Beaglehole, *Cook*, vol. I, pp. 115–16
31 Beaglehole, *Banks*, vol. I, pp. 311–12
32 Munkhouse's log, Mitchell Library, Sydney, CY Reel 157, Safe 1/29
33 PRO Adm. 51/4546/147–8
34 Beaglehole, *Cook*, vol. I, pp. 117
35 Beaglehole, *Banks*, vol. I, pp. 312–13
36 op. cit., pp. 313–14
37 Parkinson, p. 66
38 Beaglehole, *Cook*, vol. I, pp. 563–4
39 op. cit., p. 598
40 op. cit., p. 217, Note 1
41 op. cit., p. 215
42 Beaglehole, *Banks*, vol. I, pp. 440–1
43 Beaglehole, *Cook*, vol. I, p. 216

CHAPTER 7: PERADVENTURE

1 PRO Adm. 51/4548/145–6
2 Beaglehole, *Cook*, vol. I, p. 535
3 op. cit., pp. 565–6
4 op. cit., pp. 566–8
5 op. cit., pp. 568–9
6 op. cit., pp. 170–71
7 PRO Adm. 55/39
8 Beaglehole, *Banks*, vol. I, pp. 403–4
9 Beaglehole, *Cook*, vol. I, p. 172
10 op. cit., p. 214
11 17 August 1770; op. cit., p. 38

BIBLIOGRAPHY

Badger, G.M. (ed.), *Captain Cook: Navigator and Scientist—Papers presented at the Cook Bicentenary Symposium, Australian Academy of Science, Canberra, 1 May 1969*, Australian National University Press, Canberra, 1970

Beaglehole, J.C. (ed.), *The Endeavour Journal of Joseph Banks 1768–1771*, vol. I, Public Library of New South Wales/Angus & Robertson Ltd, Sydney, 2nd edition, 1963

——, *The* Endeavour Journal of *Joseph Banks 1768–1771*, vol. II, Public Library of New South Wales/Angus & Robertson Ltd, Sydney, 2nd edition, 1963

——, *The Journals of Captain James Cook on His Voyages of Discovery*, vol. I: *The Voyage of the* Endeavour *1768–1771*, Cambridge University Press for the Hakluyt Society, London, 1955

——, *The Journals of Captain James Cook on His Voyages of Discovery*, vol. IV: *The Life of Captain James Cook*, The Hakluyt Society c/o The British Museum, London,1974

Chapman, F. af, *Architectura Navalis Mercatoria* (1768), reprinted by Adlard Coles Ltd, London, 1971

Chapelle, H. I., *The History of the American Sailing Navy: the ships and their development*, Bonanza Books, New York, 1949?

Encyclopaedia Britannica, vol. III (M–Z), Edinburgh, 1771

Falconer's Marine Dictionary (1780), William Falconer, reprinted by David & Charles (Publishers) Limited, Devon, United Kingdom, 1970

Forbes, E.G., *The Birth of Navigational Science*, Maritime Monographs and Reports, No. 10—1974, National Maritime Museum, Greenwich, London

Knight, C., 'H.M. Bark *Endeavour*', in *The Mariner's Mirror*, vol. XIX, The Society for Nautical Research, London, 1933

New Universal Dictionary of the Marine, originally compiled by William Falconer, modernized and enlarged by William Burney (1815), reprinted by Library Editions Ltd, New York, 1970

Parkinson, S., *A Journal of a Voyage to the South Seas* (1773), Australiana Facsimile Editions No. A34, the Libraries Board of South Australia, Adelaide, 1972

Problems of Medicine at Sea, Maritime Monographs and Reports, No. 12, National Maritime Museum, Greenwich, London, 1974

Rees, A., *Naval Architecture (1819–20): the cyclopaedia; or universal dictionary of arts, sciences and literature*, reprinted by David & Charles (Publishers) Limited, Devon, United Kingdom, 1970

Runciman, W., *Collier Brigs and Their Sailors*, T. Fisher Unwin Ltd, London, 1926

Smith, Captain J., *A Sea Grammar*, 1627, ed. Kermit Goell, Michael Joseph, London, 1970

Stanbury, D. (ed.), *A Narrative of the Voyage of H.M.S. Beagle*, The Folio Society, London, 1977

Surgeon's Mate: the diary of John Knyveton, surgeon in the British Fleet during the Seven Years War, 1756–1762, ed. and transcr. Ernest Gray, Robert Hale Limited, London, 1942

Taylor, E.G.R., *Navigation in the Days of Captain Cook*, Maritime Monographs and Reports, No. 18—1974, National Maritime Museum, Greenwich, London, 1975

Villiers, A., *Captain Cook, the Seamen's Seaman*, Penguin, Harmondsworth, 1969

INDEX OF INDIVIDUALS AND LOCATIONS

Occupations of the crew of *Endeavour* are shown in parentheses beside names. 'A.B.' refers to Able Bodied Seaman.

References to illustrations are in italics.

'153', 196, 210, 414, 440, 444

Abbot Point, 283
Aborigines, 167–8, 177–8, 221, 433, 440–2, 449–54
  aggressive incidents involving, 184–5, 191, 194–6
  at Botany Bay, 180–97, 200, 203
  at Bustard Bay, 243–6
  at Endeavour River, 342, 347, 350, 353–4, 356–8, 361, 365–6, 374, 388–90
  at Halifax Bay, 292
  at Thirsty Sound, 265
  canoes, *193*, 356
  fires, 174, 216, 328, 367–70
  huts, 185
  language, 452–3
  on the Family Isles, 293
Admiralty Bay, 147
Anderson, Robert (Quartermaster), 96, 106, 119–20
Archer Point, 323
Asolphus Islands, 437

Banks, Joseph (Naturalist), 98
  attitude to Aborigines, 181, 186–7, 196–7
  botanical work, 197, 199, 201, 203, 329, 449
  cabin, 80, 84
  effect on Cook, 59, 419
  hunting, 49, 191
  in New Zealand, 131
  journal of, 28, 30, 31, 32, 107–8, 142
    Aborigines, 292, 358–9, 366
    arrival in New Holland, 158
    Botany Bay, 182–6, 188–90, 192–6, 199, 203
    confirms Parkinson's drawing, 26
    deaths of Buchan, Greenslade and Reading 113–14
    departure from Endeavour River, 383–5, 394, 396–8, 400, 402–6, 410
    Endeavour Reef, 302–4, 312–14,
    Endeavour River, 325–32, 334–42, 344–50, 352–9, 362–6, 368–81
    kangaroos, 336
    New Zealand, 128–30, 135–6, 148–9, 152–7
    Point Hicks to Botany Bay, 160–1, 167–9, 171, 174–6, 178
    Port Jackson to Sandy Cape, 202, 206–8, 211, 213, 215–16, 219, 221, 223, 226, 229–33
    Reef to Booby Island, 413, 416–18, 422–3, 425, 427, 433–4, 436, 440, 445
    Tahiti, 124–7
    Thirsty Sound to Trinity Bay, 269, 273, 275–6, 278, 280, 284, 287–8, 292, 295–8
    worship, 115–16
  misadventure on Tierra del Fuego, 111–13
  on discipline, 121
  on provisions, 94–5
  opinion of Parkinson, 13–16,
  opinion of the *Endeavour*, 69
  retinue, 71, 76, 79–80, 102
Bare Island, 189
Bare Islet, 201
Barren Head, 287
Barren Isles, 269
Barrenjoey Head, 210
Batavia, 108
Bateman Bay, 166

Batts, Elizabeth, 65
Bay of Islets, 273–4
Beaglehole, J.C., 5–6, 59–60, 176, 246, 429
Bedwell Group, 270, 273
Bellambi Point, 174
Bird Island (Isles), 433–4
Bisset, 63–4
Black Head, 214
Blackbird Patches, 326
Blackwood Shoals, 276, 278
Bligh, Captain William, 172
Bligh Reef, 419
Bolt Head, 427, 430
Booby Island, 446, 448
Boomerang Shoal, 269
Boondelabah Island, 214
Bootie, John (Midshipman), 96
  journal of, 195, 207, 262, 377, 401, 420, 424, 426, 438, 444
Booty Island, 429
Botany Bay, 180–203, 448–9
Boulder Reef, 364, 392; *see also* Turtle Reef
Bowles, John (Marine), 98
Boydong Cays, 433–4
Brampton Island, 276
Break Sea Spit, 234, 236–7
Briscoe, Peter (Banks's Footman), 32, 98, 103, 111–13
  journal of, 99, 219
Broad Sound, 266, 269–70, 274
Broad Sound Channel, 260, 276
Broken Bay, 206, 210
Brook Islands, 293
Broughton Island, 214
Brown, Robert, 99
Brush Island, 167
Buchan, Alexander (Landscape Artist), 98, 103–4, 111–14
Buchan Rock, 429
Bulli, 174
Burnett River, 238
Bushy Island, 435–6
Bustard Bay, 243–5
Bustard Head, 247

Cabbage Tree Island, 214
Cairncross Islets, 435–6
Cairns Reef, 323
Caloundra Head, 226
Cape Banks, 191
Cape Bedford, 323, 385, 402
Cape Bowling Green, 285
Cape Byron, 220–1
Cape Capricorn, 248–9
Cape Cleveland, 287, 291
Cape Clinton, 259
Cape Conway, 278–9
Cape Cornwell, 442
Cape Dromedary, 165
Cape Farewell, 149–50
Cape Flattery, 401–2, 404
Cape Gloucester, 280, 283–4
Cape Grafton, 295–8
Cape Grenville, 427, 429, 434
Cape Hawke, 213
Cape Hillsborough, 275–6, 278
Cape Howe, 160–3
Cape Keppel, 253
Cape Kidnappers, 138
Cape Kimberley, 298
Cape Manyfold, 256–9
Cape Morton, 213, 225
Cape Palmerston, 273–4
Cape Sandwich, 291, 293
Cape Solander, 191
Cape St George, 171–3
Cape Three Points, 206, 208
Cape Townshend, 258–9, 263, 273–4
Cape Tribulation, 297–8, 304
Cape Upstart, 284–5
Cape Weymouth, 422
Cape York, 435, 437
Carpentaria, 446
Charco Harbour, 331; *see also* Endeavour River
Charlton, John (Captain's Servant), 97, 100
Childs, Josiah (Captain's Cook), 97
Clarence River, 221
Clerke, Charles (Master's Mate), 96, 100
  journal of, 198, 293
Clerke Island, 429
Cleveland Bay, 285
Coaster Channel, 276
Cockburn Isles, 427, 429
Cockburn Reef, 429, 431
Collett, William (Barber), 97
Colville, Lord, 65
Cook, James, 32, 58–63, 96, 418–19
  and Aborigines, 187, 190, 358–9, 366, 390, 449–50
  as purser, 90–1
  as teacher of Bligh, 172
  biography, 63–7
  children of, 66–7, 115
  discipline, 117–23
  journal of, 43, 106–7, 138
    arrival in New Holland, 158
    Botany Bay, 180–2, 187–8, 191–5, 198, 201–2
    death of Buchan, 114
    departure from Endeavour River, 382–6, 391–8, 400, 402–10
    Endeavour Reef, 300–2, 311–12, 320–1,

Endeavour River, 325, 327–35, 337–52, 354–8, 361–3, 365–8, 371–2, 374–81
Endeavour's boats, 30
New Zealand, 128–30, 132, 134–7, 147–8, 151–7
Point Hicks to Botany Bay, 160, 163–7, 169, 171, 173, 175–7
Port Jackson to Sandy Cape, 205–8, 211, 213–20, 222–33
Reef to Booby Island, 413–16, 421–2, 424–7, 431–3, 435–6, 441–2, 445–7
summary and Aboriginal lexicon, 448–54
Tahiti, 123–5
Thirsty Sound to Trinity Bay, 267, 270–3, 275, 277–80, 284–8, 291–2, 295, 297
marriage, 66
observations, 342–3
opinion of the *Endeavour*, 70, 74
promoted to Lieutenant, 72
relations with crew, 48, 106–8, 323, 372
relations with the Maori, 128–33
Cook's Passage, 51, 408, 411
Cooktown, 317
Cowlishaw Reef, 326
Cox, Matthew (A.B.), 98, 130
Cumberland Isles, 278, 280
Currockbilly, 167
Curtis Island, 249

Dalrymple, 304
Dalton, George (Banks' Servant), 98, 104, 111–13
Dampier's Strait, 149
Dawson, William (Cooper's Steward), 97
Dawson Reef, 326
Dent Island, 282
Disaster Bay, 163
Divided Island, 253
Dolphin Point, 282
Donovan Shoal, 260
Dootaha, *see* Tutuhah
Double Cone Island, 282
Double Island Point, 227–9
Double Point, 296
Dozey, John (A.B.), 98, 102
Duke Islands, 266, 269
Dunk Island (Isle), 293, 296
Dunster, Thomas (Marine), 98, 119, 288–90

Eagle Islet (Island), 402, 405–6
Eagle Reef, 402
East Islets, 433–4, 436
Ebora Island, 435
Edgecumbe, John (Marine Sargeant), 98, 188
Edgecumbe Bay, 280, 283
Endeavour reef, 73, 306–20, 313
Endeavour River, 28, 324–69, *330*, 385–6, 408, 449–51
Endeavour Strait, 440, 446
Esk Island, 290
Eva Island, 293
Evans, Samuel (Quartermaster), 96, 131, 348

Facing Island, 249
Fairway Rock, 249
False Cape, 298
Family Isles, 293
Fantome Island, 292
Fiddle Head, 227
Fingal Head, 223
First Stony Point, 430
Fitzroy, Captain Robert, 121
Fitzroy Island, 296
Fitzroy River, 249, 253
Five Islands, 179
Flat Isles, 269
Flat Islet, 257
Flat Rock, 226
Flinders, Matthew, 170, 172, 249, 260, 343
Flowers, Peter (A.B.), 97, 100, 102, 111
Forbes's Isles, 427, 429
Forrester Reef, 394, 397
Forwood, Stephen (Gunner), 81, 96, 128
journal of, 182, 195, 199, 207, 379, 401, 440
Forwood Reef, 429
Frankland Isles, 295–6
Fraser Island, 229, 238
Funchal, Madiera, 110

Gabo Island, 160–3
Gathrey, John (Boatswain), 30, 80
Georges River, 196
Gibson, Samuel (Marine), 98, 106, 123–6, 128
Glasshouse Bay, 226
Glasshouse Mountains, 225, 226
Gloucester Head, 283
Gloucester Island, 283
Gloucester Passage, 283
Gold Coast, 223
Goodjohn, John (Cooper's Mate), 97
Gore, John (Second Lieutenant), 81, 96, 101, 449
and Aborigines, 190–1, 342
at Endeavour River, 355–7
hunting, 49, 191, 196, 266, 343, 361, 378
journal of, 131–2
Gore Island, 429
Grassy Hill, 344
Gray, James (A.B.), 97
Great Barrier Reef, 31, 51, 282, 298, 305, 367, 410
Great Keppel Island, 254, 256–7
Great Palm Island, 287, 290

Green Cape, 163
Green, Charles (Astronomer), 62, 67, 98, 99, 101, 351, 374
  illness, 328, 331
  in New Zealand, 132–4
  journal of, 142, 182, 220–1, 229, 378, 407, 412, 414
  misadventure on Tierra del Fuego, 111–13
  observations, 165, 342–3, 407, 412, 414, 420, 447
Green Island, 276, 297–8, 304
Greenslade, William (Marine), 83, 98
  death, 113–14

Haggerstone Island, 429
Haite, Francis (Carpenter's Crew), 97, 100
Halfway Islets (Isle), 433–4, 436
Halifax Bay, 288, 291, 293
Hamilton Island, 282
Hardmand, Thomas (Bos'ns Mate), 97
Harvey, William (First Lieutenant's Mate), 97
Harvey Island, 429
Hat Hill, 173
Havannah Island, 290
Hawkes Bay, 137–8
Hayman Island, 282
Hervey('s) Bay, 236, 238
Hervey Isles, 259
Hickes, Zachary (First Lieutenant), 81, 96, 101, 124, 187
  journal of,
    Botany Bay, 191–2
    death of Reading, 114
    Endeavour River, 327, 330, 381, 383
    New Zealand, 128–30
    Reef to Booby Island, 414, 440, 444
    Tahiti, 126
  sights New Holland, 158
Hicks Island, 429
Hillsborough Channel, 276
Hinchinbrook Island, 293
Holburn Isle, 280
Holland, Major Samuel, 64
Home Islands, 429; *see also* Cockburn Isles
Hook Island, 282–3
Hope Islands, 304, 311, 320–1, 323
Horn Island, 435
Howson, William (Captain's Servant), 97, 100
Hughes, Richard (Carpenter's Mate), 97, 319
Hulme, Dr, 253–4
Hume, David, 317
Hummocky Island, 249
Hutchins, Richard (Bos'ns Mate), 97, 121

Indian Head, 231, 367
Inscription Point, 191
Iron Head, 291
Island Head, 259
Island Point, 298
Islands of Direction, 408

Jeffs, Henry (Butcher), 97, 121–2
Jervis Bay, 172–3
Johnson, Isaac (Cooper), 97
Jones, Samuel (A.B.), 98, 121
Jones, Thomas (A.B.), 98
Jones, Thomas (Surgeon's Servant), 97
Jordan, Benjamin (Carpenter's Mate), 98
Jordan, Thomas (Ship's Cook's Servant), 97
Judge, William (Marine Private), 98, 119–20
Jumpin Pin, 223

Kauffman, Dr Virgil, 317
Kennedy Sound, 279
Keppel Bay, 213, 249, 256
Keppel Isles, 305
Knight, Thomas (Lieutenants' Cook), 97
Knyveton, John, 87–8, 92, 116–18
Kurnell, 188, 203

Labyrinth, 237
Labyrinth Harbour, 262
Laguna Bay, 226
Lake Shoals, 270, 273
Lark Reef, 392
Laurel Reef, 429
Lind, Dr James, 86–9 (*passim*)
Little Island, 214
Littleboy, Michael (A.B.), 98
Littleboy, Richard (A.B.), 98, 128
Lizard Island, 403–8
Long Island, 266, 282
Long Nose, 173
Low Wooded Island, 400

Magnetic(al) Head, 285–7
Magnetic Island, 287
Magra, James (A.B.), 97, 102, 342
  assault on Mr Orton, 242, 245–6, 325
Magra Island, 429
Manley, Isaac George (Master's Servant), 97, 108, 374
Manley Island, 429
Marble Island, 266
Martin Reef, 402
Maskelyne, Rev. Nevil, 62
Mason Reef, 429
Mathews, Thomas (Ship's Cook's Servant), 97
Mayer, Tobias, 61–2
McBride, Dr David, 88, 89
Merimbula, 163
Mid Rock, 437
Middle Brother, 215
Mission Bay, 298
Molyneux, Robert (Master), 81, 96, 100, 347–8, 374

advice to Cook, 395, 406
examines *Endeavour*'s bottom, 339
log of, 27, 113, 116
New Zealand, 135–7
on discipline, 121–2
on Tupia and Tarheto, 128
Tahiti, 123
turtle hunting, 355, 357
Moody, Samuel (Carpenter's Crew), 97
Moody Reef, 429
Moreton Bay (present day), 226
Moreton Island, 226
Morey, Nathaniel (Second Lieutenant's Mate), 97
Morton Bay (as named by Cook), 224–6
Mount Adolphus, 435, 437
Mount Beerwah, 226
Mount Bertha, 283
Mount Budawang, 167
Mount Coonowrin, 226
Mount Dromedary, 160, 165, 167–8
Mount Kembla, 173
Mount Millman, 364
Mount Proserpine, 278
Mount Saunders, 364
Mount Tibrogargan, 226
Mount Warning, 221–2
Munkhouse, Jonathan (Midshipman), 33, 81, 92, 96, 101, 124, 191
journal of, 126
repairs *Endeavour* leak, 321–3
Munkhouse, William Brougham (Surgeon), 96, 101, 106, 116
New Zealand, 131–2
journal of, 132–4
misadventure on Tierra del Fuego, 111–13

Nambucca Heads, 216
New Castle Bay, 436
New Guinea, 149
New Holland, 149, 158–9, 441–2
New South Wales, 442–3
New Wales, 442, 447
New Zealand
crew's relations with the Maori of, 128–38
departure from, 147–50
need for security in, 49
Newcastle Harbour, 212
Nicholson, James (A.B.), 98, 122–3
Nobbys Head, 212
Nomad Reef, 429
Noosa Head, 227
North Barnard Island, 296
North Brother, 215
North Head, 247
North Keppel Island, 254, 256–7
North Molle Island, 282
North Point Islands, 269–70
North Stradbroke Island, 223, 226

Northumberland Isles, 260, 266
Nowell, George (Carpenter's Crew), 97, 350

Obreea, 123–6
Onrust Island, 351
Orfordness, 434
Orton, Richard (Captain's Clerk), 81, 96, 102, 242–6
Orton Island, 429
Outer Rock, 257

Palliser, Captain Hugh, 63–4
Palm Islands, 290, 292
Paluma Range, 288, 291
Parker, Isaac (Bos'ns Mate), 97, 115
Parkinson, Sydney (Botanical Artist), 98, 103, 114
and Aborigines, 390
botanical drawings, 215
drawings of *Endeavour* and boats, 12–34
journal of, 110, 142
arrival in New Holland, 158
assault on Mr Orton, 245–6
attitudes to Aborigines, 187
Botany Bay, 186, 199–200, 202
Bustard Bay to Sandy Point, 245, 247, 249, 253, 257, 259, 262, 265
departure from Endeavour River, 394, 401
Endeavour Reef, 303, 314, 322
Endeavour River, 326, 331, 336, 350, 385, 387–90
New Zealand, 149, 157
Point Hicks to Botany Bay, 161, 165–6, 169, 174, 176
Port Jackson to Bustard Bay, 208, 211–13, 219, 221, 226, 229, 233–4, 237, 241
Reef to Booby Island, 418, 423, 425, 440–1, 444–5
Tahiti, 123, 126–7
Thirsty Sound to Trinity Bay, 273, 276, 278, 280–2, 288–90, 292
Paul, Henry (Marine), 98
Peak Island, 253
Peaked Islet, 257, 259
Peckover, William (A.B.), 98
Pelican Island, 253
Pelorus Islands, 292
Pentecost Island, 279
Periera, Manoel (A.B.), 98, 102, 111, 128–30
Perry, William (Surgeon's Mate), 96, 101
Perry Island, 429
Pickersgill, Richard (Master's Mate), 96, 101, 374
journal of, 160, 165, 167, 178,
Botany Bay 189, 192, 195, 198–9
departure from Endeavour River, 398
Endeavour Bay, 300
Endeavour Reef, 314

Endeavour River, 341–2, 362–3, 366, 368, 370, 375, 378, 380–1
Reef to Booby Island, 414, 420, 426
Pickersgill Reef, 305, 320
Pier Head, 266–7, 270
Pigeon–house Hill, 163, 165, 167–8
Pine Island, 282
Point Danger, 223
Point Hicks, 143, 158
Point Hillock, 291, 293
Point Kepple, 213
Point Lookout (on Stradbroke Island), 224–6
Point Lookout, 402
Point Slade, 276
Point Solander, 191
Point Stephens, 213
Point Sutherland, 188
Point Upright, 167
Ponto, Antonio (A.B.), 98, 102
Port Clinton, 259
Port Curtis, 249
Port Denison, 283
Port Hacking, 175
Port Jackson, 202
Port Kembla, 179
Port Stephens, 213–14
Possession Island, 442, 446
Poverty Bay, 131
Preston, Daniel (Marine), 98
Prince of Wales's Islands, 446
Proserpine River, 278
Providential Channel, 422
Pullen Reef, 392

Quail Island, 266
Quetta Rock, 437–8
Quoin Island, 259

Ram Head, 158
Ramsay, John (A.B.), 98
Ravenhill, John (Sailmaker), 49, 96
Reading, John Kinsale (Bos'ns Mate), 96, 114–15, 119–21
Reardon, Timothy (Bos'ns Yeoman), 97
Red Point, 173, 179
Repulse Bay, 278, 280
Repulse Islands, 278–9
Reynolds, John (Green's Servant), 98
Richmond, Thomas (Banks' Servant), 98, 104, 111–13
Richmond River, 221
Rio de Janeiro, 111
Roberts, Daniel (Gunner's Servant), 97
Roberts, James (Banks' Footman), 32, 98, 103, 111–13
journal of, 99, 122, 202, 213, 215, 219
Rockingham Bay, 291, 293
Rocky Mount, 367
Ross River, 287
Rossiter, Thomas (Marine Drummer), 98, 128
Rothsay Banks, 446
Round Hill Creek, 242
Round Hill Head, 247
Rundle Island, 249

St Lawrence River, 64–5
Sandy Cape, 233
Sandy Shoal, 276
Satterly, John (Carpenter), 80, 96, 313, 319, 351
Saunders, Patrick (Midshipman), 96, 246
Saunders Island, 429
Scott, Captain, 87–8
Seventy–Five Mile Beach, 229
Ship Rock, 249
Shoalwater Bay, 260, 266, 274
Shortland Reef, 437
Simcoe, Captain John, 64
Simmonds, Thomas (A.B.), 98
Simpson, Alexander (A.B.), 98, 128
Sir Charles Hardys Isles, 427, 429
Sir James Smith Group, 278
Smith, Isaac (A.B.), 97, 100, 108, 187
Smith, Captain John, 86
Smo(o)ky Cape, 216–17
Smythe Shoals, 274
Snapper Island, 298
Solander, Dr Daniel (Naturalist) 32, 80, 92, 98, 102–3
and Aborigines, 190, 365–6
botanical work, 199, 201, 203, 329, 449
misadventure on Terra del Fuego, 111–13
New Zealand, 131
Solitary Islands, 221
South Brother, 215
South Head, 247
South Ledge Reef, 435, 437
South Stradbroke Island, 223
Southport, 223
Spöring, Herman (Asst. Naturalist), 98, 103
Stainsby, Robert (A.B.), 98, 138
Startle Reef, 394, 397
Stephens, Henry (A.B.), 98, 119, 128–30
Still, John (Gunner's Servant), 97
Stingray Bay, 190, 198–9; *see also* Botany Bay; Stingray Harbour
Stingray Harbour, 190, 203, 287; *see also* Botany Bay; Stingray Bay
Stony Shoal, 276
Strong Tide Passage, 260
Sutherland, 191
Sutherland, Forby (Poulterer), 97, 188, 190–1
Sutherland Point, 191
Swinger Reef, 392

Tahiti, 95, 106–7, 114, 115, 121–8
Tarheto (Tupia's Boy Servant), 98, 126–7, 138

Tasmania, *see* Van Diemen's Land
Taylor, Robert (Armourer), 96
Telegraph Point, 161–3
Temple Bay, 427, 429–30
Terrell, Edward (Carpenter's Crew), 97
Thirsty Sound, 263, 266–70, 273, 448
Thompson John (Ship's Cook), 81, 96, 99–100
Three Brothers, 214–15
Thurman (Thurmond), John (Sailmaker's Mate), 97, 110–11, 119, 122–3
Tiato, see Tarheto
Tierra del Fuego, 111–13
Tom Thumb Lagoon, 179
Tom Ugly's Point, 196
Torch Shoal, 276
Townshend Island, 260
Trinity Bay, 297–8
Tropic of Capricorn, 248
Truslove, John (Marine Corporal), 98, 124
Tunley, James (A.B.), 98
Tupia (Interpreter), 98, 126–7, 132–5, 137, 353
  and Aborigines, 190, 193, 363
  cooking, 341
  illness, 328, 330
Turtle Reef, 364, 385, 392, 395
Tutuhah, 123–6
Tweed Heads, 223
Two Brothers, 257, 259
Two Round Rocks, 269
Twofold Bay, 163

Upstart Bay, 284

Van Diemen's Land, 148
Viking Reef, 433–4
Viscount Shoal, 276
Vlasoff, Vince, 317

Waddy Point, 231
Walker Bay, 326
Wallice's Isles, 442, 446
Wallis, Captain, 95, 122
Walter, Richard, 86
Wattamolla, 175
Webb, Clement (Gun Room Steward), 98, 123–6, 128
Wedge Island, 253
Weir, Alexander (Quartermaster), 96, 110
Weymouth Bay, 422
Whitsunday Islands, 282
Whitsunday(s) Passage, 269, 276, 279–80, 282–3
Wide Bay, 227–9
Wild Duck Island, 269
Wilkinson, Francis (Master's Mate), 96, 101,
  journal of, 116, 189, 192, 207,
    departure from Endeavour River, 382, 384
    Endeavour River, 332, 335, 354, 358, 361, 363, 365–6, 373–4, 377, 381
Williams, Charles (A.B.), 98
Williamson Reef, 394
Wiltshire, William (Marine), 98
Wizard Reef, 433–4
Wolfe, Archibald (Tailor), 97, 122
Woodworth, John (A.B.), 98
Wrecks Rocks, 241
Wyborn Reef, 435, 437–8

Yaralla Shoal, 274, 276
Yeppoon, 254
York Isles, 435
Young, Nicholas (Surgeon's Servant), 98, 104

THE MIEGUNYAH PRESS

PUBLISHER'S EDITOR: SALLY MOSS

THIS BOOK WAS DESIGNED BY MARK DAVIS
THE BODY TEXT WAS SET IN 11 ½ POINT APOLLO
WITH 3 ½ POINTS OF LEADING

THE TEXT WAS PRINTED ON
120GSM BAI JIN 1.3 IVORY WOODFREE
IN CHINA BY 1010 PRINTING ASIA PTY LTD